GOOD
BEER
GUIDE
Belgium

Fifth Edition

TIM WEBB

CAMRA
BOOKS

To Siri-Ann, for ensuring that there is some corner of a Cambridgeshire field that is not forever Flanders.

Published by Campaign for Real Ale
230 Hatfield Road
St Albans
Hertfordshire AL1 4LW

www.camra.org.uk/books

First published 1992
Second edition 1995
Third edition 1998
US edition 1999
Fourth Edition 2002
Dutch Edition 2003
Fifth Edition 2005
Reprinted with corrections and updates 2006

ISBN 10: 1-85249-210-4   ISBN 13: 978-1-85249-210-6

A CIP catalogue record for this book is available from the British Library

Printed in Singapore by KHL Printing Co. Pte Ltd

Head of Publications: Joanna Copestick
Editorial Assistance: Emma Lloyd, Debbie Williams
Design/typography: Dale Tomlinson
Typeface: OT Versa *(Peter Verheul)*
Maps: John Macklin

Photographic Credits
CHARLES D COOK: pages 11, 37, 40, 41, 43, 47, 58, 61, 86, 127,
134, 147, 165, 173, 260, 294, 315, 335. JEREMY GRAY: pages 4, 14,
20, 42, 69, 156, 202, 204, 212, 220, 237, 242, 247, 250, 257, 258,
259, 280, 284, 286, 296, 308. CHRIS POLLARD: pages 66/67,
72, 76, 101, 105, 155. TIM WEBB: pages 64, 85, 92, 131, 167, 307.
JOHN WHITE: pages 18/19, 24, 45, 62, 74, 164, 168, 177, 186,
189, 190, 211, 218, 268, 275, 276, 289. Page 25: Paul Skinner.
Page 26: Powerstock/Chris Cheadle. Pages 51 & 320: Filip Geerts.
Page 55: JCE Bastogne. Page 71: CAMRA. Page 75: CAMRA.
Page 81: De Koninck. Page 161: Photolibrary/The Travel Library.
Page 180: Photononstop/Walter Bibikow. Page 224: SLR
Photography. Page 228: Photononstop/Gérard Guittot.
Page 310: Dean Southall. FRONT COVER: *Top:* Corbis/Bob Krist;
Bottom: Jeremy Gray.

Contents

Acknowledgements

The perpetually evolving and we hope ever-improving nature of the Guide owes a great deal to a relatively small band of dedicated beer nuts and Belgophiles, who appear to have nothing better to do with their spare time than lounge about in top rate cafés drinking the world's finest beers, enjoying top rate cuisine and great conversation, preferably to the sound of church bells.

For this great sacrifice I must thank dedicated hiker and shirt maker Chris Pollard, whose knowledge of Payottenland and Bruges is without equal; babbling trainee waiter Jeremy Gray through whose eyes we saw many a dark café; and comprehensive John White who has now swapped the oil business for a front seat in the char-a-banc.

Casimir Elsen, Yvan de Baets and Joris Pattyn influenced our path with their factual corrections, the wisdom of experience and the odd passionately held view. So did the host of Belgian brewers, beer merchants, officials, politicos and others who gave their time, analysis, advice and gossip for free and for some reason wish no acknowledgement – thank you anyway.

Mark Caygill turned shore discharge into an excuse to research Belgian beer in the UK, while Stephen D'Arcy, and colleagues Desmond Langham, Rhodri Thomas and Paul Briggs from CAMRA Brussels continued to man the trenches and advise on Beer Festivals, Brussels, Antwerp and the flight game.

Chuck Cook and the American contingent turned out in droves this time round, boldly going where no beer travellers had managed to inveigle their way before, while Steve Gale stayed at home to mind the website and became the world's greatest living home-brewer.

Thanks to Marcus Misieukiewicz for surviving the purgatory a little longer, to Hugh Shipman, Jim Dorsch and Koppelstock for keeping my cynicism levels topped up and to Filip Geerts and Danny van Tricht for trying to water them down again.

Stephen Hannigan, Martin Self, Jason Barker, Brendan Boyle, David Thornhill, Vince Murray & Phil Cotham, Geoff Green, Mark Goodair & Wakefield CAMRA, Rik Vernack, Jim Horlock, Lorenzo Dabove and Gunter Maertens all contributed valuable information beyond the call of duty.

To the, literally hundreds of unsung readers who mailed with helpful suggestions and comments, be assured that I was grateful for every one, even if replies were rare.

Finally, thanks to Siobhan, Theresa and Joyce for your complicity, to Jo for taking the idea seriously and to Dale for seeing the dawn up in front of the Apple Mac.

Introduction

Welcome to the Good Beer Guide to Belgium, the best-informed, most comprehensive guide in any language for travellers to the world's most interesting beer country and lovers of the world's most distinctive beers.

THE GROWING INTERNATIONAL reputation of Belgian beers draws over a million visitors each year to this historically fascinating and endearingly daft little kingdom at the heart of Europe. With over 40% of Belgian beer now exported, many millions more are enjoying the trip without moving from the comfort of home.

All touring goes better with a guidebook and we are the one for such a journey. Don't bother to compare, you won't find anything like us elsewhere.

Going up in the world
Regular readers will spot that we have changed a bit.

Our descriptions have always been colourful but now our pages are too. We have dropped our coverage of the Netherlands, which has made space for a thorough revision of the rest of the Guide.

Our all-important chapter on the Beer Styles of Belgium has been completely rewritten to reflect modern trends and our increasing understanding. Our thorough descriptions of Belgium's 120 working breweries and notes on over 800 of their beers are based on fifteen years' work.

We have expanded our sections on everything a beer traveller needs to know to get the best out of a visit, be it a day trip on Eurostar to Brussels or the month-long pilgrimage that we know some readers make.

As well as advising on practical stuff like how to get around, what to eat and where to go, we have brought together a full calendar of regular beer festivals and brewing events, and a complete list of beer-related tourist sites. Our hotel tips also grow with our inspectors' experience.

The 515 hand-picked cafés, taverns, restaurants and hotels we list are the best in Belgium, not just for sampling beer but for experiencing daily life. We guarantee they will make you want to return time and again, bringing your friends along for the ride.

If those friends need persuading, we have revised and significantly expanded our sections on buying beer to bring home and the places in the UK that specialise in selling Belgian beers.

A word in your ear
Regular readers will know that this is a Guide with an attitude. We do not do cheery-beery.

All too many books and articles written about beer makers and their brews hover in the comfort zone between laddish laughs and relaxed contemplation, often draped in pseudo-historical imagery with the odd business fact thrown in. The Guide does not do this.

We will not sing the praises of companies that relentlessly create smooth images for dull products so that their cut-price methods of production are accepted as mainstream. We do not write nice things for people who lie to us about what they do or who take our readers to be naïve idiots.

The Guide's opinions are laced throughout its pages.

For example, if you want to know our view on the effect globalisation is having on the brewing industry and its consequences for consumers, see our intro to "Global Beer Makers" on page 148. For our take on the dilemmas facing the monastic breweries and small lambic producers of the Senne Valley, turn to Beer Styles on pages 73 and 66.

Some of our best friends are brewers

The Guide is not anti-brewer. Many professionals in the brewing industry provide us with the background facts, thoughtful analysis and juicy bits of gossip essential to our credibility. But they know we are critical friends. We do not stay silent when we think that brewers get it wrong.

Sadly, the last few years have given us more than enough cause to speak.

In 2004 Interbrew, the company that owned the bulk of Belgian brewing and beer retailing for decades, merged with the South American giant AmBev, to form the unfortunately named InBev. It became obvious that Belgian influence was no longer central in its operations when it chose a corporate name that in Antwerp slang means, roughly, engaged in an act of oral sex.

Meanwhile, global rivals Anheuser-Busch, who make Budweiser and other drinks for the aesthetically challenged, showed just how petty these detached corporations can become by moving to bar Belgium's Dubuisson brewery from using its long-established brand name, Bush. (For the Guide's solution see page 113).

A more worrying development for lovers of serious beers was the collective abandonment of quality brewing techniques by many smaller independent producers. In an effort to compete on price, one company after another appeared to start making "fast beer", the brewers' equivalent of fast food.

Cheap and nasty

We commented in our last edition about the increasing substitution of cheap sugar sources for malted barley and the replacement of hops with hop extracts. This has continued to a noticeable extent. To add to the problem many breweries have speeded up the process of brewing, fermenting and conditioning.

Something somewhere is having a bad effect on beer character.

A whole generation of brewing engineers – the industry term for what used to be called brewers – seems both blind and deaf to the accusation that this has a bad effect on beer quality. Though maybe this is why they have started to flavour their products a lot more with spices, fruit syrups and extra alcohol.

Ignoring the problem fails to address the international groundswell of support for food and drink of greater not lesser character. The growth in popularity of traditionally made hams and cheeses, organically grown vegetables, fine wines and single malt whiskies are all examples of this trend.

With 40% of Belgian beer already bound for export and with the nation earning a cache for quality, Belgium's brewery companies are well set for supplying the world's thirst for characterful and enjoyable beers.

But not if they carry on creating joke brands for adolescents.

The local view

The Guide enjoys a lot of support among Belgian beer lovers and this time around we asked a few of them to write about what is happening to their nation's beer scene.

Brussels-based beer connoisseur turned brewer Yvan de Baets uses the opportunity to rail against what he sees as a new mediocrity in Belgian brewing.

Flanders-based connoisseur and beer judge Joris Pattyn dissects the reasons why there may be a downturn in Belgian beer tastes.

And the retiring editor of Zytholoog magazine, Limburg-based Casimir Elsen plots the decline in craft brewing through the 20th century.

But first, a brief résumé of a simple issue that lies at the heart of all consumer deception – what the customer should be entitled to know.

What do we tell the poor dears?

The Belgian beer consumer group Zythos is spearheading a campaign in Belgium and the EU that seeks to revolutionise beer labelling and make it of far greater use to consumers.

The current law
Under Belgian law the label on a beer must say that it is a beer. It must state the alcohol strength (if over 1.2%) and within arcane limits the class of beer. Fruit additions must be listed, as must the presence of certain sweeteners.

Zythos wants labels to state what type of beer it is, what it contains, who makes it and how you should look after it

They would like to see the label state the type of fermentation (top, bottom or spontaneous), whether the beer is bottle-conditioned, filtered or pasteurised and within clearer guidelines whether it is a Pils, wheat beer, old brown, dubbel, tripel, ambrée, Scotch, oude gueuze or whatever.

What is in it?
The list of ingredients is already compulsory on animal feeds, so it seems reasonable to expect it on a product designed mainly for humans.

A good start would be the proportions of grain used (barley malt, wheat, maize, rice, sorgrum) and their form (whole grain, flour, syrup), and the hop varieties (Saaz, Hallertau, Goldings) and their form (whole hops, pellets, extract, oil). Adjuncts (sugars, fruit syrups, starch, vegetable extracts) should be listed, along with named spices, essences, flavourings and E-numbers.

Alcohol content should be stated as both percentage by volume and the total units of alcohol in the bottle.

Who made it?
They have called for an end to the practice of brewery companies trying to be people they are not. At present the label does not have to state the producer. Zythos wants to see it state the name and location of the brewery where the beer was brewed and where it is a subsidiary, the name of the parent company.

Where the beer is a relabelled version of an existing brand, the identity of the original brand should be stated.

How do you look after me?
They want to see an end to the compulsory use of "best before" dates for beers that can age delightfully in the cellar over many years. They believe it is more intelligent to state the date of bottling.

Finally, they have suggested a simple code for storing and pouring advice and the type of glass in which the beer is best presented, to be added to the symbols that distinguish bottles for returning or recycling.

Sensible and simple
If a uniform system for approving and displaying the organic or eco-friendly credentials of the beer and its brewery of origin can be agreed then you have all the information the discerning consumer needs to make their choice.

Sensible and simple?

To understand the reasons why the brewing establishment in Belgium and around the world will fight each and every one of these suggestions in tooth and claw, you will need to read the rest of the Guide.

Mediocrity... it's the new Classic!

The sales pitch for Belgium says ours is the Beer Paradise™, because we have the greatest diversity of beers in the world. Even InBev says this – so it must be true.

But look closely and you will see a trick.

Rediscovered history

Belgian brewing was in decline for the same reasons as the rest of agribusiness – increasing industrialisation, easy-to-please consumers, small family companies taken over by conglomerates and so on.

At the beginning of the Eighties this decline seemed to stop for a time. Foreign writers brought attention to our brewery inheritance, some even writing books on the subject. Gradually, Belgian beer forged a world reputation, led by the "Belgian classics", as defined by the world's top beer writer Michael Jackson.

There was renewed interest in "traditional country products" and this led to greater interest in special beers produced by small or regional breweries. New breweries were even born. Local passion and international recognition undoubtedly saved many small breweries and gave a new image, more "noble", to our country's beers.

Turning history into profit

Since then however, certain brewers carried by this wave, have gone for the money, modifying their beers to make them "easier to drink" while continuing to portray them as being the originals.

The breweries that led this decline in the early Nineties were important ones, in terms of their production and appreciable financial resources. And because they were famous their behaviour influenced others.

No type of brewery escaped. Not even the famous Trappists.

The sirens of easy profit triumphed over authentic beer-makers. In modern Belgium the term "gueuze", for instance, can describe the best and worst of beers. There are now breweries of all sizes and types that are second rate.

A product of little importance

In Belgium, beer is often regarded as a consumer commodity of little importance, by those who produce it as much as by those who drink it. The marketing of beers sometimes uses noble imagery, but often to promote a cheapskate product.

The reputation of French wine was not made by *vin ordinaire* but by *grand cru*. So why does Belgian beer choose to build a reputation using ordinary products? Are some brewers ashamed to produce "only" a beer?

Plus ça change

Although diverse tendencies are found in the Belgian brewing scene, all lead to standardisation or regression of taste.

First is the tendency to make sweet beers. Goodbye to bitterness or acidity because "the consumer does not like these extreme tastes". What these brewers mean is that they still want to follow the processed food industry's "push to sugar".

Sweet tastes are basic, for attracting animals. Bitterness and sourness are cultured and belong to human evolution. The development of taste in human beings, requires education. It seems to me that one duty of a brewer should be to defend cultured tastes and, when necessary, educate the customer.

Yet we see a decline in recent years in the quantity of hops employed in making beers. And finding an authentic lambic beer in a pub is easier in Helsinki than in Brussels!

Three big mistakes

Fruitiness can come from the use of real fruits (rarely found nowadays) or the use of certain yeast strains. But it can also come from using awful artificial essences that make a jam. The subtle use of a spice can, in certain recipes, bring more aromatic complexity to a beer. But increasingly Belgian ale *à la mode* tastes like coriander soup.

Another annoying tendency is to produce the strongest possible beers. If stricter driving laws restrict the number of beers you can drink before you go home, then make them strong ones!

Though there are some excellent strong beers, alcoholic strength is now rarely supported by complexity of flavour. Sweetness, spiciness, fruitiness and alcoholic strength all hide subtle aromas more than revealing them.

The thin film of lead

So a dreadful parody descends like a thin film of lead on our beautiful country. We see the appearance of the Belgian Special Beer product. Just like beer but with added sugar, spice, fruit or alcohol – the magical formula of the new mediocrity.

So why does the Belgian consumer buy this?

Well firstly, it is not easy to live in a country in which one huge brewery group define the market. Industrial products are imposed everywhere, educating the public taste to follow the formatted easy qualities of their beers and those of a growing number of small breweries.

It helps that we package our myth with the image of a jolly monk or a beautiful forest creature but this consumer also has a psychological handicap, which takes the form:

I am Belgian ... Belgium is the country of beer ... therefore I know about beer.

This is the certainty that undermines the curiosity of the amateur, along with their critical spirit. They become satisfied with the ordinary product found in any café in Belgium.

Why go further? Why not enjoy the cage for its certainty?

The lost classics

So Belgium loses the desire to defend its great beers, leaving the field free for simple-minded brewers to change them. A majority of what were formerly "Belgian Classics" have been sacrificed. Their bitterness reduced, their acidity neutralised, their production standardised, their fermentation speeded up, only their names unchanged.

You put something in the mainstream if you want it washed away.

The current idolatry of the Belgian Special Beer product, without discernment or discretion endangers our really fine beers.

Yet hope remains. Belgium still shelters some irrepressible brewers, determined to continue to make authentic products. To discover them is still an enthralling adventure. In these beers you still find the spirit that made the fallen classics.

Where greatness lies

It is difficult to put into words the subjective sensations that differentiate authentic character in a beer from that which is not. These are deep things, borne of fundamental values, such as ecology, humanity, love of a job well done and respect for time. It always takes time to make a good beer.

These beers come from brewers who do not have anything to hide. No mysterious recipes with secret ingredients, rediscovered in some pseudo-archive from the Middle Ages. Beers crafted from real work, from respect for those traditions that have stood the tests of time and with a clear vision of what a good beer must be.

A great beer combines intricacy with forcefulness. Its simplicity in composition should defy its complexity of character. These are beers that do not leave one indifferent, of which one never wearies. Offering with each mouthful something to discover again, when one believed one knew them so well.

This is what justifies Belgium still being a beer paradise. For how long is another question...   YVAN DE BAETS
Brussels

Sugar and spice and all things nice

If one follows the pulse of the beer-related Internet closely in the way I have done for some years, a few themes keep recurring. One controversial issue is that of the "dumbing down" of top Belgian beers, even by monastery-related breweries.

There is a small but solid band of people who deny categorically that any such thing has happened. They argue that during the life of a beer taster, the senses get sharpened. One's taste becomes more astute and so the beer that was once so wonderfully beckoning when discovered, turns out to be pretty average after all.

The cost of savings
Another argument pops up whenever critical beer tasters attack contemporary brewing methods, techniques and equipment. This says that changing to newer, better, cost-saving brewing techniques that are easier to control is something that was ever-present. The brewing methods of the 17th century Netherlands, although famous across Europe became unpalatable to people when they read Pasteur's' new research on micro-organisms.

Yet most people in the world of brewing admit, at least privately that the quality of a number of acclaimed Belgian brews is no longer what it was.

Changing tastes
The drinking habits of the public seem to move towards sweeter, stronger and more "obvious" beers, veering away from difficult, complex and subtle ones. The trend is not new. It has been going on for thirty years.

Part of the explanation may lie with the methods of bigger brewing concerns.

If such a company does a survey, it will ask as varied and large a group as possible for its opinion. Extreme tastes – in beer this means mainly sharp and bitter flavours – will offend people more often than bland, sweet or fruity tastes. So they make their beers for people of bland tastes.

Fruit tastes pose an additional problem. Real fruit sugars are easily fermented away by *saccharomyces* yeast but the use of real fruit is not only unwieldy, expensive and cumbersome, it also results in what the bigger brewers' survey groups perceive as unwanted, i.e. sharp and acidic tastes.

The appliance of science
The fruit agents added are diluted, sugared concentrates and laboratory-derived fruit esters. The result is sweet, syrupy, and often artificial tasting, brightly coloured concoctions that bear little resemblance to the superbly complex, satisfying experience of a real fruit-enriched beer.

Sad to say, in order to compete, a lot of smaller brewers have aligned themselves with the trend.

Yet it is not just non-discriminating beer drinkers, staunchly defended by cost-conscious brewers, who fête these beers. So do the beer geeks, set on encouraging a flood of strange and sometimes ridiculous flavoured beers onto the market.

Worse, "enlightened" beer connoisseurs pay lip service, maintaining that the production of these beers means a more confident future for "real" fruit beers.

The argument is inherently false. As long as these laughable concoctions exist, the inherent laziness of general taste will stay focused on them. Why let your palate venture outside the safe boundaries of syrup?

Unnatural fluids

The zealous search for new and exciting tastes encourages new microbrewers in an erroneous belief that "more is better", or "a special taste is always a bonus".

I have tasted beers that have the flavour of dentists' mouthwash, of the *pot pourri* that perfumes bathrooms, and of the candles burned by followers of Zen. There is little joy in those beers. Served at a blind tasting, their defenders might reasonably invoke eternal damnation over their perpetrators, for the crime of creating unnatural fluids.

Perhaps this all began some decades ago with the inoffensive coriander seed. (Before my good friend and icon Pierre Celis has a heart attack, I must say that the addition of ground coriander to *witbier* is historically completely defensible and helped to resurrect the Hoegaarden-style wit, a bonus for the array of Belgian beers. And for our export figures.)

The inherent characteristic of coriander seed lies in its perfuming qualities. This is why it goes admirably well in spicy cuisine such as Indian or Indonesian. However, in a regular beer the citrus perfume becomes rapidly oppressive and overpowering, rendering it like an unsalted soup or an exotic sauce, with no remaining refreshing qualities whatever.

Joris Pattyn, beer judge, at work.

A new law

I have a personal ambition to make a new law. This will stipulate that no brewer may legally purchase coriander seed until they have been licensed to brew for so many years. Even then only carefully weighed quantities may be bought, governed by the annual output of approved beers.

Today, any brewer wanting to boost a beer feels free to add indiscriminate amounts of coriander to beers of styles that ought never to see this obnoxious weed. Worse, in their endeavour to honour Belgian beers by copying them, some North American brewers make coriander infusions disguised as beer, which are totally undrinkable.

The use of spices in beer brewing ought to be circumspect and preferably in low doses. Making, say, a lemongrass lager because it has been designed to accompany some Thai dish, is not an enjoyable thought. This new concept, which is becoming popular in the UK, to make beers to match to specific food – instead of carefully choosing which pairing is most successful – is alarming and should be nipped in the bud.

Impress me

If you want to make a beer to impress me, give me one that tastes OK in its own right, which satisfies me, and even better, by its complexity poses me a riddle as to what subtle additions and touches have been adopted by its creator.

I want to be intrigued, not bowled over by a punch in the mouth that puts me off my food for the next couple of days. Imposing a character on a beer makes an ominous promise of what beer is going to be, instead of building on what it ought to be.

JORIS PATTYN
East Flanders

11

New wars for old

The Belgian brewing sector has undergone an enormous evolution in the course of the past hundred years. 3,223 breweries were active in Belgium in the year 1900. A century later there are 120. So what caused this deforestation?

We can trace three main factors that have had a distinct impact – the two large wars on Belgian territory in the first half of the 20th century, the emergence of Pilsener beers and the evolution of small local businesses into industrial concerns.

The spoils of war

The periods 1914–1918 and 1940–1945 were disastrous times for Belgian breweries. Many restrictions were imposed by the German occupiers and the shortage of basic ingredients meant it was soon impossible for many brewers to brew at all, let alone well.

Brewhouses were plundered. Equipment was seized and dismantled, coppers often being claimed and removed. Hundreds had to close their doors and after the armistice did not re-open. 1,908 breweries survived to 1920, only 775 to 1946.

Some owners had lost the courage for business while others had found different work. Many who wanted to restart lacked the money to do so.

The outbreak of Pils

With only a few exceptions the breweries of 1900 brewed exclusively top fermentation beers (ales). With import duties relatively low, more and more bottom fermentation beers (lagers), were introduced from abroad and became popular.

The switch from ale to lager production demanded considerable financial investment and this was not possible for many small breweries. The companies that could make the move found much success and developed into the large industrial firms supplying a new market with Pils beers. So smaller breweries were marginalized or else had to sell up to bigger concerns.

The evolution from small businesses

There was no real brewing "industry" in Belgium at the beginning of the 20th century. Breweries were generally small concerns with old-fashioned methods, farm-based or serving a few cafés.

Additional increases in costs came as a result of new social laws and other influences. Already in 1909, Louis Van Hulle, director of the *Institut Supérieur de Brasserie* in Ghent, was advising: "Take all your old breweries and form a large central brewery that can service all your customers."

The economic crisis between the two wars did the sector no favours. Closures, mergers and concentration indeed became the order of the day. After the second war the process simply accelerated.

The second half of the 20th century saw the emergence of large brewery concerns. Breweries that were no longer viable were absorbed and closed at a relentless pace. Activities spread beyond the Belgian market to become multinational.

The great efficiency

Although the number of breweries was for a hundred years in free fall, the volume of beer produced gives a different picture. The breweries of 1900 produced 14,617,000 hl of beer for Belgium's 6.7 million inhabitants. In 2000 they made more or less the same amount, 14,734,000 hl for a population of 10.2 million.

In fact the picture is worse. Of the beer produced in 1900, only 5,000 hl was exported, while an additional 5,000,000 hl was imported. In 2000, over 4,000,000 hl of the beer produced went abroad, while only 800,000 hl arrived. Annual consumption per head had fallen from over 220 litres to less than 100.

The efficiency of having 96% fewer breweries had led to an increase in output of less that 1%. And even this came at a cost.

Loss of character

The brewer of 1900 was a local character. With few exceptions breweries were very small and only brewed for the village or local area. They brewed beer to a local taste. Few made the beers of elsewhere.

Specific discernible styles existed, named after a certain village or city. Leuven, Aarschot, Aalst, Mechelen and Diest all produced ale styles unique to their area. As mobility improved and customers' horizons broadened so people came to know other regions and beer styles. So local variations were suppressed and in time disappeared entirely.

In general, modern beers that are said to be in a local style rarely have affinity with the original product.

The Coca Cola culture

It is an unmistakable fact, especially since the end of the second war that there has been a sweetening of the public taste. The "Coca Cola culture" has ensured that bitter and sour tastes are less appreciated, especially by young people.

The impact of this on the beer market is considerable. Traditional characteristic beer tastes, as found in Flemish old brown and red beers or traditional lambics and gueuze, are put at a bad disadvantage. Even the revival of interest in some styles in recent years has involved only marginal sales in comparison with former glories.

And yet Belgium still enjoys the reputation of a beer paradise, with an enviable variety of styles. Nowadays this comes due to the small breweries that survive or which have been set up in recent years.

Survivors of a lost era

The 120 breweries that still exist are very varied in size and the Belgian beer market is unbalanced. Two large concerns – InBev and Alken-Maes – control over 80% of the market. A further 15% is taken by just ten medium-sized breweries.

These producers brew a large volume of beers that are aimed at the large mass of people who are easily pleased. Mainstream products, technically perfect but mostly characterless and predictable and worthy of little note.

The hundred other breweries must satisfy themselves with less than 5% of the market. This is at the same time their weakness and their strength. Weakness because their fate is controlled by the financial power of the big beer buyers. Strength because nobody can stop them from experimenting with small-scale character beers, with pronounced, characteristic tastes.

It is the small brewers that are best equipped to supply the beers that entertain real beer lovers, a market that is not interesting for larger brewers who must have volume.

The future

In one century much has disappeared from the Belgian brewing world. The process of enlargement has, put gently, not always had a positive impact. The growth of industrial brewing brought decisive financial and economic changes but to the detriment of respect for beer.

Management of the firm became more important than brewing well. The beers became relegated to the status of products that appear in the business's annual results sheets.

But everything is not yet lost. More than half of the breweries that now exist were set up during the last 25 years. In these small enterprises highly creative brewers prefer to make original and outspoken flavours rather than high volumes.

And as long as they can maintain themselves – David against Goliath – the consumer will always find a rich palette of fragrances, colours and tastes on the Belgian beer market. How Belgian beer will fare in the world in the long run will depend on them, and not on the mass producers.

CASIMIR ELSEN
Limburg

Belgium and its history

"Belgium is a country invented by the British to annoy the French."

CHARLES DE GAULLE, *President of France*

THE KINGDOM OF BELGIUM was founded as the result of a riot in Brussels in 1830 and a conference in London in 1831. In the eight centuries before its creation the lands within its current borders had been invaded, claimed and occupied dozens of times. Since it became a nation this has only happened twice.

Nowadays the only major threat to its integrity is from within. Despite being the home of the European Union, the country itself is more divided down linguistic lines that at any time since it achieved statehood.

BELGIUM

POPULATION (2002): **10,250,000**
AREA: **30,520 km²**
BREWERIES (1.4.05): **120**

Belgium is an unlikely idea. From the outset this was a nation of two halves – Dutch-speaking and French-speaking. As time passed it added a German quarter and the capital Brussels became a law unto itself.

Its diversity is illustrated in its intricate electoral system. In the 2004 elections, Belgium's 7.5 million electors were called upon to elect 313 deputies. Of these, 124 had to be Flemish, 75 Wallonian, 25 German-speaking and 89 from Brussels (of whom 72 must be French-speaking and 17 Dutch-speaking). 99,000 officials oversaw this commitment to democracy and people who did not vote were fined up to €150.

Around Flanders

Tourism website: www.toervl.be

Modern Flanders (Du: *Vlaanderen*) consists of the five provinces of northern Belgium – *West-Vlaanderen* (West Flanders), *Oost-Vlaanderen*

(East Flanders), *Vlaams-Brabant* (Flemish Brabant), *Antwerpen* (Antwerp) and Limburg. Its regional parliament sits in Brussels.

Flanders is flat. Cycle from the hopfields and war graves near the French border of West Flanders, along the do-in-a-day North Sea coast, hook back into the mediaeval splendour of Bruges, along the Albert Canal to beautiful Ghent, down the valley of the Schelde to the port of Antwerp and you will be dismounting for traffic lights, not hills.

Even along the forest tracks of Limburg, across the gentle plain of Brabant, down through Payottenland and into the Flemish Ardennes of southern East Flanders, you will not be using the gears much.

Bruges is essential and so is Ghent. Visit the port of Antwerp for old times' sake but consider other places too. Mechelen and Leuven have small but majestic centres and a growing beer culture. Hasselt makes an excellent base for exploring the emerging talents of Limburg. Aalst is another useful touring base and we confess a soft spot for the area around Geraardsbergen and its quiet country station with trains to everywhere.

Around Wallonia

Tourism website: www.belgium-tourism.net

Wallonia (Fr: *Wallonnie*) is the French-speaking region of southern Belgium and also consists of five provinces – Hainaut, *Brabant-Wallonnie* (Wallonian Brabant), Namur, Liège and Luxembourg. The last of these was gifted by the Grand Duke of Luxembourg, as part of the deal by which his eastern lands gained full nationhood. The Wallonian parliament sits in Namur.

If the tourist authorities got their way the region would be renamed the Ardennes, after the area of outstanding natural beauty that was once and in places still is the Ardennes Forest. This is a land of rolling hills and steep river valleys, old woodland and high moors, running from north-eastern France and on into Luxembourg and Germany.

But not all of Wallonia is so cute. In its northern parts this was modern Belgium's industrial heartland until the crash of heavy industry across most of northern Europe in the 1970s. Thirty years on the slagheaps have been turned to forest, and the mines and canal lifts are now pieces of "industrial archaeology", their magnificence all the more visible for their disuse.

Wallonia is almost virgin tourist country. Use our pages to plot your route but consider the compact pleasures of Mons, Namur and even Charleroi in the north, the run of brewery cafés between Tournai and Enghien and the pleasures of a rural journey from the Semois valley to Arlon in the deep south. And try to spend a day of gastro-tourism southwest of Mons.

Ancient history

The language divide has its roots at the very beginning of Belgian history.

Ancient Gaul was divided into three parts. At its north-eastern end the Belgae under Ambiorix defended their lands vigorously against Caesar. Nonetheless *Gallia Belgica* fell to Roman rule and remained that way for five hundred years. Latin became the local language.

One of the Romans' more impressive creations was a great highway that ran in modern terms from Köln (Cologne) via Tongeren to Bavay in France. When the Roman Empire began to collapse it was this highway that enabled the Germanic tribe, the Franks to take control of the region for a time, making their capital in Tournai, and in effect ruling part of northern France.

Holy Romans and the rise of Flanders

The Holy Roman Empire brought a sort of stability to Europe but essentially real power lay increasing with local potentates whose families ceased control of discreet pockets of territory – Count Sigefroi in Luxembourg,

Prince-Bishop Notger in Liège and Count Baldwin the Iron Arm in Flanders.

The earliest rough equivalent of modern Wallonia was created following the death of the mightiest of the Holy Roman Emperors, Charlemagne. A broad strip of nations was created between the Mediterranean and the North Sea to keep France apart from Germania. The southern peninsula was called Italy, the central part Burgundy and the northern lands Lotharingia.

Baldwin had made a strange alliance with France by marrying the King's daughter, though he had to kidnap her first. Their son, another Baldwin, married a daughter of the English King, Alfred the Great, in marginally more consensual circumstances. The family ruled over Flanders from their castle fortress in Ghent for over three hundred years.

Trade wars

By the 13th century towns like Ieper, Bruges and Ghent were prosperous city-states in their own right. But tensions between the ruling merchant classes who took most of the money and the artisan classes who made it for them began to get out of hand.

England's King John and Germany's Emperor Otto IV thought the Flemish craftsmen had a point but the French came to the aid of the ruling elite and suppressed the revolt at the Battle of Bouvines in 1214. France began to offer Flanders "protection".

In 1300 the French King Philip the Fair decided to be damned with fairness and annexed the region. This was not a good idea. Following a bloody tax revolt by weavers in Bruges earlier in the year, the Battle of the Golden Spurs near Kortrijk in 1302 saw a bunch of Flemish peasant soldiers literally sink the cream of the French chevaliers and inflict such a blow on France that the protection ceased and prosperity returned.

Flanders took England's side in their Hundred Years' war with the French.

By 1340 Ghent was the second largest city in Europe after Paris. Leuven, Mechelen, Brussels and Tournai had joined in the previously unequalled wealth creation. Much magnificent architecture of the time survives today.

The House of Burgundy

The marriage of the daughter of the Count of Flanders to Duke Philip the Bold of Burgundy led to a period in Belgian history of such success that to this day modern Belgians refer to a life of good food, comfortable living, sophisticated company and cultural appreciation as "Burgundian".

Philip the Bold's son, Philip the Good was the richest man in Europe ruling his Duchy not from his palace in Dijon but from his satellite court in Brussels. The arts thrived. Painters like Jan Van Eyck and Hans Memling became the Flemish Masters. He commissioned Brussels' magnificent Grand'Place and created the university at Leuven.

Burgundian rule came to an end when Mary, Duchess of Burgundy married Emperor Maximilian of Austria and then promptly died. Sadly, her grieving widower did not like the lands he called the Low Countries (as opposed to the High Countries of modern-day Germany and Austria), so he gave them to his son Philip the Handsome to rule.

In 1496 Philip married the King of Spain's daughter Joanna. In 1500 they had a son, who as Emperor Charles V of the Hapsburg Empire would become the most powerful man the world had ever known.

The Hapsburg Empire

Charles was born in Ghent and raised in Mechelen. He was just six years old when his father died and he inherited the Low Countries. His aunt, Margaret of Austria, who was largely responsible for raising him, spiritually assisted by the humanist scholar Erasmus, governed the provinces on his behalf.

At 19, on the death of his grandfather, Charles became Emperor of Austria and, through his mother's line, the ruler of Spain and all its American and Asian dominions. The global nature of the Hapsburg lands at this time was summed up in the famous geographical observation that his was an Empire "on which the sun never sets". Trade expanded so extensively that Antwerp grew to be the world's largest port.

In 1555, Charles grew weary of power and abdicated control of the Low Countries to his son King Philip II of Spain – the one Sir Francis Drake had trouble with. Where Charles was at heart a Burgundian Catholic with an instinct to tolerate the rise of Protestantism and the Reformation, Philip was an impassioned Spaniard, who saw it as the work of the devil and focussed considerable firepower on its destruction.

In 1567, in a move that is rarely a good one, he unleashed a psychopath into the situation. The awful Duke of Alba did for the Low Countries what Cromwell did for Ireland and in doing so defined the borders of modern Belgium.

In 1585, Brussels was declared the capital of the Spanish Netherlands. Protestants moved north to the Republic of the United Provinces, roughly equivalent to modern Holland.

War and peace

In the first half of the 17th century, while Catholicism, Protestantism and the royal households of Europe were slogging it out in the Thirty Years' War, Belgian territory changed hands several times but there were few battles of any significance on Belgian soil. This was instead a time in which culture blossomed, with the arrival of Baroque architecture and the painter Pieter Paul Rubens of Antwerp.

Indeed the peace proved far worse than the war. The signing of the Treaty of Westphalia in Münster, which recognised the Protestant states, had two unfortunate side-effects. First, it compromised the port of Antwerp to such an extent that most trade shifted to Amsterdam. Second, it created in Belgium a buffer zone between Protestant Holland and Catholic France – like that was going to work!

The decades of warring that followed saw the building of the Citadel at Namur, the fortifications at Huy and the ramparts of Luxembourg. The worst fighting was in the war of the Spanish Succession between 1701 and 1713, fought almost entirely on Belgian soil with the Duke of Marlborough featuring prominently on behalf of the Protestant English king. Belgian cities changed hands like cards in a game of Happy Families.

When the dust settled, the Protestants still ruled Holland but the Austrians had taken back Belgium from the French. There

followed the Age of Enlightenment, in which religious freedoms were re-learnt. And so it remained, with just the odd French invasion here and there, throughout most of the 18th century. Until 1794 to be precise, when Napoleon Bonaparte took control.

From Napoleon to independence

Aware of local disquiet with aloof Austrian dominance, best expressed in the Brabantine Revolt of 1789, Bonaparte used victory in battles at Jemappes (1792) and Fleurus (1794) to boot the Austrians out and take back the nine *départements* of the Southern Netherlands, into French hands. He was clearly disappointed by the locals' lack of gratitude, suggesting he had little appreciation of history.

The many-phased defeat of Bonaparte reached its Waterloo near Waterloo, south of Brussels, in June 1815. The consequences were as big a hash as the battle itself. The Prussians took eastern Liège, Luxembourg became a Grand Duchy and the rest of Belgium was amalgamated with the Protestant states to become the United Kingdom of the Netherlands under a new king, William I. The first and only as it turned out.

The next fifteen years saw predictable wrangling between the Dutch and the Flemish, who believed they were playing the underdog in a Greater Netherlands. Meanwhile the largely Catholic population of Wallonia, who could not even speak the language, were getting equally peeved. The two aggrieved parties rioted in Brussels in 1830. At which point the British intervened, with a cunning plan.

The London Conference of 1830 and eventual Treaty of 1839 made Belgium an independent monarchy for the first time in its history. Its first King was an Englishman, albeit a naturalised one. Leopold of Saxe-Cobourg-Gotha would have been the Prince Consort to Queen Charlotte of Great Britain and Ireland had his wife, Queen Victoria's older sister, not died before the throne was vacant.

Belgium the early years

Leopold I was a great King. He not only established his new country's independence and neutrality, he also steered his ministers

to overcome a three-year famine in Flanders (1845–48) and build a nation fit to forge its own economic future. His son, Leopold II, who became King in 1865 was a conniving and ignorant man dedicated to self-aggrandisement and the exploitation of the Congo.

Leopold II's indolence did not stop Belgium ending the 19th century and beginning the 20th with the confidant air of a place at the cutting edge of fashion. The grand promenades along its coast, the Art Nouveau architecture of Victor Horta in Brussels, the glamour of the *belle époque* and the majesty of the great industrial constructions of the Canal du Centre were all faces of a confident nation with great aspirations.

The industrial powerhouse that was the blast furnaces of Liège, the coalfields of the Borinage around Mons and the heavy industrial belt of the Centre shifted the economic focus of Belgium in a southerly direction, for the first time. No longer the opportunist agrarian economy of Europe's favourite battlegrounds, Wallonia started to make the wealth for the new nation.

It was all going swimmingly.

The war of two parts

Then came Kaiser Wilhelm of Germany, and the last big bust-up of the agents of the European royal houses. The 1914–18 war was, once again played out largely on Belgian soil, in Flanders Field, along Plug Street and

mine for some while to come. The only major fighting on Belgian soil came with the last offensive of the defeated German army, the Battle of the Ardennes, in 1944.

The emergence of present day Belgium

After the 1939–45 war political minds less affected by the obsessions of the wealthy determined that Europe required a different future from its past. Some say it was the positioning of Brussels at the heart of the new Europe that gave post-war Belgium back its assurance. But EXPO Brussels 1958 must have helped, with the Atomium, the songs of Jacques Brel and *kip aan 't spit*.

In 1948, BElgium, the NEtherlands and LUXembourg had got together to form a Customs and Excise Union that they called Benelux. This small experiment in how to build the new Europe boosted Brussels' claim to become the seat of the European Commission and then the European Union. In 1967 it acquired NATO too, then SHAPE and a host of other organisations that live and breathe international co-operation.

But the acquisition of a great new role may have overstretched the Belgian political elite. Whereas their neighbours the Dutch foresaw the collapse of heavy industry in the 1970s and trained their miners and furnacemen to be engineers and computer operators, Belgium tried to ride the punch by taking subsidies and increasing taxes. Flanders meanwhile became a tourist spot.

The present day

The first decade of the new millennium sees Belgium in a bit of a fix. While all around are moving to a world of collaboration and respect, the descendants of the Belgae and the Franks once more wish to go their separate ways. Flanders nearly elected a right wing separatist government in 2004.

A German politician said a few years ago: "Nations are now useless – too small for the decisions that shape the world, too big to decide the matters of daily life. It is time to become regions of a single Europe and glory in diversity." Let us hope for Belgium's sake that he was right.

Time for a beer.

around the hill town of Mons. Only this time the numbers were so much bigger and, like the list of names carved on the Menin Gate, unburied but Known unto God.

As part of the Treaty of Versailles in 1919, Germany gave back eastern Liège to Belgium as a way of saying sorry. The country became officially tri-lingual. But nobody thought to repair Germany.

In the brief interlude before the next round, nowhere was quicker than Belgium to pick up on the new Art Deco, the phrase coined to describe the modern-on-ancient designs at the International Exhibition of Decorative Arts at Paris in 1925. René Magritte and Paul Delvaux painted surreally. Brussels got style and Agatha Christie immortalised Hercule Poirot.

Popular King Albert I died in a climbing accident in the Meuse Valley in 1934. He was succeeded by his son Leopold III, whose beautiful young wife Astrid died the following year, Diana-like, in a car smash in Switzerland. Postage stamps with her portrait in photo-gravure, already intended to raise money for charity, were issued with a black border. Four years later, Europe was at war again.

In 1940 the still young King agreed to a murky deal allowing Rommel's tanks to roll through Belgium in a matter of days. Whether this was a disgraceful act of capitulation or a move of extreme political realism that saved a million Belgian lives, history will not deter-

SAMPLE SOME OF BRUSSELS'
FAMOUS BEERS

ENJOY REAL BELGIAN BEER IN REAL BELGIA
BARS FROM JUST £59 RETURN
VISIT THE TRAVEL CENTRE BELOW

Getting there

Travelling to Belgium from the UK can involve a train, car transporter, ferry, high-speed ship or plane. No-frills airlines and the Channel Tunnel have made hopping across the water for a couple of beers a lot cheaper in recent years. This is our attempt at a comprehensive list of options.

First choose your mode of travel.

Flying can now be the cheaper option for lone travellers and couples, though the budget options are far more limited than for, say, Amsterdam, Paris or most of Germany and Italy.

Ferry companies have marginalized Belgium in recent years with P&O North Sea Ferries' Hull–Zeebrugge and TransEuropa's new Ramsgate-Ostend routes being the only ones to dock in Belgian ports.

The easiest way from London to Brussels is by train.

The tunnel and ferry links to the French Channel ports are far more frequent. However, although the E40 coastal motorway runs directly past Calais and Dunkerque into the Belgian motorway system for Ostend, Bruges, Ghent, Brussels and beyond, it is of little use to Belgium-bound foot passengers and cyclists.

Travellers to Antwerp, Limburg and Liège should consider taking one of the routes to the Dutch ports of Hoek van Holland or Rotterdam Europoort.

Travelling from North America

The only airport in Belgium with direct trans-Atlantic flights is Brussels but consider other options.

Although Amsterdam, Paris, London and Frankfurt are in other countries, all those cities have direct trains to Brussels and may be subject to better deals. A few carriers also fly to Luxembourg and Düsseldorf, which are even closer.

All of those cities offer good opportunities for a stopover in a different beer culture.

Overall, travel has never been easier but calculating the best deal for your trip is complicated. Not least you have to cost how much you will spend on your journey – on meals,

drinks, fuel and those little purchases that were a good idea at the time – and the price you put on not being where you want to be.

The Guide's most frequent travellers advise:

- shop around for every trip
- the best flight deals are usually found by booking at least four months ahead
- the best ferry deals are usually found by waiting until the last four weeks
- higher mid-July to late August prices can be off-set by lower business hotel prices
- some travel company all-in deals are cheaper than you can get by booking direct
- seriously consider travelling round by bicycle and train
- if you want to drive consider fly-drive deals, especially on weekends and public holidays

SURFACE ROUTES

Tunnel

Eurostar passenger trains
www.eurostar.com
Depart: London Waterloo or Ashford
Arrive: EuroLille or Brussels South
Advantages: simple, comfortable and frequent; quick from Ashford to Brussels (100 mins); city centre terminals; easier to work on board; free connection to all Belgian stations.
Disadvantages: priced to compete with air travel; no night service; no through trains beyond London; check-in times as for ferries; bicycles subtly discouraged.
Tips: Ashford has a huge car park; stop over in beery Lille; links from SNCF Lille to many Belgian stations are faster than via Brussels.

Le Shuttle: car transporter
www.eurotunnel.co.uk
Depart: M20 near Folkestone
Arrive: E40 near Calais
Advantages: efficient; good quality terminals; usually the fastest way from the M20 to the E40.
Disadvantages: nothing to do or see on board; still tends to take at least 90 mins from road to road; rarely the cheapest; no pedestrians; bicycles only twice daily each way.
Tips: take your iPod or a good book and some sandwiches.

Ferries

TransEuropa Ferries
www.transeuropaferries.com
T 01843 595522 (UK); 059 340 261 (Belgium)
Depart: Ramsgate
Arrive: Ostend
Advantages: the only ferry from southern England direct to Belgian soil; three sensibly timed services per day; Ramsgate and Ostend are both great seaside towns.
Disadvantages: no access to either port for cyclists or foot passengers; the summer-only night crossing arrives in Ostend at 03.30; adequate rather than luxurious.
Tips: hefty peak time discounts with payment in advance; these are truckers' boats adapted to take additional car passengers; restricted use of credit cards.

P&O North Sea Ferries
www.poferries.com
T 0870 598 0333 (UK); 070 70 77 71 (Belgium)
Depart: Hull
Arrive: Zeebrugge
Advantages: by far the most sophisticated boats in service; excellent quality dining and a full range of cabins; saves long drives from northern England; lands on Belgian soil, a bus ride from Bruges; civilised arrival times.
Disadvantages: only one boat per day; long crossing (11–13 hrs); limited public transport at both terminals.
Tips: pre-book the excellent dinner and substantial breakfast; no plumbing in the cheapest cabins; consider the voyage to be part of the holiday.

Norfolk Lines
www.norfolkline.com
T 01304 218400 (UK); 0328 289550 (France)
Depart: Dover
Arrive: Dunkerque
Advantages: 20 mins closer to Belgium; fewer queues; no coaches or jolly drunks; wine and beer shop near the port at Dunkerque; some extraordinary deals.
Disadvantages: no foot passengers; limited facilities on board.
Tips: take your own entertainment; after dark they dim the lights so take a torch.

P&O Ferries
www.poferries.com
T 0870 598 0333 (UK); 070 70 77 71 (Belgium); 0825 120 156 (France)
Depart: Dover
Arrive: Calais
Advantages: shortest sea route (75–90 mins); ships every 45 minutes; numerous deals; sea travel is the natural way of the British.
Disadvantages: poor public transport from Calais to Belgium; fare prices can be chaotic.
Tips: Priorité (first-on first-off) is worth it at crowded times; Club Class and Langan's Brasserie are havens of peace for civilised grown-ups; always buy tickets before you get to the port; buy P&O stock and they offer a 50% discount on regular fares.

Seafrance
www.seafrance.com
T 08705 711711 (UK); 0321 468000 (France)
Depart: Dover
Arrive: Calais
Advantages: shortest sea route (75–90 mins); regular crossings; big boats.
Disadvantages: poor public transport from Calais to Belgium.
Tips: always check for deals; look out for the odd micro brew unadvertised behind the bar.

Stena
www.stenaline.co.uk
T 0870 570 7070 (UK).
Depart: Harwich
Arrive: Hook of Holland (Hoek van Holland)
Advantages: the last of the night boats; bikes go free; dinner and breakfast included in the fares; 07.30 unloading at the Hook.

Disadvantages: no foot passengers.

Tips: can be useful for Antwerp, Limburg and northern Liège; early loading for people who want the best seats in the bar; Dutch police occasionally breathalyse incoming drivers; bikes cannot be booked on-line.

Faster craft

Hoverspeed Seacat
www.hoverspeed.co.uk
Depart: Dover
Arrive: Calais
Advantages: fast crossing (45 mins); efficient.
Disadvantages: it's still Calais; not the cheapest.
Tips: do a thorough time-enjoyment cost analysis.

Stena HSS
Depart: Harwich
www.stenaline.co.uk
T 0870 570 7070 (UK).
Arrive: Hook of Holland (Hoek van Holland)
Advantages: a faster way to the southern Netherlands.
Disadvantages: not always fun in bad weather; relatively expensive; limited timetable; little escape from the clutter of humanity; club class not much better.
Tips: Dutch police may breathalyse incoming drivers; for decadent survival take in movie, then dine in the neatly hidden à la carte restaurant.

AIR ROUTES

The emergence of successful low-cost airlines, hand in hand with the expansion of smaller regional airports, had made top value tickets for flights between the UK and Belgium much easier to find for a while. However, following a bust-up between the Belgian authorities and RyanAir, over the use of subsidies to develop Belgian regional airports this all but disappeared.

At the time of going to press the most likely routes to offer cheap fares were these:

BMI

www.flybmi.com
The airline formerly known as British Midland often offers discount flights to Brussels from London Heathrow, Edinburgh, Leeds and Nottingham, separately from their economy operation, Bmi Baby.

RyanAir

www.ryanair.com
Still fly from Prestwick (between Glasgow and Ayr) to Charleroi. They also fly to Eindhoven in the southern Netherlands from London Stansted, which can be of use for Liège and Antwerp.

VLM

www.flyvlm.com
Although it is primarily a business airline VLM often has useful deals from London City to

Air links (Summer 2005)

from to	Antwerp	Brussels	Charleroi	Luxembourg
Birmingham		BA/Sabena		
Bristol		BA/Sabena		
Edinburgh		BMI		
Glasgow International		BA/Sabena		
Glasgow Prestwick			Ryanair	
Leeds Bradford		BMI		
London City	VLM	VLM		Luxair & VLM
London Gatwick		BA/Sabena		BA
London Heathrow		BMI & BA		Luxair
Manchester		BA/Sabena		Luxair
Newcastle		BA/Sabena		
Nottingham East Midlands		BMI		
Southampton		VLM		

Brussels, Antwerp and Luxembourg. They also have a new service from Southampton to Brussels.

A lot more airlines fly to Amsterdam Schiphol, from where there is a direct train to Antwerp and Brussels. Competition is fiercer and so deals come and go, though Easyjet (**www.easyjet.com**) is a good place to start.

International airports are still run mainly for businessmen in a hurry, while regional airports can be social clubs with runways. If you are in luck you might find a J D Weatherspoon's outlet. At Brussels Zaventem the European terminal has no decent beer but the transatlantic terminal has quite a few in its bar and duty free shops.

RECOMMENDED ROUTES

For speed, value and efficiency it is a question of doing your own research for what suits you best. If you actually enjoy travel and are looking for a good all-round experience, we recommend:

- for speed and decadence, first class on Eurostar trains London or Ashford–Brussels
- for the best all-in travel experience, P&O North Sea Ferries Hull–Zeebrugge
- for affordable comfort, P&O club class Dover–Calais
- for cheap speed, VLM Airlines from London City to Brussels off peak

TOUR COMPANIES

As yet no mainstream UK tour company offers packaged tours to the beery delights of Belgium. Two of the Guide's most fervent contributors do operate private tours several times a year to the sort of hand-picked beer emporia that professional tour operators would never persuade to open their doors.

Podge's Belgian Beer Tours

T 01245 354677
E podgehome@blueyonder.co.uk

Although not strictly a tour company, Podge started running annual beer trips from the UK to Belgium in 1994 and from there it snowballed. He now organises tours for friends and friends of friends around five times a year. A typical trip will take in breweries, top cafés, good hotels and restaurants, drawing on an encyclopaedic knowledge of Belgian beer culture and where you can park a coach. Forthcoming tours are known roughly a year ahead and they do speak American, albeit with a Lancashire accent.

White Beer Travels

2 Grasby Crescent, Grimsby DN37 9HE
T 01472 884768   **F** 0800 781 6187
E john@whitebeertravels.com
www.whitebeertravels.com

John White's comprehensive knowledge of the Belgian brewing scene is well illustrated on his company's website. Since retiring from the oil industry he has determined that his latter years will be spent introducing as many foreigners as possible to the European beer scene, with Belgium a particular favourite. White Beer Travels organises tour groups to various European destinations to visit beer festivals, breweries, fine restaurants and beer warehouses with the evening spent crawling round the best beer cafés in town. The exhaustive guides that accompany all this can be downloaded from the website. John will also organise bespoke tours for groups or individuals travelling from abroad for the cost of a deposit.

White Beer Travels on tour

The year of the beer

2005 was designated "Year of the Beer" in the French-speaking parts of Belgium. The effect of this in bolstering the confidence of some breweries is palpable. Businesses previously focussed on cutting each others throats in a post-industrial market that was shrinking, have turned into "farmhouse brewers" with 21st century business plans, encouraging visitors to come to their breweries and strutting their stuff collaboratively at international trade fairs.

Ironically sales of beer in Belgium are unlikely to rise in 2005 despite this initiative. The truth is that in many of the established beer-drinking nations people are drinking less beer. It is significant that in Belgium, as in most other countries, better beers are seeing an increase in sales.

There are early but clear indications that in future, people will be drinking less but drinking smarter. Tomorrow's world may have little place for dull beer. The Guide likes to believe that it is simply ahead of the times.

Being there

This is northern Europe, not outer space. Travelling is easy, local people are generally welcoming and polite but there are enough differences from life at home to make the journeying memorable. For people whose only experience of Belgium has been its motorway system, trust us that the closer you get, the more you will like it.

BASICS

Language

English-speaking tourists should not have too many difficulties being understood in most places. Indeed, cultural awareness is so strong in some areas, such as West Flanders, that you may encounter what is perceived to be fluent Home Counties slang, lor' luvva duck mate.

The language of Belgium's five northern provinces is known correctly as Dutch, though the affectation of calling the folksy Belgian dialect Flemish has caught on in some right-thinking parts.

The language of the five southern provinces of Belgium is an equally folksy version of French. It says something about how this is seen in France that when the BBC series "Allo Allo" was dubbed for a French audience, its producers gave the characters Belgian accents.

There is a German-speaking area in eastern Liège, around Eupen. You may also become aware of a variety of other strangely unrecognisable languages.

In the rural Ardennes, the Walloni dialect survives along with some unique combinations of consonants, accents and vowel sounds. In Luxembourg you may hear Letzebuergisch, a form of Middle German that allows for exclusivity in the Grand Duchy and part of its old Belgian lands. In parts of Brussels and Payottenland they speak a unique patois that is about as comprehensible as Glaswegian or Texan.

Money matters

In most of mainland Europe 1st January 2002 saw the arrival of the Euro (€), similar to the UK pound (£) but exchangeable in more countries, and worth a third less. Like a US Dollar but with a rising value (oops).

Coinage comes as 1, 2 and 5 cents in coppers, 10, 20 and 50 cents in dull brass, and 1 and 2 Euros in twin-tone. All coins are valid throughout the Euro zone, though each nation displays its nationhood on one side.

Notes come at 5, 10, 20, 50, 100, 200 and 500 Euros. Shop and café owners will not thank you for the bigger stuff, which was invented mainly to make life easier for tax evaders, drug traffickers and money launderers.

The best exchange rates are at home banks before you travel. Hole-in-the-wall cash dispensers are everywhere and usually, though not invariably, take UK and US cashcards. If yours displays a Visa, Delta or Maestro you should have few problems.

If the cost of changing money tops 3% then you are being ripped off. Moneychangers (Du: *wissel*; Fr: *bureau de change*) will try it on, particularly in large cities like Bruges and Brussels. The Guide's record was 12.5% in commission, service and bad exchange rate.

Major credit cards are taken in most restaurants and hotels but not always in shops – and facilities may be denied for amounts under €20. It remains rare to find a beer wholesaler that takes any form of credit card.

The expression: "Sorry, our computer only accepts cards from Belgian banks" translates roughly as: "We don't trust foreigners generally and you in particular, so we are only accepting cash." Excessively polite assertiveness will usually rectify the machine's faulty programming.

To open a Belgian bank account is easy if you have a Belgian address but generally requires a €1500 untouchable deposit if you live elsewhere in the EU. For regular travellers it can still pay its way.

Tourist Information

Services for tourism in Belgium are organised nationally, regionally, provincially and town-by-town. With such a wealth of organisation it comes as no surprise that it is often not organised at all, though it is getting a lot better.

Before you set out, www.visitbelgium.com will show you what Americans are offered to entice them over, then log onto www.visitbelgium.co.uk to find what Flanders thinks the British will like.

Down south, it goes without saying that they do things differently. The most impressive and useful sites are the ones run by individual provinces, which we have listed in our section on Specialist Beer Bars.

ACCOMMODATION

In our café sections, the Guide recommends some individual hotels. Our aim is to direct readers to a few places that have impressed inspectors or friends with the comfort or individuality on offer for the price. The Guide grades these roughly as follows:

★ = budget hotels with basic facilities
★★ = typical small hotels, usually family run
★★★ = middle cost comfortable hotels

Helpful hotel websites

www.hotellerie.be is the only site we know that lists every licensed hotel in Belgium. It will give you the address, phone, fax and website details and allow e-mail contact, where these are available. Sadly it does not list their star rating but it is a good place to start. www.toervl.be and www.belgiumtheplaceto.be are the regional tourist office sites.

www.horeca.be and www.horest.be select better quality places with an emphasis on independent ownership.

The net is full of companies that claim to get the best hotel deals in the known universe. Surf as you will. One site we have found to deliver fairly consistently over the last few is www.hotels-belgium.com.

We like family-run small hotels with a bit of personal flare and attention. We rarely include business or luxury hotels as we consider these places are big enough to make their own publicity and in any case tend to be overpriced and disappointing for folks who are really just interested in a place to store their luggage while they tour a few bars and the odd brewery.

The Guide does not consider itself expert at finding or even defining great hotels but if you get a bad deal or come across exceptional accommodation we are always pleased to hear from you on BelgiumGBG@aol.com.

Belgian Hotels

There are over 1,850 licensed hotels in Belgium and most are registered using a clearly defined star-rating system. Unregistered hotels are no longer illegal but tend to be quirky, either not reaching comfort standards or else catering to particular groups.

Licensed hotels display a white "h" on a blue background, plus the official star rating. Unstarred hotels are basic but safe. Five star hotels are international luxury standard. In between the star ratings are determined by a complicated scoring system measuring facilities.

The cheapest rooms encountered while researching this edition cost €30 single, €40 double and were pretty basic. A typical price for a comfortable room with good facilities was €55 single, €75 double, with VAT, service and breakfast included in the price, though some are charged room only.

It is best to book ahead whenever possible. In school holidays places can be full, while in school terms small hotels may take a night off if there are no guests.

Brussels hotels go down in price significantly at weekends and in high summer, when the EU takes a break.

The Ardennes is awash with hotels that are full in July and August and delighted to see you the rest of the time. Some of the better hotels rely heavily on enticing visitors throughout the year for gourmet weekend breaks – with some of these deals little short of astonishing.

Gîtes, Pensions & Holiday Villages

The last two decades have seen the arrival in Wallonia of French-style gîtes and small farmhouses for rent by the week or weekend. The top agency is Belsud (**www.wallonie-tourisme.be**) and their brochure is available direct from all Belgian tourist offices.

Self-contained holiday villages seem to be popping up all over the south of Belgium to complement the longstanding SunParks on the Belgian coast. Standards vary, so read the websites and brochures with a critical eye.

GETTING AROUND

Public transport

A beer tourist who cannot drink because they are driving is a sad sight.

Fortunately train, bus and tram services in most of Benelux are so good that even the most ambitious journey is possible at an efficient speed.

Few tourists who leave the car at home regret it. Most come to understand better just what a shambles the British transport network became between the time of Beeching and the present day.

Belgian Trains

Compared to the UK, trains in Belgium are usually slower, just as tatty, much more frequent and go to lots more places. They do not reach the more obsessive standards of many German, Dutch or French trains.

Timetabling is not as obsessively neat and logical either, except on www.b-rail.be, the generally very navigable English language version of the national network's website. Comprehensive maps of the train system are like hens' teeth. We do not believe one can even be accessed on the website. A complete timetable is the size of a small telephone directory. The pocket ones only deal with main lines.

At stations two timetables are displayed – one for weekdays and the other for weekends and bank holidays. Dutch language timetables often list Wallonian stations by their obscure and largely disused French names and vice versa.

Few trains run after midnight and the few lines serving the Ardennes run only occasional trains. Some services, particularly round Brussels, do not run at all at weekends.

A lot of the saver ticket deals were done away with in 2004 but there are still excellent group tickets for parties of up to five on weekends, public holidays and for the two weeks over Christmas and New Year.

An unhelpful legacy of the old Europe is that trains are not good at crossing national frontiers. You can only cross the Belgian-Dutch border on the Maastricht-Liège and Antwerp-Roosendaal lines. Belgium into Luxembourg is mainly via Brussels-Arlon, with an additional country route going via Liège-Malmedy.

Belgian-French border crossing is easier since the Eurostar and TGV links to Lille. However, there remains no coastal link to the French channel ports. Lille's regular station (Lille Flandres SNCF) has direct trains to Ostend, Kortrijk, Ghent, Antwerp, Mons, Charleroi, Namur and Liège.

The Lille train to Brussels has been replaced by the 38-minute Eurostar jaunt between Brussels South and Euro-Lille. The Thalys high-speed train network runs services on the Paris-Mons-Charleroi-Namur-Liège-Aachen-Cologne, Brussels-Antwerp-Amsterdam and Brussels-Liège-Aachen-Cologne lines. Paris can be reached non-stop from Brussels too.

Buses and Trams

As older British readers may remember, the secret of a successful public transport system is to get bus and rail operators to act in collaboration with each other.

The most obvious manifestation of this approach in Belgium is combined bus, tram and metro tickets found in most large cities. Ordinary tickets usually last an hour, with one-day *stad* passes also available.

The bus and tram network is best reserved for awkward short journeys, rather than long distance hauls. In most places it is likely there will be a bus to within reasonable walking distance of where you want to go, in the not too distant future. Finding it and being sure you got the right one can get interesting.

The Flemish bus company, De Lijn, has a

cumbersome but knowledgeable website in Dutch (**www.delijn.be**). Its Wallonian equivalent, SRWT (TEC) has a marginally more navigable site in French (**www.tec-wl.be**).

The worst area to travel is the Ardennes, where buses are about as frequent as in some of the better parts of rural England. The best ride of the lot is the "Royal" tramway, which runs the length of the Belgian coast from Adinkerke to Knokke, stopping at every resort on the way.

In Flanders, getting to the most remote locations is made easier by the extraordinary Belbus system. This is a minibus that follows a regular route but only runs if at least one customer has booked at least two hours in advance. You tell the operator when you want to travel and where you are headed. They will tell you the exact time you have to be at which stop.

Booking can be quite a pally event. One reader reported using the service to visit Watou from Poperinge. When he told the operator his destination she guessed, correctly that he must be having lunch at the Hommelhof, which she assured him was a good choice. When he proposed returning on the 14.10 bus she politely overruled him on the grounds that he would never finish by then.

Belbus routes can be checked on **www. delijn.be** – follow the province and then *openbaar vervoer*.

The importance of buying a ticket

The only "don't" on Belgian public transport is "don't forget to pay". Late one evening on the coastal tram route your editor encountered the hit squad. On the station platform these guys looked like regular scruffy punters in baggy jackets and denims. When the tram rolled out of the station however, they revealed their true colours, checking tickets with the precision of that Gestapo officer who did for Dickie Attenborough's sidekick in the Great Escape. Two of them were carrying weapons of the bullet-shooting variety, relative safety coming only after the first sixteen rounds. Getting the right ticket has become second nature since then.

Bookings are made on the following numbers:

ANTWERP: **T** 03 218 14 94
EAST FLANDERS: **T** 09 210 94 94
FLEMISH BRABANT: **T** 016 31 37 00
LIMBURG: **T** 011 85 03 00
WEST FLANDERS: **T** 078 15 11 15

We do not know of a similar system down south.

Driving

The speed limits in Belgium are 120 kph (75 mph) on motorways, 90 kph (56 mph) on country roads and 50 kph (31 mph) in the town. Less well known is that there is a minimum speed rule on motorways of 70 kph (45 mph).

For some years, the UK has enjoyed the most expensive fuel in Europe, though the strengthening Euro is helping Belgium to catch up. It still pays to fill up on the way back rather than the way out, especially if you use diesel, which is about 15% cheaper than petrol in much of mainland Europe.

Most of the Belgian economy still closes for business on Sunday, including a substantial majority of filling stations. Automatic dispense is available but often only to holders of obscure Belgian cash cards or, increasingly rarely, bank notes in good condition.

Luxembourg has the cheapest fuel in Europe. If you like obscure tourism, visit the small market town of Martelange, draped along the border between Belgium and Luxembourg. The eastern side of its high street consists of wall-to-wall filling stations, celebrating the fact that fuel tax is 30% lower than over the road.

You will find fuel at all hours in a motorway service area, costing the same as in the rest of Belgium.

Unlike the disgraceful accretion of meaningless brand names that conspire in institutional overpricing at British motorway services, the Belgian equivalents can offer surprisingly good food and facilities at unexpectedly sharp prices. A large play area, well-designed restaurant, prompt polite service, a tourist office, crafts shop or even a comfortable hotel may feature too.

Belgium's major highways are generally well designed and maintained. With the exception of the Brussels Ring, they are rarely inundated with traffic unless there has been an accident. Belgian drivers generally stick to the inside lane and only use the second and third lanes for overtaking. An average speed on long journeys of over 110 kph is usually possible.

The country is also criss-crossed by trunk roads, often long and straight, linking market towns. These "stone roads" (Du: *steenwegen*) used to be cobbled. Some still feel as if they are, being laid in twenty metre rectangles of flat concrete, set at subtly uneven heights so as to rattle even the smoothest suspension. Designed for the 1860s, they had become inadequate by the 1960s and an average speed of 40 kph (25 mph) is more realistic.

Trunk road repairs occur one pothole at a time. Road menders are specially trained to add a little too much tar to sign off their work. For larger repair jobs councils like to mend things one town at a time, cutting off the whole community from the outside world for a month or two. Most repairs happen between May and September, with a long break in the middle for the summer holidays.

The saving grace of trunk roads is that they are often littered liberally with chip shops, flower sellers and fruit and vegetable stalls. On roads frequented by lorry drivers and American troops, you may also find small drive-in bordellos, a concept that could breathe new life into the British notion of a lay-by.

Belgian towns protect themselves from invasion by foreigners through the careful use of road signs. Black writing on an orange background, with a red border means that you have just entered the parish. You only reach the town boundary when you pass a sign with dark blue lettering on a white background. The town should follow in the next half hour or so.

Bilingual town names

The politics of language in Belgium is terribly delicate. The national compromise on who has the right to call where what does not include a rule that foreign drivers should get the odd hint at to where they are. North of the linguistic border town names are expressed in Dutch, while south of it they are in French.

These are the examples we have collected so far of towns with a double identity.

The locally preferred name in **bold** print:

DUTCH	FRENCH
Aalst	Alost
Aat	**Ath**
's Gravenbrakel	**Braine-le-Comte**
Brugge	Bruges
Dendermonde	Termonde
Edinge	**Enghien**
Vloesberg	**Flobecq**
Geraardsbegen	Gramont
's Gravenvoeren	Fouron-le-Comte
Halle	Hal
Hoei	**Huy**
Ieper	Ypres
Kortrijk	Courtrai
Lessen	**Lessines**
Leuven	Louvain
Lier	Lierre
Luik	**Liège**
Rijsel	**Lille**
Mechelen	Malines
Bergen	**Mons**
Moeskroen	**Mouscron**
Namen	**Namur**
Nijvel	**Nivelles**
Oudenaarde	Audenarde
Roeselare	Roulers
Ronse	Renaix
Sint Truiden	Saint Trond
Zinnik	**Soignies**
Tienen	Tirlemont
Tongeren	Tongres
Doornik	**Tournai**
Tubeke	**Tubize**
Veurne	Furnes

The situation is complicated further by the Imperial insistence of the English speaking nations that we can rename the great cities of the world as we see fit if we do not like the local version. Thus we abuse Antwerp (Du: *Antwerpen*: Fr: *Anvers*), Brussels (Du: **Brussel**; Fr: **Bruxelles**), Ghent (Du: **Gent**: Fr: *Gand*) and Ostend (Du: **Oostende**: Fr: *Ostende*), and insist on using the French names *Bruges* and *Ypres* for the correctly Flemish **Brugge** and **Ieper**.

The coastal resort of *De Haan* once gloried in the French name of *Coq-sur-Mer*, which of course means Chicken-on-Sea.

Bicycling

In 1830, when God created Belgium, He was already working on the bicycle.

Cycling in a flat country is a cheap, effective way of getting around. It also burns off the beer and avoids the risk of losing your driving licence, or worse. Even if cycling is not usually your thing, consider it. The rewards are seeing, hearing and smelling the environment while moving through it three or four times faster than on foot, and in many towns faster than you can drive.

Combining it with train travel makes grand touring by pedal power a feasible reality.

Taking your own bike to and from the UK can be tiresome. Some British train operators deserve a big hug, while others may need squeezing in a more focussed way. At ports like Dover and Calais the station is some way from the docks and Ramsgate will need completely re-designing before they let cyclists play among the artics.

Ferry operators usually carry bikes free of charge but some carriers are a problem. The Seacats charge a little while Eurostar charges a lot (unless it is a foldaway) and, for obscure reasons makes you wait a day to load or unload it.

Airlines place the risk with the rider but still charge a special carriage rate of around £10.00–15.00. To acquire least damage in the hold, deflate your tyres, take off the saddle plus any detachable wheels or pedals, and straighten the handlebars, otherwise stick it in a carriage bag. Bubble wrap can protect sharp edges.

Leaving your own bike at home and hiring in Belgium is feasible but can be a bit hit-and-miss. Some local shops offer excellent machines at reasonable prices, while others see travellers as cash cows and rent them basic and old machines for as much per day as they could get for selling them.

Some large and medium size railway stations hire bikes (Du: *fietsverhuur*) with offices open daily from 07.00 to 20.00. Blankenberge, Dendermonde, Brugge *(Bruges)*, Diksmuide, Dinant, Essen, Gent Sint Pieters, Ieper, Herentals, Lobbes, Knokke-Heist, Lier, Oostende *(Ostend)*, Oudenaarde, Puurs, Torhout and Veurne stations are the most reliable. Spa and Vielsalm hire mountain bikes.

You will need ID (passport or equivalent) and a deposit. Hired bikes are usually in excellent mechanical condition but vary from professional to basic.

Railway stations may have lifts and escalators but grooved ramps running alongside flights of stairs are more common. A few do not even bother with these. Brussels Central dislikes cyclists.

Carriage on trains requires a day ticket (Du: *fietskaart*), which costs the same regardless of how far you are going. You are not allowed to carry your bike on with you. A guard must rack it in a special compartment at one end of the train. This involves catching the guard's eye and helping him lift it on board. If anyone knows how you guess which end of the train the guard and this compartment will be, please let us know.

Bikes are barred from commuter trains during the morning and evening rush hours. There is also a maximum number of bikes allowed on board – usually four. Guards are discouraged from allowing more. Questioning their parentage or offering bribes is counterproductive. A sincere and reasoned explanation that a delay will cause you to miss your plane, fail to see your dying grandmother for the last time or else bring untold worry to your young children is also a waste of breath.

In towns and cities, bicycle racks, shelters and other parking places are plentiful. There are far fewer no-go areas and one-way streets than for cars and protected lanes on many major roads. Even in the most heavily pedestrianised areas it is rare to have to get off and push.

In rural areas cycle paths (Du: *fietspad*) abound, particularly alongside rivers and canals, or through woods. These can take you down attractive, fume-free by-ways from town to town often to a more direct route than the main roads. There are maps to cycle ways in every Belgian province (see Guidebooks).

Being drunk in charge of a bicycle is an offence under Belgian law. However, police enforcement is rare unless a cyclist is clearly drunk and dangerous, chooses to behave obnoxiously to others or else causes actual damage. It is far more difficult to kill someone with a bicycle that with a ton of motorised steel.

Boating

Considering the maze of canals and rivers that exists in northern Belgium, it is remarkable that there is so little tradition of pleasure cruising. This is mainly because these are still commercial waterways, albeit in decline.

Freighters up to 7,000 tonnes and strings of massive coal barges can still be seen carrying goods into France and Germany down the Rhine, Meuse and Schelde and along the Albert Canal and others.

Boats over three tonnes cannot legally be barred from the network, though in Belgium lighter boats within this category are only allowed on sufferance and entry to various waterways may be delayed by the local engineers on pretty spurious grounds.

Since the last edition the British company Hoseasons (www.hoseasons.co.uk) has begun to pioneer boat hire in Belgium. Operating out of Nieuwpoort on the coast they recommend week-long and fortnight-long round tours of West and East Flanders, encompassing Ieper, Bruges, Ghent and Kortrijk, plus a small foray into north-eastern France.

Home sickness

Stay in touch with the UK via BBC World, plus BBC 1 & 2 in most three-star hotels. Radio 4 Long Wave (198 KHz AM), Radio 5 Live medium wave (909 KHz AM and others) and the World Service (648 KHz AM) will ensure that you do not lose track of the cricket. Reception is generally poor south of Brussels and east of Leuven.

For those who are missing their Radio 3 or Classic FM, there in a classical radio station in Belgium that sounds remarkably like a hybrid of the two.

You will not need a degree in modern languages to follow most of the rest of the Belgian radio network broadcasts. You learn that awful, repetitive, cynically exploited bland popular songs are also written and performed in French, Dutch and German. What is perhaps more surprising is that you can also follow the purposeless drivel interspersed between tracks without understanding a word of it.

General guides

Every major guidebook producer covers Belgium in one form or another, though some concentrate on the big cities only. Single country guides generally lump Luxembourg in with Belgium. Benelux guides add in the Netherlands.

For basic good quality travel advice you still cannot beat the much-travelled *Rough Guide to Belgium & Luxembourg*, compiled by co-founder Martin Dunford and travel writer Phil Lee, even if they did ask Michael Jackson to write the section on beer last time.

The much improved latest edition of *Lonely Planet Belgium & Luxembourg* is now written by an Australo-Belgian couple, Leanne Logan and Geert Cole, who do not currently employ a major Belgian beer expert to write their frankly rather underpowered section on beer.

For more formally bibbed and tucked information about the region, we recommend the **Michelin Green** guide if you like to see things with a French bias. The German **Baedeker's** guide, published in Britain by AA, is perhaps more balanced in its favours and reliable too.

Although there are numerous other guides on the market – and we try to plagiarise from them all in equal measure if we can – most seem to lack the cosy details, relying more on the recommendations of friendly commercial companies about what to visit.

Most guides approach the subject of beer with bedazzlement or else restrict themselves to saying something naïve about the top InBev lines and a couple of other mass market brews.

Even **Routard**, which generally knows a bit about getting fed and watered, still mentions beer as an amusing aside in what it clearly sees as a country dedicated to drinking imported wines.

The Guide is delighted to be able to continue to claim with some sincerity that it remains unwise for any serious beer lover to step onto Belgian soil without us.

Maps

They are still building new roads in Belgium so, if you are driving, an up-to-date road map is a good idea. Another reason is that accuracy has got a lot better in recent years.

Geocart and **Michelin** tend to come up with the most readable and inclusive road maps in our experience though they come in a variety of scales.

For professional drivers and real obsessives such as the Guide's editor and top contributors, the gold standard atlas is the **Travelmanager Auto-Atlas**, sponsored by TNT and published by Andes of Eindhoven. Thicker than War and Peace and with just as many gags, it lists and shows every street in the country.

Geocart also publishes two sets of province-by-province maps for the cyclist (Du: *fietskaart*; Fr: *carte cycliste*). The simpler ones mark cycle routes on a plain road map. The posher ones add a blow by blow account of the route in much clearer detail.

The railway network produces a timetable and map of the whole system that is essential if you seek to use rail travel a lot. Get it from the information office at larger stations. You may need to use charm and a certain unflappable determination.

Beer books and magazines

There are remarkably few publications in English about Belgian beer.

The Great Beers of Belgium (4th edition – 2001) by Michael Jackson, is a beautifully illustrated, delightfully written book detailing the thoughts of the world's best known beer writer on the world's most interesting ales. Published by the same people as Beer Passion magazine (below), the best purchase price is available via their website on www.beerpassion.com. The magazine itself is no longer published in English but its publishers do mount a successful annual beer festival in Antwerp at the end of June (see Beer Events).

Unterwegs auf den Spuren des Belgischen Bieren (2005 – Grenz Echo Verlag – ISBN 90 5433 201 8) by Ann-Marie Bernardt, is hopefully a portent of things to come. This is the first guide to Belgian beer for the German market. Its 240 pages are well illustrated and packed with information on the history of Belgian beer, the part it plays in the economy and the story of some of the characters on the scene. Numerous beer tours, with maps, show readers around in a practical way.

For the best of the rest you need to be willing to master Dutch.

The Belgian consumer group Zythos publish *Zytholoog* magazine quarterly. It is available to members only with membership available via one of the local branches of the organisation (see Consumer Groups). It lists new beers, keeps up to date with new breweries with reports on their progress and carries news of forthcoming beer festivals. Those who read Dutch will also appreciate that it packs quite a campaigning punch too.

One beautiful book to consider buying in Dutch or French is Jef van den Steen's *Trappist: het Bier en de Monikken* (175pp, Davidsfons of Leuven, €35 plus postage) which outlines the history of Trappist beers and breweries in the context of Belgian history and the monastic tradition.

Café guides

In a bit of blatant self-promotion by its editor the Guide is delighted to recommend readers to *LambicLand* (Cogan & Mater; www.booksaboutbeer.com), the most obscure pub guide ever compiled. Written by Tim Webb and Chris Pollard, with help from Flemish beer writer Joris Pattyn this two-language, full colour book is the only comprehensive guide to the lambic cafés of Brussels and Payottenland and the beer found in them.

There is no strong tradition of beer and café guides in Belgium. Dutch is the first language of only twenty million people worldwide and many of these speak and read English well. French speakers are not yet sufficiently renowned for their love of beer, so publishers duck the challenge.

The one exception is the pair of books published in alternate years by Flemish beer salesman and guide compiler Bob Hendrickx.

Originele Cafés in Vlaanderen (6th edition due in 2005) demands advance purchase of books from cafés who wish to be included. However, Bob only approaches cafés of a pretty high standard. Very few entries disappoint, though only a small proportion have top-rate beer lists. Covers mainly Flanders with a handful in Wallonia, the Netherlands and, for 2005–06, the UK. Cheeky bastard.

The original guide expanded so rapidly that in 2002 he decided to split it in two. *Eetcafés in Vlaanderen* (2nd edition: 2004) follows the same principles and format as the original but features only taverns, brasseries and restaurants, with the emphasis on their food. Both books are written in Dutch but the layout makes them easy to follow. There is always a two-for-one offer on your first beer at any entry.

The only local guide in English worth seeking out is the *Selective Guide to Brussels Bars* by Stephen D'Arcy. Compiled for CAMRA Brussels, it is a constantly up-dated A4 printout (currently 36 pages) about bars, restaurants, off-licences, museums, beer festivals, tram museums, German sausage suppliers, Breton cider and anything else that its editor thinks will amuse a visitor to the Belgian capital.

D'Arcy writes with attitude. We particularly like the advice on how to get to one café a few hundred metres off the beaten track, which is "Walk, you idle sod." Available to UK readers by sending a UK bank cheque for £5.00, payable to "CAMRA Brussels" (for Eurozone send €5.00 cash; for North America US$10.00 cash) to Stephen D'Arcy at 16 Rue Willems (#2013), 1210 Brussels, Belgium.

We have probably seen a dozen national and local books purporting to list the best Belgian beer cafés in the last ten years. The ones that simply plagiarise our listings from previous editions are taken as compliments (though acknowledgement would have been polite, ladies and gentlemen).

The other ones are frankly not up to much with the exception of *Le Guide des Estaminets* (2003) by Amandine Lefèbvre, Dorothée Delecourt and Véronique Boupian-Lelieur. This café guide in French covered the western part of West Flanders and the French border areas of Picardie and Pas de Calais in magazine style. It was packed with useful information, including a list of thirty plus breweries in "French Flanders". Available

from local bookshops and tourist offices for €10.00 if you can still find it. Published by PdN Editions, 229 Rue Salférino, 59000 Lille.

Other books

Quite simply the funniest book ever written about Belgium through the eye of a visitor is Harry Pearson's *A Tall Man in a Low Land: some time among the Belgians* (2000). Pearson writes like a Belgophile. His semi-detached observations on Belgian customs, the habits of the local residents, the history of the country and the national obsession with DIY are hilarious, disparaging and deeply respectful in equal measure. If Amazon ever runs out, steal it from a friend.

FOOD AND DRINK

"*In Belgium they make hundreds of different types of cheese, orange white and blue, hard, soft, goat's cheese and no-one has ever heard of them. In the Netherlands they make two very boring sorts of cheese and the whole world knows about them.*"

HARRY PEARSON, A Tall Man in a Low Land

Belgium may be developing an enviable reputation for its beers but its food remains one of Europe's better-kept secrets. The insularity of local brewing habits extends to culinary traditions too. Couple this with a natural insistence on fresh local ingredients and centuries of respect for the profession of chef and the ultimate result is a gourmet's paradise with a nice sideline in much-loved unique local bar snacks.

The cartoon version of Belgian cooking is that it is all about mussels and chips, topped with mayonnaise and followed by white chocolate truffles. In fact, as you would expect in a country that has been invaded so often by nations of great cooks, the regional styles of Belgian cooking combine many fine culinary traditions. From the simplest pub snack to the seven-course banquet, Belgians know how to eat well.

When touring you only see the public face of a nation's cuisine. Even so the abiding memory brought home by many beer lovers is of "that meal in the restaurant by that fountain place."

Breakfast

Just as Belgium finds itself geographically between France on the Netherlands, so it finds itself also wedged between the traditional Dutch breakfast of cheese, cold meat, bread, sweet spreads and the compulsory egg and the French version of coffee and a roll. If there is a weak spot in Belgian cuisine then this is it.

Breakfast tends to diminish in size and complexity the closer you get to the French border, which can be a blessing. Thinly-sized rubbery cheese, some polluted with caraway seeds, vies with even thinner slices of tasteless processed hams to protect softer palates from rough, dry bread that dries quicker for being pre-sliced at the bakery. A fresh egg is a rare luxury. Maybe it is the purpose of Belgian breakfasts to be dull.

The light lunch

The staple fare of most Belgian cafés is a limited range of pasta, omelettes, croque monsieur and the like. Chilli and tandoori are the emerging British contributions to the list. The international catering affliction called barbecued ribs (Du: *ribbetjes*) has reached Belgian griddle pans along with various forms of kebab (Fr: *brochette*).

Equally dull but more traditional is *uitsmijter*, slices of cold ham on bread, often with mayonnaise and salad, sometimes with cheese and usually topped with three fried eggs. Older British readers may get a flash of nostalgia when seeing an orange yolk, reminiscent of the days when chickens still had feathers.

More exciting is the national version of steak tartare (Du: *cannibaal*, Fr: *Americaine*). This is raw beefsteak pulped in mayonnaise and spread on toast, usually served with pickles, raw vegetables and Worcester sauce, sometimes accompanied by a raw egg yolk. No E coli or BSE here then.

Local variants on cooked dry sausage (Fr: *saucisson sec*) appear everywhere and are a constant source of delight and occasional amazement. Flemish cafés often offer strings of beer sausage (Du: *bierwurst*), best when dried over a frame at the back of the bar.

One of the great joys of light lunching in Belgium is the chance to try local specialities. These are usually modern versions of peasant dishes that gained local popularity through the activity of a few local bakers or pork butchers.

The great Brussels café delicacy is a chicken-based brawn called *kip-kap* – imagine pet food with crunchy vegetable inlay. Calf's head (Fr: *tête de veau*) and pig's head (Fr: *tête pressée*), both brawns made from tongue and cheek, are popular all across the south of Belgium.

Internationally the name "Ardennes" is associated with coarse pâté and thin-sliced, cured ham. In the region itself the array of cold meats is far broader. Indeed traditional Ardennes pâtés contained goose and wild boar. A visit to a specialist shop (Fr: *salaisons*) is a real tourist treat. You should find several dozen varieties of sausage, ham, gammon, bacon, pâté, mousse, brawn, terrine, hash, meatloaf, trotter and hock.

In some parts of the country every market town will have its own take on preparing cooked sausage. One favourite, from Florenville, is made with Orval beer. Others features strong spices, dried fruit, grain or even vegetables.

The French-speaking parts of Belgium have *boudin noir* – that's "noir" as in black and "boudin" as in pudding – a plain blood sausage. The Flemish equivalent *bloedpans* tends to contain bacon. In the north of Liège province they produce a sausage called *lev' gos* in a black pudding style, sweetened with currants.

Boudin blanc is white sausage made with minced pork. Boudins are typically either eaten cold or else heated and served with sprouts, puréed potatoes and a sharp applesauce.

But it is not just the Ardennes that has cold meat specialities. Round West Flanders they have a variety of terrines and jellied meats with names like *potjesvlees*, *tapjesvlees* and *hennepot*. In our experience the use of these terms changes from town to town and café to café. The common theme is that these are usually cold dishes featuring jellied potted chicken, pork and/or rabbit. The jelly is usually some variant on lemon aspic, additional vegetables are optional, and they are sometimes encased in pastry.

Across the Ardennes and in particular around southern Hainaut they have a fishy equivalent to this called *escavêches*. This is a hang-on from the Spanish era, when homesick Galicians used to preserve fish by steeping it in barrels with vinegar, lemon juice and onions. Nowadays the fish tends to be eel or trout. Whether you take it hot or cold, expect a challenge.

Street food

The street snack for which Belgium is most famous is chips (Du: *friten*; Fr: *frites*). These are thin cut, parboiled, lightly salted and then double fried. Although they gave birth to the American concept of "French fries", their quality generally puts the upstart version to shame.

Although *frites* are famously served with mayonnaise, the kiosks that sell them tend to offer a whole range of sauces to dab, squirt or ladle on the top. Particularly in Flanders some will offer stewed meat (Du: *stoofvlees*) as an accompaniment, traditionally made by slow-cooking beef or horsemeat in brown beer.

In some parts of Limburg and Antwerp Dutch-style fish stalls have taken to appearing at local markets. The top local delicacy is raw herring (Du: *maatjes* or *nieuwe haring*). This is typically eaten straight, with chopped raw onion or with pickled dill. Dutch gentlemen of a certain age see it as a natural form of Viagra and ensure they take a single daily dose by mid-morning. Similar stalls on the Belgian coast may feature a pot of hot whelks (Du: *wulken*).

Restaurant food

It is the sign of a great cook that they can make a mean soup from virtually anything. Sadly, soups are out of fashion in modern day Belgian cafés but you may still come across a thick Brabantine vegetable soup (Fr: *potage Brabançon*) made from sprouts, onion, celery, potatoes, rice, eggs, bacon and light ale.

Mechelen has a cauliflower broth, usually prepared with nutmeg.

The Belgians like their little grey shrimps, tiny prawn-like creatures found in inshore waters. A dish that includes them will often take the name *Ostendaise*. The simplest such preparation is a tomato stuffed with grey shrimps in mayonnaise, usually called *tomate crevette*.

Originally from the Netherlands but now taken as Flemish are shrimp croquettes (Du: *garnalenkroketten*), pulped grey shrimps with mayonnaise, covered in breadcrumbs and deep-fried. Huge efforts sometimes go into the preparation of these popular items and despite appearances this is not fast food.

The more famous Belgian obsession with shellfish has more emphasis on the shell.

Mussels (Du: *mosselen*; Fr: *moules*) are prepared in numerous ways, the best known involving them being steamed by the kilo in large pots, in their shells. The stock that brings out their character best contains celery, carrot and onion, usually accompanied by a mix of herbs. Many chefs balance the earthiness of this with the malty sweetness of a blond or amber ale.

Belgian salmon (Du: *zalm*; Fr: *saumon*) and trout (Du: *forel*; Fr: *truite*) tend to be farmed. The more traditional pike (Du: *snoek*; Fr: *brochet*) in sometimes found marinaded then cooked in gueuze.

Eel (Du: *paling*; Fr: *anguille*) is extremely popular on the Belgian coast and comes *Provençale*, in a cream sauce (Du: *roomsaus*; Fr: *à la crème*), or in a traditional chervil sauce (Du: *in 't groen*; Fr: *au vert*).

Monkfish (Du: *zeeduivel* or *staartvis*; Fr: *lotte*) is prized as the chewiest tasty sea fish and is most traditionally cooked in garlic, with vegetables or in a variety of cream sauces. Cod (Du: *kabeljauw*; Fr: *cabillaud*) is less prized in Belgium but ends up chopped and fried in a variety of ways by fish stalls and restaurateurs in Limburg. Sea bass (Du: *zeewolf*) can often be found much cheaper than in the UK, though you may find catfish sold under the same name.

Flat fishes like turbot (Du: *tarbot*) and Dover sole (Du: *zeetong*) are highly rated but rarely found. The traditional Antwerp way of cooking turbot is with chicory in a honey sauce. Plaice (Du: *schol*) and halibut (Du: *heilbot*) tend to be left in the sea for the British to catch.

In Belgium they take a lean cut of beef, expose its edges to volcanic heat for twenty seconds and consider it suitable for consumption. The old British way of preferring steaks grey or cremated brings heartache to most Belgian chefs. So much so that they have invented some cuts of beef that make "cooked through" a physical impossibility.

Côte à l'Os is a lop-sided pyramid of cow that defies all attempts to turn its inside even vaguely pink. *Pavé* is a thick, chunky steak.

The five big sauces to eat with steak and chips in Belgium are *Béarnaise* (a butter sauce with tarragon), *Provençale* (tomato, pepper, onions and garlic), *Archiduc* (mushrooms in cream), *Poivre Vert* (green peppercorns, brandy and cream) and *Roquefort* (blue cheese, sometimes with beer).

Lamb (Du: *lamsvlees*; Fr: *agneau*) is more often found in southern Belgium, usually with garlic and rosemary. Pork (Du: *varkenvlees*; Fr: *porc*) is making a comeback in better restaurants due largely to the perception of hard times. The Belgians have not yet mastered crackling.

Offal is still found on the menus of more traditional restaurants, again with local variants.

Liège specialises in kidneys (Fr: *rognons Liègeois*). The old-fashioned version was a stew made with smoked gammon strips, juniper berries and the local spirit, pékèts. The modern way is to present these in a mustard cream sauce, sometimes including shallots or stewed garlic cloves, sometimes termed *Dijonnais* or *Jamboise*.

In Brussels, *choesels* is calf's pancreas, typically marinaded in Madeira then stewed with oxtail and lambic. Be warned that *cerveilles* means brains, usually from sheep, and that *raie* means thyroid, usually from bulls. Liver is what you put in pâtés.

Some parts of Flanders are very keen on what they term "grandmother's cooking". The cartoon version of this is to use a lot of lard and then stewed at a low temperature for eons. *Carbonnade* is loosely a restaurant version of the chip stall's *stoofvlees* (above), with a heavy brown ale added an hour or so before completion.

Ragoût was originally a stew made from offal and meat scraps. *Hochepôt* or *hutsepot*, much like the British hotpot, is a winter vegetable stew, typically made with salt pork belly, stewing beef or shoulder of mutton.

Waterzooi is a Ghent dish, featuring chicken boiled in an aromatic broth, eaten with boiled potatoes or bread. Goose (Du: *gans*; Fr: *oie*) can be cooked in the same way. Fish waterzooi is probably a more recent invention, though food historians have rows about this.

Game

If God means it to live wild the Belgians will protect the lands it lives in, ensure it has shelter and feed, then let it free, shoot it and cook it in a really great sauce.

The Ardennes is famed for its game. All manner of species can appear on a full Ardennaise menu. This might include wild boar (Du: *everzwijn*, Fr: *marcassin*), rabbit (Du: *konijn*, Fr: *lapin*), hare (Du: *haas*; Fr: *lièvre*), venison (Du: *wildbraad*; Fr: *cerf*), roe deer (Du: *ree*; Fr: *chevreuil*); pheasant (Du: *fazant*; Fr: *faisan*), partridge (Du: *patrijs*; Fr: *perdrix*), snipe (Du: *snip*; Fr: *bécassine*), quail (Du: *kwartel*; Fr: *caille*) and wild duck (Du: *wilde eend*; Fr: *canard*).

The typical ways of serving game will be either stewed until hard and blackened, or else fast roast till crisp outside but blood red throughout.

For deer, there are different recipes and styles of cooking for buck and roe.

Pheasant is sometimes stuffed with and accompanied by chicory.

Hare can also come stuffed but the more usual way to cook it is as *hazepeper*. Pieces of hare are quick-roasted, covered in black pepper, salted, thyme and laurel, then stewed with shallots, cream and red wine. We have seen it also "jugged" British style with redcurrant jelly and brown ale.

Rabbit in mustard is very Ghent. In Payottenland it is cooked in gueuze.

Poultry

The most popular way to cook chicken (Du: *kip*; Fr: *poulet*) in recent years has been on a spit, often vertically, and then serve it with apple sauce.

Chicken breast cooked in a pan is served with various butter, cream or other sauces.

The Belgians like their not-so-wild duck cooked pink with a juniper (Du: *jeneverbes*; Fr: *genièvre*), orange or redcurrant sauce. A favourite in Payottenland is *magret* of duck cooked in cherries and a cherry lambic. Orange is another popular fruit sauce.

As in France, *confit d'oie* and *confit de canard* suggests preserved goose or duck meat, stewed in its own fat. One of the worlds' top recipes for poultry, but perhaps not one for the diet. Turkey does not feature often but you will see stewed, roasted and baked guinea-fowl (Du: *parelhoen*; Fr: *pintadeau*) on some menus.

Vegetables

Being vegetarian in Belgium is not easy. On the other hand, eating amazingly created vegetables is no bother.

In the Ardennes, vegetables are typically parboiled then tossed and cooked in butter. One meal we ate, for example, was accompanied by green beans wrapped in thin ham, a single Brussels sprout in nutmeg, a purée of artichoke, two carved parsnip pieces, a Julienne of shredded leek and carrot, a sticky red cabbage jam and a couple of small balls of mashed potato deep fried in batter.

White chicory (Du: *witloof*; Fr: *endive*) was originally cultivated by Belgian farmers between Brussels and Mechelen. It can be chopped and braised in butter, stuffed with chopped meat or wrapped in ham and roasted, often then served in a cheese sauce.

Brussels sprouts, ironically less authentically Belgian, are picked large, as they still are in some parts of northern England. They are parboiled then browned in butter or pork dripping and baked. They can come with chopped bacon and maybe some nutmeg too.

Asparagus is preferred white. Cooking it in the Flemish way (Du: *Vlaamse asperge*; Fr: *asperges à la Flamande*), the spears are steeped in melted butter and onion before boiling. They are then served with chopped egg, parsley and melted butter or a butter sauce.

Aalst is famous for its onions and *Aalsterse brei* is onions boiled in milk and beef stock.

Hop shoots (Du: *hoppescheuten*; Fr: *jets d'houblon*) are a Poperinge speciality in March and early spring. They are served raw in salads. Alternatively they can be boiled and served in a mouseline sauce with poached eggs or butter and cream. In the West Flanders hop fields they are called *jonge hommelen*.

Stoemp is classic Bruxellois pub grub, mashed potato with swede, carrot, parsnip and/or turnip.

Pastries and puddings

Both Belgian pâtisseries and restaurants do puddings and deserts big time. However, these tend to be a conglomerate from the best in Europe and few are typical of the country.

Waffles (Du: *wafelen*; Fr: *gauffres*) are found everywhere but are best in Brussels. Pancakes (Du: *pannekoeken*; Fr: *crêpes*) are good everywhere. Both are just excuses for a huge variety of sauces, some of which are savoury. Homemade ice creams are not quite up to Italian standards but get close.

Geraardsbergen has the *mattetaart* while Wallonia has the *matton*, a sweetish baked cheesecake tart.

The *marzarine* of West Flanders is a cake-like desert served in a cinnamon butter sauce.

Black côrin is dried fruits cooked with sugar. In *white côrin* they are cooked with rice and cream cheese.

Cheese

Any reader who shares the aim of your editor's daughters to try every cheese in the world before Christmas will have their work cut out in Belgium. Although the country may well manufacture many hundreds of varieties few are sold widely and so exploration involves mainly lucky discovery in specialist local shops.

Of those that are marketed with a little more consistency, few are exported and so the imagery is made familiar.

You will find semi-soft cheeses, often of the orange-rinded Port Salut style, from *Chimay, Orval, Westmalle* and *Westvleteren*, plus *Postel, Affligem, Floreffe, Maredsous, Corsendonk* and *Val-Dieu.* Any names ring a bell? The term Abbey cheese comes to mind.

Chimay is keen to export its four cheeses, the original, a *lait cru*, an aged cheese and a beer cheese, along with its beers. They are experimenting with a goat's cheese.

Fromage de Bruxelles is a strongly salty cream cheese eaten traditionally with stronger flavoured beers. Radishes, spring onion and thinly sliced horseradish (Du: *ramenas*; Fr: *radis noir*) might accompany cream cheeses eaten with lambic.

Maandjeskaas comes from Beersel, *schepkaas* from St. Pieters-Leeuw and *betchée* from Jodoigne

The cheese that is coming to epitomise Belgian country cheeses is *Herve*, from northern Liège. Somewhere along the lines of an epoisse, this square-set soft cheese with its natural washed rind has such a, shall we say characteristic aroma that it is impossible to bring home unless you are willing to have the car valeted and all passengers steam-cleaned before returning to work. Try to catch it locally, typically serve with a double-cooked apple and pear syrup as *romedoe met stroop*.

Others to look out for include soft cheeses called *Madreret, Paillardin* and *Trou d'Sottai*, hard cheeses called *Beauvoorde, Ambiorix* and *Sezoen*, and blue cheeses such as *Bleu de Franchimont* and *Château d'Arville*.

Matching beer to food

If wines can be matched to foods then why not beers? And where better than the nation of four hundred beer styles?

The traditional accompaniment to authentic lambic is soft cheese and radishes. For Ardennaise game stews we recommend a heavy brown ale.

Chimay beers are said to do well with basil, Orval with sage, Rochefort with juniper, Westvleteren with ginger and Westmalle with thyme.

But a word for the unwary.

Readers may or may not known that the great British tradition of the Ploughman's Lunch, whereby Cheddar cheese and a crusty loaf became the natural accompaniment of a pint of best bitter, was actually invented by a Government agency, the Milk Marketing Board, in collaboration with a national brewery, through a clever promotion over some years in the licensed trade.

So the suggestion that an awful lot of this beer-food pairing stuff is just a lot of self-serving hooey might not be entirely off the mark. The Guide is genuinely undecided. If you hit a pairing that really works for you, let us know on BelgiumGBG@aol.com.

Coffee

The drink they named Belgian pubs after.

It may he hard to believe but coffee is the mainstay of Guide café inspectors. One memorable inspection trip some years ago, to the then uncharted rural parts of Hainaut featured your editor developing visual hallucinations while marvelling at the pitifully slow reaction times of other drivers. That is what seventeen cups in a day can do.

While the coffee is strong and repetitive, tea tends to be flabby in quality but substantial in variety. And Belgians still do not understand that dipping a tea bag in a cup of warm water is not really what it is about.

Genever and other spirits

The British have gin, infused with extracts of juniper and dried orange peel and the Dutch have jenever, a clear grain-based spirit served from stone bottles. These translate into *genever* in Flanders (Fr: *genièvre*) and *pékèts* in Wallonia.

Genevers are mainly produced by one large distillery (Smeets of Hasselt), which sponsors the excellent Nationaal Jenevermuseum in the town (see Beer Tourism).

The tendency over the years has been to downgrade the ingredients, quicken brewing and distillation methods and produce a clearer spirit that is increasingly "clean", or tasteless if you prefer. Craft genevers still exist and the best examples come from the older, smaller producers, of which only a few remain.

Names to look out for are St Pol of Kortrijk in West Flanders, Filliers of Bachte-Maria-Leerne near Deinze in East Flanders and Van Damme of Balegem, also in East Flanders.

Down south the only company still making *pékèts de Wallonie* is the Biercée distillery in the town of the same name, south-west of Charleroi in northern Hainaut, where tours and tastings are possible.

The Radermacher distillery, at Raeren in the German-speaking canton of eastern Liège, makes a juniper-based genever that is close to English style gin, as well as a range of fruit spirits. It also commissions a range of juniper-spiked beers from the Val-Dieu brewery in nearby Aubel.

Eaux de vie, fruit genevers and a variety of liqueurs (Du: *likeurs*) also appear. The best of these are based on the spirits made by the genever distilleries, though other spirits-blending companies are also in on the act, buying in alcohols and mixing them with flavour concentrates to create image drinks for the gullible classes, as British and American spirits manufacturers do.

Wines

The Belgian wine industry officially died out in the late 20th century. However, recent years have seen a resprouting of vine cultivation in Hageland (Brabant), Haspengouw (Limburg), Heuvelland (West Flanders) and Pays de Gaume (Luxembourg). Local wines have found a sympathetic audience, much as English wines have, with some better quality vintages emerging.

Fruit wines crop up over an increasing area of the Ardennes. There is a commercial but catchy strawberry wine made in Wépion, south of Namur and we have seen a variety of interesting fruit wines in western Hainaut.

The Guide is always interested to hear of new craft wines, ciders and spirits, locally made cheeses and other local delicacies on BelgiumGBG@aol.com.

Beer tourism

THE INCREASING INTEREST in quality Belgian beers across Europe and the rest of the world is reflected in the many beer-related tourist attractions that are springing up across the country. They range from the mundane via the quirky to the spectacular and may deal with their subject in all ways from the bland and superficial to the meticulously technical.

Specialist museums

It is a good rule in Belgium that if something has been around for more than twenty years, there will be a museum dedicated to its history and the celebration of its diversity. And so, inevitably, brewing has more than its fair share of museums.

Most are either extensions of a brewery or some other commercial enterprise in the beer business. Others are the weekend obsessions of collectors. Some are badly in need of a makeover, particularly in how they present interesting facts and the relevance of their exhibits.

Enthusiasm usually shines through and many are run by the most extraordinary characters. Communication is not always reliant on words. We welcome feedback on BelgiumGBG@aol.com

Brewery visits

Breweries were once keen to keep people away from their premises, believing that the magic spell of their products might be ruined if drinkers saw the stark industrial reality of how they are produced. However, although some understandable reservations remain about revealing industrial secrets and acquiring people-borne brewing infections, most companies now see visits by the public as good public relations.

For many smaller companies visits are also seen as a chance to sell some beer.

There are many ways of visiting breweries. Most will welcome tour groups. Some have regular tours at fixed times of the week to which you can just roll up. Increasingly popular are brewery open days, sometimes involving a brewing demonstration.

In regard to information gleaned from such trips, an old friend who had studied philosophy used to ask the question "When is a fact not a fact?" to which the best answer was always "When it is a fact."

If you cannot get to see a brewery the next best thing is often to visit the brewery tap (Du: *proeflokaal*). This is typically a café or sampling room inside, at or near the brewery's front gate. The Guide lists all known brewery taps under "Brewery cafés" in its province-by-province café listings.

THE BREWERY VISITOR'S CODE

This agreement is held unofficially but unerringly to pertain to the behaviour of the parties of the first part and parties of the second part in the matter of visiting breweries. The code imposes no duties on either party but should be ignored at your peril.

I the undersigned, hereinafter referred to as the visitor, hereby agree that I shall **never**:

- Turn up intoxicated, talking loudly and knowledgeably to my friends throughout the tour
- Allow my children to run off and play with the malt grinder or throw gum in the kettles
- Demonstrate by facile questions that this is the third brewery I have visited this trip
- Remove any brewery artefacts whatsoever
- Demonstrate anything but surprise and huge appreciation when offered a beer at the end of the tour
- Believe a word uttered by any tour guide not responsible for making the stuff themselves
- End the tour by asking the brewer how much syrup they add to their beers
- Refuse to buy the attractively positioned mixed case of the most drinkable beers in the place.

I the undersigned, hereinafter referred to as the brewer, hereby agree that I shall **always**:

- Start the tour by gauging how much bull this particular group is likely to swallow
- Take extreme liberties with the factual description of my family, its brewery and our products
- Look hurt and offended when anyone suggests I use 30% maize flour in my mash
- Precede all examples of out-and-out lying with the phrase "I will tell you honestly..."
- Completely ignore long-suffering stragglers who just want to get to the bar and sit down
- Treat with extreme caution any visitor carrying a copy of the *Good Beer Guide to Belgium*
- Appear humbled by the generosity of any visitor who buys a mixed case of my beer to take away
- Remember that I need to hire some nice bimbette from the tourist office to do these tours in future.

The bearer agrees that all is fair in love, war and commerce and that any information or opinion that passes between us will be strenuously denied, particularly when it was exchanged in the tasting room many hours after the tour had finished.

We love each other. You are my best friend.

_____ (VISITOR) _____ (BREWER)

ANTWERP

BREENDONK

Brouwerij Duvel Moortgat
65 Breendonkdorp
T 03 860 94 00   **E** info@duvel.be
www.duvel.be

Although the brewery visit slots are strictly for groups the company is happy to slip a few extra people into the tour, if you ring or e-mail in advance. Which is fine unless you manage, like one reader, to get on the only Polish-speaking trip of the year. The new tasting room will come on stream in 2006. Entry €1.00 (2004) includes a beer.
Mon–Fri 09.00, 14.30 & 18.30

MECHELEN

Brouwerij Het Anker
49 Guido Gezellelaan
T 015 28 71 44   **E** het.anker@pandora.be
www.hetanker.be

There are no fixed times for brewery tours here but ring up in advance and they can usually suggest one. The old brewhouse is a living museum. Entry €3.50 (2004) includes a beer.

BRUSSELS

BRUSSELS (CITY CENTRE)

National Brewery Museum of Belgian Brewers
Maison des Brasseurs, 10 Grand'Place
T 02 511 49 87
E belgian.brewers@beerparadise.be
www.beerparadise.be

The brewers' guild house on Brussels' magnificent Grand'Place housed until recently the national organisation that represented Belgium's brewers. Following its demise a more independent organisation was formed by several of the old management team, who continue to do an excellent job of promoting Belgian beers around the world. They continue to run the small museum in its basement, where both craft and high-tech brewing are explained in a short presentation. Entry €3.00.
Daily 10.00–17.00

BRUSSELS (ANDERLECHT)

Cantillon Brewery & Museum of Gueuze
56 Rue Gheude
T 02 521 49 28   **E** info@cantillon.be
www.cantillon.be

Cantillon may appear to be a brewery and do indeed brew and store top-rate lambic beers but according to the authorities they are a museum and preserved monument. In practice you can roll up and wander round at most of the times listed below. If anyone is around they may give you a guided tour. Ring ahead to be sure. View the brewing equipment, the partly open roof above the cooling vessel, and the rows of oak tuns in which the lambic ferments. There is a small drinking area and an informal shop selling the beers and other lambic-based products. Entry €3.50 (2004) includes a beer. The best visits are on the public brewing days, usually on the first or second Saturday in March and November, with activities running from 06.00 to 18.00. There are occasionally other events through the year.   CLOSED SUNDAY
Sat 10.00–17.00; *Other days* 09.00–17.00

Cantillon's Van Roy father and son

BRUSSELS (SCHAERBEEK)

Schaerbeek Beer Museum
33–35 Avenue Louis Bertrand
T 02 734 63 66

Small beer museum north of the city centre, with collections of bottles, glasses, beer mats, advertising materials, brewing equipment and a dray. Entry €3.00 (2004) includes a beer. €15.00 buys you membership of its league of friends. Group tours by arrangement.
Wed & Sat 14.00–18.00

EAST FLANDERS

BELSELE

Huisbrouwerij Boelens
Kerkstraat 7, 9111 Belsele   T 03 772 32 00
E brouwerij.boelens@pandora.be
www.proximedia.com/web/boelens.html

They brew on Saturdays and don't mind people watching. Call in advance to check it is happening. Their beer warehouse also has a tasting facility (closed Su&Mo; others 13.30–18.00; Sa only 09.00–12.00).

BRAKEL

Brouwerij De Graal
Warande 15
T 055 42 47 90   E info@degraal.be
www.degraal.be

Roll up to watch brewing most Saturdays of the year. The best action is usually in the morning. Attendance with an explanation costs €5.00 and includes at least one beer.
Sun 09.00–16.00

ERTVELDE

Biermuseum
36 Kuipstraat   T 09 344 81 47

Small café in the basement of a house in a residential street off the N458 to Kluizen, serving about 30 beers. The big attraction is the display of over 6000 glasses and 5000 beer bottles from around the world.
CLOSED TUEDAY & WEDNESDAY
Sat 14.00 onwards; *Sun* 10.00 onwards
Other days 18.00 onwards

FLEMISH BRABANT

EIZERINGEN

In de Verzekering Tegen de Grote Dorst
45 Frans Baetensstraat   T 02 532 58 58
www.dorst.be

Marguerite decided to retire on Christmas Eve 1999, at the age of 85, closing the doors of the little lambic café she had run for fifty-one years. And that would have been the end of the story had the Paneel brothers not set about preserving its former simplicity for future generations. Five years and one

potentially terminal fire later, the rebirth of the "Insurance Against Great Thirst" has now been completed. Its two magnificently restored old bars only open to the public on Sundays and public holidays though they take booking for private functions, tour groups and funerals at St Ursula's Church opposite. The bar stocks perhaps the best range of lambic beers on the planet.
Sun 10.00–13.30

GOOIK

De Cam Cultureel Centrum
67a Dorp   T 02 532 21 32

This museum of village life houses the impressive old Pilsener Urquell oak casks of the newest gueuze blender and lambic fermenter. There is a café on site selling all the beers as well as there being two other beer-loving cafés in the parish (see Flemish Brabant).
CLOSED MONDAY; *Other days* 11.00–18.00

LEMBEEK

Brouwerij Boon
65 Fonteinstraat   T 02 356 66 44

One from the informative end of the spectrum. Meet at the Kring café (see Flemish Brabant) on a Wednesday afternoon in July or August and you can join a tour of this extraordinary brewery and lambic store. With luck this will be conducted by the man himself, a walking encyclopaedia of brewing and all things lambic. Be warned not to ask a question to which you do not want a comprehensive answer. We are talking a potent combination of passion and knowledge here. Entry €5.00 (2004) includes a beer.   *Wed* 15.00 *(Jul&Aug)*

HAINAUT

BAILEUX

Bières de Chimay
8 Route Charlemagne   T 060 21 03 11
E info@chimay.com   www.chimay.com

The brewery at the Abbaye de Scourmont may not be visited. The Chimay bottling plant in nearby Baileux is open to casual visitors in the Easter holidays *(Tu–Fr* 10.00–13.30).

ECAUSSINNES

Brasserie d'Ecaussinnes
118 Rue de Restaumont
T 067 34 22 77   **E** bras.ultra@skynet.be
www.brasserieecaussinnes.be

Regular brewery tours throughout opening hours (see Hainaut: Brewery cafés) include the brewhouse, the lagering tanks and the new bottling line. Entry €3.00 (2004) includes a beer.

ELLEZELLES

Brasserie Ellezelloise
75 Rue Guinaumont
T 068 54 31 60   **E** ellezelloisbr@tiscalinet.be
www.brasserie-ellezelloise.be

This unusual brewery in the rural part of northern Hainaut keeps a real open door policy. You are more likely to get shown round the brewery if you are there in the afternoon and if you ring in advance. Just as a hint, there is a drive-in loading area just next to the brewhouse and a café upstairs (see Hainaut: Brewery cafés). Entry €2.50 (2004) includes a beer.
Sun 09.00–12.00; 15.00–19.00
Other days 09.00–19.00

PIPAIX

Brasserie Dubuisson
28 Chaussée de Mons
T 069 67 22 22   **E** info@br-dubuisson.com
www.br-dubuisson.com

There is a turn-up-and-pay tour round the brewery every Saturday throughout the year, starting in the new café (see Hainaut: Brewery cafés). The visit includes the small museum. Entry €5.00 or €6.50 (2004), depending on how seriously you want to investigate the product.   *Sat* 15.00

Brasserie à Vapeur
Rue de Maréchal 1, 7904 Pipaix-Leuze
T 069 66 20 47   **E** info@vapeur.com
www.vapeur.com

To see what is probably the last fully operational steam-powered brewery in the world in action turn up on the last Saturday of each month at 09.00. The highlight is the 12-HP

Pukkah foudres at Dubuisson

steam generator that powers the water pump, gristmill, mash stirrer and virtually every other moving part in the brewing process. Alternatively join a guided tour on Sunday. Entry to either costs €4.00 and includes a beer. Book ahead and they will offer lunch with a full *dégustation* of all the beers for €20.00 a head. They are phone-call and e-mail friendly.   *Sun* 11.00

RAGNIES

Distillerie de Biercée
Ferme de la Cour, 36 Rue de la Roquette
T 071 50 00 50
E info@distilleriedebiercee.com
www.distilleriedebiercee.com

The Wallonian distillery that is responsible for most of Belgium's fruit liqueurs, *eaux de vie* and those "*pékèts*" so beloved of the Liège. It only agreed to open its doors to the public in Spring 2004, as part of a new approach to business. They pose the question "How does 10 kg of fruit get turned into one bottle of spirits?" and then answer it. Guided tours at 11.00 and 15.00 (plus 14.00 & 16.00, Jul-Aug). Group visits by arrangement at other times.
CLOSED OCTOBER TO MARCH
CLOSED MONDAY (*Sep-Jun*)
Other days 10.00–18.00

WARNETON

Museum of the Brasserie de la Poste
Rue Pierre de Simpel   T 056 55 54 04

We know very little about this museum except that it is a recreation of the "Post Office" brewery, built in 1857 by the Vanwindekens family, who had been brewing since the 17th century. It was destroyed in the First World War but rebuilt and enlarged on the same site. All the equipment is said to be still in place and there is a project underway to restore the building. We believe it can be visited but apologise if we have sent you on a wild goose chase.

LIÈGE

ANTHISNES

Avouerie d'Anthisnes
19 Avenue de l'Abbaye   T 04 383 63 90

The "avouerie" was the home of an old-time man of law. The collection of breweriana is at present housed in one large room but in a few years it is hoped to re-open the old brewhouse (Fr: *brassine*) in another wing, to house the rest of the artefacts. The museum commissions two unusual special beers via Corman-Collins from Silly brewery. The best bit is the drive to get here, through one of the hilliest and prettiest parts of the Ardennes.
CLOSED JANUARY; CLOSED MONDAY
Other days 12.00–18.00

LIMBURG

BOCHOLT

Bocholter Brouwerijmuseum
53 Dorpsstraat
T 089 48 04 80 (group visits)
T 089 46 04 94 (summer visitors)
E info@bocholterbrouwerijmuseum.be
www.bocholterbrouwerijmuseum.be

The best of all Belgium's museums of brewing is sadly kept behind closed doors for most of the year, unless you book as a group of 20 or more or use the conference facilities on the site. However, in high summer this much-praised collection has now been opened up

for public viewing by its owners, Martens brewery. There are lengthy guided tours at 13.30 and 15.30, which end with a tasting. Entry €4.95 includes a beer.
Daily 13.00–18.00 (Jul & Aug only)

HASSELT

Nationaal Jenevermuseum
19 Witte Nonnenstraat
T 011 23 98 60   www.hasselt.be

Not a beer in sight, in this beautifully restored 19th century distillery. The splendidly laid out museum tells the story of distillation in the home town of the country's largest genever distiller, Smeets. Its shop is reputed to sell every known brand of Belgian genever including its own brand and a cherry brandy (Du: *kriekgenever*). Entry €3.00 (2004) includes a shot, €1.00 (aged 12 to 18), younger children free. There is a restaurant opposite called the Borrelhuys, which specialises in cooking with the stuff!
CLOSED MONDAY
Sat & Sun 13.00–17.00 (Nov–Mar)
Other days 10.00–17.00

HELCHTEREN

Kasteelbrouwerij De Dool
21 Eikendreef
T 011 60 69 99   E info@terdolen.be
www.terdolen.be

The café at the Dool brewery is open throughout the week in summer (see Limburg: Brewery cafés) and group tours of the brewery are available by arrangement on most days. There are also two pay-on-the door tours at weekends all year, as shown. Entry €5.00 (2004) includes a beer.   *Sat & Sun* 15.00

LUXEMBOURG

ACHOUFFE

Brasserie d'Achouffe
32 Achouffe
T 061 28 94 55   E info@achouffe.be
www.achouffe.be

There is a tour slot every morning at 10.30. Theoretically these are for groups of at least

10 people but they are practical at Achouffe and a quick word with Jean-Luc on the above number will tell you whether there is a group you can latch onto. Turning up on spec is risky. Entry €5.00 (2004) includes a beer, a glass and a postcard home.

BOUILLON

Brasserie de Bouillon
Grand' Rue 22, 6830 Bouillon
E brasserie.de.bouillon@belgacom.net
T 061 46 89 40

The real reason to come here is the excellent range of beers on sale in the Marché de Nathalie beer shop that was a forerunner to the microbrewery at the rear. The sideshow is that brewing and bottling can go on at any time. Phoning or mailing ahead might be a good idea. The new brewery will cater better for touring.
CLOSED MONDAY TO WEDNESDAY (Sep–Jun)
Others days 09.00–18.30

NAMUR

FAMIGNOUL

Brasserie Caracole
Côte Marie-Thérèse 86
T 082 74 40 80   E caracole@namur.be

Individual visitors can tour on any day in July and August, with guided visits in French, Dutch and English at 14.00, 15.00, 16.00 and 17.00 every day. Group tours can be arranged all year round. The tasting room is open to all on Saturdays and you might be able to latch on to a tour. Entry €5.00 (2005) includes a taste of all four beers.   Sat 14.00–19.00 (all year)
Daily 13.00–19.00 (Jul & Aug)

LUSTIN

Musée des Bières Belges
19 Rue de la Gare   T 081 41 11 02
www.museebieresbelges.centerall.com

This extraordinary collection of over 13,000 old bottles and glasses maps the history of brewing in Belgium. Housed in a converted pub (see Namur) and run by amiable fanatics. There is a beer tasting on the third weekend

of the month and they hold breweriana fairs. Entry €1.50 (2002) includes a beer, €1.00 for children includes a soft drink. Group visits by arrangement can include cooking with beer. Also open when there is a bank holiday, plus Fridays in school holidays. Sadly family illness is limiting some visits so try to phone ahead.
CLOSED MONDAY TO THURSDAY (Sep–Jun)
Other days 11.00–9.30

MARIEMBOURG

Brasserie des Fagnes
26 Route de Nismes
T 060 31 39 19   E mail@brasseriedesfagnes.be
www.fagnes.com

This large modern house brewery has a bit of a prefabricated feel to it but houses relics of the old Degauquier brewery of Chimay. The spanking new, squeaky-clean brewhouse that produces the small run beers for the attached café (see Namur: Brewery cafés) is in sharp contrast. Guided tours are for groups only.
CLOSED MONDAY
Tue–Thu 15.00–21.00 (Oct–Mar)
Other days 10.00–21.00

PURNODE

Brasserie du Bocq
4 Rue de la Brasserie
T 082 61 07 90   E brasserie@bocq.be
www.bocq.be

Open on Saturday and Sunday afternoons from April to the first week of November for a guided brewery tour at 15.00. Daily tours in July and August at 14.00 and 16.00. Entry €4.00 includes a beer, €3.00 for children (2004).

ROMEDENNE

Gambrinus Drivers Museum
2a Fontaine St.Pierre
T 082 67 83 48

The only museum in the world dedicated to brewery transport. If you are drawn to the eccentricities of Belgian life, come here. A unique collection from reconstructed horse-drawn drays of the middle ages to some of the more unusual petrol-driven transporters of the 20th century. Not the work of a quiet collector but the obsession of a man driven

by a passion beyond his control. Housed in a 19th century disused brewery and maltings stuffed with breweriana. Teamed with the Caracole brewery in Falmignoul (above). There is a bar and eatery. Entry €5.00 (2004).
CLOSED NOVEMBER TO MARCH
CLOSED MONDAY TO FRIDAY *(Sep–Jun)*
Other days 11.00–19.00

Just over the border in France the **Musée Européen de la Bière** (Rue de la Citadelle, Stenay – **T** 03 29 80 68 78 – closed Tu; closed Nov–Mar; others 10.00–18.00) is well worth a detour.

WEST FLANDERS

ALVERINGEM

De Snoek Mout en Brouwhuis Museum
40 Fortem   **T** 058 28 96 74
www.desnoek.be

By the Fortembrug canal bridge on the out-skirts of Alveringem. The "Pike" is a labour of love housed in a protected building that was once the old village brewery. Wander round an easy-to-follow exhibit demonstrating old-style malting and brewing processes, with written guides in Dutch, French, English and Braille. The restoration retains the original 19th century coppers and other equipment. There is a café (see West Flanders) serving a beer from every West Flanders brewery, plus snacks. Entry €3.50 includes a beer, €2.50 without, €1.50 child (2004).
CLOSED MONDAY; CLOSED TUESDAY *(Sep–Jun)*
Wed–Sat 14.00–17.30 *(Sep–Jun)*
Other days 10.30–18.30

BRUGES

De Halve Maan (Straffe Hendrik)
26 Walplein
T 050 33 26 97   **E** info@halvemaan.be
www.halvemaan.be

The currently unused brewery can be visited throughout the year. The highlights of the 45-minute tour are the Baudelot wort cooler and the view of Bruges from the top of the building. Entry €3.70 (2004) includes a Straffe Hendrik beer in the café (daily 11.00–18.00) at the end.   *Daily* 11.00–15.00

ESEN

Dolle Brouwers
12b Roeselaerestraat
T 051 50 27 81   **E** de.dolle@proximedia.be
www.dedollebrouwers.be

There is a guided tour of this interesting, restored old brewery every Sunday at 14.00 in French and English and at 15.00 in Dutch. The jokes vary depending on the language. The tours end in the bar, which includes a shop and at times an art gallery, all of which are open at weekends (see West Flanders: Brewery cafés). Entry €2.50 (2004) includes a beer.

POPERINGE

National Hop Museum
71 Gasthuisstraat
T 057 34 66 76   **E** toerisme@poperinge.be
www.poperinge.be/UK/Inex.htm

As yet the only museum in the world dedicated to the history of hop cultivation. Housed in an old hop warehouse and weigh station, it leads the visitor through the four seasons of hop growing, using hundreds of exhibits and a 1936 film of what things were like before mechanisation. Managed well by the excellent local tourist office (1 Grote Markt). Entry €3.00 includes a beer, children €1.50 (2004). Also open on bank holidays in May and June.
CLOSED OCTOBER TO APRIL
CLOSED MONDAY TO SATURDAY *(May & June)*
Other days 14.00–18.00

ROESELARE

Brouwerij Rodenbach
133–141 Spanjestraat   **T** 051 27 28 10
E visit.rodenbach@palmbreweries.com
www.rodenbach.be

The site of the world's largest collection of beer-ripening oak tuns is open for turn-up-and-pay visitors only in high summer at present, though popularity warrants three tours a day. Entry €2.50 (2004) includes a beer.
Tue–Thu 10.00, 14.00 & 15.00 *(Jul & Aug only)*

BEER FESTIVALS & EVENTS

"A train pulls in to an isolated station in an empty wilderness. Two strangers get off. They are joined by a third who has been sheltering in a crude wooden hut on the platform. Without a word they head off along a lonely road that stretches away through a windswept and desolate landscape, the horizontal rain lashing them in the face. Three British idiots are trying to get to a crowded village hall to hear a jazz band play too loudly and to drink more beer than is wise."

RHODRI THOMAS
CAMRA Brussels, on Belgian beer festivals

Surprisingly for a country of such a diverse beer culture, Belgium had until recently no tradition of holding beer festivals. Smaller Belgian breweries have often sold their wares at local carnivals but the nearest thing to German or British style beer festivals were commercial affairs designed to promote the wares of large commercial brewers.

In the Eighties the various branches of the consumer organisation OBP began putting together local gatherings of brewers eager to promote their more interesting beers to a willing audience of beer lovers. This tradition has carried on into the era of Zythos. Some local fundraisers and commercial organisations have now followed this example, particularly in areas where Zythos is not active.

Another welcome trend of recent years has been the decision by breweries, sometimes in a co-ordinated way across a whole region, to open their doors to the public. If you are lucky you will catch a live demonstration of brewing.

The Guide presents below the regular events that make up the tourist calendar of the Belgian brewing year. We apologise if the details we quote are inaccurate. Events have a habit of disappearing as elusively as they arrived. Even the regulars have a habit of changing venue, timing and local contact details with great regularity. Tracking them can be like trying to catch eels with a knitting needle.

Recommended websites for keeping up to date include **www.zythos.be**, **www.limburgsebiervrienden.be** and **www.bierfestival.be**. Alternatively, support the cause by joining the organisations that compile them (see Consumer Groups).

THE BELGIAN BEER EVENT CALENDAR

JANUARY

THE FINNISH CONNECTION

There are no regular beer events in Belgium in January. However, what is possibly the most unusual festival of Belgian beers in the world happens in **Helsinki**, Finland. Kari Likovouri, who brews a better tripel than most Belgian colleagues at the Stadin brewery in the city, assists Markku Korhonen, landlord of the **One Pint** pub (2 Santakatu, Ruoholahti, Helsinki), in hosting a festival of Belgian beers throughout January. They collect most of the beers themselves on a New Year tour of Belgium. This pair is also responsible for commissioning the special Finnish lambic from Cantillon (see Belgian Breweries). The festival runs from the end of January until the beer runs out. *More details on* www.posbeer.org *or* www.helsinkibeerfestival.com

FEBRUARY

3RD OR 4TH WEEKEND:
SOHIER (*Luxembourg*)
Cercle St Lambert, 5 Rue Basse, in the centre.
Le WEBS (*Week-End Bières Spéciales*)
Annually since 1994. A village fête, Wallonian style. Unusually there are no draught beers in the range of 120. *Fri&Sat from 20.00; Sun from 11.00. More details on* www.sohier.be

3RD OR 4TH WEEKEND:
WEERDE (*Flemish Brabant*)
Oude School, 49 Damstraat, in the centre.
Weerdse Bierproeverij
On the first weekend in May Weerde hosts a beer festival with a relatively meagre selection of beers but plenty of oompah. This altogether more serious affair features a tasting of about 60 beers. *Sat 14.00–02.00; Sun 14.00–22.00. More details on* www.weerdsebierfeesten.be

4TH WEEKEND:
PUTTE (*Antwerp*)
Parochiezaal, in the town centre.
Dolle Dagen van het Gerstenat
Run by De Putse Bierkliek, annually since 1994.

Usually around 80 beers plus the usual supports to keep you there.
Sat & Sun from 15.00.
More details on www.zythos.be

24TH OF THE MONTH:
MECHELEN (*Antwerp*)
Anker brewery opens its doors for the annual brewing of Cuvée van de Keizer, on the birthday of Emperor Charles V, whose palace was in the town and whose coinage gave this ancient brewery its brand name of Gouden Carolus.

MARCH

Belgian national beer festival

1ST WEEKEND:
SINT NIKLAAS (*East Flanders*)
Stadsfeestzalen, 67 Leopold II-Laan.
The transition of OBP into Zythos coincided with the destruction of the splendid venue in Antwerp for OBP's **24-Uur bierfestival**. Zythos had therefore to shift both the venue and the timing of their national festival of Belgian brewing. The new venue is 200 metres from the train station, which is on the main line between Antwerp and Ghent and easily accessible from Brussels and Mechelen. Be warned there are few hotels in the town and for foreign visitors, bunking down in Antwerp or Ghent is the easiest option.
Sat 12.00–24.00; Sun 10.00–22.00. More details on www.zythos.be

Easter

EASTER WEEKEND:
AARSCHOT (*Flemish Brabant*)
Parochiezaal Bekaf, Bekaflaan. Ten minutes from the station, near the centre.
Aarschots Bierfestijn
Run by the Aarschotse Bierwegers, annually since 1994. *Sat from 14.00; Sun from 13.00. More details on* www.zythos.be

APRIL

1ST SUNDAY:
PAYOTTENLAND *(Flemish Brabant)*
Toer de Geuze
The eight small lambic breweries that make up the membership of HORAL open their doors to varying extents on the day, with excursion tickets available to sample at every one of them. Buses are provided for the wise and organised, along different routes.
Sun 10.00–17.00
More details on http://welcome.to/horal

4TH WEEKEND:
BASTOGNE *(Luxembourg)*
Salle Vitrée du Petit Séminaire, 24 Place Saint-Pierre in the centre.
Marché Wallon de la Bière
First held in 2003. A festival of local produce in a converted market hall. Open to all Wallonian brewers and particularly attracting smaller brewers, with a good selection of brews. Excellent charcuterie. Beware of the enthusiastic accordionist.
Sat 14.00–20.00; Sun 14.00–18.00
More details on www.jce-bastogne.be

LAST WEEKEND
(2005 and alternate years thereafter)
LEUVEN *(Flemish Brabant)*
Ons Huis, 28 Goudbloemstraat, five minutes from the centre.
LBT Bierfestival
Run by De Leuvense Biertherapeuten, with a different name and theme every time. One year they pitched 40 Interbrew beers against 40 from small Flemish brewers. The cheek of it was much admired. *Sat 12.00–24.00.*
More details on www.lbt.be

MAY

LAST WEEKEND:
OPSTAL *(East Flanders)*
't Beukenhof, 18 Broekstraat
Weekend Der Spontane Gisting
A sedate affair run by the Bierpallieters that features every available lambic and lambic-derived beer. Gathered from official sources and, er, not so official ones. Just about walkable from Heizijde train station. One for the aficionado. *Sat from 17.00; Sun from 15.00.*
More details on www.zythos.be

JUNE

1ST WEEKEND:
IRCHONWELZ *(Hainaut)*
Brasserie des Géants, on the outskirts of Ath.
Les Bouffonneries à la Brasserie
This weekend coincides with a carnival in Ath, which features a parade of the giants from which the brewery takes its name. It also marks the first weekend of the season that the brewery opens its gates and shows off the modern equipment it has installed in its mediaeval castle. *Sat & Sun 15.00–21.00.*
More details on www.brasseriedesgeants.com

1ST WEEKEND:
VICHTE *(West Flanders)*
Zaal De Stringe, 4 Ommersheimplein.
Karakter-Bier Weekend
Run by HOP (Heerlijk Objectief Proeven), an enthusiastic bunch of beer nuts. A semi-educational beer festival of great professionalism. Noted for its wide range of beers including French ones. *Sat & Sun 14.00–23.00.*
Details in English on www.karakterbierweekend.be

3RD WEEKEND:
MIDDELKERKE *(West Flanders)*
On the seafront.
Belgische Bierweekend
Annually since 1982, with 25 breweries and rising. A commercial festival that is more of an al fresco pub-crawl down the promenade. Sponsored by a local beer distributor.
More details on www.middelkerke.be

4TH WEEKEND:
ANTWERP
Groenplaats, in the centre of the city.
Bier Passie
Run by the publishers of Beer Passion magazine, annually since 2001, aiming for forty breweries and over 100 beers. They try to include small brewers but this is difficult when you have to stay commercially viable.
Fri 14.00–22.00; Sat & Sun 13.00–22.00.
More details on www.beerpassion.com

LAST WEEKEND:
OUDENAARDE *(East Flanders)*
On the market square.
Adriaan Brouwer Bierfeesten
Annually since 1958, as part of a larger town

celebration. Features a gaggle of gustatory gastronomics.
Fri & Sat from 18.00; Sun from 15.00.
More details on **www.oudenaarde.be**

JULY

1ST WEEKEND:
MECHELEN (*Antwerp*)
Olivetenhof, 32 Olivietenvest, near the Anker brewery.
Beer Brothers' Bierdag
Run by The Beer Brothers, annually since 1996. Beers from all over are combined with a brewery open day. Sometimes on the last weekend in June. *Sat from 14.00.*
More details on **www.thebeerbrothers.be**

2ND OR 3RD WEEKEND:
OSTEND (*West Flanders*)
On the corner of Sint Paulusstraat and Sint Franciscusstraat.
Oostendse Bierjutterij
Run by De Oostendse Bierjutters. Popular with British beer lovers. Fifteen West Flanders breweries present their beers on draught.
Sat from 11.00.
More details on **www.deoostendsebierjutters.org**

3RD SATURDAY
HOTTON (*Luxembourg*)
Fête des Bières de la Province de Luxembourg
Features beers from all of the province's breweries, plus a barbecue and live music.
More details on **www.hotton.be**

4TH WEEKEND:
VERVIERS (*Liège*)
Chanteloup, 9 Rue des Champs, Stembert.
Fête de la Bière
Part of Stembert's carnival, la Kermesse Stembertois. Annually since 2002. The 2005 event should top 150 beers. Part of an event in this village-cum-suburb that rolls on from Friday into the middle of the next week.
More details on **www.stembert.be**

AUGUST

MIDDLE WEEKEND:
ANVAING (*Hainaut*)
Salle Omnisports, Place Verte.
Fête des 100 Bières

Annually since 1979. Part of the town's annual carnival, La Gayolle, with a big barbecue. All 100 beers are Wallonian. *Fri from 18.00; Sat from 19.30.* *More details on* **www.chez.com/gayolle/100bieres.html**

15TH OF THE MONTH:
ACHOUFFE (*Luxembourg*)
The Achouffe brewery holds a very beery open day on the anniversary of its first mash.

SATURDAY OF 2ND WEEK:
NINOVE (*East Flanders*)
The Slaghmuylder brewery (2 Denderhoutembaan) holds an open day at which it is possible to visit their impressive museum.

14TH & 15TH OF THE MONTH:
ZWEVEGEM (*West Flanders*)
Theophiel Toyeplein in the centre of town.
The **Internationaal Streekbierenfestival**
We are not sure who runs this one but it has been an annual event since 2001. August 15th is a national holiday in Belgium – the Assumption of the Virgin Mary. Claims to have attracted 15,000 visitors in 2004. Imagine a beer festival with a street party thrown in.
14th 18.00–02.00; 15th 11.00–02.00
More details on **www.flanderseventsvzw.be**

LAST WEEKEND:
ALSEMBERG (*Flemish Brabant*)
Cultureel Centrum De Meent, 34 Gemeenveldstraat, just off the main road to Brussels.
Biefestival van de Lambikstoempers
A friendly festival run by the local branch of Zythos in a large modern community centre. 100 beers including many lambics. Child friendly. Sandwiches and cheeses.
Sat 14.00–24.00; Sun 11.00–20.00
More details on **http://quickly.to/lambikstoempers**

SEPTEMBER

1ST OR 2ND WEEKEND:
BRUSSELS
On the Grand'Place.
Belgian Beer Weekend
Run by the organisation now called Belgian Brewers, with the City of Brussels and the Chevalerie du Fourquet des Brasseurs. This is

The beer festival of Wallonian beers in Bastogne

a real showpiece event in the heart of Brussels aimed more at high street Belgium and the general tourist than at the aficionado. Running since 1999. Possibly the only beer festival to be held in a World Heritage Site. Despite the crowds it has become a gathering of the clans, attended by brewers large and small. Even the Guide goes (in a wig and dark glasses, wearing a stab jacket).

Fri 18.00–22.00; Sat 11.00–22.00; Sun 11.00–20.00.
More details on **www.belgianbeerweekend.be**

MIDDLE WEEKEND:
TEMSE *(Antwerp)*
Parochiaal Centrum Kristus Koning.
Grote Bieren van Kleine Brouwers
Run by Objectieve Kaaischuimers van Temse, annually since 1998. Small breweries only. Free admission. Children's play area.
Sat & Sun from 17.00.
More details on **www.zythos.be**

3RD WEEKEND (every three years):
POPERINGE *(West Flanders)*
Throughout the town.

Hop Fest

The only full-blown Belgian carnival to be built on a beery theme happens every three years (2005, 2008 and on) in the hop town of Poperinge, culminating in the Hoppestoet parade (Sun from 15.00). There are smallish beer festivals on Friday and Saturday nights, demonstrations of hop-picking by hand, bands from Poperinge and its twin towns, Zatec in the Czech Republic and Wolznach in Germany. The Hop Museum opens all day. For reasons beyond comprehension the most prominent beer is Stella.
More details on **www.poperinge.be**

3RD OR 4TH WEEKEND:
GEEL *(Antwerp)*
Cultureel Centrum De Werft.
Kempisch Bierfestival
Annually since 1988. With 140 beers it boasts the largest selection of any festival in Belgium. Well-run and popular, with facilities for children. Cheese and fish plates. Table service and plenty of space.
Sat from 14.00; Sun 14.00–22.00.
More details on **www.ondertschuim.tk**

3RD OR 4TH WEEKEND:
BLEHARIES *(Hainaut)*
On the football field.
No details but we know it happens.

LAST WEEKEND:
TOURPES *(Hainaut)*
The Dupont brewery opens its beer-making and cheese-making facilities to the public.

VILLERS-DEVANT-ORVAL *(Luxembourg)*
The Orval brewery opens its doors for inspection, though its cheese factory remains closed.

Be warned that the **Dixmuide Beer Festival**, which runs most weekends in September and October and receives extensive advertising by British coach tour operators, is a commercial concern aimed at British boozer cruisers intent on getting lagered up in some corner of a foreign field. The Guide does not recommend it.

OCTOBER

1ST WEEKEND:
MARBEHAN *(Luxembourg)*
Bois des Isles football ground.
Brassigaume
Annually since 2001. Rapidly establishing itself as the Wallonian classic. Rustic as hell, with only microbreweries (<4,000 hl per annum) allowed to supply. Attendances are helped by the fact that Marbehan station is on the main line from Brussels to Luxembourg. Commended as a real campaigning event aimed straight at the general public.
Sat & Sun from 14.00.
More details on **www.brassigaume.be**

MIDDLE SATURDAY:
ZOTTEGEM *(East Flanders)*
Feestzaal Bevegemse Vivjers in Zwembadstraat.
Bierhappening
Run by BLES (Bierliefhebbers van de Egmont-stede), annually since 1994. A civilised affair, featuring 25 smaller breweries, including a Dutch guest.   *Sat from 14.00.*
More details on **www.bles.be**

LAST WEEKEND:
POPERINGE *(West Flanders)*
Palace Hotel, Ieperstraat.
Karakter Bierfestival
Long-standing beer festival that is literally in-house, in the roomy but intimate function suite at the back of the hotel, spilling out into its courtyard car park.   *Sat & Sun 15.00–23.00. More details on* www.hotelpalace.virtualave.net

LAST WEEKEND:
BERLAAR-HEIKANT *(Antwerp)*
Zaal Familia, opposite the church on the Lier to Aarschot road.
Heikantse Bierfeesten
Annually since 1988. More music-orientated than most. Good children's facilities
*Fri & Sat from 20.00; Sun from 15.00.
More details on* www.heikantsebierlefhebbers.be

LAST WEEKEND:
HERENTALS *(Antwerp)*
Zaal 't Hof, Grote Markt.
Herentalse Bierfeesten
Organised by KSJ Herentals, the local scout troop, annually since 1998. Aims to feature at least 110 beers and usually tops that.
*Sat & Sun from 12.00.
More details on* www.herentalsebierfeesten.be

NOVEMBER

2ND WEEKEND:
HASSELT *(Limburg)*
Zaal De Schakel, 43 Rechterstraat.
Weekend der Belgische Bieren
Annually since 1994. Has a reputation as one of the best local festivals in Belgium, attracting unusual beers. So well organised that they run buses round a 25 km radius of the venue.
*Fri from 18.00; Sat & Sun from 14.00.
More details on* www.delimburgse-biervrienden.be

2ND WEEKEND:
ONZE-LIEVE-VROUW OLEN *(Antwerp)*
Zaal Boekelheem.
Weekend der Belgische Bieren
Sorry no details.   *Sat from 14.00.*

DECEMBER

2ND WEEKEND:
ESSEN *(Antwerp)*
New venue for 2005.
Christmas Beer Festival
Run by OBER (Objectieve Bierproevers Essense Regio), annually since 1995. The last biggie of the year in the northernmost town on the Belgian rail network. Features just about every winter beer in all of Belgium, including some specials – 125 in 2004. A simple festival that is becoming a landmark for European beer lovers. The new venue is 1.5 km from the station – hourly trains for Antwerp and Roosendaal.
Sat&Sun from 12.00. More details on www.ober.be

BETWEEN CHRISTMAS AND NEW YEAR:
BERLAAR-HEIKANT *(Antwerp)*
Zaal Familia, opposite the church on the Lier to Aarschot road.
Kerst en Winter Bieren
Run by Heikantse Bierlefhebbers.
More details on www.heikantsebierlefhebbers.be

Trying the big beers

An increasing number of classic Belgian beers come in 75cl bottles. The yeast dynamics and character are often fuller as a result.

These are a great way to lure normally beer-wary guests into your world. Order three or four glasses and share a bottle, as you would a wine.

Sharing is also an easy way of sampling a whole tranche of rarer beers.

The most popular type of bottle is a dark green champagne-style affair, though there is also straight-sided, round-shouldered brown glass type. All are corked. Some have champagne-style corks with a wire and cap wrap, while others may be additionally crown-topped, thus requiring both corkscrew and bottle-opener.

Some drab beers have also adopted this presentation. To spot the worst, check out the base. No dimple in the bottom of a champagne-style bottle usually means no yeast inside, as the walls are not strong enough to contain the effects of bottle-conditioning.

The art of making beer

"I grow onions. Well I say I grow onions. I don't really. God does.
I just plant the seeds. Then I pick them when they're finished."

KEVIN TURVEY (*aka Rik Mayall*), "Three of a Kind"

TO BE LEGALLY CLASSIFIED as beer for sale in the European Union a drink must be made primarily from boiled grain. At least seventy per cent of its fermented sugars must derive from particular recognised cereals.

In Belgium 60% of the total must be malted barley. In addition, all the alcohol must come from fermentation rather than distillation or fortifying.

Put another way, beer is what you get when you ferment sugars that came from grain. The most popular grain in use is malted barley. The most popular additive is hops.

Ancient history

We think the first people to turn the sweet extract of boiled grain into an alcoholic drink lived in ancient Palestine some ten thousand years ago.

Much of the early history of beer making was, as with many folk arts, unrecorded and thus subject to educated guesswork and con-jecture. We assume that somewhere along the line common taste allowed that the best beers were made from malted barley. How such a discovery was made is anyone's guess.

Wheat and no doubt other grains were used commonly in ancient ales. These early types of beer would likely still taste acceptable to many modern palates, provided they were freshly made. The problem came when trying to preserve their integrity beyond the first few days.

Ancient brewers tried to stop their beers oxidising and turning to vinegar. Herbal remedies abounded for the purpose. One such, known as *gruit*, is still used occasionally by brewers, when they want to be different. Whether these mixtures of ground dried herbs and spices prevented fouling or merely masked it is a matter of opinion. Either way,

it became academic when brewers discovered the power of the humble hop.

Hops are wild weeds, the flowers of which have natural properties that prolong the life of a beer by preventing it from oxidising and fighting off infections. Although initially there was huge resistance to hopped beers, mediaeval drinkers were eventually won over by their keeping qualities. In time they came to like their bitter herbal flavours too.

Meanwhile, understanding of the last vital ingredient of beer, yeast, was subject to much scientific and spiritual exertion. Long before anyone understood that this was a living micro-organism, respect for a substance that could turn flour and water into bread, and porridge into beer, was already riding high.

The basics

Making a beer for sale involves a six-stage process.

STAGE 1

Choosing the ingredients

To brew beer to the traditional method you need only four things – water, grain, hops and yeast.

The **water** supply should be clean and plentiful. Brewing works best with a particular balance of minerals, though nowadays even the smallest commercial brewery can adjust the mineral content of its water easily. There are a few breweries that still have big problems with their water, mainly if the supply is of unpredictable quality and content.

The classic **grain** is malted barley. Pearls of harvested and sifted barley are watered and warmed in a maltings for a few days to enable germination. These seeds are then killed off by heating.

Malted barley is preferred for its high starch content, which provides more sugar for fermentation. Its hard husks make it a better grain to manage in the brewhouse, for example by draining easily and being simpler to wash away. It also gives intense background flavours that add crucially to the character of the beer.

Malt comes in many varieties, each imparting different colours and flavours. The palest type is Pilsener malt, the base malt for almost all Belgian beers, regardless of their colour. Others include Pale Ale, Münchener, and Caramalt.

The darkest are the heavily roasted chocolate malts. These add a burnt character to beer but are used mainly for colouring. A mere 5% of chocolate malt in a recipe can create a near-black stout.

A strong beer made to a 100% malt recipe has an intense character that even seasoned beer drinkers may find challenging. Most brewers will dilute this effect by using simpler sources of sugar that leave little in the way of backtastes. These include maize, corn flour, starch, sugars and syrups. 10–15% substitution is barely noticeable in a beer of 8% alcohol by volume. When it hits 30% the thinning effect is obvious.

Wheat, oats, rye and other grains have a sweetening effect on beer and impart quite strong background flavours. Brewers are not afraid to use them to create a different character in a beer but dislike using too much as they are not as manageable in the brewery.

Hops come in many varieties, each of which has different potential for adding flowery aromas, herbal flavours, bitterness and preservative strength. The hop varieties used in a beer are as important to its flavour as the grape varieties are to a wine.

For brewing they come in different forms including whole hops (usually compressed), pellets and extracts.

Many quality breweries around the world insist that compressed whole hops are essential to giving a beer a proper hoppy character. Most Belgian brewers believe that hop pellets achieve the same end, provided the hops were frozen at the time of pellet manufacture. An increasing number believe

the same of hop extract. Excellent hop character is a rarity in a Belgian beer and the Guide believes these brewers are wrong.

Brewers' **yeast** is a class of living micro-organism. Its talent is the ability to ferment sugars into alcohol and carbon dioxide gas. Strains of yeast vary in their capabilities, each working best at particular alcohol concentrations, temperatures and sugar intensities. A brewer may deliberately use more than one yeast strain to ferment a beer, each imparting a different quality to the fermentation.

STAGE 2

Preparing the sugars

To get the fermentable sugar out of whole grain, the corns must first be "cracked" in a mill to make **grist**.

Many brewers will substitute flours, starches, syrups and grain extracts as adjuncts to the mix. The simpler the source of sugar, the fewer background flavours it leaves in the beer. All get turned in largest part into alcohol.

The eventual ingredients are then mixed with the water – confusingly called "liquor" in Britain – and boiled as a **mash** for one to one and a half hours in a "mash tun".

The temperature of the mash affects the quality of the sugars that are extracted. For example, at 70°C you will extract dextrins, which will remain in the beer after fermentation. Saliva converts dextrins to sugar, sweetening the taste of the beer in the mouth. At 60°C no dextrins emerge but mashing takes longer.

A typical mash has the appearance of thin porridge. When it is completed the boiling sludge is filtered to leave a concentrated solution of sugars and suspended proteins. This brown, hazy liquid is called the **sweet wort**.

STAGE 3

Brewing

When the brewer thinks that their sweet wort is at the right strength, the hops are added and the mixture is brought to the boil again. The bitterness from hops is only liberated if you boil them.

This is the part of the process correctly referred to as **brewing**, the same term used loosely to refer to beer-making generally.

Many Belgian brewers add herbs, spices or essences to their brews at this stage. Dried peel and coriander have been used for centuries. Over forty other flavourings are in current use. Unlike malt and hops, spices do not come from the supplier ready-graded for spiciness. This accounts for why spiced beers can be delicious, distracting or undrinkable.

At the end of brewing the final product, called the **hopped wort**, is cooled and filtered to remove remaining solids prior to fermentation.

STAGE 4

Fermentation

After cooling and transfer to a fermenting vessel, yeast is added to the wort and allowed to work its little miracles.

Traditionally, **primary fermentation** took place in open-top fermenting vessels that look rather like small swimming pools. Ale would take seven to ten days to ferment and lager a little longer, as its fermentation was temperature-controlled. Yeast in the vigorously fermenting ale rose to the top and so ales were termed "top-fermented". In the more orderly lagers it sank, making them "bottom-fermented".

In the last twenty years the practice of fermentation has changed radically. Most commercial brewers now use enclosed tanks, to decrease the risk of infection. This radically affects the working of the yeast. Taller, cylindro-conical fermenters are associated with high fermentation temperatures leading to completion in a matter of a few days. The results strike many as clumsy.

The technology graduates who make up most of the professional brewing workforce are unmoved by the comments of more experienced brewers that the vital formation of esters, the chemicals that give the final beer its flavour and aroma, is impaired by the use of conical fermenters. They argue that this effect cannot be measured, as if this means it does not exist.

Of course, if fermentation good enough for the brewing director can be completed in three days, ten days becomes an awfully long time in the mind of the finance director. A few ale brewers still ferment for ten days and longer, usually with impressive results. Those who ferment in four or five days can get good results too. That is can, as in might happen.

Trying to jump from describing regular

The open mash tun at Saint Feuillien

fermentation to the concept of spontaneous fermentation is not easy, so for this we refer you to our description of lambic brewing (see Belgian Beer Styles).

Not all yeast is seen as helpful. Some spoiler yeast create yeast infection, a generally unwelcome addition to fermentation. However, tastes are mainly matters of convention. In years gone by, some small local brewers, relying more on their artistic instincts than a microscopic analysis of what was in the yeast culture, developed some pretty eccentric mixes to work on their beers.

These "perfect infections" were introduced deliberately to the fermentation process and gave their beers a character that inhabited the disputed territory between eccentricity, genius and madness. We have the good Dr Louis Pasteur to blame for their passing. The man who made kegged beer a possibility.

STAGE 5

Conditioning

Once beer has completed its primary fermentation it is filtered. The colder the beer at filtration the more flavour particles will be removed from it. Likewise the finer the filter, which in modern breweries is often a centrifuge, the more flavour is removed.

After filtration it can be prepared for sale immediately and shipped out from the brewery to the beer trade. This is what happens to British "real ale", which traditionally undergoes further (secondary) fermentation in its barrel, or cask, usually after some fresh yeast is added.

Around the world, most beers undergo some form of secondary fermentation, or **conditioning** at the brewery. This may take many forms, from storage in huge oak casks in vast warehouses for a couple of years, via sitting in cooled tanks at the brewery for a couple of months, to being bottled with some fresh year and stuck in a warm room for a couple of weeks.

The oldest and most intriguing of these is **oak-ageing**, of which we say more in our comments on lambics and oak-aged ales (see Beer Styles of Belgium). This technique is of course common to many other forms of better quality alcoholic drinks, as well as many other preserved foods.

Ageing a beer in huge oak casks or tuns for a year or two will cause it to darken and take on a dry, sharp character. This comes through lactic acidity from slow-fermenting yeast, tannin from the wood and acetic notes from slight oxidation. Simply putting the beer into steel containers and letting it age for a year or two adds no tannin and provides lactate only if additional micro-organisms are introduced.

The process of **lagering** beers was first perfected in 1842 in the Bohemian town of

Makeshift soft pegs at the Dolle Brouwers

Plzen (Pilsen). Traditionally it involved storing a beer a few degrees above freezing point in sealed vessels, to mature for between eight and sixteen weeks. The development of character can be profound.

Lagering ales sounds a contradiction in terms but is the norm for most Belgian beers, though times vary from five days to six weeks.

Lagering is expensive as it creates the need for extra space in the brewery and puts time between the outlay on ingredients and staff and the income from sales. To make it even more expensive but entertaining, you can pitch porous sacks of fresh hops into the tanks for some **dry hopping**. This is the upscale version of the old habit of chucking a handful of hops into an open cask before it leaves the brewery.

In recent years there has been a clear move back to bottling beers with active yeast in them so that they condition in the bottle. Yeast from the primary fermentation is filtered out – the beer may even be pasteurised – and a drop of freshly prepared yeast is introduced to each bottle.

Bottle conditioning usually adds significant character to a beer. The yeast may be a different strain from the brewing yeast so home-brewers trying to clone a commercial brewery's beers will be disappointed.

Many, if not most, Belgian brewers nowadays will sit the re-seeded beer in a warm chamber for a couple of weeks before allowing it out into the trade. This is usually little more that a temperature-controlled warehouse and doubles as a place of congregation for brewery workers on cold winter mornings. The "before and after" flavour differences can be profound.

One variant on conditioning that has been almost unique to Belgian craft brewers in the last hundred years is the tradition of **steeping** fruit in the beer. Traditionally this involved putting whole fruit in a cask of beer for around six months (see Beer styles of Belgium: Fruit lambic). Modern versions use juice or syrup and get it over quicker.

A modern variant on the theory of the "perfect infection" is beginning to be adopted by some brewers who use a radically different yeast culture for re-fermentation including for example *brettanomyces*, one of the slow-fermenting yeasts that give authentic gueuze its character.

There is no living tradition of cask-conditioned or "real" draught ales in Belgium. However, a number of Belgian brewers do put live yeast in some of their draught beers, despite them being in sealed kegs. Without question these continue to develop some character after leaving the brewery, though not to the same extent as occurs in bottled beers. If they did that, they would become dangerously explosive.

STAGE 6

Preparing for sale

It is a sad but true reflection on our collective idiocy as consumers that the wisdom, creativity and technical wizardry of the most adept modern brewers count for little when it comes to making a beer sellable. What really matters is what it looks like and whether its name rings the right bells.

The proportion of knowledgeable beer lovers in the beer selling business is pathetically low. This may sound daft but when you consider the proportion of knowledgeable beer lovers in the beer buying public, or knowledgeable bread lovers in the bread-buying public for that matter, it starts to make sense.

As with a theatre company producing a play, so it is with a brewer creating a beer. The vital ingredients required to put the show together eventually become just a footnote to the final presentation.

Large breweries put far more effort into the shape, size and colour of the bottle, the precise design of the bar fount, the memorable characteristics of the badge and of course, the catchy message on the advertising strapline than they put into making it taste unusually good. This is a fair reflection of customer concerns. We buy with our eyes not our brains. That is why advertising works.

The Marketing Director of one large British brewery – long since absorbed into the global soup – once confided in your editor that: "You can sell a sucker their own boots if you try hard enough."

Remember that next time you go shopping, or order a beer.

The beer styles of Belgium

"One step above the sublime makes the ridiculous,
and one step above the ridiculous makes the sublime again."

THOMAS PAINE, *The Age of Reason* (1795)

THE BELGIAN CLAIM to be the world's best country for beer is not based on the huge range of beers it produces.

While great brewing nations like Germany, Britain and the Czech Republic struggle to find more than a handful of different styles of beer in current production, Belgium has hundreds.

When does a make of beer become so distinctive that it can be said to have developed a style of its own? You can argue always, never and all points in between.

An absolute classification of beer styles would be an impossible, indulgent exercise in self-serving pedantry. See this chapter as a brief introduction to the major variations on the theme of beer that the Belgian nation endows to the world. Memorise it, then develop a whole string of objections to it and you can probably call yourself an expert. Or at least you will be able to hold your own with those that are.

The traditional top line in classifying the beers of the world is the method of fermentation. In technologically simpler times the world's beers were made up of vast oceans of bottom-fermented **lagers**, enlivened by a few surviving top-fermented **ales** and a wafer-thin legacy of spontaneously fermented **lambics**.

LAGERS

Most of the beer drunk in Belgium is lager. This is sad for Belgians and the rest of us, as lager brewing is not their industry's strong point.

Those of simple tastes are able to find identical gassy blond fluids wherever they travel. The familiar names were briefly exotic in their day.

On the whole, if you enjoy well-made premium quality lagers it is best to stay on the train and head for Germany, while it enjoys its last decade outside the clutches of InBev and their breed. Bavaria in general and Franconia in particular reward exploration. Think Münich (Ge: *München*) and Bamberg.

Pilsener

The best known name of any beer style in the world is Pilsener, often shortened to Pilsner or Pils. It derives from the town of Plzen in the Czech Republic, which was once part of greater Germany and called Pilsen. It was here that the science of slow beer-making was perfected.

Originally Pilseners were deep golden brews with a distinctive aged character. The straw-blond variants on wet air that flow from shiny bar founts round the world are more recent corruptions.

In Belgium, as elsewhere, the designation Pils should imply a blond lager, made from Pilsener malt and lightly hopped with Hallertau or other German hop varieties. Typical strength will be 4.5–5.2% abv. Few Belgian Pilseners are 100% malt, many are fast-fermented, none is lagered for more than a month or so and most are predictably drab.

Pilsener is the supermarket white crusty loaf of international brewing. It can be made in tall fermenters at high temperatures, can absorb quite a lot of non-malt sugars in its recipe and still come out smelling of ... well, not a lot actually.

Pilsener's internationally accepted image makes it a cost cutter's dream. In truth, more people want to be seen drinking a beer, to retain the common touch, than actually like beer. Five decades of positioning this variety successfully at the top of the price list have brought tidy profits.

Some Pilseners have additional designations added to them.

Luxe Pils tends to mean that the beer has been created for the airlines and business hotels' market. A bit of dry hopping, a fancier label and a thin glass help to justify a higher price tag.

Strong Pils, usually written in English, mean a slightly stronger beer, full of adjuncts, aimed at ignorant British and Scandinavian tourists who want to get drunk.

Urtyp Pilsener means original style, so should have the stewed and aged quality of an old-style Pilsener, often with the addition of some ruddier Vienna malts. These are usually of superior quality but feature little in the Belgian market.

BEST BELGIAN PILSENERS
Redor Pils *Dupont*
Strubbe Super Pils *Strubbe*
Bel Pils *Moortgat*
Slaghmuylder Paasbier *Slaghmuylder*
Slaghmuylder Kerstbier *Slaghmuylder*

Dortmunder

This style takes its name from the German city of Dortmund, which produces two styles of beer, including the stronger blond lager that has become known the world over as Dortmunder.

A Dortmunder should be a blond lager, originally lighter in colour than Pilsener though nowadays often darker. It is generally stronger, more elegant, aromatic and confident.

Where the name of Pilsener has been de-graded by overuse, Dortmunder has retained a certain cache. Though as the boundary between the two styles blurs, a cynic might claim that a brewer making a classy Pils would be better off calling it a Dort.

BEST BELGIAN DORTMUNDERS
Kerelsbier Licht *Leroy*
Sasbräu Dortmunder *Leroy*

LAMBICS

From the world's biggest and most tawdry beer style to its tiniest and most extraordinary. Of all Belgian beers only one group is unique and this is it.

The practice of producing spontaneously-fermented beers is probably thousands of years old. Certainly making beers in this way was practiced on a large scale in the 16th century. Whether this was as a presentation of folk craft or by design is anyone's guess.

Lambic beers differ from all others because their yeast source comes from the atmosphere. When air makes contact with a cooling vat of freshly brewed wort, natural yeast from that air land in the liquid and begin to ferment it, just as any pitched yeast would. Fermentation is slower as there is less and because naturally occurring yeast are not specifically bred to ferment.

The basic recipe is similar to that for wheat beer – 30% wheat, 70% barley – but the hops used are traditionally aged. This ensures that they are cheap – there is not a huge market in second-hand unused hops – but also means that their aromatic and bitter characteristics have faded, leaving only their natural preservative powers intact.

Right: *The brewery yard at Drie Fonteinen*

Romance dictates that fermentation begins when natural yeast descends from the night sky, through the brewery's open roof onto cooling wort. In practice most lambic brewers will blow air across the surface of shallow fermenting vessels. This lands more yeast on target and cools the wort slightly quicker. We believe that one commercial producer bubbles cold air through warm wort in conical fermenters.

Of course atmospheric air contains all manner of microbes, not just yeast. Many of these will send a beer rank in days. Lambic brewers have a variety of tricks to kill off these unwanted organisms before the cooled sweet mixture is laid down in oak casks for slow fermentation. What should remain is a dominant strain of *saccharomyces* yeast, the type that ferments sugar into alcohol and carbon dioxide as in other beers.

Once in its casks, fermentation of lambics appears simple. Cask sits in warehouse gathering dust. Beer ferments inside. Brewer sits and does as little at they dare. However, an immensely complex biological process is going on inside each cask.

The vigorous phase of fermentation lasts little more than two weeks before tailing off as the natural sugars are fermented out and

the *saccharomyces* run out of steam. At this stage a lambic will taste like a slightly musty real ale version of a wheat beer.

Three or four months into maturation, the action of micro-organisms in the walls of the cask will be bringing a lactic acid flavour to the beer, a classic component of oak-ageing. Taste the beer at this stage and it is has the sharp, somewhat acrid character of beer that has gone off in the pipes, against a fungal background. At this stage the beer is at its least attractive but is starting to show its potential. It is an adolescent.

With further ageing *brettanomyces* begin to take over as the dominant yeast strain. This type of yeast has little effect on alcohol production, though a little does continue. The main role of "brett" is to develop a multi-dimensional complex of tastes and aromas we call maturity, character, ageing and the like. Citrous backtastes and an afterburn like an old tobacco pouch can emerge, each producer leaving their own thumbprint.

The six to eight months of this slow fermentation develops the lambic into a drier, mustier drink of low natural carbonation, which by its first birthday is called young lambic (Du: *jong lambiek*). The transition from beer to wine is under way. This one-year-old beer is fit to put into casks and is sold in some cafés around Brussels and Payottenland by gravity dispense straight from the cask. It is also used for blending.

Meanwhile back at the brewery, the young lambic that is not used at this stage is growing older.

Cask lambic continues to mature for three years and occasionally longer. It has then graduated to become old lambic (Du: *oud lambiek*). By this stage *brettanomyces* will have left their mark in the form of strong shards of citric tang, and a more elegant, sometimes snuff-like or musky backdrop, with chemical reduction forming sherried and Madeira flavours in there too.

Old lambic will occasionally find its way into a few local cafés in its raw draught form – pan flat, clear and, well, an acquired taste. A couple are bottled and in so doing manage just enough continuing fermentation to get some fizz.

Draught lambic

The Guide refers to all beers made by the use of spontaneous fermentation as lambics, in the same sense that top-fermented beers are ales and bottom-fermented beers lagers.

In a few cafés of Brussels and Payottenland the term lambic still refers to the type of beer that is racked directly from the cask and served as a draught beer. This is a dying breed of outlet and for as comprehensive a list as exists anywhere, consult *LambicLand* (see Being there: Guidebooks).

The Guide does not star-rate draught lambics or quote an alcoholic strength, as these can vary with each cask and its age. All are rare and worth trying while you still can.

RECOMMENDED DRAUGHT LAMBICS

De Cam Lambiek *de Cam*
Cantillon 100% Lambic *Cantillon*
Drie Fonteinen Lambiek *Drie Fonteinen*
Girardin jong lambiek *Girardin*
Girardin oud lambiek *Girardin*
Boon Lambiek *Boon*

Bottled lambic

As far as we are aware only two brewers bottle their cask lambics directly. In each case they use three-year-old lambics and older. At bottling carbonation is virtually nil but minimal yeast action in the bottle usually raises a light carbonation by the time of serving.

BOTTLED LAMBICS

Broucsella Grand Cru *Cantillon*
De Cam Lambiek *de Cam*

Faro

A cask-aged lambic will tend to be flat. By adding some unrefined sugar to the cask, and sometimes a little freshly made lambic, re-fermentation in the cask can be kick-started. Because of the nature of the drink, arrangements to supply this type of beer tend to be on an individual café basis.

A couple of brewers have tried to capture the same principle in a bottle, unsuccessfully in our view.

DRAUGHT FAROS

Cantillon Faro *Cantillon*
Drie Fonteinen Faro *Drie Fonteinen*
Girardin Faro *Girardin*
Timmermans Lambic Doux *Timmermans*

BOTTLED FAROS

Pertotale Faro *Boon*
Lindemans Faro *Lindemans*

Oude Gueuze

Most old lambics are neither served on draught nor bottled in their own right. Instead they are used as the essential character-bringing cordial in the making of the most complicated beer of all, gueuze.

How is it possible to encapsulate the spirit of great gueuze in mere words? For a previous edition we managed the following and have been unable to better it since:

> "Your first encounter … *(with oude gueuze)* … can be astonishingly awful. It may make you want to send it back immediately, but then persuades you to hold on for just another mouthful. Having soldiered through the bottle and awarded yourself a gold rosette for adding painfully to your knowledge of brewing history, it should make you vow never to try it again. Then order another just in case you got it wrong."

We could easily have added "… and after your third you will never think about beer in the same way again."

Perfect traditional gueuze is served from a champagne bottle that may be covered by the dust and cobwebs of several years in the cellar. In the old days there would be no label. It would sport a sash mark in whitewash, its identity marked only by the maker's name printed on the cork.

Authentic gueuze (Du: *oude geuze* or *oude gueuze*) is made by blending lambics. A skilled blender will judge which casks to mix by using their tastebuds, not a chemistry kit. Imagine an old bloke in a flat cap getting paid to say that if it was up to him, he would shove this barrel in with those two over there, and you would be close. Though there is likely to be a lot of discussion first, over a glass of gueuze.

As a rough rule the best results come from blending a three-year-old lambic with some one-year-old. Once the contents of the casks have been mixed, the gueuze blender will add a tiny amount of sugar in order to spark re-fermentation, and then bottle the lot, usually by hand.

In the first few months after bottling, a gueuze tastes like spritzy lambic. The longer you leave it the more its character will show.

Top quality gueuze may take many years to peak. Armand Debelder from Drie Fonteinen reckons his Millennium gueuze, the oldest component of which was brewed in 1997, will be entering its prime around 2007 and may even join the classics in the brewery cellar, some of which are more than twenty years old.

The Guide used to recommend that people who are new to Belgian beer should leave authentic gueuze until they had gained significant experience to understand what diversity there is. More recent experience suggests that some people who are not great beer lovers get a real buzz out of the best gueuze and from there learn their way, backwards as it were, into more mainstream beer styles.

Great gueuze should be dry and spritzy, with only the faintest hint of bitterness. The complex character of the aged lambic base should shine through like a perfectly lit actor at a photo shoot. All brewers manage different characteristics but variations on tannin from oak-ageing, tartness from lactic effects, citrous, musky and even peppery character from *brettanomyces* are all fair play.

Whatever else you get from gueuze, you will not be alone if you find yourself thinking "I'm not sure I have ever tasted anything like that before".

Our only advice is to stick with it. Finest authentic gueuzes are in our view among the great taste experiences of the international drinking scene, holding their own with cask strength single malt Islay whiskies and Premier Cru red Bordeaux.

The use of the name Oude Gueuze in the labelling of a beer is now protected in Belgian law. An application for recognition of Brussels and Payottenland as the official place of origin is still under consideration by the EU Commission.

BEST AUTHENTIC GUEUZES

Gueuze 100% Lambic Cantillon *Cantillon*
Drie Fonteinen Oude Gueuze *Drie Fonteinen*
De Cam Oude Gueuze *de Cam*
Girardin Oude Gueuze 1882 (black label) *Girardin*
(see brewery entry for proviso)
Cantillon Iris *Cantillon*

OTHER VERY GOOD AUTHENTIC GUEUZES

Boon Oude Gueuze Mariage Parfait *Boon*
Hanssens Artisanaale Oude Gueuze *Hanssens*
Mort Subite Oude Gueuze *Mort Subite (SCAM)*

RARE AND EXPENSIVE AUTHENTIC GUEUZES

Cantillon Lou Pepe Gueuze *Cantillon*
Drie Fonteinen Millennium Gueuze *Drie Fonteinen*
50th Anniversary Gueuze *Drie Fonteinen*

Commercial gueuze

If best authentic gueuze can be compared to vintage champagne, so the commercially made versions are like cheap bottled ciders.

The Guide used to be measured about this. With gueuze being such a complex drink, maybe the world's drinkers needed a gentle introduction via some halfway product that nodded towards gueuze from a position of a mainstream beer with a dab of mustiness behind the ears. But on reflection we were talking bollocks. [For American readers, bollocks, or bow-locks, are the means by which the front oars of a boat are secured.]

The Guide has never met a single person whose love of Drie Fonteinen or Cantillon came about because they quite liked Belle Vue.

After the 1939–45 war the refining of cheap sugar sources from the developing world became a lucrative process for a food industry seeking cheap nutrition in a Europe hit by rationing. This probably led directly to the epidemic of diabetes and obesity that now afflicts the Western World, though to assert that the two are linked is to launch a fundamental assault on our so-called freedoms.

The impact of the sugar fad on traditional lambic brewing and blending was profound. Brewers with a commercial instinct started to pander to modern tastes by sweetening their beers. This could include padding out lambics with sweet pale ales or lagers, or simply adding syrups or sweeteners.

The public perception of gueuze shifted in a generation from being one of a dry and characterful drink that was the poor man's champagne to meaning a sweet blond beer with a vague backtaste of mushroom and yoghurt.

When a few small producers started to kick up a fuss in the Eighties, suggesting that the great Belgian public might have been hoodwinked into losing a whole tradition of excellence, the reaction spoke volumes about how things work in small countries when big firms get upset.

When your company chairman is the minister for agriculture and the PM is on the board of directors, some cynical beer lovers might be forgiven for thinking you have laws changed to fit in with the corporate vision.

On 31st March 1993 a Royal Decree (Du: *Konincklijk Besluit*) was passed by the Belgian parliament that allowed the use of the terms gueuze, lambic and gueuze-lambic to describe "… acid beers where spontaneous fermentation is part of the production process."

For a large producer, this was a major advance on the idea that lambics had to be produced solely by spontaneous fermentation. In effect it legitimised the marketing of bland lagers with a touch of lambic in them as being a gueuze. Apply the logic to other processed foodstuffs and you can start to appreciate the full absurdity of this law in consumer terms.

EXAMPLES OF COMMERCIAL GUEUZES
Belle Vue Gueuze *Belle Vue (InBev)*
Chapeau Gueuze *De Troch*
St. Louis Gueuze Lambic *Van Honsebrouck*
Mort Subite Gueuze *Mort Subite (SCAM)*
Jacobins Gueuze *Bockor*
Timmermans Gueuze Lambic *Timmermans*
Lindemans Gueuze *Lindemans*

Other gueuzes

Two breweries from outside the Senne Valley, Van Honsebrouck and Bockor from southern West Flanders, also claim to make spontaneously-fermented beers. Although each is primarily a maker of sweet commercial ales, they appear to have retained a *koelschip*, the open-air cooling vessel near the roof of the brewery in which wild yeast is cropped for the fermentation on a lambic beer.

The mere mention of this is enough to cause apoplexy in some Senne Valley producers. The Guide has yet to get to the bottom of the story but has seen one of the vessels in question. Spiritually we are torn between wishing to see a return of oak-aged and sour beers in West Flanders and the difficulties that a rogue producer or two causes to the Senne Valley producers' claims to an appellation contrôlée.

THE ECCENTRIC GUEUZE
Gueuze Fond Tradition St. Louis
Van Honsebrouck

THE BEER STYLES OF BELGIUM

Fruit lambics

The world of lambic has a second peasant tradition that creates magnificent taste experiences. This comes with the art of steeping fruit in casks of lambic to make a cherry lambic called *kriek*, a raspberry lambic called *framboise* and other fruit lambics.

This practice has operated for at least as long as lambic fermentation itself. Using fruit for steeping is a classic farmers' way of avoiding good produce going to waste. Inevitably therefore the most favoured fruits will be those that traditionally crop in great abundance over a short season, creating an inevitable glut for a time. And what do you do with unsold fruit? Why, you sell it off cheap of course.

There are three additional benefits to introducing fruits into lambic. First the fructose in them can assist with fermentation and when unfermentable will sweeten it a little. Second, the aromas and flavours of the fruit can be absorbed into the lambic to make an enriched taste. Third, the colouring is appealing to the eye.

The fruits most suited to the job description in Belgium were traditionally cherries and raspberries. These have strong flavours and colours and are easier to manage than larger or fleshier fruits.

The experience of centuries shows that the best fruit should be firm and flavoursome

but need not be particularly juicy or sweet. Schaarbeek cherries, named after an area of north Brussels, were the traditional favourite, though these are now rare and expensive. The variety used will show clearly in the final beer. Even a beginner can taste the differences.

The optimum time for steeping whole fruit is around six months. This imparts maximum fruit flavour without additional aged tastes. Concentrations are remarkably high with between 200 and 400 grams of fruit added per litre. Keeping the stones in the cherries will give a fuller character than using macerated fruit, which in turn is more fulsome than using juice.

Draught cherry lambic

In Brussels and Payottenland you can still find a few cafés that sell cherry lambics racked from the cask and served on draught, usually as *kriekenlambiek*.

THE AUTHENTIC KRIEKENLAMBIEKS
Girardin Kriekenlambiek *Girardin*
Drie Fonteinen Kriek van 't vat *Drie Fonteinen*
Kriekenlambiek De Cam *de Cam*

Oude kriek

In theory the only beers in Belgium that can be sold as *kriek* should be cherry lambics. Other cherry beers should be known as *kriekenbier* or *kersenbier*. Some smaller producers are starting to use the as yet unprotected term *oude kriek* to distinguish their more authentic products, daring imitators to adopt the term misleadingly.

What constitutes an authentic cherry lambic or *oude kriek* is more difficult to define than with authentic gueuze. Some cherry lambics are simply racked from the cask, filtered to remove the detritus and then bottled, usually with a little sugar added at the last moment to spark re-fermentation.

A few are traditionally blended with other fruit lambics or with young lambic before bottling. So far, so good. But what about fruit lambics that are blended with dilute lambics such as *meerts* and end up tasting of a lot of fruit but not much lambic?

Drie Fonteinen Oude Kriek *Drie Fonteinen*
Kriek 100% Lambic Cantillon *Cantillon*
Hanssens Artisanaale Oude Kriek *Hanssens*
De Cam Oude Kriek *de Cam*
Boon Oude Kriek Mariage Parfait *Boon*

RARE AND EXPENSIVE AUTHENTIC KRIEKS
Cantillon Lou Pepe Kriek *Cantillon*
Drie Fonteinen Schaerbeekse Kriek *Drie Fonteinen*

Other authentic fruit lambics

Raspberry lambics have probably been made for centuries. However, they are often now too expensive to produce in authentic form using whole fruit as the price of raspberries from local growers in Ternat and elsewhere is simply too high. Most versions of *framboise* also compromise on the use of proper lambics.

Some highly respected brewers and blenders have made authentic style beers using other fruits in recent years. Drie Fonteinen made a couple of grape lambics a few years back as an experiment. Hanssens' too have perfected the creation of a strawberry lambic, though the fruit aroma seems to fade after about a year.

But it is Cantillon that uses the most bare cheek to push back the boundaries. Their grape lambics use White Muscat, Chardonnay, Merlot, Cabernet Franc and Pinot Noir grapes. The apricot lambic is made using fruit from the La Drôme region of southeastern France.

In our last edition we made mention of their export-only product called Midnight Sun, which is made to order from cloudberries, brought directly to the brewery by the Swedish importer who commissions the beer. The cloudberry (Sv: *hjotron*) – imagine a stunted ruddy-orange blackberry and you are nearly there – is Sweden's national fruit. Now in its third year, this is a brilliant beer.

Not to be outdone, in 2004 the importer who runs Helsinki's annual festival of Belgian beers, commissioned a Finnish equivalent. We have not yet tasted the world's first ever buckthorn berry lambic – Finnish national fruit, orangey hawthorns with attitude – but very much look forward to so doing.

BEST AUTHENTIC FRAMBOISES
Rosé de Gambrinus Cantillon *Cantillon*
Cantillon Lou Pepe Framboise *Cantillon*

BEST OTHER AUTHENTIC FRUIT LAMBICS
Cuvée Fou'foune (apricot) *Cantillon*
Oud Beitje (strawberry) *Hanssens*
St. Lamvinus (red grape) *Cantillon*
Vigneronne (white grape) *Cantillon*

Commercial fruit lambics

When international fame first came, rightfully, to the authentic steeped fruit lambics of the Senne Valley in the Seventies, courtesy of Michael Jackson and other beer writers, the commercial wing of the Beer Paradise started looking at cheap ways to make look-alikes for the less discerning.

Variations on the lambic theme at Drie Fonteinen

In those days some traditional makers had been topping up the fruit content of their *krieks* with cherry juice for years, and not necessarily adding it at the beginning of six months' steeping. So the cut-price merchants reasoned that as adding cherry juice was obviously okay, what was wrong with diluted fruit concentrate, alcoholic fruit cordials and even cherry syrup.

Then they discovered dilution. Fears that lambic makers were diluting their beer with water were probably unfounded. They did not need to. They had two other cheap liquids to call on. The first was a couple of minor varieties of diluted lambics made by fermenting the liquid drained off washed down spent grain before it is fed to the pigs or whatever. The second is *mengbier*, a cheap-and-easy brew created simply for mixing.

Once the juice-syrup barrier had been breached and strength no longer mattered, the new possibilities were endless. A downturn in the authenticity of raspberry beers was accompanied by lambics containing blackcurrant, peach, banana, pineapple, strawberry, apricot, plum, date, lemon, and tea. (Two sugars no milk presumably.) The nadir was the release of a caffeinated lambic to rival Red Bull.

The excuses for this tasteless commercial exploitation of a grand tradition ranged from the desire to draw young people away from the dangers of alcopops to that of encouraging women to drink beer. Not a word of "we want to sell our national culture down the river, then get rich by selling out to a multinational and moving to a tax haven".

To be fair, some brewers embraced the devil with more relish than others and a number would love to get back to the days when then did not have to hide their tricks from visitors.

EXAMPLES OF COMMERCIAL FRUIT LAMBICS

All Chapeau fruit brands *De Troch*
All Belle Vue fruit brands *Belle Vue (InBev)*
All St Louis fruit brands *Van Honsebrouck*
All Jacobins fruit brands *Bockor*
All Mort Subite fruit brands *Mort Subite (SCAM)*
(see brewery entry for proviso)
All Lindemans fruit brands *Lindemans*
All Timmermans fruit brands *Timmermans*
Louwaege Kriek *Mort Subite (SCAM)*

ALES

Lagers may be popular and lambics unique but the group of beer styles that has made Belgian brewing famous across the world is its ales. To be more precise, the Belgian forte is bottled ales. And the very best of these are the ones that condition in the bottle.

The spectrum of ale styles is broad and the boundaries between individual styles are not always as clear as didactic beer writers and those who hold brewing competitions would like you to think. We have done our best to introduce readers to the subject in a way that we hope makes sense of the main distinctions.

Trappist ales

In Belgium there are monks who make beer. This is such an attractive fact that it can only be a matter of time before a cartoon of a monk with a mashing fork is put on the national flag.

Monastic brewing is known to have existed as far back as the 6th century. St. Benedict, on whose rules the monastic system has always been based, encouraged abbeys to contribute to their local community and the brewing of beer was a part of that work.

In the Middle Ages ale was brewed as much on public health grounds as anything else – mashing killed off any infections in the brewing water, making beer a healthier option than the local water supply. Additionally, abbeys would run simple inns where travellers could enjoy bread, beer, cheese and other home-made produce, which made for excellent relations with the travelling classes.

The abbeys were great centres of learning. In scientific terms this helped in the discovery of how the world worked, not least the fermentation of alcohol. However, with knowledge came the opportunity to wield political power and influence.

The French Revolution in 1783 put an end to this, stripping the abbeys of their wealth and the roles they had played in the support of empires. As a side-effect, all brewing ceased. It was not revived until the abbey of Westmalle near Antwerp, in newly independent Belgium, began to make beer again in 1836.

Nowadays, monastic brewing has become associated entirely with the Cistercian Order of the Strict Observance, better known as the Trappists.

The Cistercian Order traces its origins back to the abbey of Cîteaux in eastern France, where Benedict's rules were adapted to make the distinctive code of a new Order. At the abbey of La Trappe in Normandy, in 1677 under Abbot Rancé, stricter rules were adopted for religious observance, including the well-known periods of silent contemplation. The Trappist tradition was granted the status of a separate Order in 1892.

Six of the seven approved abbey breweries are in Belgium and all are Trappist.

When **Westmalle** began in 1836 there was no commercial sale of its beers. This did not begin until around 1860 whereafter production grew gently. In 1921 they formed what we would call nowadays a "not-for-profit company" to oversee sales and distribution. Westmalle Tripel was first produced in 1934, though it did not become the beer we know today until 1956.

In 1839, the abbey of St. Sixtus, near **Westvleteren** in West Flanders had begun to brew. It is not known when the beers were first put on commercial sale but by 1946 a decision was made to commission a lay brewer, St. Bernardus at nearby Watou, to make its three existing beers for public sale under the St. Sixtus label. This agreement ended in 1992, since when the abbey's own brewhouse has been responsible for brewing three wonderful if, rarely found, ales.

The abbey at Scourmont, south of **Chimay**, was founded by monks from St. Sixtus in 1850. From the time that its brewery opened in 1862 there was some commercial sale to the public. Until 1948 only one beer was brewed, a brown ale equivalent to the current Chimay Red, in 75cl bottles only. Then came the Blue, originally as a Christmas brew, sold in 33cl bottles. The White was added eventually, in 1966 and became Triple in 2003.

At the abbey of St. Rémy, near **Rochefort**, on the borders of Namur and Luxembourg provinces, brewing began in 1892, just five years after it had been re-opened. As at

Westvleteren, full commercialisation has never really occurred, though the three dark ales are produced with all the professionalism of any modern brewhouse.

The purpose of the brewery at the abbey of **Orval** at Villers-devant-Orval, on the French border in Luxembourg province, was initially to fund the re-building of the abbey. It has been a commercial concern since it began in 1931. Breaking with the traditional of brown ales, the brewery produces a single distinctive amber ale in equally distinctive bottles.

The monks who re-established the abbey at Rochefort had come from the abbey at **Achel**, bang on the Dutch border in Limburg. In 1999 brewing commenced there in what initially seemed like a sort of abbey-brewpub. The first beers were light draught ales but as the years have passed a collection of heavier bottled ales is building that is more in keeping with the monastic brewing tradition.

Brewing at all six abbeys is carried out by professional lay brewers. Westmalle has always been open about using candy sugar in their brewing. They have done this for years and see it as an integral part of their products. Westvleteren does this too. Chimay uses starch. Orval uses straightforward sugar. We do not know the position at Achel.

Westmalle is the Abbey that brought the world the idea that *dubbel* beers should be brown and *tripel* beers blond, thereby disregarding the fact that ales tend to get darker with greater strength. Until they did that, *tripel* beers had tended to be dark brown in colour.

Yet there is no distinctive style of beer that should be called Trappist. The designation of Trappist beer is a legal one.

The seventh abbey, Schaapskooi, near Tilburg in the Netherlands lost its approval between 2000 and 2005 because its operations went outside the control of the Order into the hands of a commercial Dutch brewery, Bavaria. They were recently welcomed back into the flock after passing a number of authenticity and accountability tests.

The commercial exploitation of the term "Trappist" in marketing was limited by

Belgian law in 1962 to beers brewed by the monasteries. However, this law had few teeth and so an official designation of "Authentic Trappist Product" arrived in 1992.

Products must be approved by the Vatican as legitimate abbey produce. The mark has gone not only to beers but also to cheeses, breads, liqueurs, perfumes, soaps and many other goods. It does for Trappist beers what the black cockerel does for the wines of Chianti or the Soil Association logo does for British-grown organic foods. Although it is not in fact a pre-requisite, the badge implies that a product is "wholesome and pure".

Before being approved as an "Authentic Trappist Product" a commodity must meet unbreakable three rules. First, it must have been made within the walls of a Trappist abbey. Second, it must be made by or under the supervision of the monastery community. Third, the largest part of the profit must be spent on social work.

The importance of the word "made" in this context is crucial.

In the case of Chimay, its brewery has been functioning at maximum viable capacity for years. The beers are brewed and undergo primary fermentation at the abbey at Scourmont. Tankers then transport them from the fermenters to the bottling line some eight kilometres away at Baileux. So secondary fermentation in bottles in the warming chambers is not taken as part of "making the beer".

The most authentic of the Trappist breweries are those at Westvleteren and Rochefort. At each of these a small brewing staff still includes some of the brothers helping in one capacity or another, though the idea of them lugging great sacks of hops into the gleaming coppers is fanciful nonsense.

The companies that run the Westmalle and Chimay breweries make no bones about the fact that they are commercial concerns and that they seek to be commercially successful in the international beer market. Their share-holders, the Order, are just as demanding as those of a public company, though to different ends. As everywhere else, the companies seek to drive costs down while keeping profits high.

Belgian beer lovers have worried for decades that the Trappist beers are becoming simpler than they once were. Natural spiciness, bold bitterness and great complexity in the body of these beers, now gives way to a tendency towards greater sweetness, less bitterness and poorer reliability.

Without question this is true, though it is interesting as to why this should be.

Our last edition put forward the view that the increasing use of hop extracts and adjunctive sugars in the recipes was largely to blame. We continue to harbour concerns about the high use of adjuncts and the lack of assertive hopping. With every substitution or short cut it is inevitable that the odd percent or two will be knocked off the quality of the a beer, in a way that is cumulative.

However, at that stage we were unaware of another, more worrying trend that has been spreading across the Belgian brewing industry, which is the move to faster fermentation in tall fermenters.

The position is seen at its starkest at the Chimay brewery. These beers have become very popular in recent years and are exported across the world. However, several of the standard ways of expanding production to meet the demand are not available to the brewery.

Chimay's brewhouse cannot expand as it is housed within a small and tranquil abbey. Nor can it move to 24/7 production as it is next to a place of prayer and contemplation. Operating heavy machinery in the middle of the night would rather get in the way of the main event.

The bottling line and storage space were moved off site years ago so what, if anything, can give?

What they did was to condense the space taken up by fermentation, replacing the open shallow fermenters with tall sealed ones that ferment at a higher temperature. The floor space taken up by fermentation shrank impressively and a process that used to take ten days now took four. Then they cut out the lagering period.

However, having pinned their colours to the mast of supplying the demand, what do they do to keep up next? The logical next step would be to move primary fermentation off site. But that would beg the question of whether the beer would then still be "made" at the abbey.

The Guide has sympathy with Chimay's problems but it seems the dilemma here is simple. To maximise income at a time when demand outstrips supply one has two possible ways forward. Either you make more or you charge more. If you do not have capacity to make more then the decision seems an easy one.

The popular beer lovers' website www.ratebeer.com recently voted Westvleteren Abt as the best beer in the world. At a strength of 10.3% abv it is on a par with many wines. At the abbey's café the equivalent of a wine bottle of it would cost €4.75 (£3.20). We have never encountered a Belgian restaurant that sells even the most basic wine at such a price. Can the world's greatest beers afford to be so cheap?

In a head-to-head tasting of Belgian-style abbey beers made by American microbrewers, held in Washington in early 2005, the Guide's editor was shocked to find the imitators knocking the socks off freshly imported "real" Trappist ales. A re-run on Belgian soil would be interesting.

With only two major exceptions, Trappist beers appear only in bottled versions. In view of the shortened fermentation times at the brewery, we strongly recommend laying them down somewhere cool for at least six months. Though in the case of the high non-malt sugar, low-hopped ones this is proving too much for them.

BEST TRAPPIST PALE ALES
Westvleteren Blond *Westvleteren*
Orval *Orval*

BEST TRAPPIST BROWN ALES
Westvleteren Extra 8° *Westvleteren*
Rochefort 8° *Rochefort*
Achel Bruin *Achel*

DRAUGHT TRAPPIST ALES
Chimay Triple *Chimay*
Westmalle Dubbel *Westamalle*

BEST TRAPPIST BLOND TRIPLES
Trappist Achel Blond 8.5° *Achel*
Westmalle Tripel *Westmalle*
Chimay Cinq Cents (75cl) *Chimay*

BEST TRAPPIST STRONG BROWN ALES
Westvleteren Abt 12° *Westvleteren*
Rochefort 10° *Rochefort*
Trappist Achel 9.5° *Achel*
Chimay Grande Réserve (75cl) *Chimay*

Abbey beers

The reason that use of the term Trappist was restricted by Belgian law in 1962 was that exploitation of monastic brewing traditions by commercial breweries was getting out of hand. It had become too easy to cash in on the holy beers market.

Since that time the term "abbey beers" has grown up to describe a ragbag of beers that include at least two distinct but overlapping groups. The first are the Trappist wannabes, designed to imitate the best traditions of dubbel and tripel beers on the principle that imitation is the most lucrative form of flattery. The second are beers brewed at the request of religious institutions to make a bit of money.

The way these deals work is that a commercial negotiator representing an abbey or other religious institution gets together with a brewer or wholesaler and agree a deal whereby the abbey officially licences the brewer to make beers in their name. The abbey gets some useful income, while the brewer gets the cache of a blessing for their product.

We believe that the abbey-brewery pairings that benefit in this way are:

- Affligem (*Flemish Brabant*) & Postel (*Antwerp*) – Affligem (Heineken)
- Bornem (*Antwerp*) – Van Steenberge
- Cambron (*Hainaut*) – Silly
- Dendermonde (*East Flanders*) – De Block
- Ename (*East Flanders*) – Roman
- Bonne Espèrance (*Hainaut*) & Floreffe (*Namur*) – Lefèbvre
- Grimbergen (*Flemish Brabant*) – Union (SCAM)
- Leffe (*Namur*) – Hoegaarden (InBev)
- Maredsous (*Namur*) – Moortgat
- Steenbrugge (*West Flanders*) – Palm
- Tongerlo (*Antwerp*) – Haacht
- Val-Dieu (*Liège*) – Val-Dieu

Other prominent brands sporting the names of defunct cloisters include Abbaye d'Aulne, Ciney and Corsendonk. The orders that ran these places are not thought to derive any commercial benefit from the beers that take their names.

Ironically those breweries that imply monk-ish connections to beers that have none are often the most loyal to the monastic styles. Names include:

Abbaye des Rocs & Montagnarde (Abbaye des Rocs), Moinette (Dupont), Guldenberg (de Ranke), Kapittel (Van Eecke), Augustijn (Van Steenberge), Bon-Secours (Caulier), Braven Apostel (commissioned from Proef), Divine (Silly), Karmeliet (Bosteels), Pater Lieven (Van den Bossche), St. Benoît & Triple Moine (du Bocq), St. Bernardus (St. Bernard-us), St. Gummarus (St. Jozef), St. Idesbald (Huyghe) and Witkap (Slaghmuylder).

Twenty years ago there were three main types of abbey beer. These were brown ales of 6.5–8% abv in the style of Westmalle Dubbel, blond ales of 8–9.5% abv in the style of Westmalle Tripel and brown blockbusters of 9–12% abv in the style of Chimay Bleue.

In recent years two other so-called abbey beer styles have emerged. These are ordinary blond and brown ales of 5.5–7.5% abv, usually called blond and brown. As these are indistinguishable from other medium strength beers of the same colour we will say no more about them here.

Dubbel/Double

A typical *dubbel* (Fr: *double*) should be copper-brown to dark brown in colour, contain some caramelised malts and be re-fermented in the bottle. It may have some candied sweetness. Bitterness may vary from soft to obvious.

At the sweeter, lighter end they are much like strong brown ales anywhere. The more interesting ones are black and brackish like a strong porter, with elements of stewed tea.

Tripel/Triple

A typical *tripel* (Fr: *triple*) should be strong and nowadays is blond to golden in colour. It is made with mainly lighter coloured malts and is likely to contain adjuncts in the mash that give it a candied sweetness. It will be re-fermented in the bottle. Bitterness may vary from soft to assertive.

The lightest are superannuated ordinary blonds. The style overlaps increasingly with the strong blond style of Duvel and its imitators.

BEST LIGHTER ABBEY DUBBELS
St. Bernardus Pater 6° *St. Bernardus*

BEST HEAVIER ABBEY DUBBELS
St. Bernardus Prior *St. Bernardus*
Maredsous 8 *Moortgat*
St. Feuillien Brune *St. Feuillien*

BEST LIGHTER BLOND ABBEY TRIPELS
Nounnette *Abbaye des Rocs*
Watou Tripel *St. Bernardus*
St. Bernardus Tripel *St. Bernardus*
Witkap Tripel *Slaghmuylder*

BEST HEAVIER BLOND ABBEY TRIPELS
Kerckomse Tripel *Kerkom*
St. Feuillien Triple *St. Feuillien*
La Rulles Triple *Rulles*
Reinaert Tripel *Proef*
Kameleon Tripel *Hopperd*

Wheat beers

The success of wheat beers is one of the marketing miracles of the modern age.

People have been brewing beers with wheat for as long as they have been using barley. The latter grain gained the upper hand because beers made with a high wheat mash are horribly sweet and do not clear easily. The mash can also leave a sticky residue in the brewing equipment that is hard to shift and may attract infection.

Despite the downside, wheat has always had one unassailable advantage over barley – it is almost invariably cheaper. This helped the survival of wheat beers into the 20th century, though by 1970 wheat beers had all but disappeared from commercial brewing in Europe.

Their revival in fortune can be traced back to one man, a Belgian called Pierre Celis.

In 1966 Celis bought the old De Kluis brewery in his home town of Hoegaarden because he hankered after reviving a type of beer that he had watched a local brewer making when he was a child.

The Guide's editor first encountered Celis's beer back in 1975, when it was known as Oud Hoegaards. It was sold in opaque white bottles with lettering engraved on them and dyed in blue. In those days a cloudy beer was usually a cause of complaint but this sweet, rather delicate concoction was fascinating. Lazy spicing had not taken a grip then, so coriander and dried Curaçao orange peel were racy additions.

Forty years on, Pierre and his beer style have done rather well, though whether even he thought that Hoegaarden would one day have a brewery producing nearly a million hectolitres a year of wheat beer and sending it around the globe is doubtful. And would anyone have foreseen that this revival would spread throughout Europe, to North America and maybe yet worldwide?

Wheat beers go by different identities, which can get confusing. Some are called, literally, wheat beer (Du: *tarwebier*; Fr: *bière de froment*). Others are called white beer (Du: *witbier*; Fr: *bière blanche*).

The term white beer comes about because unless the beer is spun at low temperature, it will retain a milky protein haze that creates a cloudy-looking beer in the glass.

Against the preferences of a generation ago, most modern drinkers seem to like their wheat beers cloudy. Nowadays most Belgian wheat beers retain their haze.

The mash in a commercial wheat beer contains typically 30–40% wheat. Some brewers will use a proportion of malted wheat. The rest of the grain is likely to be Pilsener malt. Wheat imparts a strong grainy flavour to beer, much like freshly baked bread. The style is not robust enough to absorb substitute sugars without wilting, though this does not stop brewers trying.

Wheat beers tend to be relatively low in alcohol (4–5.5% abv) as the higher grain concentrations required for making stronger beers clog the brew kettles, though there are some stronger wheat beers on the market.

Traditionally hopping is on the low side though a few breweries are experimenting with a more assertive hop presence. The addition of flavourings such as dried peel and coriander, is commonplace and for a change is a traditional practice.

A number of smaller producers have also experimented with using old-fashioned strains of wheat such as spelt (Fr: *épeautre*) or buckwheat (Du: *boekweit*; Fr: *sarrasin*). Others add oats (Du: *haver*; Fr: *avoine*) or rye (Du: *rogge*; Fr: *seigle*).

A recent trend to adding fruit syrups before bottling will hopefully die on its feet.

Some cafés serve wheat beers with a slice of lemon in the glass. Please yourself but we think it looks and tastes ridiculous.

BEST ORDINARY WHEAT BEERS

St. Bernardus Wit *St. Bernardus*
Saisis *Ellezelloise*
Watou's Witbier *Van Eecke*
Limburgse Witte *St. Jozef*
Augrenoise *Augrenoise*
Troublette *Caracole*

BEST UNUSUAL WHEAT BEERS

Saison de l'Épeautre *Blaugies*
Sara *Silenrieux*
Joseph *Silenrieux*
Waase Wolfbier *Boelens*

Oak-aged ales

Lambics are not the only beers in Belgium to be aged in oak casks. There is also a tradition of ageing ales in oak, mainly in the provinces of East and West Flanders, aimed at creating sharp, sour beers.

The pedigree of oak-aged beers has become blurred by history. However, present day Belgium first became famed for its ales as far back as the 14th century. In those days the reputation accrued mainly to strong brown ales served directly from the oak casks in which they had been stored for some time.

In the first half of the 20th century the standard ales of many Flemish breweries remained brown ales. Farm and factory workers would drink sour brown ales of lower gravity while taverns would sell stronger brews.

Around the East Flanders town of Oudenaarde, a small cluster of independent breweries remained until recently producing characteristic dark brown ales. The traditional way of making these included boiling the mash for up to three hours to produce a stewed effect. Thus the beers were dark in colour with a clear presence of caramelised sugars.

These beers have all but disappeared in recent years, their only residue being a number of locally produced imitations of the genre, in most cases of little pedigree.

In the southern part of West Flanders, around Kortrijk and Roeselare, the tradition of making slightly sour brown ales has survived more successfully and is showing signs of a revival.

The common thread to oak-aged ales is that after brewing they are stored in large oak tuns (Du: *foederen*; Fr: *foudres*) for prolonged maturation lasting up to two years. Conditioning in this way introduces secondary and tertiary fermentation that has some similarities with the lactic fermentation of lambic-making. It is not dissimilar from the ageing of traditional ciders or wines in large casks or barriques.

In its raw state brown ale that has been in the wood for two years is ultra-dry and a bit of a challenge. The driest are so astringent that salivary glands may spasm on first contact. Yet as with authentic gueuze, once the taste is acquired you will want to have a case in your cellar at all times.

After maturation, the beers are blended before bottling. Most commonly brewers mix their older beers with younger ones to reach a sweet and sour quality that is more acceptable to most palates. Getting it right is difficult. Too much fresh beer makes for a bland blend.

Traditionally a distinction has been drawn between the beers of West Flanders and those from round Oudenaarde. Michael Jackson coined the term Flemish Red (Du:

Vlaams rood) for the former and Flemish Old Brown (Du: *Vlaams oud bruin*) for the latter.

The two traditions are certainly related. They are not twins but whether they are brothers or cousins is a matter of opinion. In practice the browner beers use more pale ale malts, while the redder ones stick to Pilsener malt.

The eventual fate of oak-aged ales is one of the pivotal issues to the future of Belgian beer. It takes a lot of cash and even more faith to invest in regenerating a brewery that requires to be kitted out with huge, handcrafted constructions in oak.

The Eighties and Nineties saw brewers failing to renew their old kit and everyone assumed that these sour old beers would fade into history. Interbrew did not want one so therefore the beers were dead.

Some breweries decided they could age their beers just as well in steel, leaving them in a disused vessel in some quiet corner of the brewery. Others tried to imitate an ageing effect by injecting their beers with lactic acid or in one case suspending a piece of wood in them.

The largest maker of these beers, Rodenbach, was taken over by the large independent, Palm in 1998, who closed the brewery. Many of us assumed that Palm would let the oak-ageing capacity run down and would replace it by "modern methods". In practice investment in the fermentation capacity appears to have been impressive. Indeed shortly before going to press, a draught version of the beer from the fermenting hall went on sale in a pub in Roeselare, Rodenbach's home town.

Up the road in Vichte, the Verhaeghe family brewery has been developing both its beers and its marketing with sound commercial success, its faith in the future demonstrated by investment in new tuns.

The Guide is watching with interest what Bavik will do, now that it has tapped a US market for a direct bottling of its oak-aged mixer beer. Even Liefmans, who stopped producing oak-aged beers soon after the Riva takeover of 1990, has managed to do something clever with a couple of experimental runs of its Odnar in the last year or so.

Perhaps the most significant development for the tenuous survival of these marvellously unusual ales has happened not in Oudenaarde or Kortrijk but in Fort Collins, Colorado.

The New Belgium Brewing Company, under the steer of Peter Bouckaert, a former brewer at Rodenbach, has actually started making an American oak-aged ale called La Folie, in new oak tuns specially commissioned for the process. More to the point it is a remarkably fine beer.

BEST OAK-AGED ALES
Duchesse de Bourgogne *Verhaeghe*
Rodenbach Grand Cru *Rodenbach*
Vichtenaar *Verhaeghe*
Petrus Aged Ale (US import only) *Bavik*
Oud Belegen Foederbier *Rodenbach*

OTHER INTERESTING AGED ALES
Cnudde Oud Bruin *Cnudde*
Felix Oudenaards Oud Bruin *Verhaeghe*
Odnar *Liefmans*
Bios Vlaamse Bourgogne *Van Steenberge*

Blonde ales

The rising public interest of the last fifty years in light-coloured lagers such as Pilsener has led to brewers paying increasing attention to the creation of ales of a similar hue. The dominant style of blond ale (Fr: *bière blonde*) takes roughly the same form across the whole of Belgium and extends effortlessly into France and the southern Netherlands.

This is a brew of typically 5.5–7.5% abv that tends to be highly polished in appearance. Some are spiced but most are not. Where there is bottle conditioning this is usually managed by a thin film of active cells rather than the thick layer of dead ones.

The light colour is produced by the heavy, sometimes exclusive reliance on Pilsener malt. Hopping has generally been mild to moderate, though some brewers are beginning to branch out a bit by adding dry hopping with good effects.

In the German city of Köln (Cologne), they are proud to make many versions of a straw-coloured, low strength (4–5% abv) style of ale, named Kölsch after the town. Brewers there have applied for an appellation contrôlée for the style but even if this were to be accepted globally, imitations are likely to continue simply because it is such a good idea. The Netherlands has a dozen and Belgium one or two.

It is less that a hundred kilometres from Köln to Limburg, where the Guide swears there is a style of slightly stronger dry-hopped light blond ale emerging. The original was Martens Sezoens, which has interestingly just appeared in a bottle-conditioned variety called Opus. On the principle that all good beers should be respected by the maker's near neighbours, we think we see a trend in the province.

Stronger blond ales are more difficult to define in objective terms. Moortgat brewery made Duvel and then a lot of others brewers, envious of its success but aware of its excellence, followed suit. Calling such beers strong blonds sounds pathetic but is possibly better that saying "all those beers that wish they were Duvel".

In such beers any pungent bouquet should come from hops not spice. Their most disarming quality is that most are dangerously drinkable. Any delicate sediment is often best left in the bottle. We wish more were dry hopped. More assertive hopping would be a major factor in distinguishing them from the tripel style. Reliance on Pilsener malt is the other.

BEST ORDINARY BLOND ALES
La Rulles Blond *Rulles*
Affligem Paters Vat *Affligem* (Heineken)
Kapittel Blond *Van Eecke*
Gouyasse Tradition *Géants*

BEST LIMBURG BLOND ALES
Ter Dolen Blond *ter Dolen*
Sezoens Blond *Martens*
Bink Blond *Kerkom*
Ops-Ale *St. Jozef*

BEST STRONG BLOND ALES
Moinette Blonde *Dupont*
Duvel *Moortgat*
Quintine Blonde *Ellezelloise*
Hapkin *Union* (SCAM)

BEST UNUSUAL BLOND ALES
Stimulo *Slaghmuylder*
Darbyste (with fig essence) *Blaugies*
Arabier *de Dolle Brouwers*
Vlaskop *Strubbe*

Pale and amber ales

Sitting uncomfortably between the extremes of blond and brown ales are a group of beer styles that much of the world refers to as pale ales. It is a matter of opinion whether the Belgians invented pale ale and exported the idea to Britain, or vice versa, or neither.

In Belgium, the term *pale-ale* occurs as a legitimate part of the brewer's lexicon in both Dutch and French, implying a light amber beer of English character. A term that has revived somewhat in the last few years is special (Du: *speciaal*; Fr: *spéciale*). This implies a distinctly Belgian style of pale ale in the 4–5.5% abv range. For beers of 6% and above the term amber (Fr: *ambrée*) is preferred.

The big name Flemish pale ales developed in the years between the two 20th century wars. The biggest sellers, Palm Speciaal and De Koninck, date from 1928 and 1939 respectively.

The principle differences between these and their English forebears is in the hopping. The beers considered English tend towards English hop varieties such as Goldings. In Belgian pale ales bitterness is rarely a strong point at all, their character is dominated by slightly caramelised overtones and restraint the order of the day.

Down south they have a different style of pale ale altogether. As *saison* the cluster of unrelated pale ales, some made year-round, others just for summer, was never going to work as a style. French small brewers had adopted *bière de garde* to great effect, so the term "farmhouse ales" has grown in prominence in the last couple of years. The essential concept is that huge individual differences are allowed, or even expected.

If *saison* has a legitimate history it was as a light beer in which most of the sugar had been fermented through to alcohol. They needed to be thirst-quenching but at the same time resilient to warm storage. They achieved this by heavy hopping.

The Guide predicts that with their renewed confidence, Wallonian brewers will come to discover and recreate a tradition of huge hoppy beers from their localities many of which bear a remarkable resemblance to

Saison Dupont. Except for a few who might dare to produce something akin to the major league eccentricity of Vapeur.

More typical of Wallonian brewing in the last two decades has been the adoption of single brand name ranges of blonde, brune and ambrée beers, made popular by du Bocq with la Gauloise.

However, Wallonie would not be Wallonie if there were any convention about what a brewer's ambrée should be like. Some are the strongest of the range, some the weakest. A few are heavyweight classics while others are frivolous. Some are heavily spiced, others totally clean. What matters is that none is like De Konick or Palm, Bass or John Martin's.

BEST ORDINARY PALE ALES

De Koninck *De Koninck*
De Ryck Speciaal *De Ryck*
Yperman *Leroy*
Malheur 6 *Malheur*

BEST SAISONS

Saison Dupont *Dupont*
Saison Dupont Biologique *Dupont*
Saison 2000 *Ellezelloise*
Saison de Pipaix *Vapeur*

BEST ORDINARY AMBRÉES
La Médiévale Ambrée *Bouillon*
Urchon *Géants*
Kameleon Amber *Hopperd*
Artevelde Grand Cru *Huyghe*

BEST STRONG AMBRÉES
Avec les Bons Voeux *Dupont*
Guldenberg *de Ranke*
Caracole Ambrée *Caracole*
La Montagnarde *Abbaye des Rocs*

BEST UNUSUAL PALE ALES
XX Bitter *de Ranke*
Poperings Hommelbier *Van Eecke*
Tonneke *Contreras*
Cervesia *Dupont*

Brown ales and stouts

Until the 20th century, the majority of beer in the world was brown. In 1939 so was four-fifths of the beer in Belgium. By tradition, old brewing towns like Diest, Mechelen and Oudenaarde produced distinctly different styles of brown beer. While dark ales generally are making a comeback they will return to a different world.

Low-medium strength (4–5.5%) brown ales of character are fast disappearing to be replaced by stronger (5.5–7.5%) brown beers stylised into a newly created abbey brown style, which is code for "like Leffe". There is a confusion in its relationship to dubbel, unsurprisingly. But as modern drinkers use their eyes more than their noses and their palates, this may be a necessary phase.

Stout has undergone something of a revival in Belgium in recent years, not helped by the huge differences in the beers that share that name. Stout is usually regarded as a dark, bitter beer made with a relatively high proportion of chocolate malt and roasted barley.

Ireland has snaffled the reputation as the world's great stout makers with their three heavily-marketed international brands, Guinness, Murphy's and Beamish. These create the impression that stout should be dry, plain, weak and dark, with a cleverly manufactured head. This ain't necessarily so.

In Britain, milk stout and oat stout have always been sweet. This is also true in West Flanders, where stout usually means a lowish

strength (4–5%), intensely sweet ale similar to old Kentish stouts like Mackeson.

Although there are also drier Belgian stouts of ordinary strength, more are of higher strength, roughly equivalent to that of the Export Guinness (8.8%) that has been imported for over a century. So powerful is the Guinness brand that unusually it is not directly imitated though there are heavy black Belgian beers that have similarities.

It is thought that *Scotch ale* began to appear in Belgium during the 1914–18 war, as a brew for Scottish servicemen. Scottish ales have historically made up for low hopping (hops did not grow in Scotland) by adopting a fulsome malt character. Longer brewing times tended to make them darker.

Although Scotch ale had all but disappeared from Scotland by the late 1950s, it continued in Belgium, where it is a dark, sweetish, strongish beer with a highish hop count masked by lots of unfermented sugars.

In Flanders the tradition of strong dark tripels virtually disappeared once the Westmalle phenomenon took off, though it should be remembered that tripel was traditionally a style of brown ale. Many of the abbey brands from West Flanders breweries take their pedigree from this tradition.

Down south Wallonian brewers take their role model as the mighty Gauloise Brune, with the imitators sometimes finding themselves in the ascendancy since the original was cleaned up a bit too fastidiously. Wallonian *bière brune* is usually best when free of spices, rich, dark and bottle-conditioned.

BEST ORDINARY BROWN ALES
La Rulles Brune *Rulles*
Buffalo *Van den Bossche*
Bink Bruin *Kerkom*
Rochus Vlumschen Bruinen *De Ryck*

BEST STRONG BROWN ALES
Kapittel Prior *Van Eecke*
St. Bernardus Prior *St. Bernardus*
Gouden Carolus Classic *Anker*
't Smisje Dubbel Dadel *Regenboog*

BEST UNUSUAL BROWN ALES
Oerbier *de Dolle Brouwers*
Grottenbier *St. Bernardus*
Duivel Donkere *Boon*
3 Schténg *Grain d'Orge*

BEST WALLONIAN BROWN ALES
Moinette Brune Dupont
Gauloise Brune du Bocq
St. Feuillien Brune St. Feuillien
Abbaye des Rocs Abbaye des Rocs

BEST ORDINARY SWEET STOUTS
Wilson Mild Stout Van Steenberge

BEST ORDINARY DRY STOUTS
Callewaert Stout Strubbe

BEST STRONG DRY STOUTS
Hercule Ellezelloise
Dolle Extra Stout de Dolle Brouwers
Ambiorix Dubbel Slaghmuylder

BEST STRONG SWEET STOUTS
Zatte Bie de Bie
(see brewery entry for proviso)

BEST SCOTCH ALES
Scotch Silly Silly

Barley wines

The term barley wine (Du: *gerstewijn*) is used widely in the beer world. The point at which a strong ale becomes a barley wine is not yet the subject of EU legislation. Until it is, the Guide will take any beer in the 10% and over range as qualifying.

These are not beers designed to assist the alcoholically challenged on the road to oblivion – that is the job of tinned super-strength lagers.

A barley wine should be what it says, a creation that should be treated as a sipping drink made from the best of grains. Poorly made ones are more quaffable but lead to drunkenness before satisfaction. The best will make their presence felt whatever the occasion and leave you with the simple challenge "follow that then".

Barley wines tend to be sweet. Traditional brewers' yeast get killed by alcohol poisoning before they reach the dizzying heights of wine strength. On the other hand wine yeast is generally too slow to ferment a strong beer. Brewers generally mix their yeast to get the right balance.

A recent fascinating variant with a lot of potential is the beers made by the Champagne method. These were championed by Malheur and followed with remarkable foresight by

their neighbours Bosteels in 2002. Hand crafted and labour-intensive, they will never be other than expensive, but can be worth every penny.

BEST STANDARD BARLEY WINES
Bush Ambrée Dubuisson
Maredsous 10 Moortgat
St. Bernardus Abt St. Bernardus
Bush Blonde Dubuisson

BEST RARE AND EXPENSIVE BARLEY WINES
Malheur Bière Brut Malheur
Bush Prestige Dubuisson
Malheur Dark Brut Malheur

SEASONAL VARIETIES

Most beer-producing nations have a tradition of seasonal beers. Culturally, these may serve to celebrate a religious festival such as Christmas or Easter or they may derive from practical farming considerations. Disposing of a great mound of grain by brewing a stronger beer after harvest or as over-stocking becomes apparent in spring makes good sense.

In recent years, suggestions from the finance director on how to maintain cashflow have prompted the invention of new frivolities.

Winter beers

The most interesting season for special beers in Belgium is undoubtedly the winter. If you want to see the whole array in one go, visit the festival of winter beers held in mid-December at Essen, north of Antwerp (see Beer Events).

Three traditions have met under one banner – Christmas beers (Du: *kerstbieren*: Fr: *bières de Noël*), New Year's Eve beers (Du: *eindejaarsbieren*) and winter ales (Du: *winterbieren*; Fr: *bières d'hiver*).

Some Belgian cafés that take an interest in such things muster up to fifty, before you count the ones they have kept back in the cellar from previous years. One of the appeals of the stronger brews is that they are made with impressive keeping quality.

Spicing of winter ales is traditional. The commonly used ingredients are cinnamon, allspice, ginger, dried fruits and nutmeg.

Some taste suspiciously like mince pies and Christmas cake.

But by no means all of these beers are high strength. A few breweries deliberately produce wheat beers or simply up-market regular ales.

The annoying feature is the ever-changing nature of beers from year to year. The ones we particularly recommend are those that maintain the same character year on year.

BEST LIGHT WINTER BEERS
Noël Christmas Weihnacht *Verhaeghe*
De Ryck Christmas Pale Ale *De Ryck*

BEST HEAVY WINTER BEERS
Stille Nacht *de Dolle Brouwers*
Bush Premium *Dubuisson*
Kerstpater *Van den Bossche*
Abbaye des Rocs Spéciale Noël *Abbaye des Rocs*

BEST UNUSUAL WINTER BEERS
Liefmans Glühkriek *Liefmans*

Easter beers

Belgian brewers have been rather docile about welcoming the spring but fiscal needs must and a style will emerge in time. Across the Dutch and German borders this is the season of pale, malty, sweet *meibo(c)k* beers. The Danes are keen on dark brews for the season.

BEST SPRING ALES
Boskeun *de Dolle Brouwers*
Printemps de Silly *Silly*
Contreras Mars Especial *Contreras*

Summer beers

The emergence of light bitter summer ales in Britain and the US is beginning to influence Belgian brewers, though the propensity to add flowers and perfumes is not perhaps the most alluring of new trends. The Wallonian tradition of saison beers has now moved to become an all-year phenomenon and is dealt with under pale and amber ales (above).

BEST LIGHT SUMMER BEERS
Biolégère *Dupont*
Vapeur Légère *Vapeur*

BEST OTHER SUMMER BEERS
Oeral *de Dolle Brouwers*
Reuss *Kerkom*
Vlaamse Primitief *Proef*

Autumn beers

A few Belgian brewers have experimented with dark strongish beers with falling leaves type of spices in them. There is no pattern or stability as yet.

Winter beer

FLAVOURED BEERS

Until the last five years, British brewers had spent half a century shying away from deliberately flavouring beers, despite the fact that they had done so for centuries previously. The Belgians on the other hand had never stopped adding external flavours such as spices and fruit. Indeed a dab of coriander was often one of the magical ingredients that gave a Belgian ale its edge.

Spicing used to be a subtle and clever variant on the brewer's art. Unfortunately for everyone the last ten years has seen Belgian brewers in a pathetic rush towards making beers that are cartoons of special ales. Coriander soups and pre-mixed lager and black have become the order of the day, some from pioneering microbrewers, as well as the usual suspects.

The Guide hopes this is just a fad. Belgian brewing has enough problems in its export markets being saddled with InBev's cack-handed misrepresentation of the Belgium brand, without serious beer makers getting the commercial equivalent of a mid-life crisis and thinking they can take the world with tenth rate joke brews.

Spiced beers

Brewers the world over have been chucking spices into beer, overtly or otherwise, since the time of the ancient Egyptians. Cinnamon, coriander, cumin, dried peel, aniseed and vanilla have been used to add interest to beer as they do to baking. In wheat beers and winter brews they are traditional ingredients.

However, spicing is also used with less integrity to mask unpleasant flavours caused by bad beer-making technique or unclean kit allowing uncontrolled infection and bad tastes into a living beer.

Popular additives of recent times include allspice, basil, bog-myrtle, camomile, caraway seed, chicory, cloves, dill seed, ginger, ginseng, horseradish, juniper, liquorice, mint, nutmeg, pepper, vanilla, woodruff, something called "seeds of paradise" and a variety of nuts!

Spices for flavouring may be added at the brewing stage. For masking bad technique they can be added at any point up to bottling – like wearing cheap perfume instead of washing. As with cooking they can be used whole, crushed or in powdered form. For later interventions essence is better.

Changing the spice recipe in a brew is one of the tricks used by brewers to claim that brew X is unique. A hint of coriander in the background of a beer can be entertaining. A great clump of Eurospice in the middle of it is often a rip-off.

Fruit beers

The steeping of fruit in cask-aged beers is a noble art and has given the world a host of superbly different flavours and experiences. It is not restricted to lambic makers. Some brewers of oak-aged and other ales produce great examples too.

Sticking syrup into mass-production lagers and cheap ales is a blatant attempt to make money by selling crap to the ill-informed

The claim that they like it is not good enough to justify it. People like the smell of chloroform and the taste of cyanide.

In no form of beer making is the gap between the craftsman and the charlatan so apparent. If the Belgian brewing establishment wishes to pander to mediocrity in this way it deserves every hit it takes.

THE BEST NON-LAMBIC FRUIT BEERS
De Ranke Kriekbier *de Ranke*
Verhaeghe Echte Kriek *Verhaeghe*
Ducassis *Géants*

Honey beers

A new fad on which the Guide has no clear view is the habit of adding the thinnest of honeys to beer. The principle is much the same as with any other substitute sugars in that the sugar content of honey ferments quite well but residual flavours remain in the beer.

This results in the production of some sickly sweet beers while others are surprisingly full-flavoured. We think it depends on the skill of the brewer, God forbid!

BEST HONEY BEERS
Klokbier *Boelens*
Bière de Miel Bio *Dupont*

And then some

Thankfully, the beers of Belgium will never be containable to a simple matrix of characters and flavours. However hard one tries to be omniscient, some devious fellow will go and do something different or else just do the opposite of good practice and come up with a stroke of genius.

If it were ever different we would quit and write about American microbrewers instead.

The strangest grain from which we have tasted a good beer is mustard seed. We are less convinced by South American quinua.

The oddest additives in a good beer is a difficult one, though shii-take mushrooms take some beating. Pumpkin, lichen, carrots and stinging nettles are other possible contenders. We have not dared ask Dany Prignon what his more outrageous concoctions at Fantôme contain.

BEST OTHER BEERS
Vapeur en Folie *Vapeur*
Fantôme *Fantôme*
Kameleon Ginseng *Hopperd*
St. Monon Bière Spéciale des Fêtes *St. Monon*

The brewers of Belgium

"History is bunk."

HENRY FORD
Founder of the Ford Motor Company

BELGIUM IS CHAUVINISTIC ABOUT BEER. Less than 8% of the beer drunk is imported. Even the global "wet air" brands do not have a significant foothold yet.

If there were such a thing as a typical Belgian then their take on beer would involve immense pride and pitifully little knowledge.

The real reason that brewery companies like to boast about their longevity is that surviving more than a few decades is remarkable. At the beginning of 2005 there were between 118 and 124 functioning commercial breweries in Belgium, depending on your definitions. All but eight of these were independent of the global corporations.

Gains and losses

Since the 1998 edition of the *Good Beer Guide to Belgium & Holland*, Belgium lost twelve independent breweries and confirmed the demise of two others.

The biggest to go was **Sterkens**, an old-fashioned ale brewery near Antwerp, whose next generation prefer to brew in Florida. Bruges lost the **Gouden Boom** brewery and the maltings museum that went with it.

Bruges also saw a remarkable revival though, with the descendants of Henri Maes starting to brew once more at the **Halve Maan** brewery in the city, which had brewed very little since it had become Straffe Hendrik some fifteen years ago.

Rodenbach also restarted brewing at Roeselare, enabling them to stop having to trunk brown ale from Palm for fermentation in their old oak tuns.

By far the most important brewery to go was **Oud Beersel**. One of the few remaining lambic breweries it fell victim to a family disagreement, though recent developments have seen new blood well set to revive its old crafts within the next few years.

Crombé of Zottegem in East Flanders, a brewery for ten generations and maker of an extraordinary cherry beer, had not brewed since 1999 and the Gyuide does not believe it will brew again. Likewise **Facon** of Bellegem, which failed to revive its rich and aged brown ales.

Of the newer breweries particularly sad losses were **Vervifontaine**, whose gutsy ales had survived legal battles and to keep Liège province watered, **Rochefortoise**, whose remarkable growth was not sufficient to keep its owner in Europe, and **Tongrinnoise**, another new micro that had impressed beer lovers in its time but failed to survive varying levels of commitment from its shareholders.

The brewpub scene lost the **Brugse Bierkaai** in Bruges and the **Mibrana** brewery at the Artisans Brasseurs in Namur, but gained three others in Mons, Brussels and rural Luxembourg.

In all there have been fourteen newcomers of which ten have been in Wallonia and only four in Flanders. For those who like this sort of thing, check out Alvinne, Authentique, Brabant, Brasse-Temps (Mons), Cazeau, Flo, Glazen Toren, 't Hofbrouwerijke, Imprimerie, Lautenne, Millivertus, St. Canarus, St. Pieters and Trois Fourquets in our listings below.

To show just how fluid this industry is, two breweries both came and went in this time and three others are probably in production (see Future breweries, page 160).

It is interesting but not surprising that all the newcomers are ale breweries and that except for the brewpubs they mainly produce bottle-fermented beers. At least three already export to the US. A couple of others should.

Riva has rebranded itself as **Liefmans**, absorbing the Straffe Hendrik brands. The owners of the Landtsheer brewery have renamed it after its main products, **Malheur**. And the Doolen brewery has rebadged itself **ter Dolen**.

The Belgian beer market

Figures from the trade organisation CBB show that consumption of beer in Belgium fell 8% between 1993 and 2001, to just under 10 million hectolitres. Even scarier for brewers, between 1990 and 2002, the average Belgian citizen, as opposed to traveller or ex-pat, reduced their reported annual beer intake from 120 litres to just 90.

In 2003, for the first time ever, beer was relegated to fourth place in the league table of favourite drinks, after soft drinks, water and the most popular, coffee, which came in at an agitating 135 litres.

The brunt of the decline affected Pilseners, including imported varieties. At the same time wheat beers fell by 5% and, we are delighted to say, sales of the uniformly dreadful non-alcoholic beers halved. This last fall was so profound that brewers in effect stopped marketing them.

At the same time regional beers fell back only slightly, whereas consumption of abbey beers more than doubled. Stronger beers too saw three successive annual rises to 2001.

One of the reasons for the fall in sales is drink-drive laws affecting sales in cafés and restaurants. Nowadays only around 58% of beer is consumed in such places. The rest is drunk at home, bought from shops, warehouses and supermarkets. This reflects similar changes all over Europe.

Belgians now drink significantly less beer than the British (on 97 litres per head) but still more than the Dutch, whose 78.7 litres per head in 2003 continued a steady fall that has reached 15% since 1990.

Four awkward questions

The Guide aims to tell its readers about every Belgian brewery in current operation and every beer in regular year-round or seasonal production.

With such a simple and clearly defined mission you would have thought that compiling the information would be easy There are a number of complicated reasons why this is not the case.

What exactly do you mean by a brewery?
The Guide still holds on to the old-fashioned notion that a brewery is a place where beer is made. But this glib answer fails to make clear what is meant by the word "made".

Two of the best makers of gueuze and fruit lambics, de Cam and Hanssens, do not brew any beer at all. They buy in the lambics from which their beers are made, blend them and steep fruit in them. In so doing they create great beers that it would be far too pedantic to exclude.

That defines the thin end of the wedge but how much further should we go? Rodenbach does not brew either, but having received beer from its parent company brought in tankers across Flanders ferments it in for up to two years in oak tuns, helping to create one of the world's greatest beers. So we still include it.

Then again how often does a brewery need to be used before it can be said to be in current production? Here at least, Belgian law helps. In order to retain a licence for commercial brewing a plant must be used at least once a year. Which is helpfully clear, except...

Whose beer is it anyway?
British beer lovers of a certain age were brought up on the idea that a brewer's yeast was their thumbprint. No other producer could quite capture the finer nuances of a classic beer if they did not make it at the same plant, using the same kit, to the exact same recipe and using the brewery's own special yeast.

So it comes as a bit of a shock walking around some Belgian breweries to find famous brands from other brewers being brewed and fermented, even bottled and labelled, by kind permission of their friendly rival.

Sometimes this happens as an occasional favour, for example when part or all of a brewery has to close temporarily for renovation. It might be that the brewery of origin is over capacity that month and needs a hand with the extra volume. But some deals are more permanent.

A few brewers appear to have been completely open with us about who does their brewing for them. Others obfuscate. And we have proof that some brewers with high reputations in the world of quality beer, simply lie.

And what should the Guide do about a company that brews its own beers once or twice a year and gets someone else to do it the rest of the time? We know of three certain cases and suspect three more. All six are still listed here.

Like George Washington's dad, we believe everything we are told.

You did what exactly?

An increasing number of "brewery" companies have recognised that the really expensive part of the process is buying and maintaining a building full of expensive equipment, or a "brewery" if you prefer. So some design the beers required and then commission others to make them.

In the past we have tried to credit these beers to the company that brews them. However, this approach may please nobody. The beer designers often want to give the impression that they operate a brewery, which in one sense they do. The brewery owners may wish to, and often do, distance themselves from beers they did not design and consider unworthy of their talents.

And how much does a brewer have to do before it is reasonable to say that they were responsible for making a beer? We know of two long-standing examples of brewing teams that go in and take over someone else's brewery for a day, expelling its staff or else scaring them into submission, to produce beers utterly unlike and superior to those of the equipment's regular owners.

Equally, at the grubbier end of the spectrum, we know of companies that take an existing beer from a brewery and simply chuck a couple of bottles of spice mix to it a short while before packaging it as their own unique brand. Where is the skill in that?

Perhaps the ultimate development has been the Proef brewery in Lochristi. Here they engage with customers to help construct and then brew beers designed to their specific requirements.

Editorially challenging it may be but it is

leading to the emergence of a new breed of wannabe brewer, some of whom are going on to create their own breweries with the benefit of an established product range.

And whatever could be wrong in that?

What counts as a beer?

Again this begins simply enough. The Guide has a number of long-standing rules. We do not include beers brewed outside Belgium, brands that are no longer on sale from the brewery or most beers brewed for a single occasion or short-term contract.

We dislike most beers with an alcohol content of less than 3.5 per cent by volume though a few are included on individual merit. These are mainly from the dying breed of nostalgia-draped "table" beers (Du: *tafelbier*; Fr: *bière de table*). These were responsible for the early-life conditioning of generations of Belgian children, helping them become beer drinkers and café *habitués*.

We try to exclude any beer that is simply another with a different label. However, while everyone knows that no Belgian brewer or beer commissioner ever lies, they all have well-practiced ways of protecting customers from the truth.

Finally, we also dislike beers that have been mixed with other stuff just before packaging. This is the one that has caused us most difficulty while compiling this edition.

The real question is: "So when exactly do you add the reconstituted fruit concentrate / spiced sugar water/colouring to your beer then, *meneer brouwmeester/monsieur le maître-brasseur?*" And watch whether their ears blush when they answer.

The correct answers

The Guide has addressed all these issues with the scientific rigour and moral integrity that our readers have come to expect of us in the last thirteen years. This is the essential foundation stone of the respect in which the Guide's pronouncements are held.

In other words, if it was not obvious editorial whim prevailed.

Tasting notes

Beer tasting is an imprecise science.

In the course of compiling this edition, several major contributors to the Guide were, along with its editor privileged to sample a number of famous beers at different breweries that were picked at various phases of their production. We tasted the same beers at the end of primary fermentation, at bottling, after warm room conditioning, at release to the trade, and after a period of cellar ageing. We also tried them on draught.

The qualities of a particular beer vary considerably with conditioning, ageing and packaging. Draught beers lack the maturity of bottle-conditioned ones. Fresh beer tastes less interesting than cellar-aged beer.

Equally one's appreciation of a beer is in part dependent on the mood of the moment, the time of day, what you have eaten and on how many beers have preceded it. The quality of a beer is not all in the mind, but some of it is.

Call us heroes if you like but the Guide does not flinch from its duty to keep its readers informed. Since the last edition we have gone out and tasted another thousand or so beers and kept (sometimes illegible) notes about their form and character.

The editor's nightmare

These are the beer brands we know have been brewed at the Proef brewery in Lochristi. The list is incomplete. And some brands are produced in a range of styles. No need to count, there are 193...

100 Jaar Excelsior, 21e Eeuw, 700-Jaar Guldensporenslag, Alfa, Anabol, Anker, Aperitiefbier, Babbelaar, Baksjekraker, Barbier Jeugdhuis Lodejo, Beersel, Beukebier, Beverwijks Graaf Jan, Bieke, BioBen, Blabergs, Blesbier, Bloemenbier, Blues, Boekweit, Boeren, Boerinneken, Boerken, Boonbier, Boske, Braven Apostel, Burgemeester, CB That's Cool, Chiquina, Chiro Kadee, Chokier, Cibo Beer, Cluysenaer, Crammerocksken, Czaar Peter, Dale, Deerlikkerke, Den Hartogh, Devotion, Dikken van Pamel, Dinamite Explosive, Dobbele Java, Dogs & Sons, Echt IJmuider Pierebier, Eeksken, Egeltje, Eirke, Elfde Genot, Ezelenbok, Figaro, Flandresse, Flik Flak, Gageleer, Gebeuren, Goet Eynd, Gouden Pier Kloeffe, Haechtste Dribbel, Heilig Hart, Hoeksch, Hoge Mote, Hopper, Ijsbok, IQ 50, Kalkens, Kambier, Kapel van Viven, Kemelbier, Kempisch Vuur, Kestvuur, Kleppende Klipper, Klompenbier, Klonkoart, Klooster van Viven, Knijfken, Koantjes, Ko(d)jeel, Koning Honing, Kouterken 75, Krak, Kreaflora, Krullekop Triple, Kwis Bierke, Lastek, Lazarus, Leidsch, Living Tripel, Locomotion, Lootsch, Maelstrøm, Medewerkersbier, Meester Ben-bier, Meester Maerten, Meijestijd, Melse Koekoek, Merelbeeks Kb'the, Molenbier, Musketier, Muzebier, Nazareth, Nello's, Ne Nele, Nen Ronsischen, Ne Pootzak, Nog Ééntje, Noisette d'Andenne, Nonkel Odo, Ostensche Baron, Ostense Witn, Oudegodje, Pater Jaak, Pater Verbiest, Pechies Pils, Penske, Père Noël, Pieterman Leuven, Plaza Italia, Polderke, Possist, Promega, Provenier, Prov'ke, Puilt-en-Bier, Raes, Rebbentekker, Reckheimer, Reinaert, Renten(b)ierke, Reserveke, Rexroth, Reylof, Rhythm, Rick's, Roche Fontaine, Ronsischen, Schabber, Schooiersbier, Shii-take, Sikkens, Simons, Sinpalsken, Sint-Canarus, Sint-Jozef, Sjarelke, Slaapmutske, Slagerij De Smedt De Roeck, SNAB, Sneeuwbier, Sneukelbier, Sonderheighens Merkske, Speculator, Sprengen, Steeple, Stepabier, Sterre, Stichtse Heeren, Stoere Wulp, Straf Broerke, Tempus, Teusser, Tielts Tanneke, Tjots-Bier, Tower Automotive, Trek, Trofee-bier, Troubadour, Twieëduust, Unkerzak, Van den Vern Grand Cru, Van de Walle, Van Parijs-Bier, Vermeulen, Vlaamsche Leeuw, Vlaamse Primitief, Vremds Blondje, Waas Gordelbier, Wabeeks Keurebier, Waggelier, Waregemse, Wemelbier, Westvoorde, Wevelgemse, Wilderik, Wima's Birthday, Wimken Donorgaan, Witte Korneel, Witte Non, Wolvertemse Vivo, X-Porter, Zeppelin, Zeunt, Zoetzuur, Zonnegemse Zot & Zwalmse.

... so you see what we mean.

The aim of our tasting notes is to strip beers back to their bare essentials, to give the reader an idea of what they should expect to be buying. We try to keep the flowery language and snide asides to a minimum, though sometimes passion gets the better of us.

The Guide is not behoven to any brewer and is not compiled or edited by people whose livelihood depends on saying positive things about their products. We can therefore afford to be critical, however uncomfortable that may make our victims feel. Or us, when we have to meet them again.

With a few notable exceptions, what has surprised us over the fifteen years of Guide compilation has been the general lack of disagreement between experienced beer lovers from many backgrounds about judging that elusive property in a beer, quality. For this reason we aim to give as many beers as possible an agreed star rating, the the following rough criteria:

★★★★★ One of the world's great beers
★★★★/★ A classic of its kind
★★★★ Highly enjoyable and well-designed
★★★/★ An above-average performer
★★★ Good quality brew that is worth sampling
★★/★ May disappoint but should not irritate
★★ Unexciting
★ Not worth getting out your wallet

Not every beer is star-rated. There are two main reasons for this. In most cases, none of the tasters whose judgement the Guide has learned to trust has enough experience of the beer to give a measured view. For a few, opinion remains so divided that even with a crack team of EU legal draftsman no consensus statement can yet emerge.

In practice the biggest difficulty in agreeing an individual rating is trying to balance marks for technical quality against those for authenticity or originality.

A professional brewer when describing a beer as "fine" means that there are no bad tastes in it. It could be dull as dishwater but still technically excellent.

Equally, a beer nut praising the palate-pounding qualities of a new stout brewed with dried organic kumquat peel in the mash and left for a year in oak barrels rescued from the last saki fermenter in the Ryukyu Islands, may completely ignore the slight skunky backtastes caused by alien creatures, which indicate it will be undrinkable within a few weeks.

From the Guide's perspective, a beer that achieves a four-star rating should strike you as either well-made and good enough to drink at any time, or else a beautiful drink that survives some technical shortfalls. Our few five-star beers should be unblemished on all counts.

The brewery descriptions

Please take these with a pinch of salt.

We try to tell you who owns the brewery but like everything else in Belgium with tax implications, things are not always as they appear. In any case, virtually everyone in the Belgian brewery business has some sort of genetic, historical, financial or amorous tie with at least one relative of everyone else, so what does it matter?

We tell you when the brewery says that they were founded because we know you like to hear it. However, it strikes us that a lot of the older links involve so many changes of address and ownership as to make this more or less meaningless.

We have stopped quoting precise annual output figures as they were becoming impossible to obtain. We have instead batched output figues in hectolitres per annum, which makes them less precise but more accurate.

< 250 hl per annum implies a part-time or hobby brewery.
< 1,000 hl per annum covers most brewpubs and smaller microbreweries, plus a surprising number of established niche brewers.
> 20,000 hl means a regional company
> 1,000,000 hl is a leading mass-market supplier.

The beer descriptions

The Guide usually quotes the brand name as it appears on the regular Belgian label. Again this is not necessarily simple. Some names change for different markets, even within Belgium itself.

In view of the linguistic sensitivities, some beers take on completely different names north and south of the language divide. The beer known as Forbidden Fruit in the UK and US markets is *Verboden Vrucht* in Flanders and becomes *Fruit Défendu* in Wallonia.

Figures for alcohol content are always quoted in percentage by volume. All beer labels in Belgium should state this, though quoted strengths can change due to alterations in the recipe. Bottle-conditioned beers often quote higher percentages than their draught counterparts, reflecting the effect of refermentation in the bottle.

Seasonal beers, particularly winter beers, are notorious for keeping the same name year on year but changing strength and recipe. We try to make the pattern clear.

The small raised figure before the name of a seasonal beer indicates the season in which it hits the market:

[1] Beers are produced for March to May
[2] Beers are produced for June to August
[3] Beers are produced for September to November
[4] Beers are produced for December to February

INDEPENDENT BREWERY COMPANIES

One of the advantages of having your lands occupied or invaded thirty times in eight hundred years is that you learn to be culturally self-sufficient. In a practical sense this means that the way local people do things becomes the way their antecedents did them and to hell with outsiders.

Fortunately for the world's beer lovers this mentality still holds in much of Belgium's independent brewery sector. Long may it do so.

Brewing is a fickle industry. Companies are often built on the ambition, drive and aspirations of one individual and their ability to motivate a small group of family members or friends.

The independent brewing sector in Belgium is far from homogeneous. Companies like Martens and Haacht are big-time producers, Riva and Palm have been acquisitive, Moortgat and De Koninck are hardly minnows.

The most famous independent producers are the six officially designated Trappist breweries but even here the operations vary in size and authenticity. Chimay and Westmalle each produce the equivalent of forty million bottles of ale a year and rising. Production at Orval is barely a quarter of that. Rochefort and Westvleteren amount to quiet country livings in comparison, while the new arrival Achel began life as a monastic brewpub.

Close behind them in the international hall of fame, but tragically neglected in their home country, are the lambic breweries of Brussels and Payottenland. The remaining independent lambic brewers are Cantillon, Drie Fonteinen, Girardin, Boon, Lindemans, Timmermans and De Troch. Hanssens and De Cam join them in blending and maturing the lambics of others. The other lambic brewery, Mort Subite, is owned by SCAM and as such is listed under Global beer makers.

In many ways the backbone of the Belgian brewing industry, as in so many other countries, is the group of largely family-owned companies that brew local beers (Du: *streekbieren*; Fr: *bières régionales*).

Traditionally these breweries produced beers that had distinctive local character and were often unrelated to beers found elsewhere in Belgium, or for that matter any other part of the planet. Sadly, nowadays many simply mimic the styles of beer made by Interbrew Belgium (InBev). In so doing they undermine not only the ethos of Belgian brewing but also their own greatest asset, their originality.

It is heartening to see some ale breweries still flying the flag for excellence and originality. Beers made by de Ranke, Kerkom, Blaugies, Verhaeghe, Dupont, Anker, Rulles, de Dolle Brouwers, Ellezelloise, Slaghmuylder, Géants, Van Eecke, St. Feuillien (own brewery), St. Bernardus, Caracole, Contreras, Malheur, Abbaye des Rocs and others have been consistently hitting the spot for years and continue to do so.

The Eighties saw the beginning of a micro-brewery revolution in Belgium. Some of the survivors are not so micro any more. Achouffe is looking forward to annual production of 20,000 hl in 2005 and also has foreign interests. Others such as de Dolle Brouwers and Abbaye des Rocs are at least as well known in the US as they are in their home country. Handing successful firms on to the next generation has already begun.

The imitation of American-style brewpubs started in Leuven with Domus and has since spread to Antwerp (Pakhuis), Kortrijk (Old Bailey), Louvain-la-Neuve (Brasse-Temps), Mons (Brasse-Temps) and most recently Brussels (Brasseurs de la Grand'Place and Imprimerie). Similar businesses in rural areas succeed in drawing hordes of tourists to see what all the fuss is about, for example at Fagnes (in southern Namur) and Ecaussinnes (in northern Hainaut).

The smallest of the new microbreweries are little more than licensed home brewers. A couple even call themselves pico-breweries to reflect their tiny nature. Some produce extraordinarily fine ales while others have big problems with quality control. One reason for the popularity of spicing beers is that it is a good way to drown your inadequacies. History repeats itself. This is how things were at the beginning of the last century, when Belgium had over 3,200 working breweries.

Here is the role of honour.

Abbaye des Rocs

Brasserie de l'Abbaye des Rocs
Chaussée de Brunehault 37
7387 Montignies-sur-Roc
T 065 75 59 99   **E** abbaye.des.rocs@skynet.be
www.abbaye-des-rocs.com

Successful small brewery in a village near the French border in northern Hainaut, south-west of Mons. Operating since 1979. A new brewhouse was built in 1987 and there has been gradual expansion ever since. Despite the name its abbey connections are minimal. Produces bottled sediment ales in a variety of styles. The beers, most of which remain highly accomplished, have been tidied up in recent years, some becoming heavily spiced, particularly with liquorice. The draught beers are unfiltered. This was one of the first breweries in modern times to experiment with malted oats. The Christmas beer also appears as Grand Cru on draught and in large bottles. Exports to much of Europe and the US (where the brewery is known as Brasserie des Rocs). Group visits only, by arrangement.

ANNUAL OUTPUT: 2,000–10,000 hl.

REGULAR BEERS:
Blanche des Honnelles (6%: ★★★/★)
Stronger-than-average, mildly spiced wheat beer with malted oats. Has its fans.
Altitude (6%: ★★★★/★)
Increasingly complex sediment blonde ale, spicy without spices.
Nounnette (7.5%: ★★★★)
Competent, lighter, blonder triple with no obvious spicing.
Abbaye des Rocs (9%: ★★★★)
Ruddy brown brew with big caramel and coriander, plus liquorice recently.
Montagnarde (9%: ★★★★)
Amber coloured triple, simpler and spicer than previously.

SEASONAL BEER:
[4]**Abbaye des Rocs Spéciale Noël** (10%: ★★★★)
Sweet ruddy-brown ale spiced with cardoman and an ancient form of ginger.

Achel

Brouwerij der St. Benedictusabdij de Achelse Kluis, Kluis 1, 3930 Hamont-Achel
T 011 80 07 60   **E** brouwerij@achelsekluis.be
www.achelsekluis.org

The monastic world likes to have a revolution every century or so. In 1999 it was the creation of a new Trappist brewery. When the cloisters of Achel, bang on the Dutch border in the north of Limburg, added a brewery and café to their remote if impressive "hermitage". The immediate impression was that someone had built a house brewery in the vistors' canteen (see Limburg: Brewery cafés). They began with lowish alcohol draught beers with the odd monastic nuance but in recent years have progressed to produce substantial ales that are more in the traditions of Westmalle, Rochefort and other brethren. Bottling of 33cl beers occurs at St. Jozef (below), while larger bottles are filled at the abbey. The range is still evolving and quality continues to rise. Group visits by arrangement.

ANNUAL OUTPUT: 2,000–10,000 hl.

REGULAR BEERS:
Trappist Achel 5° Blond (5%: ★★★/★)
Light blond, aromatic draught ale with an appealing hoppiness.
Trappist Achel 5° Brune (5%: ★★★)
Sweetish, unassertive, light brown draught ale.
Trappist Achel Blond 8° (8%: ★★★★)
Neat but tasty, straw coloured tripel with an interesting but understated, almost peppery style of hopping.
Trappist Achel Bruin 8° (8%: ★★★★)
Gradually improving brown ale most typical of traditional monastic brews.
Trappist Achel Blond 8.5° (8%: ★★★★)
Possibly the 8° in 75cl bottles but appearing classier.
Trappist Achel 9.5° (9.5%: ★★★★/★)
Heavy, sweet and spicy ale in 75cl bottles, derived from and possibly replacing the winter beer.

SEASONAL BEER:
[4]**De Drie Wijzen** (9.5%: ★★★★)
Huge toffee-laden dark winter brew that appeared at Christmas 2002, becoming the first seasonal beer from a Trappist brewery since Chimay Bleue first appeared.

Achilles

Microbrouwerij Achilles
Dulft 9A, 2222 Itegem
T 015 24 83 64
E microbrouwerij.achilles.bvba@pandora.be
www.serafijn.be

Achilles Van de Moer is a hobby brewer with the sort of brewing kit and bottling line that you would not normally expect to see in the garage and conservatory of a neat suburban home. Opened at Itegem, south east of Antwerp in 1999. Produces unfiltered ales in monthly batches of 25hl. All are spiced, sometimes oppressively so, though this is improving. We believe that Licht is sometimes called Tarwebier. He also brews commissions for a couple of local cafés and organisations, and makes both pâté and fruit genevers on the premises.

ANNUAL OUTPUT: <1,000 hl.

REGULAR BEERS:
Celtic Angel (6.2%: ★★★/★)
  A surprisingly good take on a Franco-Irish red beer.
Serafijn Blond (6.2% ★★★)
  Spiced blond ale.
Serafijn Licht (6.2%: ★★★/★)
  Medium-spiced wheat beer from the middle of the road.
Serafijn Donker (8%: ★★/★)
  Strong brown ale drowned in spice.
Serafijn Tripel (8%: ★★/★)
  Strong blond coriander beer.

SEASONAL BEER:
[4]**Serafijn Kerstlicht** (7%: ★★★/★)
  Light amber Christmas beer, spiced into acceptability.

Achouffe

Brasserie d'Achouffe SCRL,
Achouffe 32, 6666 Achouffe
T 061 28 81 47   **E** info@achouffe.be
www.achouffe.be

Set up in 1982 in the outhouse of a farm in the then unknown hamlet of Achouffe near Houffalize. The first of the new wave of Luxembourg microbreweries and by far the biggest. The original boss, Kris Bauweraerts, remains in charge of an unlikely success story that is now a high tech operation. The beers fluctuate sometimes, when spice levels are altered or fermentation is speeded up. Recently things have improved again. The draught beers are often kegged with a little yeast. There is a bistro and shop on site (see Luxembourg: Brewery cafés). Group visits can be arranged via the website. Holds a major splurge called "Grande Choufferie" on the second weekend in August. Exports to nearly twenty countries including Europe, North America, Australia, Japan and Israel.

ANNUAL OUTPUT: 10,000–20,000 hl.

REGULAR BEERS:
La Chouffe (8%: ★★★/★)
  Well-coriandered strong pale ale.
MacChouffe (8.5%: ★★★/★)
  Dryish brown ale getting spicier again, possibly with licquorice.

SEASONAL BEERS:
[4]**N'Ice Chouffe** (10%: ★★★/★)
  Heavy, sweet, black winter brew.

COMMISSIONED BEERS:
A dry, grey-blonde ale called **La Vieille Salme** (8.3%: ★★★) is occasionally brewed for Detrembleur of Grand Halleux.

Affligem – *See Global beer makers* (Heineken)

Alken-Maes – *see Global beer makers* (SCAM)

Alvinne

Picobrouwerij Alvinne
Oostrozebekestraat 114, 8770 Ingelmunster
T 051 30 55 17
www.alvinne.be

On the same street as the Van Honsebrouck brewery (below), in the southern West Flanders market town of Ingelmunster. Licensed in 2004, the crew here had been developing beers at De Graal (below) for some while. Early efforts were drowned in aromatic spices but they are getting more confident. Two stronger blond beers, **Alvinne Blond Extra** (7.1%) and **Alvinne Tripel** have also arrived.

ANNUAL OUTPUT: <250 hl.

REGULAR BEERS:
Alvinne Blond (6%: ★★★)
Competent blond ale lost behind a cloud of aftershave.
Alvinne Bruin (6.5%)
The second brew to transfer to the new kit.
Balthazar (9%)
Ruddy-brown spiced strong ale.

Angerik

Brouwerij Angerik BVBA
Snakkaertstraat 30, 1700 Dilbeek
T 02 569 33 48   **F** 02 569 39 06

Set up in 1998 by two hobby brewers called
Angelo (Buyse) and Erik (De Kuyper), just
outside the Brussels ring road in Flemish
Brabant. Brews three beers in 900 litre
batches. Sadly we have no details about the
third. Can taste of antiseptic.

ANNUAL OUTPUT: <250 hl.

REGULAR BEERS:
Boerke Blond (6.5%: ★★★)
Aromatic with aldehydes.
Boerke Donker (6.5%: ★★/★)
Cloudy, ruddy-brown ale that needs more work.

Anker

Brouwerij Het Anker
Guido Gezellelaan 49 , 2800 Mechelen
T 015 28 71 47   **F** 015 28 71 48
E het.anker@pandora.be
www.hetanker.be

Perhaps the most re-vitalised brewery in
Belgium. They can produce records to show
that a forerunner of the "Anchor" brewery
was operating in Mechelen, between Brussels
and Antwerp, by 1369 and possibly earlier.
Two world wars did it few favours, but investment in 1945 saw a return of serious brewing.
By 1960 a strong, dark ale called Gouden
Carolus, after a coin from the reign of
Emperor Charles V, was proving particularly
popular. Attempts by the fifth generation of
the Van Breendam family to modernise the
plant involved liaisons with Riva and then
John Martins in the Nineties. Eventually in
1998, they sold up to Charles Leclef, who had
been at Anker since 1990. Since then it has
advanced on all fronts with a major revision

of the product range, restoration of the 1873
steam brewhouse and the opening of
Belgium's first brewery hotel. As well as the
regular beers there is a 75cl beer called **Cuvée
van de Keizer** (11%: ★★★★/★), based on the
Classic but brewed to a unique recipe once a
year. A fruit beer called **Boscoulis** (6.5%:
★★/★) and a lighter brown ale called **Anker
Mechels Bruin** (6.5%) appeared in 2004.
Exports to much of Europe, North America
and Japan. There is a café (see Antwerp:
Brewery cafés) and beer shop on the
premises. Group visits are easily arranged.

ANNUAL OUTPUT: 2,000–10,000 hl.

REGULAR BEERS:
Blusser (5.4%: ★★★)
*Adequate, reasonably tasty Pilsener with Kölsch-like
leanings.*
Anker Blond (6.5%)
Light blond ale aimed at the French market.
Gouden Carolus Ambrio (8%: ★★★/★)
*Ruddy-amber beer with a bit of herbal medicine to
it, not sampled since a recent rise in strength*
Gouden Carolus Classic (8.5%: ★★★★)
*Clear, beefy dark brown ale that gains a touch of the
Rocheforts with keeping.*
Gouden Carolus Tripel (9%: ★★★★)
*Clean, precise, faintly spiced, light golden tripel
that is drying out but retaining bite.*

SEASONAL BEER:
[1]**Gouden Carolus Easter Beer** (10%)
*Strong, ruddy-brown ale recommended for at least
two years cellar-ageing.*
[3]**Anker-Bok** (6.5%)
*Medium brown draught ale aimed at the Dutch
bokbier market.*
[4]**Gouden Carolus Christmas** (10%: ★★★★)
Sweet, dark barley wine with licquorice and depth.

Augrenoise

Brasserie Augrenoise
Chaussée de Bruxelles 184, 7061 Casteau
T 065 72 82 66   **E** stalfred@belgacom.net

Microbrewery in northern Hainaut between
Mons and Brussels, opened in Spring 2001.
Built in a small unit attached to a residential
home for learning disabled people. Residents
have helped with production and designed
the strangely groovy label. Brews once a

month under the auspices of Jean-Marie Rock, head brewer at Orval. Hence the use of Orval yeast. A special beer featuring a recipe that includes various root vegetables has been threatened. All beers are unfiltered, unpasteurised and in 75cl bottles.

ANNUAL OUTPUT: <250 hl.

REGULAR BEERS:

Augrenoise (6.5%: ★★★★)
Initially plain, straightforward and unspiced wheat beer with an assertive character that grows on you.

SEASONAL BEER:
[4]**Augrenoise Blonde de Noël** (9.5%)
Blond Christmas brew.

Authentique

Brasserie Authentique, Rue de Condé 5
7321 Blaton   T 069 58 07 78
E authentiquebrasserie@skynet.be
www.authentiquebrasserie.be

Tiny new brewery in central Hainaut between Tournai and Mons, not far from the French border. Opened in May 2004. An orange-infused spring beer, a light ale, a wheat beer and a strong triple have all appeared. All beers are bottle-conditioned. A tasting room should open at weekends some time in 2005.

ANNUAL OUTPUT: <250 hl.

REGULAR BEERS: All beers are called Authentique. The **Ambrée** (5%) is a lightish amber ale refermented with brown sugar, the **Blonde** (6.5%) is a wheat beer with coriander and pepper (!) and the **621** (7.5%) is a brown ale brewed to a six-malt, two-hop recipe. [4]**Blonde de Noël** (9%) was the brewery's first all-malt brew.

Bavik

NV Bavik SA , Rijksweg 33, 8531 Bavikhove
T 056 71 90 91   E info@bavik.be
www.bavik.be

Largish regional company founded in 1894 in the village of Bavikhove, north-east of Kortrijk. Now under the fourth generation of the De Brabandere family. It was not until 1950 that the trade was expanded beyond a network of local tied cafés to include beer wholesalers in West and East Flanders, and Hainaut. In the

mid Seventies they began to expand into the restaurant and tavern trade. The rather dull Pilseners are the best sellers but the wheat beers are the surprise. Petrus Oud Bruin contains 33% oak-aged ale, decanted from oak tuns. This mixer beer is bottled undiluted for the American market as **Petrus Aged Pale** (7.3%: ★★★★/★) and has a true old Rodenbach character. We do not know why it is unavailable in Belgium. Wittekerke is named after and licensed by a Flemish TV soap opera. 2004 saw a fruity hybrid called **Wittekerke Rosé** (4.3%). We think **Pony Stout** (5.5%: ★★★/★) has gone to the knacker's yard and that the Ezel brands have replaced the i.a. commissioned beers, as part of a steady revision of the product range. Exports to France, where it owns a café chain, plus Italy and the US. Group visits only by arrangement.

ANNUAL OUTPUT: 100,000–200,000 hl.

REGULAR BEERS:
Big Bavik (5%)
Despite its name, the basic Pilsener.
Wittekerke (5%: ★★★/★)
Surprisingly good, spiced wheat beer that chills well in summer.
Bavik Premium Pils (5.2%: ★★/★)
Strongish but neutral unpasteurised Pilsener.
Petrus Oud Bruin (5.5%: ★★★/★)
Pleasant blend of brown and oak-aged ale.
Petrus Speciale (5.5%: ★★★)
Unassertive, filtered amber ale.
Ezel Wit (5.8%: ★★★★)
Another chewy and above-average wheat beer.
Ezel Bruin (6.5%)
Brown ale that is not bottle-conditioned.
Pilaarbijter Bruin (6.5%)
Brown ale that is bottle-conditioned.
Pilaarbijter Blond (7.2%: ★★★/★)
Lightly-spiced bottle-conditioned sediment blond ale originally brewed for the French market but now in Belgium.
Petrus Triple (7.5%: ★★★/★)
Golden tripel, now bottle-conditioned and developing greater character.

SEASONAL BEERS:
[3]**Wittekerke Speciale** (5.8%: ★★★/★)
Heavier, spicier, autumnal wheat beer.
[4]**Petrus Winterbier** (6.5%: ★★/★)
Copper coloured spicy filtered ale, which has yet to hit the spot.

Belle Vue — *see Global beer makers* (InBev)

de Bie

Brouwerij De Bie
Dikkebusstraat 171, 8958 Loker
T 0475 23 47 95   **F** 056 61 45 13
www.brijdebie.be

The "Bee" brewery was set up in 1992 near Watou, deep in the West Flanders hop garden. This closed in 2001 and after a period when the beers were made at Deca (below) a new and much enlarged plant opened in the outbuildings of a beer café in Loker. Since then there has been a welcome expansion of the beer range but a regrettable inconsistency in quality, that tastes to us like an infection problem. Ratings have been withheld for that reason. This was a great shame as the beers have always been essentially well-designed and some have been excellent. More recently they have tasted free of yeast infection but they are thinner than we recall. Exports a bit to the Netherlands and UK. Group visits are easy to arrange.

ANNUAL OUTPUT: <1,000 hl.

REGULAR BEERS:
Hellekapelle (5%)
Light blond bittersweet ale with a suggestion of spice.
Double Bie (6%)
Dark, sweetish, ruby-brown ale.
Stoute Bie (6.5%)
Deep orangey-brown, rich, sharp, sweet stout with a lactic tinge that might be accidental.
Helleketelbier (7%)
Delicious, brandy coloured, spiced ale brewed with some maize.
Plokkersbier (7%)
Herbal pale ale that has tended to be the least reliable in the range.
Blonde Bie (8%)
A thin body for so much alcohol.
Riebedebie (8%)
An uncharacteristicly bland, sweet, unimpressive triple that may have been tainted when we tried it.
Zatte Bie (9%)
Lightly spiced, huge black beer, burnt to a frazzle like a strong stout but recently off colour.

SEASONAL BEERS:
[2]**Kriekedebie** (4.5%)
Pungently cherried light brown ale, like a best bitter drowned in fruit extract.
[4]**Kerstbie** (8%)
Spiced Christmas version of Zatte Bie.

Binchoise

Brasserie La Binchoise, 31 Avenue Leopold III
7134 Péronnes-Lez-Binche
T 064 37 01 75   **E** info@brasserielabinchoise.be
www.brasserielabinchoise.be

Hainaut microbrewery founded in 1987 at Binche, between Mons and Charleroi. Brewing continues in Binche next to the brewery café (see Hainaut: Brewery cafés) but the distribution and offices moved up the road in April 2004. Since new owners in 2001, ambitions have become more commercial. The range of regular beers is expanding, though none of the newcomers is classy. Spicing of some longer-standing brews has become too heavy. Blonde still accounts for half the production. Bière des Ours can be found as Berenbier in Flanders and the Netherlands. Group visits by arrangement. There is a weekend café-restaurant at the old brewery (see Belgian cafés: Hainaut), which may be turned into a museum. Exports to France, Switzerland, Italy, Canada, the US and Japan.

ANNUAL OUTPUT: 2,000–10,000 hl.

REGULAR BEERS:
La Binchoise Belge (5%: ★★/★)
Light amber ale with too much sugar and not enough hop.
La Binchoise Blonde (6.2%: ★★★★)
Lightly sedimented, perfumed, herbal blonde ale brewed with orange peel.
La Binchoise Brune (8.2%: ★★★/★)
Less sweet, less spiced and strangely less fun than it was but still a good brune.
La Binchoise Bière des Ours (8.4%: ★★★/★)
Honeyed prior to fermentation so less sweet than some of its ilk.

SEASONAL BEERS:
[1]**La Binchoise Flora** (7%: ★★★)
Lightly spiced, floppy amber ale brewed for Easter.
[2]**Binchoise Rose des Remparts** (4.5%: ★★/★)
Light ale with raspberry flavouring.

[4]**Binchoise Spéciale Noël** (9%: ★★★★)
Spicy, perfumed, chestnut-coloured special.

COMMISSIONED BEERS: Brands called Cistercienne have been brewed for a local wholesaler. At Christmas they make [4]**Cuvée de Trazegnies** (8.5%: ★★★★), a brown ale with Curaçao orange peel, for Lannoy of Trazegnies.

Blaugies

Brasserie de Blaugies
435 Rue de la Frontière, 7370 Dour (Blaugies)
T 065 65 03 60   E info@brasseriedeblaugies.com
www.brasseriedeblaugies.com

One of the best breweries in Belgium. Started in 1988 at Blaugies, a stone's throw from the French border, south-west of Mons in western Hainaut by Pierre-Alex Carlier and Marie-Robert Poutois. They are passing the business on to their two sons. Kevin is now the brewer, while Cédric runs the brewery's restaurant (see Hainaut: Brewery cafés), a must-visit for the Belgian tour. Their beers enjoy a well-deserved reputation for distinctive but authentic local character. As Pierre-Alex explains, "I brewed them for me to drink. If other people like them too then that is fine." The two Moneuse beers are good enough to lay down for a year or two. They are named after a highwayman who stripped his victims and burned their feet to discover their money. Marie-Robert is a descendant! All beers condition in corked bottles. Group visits only, by arrangement. Open days at Whitsun.

ANNUAL OUTPUT: 1,000–2,000 hl.

REGULAR BEERS:
Darbyste (5.8%: ★★★★)
Hazy, dry but grainy wheat beer with fig syrup that is fermented through.
Saison de l'Epeautre (6%: ★★★★★)
A saison in the sense that it is a dry aromatic hoppy beer, but made with buckwheat in the mash, so ending turbid. Unique and excellent.
La Moneuse (8%: ★★★★/★)
Punchy, strong saison with the characteristic Blaugies hopping, like a huge best bitter.

SEASONAL BEER:
[4]**La Moneuse Spéciale Noël** (8%: ★★★★)
Dry, tangy, aged, chocolatey, unspiced brown Christmas ale.

Bockor

NV Brouwerij Bockor
Kwabrugstraat 5, 8510 Bellegem-Kortrijk
T 056 23 51 71   E info@bockor.be
www.bockor.be

Regional brewery founded in 1892 south of Kortrijk in West Flanders, owned by descendents of the founding Vanderghinste family. Bockor appears to have its ambitions set on mediocrity, which the Guide believes is a mistake. Although we have never seen it we understood that they have a *koelschip* in the roof of the brewery that is somehow involved in the production of the beers that they call lambics. We also know that they possess large oak tuns of the Rodenbach variety each holding over 3000 litres of ageing beer, some steeped with cherries. So why on Earth do they go on to create such sickly sweet beers with fruit additives? This original beer was an oak-aged brown ale called Ouden Tripel. This has now become Bellegems Bruin, which we understand to be a blend of darkened lager and whatever their "lambic" is. We believe Bockor Blauw is the Pils in bigger bottles. Oh passion, oh history, where are you now when they need you. Exports to France and the US. Group visits only, by arrangement, weekday afternoons September to May (T 056 21 45 38).

ANNUAL OUTPUT: 20,000–100,000 hl.

REGULAR BEERS:
Bockor Pils (5.2%: ★★★)
Deceptively smooth Pilsener with a spiky bitterness.
Passion Max (5.2%)
Mixed fruit version of what goes below.
Bellegems Bruin (5.5%: ★★★)
Clear, slightly sour brown beer with caramel-like leanings.
Jacobins Framboise Max (5.5%: ★★)
Curious, sweet and sour concoction of raspberry and mythical lambic
Jacobins Gueuze (5.5%: ★★★)
Strange, fruity, off-mainstream pale ale without classical lambic flavours.
Jacobins Kriek Lambic (5.5%: ★★)
Sweet, dark liquid with an intense cherry flavour.

du Bocq

Brasserie du Bocq
Rue de la Brasserie 4, 5530 Purnode
T 082 61 07 80   **E** brasserie@bocq.be
www.bocq.be

Active, well-managed, independent brewery in a village above the Meuse valley, north of Dinant in Namur province. Founded by farmer Martin Belot in 1858 and now run by the sixth generation of the Belot family. Named after a local stream. A good quality commercial brewery that has a range of own brands (some with two incarnations) and touts openly for contract brewing. The standard method of ale production is to lager beers in cold tanks for several weeks before bottling, then coax them with warm room fermentation. Its most famous brands are the Gauloise range, the brune dating from the 1920s and the others from 1994. The two Régal beers came from the Marbaix-la-Tour brewery in Hainaut, which closed in 1983. The brewery is tight-lipped about who commissions beers from them but we do our best to list the ones we think emanate from here. Bottles a lot of beer for other breweries. For a number, notably St. Feuillien and Fagnes, they also brew the bigger runs, leaving the commissioning brewery to concentrate on smaller scale stuff. Exports all over Europe and to Japan but not yet North America. Open to visitors at weekends (see Beer Tourism). Group visits at other times by arrangement.

ANNUAL OUTPUT: 20,000–100,000 hl.

REGULAR BEERS:
Blanche de Namur (4.5%: ★★★/★)
Unfiltered, multiply spiced soft sweet wheat beer.
Saison Régal (5.5%: ★★★/★)
Crisp, clean, filtered copper-coloured beer in a modern saison style, possibly spiced.
La Gauloise Ambrée (5.5%: ★★★)
Bitter, dryish, light chestnut filtered amber ale.
La Gauloise Blonde/St. Benoît Blonde
(6.3%: ★★★/★). *Clean lightly sedimented sweet blonde ale with hop aroma but little bitterness.*
St. Benoît Brune (6.5%: ★★★/★)
Blackened, more bitter version of the blonde.
Deugniet/Triple Moine (7.3%: ★★★/★)
Different names for a crisp, herbal, hoppy lightweight triple.

La Gauloise Brune (8.1%: ★★★★)
Not as brown or stewed or complex as it was in its world classic days, possibly due to faster production.

SEASONAL BEERS:
[4]**Régal Christmas** (8.1%: ★★★★)
Sedate and spicy brune with licquorice and coriander.

COMMISSIONED BEERS: The **Corsendonk** warehouse of Oud Turnhout commissions their brand name brown **Pater** (7.5%: ★★★/★), blond **Agnus** (7.5%: ★★★/★) and [4]**Christmas** (8.5%). The Confrérie Li Crochon in Falaën appears to re-label their blonde ale but **Li Crochon Brune** (9%: ★★★★) is too dark and robust to be Gauloise Brune. Fagnes (below) have their two biggest selling beers, the spicy **Fagnes Blonde** (7.5%: ★★★/★) and the rather mainstream **Super des Fagnes Brune** (7.5%: ★★★/★) made here. St. Feuillien brewery (below) commissions the regular sized bottles (25–75cl) of its finely flavoured, hoppy **St. Feuillien Blonde** (7.5%: ★★★/★) and dark, heavily roasted, slightly licquoriced **St. Feuillien Brune** (8%: ★★★/★). The Vanuxeem warehouse of Ploegsteert has its spiced, bitter **Queue de Charrue Ambrée** (5.6%: ★★★) made. **Godefroy** (5.8%: ★★★) is an apple-edged amber ale for a wholesaler in Corbion.

Boelens

Huisbrouwerij Boelens
Kerkstraat 7, 9111 Belsele
T 03 772 32 00
E brouwerij.boelens@pandora.be
www.proximedia.com/web/boelens.html

Microbrewery opened in 1993 on the outskirts of St. Niklaas in East Flanders. Situated in a beer warehouse. All beers are bottle-conditioned with a penchant for honeyed, sweet, strong, foggy spiced brews. The range has now settled down and reliability has improved. They also make Heerenbier, a copper-coloured ale, for the Heeren van Liedekerke café in Denderleeuw (see East Flanders) and elsewhere. Watch them brew on Saturdays (see Beer Tourism).

ANNUAL OUTPUT: <1,000 hl.

REGULAR BEERS:
Waase Wolf (6%: ★★★★)
Thick, spicy and chewy wheat beer.

Klokbier (8.5%: ★★★★)
Amber-coloured, murky, honeyed tripel.
Bieken (8.5%: ★★★)
Firm, dark blond honey beer.
Pa-Gijs (8.5%: ★★★)
Darker spiced honey beer.

[4]**Boelens Kerstbier** (8.5%)
*A dark brown ale that replaced previous strong
wheat beers like Witte Kerst as a winter offering.*

Boon

Boon NV
Fonteinstraat 65, 1502 Lembeek
T 02 356 66 44   **E** frank.boon@pandora.be

The southernmost of the lambic brewers,
just south of Halle in Flemish Brabant. When
Frank Boon took over the De Vits lambic
brewery in 1975, he was considered either an
idealistic amateur or a crank, who had not
realised lambic was dying. Whether one sees
him as a hero trying to revive lambic brewing
or as a man whose compromises have
encouraged the popularity of sweeter lambics
(the Guide bends towards the former) there
is no denying that this is one extraordinary
bloke. In twenty years he has saved his
cobweb-covered brewery-warehouse by
increasing production 20-fold. Two-thirds of
his beer is kriek of which 98% is the filtered
variety. While both are wholesome, the more
authentic version is an obviously superior
drink. We have his assurance that if somebody
was to buy twenty times as much oude kriek
he will swap his production tomorrow.

So would any nice importer like to rise to the
challenge? The ordinary kriek and faro are
made using *meerts*, a lighter type of lambic.
Beer aficionados will like more the beers
that include "Oude" or "Mariage Parfait" in
their names. Duivel Donkere is a revival of a
beer made fifty years ago by the Pêtre brewery
and continued in a paler, lighter form by the
Vander Linden brewery in Halle till they closed
in 2002. It lies somewhere between a faro and
a Scotch and is the closest we get to seeing
Boon the ale brewer, though lambic is still
added. In the real world he is kept afloat by
his distribution deal through Palm, who see
assisting his brewery as an act of cultural
preservation. Group visits by arrangement
(also see Beer Tourism).

ANNUAL OUTPUT: <10,000 hl.

REGULAR BEERS:
Boon Kriek (4%: ★★★)
*Better drunk for its sumptuous whole fruit content
(250gm/l) than its lambic character.*
Boon Framboise (6.2%: ★★/★)
*A filtered young lambic steeped with raspberry and
a few cherries.*
Boon Faro Pertotale (6%: ★★/★)
*Pasteurised bottled beer made from lambic, meerts
and brown sugar.*
Boon Lambiek (6%)
Slightly acetic, soft draught lambic.
Boon Oude Kriek (6%: ★★★★/★)
*Traditionally made bottled kriek, with unusually
intense fruit (300gm/l) making it sweeter than most.*
Boon Oude Geuze (7%: ★★★★)
Delightfully dry, mellow, unfiltered gueuze.
Boon Oude Geuze Mariage Parfait
(8%: ★★★★/★). *Smooth and dry without huge
maturity, though traditionally made using all
three-year-old lambic.*
Boon Oude Kriek Mariage Parfait
(8%: ★★★★/★). *Lush almondy kriek with full
lambic character.*
Donkere Duivel (8%: ★★★★)
*Surprisingly good dark brown ale with lambic leanings
that are less obvious than the licquorice overlay.*

COMMISSIONED BEERS: Until the late Seventies
two beer merchants, Moriau of St. Pieters
Leeuw and De Koninck of Dworp used to
blend and bottle their own gueuze and kriek.
Nowadays De Koninck relabels Boon products
but Moriau commissions original ones.

Moriau Kriek (6.5%: ★★★★) is particularly interesting as a member of the Moriau family still steeps small quantities of kriek based on Boon lambic and this is added to the beer, making it darker than the Boon krieks, though just as fruity. **Moriau Oude Geuze** (6.5%: ★★★★) tastes just as authentic as the best Boon beers.

Bosteels

Brouwerij Bosteels
Kerkstraat 92, 9255 Buggenhout
T 052 33 23 23   **E** info@kwak.karmeliet.be
www.bestbelgianspecialbeers.be

East Flanders regional brewery, equidistant from Antwerp, Brussels and Ghent. Founded in 1791 and in the Bosteels family for six generations. Brews in an old tower brewery at the manor that was once the family home. Best known for its more recent stronger ales and splendid glasses. Not as though they may have been imitating their near neighbours Malheur (below) you understand, but 2002 saw the launch of a beer made allegedly by the Méthode Champenoise and sold in Dom Perignon bottles. It is said to take twelve months to mature, which may account for the price. At least some Karmeliet has been brewed at Van Steenberge. Beers are exported to most of Europe, North America and Japan. Group visits only, by arrangement.

ANNUAL OUTPUT: 20,000–100,000 hl.

REGULAR BEERS:
Prosit Pils (4.8%: ★★)
Flabby Pilsener tasting of adjuncts.
't Zelfde (6%: ★★★)
Clean, sweet, deep golden ale. The name means "Same Again".
Karmeliet Tripel (8%: ★★★★)
Tripel that does sweetness on the delicious scale, deliberately enhancing it with wheat and oats.
Pauwel Kwak (8%:★★★/★)
Amber ale rounded by a three malt mash, then browned and sweetened by candy sugar.
Deus Brut des Flandres (11.5%: ★★★)
Unique blond ale, like a champagne beer that has been fermented in an old Eau de Cologne barrel.

Bouillon

Brasserie de Bouillon
Grand' Rue 22, 6830 Bouillon
E brasserie.de.bouillon@belgacom.net
T 061 46 89 40

The Marché de Nathalie beer shop at Bouillon, in Luxembourg province opened a brewery in 1999. They may even break off from bottling to serve you. Over half their production is commissioned but we are not sure which beers these are. A beer called Première also exists. Brews are variations on two or three themes. All are bottle-conditioned in 33cl stubbies. The brewery is in effect always on show (see Beer Tourism) but visits will be easier when it moves (see Future Breweries). They also brew original recipe commissioned beers.

ANNUAL OUTPUT: <1,000 hl.

REGULAR BEERS:
La Blanche de Bouillon (5.5%)
A bottle-conditioned spiced wheat beer.
La Sarrasine (6%)
A bottle-conditioned wheat beer made with spelt.
La Médiévale Ambrée (6%: ★★★★)
Bottle-conditioned amber ale with a sweetish big malt character.
Cuvée de Bouillon Blonde (6.5%: ★★★★)
The regular blonde ale, again big on malt character but somehow delicate.
La Bouillonaise (7%)
An unspiced bottle-conditioned brown ale.

SEASONAL BEER:
[3]**La Saison des Chasses Blonde** (6%)
Lighter seasonal blonde ale.
[3]**La Saison des Chasses Ambrée** (7%)
Heavier autumnal amber ale.
La Spéciale des Fêtes (8.5%)
The beer they bring out for special occasions.

Brabant

La Brasserie du Brabant
59 Rue Banterlez, 1470 Baisy-Thy
T 067 79 18 79
E labrasseriedubrabant@skynet.be
http://users.skynet.be/labrasseriedubrabant

Opened near Genappe in Wallonian Brabant in October 2002. Brews once a month. Using good quality makeshift kit in an old farmhouse.

Adds sugar to the mash and ferments in five days. Still experimenting with its range. The blonde and amber have appeared in a number of strengths. All are conditioned in 75cl bottles. Although the range is not finalised, the hop recipes are clever. If bigger malt recipes were employed these could be trainee classics.

ANNUAL OUTPUT: <250 hl.

REGULAR BEERS:
La Brabançonne Ambrée (7.5%) is an unspiced amber ale, the **Blonde au Miel** (8%) is a blonde made with honey from Jodoigne and the **Brune** (9.1%) is a spiced strong brown.

SEASONAL BEERS:
At Christmas they make a strong, spiced beer called **La Moche de Noël** (9%).

Brasse-Temps (Louvain-la-Neuve)

Brasserie Dubuisson Frères
Place des Brabançons 4
1348 Louvain-la-Neuve   T 010 45 70 27
E brasse-temps@tiscalinet.be

Brewpub set up in June 2000 by Dubuisson (below). The two beers can only be found at the café (see Wallonian Brabant: Brewery cafés) or on occasions at the sister pub in Mons (below) and Dubuisson brewery café. A third beer, Cuvée des Trolls attributed to the café, is now made at the parent brewery. The installation is easy to visit.

ANNUAL OUTPUT: <1,000 hl.

REGULAR BEERS:
La Blanche Neuve (5%: ★★★)
Soft and lightly spiced wheat beer.
L'Ambrasse-Temps (5%)
Draught amber ale.

Brasse-Temps (Mons)

Microbrasserie le Brasse-Temps
Complexe Imagix, Zoning des Grands Prés
Boulevard Initialis 1, 7000 Mons
T 065 84 94 14   F 065 84 94 15

Dubuisson's second brewpub entered production in March 2003 in an entertainments complex next to a shopping mall on the outskirts of Mons. Neat draught ales from as yet dull technique and recipes. Watch them try to on Saturdays at 15.00.

ANNUAL OUTPUT: <1,000 hl.

REGULAR BEER:
Blanche de Ste. Waudru (4.5%: ★★/★)
If this beer was a person it would be a skinny nun wearing strong perfume.
La Brasse-Temps des Cerises (5%: ★★)
Reminiscent of penicillin syrup for childhood sore throats.
L'Ambrasse-Temps (5.5%: ★★★)
Soft light amber ale.

Brasseurs de la Grand'Place

Les Brasseurs de la Grand'Place
Rue de la Colline 24, 1000 Bruxelles
T 02 513 98 43   E info@brasseurs-brouwers.be
www.brasseurs-brouwers.be

Brewpub in the Au Balance building on the Grand'Place in Brussels, opened in July 2001. Good quality Meura-Delta equipment is on show and brewing happens overnight. The beers are available only on draught at the café (see Brussels: Brewery cafés). Thus far the house style has been ultra-safe.

ANNUAL OUTPUT: 1,000–2,000 hl.

REGULAR BEERS:
Grand Place Ale (5%: ★★★)
Sweetish, unassertive, slightly British pale ale.
Spéciale Grand Place (6%: ★★★)
Average brewpub top-fermented blond.

SEASONAL BEERS:
[1&2]**Grand Place White** (5%: ★★★)
Lightly doused wheat beer from April to September.
[3&4]**Grand Place Brune** (8%)
Abbey beer from October to April.

Brootcoorens

Brasserie Brootcoorens
Rue de Mauberge 197, 6560 Erquelinnes
T 071 55 86 66   E angelus.br@swing.be
www.brasserie-brootcoorens-erquelinnes.be

Enthusiastic new microbrewery opened in December 2000 at Erquelinnes, near the French border in south-eastern Hainaut. Owner Alain Brootcoorens brews ales for fermentation in 75cl bottles, in brew runs of 450 litres. Our only encounter thus far has been with aged examples of the first commercial brew runs, which had held up well. Direct sales from the brewery on Saturdays (09.00-12.00; 13.30-17.00). Brews beers for private customers on demand. Group visits by arrangemnt.

ANNUAL OUTPUT: <250 hl.

REGULAR BEERS: The two Angélus beers, **Blonde** (7%) and **Brune** (7%) are typical Wallonian brews. **La Sambresse Blonde** (8%) is the newer stronger blonde ale.

SEASONAL BEERS: **Angélus Spéciale Noël** (7%) is a winter beer with peardrop notes.

Brunehaut

Brasserie de Brunehaut
Rue des Panneries 17-19, 7623 Rongy-Brunehaut
T 069 34 64 11   **E** info@brunehaut.com
www.brunehaut.com

Set up south of Tournai, a kilometre from the French border in Hainaut province, during 1992, by a brewer trained in Zaire. Athough there was significant investment in modern kit, the concentration on technical perfection appears to have been at the expense of adventurousness. Recipes appear too thin on grain and hops, or fermentation is too fast – we do not know which. The bottled beers are pasteurised before yeast is added for conditioning. Group visits only, by arrangement.

ANNUAL OUTPUT: 2,000-10,000 hl.

REGULAR BEERS:
Brunehaut Blanche (5%: ★★★)
Dryish lightly spiced wheat beer.
Brunehaut Tradition Ambrée (6.5%: ★★★)
Sweetish, burnt, copper brown sediment ale, spoilt by unsubtle bitterness.
Brunehaut Villages Blonde (6.5%: ★★★)
Sweet, sediment blonde ale with odd backtastes.
Ne Kopstoot/Abbaye de St. Amande
(7%: ★★★) *Pleasant enough blond beer with juniper.*
St. Martin (7%: ★★)
Underpowered blonde ale brewed for Tournai.
Bière du Mont St. Aubert (8%: ★★★)
Lightly sedimented blonde ale with a bitter-sweet character.

SEASONAL BEER:
[4]**St. Martin Lumière d'Hiver** (8%: ★★/★)
Overly simple, candy-sweet caramelised brown ale.

COMMISSIONED BEERS: They brew a spicy **Ramée Ambrée** (7.5%: ★★★/★) and heavy **Ramée Blonde** (8%: ★★★/★) for Bibco of Ternat. We know there are others, especially for France but do not know if these are to original recipes.

Bruyères

Brasserie Artisanale des Bruyères
17 Rue sur les Pleins, 4020 Jupille-sur-Meuse
T 04 367 55 48

Jupille's second largest brewery was set up in 2001 as a cheeky answer to the bland outpourings of the town's other one, InBev's massive Jupiler factory. Considered serious brewers working out of a Mickey Mouse brewhouse. We believe a dry cherry beer appeared. The original plan also involved a blonde. All news welcome.

ANNUAL OUTPUT: <250 hl.

REGULAR BEERS: The only one of the brewery's La Botteresse beers subjected to official tasting was the original **Ambrée** (8.5%: ★★★/★), which impressed as a classical Wallonian ambrée spoiled by crude and unnecessary spicing. Since then a honeyed beer called **Miel** (8.5%) and a **Brune** (9.5%) have appeared.

de Cam

Gueuzestekerij De Cam
Dorpsstraat 67A, 1755 Gooik
T 02 532 21 32   **E** Karl.goddeau@worldonline.be

The first new gueuze blender for forty years, set up at the de Cam community centre in the Payottenland village of Gooik, south-west of Brussels, in 1997 (see Beer Tourism). Originally the brainchild of a successful commercial brewery director, intent on helping authentic lambic beers to survive. Taken over in 2002 by another talented brewer from the next generation, whose day job is with Slaghmuylder and who moonlights for Drie Fonteinen. Blends and steeps lambics from Lindemans, Boon, Girardin and Drie Fonteinen. The casks used were retrieved from the original Pilsener brewery in the Czech Republic. The beers fermented in them are either bottled neat or else blended to make increasingly confident and impressive oude gueuze. One to watch.

ANNUAL OUTPUT: <250 hl.

REGULAR BEERS:

Kriekenlambiek De Cam (5.2%)
Draught kriek, showing good fruit against an oaky background.

Lambiek De Cam (5%)
Often surprisingly different from its base lambic.

De Cam Oude Gueuze (6.5%: ★★★★/★)
Getting there. Reminiscent of Drie Fonteinen.

De Cam Oude Kriek (6.5%: ★★★★/★)
Cloudy, tart, traditional style bottled kriek of Royal pink hue, that loses its cherry when it ripens, so to speak.

Cantillon

Brasserie Cantillon SPRL
Rue Gheude 56, 1070 Bruxelles (Anderlecht)
T 02 521 49 28 **E** info@cantillon.be
www.cantillon.be

Founded in 1900 in the Brussels suburb of Anderlecht by the Cantillon family. Virtually unchanged in most important ways. The Van Roy branch of the family took over in 1978 and shifted generation in 2003. In fiscal terms this is a museum, so the lack of spanking new equipment is semi-deliberate. All beers are produced with whole ingredients and all gueuzes are now made entirely from organic ingredients. No syrups darken the doorsteps here. The lambics have a house thumbprint of musty lemon and a touch of grapefruit.

They are coaxed into becoming unashamedly dry gueuzes and fruit lambics by the deliberate use of ultra-traditional methods. The date on the bottle refers to the year of brewing, not bottling. Semi-retired Jean-Pierre Van Roy campaigns vigorously, sometimes outspokenly, for purist standards and decries all waivering from the most vehement appelation controlée standards, though Cantillon likes to experiment. The Lou Pepe range of beers translates roughly as "Grandpa's" and is the next generation's tribute to the great man. These beers use of the best casks of kriek, framboos and old lambic to make the gueuze equivalent of Champagne Millésimé. If we awarded a sixth star these beers would receive it. Cantillon also makes a dry-hopped bottled lambic that is allowed out by special arrangement. For example it appeared as **Cuvée des Champions** (5%: ★★★★★) when bottled for the brewer's favourite football club. There are also special fruit lambics brewed for Sweden (Midnight Sun, with cloudberries) and Finland (from buckthorn berries). Exports small quantities to lots of countries. The doors are always open to visitors (see Beer Tourism) and groups may visit by arrangement. The open brewing days are particularly entertaining (see Beer Events). Do not leave Belgium without trying these uniquely tart and traditional beers.

ANNUAL OUTPUT: <1,000 hl.

REGULAR BEERS:

Cantillon Grand Cru Bruocsella (5%: ★★★★★)
Bottled three-year-old lambic that darkens with age. Low carbonation occasionally but a classic beer.

Cantillon Iris (5%: ★★★★/★)
A spontaneously fermented beer brewed from a malt and fresh hops ale recipe, dry-hopped in the cask.

Cantillon Fou' Foune (5%: ★★★★/★)
The world's only apricot lambic in an authentic style uses organic apricots from south-east France.

Cantillon Faro (5%)
Proper draught faro is prepared on demand by adding dark sugar to a one- or two-year-old lambic.

Cantillon Gueuze 100% Lambic (5%: ★★★★★)
Highly accomplished, dry, slightly bitter, citrous gueuze that accounts for 50% of production.

Kriek 100% Lambic Cantillon (5%: ★★★★★)
Superb, dry, aromatic, deep rose-coloured bottled lambic made with a varity of cherries.

Cantillon Lambic (5%)

The naturally lemony basic ingredient, sometimes found on draught.

Rosé de Gambrinus Cantillon (5%: ★★★★★)

Flowery, pink, extra dry and delicate, bottled raspberry lambic.

Cantillon St. Lamvinus (6%: ★★★★/★)

Bottled grape lambic using Merlot and Cabernet Franc for steeping.

Cantillon Vigneronne (6%: ★★★★/★)

Bottled lambic in which Italian sweet white Muscat grapes have been steeped.

Caracole

Brasserie la Caracole
Côte Marie-Thérèse 86
5500 Falmignoul   T 082 74 40 80

This increasingly well-respected microbrewery began life in 1990 at Namur but expanded into its current premises, up the Meuse valley near Dinant, in 1994. The building had been a brewhouse for over 200 years before closure in 1971. Brewer Charles Debras is a graduate of Louvain-la-Neuve brewing school but began the "Snail" brewery as a hobby and still sees it as his weekend job. All beers are unfiltered and re-fermented in the bottle. Troublette and Saxo also come in organic forms called Bio. Nostradamus Brune was preceded for many years by a Christmas beer, Cuvée de l'An Neuf, under which label it still sometimes appears. They do occasional commissions too. Exports to the US, Netherlands, France, Italy, Switzerland and Japan. Group visits by arrangement. Casual visitors welcome in high summer (see Beer Tourism).

ANNUAL OUTPUT: 1,000–2,000 hl.

REGULAR BEERS:

Troublette (5%: ★★★★)

Interesting unfiltered lightly spiced wheat beer.

Caracole Ambrée (8%: ★★★★)

Darkish amber ale relying less nowadays on spice and more on malt character.

Saxo (8%: ★★★★)

Dryish strong golden-blonde ale that is confidently different.

Nostradamus (9.5%: ★★★★)

Rich, warming strong brown ale.

Caulier

Brasserie Caulier Frères
Rue de Sondeville 134, 7600 Péruwelz
T 069 77 24 71   E info@caulier.be
www.peruwelz.be

A peculiarly designed, three-storey brewpub and commercial brewhouse built in the oversized car park of a row of suburban shops (see Hainaut: Brewery cafés). On the outskirts of Péruwelz, half way between Mons and Tournai, near the French border. Opened in 1995 to brew the Bon-Secours brands they had commissioned for many years from other breweries. The beers used to have a strange character but in recent years have improved markedly. The Bon-Secours brand come in tall swing-top bottles. The Rochefortoise brands were taken on after the closure of that brewery in 2002. We have not sampled them enough since the transfer to give a reliable opinion.

ANNUAL OUTPUT: 2,000–10,000 hl.

REGULAR BEERS:

Perle Caulier (5%)

Blond beer brewed as a lager.

La Rochefortoise Blonde (6.2%)

La Rochefortoise Ambrée (6.2%)

Bon-Secours Blonde (8%: ★★★)

Improved in recent years to become ordinary.

Bon-Secours Ambrée (8%: ★★★)

Slightly herb-tainted amber ale.

Bon-Secours Brune (8%: ★★★/★)

Rich dark brew that is beginning to grow into a big boy.

La Rochfortoise Brune (10%)

Strong brown ale.

SEASONAL BEER:

[1]**Blanche des Sources** (5.5%)

Wheat beer with oats and rye also in the mash.

[2]**L'Ampounette** (7%: ★★★/★)

Imagine raspberry juice poured into an amber-blonde wheat beer and then fermented to dryness.

[3]**La Chaperon** (7%)

Proper beer with blackcurrant in it.

[4]**Bon-Secours Blonde de Noël** (10%: ★★★/★)

Strong, sweet, golden ale with little spicing, improving each year so far.

Cazeau

Brasserie de Cazeau SPRL
67 Rue de Cazeau, 7520 Templeuve
T 069 35 25 53

The revival of an 18th century brewery that closed in 1969. Re-opened by the last brewer's son in August 2004 at the family farm in central Hainaut, on the French border. Began production with a single blonde ale and intends to stick with that until it is perfected. The last person to tell us that was the brewer at Rulles, which bodes well. They do brewery visits for groups. Open for sales on Friday night (see Hainaut: Brewery cafés). Already exports to the Alsace region of France.

ANNUAL OUTPUT: <250 hl.

REGULAR BEER:
Tournay (7.2%: ★★★/★)
Remarkably confident unfiltered blonde ale that seems intent on ducking mainstream sweetness.

Chimay

Bières de Chimay SA – NV
Route de Charlemagne 8, 6464 Baileux
T 060 21 03 11   **E** info@chimay.be
www.chimay.be

The second largest of the Belgian "Trappist" breweries after Westmalle, contained within the Abbaye Notre Dame de Scourmont at Scourmont, ten kilometres south of the Hainaut market town after which the beers are named. The abbey was founded in 1850 and brewing commenced in 1862. The beers are brewed and undergo the first phase of fermentation at the abbey but are transported to a warehouse facility in nearby Baileux for warm-room conditioning and bottling. Somewhere between 12% and 34% of the mash, depending on whom you believe, is made up of non-malt sugars, mainly starch. Only hop extract is used in the brew. Primary fermentation takes only a few days and since 1992 has happened in taller fermenting vessels. The world's leading beer writer, Michael Jackson, ascribes their relatively recent loss of complexity to the changes in yeast dynamics brought about by that change. The Guide does not disagree but questions whether this has also exposed pre-existing shortcuts in the recipes.

Chimay is exactly the sort of brewery that the Guide would love to support in all its works. It pains us to score these beers so low. We will be the first to rejoice if and when they improve. The Blanche became Triple in 2003 with the launch of a draught version that is kegged with yeast. The three beers appear in 75cl, corked bottles as **Chimay Première** (Rouge), **Chimay Cinq Cents** (Triple) and **Chimay Grande Réserve** (Bleue). Their character is noticeably smoother. There is an official café near the abbey (see Hainaut: Brewery cafés). Group visits to the bottling line only. Exported widely across Europe, North America and elsewhere.

ANNUAL OUTPUT: 100,000–200,000 hl.

REGULAR BEERS:
Chimay Dorée (4.8%: ★★★)
Smooth, slightly spicy blonde ale, available mainly at the brewery tap.
Chimay Rouge (7%: ★★★)
Ruddy-brown beer with too little body and a rather caustic bitterness.
Chimay Triple (8%: ★★★)
Strangely less bitter when young and smoother when found on draught (★★★/★).
Chimay Bleue (9%: ★★★/★)
Once a great ale of spicy complexity, now simplified for the common good.

Cnudde

Brouwerij Cnudde
Fabriekstraat 8, 9700 Eine-Oudenaarde
T 055 31 18 34

Small East Flanders family-run brewery founded in 1919, at Eine, just north of Oudenaarde. It produces a unique aged brown ale, based on the Oudenaarde style but available only on draught. We believe it is no longer aged in oak. A cherry beer is made annually, primarily for family members, and occasionally makes public appearances. Kept afloat by the Roman brewery (below) as an act of cultural preservation. It would be interesting to see what would happen if there was re-investment in a few oak tuns and some international marketing on the boutique beer principle. In practice the beer is rarely seen outside Eine (see East Flanders: Brewery cafés).

ANNUAL OUTPUT: <250 hl.

REGULAR BEER:

Cnudde Bruin (4.7%: ★★★★)

Unique, dry, sourish, grainy and almost fruity old brown ale with lactic overtones.

Contreras

Brouwerij Contreras
Molenstraat 115, 9890 Gavere
T 09 384 27 06
E brouwerijcontreras@pandora.be

Small East Flanders artisan brewery, tracing its origins to 1818. Until recently the beers were found in painted brown bottles distinguishable only by their tops. Nowadays they come in Duvel-like stubbies with designer labelling. Son-in-law Frederick De Vrieze took over the marketing side of the business a year or two ago with some obvious immediate successes. The old style was rustic and dry, the new is sweeter but with the impression that these beers will age well to dryness in the cellar. We hope the company intends to remain a little off the mainstream. In a world of clones a character is welcome. Mars has become Especial and seems to be available more. Valeir is good enough to catch the attention. Tonneke has always been unique. One to watch.

ANNUAL OUTPUT: 2,000–10,000 hl.

REGULAR BEERS:

Contra-Pils (4.8%: ★★★/★)

Low production Pilsener for the local market.

Tonneke (4.8%: ★★★★)

Soft, slightly sweet, naturally spritzy amber ale with quiet class.

Valeir Blond (6.5%: ★★★/★)

New bottle-conditioned blond ale with a bit of rustic attitude.

SEASONAL BEER:

[1]**Contreras Mars Especial** (6.5%: ★★★★)

Unfiltered, bitter-sweet, light-copper pale ale, sweeter in recent years should age well.

De Block

Brouwerij De Block
Nieuwbaan 92, 1785 Merchtem-Peizegem
T 052 37 21 59   **F** 052 37 53 88
www.satanbeer.com

Established in 1887 at Peizegem, north-west of Brussels, in Flemish Brabant. A family-run brewery with a strong sense of history, nowadays concentrating on production of the Satan brands. Sadly they no longer brew the eccentric but wonderful Block Special. Kastaar is rarely produced. A special brew called Reservé de Block, produced in boxed 3-litre bottles, and the equally elusive St. Timothaeus Blond and Bruin have never crossed our path. Sees a good future in export, particularly to France, Italy and the Netherlands. Group visits by arrangement. There is a small brewery museum (see Beer Tourism).

ANNUAL OUTPUT: 2,000–10,000 hl.

REGULAR BEERS:

Kastaar (5%: ★★★)

Occasional dark copper ale with brown ale character.

Satan Gold (8%: ★★★)

Lightly sedimented strong off-blond ale with aldehyde backtastes.

Satan Red (8%: ★★)

Filtered, candied, sweet clear ale

Dendermonde Tripel (8%)

Newish strong blond ale.

Deca

SA Deca Services NV
Elverdingestraat 4
8640 Woesten-Vleteren
T 057 42 20 75   **F** 057 42 36 86

Independent brewery company north-west of Ieper in West Flanders, in what was until 1991 the Isebaert brewery. More a brewhouse than a beer maker. It has been used by de Ranke (below) and a couple of Dutch set-ups as a brewery for hire. Also leant itself to a project that made "own label house beers" for a time. Now that many of these have moved on it will be interesting (or nerve-racking) to see whether their own brand beers are enough to keep them going. There is a large tasting room at the brewery for pre-booked parties.

ANNUAL OUTPUT: 2,000–10,000 hl.

REGULAR BEERS:

Abdijbier Bière d'Abbaye Blonde (5%: ★★★)

Plain, bitter pale ale

Antiek Blond (7%: ★★★)

Sweet, slightly spicy, sediment amber ale

Antiek Bruin (7%: ★★★/★)
The darker version
Vleteren Alt (8%: ★★★★)
Beefy medium dark sediment ale, full of malt but lacking bitterness.
Vleteren Super 8 (8%)
An amber tripel, we think!
St. Amandus (8%)
A blonde tripel.

De Koninck

Brouwerij De Koninck NV
Mechelsesteenweg 291, 2018 Antwerpen 1
T 03 218 40 48   **E** info@dekoninck.com
www.dekoninck.be

Proudly independent family-owned brewery in the city of Antwerp. Founded in 1833 by the De Koninck family, who bowed out in 1912. Now on its fifth generation of the Van Den Bogaerts. Its ordinary beer is the classic Flemish pale ale against which all others are judged. You can drink it on draught in almost any café in Antwerp, where you ask simply for a "bolleke", a 33cl glass with 25cl of beer in it. Expansion of the product range in recent years has been followed by rebranding. Antoon has become De Koninck Blond and Cuvée is now De Koninck Tripel, both becoming more confident beers as the years roll by. Other new efforts have been seen from time to time. Exports to France, Spain, Britain, the US, Russia, China and South Africa. Group visits only, by arrangement, Monday to Saturday booked through the website.

ANNUAL OUTPUT: 100,000–200,000 hl.

REGULAR BEERS:
De Koninck (5%: ★★★★)
Soft, reliable, characterful, well-rounded, quaffable pale ale on draught, a little plainer in its filtered, bottled version.
De Koninck Blond (6%: ★★★/★)
Clear, fulsome, sweetish blond ale that annoys some with its niceness.
De Koninck Tripel (8%: ★★★/★)
Increasingly attractive clear and assertive light amber strong ale.

SEASONAL BEER:
[4]**Winterkoninck** (6.5%: ★★★)
Darkish amber ale that will be great when it has grown up.

De Ryck

Brouwerij De Ryck
Kerkstraat 24, 9550 Herzele
T 053 62 23 02
E brouwerij.de.ryck@skynet.be
www.brouwerijderyck.be

A simple but successful family brewery based between Ghent and Brussels in the East Flanders. Established in 1886, it produces straightforward ales to a high standard that gets better as the years go by. The esteemed Peter Crombecq, creator of the Flemish beer consumer movement, claimed a few years ago that the Special was his favourite beer, though to be fair one was in his hand at the time. The beers are made mainly for draught sales in local pubs or in takeaway kegs for home consumption. In 2003 they began to make 75cl bottled-conditioned versions. There are rumours of further fruit beers. The company also commissions a 40% abv spirit called Bierblomme that has extracts of hops and oranges, a cheese with hazelnuts and a pâté made with beer. Group visits only, by prior arrangement.

ANNUAL OUTPUT: 2,000–10,000 hl.

REGULAR BEERS:
Kriek Fantastiek (4.9%)
New cherry beer made from Christmas beer, using black cherries and essence.
Special De Ryck (5.5%: ★★★★/★)
As straightforward a Belgian pale ale as you will find, still getting better.
Rochus Vlumschen Bruinen (6.3%: ★★★★)
Dark, sweet and sharp brown ale with multiple overtones.

SEASONAL BEER:
[4]**De Ryck Christmas Ale** (6%: ★★★★)
Light, bitter-sweet, ruddy-amber, roasted ale of great complexity for one so small.

De Troch

Brouwerij De Troch BVBA
Langestraat 20, 1741 Wambeek
T 02 582 10 27 **E** brouwerij.detroch@skynet.be
www.detroch.be

One of the oldest surviving lambic breweries, in that part of rural Payottenland that nestles between the E40 motorway and suburbia. One Pieter De Troch ran a brewery on this site in the late 18th century and indirect family ownership has continued ever since. In the mid-1980s they swerved rapidly from making authentic lambic beers to mixing fruit syrups into some sort of young lambic, maybe *meerts*. They called these beers Chapeau. Most of the fruit beers fail to reach the Guide's inclusion criterion of 3.5% alcohol by volume, thankfully. For the record there are Chapeau variants in apricot (Abricot 3% abv), pineapple (Exotic – 1.5%), strawberry (Fraises– 3%), raspberry (Framboise–3%), cherry (Kriek – 3%), plum (Mirabelle – 3%), peach (Pêche – 3%) and banana (Tropical – 3%). Token efforts to acknowledge a market in more serious lambics have been made under duress and have tended to be not that good. Despite this, when local health inspectors tried to use obscure laws to shut the place down the full force of consumer resistance rose to their aid. Maybe if they moved out of the locality and lost their lambic appellation, they would stop being a liability for real lambic producers. Exports to much of Europe, North America and Japan. Brewery visits by arrangement.

ANNUAL OUTPUT: 2,000–10,000 hl.

REGULAR BEERS:

Chapeau Lemon (4.5%)
Like the old Guinness ad, we haven't tried it because we don't like it.

Chapeau Faro (4.8%: ★★/★)
Commercial, bottled, sugary lambic.

Chapeau Gueuze (5.5%: ★★/★)
Stronger than average but nonetheless simple commercial gueuze.

Cuvée Chapeau Oude Gueuze (5.5%: ★★★)
Very little of this rather plain and uncitrus-like supposedly authentic gueuze actually reaches the market.

ter Dolen

Brouwerij Ter Dolen NV
Eikendreef 21, 3530 Helchteren
T 011 60 69 99 **E** info@terdolen.be
www.terdolen.be

This ambitious microbrewery (see Limburg: Brewery cafés) was set up in 1994 and thought big from day one. The brewhouse is based on the sight of a restored guesthouse of the old abbey of St.Truiden. Its beers have appeared on draught in specialist beer cafés in Flanders and the southern Netherlands from the beginning and are increasingly typical of the Limburg area. Bottle-conditioned versions contain minimal sediment. Technical quality tends to be good. Bottling is done across the border at the defrocked Trappist brewery, Koningshoeven, who may brew for them occasionally. Group tours by arrangement, individual visits possible (see Beer Tourism).

ANNUAL OUTPUT: 2,000–10,000 hl.

REGULAR BEERS:

Ter Dolen Blond (6.1%: ★★★)
Decreasingly impressive former star in the Limburg style.

Ter Dolen Double Dark (7.1%: ★★★/★)
Chestnut coloured sweetish brown ale with less panache.

Ter Dolen Tripel (8.1%: ★★★★)
Orange-amber, spicy, sweet tripel that needs more assertive hopping to achieve greatness.

de Dolle Brouwers

Brouwerij De Dolle Brouwers
Roeselaerestraat 12b, 8600 Esen
T 051 50 27 81 **E** de.dolle@proximedia.be
www.dedollebrouwers.be

Add natural artistic flare to a useful streak of Flemish obstinacy and good knowledge of how to brew and you get Kris Herteleer, the driving force behind the "Mad Brewers". The Herteleer family's much-loved company took over the old Costenoble brewery in the village of Esen, near Diksmuide in West Flanders, in 1980. There had been a brewery on site since 1835, though before the takeover the beers produced were rather ordinary. With the arrival of Oerbier ("our beer") things changed.

Very little ordinary beer comes out of the front gate now. The emphasis is on best quality and fearless originality. Beers are brewed with complex malt recipes and use local Poperinge Goldings or Nugget for hopping. Although there remain some ancient areas in the brewhouse, behind the scenes equipment is modern and efficient, reflecting the professionalism of the man in the lemon yellow jacket. A few years back the brewery was threatened by the withdrawal of Rodenbach yeast from the market – friends said because Oerbier was beginning to taste better than Rodenbach. Not to be done down, the beers were reshaped and redesigned for a time, with the class still shining through. Recently there is a new way of obtaining a Rodenbach-type yeast and beers are returning to their old character. Ales are lagered in a conventional cooling room at 8 °C. The darker beers improve in the cellar for several years, while Stille Nacht, one of the most intense beers in Belgium, can last a decade and more in the cellar. Ever one to experiment, recent excellent efforts have included variants of Stille Nacht called "Reserva", oak-aged in sherry or brandy casks for eighteen months and more. All have been ★★★★★ thus far. There is a less regular beer called **Lichtervelds Blond** (8%: ★★★★/★) that enjoys greater complexity than most of its ilk and uses different yeast. The sampling room and shop are open at weekends (see West Flanders: Brewery cafés) and the brewery can be visited by groups and individuals (see Beer Tourism).

ANNUAL OUTPUT: 1,000–2,000 hl.

REGULAR BEERS:
Arabier (7%: ★★★★)
  The dry-hopped dark blond summer ale that now appears year round.
Oerbier (7.5%: ★★★★/★)
  Light ruddy-brown ale somewhere between an oak-aged ale and a sharpish dubbel, developing and redeveloping with the years.
Extra Export Stout (9%: ★★★★/★)
  Unspiced, unaromatic bitter stout, in the style of an American new wave, made initially for the American market.
Dulle Teve (10%: ★★★★)
  Sweet, strong, bitter barley wine that is more of an acquired taste than the others.

SEASONAL BEERS:
[1]**Boskeun** (8%: ★★★★/★)
  Delicious, medium-strong but heady, Easter ale with Mauritian cane sugar and Mexican honey in the mash.
[2]**Oeral** (6%: ★★★★)
  A straw-coloured summer ale with a naturally delicate character.
[4]**Stille Nacht** (12%: ★★★★/★)
  Strong, dark, sweet Christmas ale that evolves through the years but rarely lacks excellence.

COMMISSIONED BEER:
A sweet, fruity beer called **Zannekin** (8%) is brewed for Brouwerij Verlande of Lo.

Domus

Domus BVBA
Eikstraat 14, 3000 Leuven
T 016 20 14 49   **F** 016 20 64 36
www.domusleuven.be

The first of the new Belgian brewpubs, opened at Leuven in August 1985. Sadly, production has now fallen to a trickle because of the need for repairs that are considered unjustifiably expensive. We believe that most beers are brewed elsewhere and that the plant in Leuven brews only occasionally, largely to retain a legal licence.

ANNUAL OUTPUT: <250 hl.

REGULAR BEERS:
Con Domus (5%)
  Bitter aromatic unfiltered Pilsener.

Drie Fonteinen

AD Bieren bvba
Hoogstraat 2a, 1650 Beersel
T 02 306 71 03   **E** info@3fonteinen.be
www.3fonteinen.be

One of the real Belgian classics, run with passion and panache and worth flying a few thousand miles to find. The De Belder family have been steeping and blending lambics in Beersel, south of Brussels since 1953. Originally they bought the lambics from Girardin, Lindemans and Boon. In the past ten years, older brother Armand has branched out into brewing, while younger brother Guido has taken on the restaurant (see Flemish Brabant: Brewery cafés). The brewhouse opened in

1999, with help from the highly respected Willem van Herreweghen, brewing director of Palm, and was the first new lambic brewery for eighty years. More recently Armand is helped by Karel Goddeau, the head brewer at Slaghmuylder and owner of de Cam (above). Their basic lambics are becoming ever more confident as the years pass and the supply of older lambic is growing. For the restauarant a faro is made by adding sugar and the cherry lambic is available on draught. On an occasional basis, a *framboos* is made using whole raspberries, as are grape lambics using Pinot Noir and Chardonnay. A Schaerbaekse Kriek is made using real Schaerbeek cherries. (All 6%: ★★★★★). The gueuze is starting to rely more on their own lambics though some others are still involved. Our taste buds tell us that there is some cross-fertilisation with de Cam. Their **Millenium Geuze** (★★★★★) was made in 2000 and should reach the heights by about 2007. The 50th anniversary gueuze (★★★★★) was made in 2003 and is equally impressive. Most of the bottled beers improve with ageing up to five years and some for up to two decades. To raise cash, they commission one of the best Belgian Pilseners, **Beersel Lager** (5%: ★★★★/★), **Beersel Blond** (6%: ★★★★) and a couple of wheat beers to lambic recipes from Proef (below). Direct purchases are available from the brewery shop (*Thu–Sat: 09.00–19.00*).

ANNUAL OUTPUT: <1,000 hl.

REGULAR BEERS:

Drie Fonteinen Lambiek
Progressing nicely from the woody acetic tastes of the early days to something increasingly like Girardin.

Drie Fonteinen Faro (5%: ★★★★)
Amber-coloured draught lambic that Belle Vue drinkers might take to more easily.

Drie Fonteinen Kriek van't vat (5%: ★★★★/★)
Nowadays tending to be unsweetened or with minimal sugar and thus more characterful.

Drie Fonteinen Oude Gueuze (6%: ★★★★★)
Superb, distinctive, dry but slightly pungent, lemony gueuze with delicate bitterness.

Drie Fonteinen Oude Kriek (6%: ★★★★★)
Big fruit, retaining a little bitterness but embued with real lambic character – a world classic drink.

Dubuisson

Brasserie Dubuisson Frères sprl
Chaussée de Mons 28, 7904 Pipaix-Leuze
T 069 67 22 21   E info@br-dubuisson.com
www.br-dubuisson.com

One of the original Wallonian farm breweries, now under the stewardship of the eighth generation of the Dubuisson family. Based in the latest incarnation of the family farm, surrounded by fields on the N50 east of Tournai in western Hainaut. It can trace its roots to 1769, though brewing was secondary to farming until 1931. Until 1991 this was really a one-beer brewery, but what a beer! Alfred Dubuisson set out to create an ale the colour of British bitter but with a bit of Belgian oomph. To name it he Anglicised the family's name, hence "Bush Beer". Right from the start, it ranked among the strongest beers in the world. In 1991 the Christmas beer arrived, followed by a more modestly proportioned pale ale in 1994 and a strong blonde in 1998. More recently, the beers have begun to appear on draught, where they are quoted at 0.5% abv lower strength. The company has backed two brewpubs, called Brasse-Temps (above). They also helped to create New York state's Belgian-style brewery, Ommegang, now owned by Moortgat. For many years Dubuisson's beers have been called "Scaldis" in the US, so as not to be mistaken for a pappy Anheuser-Busch lager called Busch (see boxed piece below). Also exports to the Netherlands, Britain, France, Italy, Spain, Portugal, Switzerland, Greece, Canada, South Africa, Japan, Chile, Brazil and Russia. The company also runs a group of drinks wholesalers, which was, in the early 1930s, the first to market a new beer called Stella Artois. There is a café at the brewery (see Hainaut: Brewery Cafés) and brewery tours are possible (see Beer Tourism).

ANNUAL OUTPUT: 10,000–20,000 hl.

REGULAR BEERS:

Cuvée des Trolls (7%: ★★★)
Slightly sweeter take on the discontinued Bush 7 light amber ale.

Bush Blonde (10.5%: ★★★★)
Good and improving strong blonde ale with nuances of the finest Czech Pilseners of yesteryear.

Bush Ambrée (12%: ★★★★/★)

The stand alone classic amber-coloured barley wine, capable of caressing the taste buds even at the end of a long evening.

Bush Prestige (13% ★★★★★)

The rare, stately, oak-aged version of the Ambrée is found only at the various brewery taps in 75cl bottles that are expensive. Use it to win friends and influence people.

SEASONAL BEER:

[4]**Bush de Noël** (12%: ★★★/★)

Deep copper coloured barley wine with a thick caramel aftertaste some find off-putting. This is less noticeable in ...

[4]**Bush Premium** (12% ★★★★/★)

The significantly superior sediment version found in 75cl & 1.5 litre bottles.

President Scaldis, Dubuisson and the affair of the troll

Following a ruling at the International Court of Arbitration at Paris in 2004, the Dubuisson brewery is no longer allowed to call their Bush beers by their correct name, except in seven specified European countries. This follows a complaint from Anheuser-Busch, makers of Budweiser, that the name sounded similar to their Busch Beer.

So what should they call their beers now?

The obvious choice would be Dubuisson. However the company may need a brand name more suited to these monosyllabic times. The Guide thinks it has the answer.

Bush Ambrée should, we believe be renamed "Dub".

As well as capturing the modern spirit of beer marketing, this allows Dubuisson to stay with the brand name across the product range. So Bush Blonde, being paler, would become "Dub Light" and Bush Noël could be "Dub Ice".

Cuvée des Trolls is more of a problem. What do you call something that is a relative lightweight yet still dangerously powerful? Dub-ya maybe.

Dupont

Brasserie Dupont sprl
Rue Basse 5, 7904 Tourpes-Leuze
T 069 67 10 66
E contact@brasserie-dupont.com
www.brasserie-dupont.com

Established, family-run, farm brewery in the village of Tourpes, in western Hainaut. Although this is one of the most rapidly developing breweries in Belgium, there remains a clear sense of seeking to retain and develop top quality beers. The Rimaux-Deridder farm brewery had been on this site since 1844, when in 1920 Alfred Dupont bought the business as a clever investment that would deter his son Louis from emigrating to Canada. It has been in the family ever since. The Moinette brands arrived in the early Sixties and were joined by Bons Voeux. The Dupont thumbprint comes from a complex yeast mix said to involve six strains. The newer organic brands are a nice idea but can be a bit variable. Nonetheless expansion is planned. Recent years have seen many of its beers appear on draught for the first time. In one of the outhouses they make cheese for direct sale. One fifth of production is exported, mainly to the US, Canada, Japan, France, Italy and the UK. Group visits only, by arrangement.

ANNUAL OUTPUT: 10,000–20,000 hl.

REGULAR BEERS:

Biolégère (3.5%: ★★★★)

Light blonde organic ale of greater character than its strength deserves through distinctive hopping.

Blanche du Hainaut Biologique (5.5%: ★★★/★). *Plainish wheat beer with light spicing and the typical Dupont hop style.*

Saison Dupont Biologique (5.5%: ★★★★/★)

Unfiltered light blonde ale in the modern saison style, brewed with organic barley.

Redor Pils (6.2%: ★★★★)

Unfiltered Pilsener mainly for local consumption, with a good smack of hops and some eminent fans.

Saison Dupont (6.5%: ★★★★★)

Golden oak coloured, dry, herbal ale packed with hops, giving a huge aroma and lingering afterburn. The archetypal modern saison.

Moinette Biologique (7.5%: ★★★/★)

Would be a classic blonde ale if it were not some inconsistencies in storage.

Bière de Miel Bio (8%: ★★★★)
Typical strong pale ale from Dupont with an obvious honey flavour.
La Bière de Beloeil (8.5%: ★★★★)
Lightly spiced strong amber ale.
Moinette Blonde (8.5%: ★★★★/★)
The classic and unsurpassed Wallonian take on a blonde ale.
Moinette Brune (8.5%: ★★★★/★)
Slightly burnt, strongish, old-style brune with a natural spiciness.
Avec les Bons Voeux (9.5%: ★★★★/★)
This famed blond winter beer has now gone year-round. Lots of spicy hop bitterness and a yeasty background.

COMMISSIONED BEERS:
They have a long-standing contract to make a blondish ale called **Vieille des Estinnes** (7.5%: ★★★★) for Wanderpepen of Estinnes-au-Mont. They also make the extraordinary hop-free **Cervesia** (8%. ★★★★) for the Iron Age Museum at Aubechies, using a 14-herb preservative called *gruit* that predated the era of the hop.

Duysters

Duysters Brouwerij
Michel Theysstraat 58a, 3290 Diest
T 013 32 36 28   **E** weynants@belgacom.net

Tiny brewery founded in 1995 at Diest, in the eastern part of Flemish Brabant and attached to one of the big Trappist ale dealers, Weynants. Quality, recipes and even styles vary a lot. For example Loterbol appeared on draught just before we went to press in Blond and Bruin forms, each of 8%. It is generally better (★★★★ and higher) on draught. Best sampled at the brewery (see Flemish Brabant: Brewery cafés).

ANNUAL OUTPUT: < 250 hl.

REGULAR BEERS:
Loterbol (6%: ★★★/★)
Dryish, light amber ale that can be memorably excellent but tends to tire a bit in the bottle.
Drossaard (6.5%: ★★★/★)
Heavily sedimented, caramelised brown ale.

SEASONAL BEER:
[4]**Kerstbol** (8%)
The Christmas brew – no details.

Ecaussinnes

Brasserie d'Ecaussinnes
Rue de Restaumont 118
7190 Ecaussinnes d'Enghien
T 067 34 22 77   **E** bras.ultra@skynet.be
www.brasserieecaussinnes.be

A new Wallonian farmhouse brewery in an attractive part of northern Hainaut. Production has expanded massively since arriving on the scene in 2000. The business is based on exporting, which accounts for over 90% of sales. The original kit was bought from a defunct Czech brewery but is being replaced as production grows. Unusually the brewery has a bottling and kegging plant, making it one of the few wholly self-sufficient new breweries in Belgium. Concentrates on the less contemplative market but also has a few beers to tempt the serious beer lover. **Ultra Fraîche** (3.5%: ★★★/★) was a light and simple, hoppy blonde ale that appeared in summer 2004. There have been other beers containing fruit extracts and spices. There is a huge tavern and restaurant on site, open at weekends (see Hainaut: Brewery cafés). Brewery visits are possible (see Beer Tourism) with large parties a speciality. Exports to much of Europe and Japan.

ANNUAL OUTPUT: 1,000–2,000 hl.

REGULAR BEERS:
Ultramour (5%: ★★)
Tangy tonsillitis medicine with a faintly beery backdrop.
Ultra Soif (5%: ★★★)
Light blond beer with a fine pedigree but a bit of candy too.
Ultra (7%: ★★★)
Clean, lightly candied, slightly grassy amber ale.
Ultra Blonde (8%: ★★★)
Blonde-triple with a safe rather that assertive character.
Ultra Délice (8%: ★★/★)
Spiced, almost sickly sweet brown ale.
Ultra Brune (10%: ★★★★)
Serious strong brown ale in the mold of the old Gauloise Brune.

SEASONAL BEERS:
[4]**Ultra de Noël Blonde** (8.5%: ★★★)
The golden Christmas ale, heavily spiced with cinnamon, cloves and all-spice.

[4]**Ultra de Noël Brune** (8.5%: ★★★)
Sweet dark-brown spicy ale made for red-hot pokers.

Ellezelloise

Brasserie Ellezelloise
Guinaumont 75, 7890 Ellezelles
T 068 54 31 60   E info@brasserie-ellezelloise.be
www.brasserie-ellezelloise.be

Opened in 1993 at Ellezelles in the northern part of Hainaut province. A farmhouse brewery based in the attractive but rather optimisticly named Pays des Collines ("Hill Country"). The marketing gimmick is stoppered bottles but the real selling point is the skill of a brewer who produces strongly characterful beers. Claims to use no spices and says that all brewing sugars in the mash are from malt. The world-beating stout is named in honour of Hercule Poirot, the Belgian detective of the Agatha Christie whodunit novels, who is said to have come from Ellezelles. Group and individual visits by arrangement (see Beer Tourism). There is a large tasting room open daily (see Hainaut: Brewery cafés).

ANNUAL OUTPUT: 1,000–2,000 hl.

REGULAR BEERS:
Saisis (6.2%: ★★★★/★)
Clear, mellow wheat beer with with a good hoppy aroma, the impression of coriander and orange peel coming from the yeast.
Saison 2000 (6.5%: ★★★★)
Pleasant, sweetish amber-coloured ale that lacks the hoppy grit of a traditional saison.
Quintine Blonde (8%: ★★★★)
Unusually bitter for a blonde ale but big enough to stand it.
Quintine Ambrée (8.5%: ★★★/★)
The most variable of the beers in our experience, sometimes found in glorious form.
Hercule Stout (9%: ★★★★★)
Big black stout that impresses every time. Burnt to a crisp, with touches of dried prunes and authentic Irishness.

SEASONAL BEERS
[4]**Quintine Bière de Noël** tends to be the Ambrée, with or without the addition of further spices.

Fagnes

Brasserie des Fagnes
Route de Nismes 26, 5660 Mariembourg
T 060 31 39 19   E mail@brasseriedesfagnes.be
www.fagnes.com

Large scale brewpub (see Namur: Brewery cafés) created in 1998 in southern Namur to promote the Super des Fagnes brands of beer. The company is descended from the Lavaux-Riche brewery, which closed in 1963. The bulk beers Super des Fagnes Blonde and Brune, come from du Bocq (above). The smaller run house beers are made on the premises. All carry the Super des Fagnes brand and have included **Pilsner** (5.5%) with Saaz hops, **Wheat Beer** (5.5%), **Fruits des Bois** (6.5%) with blackcurrant and blackberry flavouring, **Four Cereals** (7.5%) from barley, wheat, oats and spelt, **Saison** (7%) in light amber, and the spiced **Ambrée** (8%), **Brassin d'Hiver** (8.5%) and **Triple de Noël** (9.5%). There has also been a draught table beer (1.2%) for children. Group tours by arrangement.

ANNUAL OUTPUT: 1,000–2,000 hl.

Fantôme

Brasserie Fantôme
Rue Préal 8, 6997 Soy
T 086 47 70 44   E contact@fantome.be
www.fantome.be

Microbrewery founded in 1988 at Soy, near Erezée, in the northern part of Luxembourg province. Brewer Dany Prignon is one of the great characters of the Belgian new wave and surprisingly for his image a most unassuming man. Inventive, daring and sometimes chaotic, his products divide beer lovers. With the exception of the single year-round brew and the rarely encountered light summer beers, his recipes change as often as the weather. These can be excellent, traditional and unusual beers of great character. They can also be dire, probably through the use of strange ingredients. One theory goes that the really great beers are ones that have the fruity stuff accidentally omitted. In all around fifteen beers are brewed each year. The seasonal beers, marketed as Saison d'Erezée in Belgium and Fantôme abroad vary between 6% and

9% and make use of seasonal surpluses and mystery ingredients. The steady flow of commissions have allowed a doubling of capacity to 20 hl a week. All beers are refermented in 75cl bottles. There is a sampling café at the brewery (see Luxembourg: Brewery cafés). Exports to US, UK, Finland, Sweden and Italy. Group visits welcome.

ANNUAL OUTPUT: <1,000 hl.

REGULAR BEERS:
Fantôme (8%: ★★★/★)
Usually a dryish, summery golden ale, with great chunks of apple and pear flavours.

SEASONAL BEERS:
²**Dalmatienne Blonde** (4.5%)
The rarely encountered light blonde summer ale.
²**Dalmatienne Brune** (4.5%)
The same in brown.
⁴**Fantôme de Noël** (10%: ★★★★)
Strong, dark Christmas ale that may be reaching some consistency year on year but who can say?

Ferme au Chêne

La Ferme au Chêne
Rue Comte d'Ursel 115, 6940 Durbuy
T&F 086 21 10 67

The "Oak Tree Farm" is a small café-brewery (see Luxembourg: Brewery cafés) that opened in 1989 at Durbuy, in northern Luxembourg. The brand name Marckloff was taken from a brewer that was active in the town in the 16th century. They hire Dany Prignon from Fantôme (above) to brew twice a month in summer.

ANNUAL OUTPUT: <250 hl.

REGULAR BEER:
Marckloff (6.5%: ★★★/★)
Distinctive, slightly herbal, grainy pale ale, that can vary in quality.

Flo

Brasserie Artisanale du Flo
Rue du Château 21, 4280 Blehen-Hannut
http://membres.lycos.fr/blehenvillage/brasserie.htm

The recreation of brewing in this small community in the north western corner of Liège was first signalled in 1995 but actually happened in August 2004. Opened by the "Brotherhood of the Order of St. Antoine" in the old municipal hall, its first official brew took over from previous effort commissioned from du Bocq and Van Steenberge.

ANNUAL OUTPUT: <250 hl.

REGULAR BEER:
Cuvée St. Antoine (8% ★★★/★)
A strong blond ale, with a suggestion of spicing.

't Gaverhopke

Brouwerij 't Gaverhopke
Steenbrugstraat 187
8530 Stasegem-Harelbeke
T&F 056 25 86 70
http://cmdstud.khlim.be/~hdhulster/gaverhopke/

Erik Ameye's hobby brewery opened at Stasegem in southern West Flanders in 1994. All beers are bottle-conditioned in 33cl stubbies. The easiest place to find them is at the brewery, which has a weekend café (see West Flanders: Brewery cafés).

ANNUAL OUTPUT: <250 hl.

REGULAR BEERS:
't Gaverhopke Blond (8%)
Blond ale with peardrop leanings.
't Gaverhopke Bruin 8 (8%: ★★★/★)
Ruddy brown ale with enough aged character to imitate a Flemish red.
't Gaverhopke Bruin 12 (12%)
The original beer, a dark barley wine known locally as Den Twaalf and made traditionally.

SEASONAL BEER:
²**Paasbier 't Gaverhopke** (8%)
Spiced version of the blond.
³**'t Gaverhopke Kriek** (6.5%)
Made by adding freshly pressed cherry juice to the brown ale.
⁴**Kerstbier 't Gaverhopke** (8%)
Spiced version of the bruin.

Géants

Brasserie des Géants
Rue du Castel 19, 7801 Irchonwelz (Ath)
T 068 28 79 36 E info@brasseriedesgeants.com
www.brasseriedesgeants.com

A 21st century family brewery with 19th century values, attached to a 13th century castle, on the outskirts of Ath in northern Hainaut. Only opened in 2000 but making great strides year on year. The equipment was cannibalised in part from old breweries in Flobecq (Voisin), Nismes (Avignon) and Mons (Labor). Retired family brewer Léon Voisin was so impressed that he allowed the new *maître-brasseur* Pierre Delcoigne to use the Voisin name for the saison. The brewery is gaining a high reputation for technical quality, integrity and good judgement in product range, adding one new beer per year thus far and unafraid to keep improving the established ones. Even their faddy fruit beer is made with juice, not syrup or sugar. The Triple becomes Goliath in the US. Open to the public at weekends in the summer (see Beer Tourism). Group visits by arrangement through the website.

ANNUAL OUTPUT: 1,000–2,000 hl.

REGULAR BEERS:
Saison Voisin (5%: ★★★★)
Sweetish, hoppy, amber ale, more in the mold of a Kentish bitter than a saison.
Ducassis (5.7%: ★★★/★)
Blackcurrant ale fermented through to pleasant dryness.
Gouyasse Tradition (6%: ★★★★)
Bottle-conditioned blonde ale, unspiced and confident.
Urchon (7%: ★★★★/★)
Interesting light ruddy-brown ale, caramelised but not sweet, with great structure.
Gouyasse Triple (9%: ★★★★)
The new light blonde triple has started confidently and may go on to become one of the greats.

Gigi

Brasserie Gigi sprl
Grand-Rue 96, 6769 Gérouville
T&F 063 57 75 15

Small brewery at Gérouville in the Gaume area of southern Luxembourg. Brewing since 1842 and run by the same family since 1888. Traditionally it has specialised in *bières de table* but started to produce full strength beers in 1991. When the Maire brewery closed it took over production of Gaumaise beers. The strongest of the table beers, Unic Bier, is a classic of the genre but we hear that it may have been discontinued. The full-strength ones, which were disappointing have improved in recent years, possibly because Orval yeast is now used.

ANNUAL OUTPUT: <1,000 hl.

REGULAR BEERS:
Unic Bier (3.2%: ★★★★)
A slightly sour, light ale with a delicate herbal tang.
La Gaumaise Blonde (5%: ★★/★)
A plain, sugary filtered pale ale.
La Gaumaise Brune (5%: ★★/★)
An insubstantial, easy drinking brown ale.

SEASONAL BEER:
[4]**1900 Spéciale Bon es Fêtes** (8%: ★★)
A cidery pale ale with a distinctive flavour that might have been unintentional.

Girardin

Brouwerij Girardin
Lindenbergstraat 10–12
1700 Sint-Ulriks-Kapelle
T&F 02 453 9419

The largest of the authentic lambic brewers and gueuze blenders left in the Senne Valley. A family firm that still brews on the farm. They produce clean, gentle, bitterish lambics with a slight lemon-grapefruit tang, considered by many to be the finest of all. These are also sold on to other blenders. Until recently the world-beating, unfiltered gueuze was sold under the same name as its filtered cousin but with a black label. The name has now changed slightly to include the word Oude. Just beginning to realize it makes the classic lambics of Payottenland and that a world far beyond the E40 is starting to be seriously impressed. Needs encouragement to stick with the authentic stuff. They blend a one-off dark lambic for the Rare Vos café in Schepdaal (see Lambic Country).

ANNUAL OUTPUT: 2,000–10,000 hl.

REGULAR BEERS:
Girardin Faro (5%: ★★★★)
Dark candied lambic with Madeira background, recently appearing in bottled form.

Girardin Framboise (5%: ★★★)
A highly perfumed and sweetish raspberry lambic.

Girardin Oude Gueuze 1882 (5%: ★★★★★)
A drink of exceptional excellence, the epitome of traditional gueuze, bombarding the palate with splinters of crystaline lambic character and tasting like the works of a great master.

Girardin Gueuze 1882 (5%: ★★★)
Too sweet to be serious, with more grapefruit than lemon.

Girardin Kriek 1882 (5%: ★★★/★)
The best of the slightly synthetic krieks, a fairly delicate cherry flavour off-set by a sharp background lambic.

Girardin Kriek van 't vat (5%: ★★★★/★)
The splendidly palate-tingling, refreshing draught cherry lambic is supplied mainly to a few old friends.

Girardin Lambik (5%)
Tends to be lemony, with the degree of mustiness and sourness varying with its age.

Ulricher Extra (5%: ★★)
Impressively inoffensive blond beer.

Glazen Toren

BVBA Kleinbrouwerrij Glazen Toren
Glazentorenweg 11, 9420 Erpe-Mere
T 053 83 68 17   **E** glazentoren@yahoo.com

Beer writer Jef van den Steen swapped his pen for a mashing fork when he opened his own brewery, near his home in East Flanders, on Armistice Day 2004. Neither his beers nor his approach were ever likely to be dull. He began with what he called a Flemish saison and has since followed up with his version of a Scottish winter brew called Canaster Winter-scotch, and Ondineke Oilsjtersen Tripel. There will doubtless be many more before the range settles. All are in 75cl bottles so far. Quality is heading upwards. One to watch.

ANNUAL OUTPUT: <250 hl.

REGULAR BEER:
Saison d'Erpe Mere (6.5%: ★★★★)
Sturdy saison-style beer heading in the crisp and hoppy direction of Dupont.

> The Guide gets a high proportion of its new leads and information from readers. If you discover something you think we need to know mail us on **BelgiumGBG@aol.com**

de Graal

Brouwerij De Graal
Warande 15, 9660 Brakel
T 055 42 47 90   **E** info@degraal.be
www.degraal.be

Enthusiastic microbrewery opened in 2002 at Brakel, in southern East Flanders. Too much adulation for the sweeter, spicier beers may have stunted its growth a bit but the brewing quality gives the impression that better things could come. Investment in an expensive bottling machine suggests he intends to stay around. A brown ale called **De Graal Speciale** (8%) is being trialed. Hosted the early brewing of Alvinne (above). Will brew commissions of 500 litres. Group tours by arrangement. Opens to the public on Saturdays (see Beer Tourism).

ANNUAL OUTPUT: <1,000 hl.

REGULAR BEERS:
De Graal Blond (6.5%)
Dry-hopped blond ale.

De Graal Dubbel (6.5%: ★★/★)
Highly spiced brown ale drowned in licquorice.

Triverius (6.8%)
Dryish, strongish, bitterish wheat beer with the usual spices.

De Graal Gember (8%: ★★★)
A ginger-flavoured sweet blond ale.

De Graal Tripel (9%)
A new blond tripel that has had good reviews.

Grain d'Orge

Brasserie Grain d'Orge
Centre 16
4852 Hombourg (Plombières)
T 087 78 77 84   **E** info@drielandenpunt.org
www.hombourg.be/graindorge

Microbrewery added on to a specialist beer café in northern Liège, early in 2002. Constructed from bits of recent Liègeois brewing history. Brewer Benoît Johnen came from Piron brewery in nearby Aubel, while his kit came from the equally deceased Tour and Ruwet breweries. 3 Schténg is the name in local Limburg dialect of the "Three Stones" that mark the place where Belgium, Germany and the Netherlands meet, a few kilometres up the road. That is the language on the label too. All beers are available at their café (see

Liège: Brewery cafés). Groups visits by arrangement.

ANNUAL OUTPUT: <1,000 hl.

REGULAR BEERS:

3 Schténg (6%: ★★★★)
Unusual, workmanlike deep chestnut ale, something like a porter. Dry character and sweet spices.

Aubel Blonde (6.5%: ★★★)
Spiced blonde ale dominated by ginger, with an apple taste in the background.

Aubel Brune (6.5%: ★★★/★)
Brown ale with less intense spicing.

Brice (7.5% ★★★/★)
Overtly spiced, fruitily laced orange-blonde ale.

Joup (7.5% ★★★)
A less memorable oddly-spiced strong brown ale.

Haacht

Brouwerij Haacht NV
Provinciesteenweg 28, 3190 Boortmeerbeek
T 016 60 15 01   **E** info@haacht.com
www.haacht.com

Established in 1898 at Boortmeerbeek, north of Leuven in Flemish Brabant. The largest independent brewery in Belgium, the family having bought back the 35% stake aquired by Interbrew in the Nineties. Not that independence has benefited the consumer much. 90% of the production is mass-market blond lager and most of the ales are pretty drab. Not as though the brewery appears to care much about that – their website does not even mention them. We heard a whisper that they don't even brew them any more but farm them out elsewhere. None of this would matter if the company did not own over 5,000 cafés. There is a brewery tap (see Flemish Brabant: Brewery cafés).

ANNUAL OUTPUT: >1,000,000 hl.

REGULAR BEERS:

Witbier Haecht (4.8%: ★★★)
Gentle, sweet, slightly perfumed wheat beer with coriander and curaçao.

Primus (5%: ★★)
Standard Belgian Pils.

Adler (6%: ★★★)
Stronger, sweeter, Dortmunder, lager.

Tongerlo Dubbel Blond (6%: ★★/★)
Rather disappointing blond ale.

Tongerlo Dubbel Bruin (6%: ★★★)
Ruddy chestnut, bottle-condition brown ale with a burnt sugar character.

Gildenbier (7%: ★★★/★)
Sweet, heavily caramelised, clean, walnut-coloured ale, inherited from Cerckel brewery of Diest.

Tongerlo Tripel Blond (8%: ★★)
Thin tasting, filtered tripel.

Keizer Karel (9%: ★★★)
Dark sweet, strong ale of insufficient character for its strength.

SEASONAL BEER:

[4]**Tongerlo Christmas** (6.5%)
Not encountered since 2002.

Halve Maan

Huisbrouwerij De Halve Maan
Walplein 26, 8000 Brugge
T 050 33 26 97
F 050 34 59 35
E info@halvemaan.be
www.halvemaan.be

When we started researching the first edition of the Guide back in 1988 this old Bruges brewery, founded in 1856, was called Henri Maes. It had just re-opened to brew a beer called Straffe Hendrik. Within a few years it became part of the Riva group thpugh the family retained ownership. When Riva changed hands and became Liefmans, the brands stayed with them but Xavier Vanneste, descendant of Henri Maes and graduate of a Ghent brewing school, decided to breathe life into the brewery. With a touch of Flemish irony his new beers are called "Bruges Lunatic". Found in loads of cafés in the town including the brewery tap (see West Flanders: Brewery cafés). Tours are plentiful (see Brewery Tourism).

ANNUAL OUTPUT: <1,000 hl.

REGULAR BEERS:

Brugse Zot (6%: ★★★/★)
An inoffensive, soft pale ale that will no doubt develop in time.

Brugse Zot Dubbel (7.5%: ★★★)
Another inoffensive effort, launched in Spring 2006.

Hanssens

Hanssens Artisanaal
Vroenenbosstraat 15, 1653 Dworp
T 02 380 31 33
E hanssens.artisanaal@proximedia.be
www.proximedia.com/web/hanssens.html

Hanssens do not brew. They blend gueuze and steep fruit lambics. Based in the urban Payottenland village of Dworp, just south of Brussels, since 1871. They moved to this address in 1896. There was a brewery until the German army stole the copper during the 1914–18 war. Lambics were traditionally from Girardin and Lindemans but we suspect they buy more broadly now. The gueuze is all made to a traditional method using 100% lambic in the blends. The fruit lambics use whole fruit, though we suspect not exclusively. Strawberries are steeped for over six months before the single lambic is bottled directly. The Kriek is made from a blend of cherry lambics of different vintages, rather like a gueuze. Connoisseurs swear that there is something a little too sweet about these lambics but the Guide is unconvinced. With the exception of Oudbeitje, which loses its aroma by the following year, laying these beers down in the cellar is strongly recommended. Two years brings a marked improvement, five years even better. There is a backdrop of woodsmoke and fresh tobacco in them then. Opens to the public for direct sales on Friday (08.00–17.00) and Saturday (08.00–14.00).

ANNUAL OUTPUT: <1,000 hl.

REGULAR BEERS:
Oudbeitje (6%: ★★★★)
Unique strawberry lambic, brewed in November, steeped in June and bottled the following March for enjoying ice cold in the garden before supper.
Hanssens Artisanaale Oude Gueuze
(6%: ★★★★/★). *An authentic gueuze falling just short of greatness but improved by ageing in the cellar*
Hanssens Artisanaale Oude Kriek
(6%: ★★★★/★). *Slightly harsh balance of lambic and cherry flavours when young but improves in the third year of keeping.*

Hoegaarden *– see Global beer makers (InBev)*

't Hofbrouwerijke

't Hofbrouwerijke
Hoogstraat 151, 2580 Beerzel
T 015 75 77 07
E info@thofbrouwerijke.be
www.thofbrouwerijke.be

One man band Jef Goetelen got the license for his small plant near Heist-op-den-Berg in southern Antwerp at the end of 2005. This is still early days but seasoned observers have been as impressed with the clear business plan as with the well-crafted beers. Efforts are concentrating on perfecting six beers he created while a home brewer. Numbers three to six will be **Hofblues**, a 5.5% stout, **Hofelf** a 7% wheat beer, **Blondelle** a 7% blond and **Hofpint** a 5% unfiltered Pils.

ANNUAL OUTPUT: <250 hl.

REGULAR BEERS:
't Hofbrouwerijke Hoftrol (6.2%: ★★★★)
Highly creditable 100% malt, darkish amber ale, archetypal of the Antwerp style.
't Hofbrouwerijke Bosprotter (8.5%: ★★★★)
At last, a really bitter, lush tripel – a way to go but excellent early efforts.

Hopperd

Brouwerij Den Hopperd
Netestraat 67, 2235 Westmeerbeek
T 016 68 09 78 **E** denhopperd@tiscali.be

Microbrewery set up in 1996 in the south-east of Antwerp province by a graduate of one of the Ghent brewing schools. Brews well-respected ales in slightly off-beat ways. All very organic and not afraid to experiment. Difficult to find in our experience but must be doing something right as they have recently moved to expanded premises.

ANNUAL OUTPUT: <1,000 hl.

REGULAR BEERS:
Kameleon Amber (6%: ★★★★)
Full and rounded, hoppy pale ale.
Kameleon Ginseng (6.5%: ★★★★)
Well-brewed beer with one of those special ingredients much loved by healthy ex hippies.
Kameleon Tripel (8.5%: ★★★★)
Bigger, beefier but equally well-balanced strong pale ale.

SEASONAL BEER:
[1]Karmeleon Paasbier (7%)
Never spotted but out at Easter.

Huyghe

Brouwerij Huyghe
Brusselsesteenweg 256, 9090 Melle
T 09 252 15 01   **E** info@delirium.be
www.delirium.be

Ever had an eager colleague at work, or a family member, for whom nothing is too big a challenge or causes any inconvenience? Permanently rushed off their feet being helpful but achieving remarkably little of lasting value? You do? Well maybe they can understand what drives the Huyghe brewery. Founded in 1906 and rebuilt in 1939, on the outskirts of Ghent in East Flanders. In the mid-Eighties Huyghe (Hughes in English) began a mad chase for ale brands. The current list of thirty-three own brands is a reduction. Some of these beers seem identical but we apologise if we guessed wrong. At least three beers are contenders for the worst in Belgium, yet they also brew a few excellent and reliable straightforward beers. We think Rubbel Sexy Lager is probably the same as Campus Premium. We have not listed the collection of Floris brands, which appear to us to be wheat beers diluted with syrups – raspberry, strawberry, apple, passion fruit, cherry, chocolate, honey and mixed fruit (called "ninkeberry" for some reason). Numerous brands derive from deceased breweries, including St Idesbald (Damy), Campus (Biertoren) and Villers (Vieille Villers). Exports to a dozen countries including the UK and Japan. In North America the St Idesbald brands are known as Duinen. Group visits via the website include a peek at the museum they are developing.

ANNUAL OUTPUT: 20,000–100,000 hl.

REGULAR BEERS:
Minty (4.3%: ★)
Peppermint infused ale that is among the worst-tasting fluids in the world. Only brewed to annoy us.
Manacas (4.8%)
Pale ale with cane sugar. Sounds equally appalling. Never encountered, thankfully.

Blanche des Neiges/Floris Wit (5%: ★★★)
A sweetish, spiced but sweaty, unfiltered wheat beer.
Campus Premium (5%: ★★★)
The re-badged company Pilsener.
Artevelde (5.4%: ★★★/★)
A much improved pale ale. Imagine Palm with backbone.
Campus Gold/St Idesbald Blond (6.2%:★★)
Strangely sugary blond ales.
McGregor (6.5%: ★★)
Sweet pale ale brewed from whiskey malt.
Campus/Villers Oud (7%: ★★★)
Pleasant but sweet copper-coloured ales.
Artevelde Grand Cru (7.4%: ★★★★)
Accomplished strong pale ale with no funny stuff.
La Poiluchette Blonde (7.5%: ★★★)
Spiced ale in blonde.
La Poiluchette Brune (7.5%: ★★★/★)
Spiced ale in brown.
St. Idesbald Dubbel (8%)
Not tasted since a recent hike in strength.
Villers Trippel (8.5%)
Spiced tripel, not yet encountered.
St. Idesbald Tripel (9%: ★★/★)
A sweet, spiced blond beer that has usually disappointed.
Delirium Nocturnum (9%: ★★★)
A darker, more bitter, less overtly spicy version of....
Delirium Tremens (9%: ★★★/★)
Spiced and spiked beer that ought to be dreadful but sadly is not.
La Guillotine (9.3%: ★★★/★)
Suped up Delirium Tremens.
La Bière du Corsaire (9.4%: ★★★)
The least impressive of the strong spicy numbers.

SEASONAL BEERS:
[4]La Mère Noël (9%)
Blond Christmas beer said to be fermented three times, whatever that means.
[4]Delirium Christmas Noël (9%: ★★★)
A light brown ale spiced to murkiness.

COMMISSIONED BEERS:
Under the Mongozo brand, they brew three beers that contain extracts of banana (4.8%), a cheap South American grain called quinua (5.9%) and palm nut (7%), all of which attract the Fair Trade badge. Other beers appear from time to time. **Bobeline** (8.5%), for the town of Spa, has survived the years. They also make **Ambrel** (6%), an amber beer, for Duwac of Mouscron.

Imprimerie

Brasserie de l'Imprimerie
Chaussée de St-Job 666, 1180 Uccle
T 02 372 93 25   **F** 02 372 93 26
www.limprimerie.be

This brewpub in an outer Brussels suburb, opened in June 2003. The recipes are based on four beers brewed by the Vandenheuvel brewery, whose original brewery buildings can still be seen on Ninoofsesteenweg. The owner is the son of Vanderheuvel's last manager before the takeover. All are available on draught at the pub (see Brussels: Brewery cafés). A bottled version of each has appeared. Our tastings were in the early days so the ratings are probably mean.

ANNUAL OUTPUT: <1,000 hl.

Blanche de St Job (4.5%: ★★★/★)
Hit the ground running, as dusty, aromatic wheat beers often do.
Ekla (4.8%: ★★/★)
A light blond ale that looks like a lager.
Stout Vandenheuvel (5.8%: ★★★/★)
Dark but not yet confident enough to go dry and bitter.
Double Export (6.4%: ★★★)
Amber ale that should get better with practice.

Interbrew (Jupille-sur-Meuse & Leuven)

– see Global beer makers (Inbev)

Kerkom

Brouwerij Kerkom
Naamsesteenweg 469
3800 Kerkom-Sint-Truiden
T 011 68 20 87
E info@brouwerijkerkom.be
www.brouwerijkerkom.be

There has been a small brewery at this farmstead in the village of Kerkom in south-western Limburg since 1878. The original closed in 1968 but re-opened in 1988 with new kit. Until 1996 production was limited to a single pale ale. When Marc Limet and Marina Siongers took over in 1999, the story changed. The quality and consistency of beers improved markedly, as did the imagination behind them. The blond beers are a real triumph. Reuss was made from blond ale

mixed with three-year-old lambic. They also make original recipe commissioned beers for special customers. Kerkom is one of the new stars of Belgian brewing and possesses unarguably the cutest sampling café in Belgium (see Beer Tourism). Group visits by arrangement. **Adelardus Tripel** (9%: ★★★★) is a second triple in small bottles.

ANNUAL OUTPUT: <1,000 hl.

REGULAR BEERS:
Bink Blond (5.5%: ★★★★/★)
Light oak-coloured, dryish, aromatic bitter blond in the Limburg style.
Bink Bruin (5.5%: ★★★/★)
Smooth, dryish brown ale.
Adelardus Dubbel (7%: ★★★/★)
Dark dry brown ale in the dubbel style, with a touch of medicinal herbs.
Kerckomse Tripel (9%: ★★★★/★)
The best of an improving range, straight in at the top of the range of fulsome golden triples. Appears in the US as Bink Tripel.

SEASONAL BEERS:
[1&2]**Bloesembink** (7.1%:★★★/★)
Honeyed summer ale spiked with pear syrup – a bit of an acquired taste.
[2]**Reuss** (5.8%: ★★★★)
An old style of "mixed" beer that tastes as if it were a hoppy, dry, spritzy wheat beer.
[4]**Winterkoninkske** (8.3%: ★★★★)
Big ruby-brown, bittersweet winter ale that can be seriously impressive.

Lautenne

Brasserie de Lautenne
Rue du Bois Lorain 13, 5600 Lautenne
T 071 48 76 66
E info@ls-print.com

Brewer Laurent Scotto obtained a commercial license for his microbrewery, near Philippe-ville in western Namur, in 2002. The address changed in 2005 but the brewery did not move. Ask the town planners!

ANNUAL OUTPUT: < 250 hl.

REGULAR BEERS:
Dindon (7% : ★★★/★)
Sam Adams meets Moinette, a classic Wallonian blonde beer with odd hopping.

Lefèbvre

Brasserie Lefèbvre SA
Chemin du Croly 52, 1430 Quenast
T 067 67 07 66   **E** info@brasserielefebvre.be
www.brasserielefebvre.be

Established in 1876 at Quenast, in Wallonian Brabant. Best known for its Floreffe brands, brewed for the Abbaye de Floreffe, southwest of Namur. Let us start with the good news. This is one of the most efficient brewing plants in Belgium. They can brew 24/7 and their kegging and bottling capacity is wonderful. The bad news is that their beers have become soulless. They have always been a touch soft. Nowadays they are drifting into blandness. You want to give them a serious lecture about stylishness and how to acquire it. We assume the brewing staff all have hop allergies. There are beers called **Belgian Kriek** and **Belgian Pêches**, both 3.5% abv, which we hope will go away. **Newton** (3.5%) is a blend of wheat beer and cider that did not involve standing on the shoulders of giants. They may be currently responsible for the Jamboise beers, made with mustard flour. Group visits only, arranged through the local Syndicat d'Initiative (**T** 067 63 82 32).

ANNUAL OUTPUT: 20,000–100,000 hl.

REGULAR BEERS:
Blanche de Bruxelles/Floreffe Blanche
(4.5%: ★★★). *Cloudy sweet wheat beer with coriander and orange peel.*
Saison 1900 (5.2%: ★★★)
Sweet, fruity, filtered saison with an aftertaste of woodsmoke.
Floreffe Blonde (6.3%: ★★★)
Filtered Wallonian blonde.
Floreffe Double (6.3%: ★★★)
Filtered spicy, medium brown ale that aspires to the heights of Leffe but not beyond, sadly.
Floreffe Triple (7.5%: ★★★)
Soft, smooth, underpowered triple, more like a fluffy blonde.
Abbaye de Bonne-Espérance (7.8%: ★★★)
Sharpish, light amber ale that has transformed many times over the years.
Abbaye de Gembloux (8%)
Originally made for the agriculture college at Gembloux but now an official abbey beer.
Moeder Overste (8%: ★★★)
Workaday strong pale ale, somewhere between a blond and an amber.

Barbãr (8%: ★★★)
Pale ale with honey syrup in it.
Floreffe Prima Melior (8%: ★★★/★)
A strong brown ale with aniseed in it.

SEASONAL BEERS:
[3&4]**Barbãr Winterbok/Barbãr de Noël**
(8%: ★★★/★). *Brown ale with honey syrup in it.*

Leroy

Brouwerij Leroy
Diksmuideseweg 406, 8904 Boezinge
T 057 42 20 05   **F** 057 42 39 70

Old-fashioned brewery near Ieper in West Flanders, founded in 1720 and generally out of the limelight. The family also owns Van Eecke (below), though they operate as separate companies. Concentrates on making above-average blond lagers, an odd pursuit for a Belgian brewer. We are not sure how many different ones are made and whether Peter Benoit and the surviving Felix lagers are just labels now. The bottle-conditioned beers are the best. It is surprising they are not better known They deserve to be.

ANNUAL OUTPUT: 20,000–100,000 hl.

REGULAR BEERS:
Sas Pils (4.7%: ★★★)
Bittersweet and gaining a little character.
Leroy Stout (5%: ★★★)
Dark ruddy-brown, sweet and innocent.
Special Katje (5%: ★★★)
Pleasant but unassertive, darkish pale ale.
Paulus (5%: ★★★)
Bitter, aged brown ale with a clinical sourness that suggests no oak.
Yperman (5.5%: ★★★★)
Ginger-coloured, caramelised, bottle-conditioned, unmistakably Flemish pale ale.
Sasbräu Dortmunder (6%: ★★★★/★)
Top quality blond lager that annoys Belgian ale fanatics by its excellence.
Old Musketeer (7%: ★★★)
Sweetish, firm, well-hopped and distinctly Flemish filtered pale ale.

SEASONAL BEER:
[4]**Christmas** (7%: ★★★)
Based on Musketeer – significantly better (★★★★) when found refermented in 75cl bottles.

COMMISSIONED BEERS:

They make two styles of **Kerelsbier** for the Neve Jan beer warehouse in Krombeke. The **Licht** (6.4%: ★★★★) is a Dortmunder based no doubt on Sasbräu, while **Donker** (6%: ★★★) is a plain, chocolatey brown ale.

Liefmans

Liefmans Breweries
Wontergemstraat 42, 8720 Dentergem
T 051 63 36 81   **E** info@liefmans.be
www.liefmans.be

Liefmans was a lovely old brewery in Oudenaarde, East Flanders, that dated back to 1679. In 1990 it was taken over by Riva NV, the newest incarnation of the De Splenter family's brewery, founded in 1896 at Dentergem, just over the West Flanders border. In 1988 they had formed a partnership with the Straffe Hendrik brewery in Bruges. A seriously rocky period in 2002 led to what was effectively a takeover by the Belgian-born team that had been responsible in large part for the runaway success of the Québec's Unibroue. The range was reviewed, with improvements to the cherry beers and to Lucifer. Medium term plans are in place to sharpen up the brown beers, with an annual release of aged Goudenband flagged. A new range of **Abdis** beers is coming on stream too. Serious drinkers are unlikely to like the Fruitesse range. A way to go but getting there.

ANNUAL OUTPUT: 20,000–100,000 hl.

REGULAR BEERS:

Liefmans Odnar (4%: ★★★/★)
Oudenaarde's slightly sour local brown ale, recently improved in limited quantities.

Liefmans Frambozen Bier (4.5%: ★★★)
Brown ale with sweet raspberry something added to hike the price.

Dentergems (5%: ★★★)
Cloudy, lightly spiced dryish wheat beer, that also comes in Biological.

Liefmans Oud Bruin (5%: ★★★)
Brown ale subject to long lagering in steel.

Liefmans Jan van Gent (5.5%: ★★★/★)
Sweetish copper-coloured ale with a fruity, grainy character.

Brugse Straffe Hendrik Blond (6%: ★★★/★)
Blondish pale ale that has lost its hop panache in recent years but still drinks well.

Liefmans Kriekbier (6%: ★★★/★)
Sweet medium-brown ale with strong cherry presence.

Liefmans Abdis Bruin (6.5%: ★★★/★)
A middle-of-the road brown ale with a touch of the dubbels to it.

St. Arnoldus Triple (7.5%: ★★)
Copper-coloured filtered pale ale with little of the tripel about it.

Liefmans Goudenband (8%: ★★★/★)
Once great brown ale that now manages an aged quality without tannin. Fur coat, no knickers.

Vondel (8%: ★★★/★)
Sweet, slightly spicy, chestnut ale, like a less lagered Goudenband.

Brugse Straffe Hendrik Bruin (8.5%: ★★★/★)
A deep, rich, strong clear brown ale.

Lucifer (8.5%: ★★★/★)
Almost a double for Duvel.

SEASONAL BEERS:

[4]**Liefmans Glühkriek** (6%: ★★★)
Sweet, cherried brown ale with spices, drunk warm.

Lindemans

Brouwerij Lindemans
Lenniksebaan 1479, 1602 Vlezenbeek
T 02 569 03 90   **E** info@lindemans.be
www.lindemans.be

Arguably the brewery that benefited most from and contributed least to the thirty-year love-in between international drinkers and Belgian beer makers. Based in Vlezenbeek in the semi-rural part of Payottenland, the brewery has transformed its farmhouse origins into a small industrial estate. Eight generations of Lindemans have made lambic beers since 1809. Whether the ninth will depends on your definition of lambic. The move towards commercialism came, along with several new fruit beers, in the Eighties, in order to save the business. Unfortunately, in the process they forgot their roots and now appear to wish to be a sweetshop brewer. And why should they not? The new brewery built in 1991 had to double its capacity in 2003. Cuvée René was the aggressively dry, oude gueuze that, it was hoped, would herald the production of more beers in the authentic styles. The arrival on site of new wooden tuns for traditional lambic fermentation in late 2005 may herald a swing back to some more traditional production. No draught lambic at present. They make a drink from lambic, tea and lemon called Tea Beer and others with peach juice and raspberry juice, called Pêcheresse and Framboise. The tragedy of the Belgian beer market is epitomised by the fact that people buy them.

ANNUAL OUTPUT: 20,000–100,000 hl.

REGULAR BEERS:

Lindemans Cassis (4%: ★★)
Increasingly flabby lambic drowned in blackcurrant syrup.

Lindemans Kriek (4%: ★★★)
Loud, brassy cherry-flavoured drink with a tang that stays in the pipes after you wash them.

Lindemans Faro Lambic (4.8%: ★★/★)
Darkish, filtered, sweetened quencher.

Lindemans Cuvée René (5%: ★★★/★)
Oude gueuze Lite? Lacks the old Lindemans citric bite and does not keep well any more .

Lindemans Gueuze (5%: ★★/★)
A sweetish drink tasting of sharp lager and old fruit, also found on draught.

Malheur

Malheur Bieren
Mandekensstraat 179, 9255 Buggenhout
T 052 33 39 11   **E** de-landtsheer@malheur.be
www.malheur.be

Founded in 1997 at Buggenhout in East Flanders as Landtsheer, by an experienced operator in the beer selling business, whose family were once in brewing. From the start, the company's talents have been sharp marketing and fulsome recipes, making them an interesting prospect. All-malt brews are the norm, even at the highest gravities. They usually brew with whole hops but have experimented with herbal alternatives. A keen eye for the commercial is mixed with a daring willingness to experiment. In 2001 their first attempt at Champagne beer, called then Brut Réserve, knocked the socks off its only competitor and provoked some normally sensible beer buffs to use language usually reserved to their effete counterparts on the bin end counter. The only annoying thing is their tendency to keep changing their beer range. Group tours only, by arrangement, weekday afternoons and some evenings.

ANNUAL OUTPUT: 10,000–20,000 hl.

REGULAR BEERS:

Malheur 6 (6%: ★★★★)
Unfiltered amber beer with the character of a terribly English pale ale.

Malheur 8 (8%)
All-malt bottle-conditioned tripel exclusively for the export market thus far.

Malheur 10 (10%)
Strong golden barley wine that divides pundits to the extent the guide ducks a rating – you decide.

Malheur Bière Brut (11%: ★★★★★)
Massive blond beer of great complexity, made using Champagne yeast in its second phase of slow fermentation.

Malheur 12 (12%: ★★★★)
A dark barley wine, smooth and fulsome with the best but not leaving a massive presence on the palate.

Malheur Dark Brut (12%: ★★★★/★)
Not as settled as its blond sister but another classy beer cast by the Champagne method.

Martens

Brouwerij Martens NV
Reppelerweg 1, 3950 Bocholt
T 089 47 29 80   **E** info@martens.be
www.martens.be

One of the largest independent brewery companies in Belgium. Founded in 1758 at Bocholt, near the Dutch border in Limburg, halfway between Maastricht and Eindhoven. Despite its size it remains substantially under the family's influence. The company suffered a glitch when it fell foul of German bottle-recycling laws but now supplies enormous quantities of beer to the Aldi supermarket chain among others. Although mass-market Pils is the main business they have an interesting and slowly expanding range of more interesting beers. They market Limburgse Witte from St. Jozef (below). Sezoens Blond is the classic Limburg pale ale. They still make Tafelstout, a dark sweet table beer for children and invalids. Martens Pils is sold in France as Kwik Pils. No brewery tours but visits are possible to the brewery's conference centre, which houses the excellent Bocholter Brouwerijmuseum (see Beer Tourism).

ANNUAL OUTPUT: >1,000,000 hl.

REGULAR BEERS:

Martens Pils (5%: ★★/★)
Dryish and without distinction.

Sezoens Blond (6%: ★★★★)
A crisp and polished, dry-hopped, aromatic and highly drinkable light golden ale.

Sezoens Quattro (8%: ★★★/★)
A sweetish, copper coloured, dry-hopped but fruity ale, quite intense for its strength.

SEASONAL BEER:

²**Opus** (6.5%)
A grand cru bottle-conditioned version of Sezoens, made each spring "in the old way" for the museum.

Millevertus

Brasserie Artisanale de Toernich
8 Ruelle de la Fiels, 6700 Toernich
T 063 22 34 97 **E** info@millevertus.be
www.millevertus.be

New microbrewery, opened in July 2004 in a small village south of Arlon in Luxembourg province. Early efforts suggest they need more confidence but have all the basic skills. They brew beers to commission, such as **FFFado** (5.5%) an amber beer made for the local Portuguese community. Group visits welcome.

ANNUAL OUTPUT: <250 hl.

REGULAR BEERS:

Blanchette de Toernich (5%)
Wheat beer brewed to a 3-malt 3-hop recipe.

Mousse de Toernich (5.5%: ★★★)
Darkish, heavily spiced blonde ale brewed to an equally complex recipe.

Toernichoise (6.5%: ★★★)
The poshest of the early efforts is a dark ambrée brewed with four malts and three hop varieties.

Moortgat

Brouwerij Duvel Moortgat NV
Breendonkdorp 58, 2870 Breendonk-Puurs
T 03 886 71 21 **E** info@duvel.be
www.duvel.be

One of the very few breweries around the world to breach the political drinking mantra that bigger breweries make duller beers. Large producer with a modern, high production plant. Despite this, its beers are consistently well above average. This was originally a farm brewery, founded by the Moortgat family in 1871 at Breendonk, between Antwerp and Brussels. It remains over 70% family owned, the board including some fourth generation Moortgats. The brewery's *pièce de résistance* is held to be Duvel (the Dutch for "devil"), the ale most likely to infiltrate the otherwise dire beer list at your posh hotel or restaurant. Duvel is credited with being the first beer of a strong blond style, one step removed from tripel. It was first brewed in 1923, when it was darker than today, using yeast commandeered from Scotland. It went ultrablond about the same time as Jean Harlow and built a reputation steadily in the post-war era. By the Seventies it had spawned a host of imitators. Although its huge hop aroma of twenty years ago has gone – an organic dry-hopped version would be entertaining – it remains top of its class. The Maredsous brands, licensed by the abbey of Maredsous near Dinant, are increasingly impressive, as are the lagers, relatively. A soft blond ale called Passendaele proved too subtle and has been withdrawn. The "house" wheat beer is Steen-donk, which they co-own with its producers, Palm. The company has made adventurous foreign investments, now owning the embarrassingly good Ommegang brewery in New York state, the Bernard brewery in the Czech Republic and the Frères Berthom café chain in France. They export to over forty countries in Europe, North America and the Far East, with brands widely available in the UK and US. They are the first foreign company in which the CAMRA Investments Group has taken a shareholding. Group visits via the website. For individual visits see Beer Tourism.

ANNUAL OUTPUT: 200,000–1,000,000 hl.

REGULAR BEERS:

Vedette (5%: ★★)
Utterly uninspiring beer with money behind it.

Bel Pils (5.3%: ★★★/★)
Surprisingly good Pilsener that retains its hop character throughout.

Maredsous 6 (6%: ★★★★)
Much improved bottle-conditioned blond ale with a balance of graininess and aromatic hop.

Duvel Gefilterd (8%: ★★★)
The pasteurised "green label" version of Duvel found in skinny bottles.

Maredsous 8 (8%: ★★★★)
Well-made, strong dubbel with a demerera sweetness that ages delectably to become more stout-like.

Duvel Rood (8.5%: ★★★★)
Usually known simply as Duvel, a deceptively drink-able, straw-coloured strong ale with a light sediment, lifetime favourite of some and one of the few good beers you are likely to find in most Belgian cafés.

Maredsous 10 (10%: ★★★★/★)
Increasingly confident, orangey-blond, big, sweet triple nudging into a barley wine.

Mort Subite – *see Global beer makers* (SCAM)

Mortal's

Brasserie Mortal's Beers
Belle Ruelle 47a, 5600 Jamagne
T 032 71 61 57   **E** mortalsbeers@skynet.be
www.mortalsbeers.be

A garage microbrewery that started commer-cial production at Jamagne, just north of Philippeville in western Namur, in March 2003. The range of other regular beers has yet to settle, though **Black Mortal** (8%) with oak bark, **Season Mortal** (7.2%) with special hopping, **Sun Mortal** (5.6%) with fruit stuff and **Kool Mortal** (5.2%), with lavender and honey may be added.

ANNUAL OUTPUT: <250 hl.

REGULAR BEERS:
Special Mortal (5.3%)
Deep amber brew that is becoming the regular ale.
Yellow Mortal (7.2%: ★★★)
Spiced orange-coloured beer that is still developing.

SEASONAL BEER:
[4]**Christmas Mortal** (8%)
Spiced brown ale that dropped from 9.5% in 2003.

Old Bailey

Brouwerij Old Bailey
Kerkplein 5, 8880 St. Eloois-Winkel
T 056 50 07 28   **F** 056 50 48 38

Brewpub opened in February 1996, north of Kortrijk in West Flanders. Used as a sales pitch for selling in-house breweries to the world. The beers are found on draught at the café (see West Flanders: Brewery cafés). The Guide has completely lost track of what they produce

regularly and has been told that brewing only occurs on an occasional basis. Bottled beers such as St Honoré Blond (8.5%) and Bruin (8.5%) appear to come from Riva (below) but where they are brewed is a mystery.

ANNUAL OUTPUT: <250 hl.

Orval

Brasserie de l'Abbaye Notre-Dame d'Orval SA
Orval 2, 6823 Villers-devant-Orval
T 061 31 12 61   **E** brasserie@orval.be
www.orval.be

The abbey at Orval, in the far south-west of Luxembourg province was founded by Cistercians in 1132, sacked by Napoleon in 1793 and reconstructed wilfully in 1926. Its brewery opened in 1931 to help repay the costs of construction and maintenance. The entirely lay workforce is led by an experienced professional brewer, who enjoys working in a small corner of heaven on Earth. The single beer in its unique bottle remains one of the finest pale ales in the world despite the corners that are cut. The brewery has been open with the Guide and told us that the recipe is way off the Reinheitsgebot standard. 20% of the grain is replaced with sugar and hopping comes 80% from extract, 20% from pellets. Primary fermentation takes only five days. However, hop varieties are chosen for pungency and during the three weeks of lagering great sacks of whole hop flowers are added for aromatic effect. Brettanomycis fermentation is now restricted entirely to the bottle, which might explain why it needs a year in the cellar at home to get the classic (★★★★★) Orval taste nowadays. When a new brewhouse arrives in 2008 capacity will rise from 40,000 to 60,000 hl per annum and the temptation to make a draught version will be great. The experimental draught does not leave the brewery sampling room but has a wholly different, fresher character, as it misses out on the brettanomycis. A second, lighter beer with a green label called **Petit Orval** (3.2%: ★★★★) is made by dilution, only for the brothers, though it makes an appearance at the brewery tap (see Luxembourg: Brewery cafés). The ruins of the old abbey can be visited and there is accommodation for

The brewhouse at Orval

those seeking an opportunity for prayer. A cheese factory next to the brewery makes a commercial cheese in the Port Salut style plus a small amount of an extremely expensive grand cru. A shop at the abbey sells both cheese and beer. Exports to much of Europe, North America and Japan. Group visits by arrangement on Tuesday and Thursday afternoons. They hold occasional open days.

ANNUAL OUTPUT: 20,000–100,000 hl.

REGULAR BEER:

Orval (6.2%: ★★★★/★)
Distinctive and delightful amber ale, aromatically hoppy though no longer as bitter, with lambic overtones from brettanomyces *conditioning. Improves crucially with ageing in the cellar for a year.*

Paeleman

Brouwerij Paeleman
Boekakker 1, 9230 Wetteren
T 09 369 50 97   E paeleman@worldonline.be

Started in October 1996 by keen home brewer André Paeleman, at Wetteren in East Flanders. After taking on the Warande beer café in Wetteren (see East Flanders) brewing of the Uitzet brands has reduced to a minimum with most beers commissioned from Van Steenberge (below).

ANNUAL OUTPUT: <250 hl.

Pakhuis

Huisbrouwerij 't Pakhuis NV
Vlaamse Kaai 76, 2000 Antwerpen
T 03 238 12 40   E pakhuis@pandora.be
www.pakhuis.info

Massive brewpub opened in August 1996 at a converted warehouse near the Schelde quay in the city of Antwerp (see Antwerp: Brewery cafés). The brewing equipment is easily viewed. Most beer is draught, with a little produced in large stoppered bottles. They have started experimenting with seasonal beers.

ANNUAL OUTPUT: 1,000–2,000 hl.

REGULAR BEERS:

Antwerps Blond (5.1%: ★★★)
Clinically clean but unfiltered blond ale.
Antwerps Bruin (5.5%: ★★★)
Equally obsessive, crystal clear brown ale.
Nen Bangelijke (9.5%: ★★★/★)
Sweetish but workmanlike strong filtered tripel.

Palm

Brouwerij Palm
Steenhuffeldorp 3, 1840 Steenhuffel
T 052 31 74 11   E info@palmbreweries.com
www.palmbreweries.com

There has been a brewery in the village of Steenhuffel, near Londerzeel in Flemish Brabant, since 1747. The expansion that took it from village brewhouse to one of the largest independent breweries in Belgium began after the 1914–18 war. The Guide has been watching Palm for ages. It is like studying a twenty-year-old virgin trying to work out if they are gay. Should they go with the crowd or experiment a bit? Thus far, no decision is apparent. Palm's every natural instinct is to remain an independent business under family control. Yet they are obsessed with playing in the big boys' games, where they are not well equipped. Their big products are too mainstream to appeal to beer buffs, while remaining a bit *risqué* for the generations raised on Jupiler and alcopops. Of course those who crave their own independence do not necessarily respect that of others. The Gouden Boom brewery in Bruges, taken over by Palm a few years back, brewed its last beer in 2004. Its coppers were removed in the week before the Guide went to press. After taking over Rodenbach in 1998 Palm had closed its brewhouse but has now invested heavily in reconditioning its "temple room" of massive oak tuns, where all the oak-ageing goes on. Their relationship with Boon (above) appears more charitably inclined, though it sounds like the benificence of the lion to the mouse, with Palm controlling all the distribution and presumably bringing in the bulk of the contracts. 2005 sees Palm looking at an interesting portfolio of beers. Its top sellers are dull, its best speciality beers have been evicted from their natural homes and its one real star, Rodenbach Grand Cru, is possibly the most difficult beer in the world to sell. It is their good fortune to have attracted contract brewing from John Martins for the Gordons "Scottish" brands, which buys them time. The signs are that they are at least considering taking a few risks, though they will need to buck up their ideas about bottle conditioning and extremes of flavour if they really want to make a splash. They have developed one or two variants on beers for their export markets such as **Palm Belge** (6%) for France and **Palm Export** (6%) for everywhere else. Their biggest export market is the Netherlands where they supply a quarter of the special beers. The group tours come highly recommended and include a trip round Diepensteyn Castle. If you cannot join one make do with the brewery tap (see Flemish Brabant: Brewery cafés).

ANNUAL OUTPUT: 200,000–1,000,000 hl.

REGULAR BEERS:

Steendonk (4.5%: ★★★/★)
The sweetest, most mellow of the mainstream wheat beers, co-owned with Moortgat.

Bock Premium Pils (5%: ★★/★)
The company Pilsener never really cuts it in the advertising stakes.

Palm Speciale (5.1%: ★★★)
Well-made, clean pale ale, known simply as Palm, the popularity of which outstrips its depth.

Brugge Blond (6.5%: ★★★/★)
Clear, filtered, blonde ale that is solid but without distinction.

Steenbrugge Dubbel (6.5%: ★★★)
Chestnut-coloured, caramelised dubbel, smoother but less flavoursome on draught than in bottle.

Royal (7%: ★★★/★)
Smooth, ultraclean, sweetish amber blond ale that has a certain something

Brugge Tripel (8.2%: ★★★)
Amber-colured tripel with less to say than most.

Steenbrugge Tripel (8.5%: ★★★)
Sweeter, less English-tasting tripel.

SEASONAL BEER:
[4]**Dobbel Palm** (5.5%: ★★★)
Darker, fruitier ale brewed for the winter, that is better (★★★/★) when bottle-conditioned.

COMMISSIONED BEERS:
The Guide believes they probably brew most of the ales for John Martin SA (see Brewers without breweries), including the Gordon range.

Proef

BVBA Andelot
Doornzelestraat 20, 9080 Lochristi
T 09 356 71 02   E info@proefbrouwerij.com
www.proefbrouwerij.com

And now for something completely different. Founded in 1996 at Lochristi, in East Flanders, this purpose-built modern microbrewery is a Guide editor's nightmare, particularly as most of the beers that leave its gates are pretty good. The founders are brewing engineers, who decided to take the "brewery hirer" idea to its logical extreme. If a customer wants to have their own beer the team at Proef will sit down with them and design it, test brew it and then produce it in whatever quantity is required. Their kit is exceptional. They also act as a commercial playground for one of the brewing schools in Ghent. Customers range from cafés and wholesalers, via private individuals and wannabe brewers to commercial brewers who want to try something experimental on a small scale. They also make house beers of the Reinaert range, which are commercialised by their backing company, Andelot. The products we list here are marketed by the parent company.

ANNUAL OUTPUT: 2,000–10,000 hl.

REGULAR BEERS:

Reinaert Amber (7%: ★★★★)
Archetypal Flemish amber ale, technically excellent but a bit too clean.

Gageleer (7.5% ★★★)
Pale ale infused with bog myrtle.

Reinaert Grand Cru (9%: ★★★★)
Ruddy brown strong ale with faintly aged overtones.

Reinaert Tripel (9%: ★★★★/★)
Robust tripel said to be brewed from a 100% malt recipe, nudging greatness at times.

SEASONAL BEERS:

[2]**Vlaamse Primitief** (7.5%: ★★★★)
Unusual summer beer that included some brettanomyces in its yeast culture.

[4]**Lootsch Winterbier** (11%: ★★★/★)
Winter barley wine that can taste strongly of alcohol.

COMMISSIONED BEERS:
For the full list of brand names see the Brewers of Belgium, page 90. For Beersel brands see Drie Fonteinen, page 112.

de Ranke

Brouwerij De Ranke
Rue Petit Tourcoing 1 A, 7711 Dottignies
T&F 056 41 82 41
www.deranke.be

Nino Bacelle and Guido Devos have been making beer for over a decade, for sale through a beer shop in Wevelgem, West Flanders. Until 2005 this involved hiring the Deca brewery (above) and making it do some extraordinary un-Deca-like things. As the Guide appears, their own new brewery will open at Dottignies, near Mouscron. These are fantastic beers. De Ranke's reputation is for big, authentic and distinctive flavours.

They do not bow to the demands of the sweetshop market. When they hop, they do hops big, not just in XX Bitter – a sort of West Coast pale ale with gravitas – but also in Guldenberg, which sets a standard all of its own among triples. Seek out and enjoy. The future of Belgian brewing lies here.

ANNUAL OUTPUT: <1,000 hl.

REGULAR BEERS:

XX Bitter (6.2%: ★★★★★)
An excellent, aromatic and bitter pale ale that manages to achieve extreme delicacy despite robust hopping.

De Ranke Kriek (7%: ★★★★/★)
Big fruit and significant hopping combine to make a unique and attractive thirst-quenching kriekenbier.

Guldenberg (8.5%: ★★★★/★)
Dryish, audaciously hoppy, herbal strong pale ale that goes from strength to strength.

SEASONAL BEER:

[4]**Père Noël** (7%: ★★★/★)
Heavily sedimented dark, bitter ale.

Regenboog

Brouwerij de Regenboog
Koningin Astridlaan 134
8310 Assebroek-Brugge
T 050 37 38 33　**E** smisje@belgacom.net

Microbrewery set up in 1996 at Assebroek, on the outskirts of Bruges in West Flanders. Currently based in an old smithy (Du: *smisje*), next to a shop selling honey, and winemaking equipment. The brewery will transform into the Drie Sleutels when it moves to Mater, near Oudenaarde some time in 2005-06. Whether the beers continue to feature honey at that time remains to be seen. Spices and dried fruit show up in brews quite a lot too. Beers tend to rotate a bit. A sloe beer called **Sleedoornbier** (6%) appears irregularly. They take commissions from the US, such as **'t Smisje Calva Reserva** 2003 (12%: ★★★★) and locally. Some beers appear in Belgium with the US Surgeon General's health warning on them. A very popular brewer with some, the beers are a bit sweet for others. Exports as and when.

ANNUAL OUTPUT: <1,000 hl.

REGULAR BEERS:

Vuuve (5%: ★★★★)
Spiced, cloudy wheat beer, brewed mainly for the US.

't Smisje Honingbier (6%: ★★★)
Blond beer with a big honey aroma.

Wostyntje (7%: ★★★)
Pale ale with mustard seed in the mash.

Guido (8%: ★★★★)
Mid-brown, sweet and spicy dubbel.

't Smisje Dubbel Dadel (9%: ★★★★)
Big black brew that tastes pleasantly stewed due to the presence of dates.

't Smisje Tripel (9%: ★★★/★)
Reasonable tripel that has started to gain weight.

SEASONAL BEERS:

[3]**Halloween** (10.5%: ★★★★)
A big sweet, surprisingly pleasant red-amber ale brewed with pumpkin, mainly for Americans.

[4]**'t Smisje Kerst** (11%: ★★★★)
Massive Christmas ale, made in high summer for cold winter nights. Improving year on year.

Riva — *see Liefmans (above)*

Rochefort

Brasserie de Rochefort
Abbaye Notre Dame de St. Rémy
Rue de l'Abbaye 8, 5580 Rochefort
T 084 21 31 81   **F** 084 22 10 75

Inside Rochefort's abbey

After Westvleteren, the most traditional of the Trappist breweries, set in the Ardennes Namuroises near the border with Luxembourg province. The abbey was founded in 1230 as a convent but exchanged roles in 1464 with the abbey of Phelipré, near Givet, to become a Cistercian monastery. Although there was a brewery here from the late 16th century, it closed along with the abbey in 1794. The abbey became Trappist when it was re-occupied in 1887. Monks came from Achel in 1899 and opened a small-scale brewery that only expanded after the 1939–45 war. Its three ales are sold under the name Trappistes Rochefort and did not acquire labels until 1998. The recipes include significant quantities of non-malt sugars but benefit from seven to ten days of primary fermentation, albeit in tallish fermenters. We think there is a tiny smattering of coriander added to the mash. A bit of edge has been lost since the decision to spin-filter the beers and cut out the lagering phase. Secondary fermentation is now only in the bottle. The 8° and 10° improve to ★★★★★ after at least six months in the cellar and remain drinkable for decades. Production is under the control of a modern-thinking brewery engineer but the commercial operation from the purchase of ingredients to the sale of stock is overseen by the timeless Frère Pierre. All distribution is via a small number of distributors, who constitute the brewery's

only customers. The twenty or so monks of the abbey are allowed one beer every day but tend only to use this privilege on special occasions in the Christian calendar. Like the works of our Lord, exports move in mysterious ways.

ANNUAL OUTPUT: 10,000–20,000 hl.

REGULAR BEERS:
Rochefort 6 (7.5%: ★★★★)
A dark, dryish and surprisingly easy drinking double brewed only occasionally.
Rochefort 8 (9.2%: ★★★★/★)
The staple brew of the abbey, a ruddy brown, well-rounded ale with chocolate backtastes.
Rochefort 10 (11.3%: ★★★★/★)
One for the fireside before bedtime. A big, rich contemplative brew, the coloured of stewed tea.

Rodenbach

NV Brouwerij Rodenbach
Spanjestraat 133–141, 8800 Roeselare
T 051 22 34 00   **E** webmaster@rodenbach.be
www.rodenbach.be

One of the world's most unusual beer-makers, preserving and promoting a classical old style of oak-aged ale. Founded in 1836 at Roeselare in West Flanders and part of Palm (below) since 1998. After primary fermentation, some of the beer will be racked into one of three hundred massive oak tuns (Du: *foederen*; Fr: *foudres*) where it will condition for up to two years. This is eventually blended with fresh beer to make different versions of the brand. Soon after takeover the brewhouse was closed and parts of the site converted to a conference centre. The Guide and others feared this was the end but to their eternal credit Palm ploughed a considerable amount of money into a major clean up and sort out. The ageing tuns were refurbished and the old brewhouse replaced with a state-of-the-art version. Regular Rodenbach remains an off-beat brown ale made by blending a small amount of oak-aged ale into a fresh brew. Old-timers go apoplectic over Redbach, though we think it could be a whole lot worse. The classic product is the Grand Cru, which has regained its old tang and is back in the Premier Division of world beers. More recently

the sharp, ultra-dry draught taken straight from the tuns, appeared as Foederbier in one local café (see West Flanders: Brewery cafés). Group visits all year round by arrangement. Individual visits in summer (see Beer Tourism).

ANNUAL OUTPUT: 20,000–100,000 hl.

REGULAR BEERS:
Redbach (3.5%: ★★★)
Dilute Rodenbach mixed with Boon Kriek and sold in American bottles for youngsters.
Rodenbach (5%: ★★★)
The oak-aged beer blended with the ordinary brown ale approximate one part to three.
Rodenbach Grand Cru (6%: ★★★★/★)
We think that Grand Cru is now a blend of the oak-aged beer with some younger beer, though it remains a beautifully tangy drink and strangely has regained some of its old swagger.
Oud Belegen Foederbier (6.5%: ★★★★)
Like a raw, unpolished version of Grand Cru, with a rasping tannic edge that some will hate but many connoisseurs will adore.

Roman

Brouwerij Roman NV
Hauwaart 105, 9700 Mater-Oudenaarde
T 055 45 54 01   **E** info@roman.be
www.roman.be

This independent family-run brewery can trace its brewing activities back twelve generations to 1545. Over four hundred years later, Mater remains a small village just outside Oudenaarde in southern East Flanders. The company went public in 1927 and built its handsome, modern brewery in 1930. Bits have been added from time to time to such an extent that they stage concerts. Ironically for the brewery with the most convincing claim to be the oldest in Belgium, Roman produces beers that lack real pedigree and a clear thumbprint. As by far the largest brewery left near the town they are uniquely placed to produce an oak-aged ale in the old Oudenaard style but there is no sign of this occurring. Even the Ename range, which seems to be their main pitch to the speciality beer market, is a bit limp. They export to the Netherlands, Britain, France, Italy and Spain. A honey beer called Cervoise is made exclusively for the French. The company also produces mineral waters and soft drinks. Group visits only, by arrangement (Tue–Thu).

ANNUAL OUTPUT: 100,000–200,000 hl.

REGULAR BEERS:

Mater (5%: ★★★)
Unfiltered, unspiced wheat beer.

Adriaan Brouwer (5%)
Sweetish easy-drinking brown ale that replaced Oudenaards Bruin in 2003

Romy Pils (5.1%: ★★/★)
Clean but unmemorable Pilsener.

Special Roman (5.5%: ★★)
Dreary and predictable brown ale.

Romy Luxe (5.6%: ★★★)
Bigger, better rounded Pilsener.

Ename Blond (6.5%: ★★★/★)
Competently assembled unfiltered blond ale you could drink all night.

Ename Dubbel (6.5%: ★★★)
Dark, sweetish middle-of-the-road abbey beer.

Sloeber (7.5%: ★★★)
Surprisingly ordinary amber-blond ale with a mottled malt background and a shortage of hops.

Ename Tripel (9%: ★★★/★)
Light blond, unspiced, strong pale ale that varies from dull to bordering on excellent.

SEASONAL BEERS:
[4]**Cuvée 974** (7%: ★★★/★)
Filtered, ruddy amber ale, solid but on the sweet side.

Rulles

Brasserie Artisanale de Rulles SPRL
Rue Maurice Grévisse 36, 6724 Rulles-Habay
T 063 41 18 38   **E** larulles@hotmail.com
www.larulles.be

Rural microbrewery, tottering along since the end of 1998 and taking off early in 2001. The most interesting of the new contenders in Luxembourg province. Brews with Orval yeast, torrified malt and American Amarillo hops. Brewer Grégory Verhelst swore initially that he would concentrate on one beer, his blonde, but fortunately in recent years has forgotten this. The range has yet to settle but new beers are rarely dull and sometimes excellent. Success has been focussed on sales in the Pays de Gaume, the idiosyncratic area

where the brewery is based – hence their strapline "Bière de Gaume" – though 15% of production is exported and this is set to rise following a deal with an American importer. Well-deserved success has allowed a new brewhouse to be commissioned for 2005. Thus far there have been no compromises with quality. On the principle that if you want a job done you ask a busy man, Grégory pulls together the Brassigaume beer festival at nearby Marbehan each year (see Beer Events) with a friend from the unofficial brewery tap (see Luxembourg: Brewery cafés).

ANNUAL OUTPUT: <1,000 hl.

REGULAR BEERS:

La Rulles Estivale (5.2%: ★★★★/★)
Punchy, hoppy light amber ale with instant appeal, keeping its character throughout a session.

La Rulles Brune (6.5%: ★★★★)
Plain, workmanlike, unspiced brown ale that gets better with practice.

La Rulles Blonde (7%: ★★★★/★)
Well-made, unfiltered blonde ale that also grows more characterful as time goes by.

La Rulles Triple (8.3%: ★★★★/★)
Confident, well-rounded triple that started well and is set to become a classic of the genre.

SEASONAL BEER:
[2]**La Maitresse** (6.5%: ★★★/★)
Blond ale perfumed with aspérule, the floral herb used to flavour the local maitrank.

[4]**La Rulles Cuvée Meilleurs Vœux** (6.2%)
The winter offering changes each year but ducks major spicing.

Sainte Hélène

Microbrasserie Sainte-Hélène
Rue des Collines 21, 6760 Ethe
T 063 43 48 64   **E** saintehelene@skynet.be
www.sainte-helene.be

We assume Eddy Pourtois' brewing career is taking off as he now opens his microbrewery, in the far south of Luxembourg province, three times a week for direct sales. Opened in April 1998 and constructed from school kitchen equipment, allegedly. Beers have thus far varied in quality from impressive to not. Ring him in the Easter holidays and with luck he will show you round. The brewhouse has moved three times so far. Another brewer allowed to use Orval yeast.

ANNUAL OUTPUT: <250 hl.

REGULAR BEERS:

Bière Blanche La Gaumette (5.2%: ★★★)
Variable wheat beer, occasionally splendid.

La Marquise du Pont d'Oye (6%: ★★★/★)
Nicely balanced spiced lightish brown ale.

La Sainte Hélène Blonde (6.5%)
The newest of the beers, not yet tried.

La Sainte Hélène Ambrée (8.5%: ★★★/★)
A strong ruddy amber ale that is pretty good when on form.

Saint Feuillien

Brasserie Saint-Feuillien
Rue d'Houdeng 20, 7070 Le Roeulx
T 064 64 18 18   **E** info@st-feuillien.com
www.st-feuillien.com

Founded in 1873 at Le Roeulx, between Charleroi and Mons. The Brewery closed between 1977 and 1988. When it re-opened, it was Brasserie Friart after the family who have owned it for five generations. In 2000 the business divided, with brewing coming under the control of big sister Dominique and the warehouse falling to little brother.

Putting champagne bottles to better use

Many Belgian breweries have taken to producing their beers in the sort of large bottles that are usually reserved for champagne. This brings subtle changes to flavour through different yeast dynamics. They also make great presents.

St. Feuillien is famous for its use of huge champagne bottles, purchased from St. Gobin in France, in direct competition with champagne producers. Orders often have to be placed over a year in advance. The bottles are eventually filled by hand.

As a general rule the largest bottle seen is the three-litre double-magnum or Jeroboam. However, bottles do appear up to 12 litres. Forget about trying to pour in a way that keeps the sediment in the bottle!

15 litres	Nebuchadnezzar	King of Babylon, 605–562 BC
12 litres	Balthazar	Wise man two, who brought frankincense to Bethlehem
9 litres	Salmanazar	King of Assyria, 859–824 BC
6 litres	Methuselah	Biblical patriarch who lived to the age of 969
4.5 litres	Rehoboam	Son of King Solomon of Judeah, 922–908 BC
3 litres	Jeroboam	Founder and first king of Israel, 931–910 BC
1.5 litres	Magnum	American TV private investigator, 1980–1988

The largest bottles in regular use are the 9- and 12-litre, bigger ones tending to explode. Historically a 20-litre bottle called a Solomon (or Melchior) and a 27-litre bottle called a Primat have been made.

Beers in large bottles tend to be more expensive, as the bottles are made to order and need to be hand-filled, a labour-intensive process. Don't assume everyone considers them a collector's item though. St. Feuillien regularly gets people coming back to re-claim the deposit.

The brewery became St. Feuillien, in honour of its abbey beer brand, named after a nearby ruin. The company is completely open about its arrangement with du Bocq and Affligem breweries, and about the advantages and disadvantages of these. At Le Roeulx they make all their draught beers (except Noël) and everything that appears in supersize bottles – which means 150cl and upwards. All of the excellent Triple is made here, plus an Easter beer (7.5%: ★★★★) made initially for the Danish market. Although the brewery denies much discernible taste difference when compared with the brews from du Bocq, we suspect it will not have escaped them that their own brews always taste better. Clearly bucking the Belgian trend by improving year by year. Exports to the UK, France, Italy, the Netherlands, Denmark, Finland, Sweden, Switzerland, the US, Japan and Brazil. Group tours only, via the website. We describe the Grisette brand under Affligem (see Global beer makers).

ANNUAL OUTPUT: 20,000–100,000 hl.

REGULAR BEERS:

St. Feuillien Blonde (7.5%: ★★★★)
This draught blonde ale took the trade by storm in 2003–04.

St. Feuillien Brune (7.5%: ★★★★/★)
Striking, sweetish, burnt bière brune with a friendly welcome.

St. Feuillien Triple (8.5%: ★★★★/★)
Blonde beer of tantalising complexity that has ignored the trend for triple to go sweet and has headed for hop ascendancy. Thoroughly recommended and close to a full five-star rating.

SEASONAL BEER:

[4]**St. Feuillien Cuvée de Noël** (9%: ★★★★)
An umber coloured, lush, over-spiced winter ale that gets noticeably better (★★★★/★) in large bottles and keeps well.

Saint Monon

Brasserie Saint-Monon
Rue Principale 41, 6953 Ambly
T 084 21 46 32   **E** pierrejacob@busmail.net

Founded in 1996, near Marche-en-Famenne in the north of Luxembourg, as a sort of new wave farm brewery. Owner-brewer Pierre Jacob built his brewery in the annex of his parents' farm. The beers tend to be well made but are often spoiled by heavy spicing. All the regular beers are available filtered on draught, or bottled with sediment. Some commissioned beers appear with original recipes. Named after a 7th century Scottish monk who wound up in Rochefort. Group visits by arrangement. They run a weekend tasting room in summer (see Luxembourg: Brewery cafés).

ANNUAL OUTPUT: <1,000 hl.

REGULAR BEERS:

St. Monon Ambrée (6.5%: ★★★/★)
Soft, sweetish sediment ambrée, lightly spiced.

St. Monon Brune (7.5%: ★★★/★)
Sweet and heavily coriandered sediment brune.

St. Monon au Miel (8%: ★★★/★)
Lusciously sweet amber beer with some spiciness.

St. Monon Elmesinde (8%: ★★★/★)
Amber ale drowned in spice.

SEASONAL BEERS:

[2]**Saison de Mai** (8.3%: ★★★)
Amber blond ale brewed for Arlon and laced with aspèrule, the herb used to make maitrank.

St. Monon Bière Spéciale des Fêtes (7.5%: ★★★★). Special occasions beer that tastes like concentrated dandelion and burdock with a splash of Thai whisky.

[4]**Nectar de Noël** (7.5%)
The Christmas brew, with thyme and honey.

Schuur

Brouwerij de Schuur
Wolvendreef 30, 3120 Linden
T 016 62 13 58

The smallest commercially licenced brewery in Belgium. Hobby brewer Jan Symons began in 1995, closed in 1999 and re-opened in the cellars of the family home in 2000. He makes beers on demand for private customers, including the Hof café in Linden (see Flemish Brabant: Brewery cafés). A black Kerstbier appeared in 2003 and a Paasbier comes out at Easter. The most regular brews are **Meneer** (7.5%) and **Nikolaas Tripel** (9%).

ANNUAL OUTPUT: <250 hl.

Silenrieux

SA Brasserie de Silenrieux
Rue Naupré 1, 5630 Silenrieux
T 071 63 32 01
E brasserie.silenrieux@belgacom.net
http://users.belgacom.net/gc195540/

Opened in 1991 at Silenrieux, just by the Hainaut border in the southern part of Namur. Originally formed as a co-operative but later bought out by a group of small businessmen. The original aim was to promote ancient grain varieties in brewing, by producing the first wheat beers brewed with buckwheat and spelt. Le Pavé de l'Ours is brewed under a contract that moves brewery from time to time. Other contract and label beers exist. Regular beers are exported to France, the Netherlands, Switzerland, Spain and California. Group visits by arrangement.

Annual output: <1,000 hl.

Regular beers:
Joseph (6%: ★★★★)
Offbeat wheat beer brewed with spelt, managing an elusive, dryish character.
Sara (6%: ★★★★)
Spicy, sweetish, unusual variant of wheat beer made using buckwheat.
Le Pavé de l'Ours (8.5%: ★★★)
Overly sweet honey beer that has done the rounds.

Seasonal beer:
[4]**Noël de Silenrieux** (7.5%)
Red-brown all-malt Christmas brew.

Silly

Brasserie de Silly SA
Rue Ville Basse 2, 7830 Silly
T 068 55 16 95
E silly@silly-beer.com
www.silly-beer.com

A family-owned brewery based in the town of Silly, north of Mons in northern Hainaut. Founded in 1850 and now owned by the fifth generation. Farming remained the main business until after the 1939–45 war. In 1950 they bought a string of local cafés and produced their first lager. Known until 1974 as both Mynsbrugen and Meynsbrughen. In the following year they bought the Tennstedt-Decroes brewery in Enghien and acquired the Double Enghien brands. After several years of inconsistency, rekitting the brewhouse has created far greater reliability. Ironically this has led to the merging of several beers into a similar polished blond style. The Blonde, Noël and Printemps seem only to vary in their water content. Whichever marketing guru suggested they make Pink Killer should be pickled in the stuff – it is a contender for worst beer in Belgium. All the beers would benefit from slower fermentation and the darker ones need longer maturation, as demonstrated by the quality of a few of the specially aged commissioned beers. Exports to much of western Europe including Britain, plus North America. Group visits only, by arrangement. There are direct sales from the brewery during the week.

Annual output: 10,000–20,000 hl.

Regular beers:
Titje Blanche (4.7%: ★★★)
Spiced wheat beer with oats that has become drier over the years.
Pink Killer (5%: ★★)
Beer flavoured with pink grapefruit, for some reason.
Silly Pils (5%: ★★)
Standard light-coloured Pilsener.
Super 64 (5.2%: ★★★)
English-type pale ale relabelled as Abbaye de Cambron.
Saison de Silly (5.3%: ★★★)
Absurdly fruity but unusual, gentle beer billed as an old brown and unlike other saisons.
Double Enghien Blonde (7.5%: ★★★/★)
Filtered blonde with above average character, tasting spiced though not officially so.
Double Enghien Brune (8%: ★★★)
Copper-coloured beer with the full malt character of a traditional strong brown ale.
Scotch Silly (8%: ★★★★)
Superbly rounded, warming, sweet, filtered, chestnut-coloured ale with clear Scotch character.
La Divine (9.5%: ★★★/★)
A powerful ambrée of great character but a bit short on panache.

Seasonal beers:
[1]**Printemps de Silly** (6.5%: ★★★★/★)
Light, dryish blonde beer with unusual and appealing hopping that stays throughout the glass.

[4]**Enghien de Noël** (9%: ★★★/★)
Largely unspiced, classy triple-style blond beer.

COMMISSIONED BEERS:
Unusually, Silly saves some of its best efforts for its longer standing commissions. The Corman-Collins warehouse of Battice, near Liège, commission two beers associated with the Avouerie d'Anthisnes beer museum. Its **Cervoise** (6%: ★★★★) is a distinctive amber ale, with a cave-aged, slightly musty character, while the **Cuvée des Hauts Voués** (8%: ★★★★) is a less obviously aged strong deep amber ale. They also buy in **La Gueule Noire/ Koempelbier** (8%: ★★★), a caramelised, slightly fruity, bittersweet, black beer and **St. Christophe** (8%: ★★★★/★), a richly candied ruby-brown bottle-conditioned beer of great character, perfect to accompany roast lamb. They also brew two Villers St. Ghislain brands for Michaux Seconde of St. Symphorien. The **Blonde Spéciale** (7.2%: ★★★★) is like a strangely perfumed version of Duvel-ish, while the **Brune Spéciale** (8%: ★★★) is a bittersweet chestnut ale.

Sint Bernardus

Brouwerij St. Bernard
Trappistenweg 23, 8978 Watou
T 057 38 80 21
E info@sintbernardus.be
www.sintbernardus.be

Evarist Deconinck was a cheese maker who became a brewer. He started making cheese for the French monks of the Refuge Notre Dame de St. Bernard in 1934 and did so until 1959. This history of co-operation with one abbey led in 1946 to co-operation with another, when he created a brewery at Watou, near the French border in West Flanders. For nearly fifty years its main purpose was to produce and distribute a range of beers called St. Sixtus, which were licensed imitations of the three brews produced on a tiny scale at the eponymous abbey in nearby Westvleteren. In 1992 in effect the licence came to an end and the brewery had to prepare itself for the market place, essentially stripped of its brands. Rather than admit defeat the company rose to the challenge and began to produce a range of St. Bernardus beers, initially direct counter-

parts of the three beers they had made for ages but soon developing steadily from strength to strength. Primary fermentation of a decent length is followed by prolonged lagering to produce beers of great maturity, which improve further with keeping for a year or two. In 2002 they were awarded multiple accolades at the American brewing awards in Chicago. They were also blessed by another saintly benefactor, Pierre Celis, who gifted them the contract to brew his Grottenbier (see Brewers without Breweries). If you stay at the brewer's elegant home (see West Flanders: Brewery cafés) you might get a chance to visit this most utilitarian of post-war breweries and its handsome new bottling machine, a wonder of the modern age. Exports to the UK, France, the Netherlands, Japan and the US.

ANNUAL OUTPUT: 10,000–20,000 hl.

REGULAR BEERS:
St. Bernardus Wit (5.5%: ★★★★/★)
Spicy wheat beer of unusually strong character.
St. Bernardus Pater 6° (6.7%: ★★★★)
Fruity, dark brown, sweetish roasted dubbel that punches big.
Watou Tripel (7%: ★★★★)
The lighter of two triples, brewed originally for France to a different recipe from…
St. Bernardus Tripel (7.5%: ★★★★)
Blonde, mellow-bitter bottle-conditioned tripel that varies from good to superb.
St. Bernardus Prior 8° (8%: ★★★★/★)
A dark, sweet, mellow ale with a strong peardrop presence.
St. Bernardus Abt 12° (10.5%: ★★★★/★)
Mellow barley wine with the character of a golden brown version of Rochefort.

COMMISSIONED BEER:
For Pierre Celis they make **Grottenbier** (6.5%: ★★★★/★), a lightly spiced brown ale with a strangely pleasant flavour brought about by storing it in caves near the Dutch border. It tastes like a beer with a gadget in it. It should get a blond sister in summer 2005.

Sint Jozef

Brouwerij Sint Jozef
Itterplein 19, 3690 Opitter-Bree
T 011 86 47 11　**E** bsj@sintjozef.skynet.be
www.brouwerijsintjozef.be

Family brewery at Opitter, on the outskirts of Bree, near the Dutch border in the far north-eastern corner of Limburg. Definitely brewing in 1900 and possibly earlier. Since the latest generation of the Cornelissen family took over in 1981, production has increased five-fold. This is helped by the fact that Limburgse Witte is the wheat beer for Martens also (see above). The Guide remains resolutely rude about the fruit beers but holds the other products in growing regard, even if they are a bit clean for us. St. Gummarus was brewed originally for the Bokrijk Museum. Group visits only, by arrangement.

ANNUAL OUTPUT: 20,000–100,000 hl.

REGULAR BEERS:

Bosbier (4.5%: ★★)
Lager and black ready mixed.

Limburgse Witte (5%: ★★★★)
Gently assertive, grainy, slightly dry, milky wheat beer which is claimed to be brewed twice.

Pax Pils (5%: ★★/★)
The regular Pilsener.

St. Jozef Kriekenbier (5%: ★★)
Lager with cherry syrup.

Ops-Ale (5.5%: ★★★/★)
Pungent Limburg-style straw-coloured ale in the Sezoens tradition.

Bokkereyer (5.8%: ★★★/★)
Reddish, neutral, pale beer said by the brewery to be a lager but by Belgian beer experts to be an ale.

St. Gummarus Dubbel (7%: ★★★/★)
Well-attenuated medium-dark dubbel with a scalded sugar backtaste.

St. Gummarus Tripel (8%: ★★★)
Bright, clean, golden tripel that is improving with practice.

Sint Pieters

Brouwerij Sint Pieters
Victor Nonnemansstraat 40a
1600 Sint-Pieters-Leeuw
T 0497 93 23 75   **E** zinnebir@hotmail.com
www.zinnebir.be

Based in the buildings of the old Moriau drinks depot at St Pieters-Leeuw in Payottenland, south west of Brussels. Opened in autumn 2004. The first efforts were none too bad and recent ones are better. Some well-trusted friends rate them highly. One to watch.

ANNUAL OUTPUT: <250 hl.

REGULAR BEER:

Zinnebir (6%: ★★★★)
An increasingly confident, cleverly hopped pale ale, better without its sediment.

SEASONAL BEER:

[4]**Xmas Zinnebir** (6.6%: ★★★/★)
The first year's effort was dark, dryish and safe, achieving spiceless spiciness.

Slaghmuylder

Brouwerij Slaghmuylder
Denderhoutembaan 2, 9400 Ninove
T 054 33 18 31   **F** 054 33 84 45

A traditional, almost shy family brewery dating from 1860, based at Ninove, west of Brussels in eastern East Flanders. The current brewhouse dates from 1925. Their Witkap range of abbey beers have always rated among the best, managing spicy tastes without the addition of spices, despite relatively fast primary fermentation. Witkap were the first ever abbey beers, created by a former brewer at Westmalle, Henrik Verlinden, for his Drie Linden brewery at Brasschaat in the 1920s. Slaghmuylder took over brewing them in 1979 and bought the brand two years later. Their other claim to fame is that they produce unusually good lagers, for Belgium. They also brew two tafelbiers. Group visits by arrangement include a visit to the brewery's museum.

ANNUAL OUTPUT: <10,000 hl.

REGULAR BEERS:

Helles Lager Beer (4%)
Light lager.

Slag Lager Beer (5%: ★★★)
Slag means "cream". This light but enjoyable Pilsener, is notably better (★★★★) locally on draught.

Witkap Stimulo (6%: ★★★★/★)
Aromatic, light blond ale, impressive on draught and fruity when bottle-conditioned.

Witkap Dubbele Pater (7.2%: ★★★)
Medium brown, burnt and bitter ale.

Witkap Tripel (7.5%: ★★★★)
Unusual, spicy but unspiced, straw-coloured.

Ambiorix (8%: ★★★★)
Dark brown, dryish strong porter or stout, with a rasping bitterness and strong burnt caramel afterburn.

SEASONAL BEERS:

[1]**Slaghmuylder Paasbier** (6%: ★★★★/★)
One of the few really special Belgian lagers, lonely among a sea of fine ales.

[4]**Slaghmuylder Kerstbier** (6%: ★★★★/★)
Possibly the best Pilsener brewed in Belgium. It will carve its way through the Christmas turkey as well as any dark spicy ale. Year-round production would wake up all the others.

Strubbe

Brouwerij Strubbe
Markt 1, 8480 Ichtegem
T 051 58 81 16   **E** info@brouwerij-strubbe.be
www.brouwerij-strubbe.be

Smallish family-run brewery as old as Belgium itself. Founded in 1830 at Ichtegem, south of Ostend, as an extension of the family farm. Now run by cousins of the sixth generation. The range of beers is broad but congregates around lower strength ales. As well as those listed there is a reasonable non-alcoholic lager called Edel-Bräu and a traditional table beer called Oud Bier. Couckelaerschen Doedel is a hang-on from Lootens brewery of Koekelare (closed 1972). Group tours by arrangement.

ANNUAL OUTPUT: 10,000–20,000 hl.

REGULAR BEERS:

Krieken Bier (4.5%: ★★)
Brown ale with cherry flavouring.

Ichtegems Oud Bruin (4.9%: ★★★/★)
Passable, easy-drinking Flemish old red, made with 20% aged beer.

Strubbe Super Pils (5%: ★★★★)
Unusually well-hopped Pilsener, among Belgium's best.

Vlaskop (5.5%: ★★★★)
Unusual beer made from unmalted barley.

Couckelaerschen Doedel (6%: ★★★)
Pleasant, bottle-conditioned, bitter-sweet, spiced amber ale with a name that means "Cock-a-doodle do".

Dikke Mathile (6%: ★★★)
Plain but pleasant amber ale, lagered for six weeks.

Houten Kop (6.5%: ★★★★)
Darkish, spiced pale ale that used to be brewed by a private brewer but is now a mainstream beer.

COMMISSIONED BEERS:

They brew the delicious dry black **Callewaert Stout** (5.5%: ★★★★) for a drinks warehouse in Zwevezele that had its own brewery until 1991, plus variants of it for other local cafés. For a small chain of drinks warehouses round Aalst they brew three Pee Klak brands, a wheaty pale ale called **Moorsels Bier** (5.4%: ★★★/★), a fruity amber ale called **Hoeve Bier** (6.5%: ★★★★) and an occasional brew called **Royal** (7.8%). For a beer merchant in Oostkamp they make a spicy blond ale called **Wittoen Tripel** (7%). They were brewing beers for the defunct Crombé brewery in Zottegem but we have not heard of these lately.

Timmermans

Timmermans – John Martin NV
Kerkstraat 11, 1701 Itterbeek
T 02 569 03 57   **F** 02 569 01 98

One of the larger lambic brewers and gueuze blenders, founded in 1850 at Itterbeek on the outskirts of Brussels. Taken over in 1993 by the beer distributor, John Martin. The Guide does not believe that they produce any gueuze or kriek that is allowed to call itself "oude". The beers range from the squidgy soft commercial fruit stuff to a couple that are within wishing distance of authenticity. They have the most confusing branding system in Belgium. Quite what they mean by "Tradition" is anyone's guess. The basic lambics still exist but we believe are never sold commercially. Maybe they are not very good. More likely they are from the *meerts* end of the spectrum. Someone give this brewery a strategy, please. Group visits only, by arrangement.

ANNUAL OUTPUT: 10,000–20,000 hl.

REGULAR BEERS:

Timmermans Faro (3.5%: ★★)
Bottled lambic with candy sugar.

Timmermans Cassis Lambic (4%: ★★)
Dull blackcurrant lambic drink.

Timmermans Framboise Lambic (4%: ★★★)
Not horrifically sweet and tasting of raspberries not cough medicine.

Timmermans Pêche Lambic (4%: ★★★)
The peachy one.

Timmermans Lambicus Blanche (4.5%: ★★★/★). *Mix of lambic and a wheat beer of variable sweetness.*

Timmermans Gueuze Lambic (5%: ★★)
Commercial, sweet, filtered beer that may have other words added to its name.

Timmermans Kriek Lambic (5%: ★★★)
Sweet but fruity commercial cherry lambic.
Timmermans Doux Lambic (5.5%: ★★★/★)
Pleasant flat fruity faro made mainly for the Bécasse café in Brussels.
Bourgogne des Flandres (5.5%: ★★★)
Fruity lambic-based imitation of an oak-aged Flemish brown ale.
Timmermans Gueuze Caveau (5.5%:★★★/★)
The slightly sour, compromised, semi-traditional, filtered gueuze.

Touffe

Brasserie de la Touffe
Rue de l'Ermitage 141, 1450 Gentinnes
T 071 87 68 60

A hobby brewery that opened in 1998 at Gentinnes in Wallonian Brabant. Its name means "Tuft" and their beers are probably the most elusive in Belgium. Rumour has it that the brewery actually closed at the end of 2005 but we have been unable to confirm this. The regular beers appear to be **Fluppeke** (5%), **Ruine de Villers** (5.5%), **St. Jean** (5.5%), **St. David** (8%) and **St. Martin** (8%).

ANNUAL OUTPUT: <250 hl.

Trois Brasseurs

Brasserie les Trois Brasseurs
53 Rue de Rodange, 6791 Athus
T&F 063 38 31 72
www.3brasseurs.be

House brewery opened in 2000 by the same people who own the Trois Brasseurs in Lille and others. The "three countries" might be a better name as it is within an easy cycle ride of both France and the Grand Duchy. The beers are only available at the café as far as we know. 75cl bottles for take-away, otherwise on draught. Other seasonal beers are rumoured but not directly reported.

ANNUAL OUTPUT: <1,000 hl.

REGULAR BEERS:
Blanche de Lille (4.2%: ★★)
Thin wheat beer.
Blonde des Trois Brasseurs (5.2%: ★★)
Thin lager-like brew

Ambrée des Trois Brasseurs (6.2%: ★★)
Sweet pale ale.
Scotch des Trois Brasseurs (??%: ★★★)
Brown ale with a bit more character.

SEASONAL BEERS:
They make a Bière de Mars in spring and a brown Bière de Noël at Christmas.

Trois Fourquets

Brasserie les Trois Fourquets
50 Courtil, 6670 Courtil
T 080 64 38 39   **F** 080 64 38 80
www.les3fourquets.be

Restaurant brewery in a hamlet near Gouvy, in the east of Luxembourg province. Part-owned by the irrepressible Chris Bauweraerts from Achouffe (above). The aim is to get guest brewers to brew experimental beers from time to time but meanwhile to perfect a light blond wheat beer, all in 10-hectolitre batches. The first brew appeared in March 2004.

ANNUAL OUTPUT: <250 hl.

REGULAR BEER:
La Fourquette (4.5%: ★★★)
The first attempt at this unspiced wheat beer was somewhat workaday.

Union – *see Global beer makers* (SCAM)

Val de Sambre

Brasserie Val de Sambre
Rue Emile Vandervelde 273, 6534 Gozée
T 071 56 20 73   **E** contact@valdesambre.be
www.valdesambre.be

By the time Val de Sambre opened their brew-house south west of Charleroi, in December 2000, the beers of the Abbaye d'Aulne (or ADA) range had been on sale for twenty-five years, commissioned from Affligem. The abbey from which it takes its name is a ruin. Rumour has it that they still brew elsewhere. We have seen no evidence to support this though their bottle labels do not discount the possibility. The stronger beers are developing more bite as the years go by. Exports to France, Italy and Denmark.

ANNUAL OUTPUT: 2,000–10,000 hl.

REGULAR BEERS:

Blanche de Charleroi (5%: ★★★)
Soft, rather plain wheat beer.

Abbaye d'Aulne Blonde 6° (7%: ★★★/★)
Dryish blonde ale with a straightforward, unspiced character.

Abbaye d'Aulne Brune 6° (7%)
Brown abbey beer.

Abbaye d'Aulne Val de Sambre 6° (7%)
Recently suped up ambrée.

Abbaye d'Aulne Triple Blonde 9° (8%)
Blond triple.

Abbaye d'Aulne Triple Brune 9° (8%: ★★★★)
Strangely familiar, big, dryish, brown sediment ale.

SEASONAL BEER:

[4]**Abbaye d'Aulne Super Noël** (9%: ★★★★)
Dark and dryish Christmas ale related to the Triple Brune, with roasted malt in its afterburn.

Abbaye du Val-Dieu Triple (9%: ★★★/★)
Surprisingly easy-drinking likeable triple that lacks depth.

SEASONAL BEER:

[4]**Abbaye du Val Dieu Bière de Noël** (7%: ★★★)
Golden-amber, full-bodied and dryish with a hint of peach.

COMMISSIONED BEERS

They are brewing an increasing number of beers to contract, including the juniper-laced **Radermacher**, **La Ploquette** from the deceased Ruwet brewery and **La Pierreuse**, **Blonde d'Oleye** and **Solorea** from the equally ex Oleye. There are others called **Farnières** and **Houyeux**. **Merveilleuse de Chevremont** (7%: ★★★★) for Corman-Collins of Battice was described by one taster as being "like Duvel with a squirt of lemon squash".

Val-Dieu

Brasserie de l'Abbaye du Val-Dieu
Val-Dieu 225, 4880 Aubel
T 087 68 75 85   **E** info@val-dieu.com
www.val-dieu.com

Opened in 1997 on the farm of the 13th century Cistercian Abbey of Val-Dieu, near Aubel in northern Liège. Val-Dieu beers had been commissioned for years before brewing partner Benoît Humblet and sales partner Alain Pinckaers invested in some serious kit of their own and started to manage this well-organised brewery. Although beer quality is consistently good, character tends to be restrained. Somehow you want the beers to mature more and it would be nice to know what a full-on malty brew would taste like. Exports to UK, US, France, Germany, Switzerland, Italy and Canada. Excellent group visits can be arranged via the website.

ANNUAL OUTPUT: 2,000–10,000 hl.

REGULAR BEERS:

Abbaye du Val-Dieu Blanche (6%)
A wheat beer that entered the market as the style was falling from favour but which has impressed some.

Abbaye du Val-Dieu Blonde (6%: ★★★)
Well made but relatively simple sediment blonde ale.

Abbaye du Val-Dieu Brune (8%: ★★★)
More of a plain Wallonian brune than a Trappist double.

Van Den Bossche

Brouwerij Van Den Bossche
St. Lievensplein 16, 9550 Sint-Lievens-Esse
T 054 50 04 11   **E** paterlieven@skynet.be
www.paterlieven.be

Small family-owned East Flanders ale brewery whose beers are made in a protected 19th century brewhouse, on the village square at St. Lievens-Esse, south of Ghent. Preparations are being made for the brewery to pass to only the fourth generation of the Van den Bossche family to run the company since its foundation in 1897. Built its reputation on the excellence of its dark beers like Buffalo. The newer beers, such as the Pater Lieven brands, are sweeter. Appears to be playing with the range, with some experiments more pleasing than others. Despite the limited size and traditional set-up, the beers can be found in the US, UK, Netherlands, France and Italy. There is a shop on site (Mon-Fri: 09.00–17.00; Sat 09.00–12.00). Group visits only, by arrangement.

ANNUAL OUTPUT: 2,000–10,000 hl.

REGULAR BEERS:

Buffalo (5.7%: ★★★★/★)
Dry, firm, bitter, well-attenuated stout that loses a little on draught but has survived virtually unscathed since 1907!

Pater Lieven Blond (6.5%: ★★★★)
Full, golden sediment pale ale of character.
Pater Lieven Bruin (6.5%: ★★★★)
Dryish, good quality, straight brown ale.
Lamoral Tripel (8%: ★★★★)
Light amber tripel that is noticeably sweeter than...
Pater Lieven Tripel (8%: ★★★)
Clear, aromatic, spiced tripel with a bitter afterburn.

SEASONAL BEERS:
[4]**Kerstpater** (9%: ★★★★/★)
Rich, dark, sweetish, lightly spiced winter brew of surprising maturity. Among the best.
[4]**Pater Lieven Christmas** (9%: ★★★★)
Rich, red-brown, sweetish lightly spiced winter ale.

Van Eecke

Van Eecke NV
Douvieweg 2, 8978 Watou
T 057 42 20 05   **F** 057 42 39 70
www.brouwerijvaneecke.tk

An impressive producer of top quality ales in a range of styles, founded in 1862 as the Gouden Leeuw brewery at Watou, near Poperinge in West Flanders. Owned by the same family as Leroy (above) and although traditionally run as a separate business, the two sets of products dovetail neatly with each other and are seen increasingly together. The excellent Kapittel ("Chapter") range of abbey beers started in 1946 and is one of the best in Belgium. Kapittel Dubbel is a blend of Kapittel Pater, Kapittel Prior and a few flavourings. One of the breweries that is clearly improving its quality in recent years. They do some contract brewing from time to time, including Livinus Blonde and Brune, which we think are Kapittel Abt and Prior re-labelled in French. Export to the Netherlands, France, Italy, Portugal, Canada and Taiwan. Group visits by arrangement.

ANNUAL OUTPUT: 2,000–10,000 hl.

REGULAR BEERS:
Watou's Witbier (5%: ★★★★)
Slightly lemony, cloudy, refreshing wheat beer waivering between mundane and excellent.
Kapittel Blond (6.5%: ★★★★/★)
Mellow, easy-drinking and rounded but topped off with great hops.

Kapittel Pater (6.5%: ★★★★)
Fresh tasting, medium dark, simple brown ale.
Kapittel Dubbel (7%: ★★★★)
Dark, aromatic, beefy dubbel with peardrop esters in the background.
Poperings Hommelbier (7.5%: ★★★★)
Deceptively strong, filtered pale ale with clever hopping.
Kapittel Prior (9%: ★★★★★)
Full, medium dark, complex and delicious dark tripel, which ages well and rewards keeping for up to five years.
Kapittel Abt (10%: ★★★★)
Light coloured, slightly aromatic, sweetish strong ale that sometimes excels.

Van Honsebrouck

NV Brouwerij Van Honsebrouck
Oostrozebekestraat 43, 8770 Ingelmunster
T 051 33 51 60   **E** info@vanhonsebrouck.be
www.vanhonsebrouck.be

Commercially adept West Flanders brewery, at Ingelmunster near Roeselare. Founded in 1900. Along with Bockor (above) another brewery outside Brussels and Payottenland to produce so-called lambic, using a *koelschip* below an open roof to source wild yeast. All very mysterious. After years of being castigated for producing bandwagon beers, this family-owned, entrepreneurial brewery turned their own history on its head by ditching safe commercialism and going for unsubtle instead. First there was the rabidly dry, traditional-style gueuze. Then there were two barley wines for a mass market. Then it went plain silly. In 1999 a beer was produced, they claim, by sousing cherries with brown ale in oaken tuns. Having made the first oud bruin cherry beer for half a century, they gave it a robotic name (K8) and marketed it at teenagers in bright red plastic-coated bottles. Meanwhile the Beavis end of the operation experimented with a lighter alcohol cherry lambic with 25% cherry juice called **Premium Kriek** (3.2%). This ranks alongside a 3.5% peach lambic called **St Louis Pêche**. **Kasteel 7°** may be for export only. Exports to most of Europe, North America, Australia, Japan and the Dominican Republic.

ANNUAL OUTPUT: 20,000–100,000 hl.

REGULAR BEERS:

Bacchus (4.5%: ★★★)
Sweetish imitation Rodenbach.

St. Louis Cassis Kir Royal (4.5%: ★★★)
Annoyingly pleasant concoction of blackcurrant juice and home-made lambic.

St. Louis Framboise (4.5%: ★★)
Medium dry mix of raspberry juice and lambic.

St. Louis Gueuze Lambic (4.5%: ★★)
Sweet pale beer with a hint of mushrooms.

St. Louis Kriek Lambic (4.5%: ★★★)
Nice fruity drink that avoids tasting like beer.

Vlaamsch Wit (4.5%: ★★★)
Soapy, smoky, light coloured, sweet wheat beer.

Gueuze Fond Tradition St. Louis (5%: ★★★/★)
Imagine the presentation of an oude gueuze without the complex citric backtastes.

K8 (8%: ★★★)
Brown ale with a stewed fruit taste, possibly brewed to accompany school dinners.

Brigand (9%: ★★★/★)
Ruddy amber strong ale.

Kasteelbier Blond (11%: ★★★/★)
Uncompromising and unsubtle, sweet strong blond ale, sometimes sold as Gouden Tripel.

Kasteelbier Bruin (11%: ★★★/★)
Equally sweet, unsubtle, medium dark, clean but mighty barley wine.

SEASONAL BEER:

[4]**Brigand Christmas** (9%) is draught Brigand with or without herbs, for the Dutch market.

Van Steenberge

Brouwerij Van Steenberge NV
Lindenlaan 25, 9940 Ertvelde
T 09 344 50 71   **E** info@vansteenberge.com
www.vansteenberge.com

Family-owned, busy independent brewery at Ertvelde, north of Ghent in East Flanders. The first reference to a brewery on this site comes from 1784, though for the first hundred years of its existence brewing was a sideline to farming. The brewery first developed under the stewardship of Paul van Steenberge in the early 20th century. He went on to be mayor of Ertvelde and a member of the national parliament. He also changed the name of the brewery to Bios, which became renowned for its oud bruin beer, Vlaamse Bourgogne

(or "*Flemish Burgundy*"). Sadly this famous brew is now just a sideline. The Twenties saw soft drinks production arrive and the Thirties brought lager. In 1978 they acquired the right to brew Augustijn. Bornem abbey beers followed. For all its cosy village image, this is a brewery that intends to survive and, uncharacteristically for Belgium, has invested heavily in plant. Now known by the family name of Van Steenberge, it was the first independent Belgian brewery to install a fully computerised brewing system. More recently they bought a new fermenting vessel of such dimensions that the police had to divert traffic across Flanders while installing it brought village life to a halt for the day. Trippel Bornem sells as Augustijn Grand Cru in the supermarket trade. In what the Guide hopes is a lead to competitors, where a commissioned beer is based on an existing brew the "Mother Beer" is often named on the label. They export to Spain and the UK. Group visits only, Monday to Wednesday afternoons.

ANNUAL OUTPUT: 20,000–100,000 hl.

REGULAR BEERS:

Bios Kriekenbier (5%: ★★★)
Based on Vlaamse Bourgogne with cherry juice.

Sparta Pils (5%: ★★★/★)
Unpasteurised, nicely balanced and moderately bitter Pilsener for the brewery's own cafés.

Bruegel (5.2%: ★★★)
Gentle, easy drinking, fruity amber ale.

Wilson Mild Stout (5.2%: ★★★/★)
Absurdly sweet, dark brown ale with just enough burnt character to be serious.

Bios Vlaamse Bourgogne (5.5%: ★★★/★)
Sweet and sour brown ale that is tank-aged for two years before bottling. Harsher than oak-aged equivalents.

Leute Bokbier (7.5%: ★★★/★)
Reliable chocolaty brown ale that is available all year round.

Augustijn (8%: ★★★)
Rather stringy strong blond ale that is not as assertive as it used to be.

Dubbel Bornem (8%: ★★★/★)
Dark, dryish, rather sweaty dubbel.

Trippel Bornem/Augustijn Grand Cru (9%: ★★★)
Srong straw-coloured ale with insufficient body for its strength.

Piraat 9° (9%: ★★★/★)

Lighter in colour than the other Piraat. More of a Duvel-like export beer.

Piraat 10.5° Amber (10.5%: ★★★/★)

Golden ale that drinks like a barley wine.

Gulden Draak (10.5%: ★★★/★)

Dark and powerful tonic, herbal but unspiced in a white gloss bottle.

COMMISSIONED BEERS:

Their complete range of commissioned beers is unclear. In the past they have blended and relabelled beers but nowadays much prefer to brew to an original recipe, though this involves the commissioner buying a full brew run. Their best-known commissioned beer is **Corsendonk Pater** (7.5%: ★★★/★), a sweetish, medium brown abbey beer for the Corsendonk warehouse in Oud Turnhout. For Hopduvel warehouse of Ghent they make a bitter-sweet, amber-coloured tripel called **Gentse Tripel** (8%: ★★★★), a candied strong blond called **Blondine** (9%: ★★★), a fruity but flimsy brown ale called **Brunette** (9%: ★★★) and a dark brew called Stropken (9%). For another famous customer, Celis Europe NV, they make a number of fruity wheat beers under the Brussels brand name plus the flagship sweet and spicy, unfiltered wheat beer called **Celis White** (5%: ★★★★) and a clear copper-blond ale called **Celis Pale Bock** (5.5%: ★★★/★).

Bravely they lease out their brewhouse every now and then to the formidable brouwvrouw of the de Leyerth "brewery" of Hilvareenbeek in the Netherlands. The full range of her Urthel brands now includes a spiced brown ale called **Novicius Vertus** (5.9%), the original herbal amber lager **Tonicum Finiboldhus** (7.5%: ★★★/★), the gutsy tripel **Hibernus Quentum** (9%: ★★★★) and the two seasonal beers, the Dutch-style [3]**Bock** (6.5%) and the winter barley wine [4]**Samaranth Quadrium** (11.5%). Dirk Labie of the Saf café in Geraardsbergen commissions two St.Adriaans beers. The **Blond** (6.5%: ★★★/★) is a pleasantly chewy concoction while the **Bruin** (6.5%: ★★★/★) has a sour brown character. André Paeleman's brewery in Wetteren relies on them to produce most of his bittersweet blond **Uitzet 1730** (6.8%: ★★★) and **Uitzet Kriekenbier** (5.8%: ★★★),

the same beer with a cherry infusion. An abbey-approved tripel for Leuven called **Keizersburg** (9%: ★★★) also appears, and **Queue de Charrue Blonde** (6.5%: ★★★/★) for Vanuxeem.

Vapeur

Brasserie à Vapeur

Rue de Maréchal 1, 7904 Pipaix-Leuze

T 069 66 20 47   **E** brasserie@vapeur.com

www.vapeur.com

Founded in 1984 at Pipaix in western Hainaut to take over a brewery that had been operating since 1785. Now believed to be the last steam-powered brewery in the world, hence its name "By Steam". Part museum, part commercial brewery, part hobby. These are challenging beers. You know that old saying about the dividing line between genius and madness? As with Fantôme (above), Vapeur's beers divide the cogniscenti. The "pro" lobby see these as the epitome of traditional farmhouse brewing, while the others do not. The secret ingredient here is lichen, which adds an unmistakable earthiness. Why do this? Well the records of the old brewery show that they did this in the past. Since the Guide discovered this, our reverance has gone up considerably. Make your own minds up. We remain firmly on the fence. Exports to France, the US and Japan. One of the great brewery visits (see Beer Tourism).

ANNUAL OUTPUT: <1,000 hl.

REGULAR BEERS:

Vapeur Vanille (5%: ★★★)

Pale ale with vanilla essence. Could be worse.

Saison de Pipaix (6.5%: ★★★★)

Amber saison of unique character, the hop presence in which can disappear halfway through the bottle.

Vapeur en Folie (8%: ★★★★)

Sweet and dry, microbiologically odd amber-blonde ale that some find unbeatable.

Vapeur Cochonne (9%: ★★★/★)

Sweet, strong, dark golden spiced ale, with the same spritzy, sweetened dryness of the others.

SEASONAL BEER:

[2]**Vapeur Légère** (4.5%: ★★★)

Thin, light brew, not strictly a summer beer but rarely available at other times.

Verhaeghe

NV Brouwerij Verhaeghe Vichte
Beukenhofstraat 96, 8570 Vichte
T 056 77 70 32
E brouwerij.verhaeghe@proximedia.be
www.proximedia.com/web/breweryverhaeghe.html

A small West Flanders brewery founded in 1880 near Kortrijk. The brothers who have re-shaped it in the last seven years are the fourth generation of the Verhaeghe family to brew at Vichte. One has tidied up the brewing to make for better consistency across the year. The other has tidied up the marketing so that the range of products is more clearly defined. All beers undergo primary fermentation of between eight and ten days, followed by six weeks of lagering. Although they make a Pilsener and a range of pale ales the brewery's deserved and increasing reputation worldwide comes from its oak-aged brown ales. These are blends of ordinary brown ale with beers that have been aged for up to two years in one of the brewery's collection of oak tuns, bought from spirits and fortified wine manufacturers from all over Europe. The company has two functions. It supplies the local café trade and its tied pubs with a general range of drinks. The rest of the world gets the seriously good stuff. Their bottled ales can improve, in the case of **Duchesse de Bourgogne** to a full ★★★★★, with cellar storage of a year or more. The old brewhouse and fermentation rooms are a rabbit-run of new and disused equipment that no safety inspector would allow open for public visits. The business may move up the road in a few years time, taking its tuns with it. With luck the old site may become a museum – which it is kind of already. A contender for the most improved brewery in Belgium.

Annual output: 2,000–10,000 hl.

Regular beers:
Verhaeghe Ouden Bruinen (3.5%: ★★★★)
Basic oud bruin table beer, a real thirst quencher found mainly local to the brewery.
Cambrinus (5.1%: ★★★)
Typical of the dry, unspiced, filtered style of Belgian pale ale.

Verhaeghe Pilsener (5.1%: ★★★)
Hoppier than Maes or Stella but still no prize winner, sold also as Export.
Vichtenaar (5.1%: ★★★★/★)
The brewer's favourite oak-aged ale, sharp enough for interest but mainstream enough for regular imbibing.
Duchesse de Bourgogne (6.2%: ★★★★/★)
Sharp and sweet, oak-aged brown ale that starts too sweet.
Verhaeghe Echt Kriekenbier (6.8%: ★★★★/★)
Whole cherries steeped in aged brown ale make this marvellous fruity beer so alluring.
Gapersbier (7%: ★★★★)
Filtered, pale copper-blond ale, also sold as Ezelsbier and Zerewever.

Seasonal beer:
[4]**Noël Christmas Weihnacht** (7.2%: ★★★★)
Yellow ochre, slightly spicy, sweetish ale, nudging greater bitterness as years pass. Also sold as Ninoviet.

Commissioned beers:
They construct unique blends of oak-aged ales, usually mixed with younger beer, for a number of long-standing customers. For the former brewery of Clarysse at Oudenaarde they make **Felix Oud Bruin** (5.1%: ★★★★), which tastes as though it has something dark and sweet in it. **Queue de Charrue Brune** (5.4%: ★★★/★) is a sweetish, slightly acetic beer for Vanuxeem of Ploegsteert. For an old friend in Lier they make **Caves** (5.5%: ★★★★), a lighter, slightly sour brown ale with fruity undertones. And for Bevernagie of Lichtervelde they make **Piro Bruin** (5.4%).

Walrave

Brouwerij Walrave
Lepelstraat 36, 9270 Laarne
T 09 369 01 34

A quiet little brewery at Laarne, east of Ghent, founded in 1862, producing a single Pilsener using malt from its own maltings. Its future has been in the balance for the last eight years. The beer is rarely found outside a five-kilometre radius of the brewery. No visits.

Annual output: <1,000 hl.

Regular beers:
Pick-up Pils (4.8%: ★★★)
A gentle, reasonably bitter, easy-drinking Pilsener with lingering grainy flavours.

Westmalle

Brouwerij Westmalle
Abdij der Trappisten van Westmalle
Antwerpsesteenweg 496, 2390 Malle
T 03 312 92 22 **E** info@trappistwestmalle.be
www.trappistwestmalle.be

On the way from Antwerp to Turnhout. Its proper name is the "Abbey of Our Beloved Lady of the Sacred Heart" but known universally as Westmalle. The largest of the Trappist breweries and the most commercial. Unlike Chimay, there has been significant expansion, most recently to their warm cellar capacity. The dubbel and blond tripel styles of ale are said to have originated here and the Westmalle brews were once the archetypes of these styles. The split of production is 40:60 in favour of the Tripel, despite the Dubbel being one of only two Trappist beers available on draught. If someone could give us a convincing explanation for the *koelschip* in its roof we would be grateful. The Tripel is now available in 75cl bottles, which appears to give it a more delicate but deeper character. A light, gold-coloured pale ale called **Extra** (5.5%: ★★★★) is brewed once or twice a year and is only usually available to the brothers but occasionally makes it into the real world. The abbey also produces a cheese. No brewery visits but there is an officially owned brewery tap on the main road (see Antwerp: Brewery cafés). Exports to fourteen countries, mainly in western Europe and Scandinavia but also including Japan and the US.

ANNUAL OUTPUT: 100,000–200,000 hl.

REGULAR BEERS:

Westmalle Trappist Dubbel (7% ★★★/★)
  A dark ale that is noticeably drier in the bottle. Simpler than it was a few years ago.

Westmalle Tripel (9.5%: ★★★★)
  Smooth, amber-blond coloured tripel, increasingly found in poor condition. No longer ages well.

Westvleteren

Brouwerij Westvleteren
Sint Sixtus Trappistenbdij
Donkerstraat 12, 8640 Westvleteren
T 057 40 10 57
E brouwerij@sintsixtus.be
www.sintsixtus.be

The smallest and most traditional of the Trappist breweries, just outside the village of Westvleteren in West Flanders, near the French border. Founded in 1831 and brewing since 1839. These are among the best beers in the world, though they are no angels when it comes to recipes. The drive-through beer purchasing point in the abbey walls (Mo–Th & Sa 10.00–12.00; 14.00–17.00) is frequently out of stock. The abbey has never produced beer on a heavily commercial scale and is keen to avoid the sort of short cuts that have led to falling quality at other abbeys. In the guide's view their only way forward is to impose huge price rises. Wine makers do not charge the same for *grand cru* and *vin de table*. Any export is fortuitous. Tours of the brewery are bestowed on one beer writer per year only. We are contemplating quietly, we promise.

ANNUAL OUTPUT: 2,000–10,000 hl.

REGULAR BEERS:

Westvleteren Blond (5.8%: ★★★★/★)
  Confident, fulsome pale ale, with a lot of flavour for one so small.

Westvleteren Extra 8° (8%: ★★★★★)
  Chewy, liquorice-laden, strong dark dubbel or tripel, which improves with cellar ageing and drinks beyond its strength.

Westvleteren Abt 12° (10.2%: ★★★★★)
  One of the world's great barley wines, a dark, intense, vinous brew that will improve for up to ten years in the cellar and keeps well for even longer.

The Guide gets a high proportion of its new leads and information from readers. If you discover something you think we need to know mail us on **BelgiumGBG@aol.com**

The abbey at Westvleteren allows only one visit per year from a beer writer. In 2004 Charles D Cook got the call. We still speak to him. He sent us this.

Set in the flat farmland and fields of West Flanders, the abbey of Sint Sixtus stands out like a beacon to beer lovers. Within the abbey, monks seek God through a life of work and prayer, while across the street, worshippers of a different kind enthuse about the heavenly Westvleteren brews at the café called At Peace, or *In de Vrede*.

Brewery production is a little under 5,000 hl per year, of which 15% is the green-capped Blond, 35% the blue-capped 8, and the rest yellow-capped 12. Just over a quarter of production ends up at the Vrede, with the rest sold at the drive-through by the abbey walls.

The dark 6° and the 4° Dubbel, formerly the brothers' table beer, were replaced by the Blond in 1999. The monks may have this beer with their evening meal if they wish. The Blond also satisfies the demands of those wanting a lighter beer at the café.

All the beers use the same Pale and Pilsner malts. Westvleteren is the only Trappist brewery making dark and blond beers this way. All colouring in the 8 and 12 comes from dark candy sugar – they use no dark malts.

Westmalle yeast has been used since the new brewhouse was installed in 1989, which makes it harder to ferment to higher alcohol strength than with the old Westvleteren yeast. Hence the drop in declared alcohol to 10.2% abv.

Open fermenters are used. This, coupled with long times for lagering (4 to 8 weeks) and warm conditioning (a further 4 to 6 weeks) are surely large components of the complexity of Westvleteren beers.

Years ago travellers would come here on a spiritual pilgrimage. For the most knowledgeable of beer lovers it remains a religious experience.

By the end of the decade it is likely that over 90% of the world's beer will be produced by four global companies and that none will have a qualified brewer on their board. Their purpose will be to sell cheaply made beers for the highest attainable price. It is unlikely that they will ever champion consumer choice or craft brewing and as such, by definition, they must act against the interests of discerning beer lovers.

While Belgium may still have an array of small craft breweries, the majority of beer made and drunk in the country comes from a single global company, InBev.

Of the rest, a majority is made by the British-based multinational Scottish Courage.

Many people do not care who owns the brewery that makes their beer. If so, they are short-sighted.

In every nation of the brewing world the takeover of smaller brewers by larger ones has, for decades, spelt the end of fine products along with the expertise that made them. Beers that carved their reputations through panache survive only as brand names for lesser imitations.

The consumer is rarely asked their attitude to one company seizing production rights from another. Whose beer is it anyway?

2003 saw the big global players acquiring the brewing industries of Eastern Europe and Asia, with the stirring tiger of the Chinese economy a particularly prized market.

2004 saw the largest merger ever, with Belgian-based Interbrew, already owners of much of the British, Canadian, Italian, Dutch, French, Italian and Spanish brewing industries, bedding AmBev, the corporation that dominated South America.

The track record of each company in preserving and promoting top quality beers was dire. Most crafted brands disappeared by deletion or emasculation.

It is as though the existence of a beer of outstanding quality threatens a global market based on the world's drinkers necking oceans of the liquid equivalent of white sliced bread.

Yet at the same time in long-established markets, sales of regular beers are falling. The theory goes that this is because everyone is so health conscious. So why are wine sales rising then?

The fact is that the global brand called "Beer", a 5% alcohol by volume blond fizzy liquid made from a fermented grain and sugar mountain, is starting to fail.

It is inevitable that one of these global corporations will fail too. It could be seriously entertaining if when it does it takes a whole nation state with it. Such thoughts might reasonably keep serious political minds in Brussels focussed on problems more substantial than whether or not to ban the use of wooden containers in old brewhouses.

The world's top four beer makers

Currently these four companies make roughly one-third of the world's beer. Production figures become increasingly difficult to track, as takeovers, mergers and asset disposals happen so frequently and real ownership is lost in the obscurity of local company laws. Output figures are for one year and are estimated.

1	InBev	18.7 billion litres	Belgium and global
2	Anheuser-Bush	17.0 billion litres	US and spreading
3	SAB-Miller	11.5 billion litres	South Africa, Europe & US
4	Heineken	10.8 billion litres	Netherlands and global

HEINEKEN

Heineken is the world's fourth largest brewery company. It has supplied the majority of beer drinking countries in the world for decades. Belgium is one of the few countries where Heineken lager is a rare find. The Belgians seem obliged to see it as inferior to Jupiler for some reason.

Where InBev and SAB-Miller have gone at globalisation like newly married celebrity couples, Big H can afford to take a cocktail by the pool of one of their many homes, while the butler applies some Brasso to their latest lifetime achievement award.

Nonetheless it must have irked the normally businesslike Dutch not to have even a toe-hold in the homeland of their country cousins down south. What a good job that the De Smedt family of Affligem needed the money.

Affligem

Affligem Brouwerij BDS
Ringlaan 18, 1745 Opwijk
T 052 35 99 11   **F** 052 35 83 57
www.affligembeer.be

Founded in 1790 at Opwijk, north-west of Brussels, in Flemish Brabant. Owned and run by the De Smedt family until 1984, when the current manager, the highly respected Theo Vervloet, bought 50% and took over day-to-day running of most of the operation. Heineken bought a 50% stake in July 1999 and took over marketing and distribution. In April 2001 they expanded their shareholding to 95% and announced plans to make the Affligem brands international. The brewery markets directly in Belgium and sells everything else through Heineken Export in the Netherlands. When they dropped the maize content of recipes below 15%, sales started to fall away. Affligem abbey owns the brand name and has assurances that the beer will be brewed in Belgium until 2031 at the earliest. 40% of production is draught Affligem Blond, taken by tanker to Lille for kegging by Heineken France. Most unbiased observers agree there has been an improvement in brewing quality since Heineken's involve-

ment. Evidence of this is found in the number of independent brewers willing to entrust some of their production to the brewery here. The test of longer term intentions will come when Theo Vervloet retires. All their own beers are now bottle-conditioned. Paters' Vat is the Blond with double hopping, brewed in September for November release. The Postel beers are brewed to the same methods as their Affligem counterparts but to slightly different grain and hop recipes. Production has doubled since Heineken took over and clever expansion within the brewery could double production again.

ANNUAL OUTPUT: 100,000–300,000 hl.
REGULAR BEERS:
Op-Ale (5%: ★★★/★)
Surprisingly tasty, bittersweet filtered light ale.
Affligem Blond (6.8%: ★★★/★)
Typical, reliable, clear sweetish Belgian blonde ale.
Affligem Dubbel (6.8%: ★★★)
Brown ale with absolutely nothing offensive or distinctive about it.
Affligem Tripel (8.5%: ★★★★)
Clean, slightly bitter, blond tripel that manages character without swagger.

SEASONAL BEERS:
[3]**Affligem Paters Vat** (7%: ★★★★/★)
Delicately balanced pale ale with definite hop presence, upgraded to bottle fermented in 2004.
[4]**Affligem Christmas** (8.5%: ★★★/★)
Dark, lightly aged winter beer.

COMMISSIONED BEERS:
For St. Feuillien brewery of Le Roeulx they brew the Grisette brands. The **Blonde** (4.5%: ★★★) is dry and light, while the **Ambrée** (5%: ★★★/★) has citrus notes. We have not tried the **Blanche** (4.5%). The less said about the **Fruits des Bois** (4.5%: ★★) the better. They also brewed the 75cl version of their spiced brown **St Feuillien Cuvée de Noël** (9%: ★★★★). For the abbey at Postel in rural Antwerp they make variants on the Affligem abbey beers. **Postel Dobbel** (7%: ★★★) is a bitter-sweet dubbel, while the **Tripel** (8.5%: ★★★/★) gives the impression that it would improve with bottle-conditioning, which it may now have. There is also a Christmas brew called **Kerstbier** (8.5%). They make the Christmas brew for the Delhaize supermarket chain, called Florival Winter (9%).

INBEV

InBev
Brouwerijplein 1
3000 Leuven
T 016 27 61 11   **F** 016 50 61 11
www.inbev.com

You have to admit that it is a great address. On the other hand, you can tell that the Belgians are no longer in charge at InBev because if they had been, someone's nephew would have pointed out that in Antwerp slang the company's name means "going down", and not in the sinking sense.

Formed in spring 2004 from the coupling of Belgian giant Interbrew with the equally proportioned AmBev of South America. The new board signalled its political intentions via the business pages of newspapers like the Financial Times with the news that corporate HQ might be moved away from Belgium unless the country lowered its business taxes.

Remarkably nearly half of this massive business is still owned directly by a small number of super-rich Belgian families from clans like De Spoelberch, De Mévius and Van Damme. Around one-third of their share is in direct holdings, with the rest through a holdings company. Just over half the company is owned by other shareholders, a half of these having been shareholders in AmBev.

They seem to have got round the brouhaha about tax by basing the holdings companies in Luxembourg. So corporate HQ wound up in Leuven, east of Brussels, the city that had been home to the Artois brewery for many years.

Only five of the fourteen original board members were Belgian and none had a qualification in brewing.

One helpful decision of the first few months was to stop using their predecessor's faintly potty claim to be "The World's Local Brewer". This saved the cost of countless challenges in international courts about trades descriptions and the correct use of English.

Indeed the new beast is not only responsible for brewing one pint in every gallon of the world's beer production, it also markets mouth-watering local delicacies such as Budweiser, Bud Light and Castlemaine XXXX, in parts of the world its rivals cannot yet reach.

It's a dog lick dog world out there in global capitalism!

In its dowry InBev was gifted control of at least two-thirds of the Belgian beer market and a particularly nasty attitude to retaining it. The Guide has lost count over the years of the ways in which power and influence were used to promote company interests and obliterate all opposition. No target was too small.

There were the café owners on the Belgian coast who were told that their lager pumps would be removed if they sold a certain rival's pale ale.

Then there were the independent beer warehouse owners who were barred from buying mainstream brands of beer at proper wholesale discount if they stocked too many other beers. To continue attracting trade customers they would have to sell them for less than they cost.

When the De Wolf Cosijns specialist maltings in Aalst became surplus to requirements in 2002, it was not put up for sale but simply closed. The fact that many small Belgian brewers depended on it for supplies of specialist malt was just a bonus. So special malts became more difficult to find and special beers are more difficult to make. Where's the problem?

When people started to point out that the commercial lambic beers associated with names like Belle Vue seemed to have lost all connection with their roots in lambic brewing, helpful laws were passed to explain that they were actually just fine. The fact that the Prime Minister of the time later became a non-executive director of the company was entirely unconnected.

And when the EU finally got round to passing laws to outlaw the sort of stranglehold that companies like Interbrew had on the rights of cafés to sell other brewers beers, well they just transferred the stranglehold onto the suppliers instead.

Thank goodness all that will stop, now that we have some decent clean-living

Americans in charge at last. Let us put history where it belongs, in the dustbin, and see what the company says about its future.

"At InBev, our brands are the foundation of the company, the cornerstone of our relationships with consumers, and the key to our long-term success. Our brand portfolio, our enduring bonds with consumers, and our partnerships with customers are our most important assets. We will invest in our brands to create long-term, sustainable, competitive advantage, by meeting the beverage needs of consumers around the world, and by developing leading brand positions in every market in which we operate."

Was it slaves who had bonds?
So, what are these brands of which they speak?
The main ones are three remarkably similar looking blond lagers called Stella Artois, Brahma and Beck's – that is the one that used to be brewed to the Reinheitsgebot beer purity law in Germany. Is it still, we wonder?
Then there are the global speciality brands – four Leffes and a Hoegaarden.
According to InBev Hoegaarden is:

"...totally different – by nature. It is different from virtually any other beer or beverage experience in the world – different in the kind of beverage that it is, and in the naturally refreshing taste experience."

... except of course it is just a wheat beer and not that dissimilar from the two hundred or so other unfiltered wheat beers in the world about. Even Americans brew wheat beers for goodness sake.
The company's declared aim is to be one of the top two brewers in every country on Earth. They have an endearing habit of posting on their website the only beers they are aware of in their empire, which is not a lot.
This horrid vision of the future of beer making has come about through the sort of violent fermentation often found in the company's vessels.
Interbrew was formed in 1988 by a merger between Artois and Piedboeuf. The producers of the conveniently French-sounding Stella Artois from Flanders joined marriage with those that made the conveniently Dutch-

sounding Jupiler from Wallonia. Belgium's favourite Pils brands, like Wiels, Safir, Krüger and Lamot, followed the procession out of the church to the graveyard.
Many more breweries were acquired but few survived and those that did were only in cartoon format.
Interbrew's global ambitions first showed themselves clearly in 1995, when it acquired the Canadian giant Labatt. Thereafter it began a long march through the brewing heritages of the UK (Bass and Whitbread), Germany (Becks and a dozen others), the Netherlands (Oranjeboom), Italy (Peroni and others) and many others.
Interbrew used to pride itself, disingenuously, on its devotion to "speciality beers". InBev does not need such coy gestures as it has no illusion of loyalty to the old country. But there may be a problem here.
Sales of beer in Belgium are falling. The steepest falls are in Pilsener and wheat beers. Sales of special beers and other interesting alcoholic drinks are tending to rise. So are ordinary drinkers starting to object to being fed pap? If they are, then the current InBev portfolio of Belgian beers looks a little thin.
Industry pundits say that consumer resistance is useless but then so are most of the beers and you can't have it both ways. Watching a global corporation having to re-create brews of substance in order to keep up with the "beverage needs" of consumers seems a little far-fetched. But you have to admit it would be a good laugh.

Belle Vue

Brasserie Belle Vue
Bergensesteenweg 144
1600 Sint-Pieters-Leeuw
T 02 371 43 12   **F** 02 371 43 22

The largest producer of lambic-based beers in the known universe. Its old Brussels brewery and lambic store is now a museum, beer having last been brewed there in 1998. The Guide is not convinced that the company's only authentic lambic beer, a gueuze called Belle Vue Sélection Lambic has been produced since, so we no longer list it. Most of the production is bland and inoffensive but has little if anything in common with 100% lambic beers. Those cafés that were still picking up draught lambic from the old brewery when we visited in 1998 now have other suppliers. The Guide has a rough idea how the beers here are made but without signed statements, witnessed accounts or photographs we will not say. We have however sampled the draught kriekenlambic and can reveal that it is not red and does not taste of cherries. Rather it is faintly pinky brown, with a dab of cherry. We think they do the rest with make-up. There is also a low alcohol cherry beer called Kriek LA (1.2%). We notice that Belle Vue brands have disappeared from the published future world plan for InBev.

ANNUAL OUTPUT: 300,000 hl.

REGULAR BEERS:
Belle-Vue Kriek Extra (4.3%)
New one on us.
Jack-Op (5%: ★★★)
Palatable mess of partially soured pale ale.
Belle Vue Framboise (5.2%: ★★)
Perfumed, sweet, raspberry drink,
Belle Vue Gueuze (5.2%: ★★)
Sweet-tasting, rather wheaty commercial gueuze.
Belle Vue Kriek (5.2%: ★★)
Sweet, dark, undemanding, cherry drink.

Hoegaarden

Early in 2006 InBev announced that they were to close this iconic brewery, with the loss of a bucketful of jobs and an ocean of good will.

The old De Kluis brewery in Hoegaarden, in Flemish Brabant, was famously revived in 1966 by Pierre Celis, who had grown up next door to the town's Tomsin brewery and been shown how to brew as a child. He determined to re-create the type of wheat beer that had virtually disappeared from modern Belgian brewing. He succeeded so well that after an unfortunate brewery fire, Interbrew stepped in with some generous technical assistance and eventually went on to buy the spanking new plant they had virtually re-built. The current success of light, cloudy, lightly spiced wheat beers throughout the western world finds its origins here. Initially the brouhaha focussed on the cavalier way in which a

global corporation could stamp on a town's pride and disregard its host nation. When that died down however a more prosaic problem remained. The cloth-heads who sanctioned this PR masterpiece appear to have forgotten that Hoegaarden was the only plant in Belgium where InBev could produce beers for reconditioning in the bottle.

Julius has definitely gone. Leffe Triple has probably been replaced with brewery-conditioned Leffe 90. The Guide cannot see how Hougaerdse DAS, Hoegaarden Grand Cru, Hoegaarden Speciale or Forbidden Fruit / Verboden Vrucht / Fruit Defendu can survive either.

True to the company name. sales of Hoegaarden in Belgium have been going down. We have withdrawn star ratings on those whose futures are unclear.

ANNUAL OUTPUT: 1,000,000 hl.

REGULAR BEERS:
Hoegaarden (5%: ★★★)
Despite our cynicism, still an adequate wheat beer and an international ambassador of the unusual.
Hougaerdse DAS (5%: ★★★)
A clean and pleasant beer pitched somewhere between a blond and a filtered wheat beer.
Leffe Triple (8.4%: ★★★)
Bottle-conditioned tripel that can still be found in reasonable working order.
Hoegaarden Grand Cru (8.7%: ★★/★)
Once a big bold amber-blond bruiser of a beer, but gone to seed.
Julius (8.8%: ★★)
The best newcomer of '85 has turned into a perfumed old slapper.
Verboden Vrucht/Fruit Defendu (8.8%: ★★★)
Strong brown ale from another championship stable, gone down with depression.

SEASONAL BEER:
3&4**Hoegaarden Speciale** (5.6%: ★★★)
Beefier winter wheat beer with an adjusted blend of spices.

Interbrew (Jupille-sur-Meuse)

SA Interbrew Belgium NV
Rue des A. Houblonnières 2
4020 Jupille-sur-Meuse
T 04 345 84 66   **F** 04 345 85 12

The last of the Piedboeuf beer factories, churning out huge quantities of the lager to which it gave its name and we suspect others too. The brewery survives through national politics. Closure might destabilise nationhood. If only Jupiler were a beer about which something good could be said, beyond "it is consistent". They make two other table beers, Piedboeuf Blond (1.5% abv) and Piedboeuf Brune (1.5% abv) plus the non-alcoholic Jupiler NA (0.5%).

ANNUAL OUTPUT: 2,200,000 hl.

REGULAR BEERS:

Piedboeuf Triple (3.8%: ★★)
Technically tip-top table beer from which all character has been removed.

Hoegaarden (5%: ★★/★)
A grey and watery beer that lacks flair, passion or authority. A fallen angel.

Jupiler (5.2%: ★★)
The lager without which there would be no café signs in half of Belgium.

Interbrew (Leuven)

SA Interbrew Belgium NV
Vaartkom 31, 3000 Leuven
T 016 24 71 11   **E** info.belgium@interbrew.com
www.inbev.com

Founded in 1349, though nobody seriously believes that. This massive beer factory is responsible for producing huge quantities of run-of-the-mill ales and lagers. Other lager brands include the sadly drab **Krüger Export** (4.8%: ★★), the nostalgic **Safir** (5.2%: ★★) and the once posh luxe **Pils Loburg** (5.7%: ★★★). There are four low volume pale ale brands, the ultra-bland **Vieux Temps** (5%: ★★), the equally dull **Horse-Ale** (5%: ★★), the occasionally seen **Ginder Ale** (5.1%: ★★) and the Belgian version of **Bass Pale Ale** (5.2%: ★★). They also make two darker, stronger Scotch ales called **Scotch CTS** (7.2%: ★★) and **Campbell's Scotch Ale** (7.3%: ★★/★). We remain to be convinced that any of these has a future, except possibly the Bass. None appears to have been revitalised since the takeover and the company philosophy does not encourage diversity. The Guide would be delighted to be proved wrong. They also make **Club de Stella Artois** (5.9%), [4]**Stella Artois de Noël** and [4]**Leffe de Noël**

(6.5%) exclusively for the French market and **Stella Artois Light** (3.4%) and **Stella Artois NA** (0.5%).

ANNUAL OUTPUT: 4,800,000 hl.

REGULAR BEERS:

Stella Artois (5.2%: ★★/★)
The ordinary lager, invented long after the adverts imply.

Artois Bock (6.2%: ★★)
Leffe Amber? Like a suped up version of Watneys Red made especially for the UK market.

Leffe Brune (6.5%: ★★★)
Tasty but safe, typically Belgian brown ale.

Leffe Blonde (6.6%: ★★★)
Sweetish possibly lightly spiced blond ale of increasing reliability.

Leffe Radieuse (8.2%: ★★★)
Light chestnut ale with too little character for its strength.

Leffe 9° (9%: ★★★)
Strong, filtered, sweet, ruddy-brown ale – as good as triple can be with few hops and no yeast.

SEASONAL BEER:

Leffe de Noël (6.5%: ★★★/★)
It breaks our heart to admit it but this dark copper ale with distinctive spicing built round nutmeg was really rather pleasant in 2005–06.

Whitbread beers in Belgium

In 1904 the Whitbread brewery created an import business in Brussels. The beer came from London via the river Schelde in double hogsheads – 112-gallon barrels. It was bottled a few days later. Whitbread Stout and Pale Ale were then matured for about a month before leaving the warehouse. Initially most sales were in Hainaut but the beers proved popular and warehouses opened to serve Antwerp (1906), Liège (1910) and Ghent (1930).

In 1954 Whitbread swapped to tanker delivery, the lorries bringing the beer over on the Dover – Dunkerque ferry. Eventually production was shifted in 1979 to the Martinas brewery in Merchtem, near Brussels and moved in 1990 to Leuven, where they were still brewed until the InBev takeover.

In the Nineties these were still surprisingly interesting beers. They are currently missing in action.

SCOTTISH COURAGE
ALKEN-MAES (SCAM)

The second largest beer producer in Belgium is now Scottish-owned. But whereas the global player appears to be making plans to homogenise quality at the acceptable end of dull, this multinational is playing games. It remains to be seen whether the revival of their authentic gueuze was a more or less wacky idea than creating a new breed of table beer.

Alken brewery made its reputation from Cristal Alken, the first Pilsener in significant production in Belgium, in 1928. They were also the first brewers to introduce small, 25cl bottles for their beers, in 1936. Maes was a family-owned brewery that, until 1946, produced mainly ales. Maes Pils did not arrive until post-war austerity. Maes added the Grimbergen abbey beers, Dubbel and Tripel, in 1962.

By 1988 they had become Alken-Maes and been bought by the French glass maker BSN, who became part of the Danone group – remember that cacky yoghurt? Meanwhile, the Mort Subite lambic brewery signed an exclusive marketing deal with the group and another lambic maker, Eylenbosch was taken over.

The Maes family remained big players until about 1993 but by 1996 Danone was in charge of the lot.

In 2000, just as Interbrew was buying the English brewing industry, the British hotels and brewing group Scottish & Newcastle agreed the sort of merger with Danone that lay people might call a take-over, though the deal was so complicated that it was not complete until the end of 2002.

By this stage, if you had being working in the yard at Alken brewery for fourteen years you would have worked for six different companies. Your latest employer was called Scottish Courage (Alken-Maes) or SCAM for short.

Since the latest takeover, SCAM has closed the Maes family's old plant at Waarloos and consolidated the Alken plant. They bought and closed the Louwaege brewery in Kortemark, West Flanders because it was a good price and they could do with the pubs.

Hapkin was also an inherently better beer than the dreary Judas.

They have yet to sort out the brands at Union, though they have focussed them down onto Grimbergen and Ciney plus a few privileged friends. Things were so dire that the bottle-conditioned beers appear to have to go to Roman for bottling.

The seriously interesting developments are at Mort Subite, which remains an up-scale version of quite a traditional lambic brewery, despite the all-syrup-and-colouring image of the Mort Subite brands in the years before the Scottish invasion. In sharp contrast to prime rivals Belle Vue, the commercial brands have been improved and production of the virtually defunct oude gueuze has been increased.

The group's wheat beer, rebranded simply Brugs may be made at the group's plant in Champigneulles in France. It remains to be seen which side of the national border ale production will eventually be located. Presumably if they want the Union brewery to create top ales again they will have to put the brewers through debriefing.

We may have been a bit mean with our ratings as we are behind with the progress in cleaning up the brands.

Alken-Maes

Alken-Maes
Stationstraat 2, 3570 Alken
T 011 59 03 00　　**E** info@alken-maes.com
www.alkenmaes.be

The Alken brewery at Alken, near Hasselt in Limburg, was founded in 1880. Cristal Alken, created in 1928, was the first blond Pilsener-style lager to be brewed in Belgium on a commercial scale. Three-quarters of a century later the plant still concentrates on making the group's Belgian lagers under a variety of names. We think that ordinary Kronenbourg, Anglo Pils and Golding Campina have either gone off the market or are label beers. **Maes Nature** (1.5%) is a new weak, spicy beer made on the table beer principle. Group visits for 20–40 people on some weekday afternoons.

ANNUAL OUTPUT: 1,700,000 hl.

Brasserie Mort Subite and its brewery tap

Foster's (4.3%: ★)
Dull Australian lager brewed the Belgian way.
Brugs (4.8%: ★★★)
Big production wheat beer, not tasted since the name change
Cristal Alken (4.8%: ★★★)
Softish but bitter light Pils.
Maes Pils (4.9%: ★★/★)
Dryish, lightly bitter Pils.
Kronenbourg 1664 (5%: ★★/★)
Pitched in against Stella in the puffed up tedium market, though it claims to be 100% malt.

Mort Subite

Brouwerij Mort Subite
Lierput 1, 1730 Kobbegem
T 02 454 11 11   **F** 02 452 43 10

Now named after its brand name, Mort Subite, the most northerly of the Payottenland lambic makers and a remarkably traditional brewery. The new owners appear to be reviewing these beers, with a few rewards for serious beer lovers, among whom the brand had previously been the subject of some derision. Until recently there was an excellent but anonymous oude gueuze, served by the truckload at the café Mort Subite in Brussels (see Belgian cafés: Brussels) but rarely found elsewhere. This shyness is changing, though it is still not advertised on the company website. The real fruit content of the Kriek has been improved and we hear a rumour that an authentic oude kriek is being considered. The more commercial fruit beers are also under revision so we have held back ratings, though experience tells us that we are only looking at the difference between two and three stars. The oude gueuze is bottled here. Everything else goes to Alken.

ANNUAL OUTPUT: 50,000 hl.

REGULAR BEERS:

Louwaege Kriek (4.5%: ★★★)
Tangy drink tasting strongly of cherry but not a lot of beer.

Mort Subite Cassis (4.5%)
Dryish blackcurrant drink with lambic in it.

Mort Subite Framboise (4.5%)
Perfumed commercial framboise.

Mort Subite Gueuze (4.5%)
Fruity gueuze that is possibly drier than it was.

Mort Subite Kriek (4.5%)
Colourful commercial kriek.

Mort Subite Pêche (4.5%)
The same thing with peach syrup.

Mort Subite Fond Gueuze (6%: ★★★★/★)
The rare but authentic and increasingly available oude gueuze.

Union

Brasserie de l'Union
Rue Derbêque 7, 6040 Jumet
T 071 34 02 22 **F** 071 34 02 34

Founded in 1864 and once a prize-winning ale brewery. Now the ale production plant for the Belgian bit of the group. When SCAM took over, the beers here ranged in quality from dire via distorted to acceptable. The product range was a mess. What seems to be happening is a rationalisation of the range, focussing on big brands like Grimbergen and Ciney (some of the brews that gave abbey beers a bad name) a few old timers like Judas and Zulte and the new boy, Hapkin. The bastards killed off Watneys Red, the Scotch may go too. The same quality improvement nudges are discernable as at Mort Subite

(above) and the Guide awaits developments with interest. The star ratings listed largely reflect the old days.

ANNUAL OUTPUT: 100,000–300,000 hl.

REGULAR BEERS:

Zulte (4.7%: ★★)
The ultimate test for SCAM's authenticity drive will be whether oak-aged ale is ever blended into this brown ale.

Grimbergen Dubbel (6.5%: ★★★)
Burnt brown ale of little brain.

Grimbergen Blond 6.7%: ★★)
Pepped up recently and possibly improved.

Ciney Blonde (7%: ★★)
Absurdly sweet, dead blonde ale.

Ciney Brune (7%: ★★)
Burnt sweet dead brown ale.

Grimbergen Cuvée de l'Ermitage (7.5%: ★★)
Ruddy-brown abbey beer that has acquired the scorched sugar thumbprint of dull Union brews.

Hapkin (8.5%: ★★★/★)
A bit more Duvel-like than when it used to be brewed at Louwaege.

Judas (8.5%: ★★/★)
Always an unimpressive golden ale but now being bottle-conditioned.

Ciney Spéciale (9%: ★★★/★)
Likeable, bottle-conditioned deep brown ale with Madeira notes.

Grimbergen Tripel (9%: ★★★)
Variable golden tripel that occasionally impresses.

Grimbergen Optimo Bruno (10%: ★★★)
Surprisingly plain for such a big brown barley wine.

The most expensive part of making beer commercially is buying, running and maintaining the kit and buildings that are essential to your enterprise. One way to get round this is to use someone else's. This not only cuts your overheads, it helps share theirs too.

This new economic reality has opened the field for keen young brewers and marketing whizzes to develop unique portfolios of great new beers. Some of the best will sit down with the host brewer and hammer out an original concept, from malt recipe through to final conditioning.

The Proef brewery in Lochristi was created for just this purpose. Other commercial brewers such as Deca and Van Steenberge allow brewers to come in and take over for a day. Of course it also offers great opportunities for the ethically challenged to buy up beer in bulk, change its label and try to flog it as an imaginary new beer at a hiked up price.

Under what passes for Belgian consumer law the practice of re-labelling remains legal, as does claiming your company is a brewery when actually it only exists in cyberspace. These dishonest practices hoodwink the beer drinker. It is only an innocent deceit if they know nothing about beer. And even then is that not called exploitation?

Other dodgy practices include the creation of "new" beers by blending, diluting or adding flavourings to existing beers and then claiming they are original.

Quite how far the Guide should go in trying to list these products is an interesting conundrum, both ethically and practically.

The ethical dilemma is balancing the amount of positive publicity some beer designers deserve for their originality against the danger of promoting products that took little effort to create. The practical dilemma is that many brewery owners and beer commissioners are remarkably shy about their practices.

Our compromise is to attempt to list the better or more famous attempts that you are likely to encounter on your travels.

Braven Apostel

Brouwerij Braven Apostel
Muizelstraat 16, 9041 Oostakker
T 09 251 05 99

A single beer brewed at Proef by a private owner but licensed for sale in the trade and sometimes even found in the export trade.

REGULAR BEER:

Braven Apostel (8%: ★★★/★)
  A lusciously spiced blond malt 'n' wheat tripel.

Celis

Celis Europe NV

The artist is making a joke. But having reached his eightieth birthday with an autobiography on the way, why should he not? Pierre Celis may or may not have made his own luck. But he has had it in abundance. Since he personally recreated the wheat beer style in the late Sixties, he has spawned companies the size of minnows and sold them on as trainee whales. Oh that we could all have such a life. Respect bro. And deep envy too. Now in his dotage we have Celis Europe NV, for which the Guide can find no address.

REGULAR BEERS:

Celis White and **Pale Bock**, plus some wheat beers with fruit juice are made by Van Steenberge. **Grottenbier** is made by St. Bernardus, with a blond version promised for summer 2005.

Corman-Collins

SA Corman-Collins
1a Xhéneumont, 4651 Battice   **T** 087 674296

This long-established wholesaler north of Liège is one of the more interesting commissioners of original beers. Several in the past have gone on to be the mainstay of a new brewery. Numerous others remain interesting and unusual. There is a shop and sampling room at the front of the warehouse.

REGULAR BEERS:

Cervoise de l'Avouerie d'Anthisnes and **Cuvée des Hauts Voués de l'Avouerie d'Anthisnes** are commissioned for the museum of that name in Anthisnes (see Beer

Tourism). As with **La Geule Noire** and **St. Christophe** these are commissioned from Silly. **Merveilleuse de Chèvremont** is from Val-Dieu.

Corsendonk

NV Brouwerij Corsendonk
Slachthuisstraat 27, 2360 Oud Turnhout
T 014 45 33 11   **E** corsendonk@corsendonk.com

The old Corsendonk Priory is now a hotel and conference centre. We have no idea whether it has any business connection with this large and enterprising beer wholesaler in northern Antwerp, which is the most successful purveyor of abbey style commissioned beers. The beer range in recent years has included some experiments with a Blond, which we believe came to nothing. The draught beers have however been renamed Premium Blond and Bruin Dark. Corsendonk invests heavily in some cafés and owns some. It is big enough to have been given a national contract for distributing Pilsener Urquell and the ghastly Bud. They are a bit naughty about suggesting that they brew.

REGULAR BEERS:
Corsendonk Pater/Bruin Dark is brewed by Van Steenberge. **Agnus/Premium Blond** and the spiced **Christmas** (8.5%) are from du Bocq.

John Martin's

John Martin SA
Rue du Cerf 191, 1332 Genval
T 02 655 6213   **F** 02 655 6297
www.johnmartin.be

The original John Martin was an Englishman, who emigrated from Newmarket (Suffolk) to Antwerp in 1909 to run a citrus fruit importing business. His import-export ambitions grew and over the years he became a beer importer. The beers came in such volume that Belgian drinkers began to develop opinions about their value that were at odds with the preferences back home. So when Export Guinness in the UK dropped from 8.8% abv to around half of that, the Belgain contract continued at its old strength. Similarly, John Martin's Special continued as a thriving beer long after its English version, Courage Bulldog had

become a neglected niche product. Martin's remains a family-run company, with three Anglo-Belgian grandsons sharing the helm, though their interests have spread to include a hotel group. There is a rumour that the group will split with the beer empire changing its name slightly. Currently they hold a controlling share in Timmermans' lambic brewery and own the Gordon brands of "Scotch" ales among others. The irony is that the original maker of these brands now owns Belgium's Alken-Maes. However, although they own the rights to the Scotch ale named after the defunct London brewer Watneys they could only sell their old beers if they bought them from Martins. We do not list Cubana '59 and other proto-beers as we believe they are spiked with spirits.

REGULAR BEERS:
John Martins Pale Ale (6%: ★★★/★) is a re-working of the old Courage Bulldog but nowadays tastes more like an American cream ale. **Blond Ale** (6%: ★★★) is found in France. The Gordon brand has two lives. **Highland Scotch Ale** (8.6%: ★★★/★) is a dark, sweet ale with a lovely glass, with **X-mas** (8.6%: ★★★/★) its older-tasting seasonal version. Then there is a range of three or four "Gordon Finest", which are strong ales sold in 50cl tins. In Britain this type of beer is known as a "student and tramp brand". **Finest Silver** (7.7%) is the blond version. **Finest Red** (8%: ★★) was originally made for the Italian market. **Finest Gold** (10%: ★★) used to be the ghastly Kestrel Superstrength though it is supposed to have improved a bit. A new beer called **Finest Platinum** (12%) has yet to be encountered though a friend found a supply at a car boot sale. We think the "Finest" brands are brewed in Holland but the others at Palm.

De Cock

De Cock Meesterbrouwers BVBA
Potterstraat 10, 9170 Sint Pauwels
T 03 777 98 27   **F** 03 778 23 60
E info@brouwerijdecock.com
www.brouwerijdecock.com

Another company set up specifically to commission beers, initially from Proef but now we believe from Van Steenberge. Doing so since 1996. Sinpals is the local dialect for Sint-Pauwels

REGULAR BEERS:
Sinpalsken Blond (8.5%) and **Sinpalsken Donker** (8.5%) appear year-round and Sinpalsken Winterbier only in winter.

Musketiers

Brouwerij de Musketiers
Tramstraat 8, 9910 Ursel   **T** 09 226 42 76
E info@brouwerijdemusketiers.com
www.brouwerijdemusketiers.com

Small company set up in 2000 by three former brewing engineers who went on to better things but still like to brew as a hobby. Their beers are brewed at Proef and sometimes get into the export trade.

REGULAR BEERS:
Troubadour Blond (6.5%: ★★★/★) is a spiced, fruity, hazy blond ale. The stronger brown ale **Troubadour Obscura** (8.5%) has not been encountered yet.

Slaapmutske

Brouwerij Slaapmutske
Oefenpleinstraat 15, 9090 Melle
T&F 09 231 93 86
E brouwerijslaapmutske@tiscali.be
http://home.tiscali.be/slaapmutske

Small company set up in 2000 with a view to designing and commissioning interesting beers from Proef brewery. Exports to the Netherlands and South Africa.

REGULAR BEERS:
Slaapmutske Bruin (6%), **Slaapmutske Blond** (6.4%) and **Slaapmutske Tripel** (8.1%) are talked about a lot by Flemish beer geeks but we have yet to see them on sale.

Vanuxeem

Brasserie Vanuxeem
150 Rue d'Armentières, 7782 Ploegsteert
T 056 58 89 23   **F** 056 58 75 59

Another wholesaler that masquerades as a brewery. Based around a rather good warehouse (see Beer Shops & Warehouses) in the French-speaking enclave of Hainaut surrounded by West Flanders. Unusually, its three beers are commissioned from three different breweries. The brand name is a rough translation of Ploegsteert into French. Tommy Atkins called it Plug Street.

REGULAR BEERS:
Queue de Charrue Brune (see Verhaege); **Queue de Charrue Amber** (see du Bocq); and **Queue de Charrue Blond** (see Van Steenberge).

The Belgian consumer group Zythos has recently dipped a toe into the water by granting a kind of approval to particular brewery-less beer makers. Yet even they have found this area to be fraught with difficulty. What can you do when former brewers such as Crombé, Facon, Clarysse and Sterkens are reluctant to accept that they no are no longer brewers in the true sense but keep old brands going via surviving breweries, with varying degrees of authenticity to the original?

The Guide's editorial policy is that it is under no obligation whatever to publicise brews made by people who just sit there and press the occasional knob on a console. Unless by so doing they make something particularly nice.

Barrel sizes

Various sizes of beer barrel (Du: *vat*; Fr: *tonneau*) have developed traditional names in Britian over the centuries, such as a pin (4.5 gallons), a firkin (9), kilderkin (18), barrel (36) and hogshead (54).

French- and Dutch-speaking barrels have names too.

The official Dutch definition of a *"barrel"* is 220 litres. A *vat*, as in the expression *"van 't vat"* or *"from the barrel"* has no legal definition but used to be taken to mean 100 litres.

A French *tonne* should contain 250 litres (about 56 gallons), unlike the British "tun", which traditionally held 252 or 256 gallons.

A *pipe* should hold 650 litres (about 144 gallons). A British cask of the same name that largely died out in the 19th century held between 90 and 120 gallons.

A *foudre* contains 3,000 litres (660 gallons).

In Belgium, rumours of a new brewery can come decades before it opens. Beers are often commissioned by the potential owner from other breweries to test the market. Indeed some potential brewers give up at this stage, calculating that it would be daft to risk a lucrative distribution business in order to buy some fancy kit that they may not be that good at using.

Brasserie La Barbiot (27 Rue du Coron, 7070 Ville-sur-Haine – T&F 065 87 37 23) opened in 2005 between Mons and La Louvière in northern Hainaut. Its early efforts have included **La Barbiot Blonde** (7%: ★★★/★), a workmanlike unspiced blonde, **La Barbiot Ambrée** (9.5%: ★★★), an overly strong amber with a touch of the home-brews, and a wheat beer. There are plans for a tasting room on site.

Huisbrouwerij Sint Canarus (Polderweg 2, 9800 Gottem-Deinze – T 051 63 69 31; E sintcanarus@hotmail.com; www.canarus. be) first opened in 2004 then closed while brewer Piet Meirhaeghe transferred his kit to a larger brewhouse. This is a boutique brewery, well set to produce commissioned beers, with good quality right from the word go. One to watch, especially on Sundays. **Sint Canarus Tripel** (7.5%: ★★★★) is a clever, characterful strong blond and **Potteloereke** (8%: ★★★★) is an impressively big, soft brown ale that is a little too sweet still.

Brasserie Artisanale La Frasnoise (Rue Basse 5, 7911 Frasnes-Lez-Buissenal – T 0495 42 60 38) is a squeaky clean new microbrewery set up by Bruno Delroisse between Ath and Tournai in northern Hainaut around autumn 2005. His first beer, **Cuvée Frasnoise** (6.3%), is spiced with wild sunflower (Fr: *aunée*), known correctly in English as elecampane or, more entertainingly, scabwort. At least two other beers are planned.

Brasserie des Monts (Haillemont 15, 7890 Wodecq – T&F 068 84 39 04 ; E thierry@brasseriedesmonts.be; www.brasseriedesmonts.be) is a microbrewey opened by Thierry Vanbeselaere between Ellezelles and Lessines in northern Hainaut in the late summer of 2005. His first beer was a strong ambrée called **Cuvée des Monts** (8%), followed at the end of the year by a blond called **Blancs Mongnîs** (6.5%). The brewery is usually open for sales and nosing around on Saturday (10.00–14.00).

The last three years has seen a run of beer commissioning companies presenting themselves on websites as if they own and run a brewery. A few ended up in gaol while others have changed their Philosophy. The more honourable ones are doing this in the run-up to launching their own place, and already have their proposed beers produced by another brewery. One such is **Mont-Saint-Guibert** in the town of the same name in Walloon Brabant that was once home to the makers of Leffe beers. We hope they will grow into a brewery shortly. The **Struise Brouwers** at Lo in West Flanders are in a similarly unclear position, their beers coming currently from Caulier.

Our favourite current rumour is that an old fortress and vacated monastic community near Liège, called **La Chartreuse**, is being sold by a religious order called the Nuns of Poverty (Du: *Zusterkens der Armen*) with a plan to create a new community on the land, complete with a farm and house brewery. Only in Belgium, as we are fond of saying.

Specialist beer bars

In 1880 Belgium had around 140,000 cafés. By 1994 there were fewer than 30,000 and by the year 2000 the number had fallen again to less than 25,000. This nearly matched the number of restaurants in the country.

In 2003 the EU declared that the 10,000 cafés that had previously been tied to selling the beers of Interbrew should be allowed to buy most beers from the brewery of their choice. Whether this reverses the fortunes of the Belgian café has yet to be seen.

Belgium's network of licensed premises is usually referred to as the HORECA, which stands for HOtels, REstaurants and CAfés.

The licensing system goes on to divide cafés into those that serve mainly drinks and more elaborate businesses that sell food too. These tend to be called a *taverne* in the north and, confusingly, a *brasserie* in Brussels and the south. The class of establishment determines the level of tax paid and the qualifications required to run the business.

The distribution of cafés varies greatly from province to province. West Flanders has one for every 300 inhabitants, whereas Liège has only one per 540, though in largest part this reflects the ratio of different types of licence. Areas with fewer cafés have more restaurants and vice versa.

As a customer, the distinction between outlets is largely academic when the beer list stretches into the hundreds. Eating is only a restaurant requirement.

Many cafés remain tied to smaller breweries. Paradoxically their owners often have to pay up to twenty per cent more for their beer than cafés that are free of tie. So the customer has to pay more for the privilege of having a smaller choice of beers.

The EU Commission's 2003 ruling on the Interbrew tie has yet to bed down. On the surface, this is the first big favour from the

HOW WE CHOOSE OUR CAFÉS

The Guide learns about cafés from over fifty different regular sources. Watching the scene for twenty-five years has its advantages.

When we get a good lead, an inspector calls, without mentioning the Guide. Where there are inconsistencies in what we find, the editor will pop in, always anonymously. Anonymity means that we see a place as any customer will see it. Café owners will not put on a special show for you but they might for us if we say who we are.

What our inspectors like is a clear commitment to Belgian beer culture.

In most of the country we want to see a list of at least 60 different beers. Occasionally we will accept fewer if there are signs of specialisation in one or two types of beer or a particularly intelligent list. We also reserve the right to include a few extra entries in places of special interest to tourists, ex-pats or business travellers, and in a few parts of the country where the beer culture needs some encouragement.

The Guide is not impressed by a long list of well-known beers from larger producers. Half a dozen brews from a couple of local microbreweries are far more likely to make an impact on inspectors than fifty better known names.

We do not care about the type of bar it is. All sorts of premises from village smoking rooms to Michelin star restaurants have graced these pages and will continue to do so. We do expect it to try to be good at whatever it does, be that a one-room local or a multi-storey museum of Art Deco. We do expect owners to show skill in choosing and presenting their beers.

One of our best sources of information is recommendation by readers. Nearly half the cafés in this book originally came to our attention through amateur sleuths who took time to tell us what they found.

So if you come across an undiscovered gem with a good beer list that you thinks fits the Guide's criteria, let us know on **BelgiumGBG@aol.com** or else through CAMRA Books. New finds that are good enough to get a full entry will earn you a free copy of the next edition.
TIM WEBB, Editor

EU to Belgium's beer lovers. However, as yet the effect on the Belgian's market squares and village high streets has been muted.

Sadly, as everywhere, most bar owners and staff have little real knowledge about the beers they sell or the breweries that make them. In a world of tied houses such knowledge is unnecessary. There is no need for battery hens to understand pellet production.

Equally predictably lack of knowledge does not stop said owner and staff making up the answers to your polite enquiries anyway. Approach all conflicting facts with care. The Guide is rarely wrong.

Café listings

The Guide lists recommended cafés province by province, in alphabetical order.

We have anglicised the provinces' names, which makes the running order Antwerp, Brussels, East Flanders, Flemish Brabant, Hainaut, Liège, Limburg, Luxembourg, Namur, Wallonian Brabant and West Flanders.

Within each province, town and village names are listed in alphabetical order. We have only anglicised five city names, which are Antwerp (for Antwerpen), Bruges (for Brugge), Brussels (for Brussel/Bruxelles), Ghent (for Gent) and Ostend (for Oostende). In all other cases we have used the place name as in appears in its local language.

Café names exclude the definite article, most designations such as "Café", "Taverne", "Brasserie", "Eethuis", "Hotel", "Pub", "Bistro", and a majority of those "at the house of" tags such as "Aux", "In de" and "Chez". Hence the In de Vrede becomes the *Vrede*, the Café de la Paix becomes the *Paix*, and the Hôtel aux Ardennes becomes the *Ardennes*.

How to get there

Belgium excels at local government, deleting villages and amalgamating towns by the stroke of a pen, usually without consulting either the people who live there or those who draw up maps.

Because the Guide is written for consumers not district officials, we sometimes give the real location rather than the official one. Villages and towns are named as they appear on road signs and maps, not as on the communal register. Suburbs appear bracketed after the name of their city.

For the benefits of cyclists and walkers, whenever there is an SNCB railway station within five kilometres we give you its name, the lines it is on and how far it is from where you are heading.

[IC] after a station's name means that it is a major railway terminal for intercity trains. *[IR]* means that the station is a regional transport hub where several lines meet.

Opening times and closing days

The Guide quotes café opening hours by the 24-hour clock, so 13.00 is 1.00 pm and 24.00 is midnight.

The Belgian take on café opening hours says a great deal about the values and priorities of its people.

When we say a café is open from a given time *onwards* this means that it will close when the owner chooses to close it. This may mean any time from an early supper to an early breakfast and may well vary from day to day. Even when a set closing time is stated, this is rarely more than a statement of intent. Belgian café owners are emotional beings and often like to go with the flow.

Do NOT treat the times we list as anything more that an approximation. Belgian licensing authorities rarely impose restrictions on opening hours, though they can and will do, for example if a café is near a school or hospital. We try to list a telephone number for every entry, so if your visit takes you well out of your way, phone ahead. Most owners speak some English and a few even know when they plan to be open.

One delightful if frustrating tradition is that of the weekly closing day. Many smaller towns still have a half-day closing tradition and it can be that every café in town is closed on that day. Many rural taverns do not bother to open in the week and some city centre ones will not open much at weekends. In recent years it has become increasingly difficult to find cafés open on a Monday or Tuesday.

A similar attitude may prevail when it comes to the owner's annual holiday. Many simply close their business down while they go away. When they have school age children this can mean shutting down for a couple of weeks at the height of the tourist season. So what? Which is more important to a good Catholic, his business or his family? No competition!

This is all about people getting their priorities right and the world is probably a better place for it. Though you may not see it that way when you have just trudged all the way from Santa Monica or Sunderland just to stand outside the inexplicably locked door of a world-beating bar.

With so many variables at play you might think that displaying a place's opening hours on the front door would be a common practice. But then you are probably not Belgian. While in recent years this practice has become more common, it is still a minority of cafés and restaurants that indulge potential customers in this way.

In the Belgian psyche, telling people when your café is going to be open would oblige you to be open at that time. This would be an intolerable responsibility and so makes no sense. British and American tourists may think it is stupid but what do they know? They close their bars when they are full and make them open when nobody wants to go there. Who are the crazy ones, eh?

Public holidays

It is a little known fact that the EU insists that member nations take eleven days of public holiday per year. Café opening hours on public holidays (Du: *feestdagen*; Fr: *jours fériés*) including Christmas week, are completely unpredictable. They vary from place to place, from holiday to holiday and from year to year.

In Belgium the dates of public holidays are:

New Year's Day	*1st January*
Easter Monday	*variable (March/April)*
Labour Day	*1st May*
Ascension Day	*40 days after Easter*
Whit Monday	*7th Monday after* Easter
Festival of Flanders	*11th July (north only)*
Independence Day	*21st July*
Assumption Day	*15th August*
Festival of Wallonia	*27th September (south only)*
All Saints' Day	*1st November*
Armistice Day	*11th November*
Christmas Day	*25th December*

The new tradition of the fortnight-long Christmas and New Year run-down that is popular in the UK is starting to take a hold in Belgium too.

Children in cafés

The legal age for the purchase or consumption of alcohol in a Belgian bar is sixteen.

The real limitation to taking a child into a bar is not any legal restriction but the owner's preference. Many Belgian pubs, particularly in rural settings, attract hordes of families at weekends and in the school holidays. Others, such as the typical brown café (Du: *kroeg*) actively discourage children and may ask them to leave.

Do what the locals do, use common sense and if in doubt, ask. Reticence is not a major failing for most café owners.

As a general rule younger children are rarely welcome in any bar beyond 21.00. Whatever the time, they are expected to be supervised, behave reasonably and not disturb other customers – quite a challenge for those bred on fast food additives, caffeine and thuggery.

Belgian parents take their younger ones to the pub to teach them how to behave in future years. Many of the Guide's regular contributors have witnessed rowdy families being evicted from cafés and restaurants, often to an audible show of appreciation from other customers that may include cheering.

Service and tipping

Service charge, tax (Du: *BTW*; Fr: *TVA*) and any local add-ons are always included in the quoted menu and bar tariffs. No tip is expected.

This gives the customer some leeway to show real appreciation for courteous and efficient service. The Belgian thing is to round a small bill up to the nearest Euro and a larger one, such as a major splurge with food, to the nearest five or ten Euros.

Most cafés offer service at your table. This is almost invariably the case outdoors but applies to most indoor areas too. Service at the counter is still mainly for people who wish to sit or stand at the bar counter. Do not get embarrassed if you are not clear what to do in a particular café. Guide regulars still get confused at times and so do most Belgians.

How to pour a beer

The English method of pouring a sediment beer involves lacing it gently down the side of the glass to leave as much yeast as possible in a final millimetre or two of liquid in the bottle. This is seen by Belgian beer lovers as skilful but misguided, though few will embarrass you by saying so.

The correct way to pour a beer, Belgian style, is to empty most of its contents down the side of the glass as fast as you dare with a single move of the wrist. Done properly this will allow the formation of a controlled head. It should also stop at the point when there is about a centimetre of yeasty beer left in the bottle.

In the case of wheat beers this final centimetre should be agitated vigorously and then added to the beer before drinking. For all others you are left with the choice of discarding the yeast altogether, adding it to the beer at the outset or else saving it to the end and consuming it separately – "for the vitamins".

Nowadays only a minority of bar staff have a clue about how to pour a beer. It is common to find a neatly turned out waiter who pours half a beer into the glass and leaves the rest to cloud in the bottle. If they goofed the first one, be assertive and show them how it should be done.

A similarly assertive approach should be adopted to the increasing tendency among ignorant café owners to chill beers that are designed to be served at room temperature. Refrigeration ruins great ales. If your first was frozen, ask for the next one at room temperature (Du: *kamertemperatuur*; Fr: *chambrée*) or cellar temperature (Du: *kellertemperatuur*). If they fail to understand, look foreign but determined.

By our collective will shall we teach them the error of their ways.

Patrich D'Hane of the Bier Circus in Brussels

On the question of food

The Guide lists bars of every kind and so the food on offer varies from zero to the full à la carte, gourmet restaurant experience, via all points in between.

You will not be long in Belgium before you realise that the appearance of a place has little to do with either the availability or quality of the food it serves.

We know some splendid-looking style emporia that offer the same dull, microwaved international fast food that threatens quality dining the world over. On the other hand, we have eaten exquisitely in some of the roughest-looking dives imaginable. In small family businesses, wizards of the kitchen do not necessarily know anything about décor, and vice versa.

Where the Guide comments on food quality this is because one of a small number of inspectors with reliable tastebuds has eaten there and reported back. For all other circumstances we suggest you watch what the older locals eat – after all, they are still alive – or failing that go for the local specialities.

Eating safely in Belgium could cost you the gastronomic experience of a lifetime.

All those glasses

The Guide is not a fan of fancy glasses, which fact its Belgian supporters greet with shaking heads. Almost every Belgian beer nowadays has its own glass. This is almost entirely a sales ploy. Furthermore, it is a lot cleverer than it looks. A few standard glasses with attractive multi-purpose logos saying "*Echte Bier*" or "*Bière Supérieure*" would be a welcome addition to café life.

There is no doubt that a distinctive glass makes your beer look nicer. It also has a cuckoo's egg effect on other brewers' glasses, knocking them off the overcrowded shelves. Couple that with the cost of providing the damn things and posh glasses put a significant barrier between brewer and drinker.

The design of a particular glass is not always complete hooey but most owe far more to marketing than to sound science. The generation that took to wearing labels on the outside of its trousers will always be fresh meat for salesmen.

A fluted glass (Du: *fluit*; Fr: *flûte*) will tend to preserve fizz and is often used for lager or gueuze. The British mug (Du & Fr: *pul*) is generally reserved for draught beers. A thick frozen tumbler will keep a summer beer colder for longer, so may be used for wheat beers.

A bowl-shaped glass on a stem will warm a beer as it rests in the palm of a hand so is better for winter beers and barley wines, while a narrow-based, broad-rimmed glass will allow a beer to breathe. Both are well suited to serving bottle-conditioned beers.

Chimay have their beers served in a straight-sided goblet called a *bokaal*, while most other Trappist and abbey beers are served by preference in the curved bowl of a chalice (Du: *kelk*; Fr: *calice*). Orval produces a memorable and stylish broad-stemmed bowl that has no special name as far as we are aware.

Duvel would not be Duvel without its balloon glass (Du & Fr: *ballon*). The Antwerp "little bowl" (Du: *bolleke*) is a symbol of its city.

Undoubtedly, a few of these glasses are striking and some would count as beautiful. The John Martin thistle glass for Scotch ales is one such, though nobody seriously believes its design improves its function. Bosteels have made two different kitsch classics for their Kwak and Karmeliet beers, the former being a sort of "foot of ale" with its own wooden stand.

Collectors have been known to pay upward of a hundred Euros for rare old beer glasses in pristine condition.

Paying the bill

It is common for a café to run a tab for you and present a bill as you leave. This can be disconcerting for British drinkers used to paying for drinks before they have drunk them and for food they have not even seen. (How ever did we agree to that, by the way?)

It is becoming the norm to pay as you go on streetside terraces, largely because of modern man doing a runner. People who deliberately walk out without paying are prosecuted, though the electric chair would be too good for them in the Guide's view.

If you forget to pay accidentally be prepared for a look of withering disdain, familiar to anyone who has been an English customer at a post office in rural Wales.

Antwerp

POPULATION (2002): **1,650,000**
MAIN TOWNS: **Antwerp** (444,000) & **Mechelen** (75,000)
TOURISM WEBSITE: **www.tpa.be** (Dutch mainly).

ANTWERP (Du: *Antwerpen*; Fr: *Anvers*) points furthest north of Belgium's provinces and makes up the middle part of its border with the Netherlands.

Its south-western third radiates from the old cities of Antwerp and Mechelen and is densely populated. The north and east of the province are called the *Kempen* after the flat heathlands that dominated here until the middle of the 20th century.

The city of Antwerp, on the Schelde estuary, remains a busy port and has Belgium's largest harbour. Antwerp was the birthplace of the Belgian beer revival in the 1980s but is going through lean times. The second city, Mechelen is nowadays almost as good a destination for beer lovers.

Being agriculturally poor, the economic base of the *Kempen* was for many years coal and mineral mining. In recent years heavy industry has given way to science parks and industrial estates. Tourism has also expanded, as tracts of maturing forest become ideal for walking and cycling and wetlands are turned into bird reserves.

In Antwerp city the best-known beer is unquestionably De Koninck, sold mainly on draft in distinctively splayed glasses – you ask for the glass, a *bolleke* (boll-ucka) and need not name the beer. Better known elsewhere in the the the world are Moortgat's Duvel and the Trappist brews from the abbey at Westmalle. Moortgat's equally good Maredsous brands appear less often. Mechelen's Anker beers are rising stars.

BREWERIES: **Achilles**, *Itegem*; **Anker**, *Mechelen*; **De Koninck**, *Antwerp*; **'t Hofbrouwerijke**, *Beerzel*; **Hopperd**, *Westmeerbeek*; **Moortgat**, *Breendonk*; **Pakhuis**, *Antwerp*; and **Westmalle**, *Malle*

BREWERY CAFÉS

Anker
This reviving, business-like brewery is conveniently close to exit 9 of the E19 Antwerp – Brussels motorway. Its on-site café, the **Anker** (49 Guido Gezellelaan, Mechelen – T 015 28 71 44 – closed We; others from 11.30) is a high-ceilinged Bohemian affair with all of the brewery's beers on draught plus an increasingly adventurous menu (11.30–15.00; 18.00–22.30). Parties by arrangement. There is also a reasonably priced, increasingly comfortable 22-room hotel on site called the **Carolus** (T 015 28 71 41; F 015 28 71 42; E hotel@hetanker.be), plus a beer shop.

De Koninck
The unofficial brewery tap is the **Pilgrim** (8 Boomgardstraat, Antwerp – closed Su), a smallish café just by the brewery. The brewery tours end here, offering a chance to take some brewery yeast with a *bolleke*. Casual visitors give mixed reviews.

Moortgat
A new visitor's centre should open in 2006 and will include a brewery museum, shop and café complex. Until then, the café next to the brewery, the **Brouwershuis** (56 Breendonkdorp, Puurs – closed We – others 11.00–23.00) serves all the Moortgat beers but no food.

Pakhuis
Antwerp's brewpub is the **Pakhuis** (76 Vlaamse Kaai – T 03 238 12 40 – daily from 11.00) a massive, former warehouse (Du: *pakhuis*), two blocks off the Schelde half way between the Museum of Fine Arts and the Museum of Contemporary Art (MUHKA). Food (to 22.00, snacks thereafter) is plentiful, reliable and

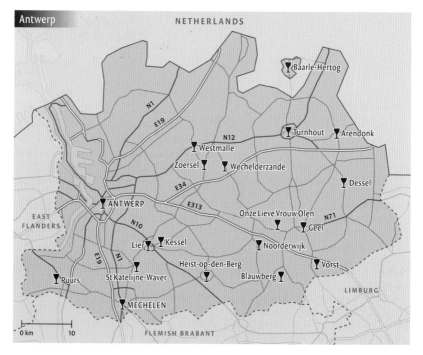

mainstream Flemish. There are seats at the bar and a less foody lounge upstairs.

Westmalle

On the Antwerp road out of Westmalle, opposite the imposing old abbey and its brewery, is a roadside tavern called the **Trappisten** (487 Antwerpsesteenweg – **T** 03 312 05 02 – daily 09.00–24.00). This is the abbey's official "taphouse" and is popular with daytrippers. A 20-minute video about brewing and cheese-making at the abbey is on show. Last time we visited they had taken the bottled dubbel off menu and were offering the draught version with grenadine. On the other hand they occasionally get the light beer, Extra.

ANTWERP

🚉 Antwerpen-Centraal *[IC]*

Antwerp is historically Belgium's most multi-cultural city, though the new-fangled Belgian politicos who invent and then espouse tribal elitism are a mite uncomfortable with that.

The old links with Spain linger on in the semi-affectionate designation of the locals as *Sinjoren*.

Belgium's second largest city (pop. 444,000) is a major harbour and business community, built around an old town centre that retains its architectural grandure. Its commercial success came from shipping and the diamond trade. It is home to the largest orthodox Jewish population outside Israel.

Centraal Station should receive the high-speed TGV train from around 2008. Its stunning structure, straight out of the golden age of steam, with Hercule Poirot threatening an entry from each portico has been poshed up to make the most of this opportunity. This is the "New" town, where cut-price gems lure the unwary. Next door to the station is the world-famous zoo.

For beer and the famous sites head for the "Old" town, centred round the massive Gothic cathedral, a fifteen-minute walk or five-minute tram ride down Keyserlei. The cathedral has four masterpieces by local boy Pieter Paul Rubens. Born in Germany to Flemish parents Rubens did much of his painting when he lived in a grand townhouse on Wapper, just off Meir, which is now a popular museum.

Antwerp was also one of the cities that led the world in the development of printing. The Plantin-Moretus museum (22 Vrijdagmarkt) is an imposing former merchant's house holding a collection that reflects the history of printing itself and of the family of printers who lived here for centuries.

The Royal Museum of Fine Arts (Leopold De Waelplaats) contains over 1,000 paintings, from Flemish masters to modern stuff. This is the sort of collection that needs you to buy a guidebook and take a sleeping bag.

For big industrial tourism, take a boat or bus through the port area north of the city along the Schelde estuary. Failing that, at least meander down to the quay and get a sense of the enormity of the waterfront.

For all its recently acquired xenophobia, one of Antwerp's great attractions is its array of high quality cooking styles from around the world, in bistros and restaurants that lack the usual pretensions.

It is a matter of extreme regret that although the city was the cradle of the beer revival in Belgium in the Eighties, recent years have seen a steady decline in the willingness of cafés to experiment.

Most hotels and tourist spots have give-away maps of the city centre, which are essential if you wish to find your way round the maze of old streets. If you find a means of acquiring a map that tells you where the trams go we would love to know!

Hotel tips: there are over forty hotels in the city. Try www.visitantwerp.be. The cheaper ones are around the New Town or on the edge of the docklands. At the weekend you may get an excellent deal at one of the top end hotels such as the SAS Radisson by the park, the Hilton on Groenenplein or the Astrid Park Plaza by the station. Otherwise settle for the ever-reliable **Florida★★**, 59 De Keyserlei (**T** 03 232 14 43; **F** 03 233 08 35; www.hotelflorida. be) opposite the station or the equally non-prize-winning **Ibis★★**, 39 Meistraat (**T** 03 231 88 30; **F** 03 234 29 21) near the Rubens Museum.

The Internationaal **Zeemanshuis★**, 21 Falconrui (**T** 03 227 54 33; **F** 03 234 26 03) is plain to the point of basic but central and cheap while the **Rubenshof★**, 115 Amerikalei (**T** 03 237 07 89) combines basic rooms with a classic Jugendstijl lounge and dining area.

Berenbak
17 Minderbroedersstraat   **T** 03 231 11 73

Away from the madding crowd. From Grote Markt take Minderbroedersrui until you find Minderbroedersstraat by the side of the school of fine arts. The "Bear's Case" (though it also means "Trough") is a pleasant, reliable, old-fashioned, well-managed café dating from 1732. It stocks 55 beers with few surprises, plus a simple menu (12.00–14.00; 18.00–24.00) that includes scampi, brochettes and steaks. There is a collection of ties to which they are happy to receive donations from customers.
CLOSED SUNDAY
Sat 12.00 onwards; *Other days* 11.00 onwards

Kulminator
32 Vleminckveld   **T** 03 232 45 38

One of the world's best-known specialist beer cafés. At the south-eastern edge of the old town. The Kulminator is one of Belgium's most famous beer cafés. Although its range is legend, the number of current beers in stock may well be under 100. This is because its big thing is cellar-aged beers. Countless hundreds of the things, listed on a beer menu the size of a small town telephone directory. There are ancient gueuzes from long-lost lambic blenders. In some cases you can taste the same beer as it has survived from every year since the early Eighties. The beer menu reads like a role-call of Belgian brewing history. The café layout enables quiet conversation and pockets of beer geekery. There is an open fire in winter and candlelight all year round. Music tends to be classical. Lager and food are alien concepts. So is politeness among some of the miserable bunch of regulars who hang around the bar. Closes for two weeks in high summer and over Christmas/New Year.
CLOSED SUNDAY; *Mon* 20.15 onwards
Tue–Fri 12.00–00.30; *Sat* 17.00 onwards

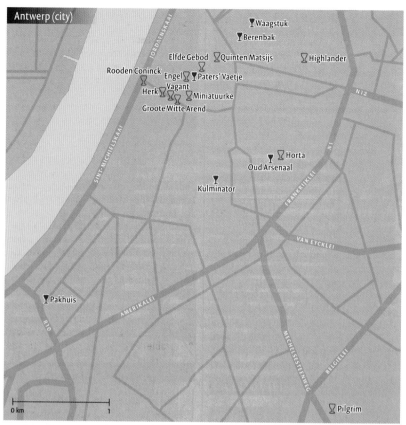

Antwerp (city)

Waagstuk
Berenbak
Elfde Gebod Quinten Matsijs Highlander
Rooden Coninck
Engel Paters' Vaetje
Herk Vagant
Miniatuurke
Groote Witte Arend

Horta
Oud Arsenaal
Kulminator

Pakhuis

Pilgrim

0 km 1

Oud Arsenaal

4 Maria Pijpelincxstraat   **T** 03 232 97 54

Conveniently close to Rubens' House, this 1929 café of classical interwar design is the archetypal Belgian café of a certain era. Though the list stops at 60, there can be lots of surprises. It enjoys growing fame for stocking rare and excellent ales and lambics. The range depends on the landlord's latest passions. Antwerpers still comfortably outnumber the growing clientele of beer travellers but seem to drink Stella. It is connected with the nearby Dorstvlegel beer shop. Do not be surprised to find obscure winter beers or lambics from De Cam or Drie Fonteinen. Loads of enamel adverts, tiled floor, carved oak in abundance, smoke-stained everything, marble top bar and nice bits of minor Art Nouveau. There is a small seating area at the front. No food but it is opposite Horta (below). Closes early, except on Fridays.   **CLOSED THURSDAY**
Sat&Sun 07.30–19.30; *Other days* 09.00 onwards

Paters' Vaetje

1 Blauwmoezelstraat   **T** 03 231 84 76

The "Monks' Casket" sits directly opposite the base of the spire of Antwerp cathedral. Its beer range nowadays hovers around 80. The single old-fashioned small main bar with an even smaller gallery upstairs has become well-known to beer travellers from around the world, though the café increasingly plays down its beer list. A small terrace area at the front allows you to be drowned by the free carillon concerts on Monday evenings and Friday lunchtimes in summer. Snacks, like the smiles of welcome, are small.
Sun–Thu 11.00–03.00; *Fri&Sat* 11.00–05.00

Waagstuk

20 Stadswaag T 03 225 02 19

The last of Antwerp's established specialist beer cafés is a former coaching inn, at the corner of a recently gentrified square, behind the school of fine arts. It is on the way from the cathedral to the red light district so gets a varied trade. The building dates from 1548 and contains some original wall paintings that artists and historians may visit at quiet times. The regular beer list of 80 rises in summer and usually has enough to interest a visitor for a whole evening. There are several traditional gueuzes and krieks plus some better regional beers. Try the **Zeppelin** (8%: ★★★★), a roasted, strong sweet stout they commission from Proef. Ironically it has the character of a German schwarzbier. A wide range of reliable bar snacks includes a few local specialities. Under new management but doing better that most.

Mon–Fri 10.00–02.00; *Sat&Sun* 14.00–02.00

Lambics at the Oud Arsenaal

The **Elfde Gebod** (10 Torfbrug), behind the cathedral, is famous for housing a unique collection of religious paraphernalia, from statues and a pulpit to pieces of kitsch religious art. A partial revamp just before we went to press appears to have included replacing some of the more miserable staff.

The **Quinten Matsijs** (17 Moriaanstraat – closed Mo; others from 12.00), just north of the cathedral, is Belgium's oldest continuously licensed café, built in 1565. Excellent on Sunday (to 20.00) when the elders gather for a natter. Thirty-something beers, with good food and service.

The **Highlander** (2 Pieter van Hobokenstraat – closed Mo&Tu; Sa from 14.00; others from 11.00) is a spick and span backstreet café with a Scottish theme that includes a list of nearly a hundred whiskies, many top rate, plus a list of over forty beers including Scottish imports.

The smallest pub in Antwerp is a cutie called the **Miniatuurke** (11 Oude Koornmarkt). Barely able to admit a football team it nonetheless has two storeys.

The road that leads from the tram terminus on Groenplaats to the quay on the Schelde river has a good array of interesting old pubs. The **Groote Witte Arend** (18 Reyndersstraat) is a courtyard bar of classical proportions, now concentrating on food and Moortgat beers. On the next corner is the **Vagant** (21 Reyndersstraat – daily 11.00–02.00), a pleasant saloon bar with one of the best selections of Belgian genevers in the country. Just down the way is the **Herk** (33 Reyndersstraat), an atmospheric three-roomed, candle-lit old bar, with a lived-in feel and almost enough beers for a full listing. In the next block is the **Rooden Coninck** (31 Vlasmarkt) is an ordinary café with a 13th century cellar downstairs.

Out near the Rubens Museum, the **Horta** (2 Hopland) is a bistro on the grand scale, constructed from the remains of the steel infrastructure of the Horta-designed Volkshuis in Brussels, rediscovered rotting in a station scrapyard thirty years after its destruction. The food is accomplished but unfiltered Palm and Boon Lambic are too often "off today sir".

For some reason lots of British and American beer travellers describe the **Engel** (3 Grote Markt) as their favourite café in Antwerp. Classical in its long bar design and usually with a bustling atmosphere, they plead endlessly with the Guide to mention it. So we have mentioned it, OK?

See also Brewery cafés above: De Koninck and Pakhuis.

ANTWERP (Berchem)

🚆 Antwerpen-Berchem *[IC]*

Berchem straddles the Kleine Ring dual carriageway that encloses most of inner Antwerp. Its busy railway station is the place where many intercity trains drop their Antwerp passengers. The three-minute connection to Centraal station, is the simplest way to get there.

Camargue
34 Statiestraat **T** 03 230 01 00

Statiestraat is opposite the rear exit of Berchem station. The Camargue is six hundred metres down on the right. The single long bar room has a small enclosed terrace at the back. A successful mix of bistro and brown café, its beer list is now down to about 110. The wide-ranging menu is strong on vegetarian food and fish. It also gets fads of things, from fruit wines via herbal teas to cheeses. They light the stove in winter. Music can be intrusive. May close for four weeks in high summer. CLOSED SUNDAY; *Other days* 11.30–01.00

ARENDONK

5km E of Turnhout on N118 & N129, off E34 exit 26

🚆 Turnhout *[Lier–Turnhout]* – 5km

Small windmilled town off the Antwerp to Eindhoven motorway.

Verdiep
36 Vrijheid **T** 0474 73 95 85

The "Levels" is a newly converted café on the corner of the village square. It takes its name from the three-level layout in one bare-brick large room. Big on music and interior design, it also has a solid beer list that has nudged up to 60, without any surprises. No food beyond nibbles. *Daily* 19.00 onwards

BAARLE-HERTOG

12km N of Turnhout on N119

A collection of Belgian enclaves, some no larger than a field, centred on a Belgian village that is surrounded by Dutch North Brabant. It has been that way since the original Maastricht treaty of 1843, which failed to account for the two local landowners preferring to ally to different countries. Even the arrival of the Euro has not stopped some local phone calls being charged at international rates. The arrangements for postal deliveries and the electricity supply are hilarious.

Brouwershuis
42 Molenstraat **T** 014 69 94 03

Fifty metres from the centre on the road towards Turnhout. The "Brewer's House" is one of the best beer shops in Belgium (see Beer shops & warehouses). It also has café and catering areas upstairs and at the back which can cater for both individual visitors and coachloads. The theoretical beer list here runs to 700. Pre-booked parties can enjoy presentations on brewing and beer, which range from a quick video with a beer through to a five-hour boozy banquet. Will open at other times for parties. CLOSED MONDAY; *Other days* 10.00–18.00

BLAUWBERG

10km SSW of Geel off N19

🚆 Testelt *[Leuven–Hasselt]* – 5km

Village on the old pilgrims' route between the abbeys of Averbode and Tongerlo.

Hulst

4 Hulst   **T** 014 54 49 35

From the village take Witputstraat to its end and turn left onto the long straight road from Averbode to Westerlo. The "Holly Bush" is near to an ancient tree from which it and the nearby wood take their names. This dedicated beer house appeals to cyclists, walkers and locals alike. Created in a restored farmhouse, its list was getting classier as the years pass, hitting 250 and still ascending. May be descending again but as it is off the Grand Tour we get few reports. May close in the second half of August.

CLOSED MONDAY; *Other days* 09.00 onwards

DESSEL

12km SE of Turnhout on N119
Small market town near the Dutch border.

Campina

2 Markt   **T** 014 37 07 09

Well-managed café with a classic Fifties design, on the main square of this simple Kempen town. Named after the town's famous Campina brewery that was closed by Alken-Maes in 1988. Convenient for the tourist parks around the Molse Meren. The plain exterior belies an elegant interior heavy on Art Deco allusions. A centre of local life. Stocks around 60 beers. The menu extends to steaks and seafood, with ribs as the house speciality.

CLOSED TUESDAY; *Other days* 10.00 onwards

GEEL

18km S of Turnhout on N19
🚃 Geel *[Lier–Neerpelt or Hasselt]*

This relatively dreary Kempen town (pop. 34,000) operates a sort of fostering system for learning disabled and mentally ill people that brings it worldwide visitors. Its incongruously stripy parish church is dedicated to St.Dympna, an 8th century Irish princess whose abusive father tracked her down to Geel and killed her. The citizens reasoned that he must be insane and so recommended care in the community!

The gory story is told in wooden carvings in the church, which is just off Nieuwstraat.

Kelderke

12 Stationsplein   **T** 014 72 37 28

A post-war corner café on the square next to the station, typical of its type except in stocking a great range of beers. About 130 at the last count, including extremes of good taste. At our last visit there were beers from Rulles, de Ranke, Dolle Brouwers, Kerkom, St Bernardus, Malheur and Alvinne among others. Food (11.00–22.00) is mainly rolls and smaller bar snacks. Weekend closing is generally 03.00. Pool, fruit machines and smoking are popular.

CLOSED MONDAY   *Other days* 09.00 onwards

Pas de Pouffe

73 Markt   **T** 014 59 23 49

This comfortable, modern town centre café, on a corner of the main square attracts yoof by night and normal people by day. Stocks around 120 beers and the range is still rising. No food beyond soup. Good value. Friendly service. Fluent French speakers will know its name means "No sales on credit". The beer scene in Geel has been steadily improving in recent years, another place worth a peek on Sundays and footballing Saturdays is the **Drijzillenhof** (2 Drijzillen – **T** 0484 11 19 56 – Su 11.00–23.00; Sa from 18.00 if Verbroedering Geel FC are playing at home).

CLOSED WEDNESDAY; *Tue* 09.00 onwards; *Sun* 14.00 onwards; *Other days* 10.00 onwards

HEIST-OP-DEN-BERG

30km SE of Antwerp off N10
🚃 Heist op den Berg *[Lier–Aarschot]*

Market town (pop. 38,000) on the old route from Antwerp to Hasselt. Said to have a good train museum though we have never been.

Hotel tip: about a kilometre the wrong side of the station on the road to Antwerp, the **Maalderij**★★, 283 Liersesteenweg (**T** 015 25 01 38; **F** 015 25 06 57; **www.hoteldemaaderij.be**) makes a homely touring base.

Afgrond

19 Herentalsesteenweg   T 015 25 18 51

The place they call the "Abyss" is a hundred metres off Heist's high street on the Herentals road. This most basic of rustic-style small cafés has a memorable bar, a small but complex tiered garden and one of the cleverest beer lists in the country, hand-picked for high quality. Housed in a two centuries old former farm building, it was converted to a café in the late Eighties. The list of 80 beers includes good examples of just about everything, including a few aged beers. Food is cheese only. For bigger food or gentility, try the **Herlaer** (6 Broeckstraat, Hallaar – closed Mo&Tu), an altogether smarter place in the next village, with around forty beers.   **CLOSED MONDAY** *Tue–Thu* 18.00 onwards; *Fri–Sun* 14.00 onwards

KESSEL

16km SE of Antwerp on N13
Kessel *[Lier–Herentals]*

A mess of a town on the outskirts of Lier, with its church and station a way apart.

Badhuis

73 Emblemsesteenweg   T 03 480 33 52

Unusual beer café and all-round tavern, in the same family for four generations. Easy to find from the station if you head away from the town. Its name, the "Bath House" refers to its first use when built in 1897. They commissioned a centennial book to prove it. The original interior has been converted to a bistro stocking 75 beers last time we checked. A full menu (12.00 – 21.00) has been reported plus good ice cream. There is a large terrace outside in summer.

CLOSED TUESDAY; **CLOSED MONDAY** (*Nov–Mar*) *Sun* 09.00 onwards; *Other days* 11.00 onwards

LIER

17km SE of Antwerp on N10 & N14
Lier *[IR]*

A nice little town (pop. 30,000) on the route to nowhere, the historical option in the Antwerp commuter belt. There is cluster of old buildings round the Grote Markt but the must-see is the pair of clocks made by local craftsman Lodewijk Zimmer in the eponymous Zimmerplein. The Stedelijk Museum Wuyts (14 Florent van Cauwenberghstraat) has Breughel's Flemish Proverbs among its paintings. The Timmermans-Opsomerhuis, by the Werf bridge, celebrates writer Felix (T) and painter Isadore (O), both of whom lived locally.

Hotel tip: for an historical treat and some serious Flemish hospitality at affordable prices try the **Hof van Aragon ★★★**, 6 Aragonstraat (T 03 491 08 00; F 03 491 0810; **www.hofvanaragon.be**).

Oude Lier

103 Nazaretdreef   T 03 480 07 20

The sad thing about Lier is that although it would be an excellent place for a serious beer café, nobody has yet taken the plunge. Its best offering is on the outskirts of town, off the road to Kessel. Turn left before the bridge over the Nete and it is 1.5 kilometres up the lane, in a good area for walking. A former abbey smallholding with a beer list of around 50, including de Dolle Brouwers. Pancakes and waffles too. In town the most interesting drinks café is the **Sterk Water** (9 Berlaarsestraat – closed Tu; others from 11.30), which stocks over a hundred genevers. A modern café worth watching is the **Delfin** (6 Zimmerplein – closed Mo; others from 09.30), though it has barely forty beers at present.

CLOSED FRIDAY; **CLOSED MONDAY** (*Nov–Easter*) *Other days* 11.30 onwards

MECHELEN

Halfway between Antwerp & Brussels off E313 exit 9
Mechelen *[IC]* & Mechelen-Nekkerspoel *[IR]*

Mechelen (Fr: *Malines*) is the province's second city (pop. 75,000), a strange mix of Bohemia and late Gothic. Ignore the horrid urban sprawl and head straight to its old centre. Emperor Charles V was brought up here and between 1506 and 1530 the town was in effect the capital of this part of the

Hapsburg Empire. His mother, Margaret of Austria, and her mother Margaret of York, each built palaces on Keizerstraat. The latter now houses a concert hall. The tower of St. Rumbout's cathedral is the highest in Belgium. Catch its carillon bells every Monday (20.30) in summer. You will find more pomp architecture in the churches of St Pieter and Hanswijk. Mechelen was also the terminus for the world's first commercial railway, which began running to and from Brussels in 1835. It remains a major railway junction, with two mainline stations. Traditional tourists buy asparagus in season, plus the local wool and lace all year round. Modern ones remark how much nicer it is than Antwerp these days. Check www.visitmechelen.com for an enthusiastic ex-pat's guide. Children should like Planckendael Animal Park near Muizen station, just east of the city.

Hotel tips: the opulent but privately owned **Grooten Wolsack★★★**, 16 Wollemarkt (**T** 015 20 46 64; **F** 015 21 86 28) can offer excellent value at the top end but the **Carolus★★**, next to Anker brewery (see Brewery cafés above) is becoming a must-stay for the beer traveller.

Afspraak

23 Keizerstraat   **T** 015 33 17 34

A welcome addition to the growing clan of good drinking places. Keizerstraat runs from the centre of the old city out to Nekkerspoel station, passing many of the famous imperial buildings on the way. At the station end is this pleasant, high-ceilinged *fin de siécle* wooden-floored new beer café with its list of 110 beers and rising. There is food too (We–Fr 11.30–14.00; 17.00–21.00; Sa 11.30–22.00; Su 15.00–21.00) from a wide-ranging menu that includes cooking with beer. Later food on Fridays.
CLOSED MONDAY & TUESDAY
Sun 15.00 onwards; *Other days* 11.00 onwards

Stillen Genieter

9 Nauwstraat   **T** 015 21 95 04

From the cathedral take Steenweg. Nauwstraat is a short street on the right. The "Gentleman at Rest" is a dedicated beer house representing the personal quest of its taciturn owner.

At the back of this long brown café is a view across the river Dijle to the building site that was Lamot brewery and will soon be a new arts centre. The official range of beers still reaches 330, though readers report stocking problems frequently. Food is limited to snacks though these are getting more adventurous. There are good teas and coffees. The background music is popular classical. Service can be languid and regulars suggest that if it is not open you should ring the bell. Said to open on school days from 12.00 to 14.00. *Daily* 20.00 onwards

OTHER MECHELEN CAFÉS:

The **Hanekeef** (8 Keizerstraat – **T** 015 20 78 46 – Su from 13.00; others from 09.00) is less beery than it was but still just as brown and may stay open absurdly late. The **Borrel en Babbel** (2 Nieuwwerk – **T** 015 27 36 89 – closed Mo; others from 12.00 summer, 19.00 winter) claims to be Belgium's smallest café and carries an exceptional range of genevers, including the very best of Smeets plus some smaller producers. Possibly the city's most attractive bar is the **Ankertje aan de Dijle** (20 Vismarkt – **T** 015 34 60 34 – daily from 11.30), which is heavy on breweriana and cooking with beer. See also Brewery cafés above: Anker.

The Ankertje aan de Dijle

NOORDERWIJK

22km ESE of Antwerp off E313 exit 22
🚉 Herentals [IR]
Old industrial village south of Herentals.

Welkom

20 Ring
T 014 27 72 95
Despite its name, Ring is actually the main
street of this urban village, running north to
south past the church. This restored pub from
the Fifties is a recent convert to better beers –
70 and rising. Small snacks only. It has the air
of a place that intends to do serious beer.
CLOSED MONDAY
Sun 10.30 onwards; *Other days* 15.00 onwards

ONZE LIEVE VROUW OLEN

23km E of Antwerp off E313 exit 22
🚉 Olen [Lier–Neerpelt or Hasselt]

Urban village between Herentals and Geel,
wedged between the Albert and Kempisch
canals, some way from the town of Olen. Our
nearest entry to Bobbejaanland, the kiddy
spectacular at Lichtaart.

Stationneke

57 Stationstraat   **T** 0477 56 96 96

The real address is platform 1 of Olen railway
station. Far easier to find by hourly train from
Antwerp and elsewhere. The "Little Station"
is billed as a museum, of what we are unclear,
but its main attraction is a café that is typical
of an old railway station bar. The range of beers
on show in the back room is falling but still
hits 60. We have never spotted food. Popular
with the local characters of a caring community.
CLOSED MONDAY & THURSDAY
Other days 12.00–24.00

PUURS

12km SSW of Antwerp off N16
🚉 Puurs [St. Niklaas–Mechelen & Antwerp–Puurs]
See Brewery cafés: Moortgat (above)

SINT KATELIJNE WAVER

5km NE of Mechelen off N14 & N105
🚉 St.-Katelijne-Waver [Mechelen–Antwerp] – 1 km

Two-part village just up the line from Duffel,
the place that invented the coat and the bag.

Café 206

206 Stationsstraat

On the road that links the east and west
halves of the village, which host the station
and church respectively. A new beer café in
an old corner bar, next to a water tower. It
was still recovering from its previously
rather run-down state when we visited but
the beer list was already a creditable 100 with
plans to go higher. Safer brews initially. No
food as far as we know. Plans to close for the
three weeks to mid July.   *Daily* 10.00 onwards

TURNHOUT

36km ENE of Antwerp off E34 exit 24
🚉 Turnhout [Lier–Turnhout]

A typically disorganised, sprawling north
Kempen town (pop. 39,000) near the Dutch
border. Our café is the best bit, the baroque
interior of St. Peter's Church comes second
and the museum of playing cards (Du:
speelkaarten) at 28 Begijnenstraat comes a
close third. The array of 16th century
buildings reflects the glory years when it was
the seat of government for this part of the
Hapsburg empire. The law court was once
the palace of the Dukes of Brabant.

Spytighen Duvel

99 Otterstraat   **T** 014 42 35 00

Four hundred metres from the Markt, on the
road to Oud Turnhout. The "Mournful Devil"
dates from 1740 and is in a cobbled area of
the old centre of town. One of the classic
beer cafés of Belgium still managing to pack
its list of 300 with unexpected and unusual
finds. Oude gueuzes may include short run
specials. There is no beer style that is not well
represented. The range of genevers and *likeurs*
is adventurous. There are single malt whiskies

and fine cigars too. The pleasant single bar room looks as though it should serve mountains of food but in practice limits itself to sandwiches, nibbles and pickled herrings, enough to see you through a long session as you absorb the excellence of this place. Not well known to regular tourists, but becoming a legitimate target for the attentions of better-informed beer lovers from around the globe.

CLOSED MONDAY
Fri & Sat 11.00–02.00; *Other days* 11.00–01.00

VORST

20km NW of Hasselt on N141 & N126

An agglomeration of villages, just south of the E313 between exits 24 & 25.

Kruimel
3 Dikstraat   **T** 013 66 57 04

Easy to find off the motorway, near Klein Vorst church, on the Geel road. The "Crumbs" is a typical all-round café with nearly 60 beers, including more than its share of tripels. Meat, fish and venison (in season) feature on a menu more renowned for limitless pizzas. A well laid-out garden at the back leads down to a field of nervous deer. Big panoramic windows add light. May close for the second half of August.

CLOSED MONDAY & TUESDAY
Other days 11.00 onwards

WECHELDERZANDE

18km ENE of Antwerp off E34 exit 21 Village in the tourist belt of rural Antwerp

Toerist
1 Vlimmersebaan   **T** 03 309 20 94

A café since the 18th century. A kilometre north of the motorway, on the main road through the centre of the village. Convenient for various cycle routes and footpaths. The "Tourist" actually bills itself as a billiards café and its large single room is certainly dominated by two Belgian tables and a darts board. The list of 165 beers, featuring good

examples of most Belgian styles, is really just a bonus. Well-managed and courteous service. There is a small terrace. Food is limited to basic snacks.

CLOSED THURSDAY
Sat 10.00–02.00; *Other days* 10.00–01.00

WESTMALLE

20km NE of Antwerp on N12
See Brewery cafés above: Westmalle.

ZOERSEL

16km ENE of Antwerp off E34 exit 20

A small market town off the Antwerp – Eindhoven motorway, with a wood to the south made famous in a story of rustic idyll by Flemish author Hendrik Conscience.

Boshuisje
1 Boshuisweg   **T** 03 385 94 53   **F** 03 324 11 37

Trust us, you won't regret it. From the motorway head away from Zoersel town. After six hundred metres, turn right into Hooidonck, then right again at the Hunck café. Stop when you see all the cars parked. It is a short walk up the bridle path. If you come by horse you can tie up outside. The "Little House in the Wood" is a classic 18th century farmhouse pub. Its front room has a large open fire, a working boiler-cum-ironing-board, candlelight and just the right number of tables and chairs. The second room is a more recent addition but blends in nicely. Strange ephemera abound. There is a large beer garden. Around 100 beers are stocked. Food ranges from serious cuisine via standard Flemish fayre to ribs, pasta and pancakes. The weekday lunch menu is limited. Note the gentlemen's urinal. The **Wandeling** (58 Peggerstraat – **T** 03 383 13 72 – closed Mo, Sep–Jun; others from 11.00) is a young pretender a few hundred metres down the way, offering fifty beers, regional cooking and a large children's play area, plus a heated verandah for the winter.

CLOSED MONDAY TO THURSDAY (*Oct–May*)
Fri & Sat 12.00–23.00; *Other days* 12.00–22.00

Brussels

POPULATION (2002): **960,000**
TOURISM WEBSITE: **www.brusselsinternational.be**

BRUSSELS is like no other place on Earth. It is a ragbag of impoverished neighbourhoods, grand architecture, messy streets, extremes of elegance and semi-detached logic. Politics runs, like its tram system, underground-overground, round 'n round and everywhere.

Brussels is the never-ending grand project, frustrated by the constant need to update. It will be great when it is finished, as they have been saying for a century and a half.

The city is not a province but since 1997 has in effect been self-governing in its local affairs.

Government is Brussels' forte. It hosts the Flemish parliament, the national parliament, the headquarters of the European Commission and innumerable offices of multi-national assemblies governing this, that or the other aspect of global harmony.

Though officially bilingual, most of its population speak French by preference and those who speak Dutch are not what you might call your average Flemish. Many of the local population have overcome the language problem by becoming fluent in at least one other tongue and able to muddle through in another two or three, often in a single sentence.

Those locals who seek an exclusive language prefer the local dialect, *Broessels* (occasionally *Bruxellois*). Imagine how a tribe from a small Pacific island would communicate with each other if they had only ever learnt to speak Dutch taught by a French missionary, and you are three parts of the way there.

Brussels was as great a centre of lambic brewing as Payottenland in the 19th century. It is now reduced to a single brewer, the vociferously authentic Cantillon. Lambics remain the true beer of old Brussels, though to find them you will need to take the Guide with you. Its two other breweries are ambitious new brewpubs.

> **BREWERIES: Brasseurs de la Grand'Place**, *City Centre*; **Cantillon**, *Anderlecht*; and **Imprimerie**, *Uccle*.

BREWERY CAFÉS

Brasseurs de la Grand'Place

Central Brussels' first brewpub is five metres off Grand'Place. The **Brasseurs de la Grand' Place** (24 Rue de la Colline – daily 11.00–23.00) has four levels and includes bar, no-smoking and dining areas. Lots of wood, tiles and bold colours. The brewery is on show. The three terribly safe draught beers are sold by the glass or pitcher, at prices one might call "Grand'Place". If you just want one, we recommend the bottled triple. Food from bar snacks to full meals is available throughout opening hours.

Cantillon

There is no café but there are numerous options for visiting this classic "Museum of Gueuze" (see Beer Tourism), just outside the Ring in the Anderlecht neighbourhood. Sampling is possible on the premises (67 Rue Gheude) and it is possible to buy beer direct.

Imprimerie

A brewpub, restaurant and night spot, just off Place St.Job in the outer suburb of Uccle (Du: *Ukkel*). The **Imprimerie** (666 Chaussée de St.Job – T 02 372 93 25 – closed Mo; others 12.00–02.00) had a former life as a printing works. Large candelabrae help create a Bohemian atmosphere against a backdrop of brewing equipment, some of it in use. An open terrace, out the back from the upstairs exit, makes a civilised drinking spot. It evolves into a nightclub in the late evening.

BRUSSELS

🚆 Brussels North, Central & South *[IC]*

Brussels can trace its origins back to the 6th century village of Broekzele, on the banks of the now bricked-over River Senne.

The city had two golden ages in the 20th century. At the beginning it was culturally sexy as the birthplace of Art Nouveau, which took its most obvious form in the architecture of Victor Horta, whose influence spawned fifty years of bold grand design.

By the end it was the "capital of Europe", the workplace of the individuals who shape the continent's development.

If ever there was a place where you need to know your way around, then this is it. Brussels can bore the pants off weekenders, leaving a visitor feeling it is only fit for Eurocrats and migrant workers. But with a bit of inside knowledge you will love it.

Pick up a map and starter pack from the tourist office in Rue Marché aux Herbes.

The city's heart is somewhere around the obsessively ornate, Gothic guildhouses of

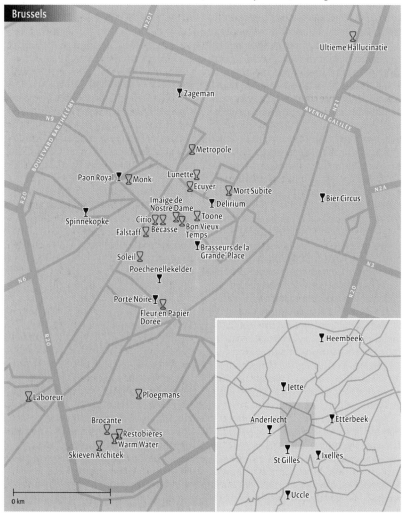

Brussels

- Ultieme Hallucinatie
- Zageman
- Metropole
- Paon Royal
- Monk
- Lunette
- Ecuyer
- Mort Subite
- Bier Circus
- Imaige de Nostre Dame
- Delirium
- Spinnekopke
- Cirio
- Toone
- Falstaff
- Bécasse
- Bon Vieux Temps
- Soleil
- Brasseurs de la Grande Place
- Poechenellekelder
- Porte Noire
- Fleur en Papier Dorée
- Laboreur
- Ploegmans
- Brocante
- Restobières
- Warm Water
- Skieven Architek
- Heembeek
- Jette
- Anderlecht
- Etterbeek
- St Gilles
- Ixelles
- Uccle

0 km   1

Grand'Place, the grey disorganised Place de Brouckère and the mess of marble and concrete that lies between the Bourse and Place de la Monnaie.

The Grand'Place is a World Heritage site. By day or night it is an amazing sight. The busiest façade is on the old Town Hall (Fr: *Hôtel de Ville*). The Brewers' Guildhouse (Fr: *Maison des Brasseurs*) is at no. 10 and houses a small museum of brewing (see Beer Tourism).

If you prefer your history obscured by time, nip next door to no. 9 and peek inside the fabulously expensive Maison du Cygne restaurant. It was here in earthier days that Marx met Engels and they set about writing the communist manifesto. They were both expelled from Belgium two months later for worrying the peasants.

Eighty years on, Brussels scared the peasants again by teaching them to wiggle the bossanova, a dance craze then exported to Brazil in the same way that New York's *spaghetti Bolognese* eventually made it to Bologna and San Francisco's chow mein to China.

The eateries of the Ilôt Sacré, along Rue des Bouchers and Rue des Petit Bouchers always deliver a bill that is double what you estimated. However, if their seafood doesn't tempt you the city has hundreds of other ways to entertain your palate.

A visit is never complete without a peek at the Manneken Pis in Rue du Chêne. First impressions are invariably disappointing. The joke is in the strapline "For You Who Pass Without Seeing Me". The disturbing undertone is the statue's adult head.

If the Guide does not persuade you that Belgium is a nation of great artists, the Royal Museum of Fine Art on Place Royale might. Its Ancient and Modern halves together represent the best collection of Belgian painting from the Breugels via Rubens to Magritte and Ensor.

One building with a different kind of wow factor is the monstrous Palace of Justice, the only one in Brussels not to house a museum. There are eighty or so that do. These are dedicated to the histories of fairground organs, puppets, office equipment, chicory and sewers.

One of the best collections is in the Comic Strips Museum (Fr: *Centre Belge de la Bande Dessinée*) in the Horta's Magasins Waucquez (20 Rue des Sables). Adjacent to Mérode metro station is a collection of collect ions – Cinquantenaire Park houses the Army & Military History Museum, the Art & History Museum, the Air Museum and the Motor Museum (Autoworld).

The metro goes as far out of town as Heysel stadium and the city's iconic landmark, the Atomium. Next door is an urban congregation of family fun called Brupark. Stop off at Bockstael station for murals of Tintin and his dog.

The city centre is generally quiet on Sunday but if you need entertaining try the old Marolles area. The daily flea market on the Place du Jeu de Balle reaches its tackiest and most fascinating on Sundays. Meanwhile, see the cosmopolitan side of the capital at the massive open-air market around Gare du Midi.

Getting about: Brussels has three main railway stations and most trains into Brussels, including the one from the airport, stop at all three. Brussels North (Fr: *Bruxelles Nord*, Du: *Brussel Noord*) is just outside the Petit Ring beyond the sex shops and chain hotels of Boulevard Adolphe Max. South station (Fr: *Bruxelles Midi*, Du: *Brussel Zuid*) is the international terminal for the TGV and Eurostar trains, set in multi-ethnic Anderlecht. Central station (Du: *Centraal*) is the smallest, dowdiest and least cycle friendly, but nearest to the Grand'Place.

The rest of the public transport system is largely unfathomable without the special four-language bus, tram and metro map. Try to find one at a tourist office, hotel or station. The easiest travel option is the day pass (Fr: *Carte d'un Jour*; Du: *Dagkaart*), valid for two at weekends. 2004 saw a brave experiment with a free discount card that includes three days of free public transport.

Surprisingly it is relatively easy to get to the centre of Brussels by car, provided you do not mind stock car style driving and obscene car parking charges. The tunnels that lead in from the E40 are particularly entertaining. With a bit of luck they might even bring you out on the Petit Ring near to the Grand'Place underground car park near Central station.

Hotel tips: Because of its political importance, Brussels' hotels are packed to the gunnels from Monday to Thursday through most of the year. However, it is quieter and cheaper in July and August. Throughout the year, relatively simple international standard hotels will ask and get €200 for a double room during the week. At the weekends prices as low as €80 for the same deal may be tracked down.

Brussels has hotels of all grades, styles and price range. There is no cheap hotel district as such. If you have arrived in town without a reservation, consider using the room finding service at Tourist Information. Alternatively, as Brussels is the transport hub of the nation, stay out of town and train it in.

BRUSSELS (City Centre)

The Guide defines the city centre as being inside the Petit Ring of boulevards sometimes known as the Pentangle, which run like a racetrack round the old town. Traditionally the Guide has been lenient towards the city centre and not insisted on making its full entries reach our usual standards for serving a broad range of beers. For this edition our noose has tightened.

Bier Circus

57 Rue de l'Enseignement   **T** 02 218 00 34

Walk up Rue des Colonies from Central station to Rue Royale and turn left for one block. Rue de l'Enseignement is at the first junction on your right. Summer 2005 saw Patrick D'Hane's beer café move fifty metres down the road and transform itself into a full-blown bistro, with *cuisine à la bière* accompanying a splendid list of over 170 beers, many from the top rank. The range varies but is usually strong on Wallonian farmhouse brews and traditional lambic beers. There are Flemish beers too with a penchant for those from Hopperd. The move was celebrated with a house beer from Cantillon called La Dernière Cuvée du 89. They may well start to open on weekday afternoons soon. The only criticism of the new premises is that the drinking area is a lot

smaller, the hope being that all will be enticed to eat.
Sat & Sun 18.00–24.00
Mon–Fri 12.00–14.30 & 18.00–24.00

Delirium

4a Impasse de la Fidélité   **T** 02 514 44 34

The Delirium beer café stocks over 2000 beers – that is two thousand not two hundred. Despite this it is a pretty good place where to date bad beers have been a rarity. Deep in the Ilôt Sacré fish restaurant area, in the same street as the Janneken Pis statuette of a young girl ... well work it out! From the Grand'Place find the Galeries Royale St. Hubert and from there turn into the pedestrianised Rue des Bouchers. The alley is on your right after fifty metres. The huge bar is downstairs and spreads onto various levels. Owner Joël Pêcheur founded the Chez Moeder Lambic chain of cafés twenty years ago but sold up in 1993. His return is proving nicely successful without getting packed to the gunnels. Many of the beers are German, though over 400 are Belgian. Every new Belgian beer that can be sourced is here. Only one Dutch café to our knowledge has so many new Dutch beers, with beers from countries we never guessed had breweries. They keep five hundred extras to cover for times when the listed brews run out. Food is limited but you could come here just for the cheese and dry sausage selection. Three dozen Belgian cheeses graced the board at our last visit, with some strictly for the unflappable. Unmissable and unique.
Sun 10.00–01.00; *Other days* 10.00–04.00

Paon Royal

6 Rue Vieux Marché aux Grains   **T** 02 513 08 68

The area around St. Catherine's church, two blocks to the wrong side of De Brouckère metro station, has become a dining zone. The "Royal Peacock" café-restaurant has been plying its trade under the same family's ownership since 1923. It is a great place for lunch (11.30–14.30) in the smart, old-fashioned salon or under the lime trees on the Place. They stock around 60 beers with highspots. The evening crowd is artier and eats less, the kitchen only opening at weekends (18.00–21.30). Note the good cartoons.

CLOSED SUNDAY & MONDAY
Other days 08.00–21.30

Poechenellekelder

5 Rue du Chêne   **T** 02 511 92 62

In the last year, the "Mannequin Cellar" has improved its beer range massively, such that the Guide would now call it unmissable. The range of authentic gueuze is without parallel in the city. They are also great ones for getting in unusual beers from smaller breweries, leading the way in introducing the new pioneers of well-hopped brews. All this is the work of an enthusiastic new cellar manager, who is a great asset. Fate has positioned this café bang opposite the statue of the Manneken Pis. Its main theme is puppetry, with many on show amid the seriously eccentric adornments and collectibles of all three storeys. The puppet maker drew many of the murals. Sitting outside on the small terrace lets you appreciate the superb joke of juxtaposing a bunch of clicking tourists alongside a pot-bellied water-passing midget, neither of which knows what all the fuss is about. Keep going with pasta, tartines and small snacks.

CLOSED MONDAY
Tue–Thu 10.00–24.00
Fri–Sun 10.00–02.00

Porte Noire

67 Rue des Alexiens   **T** 02 511 78 37

Two blocks further off Grand'Place from the Manneken Pis, take a left up the hill to find this brick-lined 16th century wine cellar. Candlelight and simplicity help to define it as something better than average. The big feature remains the list of 130 beers including brews from Ellezelloise, Van Eecke, Abbaye des Rocs and others. Food is limited to light snacks. Good range of single malts. Occasional live music at weekends. No frills, but worth the slight trek off the beaten track.

CLOSED SUNDAY
Sat 18.00–02.00
Other days 16.00–02.00

Spinnekopke

1 Place du Jardin aux Fleurs
T 02 511 86 95   **F** 02 513 24 97
www.spinnekopke.be

Our old friend the "Little Spider's Head" is a reliable traditional restaurant cum brown café famed for the culinary bias of its longtime owner Jean Rodriguez, who wrote "Cuisine Facile à la Bière". To find it, head three blocks west from Grand'Place to Rue d'Artevelde to where Rue Pletinckx and Rue des Six Jetons both bring you to the unpromising square where it lies. The list of 90 beers includes a dry, spritzy Cantillon draught lambic and may feature the rare draught Faro, as well as a good range of 75cl bottles, particularly Wallonian. Eat here (12.00–15.00; 18.00–23.00) if you like your cooking good but not prissy. Booking is advised, especially in the evenings and can be done through the website. Dropping in for a beer is acceptable in the afternoons if you want an idea of what you are missing.

CLOSED SUNDAY
Mon–Fri 11.00–23.00; *Sat* 18.00–23.00

OTHER BRUSSELS CAFÉS:

Unless stated otherwise, the cafés below sell between thirty and forty beers, with few surprises.

The **Mort Subite** (7 Rue Montagne aux Herbes Potagères – **T** 02 513 13 18 – Su 12.00–01.00; others 10.00–01.00) beyond the Galeries Royale St. Hubert from Grand'Place is named after a card game. It may be the best surviving fin de siècle long bar on the planet. Drink gueuze sur lie from Mort Subite and nibble *tête pressée* or *kip-kap*, while uniformed staff police rows of tables with a practiced disdain designed to make drinkers feel good about sitting on bench seats.

For splendour and decadence, seek out the hotel café at the **Metropole** (31 Place De Brouckère), particularly for tea and cakes in the afternoon. Opposite one side of the Bourse is the quintessentially Bruxellois Art Nouveau café called **Cirio** (20 Rue de la Bourse), while on its other side is the larger scale **Falstaff** (17 Rue Henri Maus), a sad example of what happens when *fin de siècle* authenticity meets the stupidity of a corporate beer list.

The centre has three cafés at the end of blind alleys. The **Bécasse** (off 11 Rue Tabora) is a sedate early 19th century bar that serves its own sweet draught lambic from Timmermans. The **Imaige de Nostre Dame** (Impasse des Cadeaux, off 8 Rue Marché aux Herbes) is a brightly lit but cosy, rather posh retreat from the clutter. The **Bon Vieux Temps** (Impasse St. Nicolas, off 12 Rue Marché aux Herbes) is the oldest and classiest of the three, with lots of old carvings, atmosphere and tourists.

In the Ilôt Sacré, the **Toone** (6 Impasse Schuddevelde, off Rue des Petits Bouchers – **T** 02 511 37 11 – daily 12.00–02.00) is a heavily wooded café attached to a small puppet theatre. The puppeteers perform shows (Tu 20.30; Sa 16.00 & 20.30 – **T** 02 511 71 37) mainly in the Broessels dialect, so most Belgians don't get it either! Appropriately it sells beers from Cantillon.

The **Lunette** (3 Place de la Monnaie) is a smart, long, wood-panelled, multiply-mirrored café-bistro of a type that abounded in Brussels sixty years ago. Beers are available in litre glasses called lunettes. Equally large glasses called bottes are found at the **Ecuyer** (3 Rue d'Ecuyer), a more basic bar just across the square.

An old friend that may be returning to a beerier hey-day is the **Soleil** (86 Rue Marché au Charbon – **T** 02 513 34 30), a café that always stayed cool despite its ever-changing guises. Cooler for longer is René Magritte's local, the quietly ornate **Fleur en Papier Dorée** (55 Rue des Alexiens – daily 11.00–01.00). Its beer list suggests that René was not much of an ale man, though the fixtures and fittings are classy.

Slightly further from Grand'Place you will reach the Marolles, spreading out from the Place du Jeu de Balle. On the square itself is the **Skieven Architek** (50 Place du Jeu de Balle – **T** 02 514 43 69), an attractive café named in memory of the autocratic architect who evicted hundreds of people to build the Palace of Justice. At another corner of the square the basic but enthusiastic **Brocante** (170 Rue Blaes – **T** 02 512 13 43 – *Tu-Fr* 05.00–19.00; others 05.00–18.00) hosts life-changing Sunday morning music gigs and serves loads of lambics.

Directly up the hill from here is one our absolute favourite beery restaurants. **Restobières** (32 Rue des Renards – **T** 02 502 72 51; **www.restobieres.be** – *Th&Sa* 12.00–15.00; *Fr&Sa* from 19.00; *Su* 12.00–22.00) features a shortish but excellent menu, accompanied by hand-picked beers from owner-chef Alain Fayt's latest forays into the country. Unusual beers, inspired food, great ambience, erratic opening hours so booking is essential – they speak English.

Across the street is **Warm Water** (25 Rue des Renards), a splendidly inelegant bistro that is great for Sunday brunch or any other daytime grazing. It is also the only place we know that sells draught faro from Girardin, as well as its lambic and kriekenlambic. Inelegant in a different way is the splendidly *Marollois* **Ploegmans** (148a Rue Haute), near the Palace of Justice, for a taste of the other side of Brussels culture.

Just outside the city centre, beyond the Botanical Gardens is an excellent, courtyard café called the **Ultieme Hallucinatie** (316 Rue Royale – **T** 02 217 06 14), which has an attractive plain bar, an atrociously expensive but excellent restaurant and an in-house night-club. Its beer list has seen better days but the place remains memorable for its chic.

Off Place Ste. Catherine one interesting café worth trying is the **Monk** (42 Rue Ste. Catherine – **T** 02 503 08 80 – daily

16.00–02.00). Named after Thelonius the jazz musician rather than monk the brewer, it blends classic old design with the new social fabric, helped by an intelligent list of forty beers that features Ranke. Big on multi-cultural arts, small on food.

For an up-to-date list of other interesting Brussels cafés you can do no better than CAMRA Brussels' highly informative, sometimes obstreperous but uncannily knowledgeable "Selective Guide to Brussels Bars" (see Being There: Guidebooks).

BRUSSELS (Anderlecht)

South of the Petit Ring
🚆 Brussels South *[IC]*

Anderlecht is the multicultural and rapidly developing area that spans out from Midi station. High on ethnic diversity, poor neighbourhoods and swanky office redevelopments. The Foire de Bruxelles funfair from mid-July to mid-August fans out from here. Other notable tourism includes the Museum of Gueuze at the Cantillon brewery (see Beer Tourism), and the warmer but more chilling Museum of Resistance (14 Rue Van Lint), a collection that remembers wartime resistance movements and extermination camps.

Laboureur

3 Place de la Constitution   **T** 02 520 18 59

Archetypal old Bruxellois boozer, just off the Petit Ring near the station. The "Ploughman's" is a high-ceilinged, pew-lined, pool-playing, long café with nicotine-stained walls, well-worn parquet tile flooring and something unmistakably foreign about it. Workaday Belgium with a Greek spin. Lovely. 60 beers include a sweetened lambic on draught. Food will typically include moussaka, Greek salad and mezze prepared by Greek owners, plus pasta, omelettes and pâtés. Opens on Saturdays during the Foire de Bruxelles. May close by 21.00 on quiet nights.
CLOSED SATURDAY
Daily 09.00–23.00

BRUSSELS (Etterbeek)

East of the Petit Ring
🚆 Brussels Schuman

This area, also called Euroland is dominated by the EU complex and its parts suppliers.

Galia

22 Rue de Jacques Lalaing   **T** 02 230 24 27

Parallel with Rue de la Loi, next to the British Embassy, nearer to Maalbeek than Schuman metro station. A bustling, friendly bar with a reverend range of 60 beers, including strength in Trappists. Sandwiches and lighter snacks for absorption. Terrace outside for chat. Gentle relief from the scheming all around.
CLOSED SATURDAY & SUNDAY
Mon–Fri 10.00–19.00

BRUSSELS (Heembeek)

Northern outer suburb, off exit 6 of the Ring.

Posh suburb not far from the Laeken royal palace and gardens, with their Japanese Tower, Chinese Pavilion and royal greenhouses. Divided into Neder- and Over- parts.

Achtsen Hemel

1 Place de Peter Benoit   **T** 02 262 27 49

Neither Neder nor Over, the old main square is next to the town hall and not far from the post office. Bus no. 47 will get you here from De Brouckère in twenty minutes. The "Eighth Heaven" stocks an eclectic range of 60 beers, with Vapeur, Dupont, Silly and Van den Bossche sometimes there. Good pub food, Belgian style, includes *stoemp* and *carbonnade* (12.00–14.00; 16.00–20.00). Note the business-like opening hours.
CLOSED SATURDAY & SUNDAY
Mon–Fri 11.30–22.30

Opening hours in Belgian cafés change all the time. If you spot a set of fixed opening hours posted in a café that are different from the ones we state, let us know on BelgiumGBG@aol.com.

BRUSSELS (Ixelles)

South west of the Petit Ring

Ixelles (Du: *Elsene*) is the continuation of the city centre south-west beyond the Porte de Namur and is popular with students and university types. It is also home to the Bois de la Cambre, the city's most popular park. You will need a city map to get around but the 71 bus from De Brouckère metro, Central Station or the Mort Subite and the 95 or 96 bus from outside the Bourse are useful.

Atelier

77 Rue d'Elise   **T** 02 649 19 53

To find the "Studio" take the 95 or 96 bus to La Cimitière (Ixelles cemetery) then walk down Chaussée de Boondael past Place de la Petite Suisse to Rue d'Elise. This is a large backstreet brown café with a cave-like atmosphere, close to ULB (Free University of Brussels). Tends to fill with students in the late evening but is rarely uncivilised. The beer list of over 200 features all the usual suspects but at more sensible prices than in the city centre. Occasional live music. No food.

Fri & Sat 18.00–04.00; *Other days* 16.00–03.00

Beer Mania

174 Chaussée de Wavre   **T** 02 512 17 88

This beer shop also runs a real tasting café. The principle is you get to drink beers as in a regular café – theoretically from the whole list of 400 – but with the difference that if you find ones that you like you can take some home with you. They will even ship beer around the world. Cheese and salami only. They can do larger catering for groups of ten or more with advance notice. May stay open later if there is the trade.

CLOSED SUNDAY *(Jan–Nov)*
Other days 11.00–21.00

Brassins

36 Rue Keyenveld   **T** 02 512 69 99

This new brasserie, one block west of Chaussée d'Ixelles, not far from Porte de Namur is getting a good reputation for Belgian cooking and craft beers from

Dupont, Ellezelliose, Slaghmuylder and de Ranke. All reports welcome. 60 beers.

Mon–Fri 12.00–14.30; 17.00 onwards
Sat&Sun 17.00 onwards

Ultime Atome

14 Rue St. Boniface   **T** 02 511 13 67

On the corner of Rue Solvay, one block off Chausée d'Ixelles. The "Last Atom" is walkable from the Porte de Namur or you can take the 71 bus to St. Boniface. This successful, dynamic, light brown, airy, street corner café-bistro blends open-plan modern with touches of Art Deco. Full of potted plants and white light, it stocks around 90 beers, including everything from de Dolle Brouwers. The menu (12.00–24.00) runs from light snacks to full meals and features local and national specialities plus daily specials.

Mon–Fri 09.00–01.00; *Sat & Sun* 10.00–01.00

OTHER IXELLES CAFÉS:

If you want something a bit different then the pan-African mélange at the **Horloge du Sud** (141 Rue du Trône – **T** 02 512 18 64) may fit the bill, with forty plus beers, an African menu and regular music gigs. **Stoemelings** (7 Place de Londres – **T** 02 512 43 74 – *Sa&Su* 17.00–02.00; others 11.00–02.00) is a cosy, wood-panelled brown café in a busy little square, just off Rue du Trône, stocking fifty beers and serving limited bar snacks. Another old friend is the **Châtelain** (17 Place du Châtelain – **T** 02 538 67 94 – *Sa&Su* 19.00–01.00; others 10.30–01.00), a reliable café-restaurant on tram route 93/94 from Louisa metro. Finally, many-faceted Ixelles has Brussels' first factory pub, the **Belga** (1 Place Eugène Flagey – *Fr&Sa* 09.30–03.00; others to 02.00), part of the RTB concert hall building, which is showing excellent taste on the short beer list for its huge terrace.

BRUSSELS (Jette)

Outer north-western suburb
🚃 Jette *[Brussels–Dendermonde or Aalst]*

As well as having its own train station, Jette can be reached from Simonis metro station or by taking the 94 bus from the city centre.

There is a thriving street market on Sunday morning. It is roughly on the metro route to the Atomium and Brupark.

Gele Poraa

27 Rue Jules Lahaye   **T** 02 426 58 36

The "Yellow Leek" is best reached from Jette's tiny railway station – walk past the church and Rue Lahaye runs one block parallel to its cemetery. Bills itself as Brussels' only Dutch-style brown café and that might be right. Stocks a beer list of 80 and quite a few fruit jenevers. Malt whiskies too. Bar snacks upstairs. A weirdo worth a wander is the **Barapaat** (25 Kardinaal Mercierplein – *Sa&Su* 18.00–02.00; others 12.00–01.00).
Daily 20.00 onwards

BRUSSELS (St. Gilles)

South of the Petit Ring

St. Gilles is the area beyond the Porte de Hal. More Art Nouveau buildings survive here than anywhere else in the capital. They include Horta's former home, which is now the Horta Museum (23 Rue Americaine). A map will guide a walking tour of the area that takes in the surviving high spots. Edith Cavell, the British nurse who helped troops from both sides escape from the Great War to Holland, had less fond memories of St. Gilles. She was executed here in 1915.

Moeder Lambic

68 Rue Savoie   **T** 02 539 14 19

This small, well-used, single-roomed street corner café once stocked eight hundred beers, though "Mother Lambic" has never sold draught lambic. Nowadays we have no idea how many are in stock. The days when bar staff memorised everything have gone, so you take your chances. We guess 250 on a good day. No food as such though they have cheese. If you need entertainment, browse the collection of old comic books. To get here take tram 55 from Bourse or De Brouckère to Albert. Walking down Boulevard d'Alsembург, Rue Savoie is second on the right.
Daily 16.00–04.00

For plush surroundings of the Horta variety, reasonable food but a faded beer list, try the **Porteuse d'Eau** (46 Avenue Jean Volders). On the main square of this popular residential area of inner Brussels, the **Verschueren** (11 Parvis de St. Gilles – **T** 02 539 40 68) is an excellent Thirties café with splashes of original Art Deco, which is dipping a toe in the water of special beers with Dupont, de Ranke, Ellezelloise and others at sensible prices. Another one on the beery up is **Terra Incognita** (56 Rue de Roumanie 56), which has acquired de Ranke and Hanssens and may get more beers.

Detail from the Porteuse d'Eau

BRUSSELS (Uccle)

⇥ St. Job [Halle–Vilvoorde or Mechelen (Mon–Fri) & Aalst – Braine l'Alleud]

Outer southern suburb of Brussels on the way to Payottenland.
See Brewery cafés above (Imprimerie)

East Flanders

POPULATION (2002): **1,370,000**
MAIN TOWNS: **Ghent** (222,000), **Aalst** (76,000) & **St. Niklaas** (68,000)
TOURISM WEBSITE: **www.tov.be** (*Dutch mainly*).

EAST FLANDERS (Du: *Oost-Vlaanderen*; Fr: *Flandres Orientale*) fills most of the territory between Brussels and the North Sea, though it reaches neither. Its eastern border stretches almost to the city of Antwerp but what ought to be its estuarial coast by the Schelde is part of the Dutch province of Zeeland.

The provincial capital Ghent is built where the Leie meets the Schelde. Blessed by spectacular architecture and a central position on the Belgian road and rail networks, it has been enjoying a revival of fortunes in recent years. Access for visitors has improved so much that many Belgian regulars now see it as the most enjoyable of the Flemish cities.

North of the Schelde is flat, rich pasture-land, a popular commuter belt for those who work in Brussels, Antwerp or Ghent. Cycling down the riverbank is a good way to the provincial towns.

South of the Schelde the countryside undulates and there is even the odd hill, though the expression "Flemish Ardennes" is perhaps a tad optimistic. Geraardsbergen makes an interesting touring base for its rail connections, as does Aalst.

The brewing heritage of East Flanders has been savaged in recent years. The tradition of oak-aged brown ales associated with Oudenaarde has now all but disappeared. All the province's breweries are family-owned, many with chains of cafés to their name. Touring the area is as good a way as any to find the beers of De Ryck, Slaghmuylder, Contreras, Van den Bossche and others. Better known perhaps are the products of the energetic Huyghe (Delirium Tremens), Van Steenberge (Augustijn and Bornem) and Bosteels (Kwak and Karmaliet).

BREWERIES: **Boelens**, *Belsele*; **Bosteels**, *Buggenhout*; **Cnudde**, *Eine*; **Contreras**, *Gavere*; **De Ryck**, *Herzele*; **Glazen Toren**, *Erpe-Mere*; **de Graal**, *Brakel*; **Huyghe**, *Melle*; **Malheur**, *Buggenhout*; **Paeleman**, *Wetteren*; **Proef**, *Lochristi*; **Roman**, *Oudenaarde-Mater*; **Sint Canarus**, *Gottem*; **Slaghmuylder**, *Ninove*; **Van den Bossche**, *St. Lievens-Esse*; **Van Steenberge**, *Ertevelde*; **Walrave**, *Laarne*.

BREWERY CAFÉS

Cnudde

The brewery's only café is the **Casino** (6 Eineplein, Eine), fifty metres from the brewery gate, the simplest of affairs with a single highly unusual beer. However their beers are also found at the extraordinary **Kaffee Barbier** (140 Nestor De Trièrestraat – closed Mo; Su 10.00–13.00; others 09.00–19.00), a beautifully ornate barber's shop, most suited to a gentleman's coiffeur of the *belle époque*, which doubles as a café with forty beers.

De Ryck

The delightfully straightforward beers of the De Ryck brewery are most frequently found in one of the brewery's eighty or so local cafés. The nearest to the brewery is the **Torenhof** (39 Kerkstraat, Herzele), a traditional style small town bar. The brewery is intending to open a shop selling the 75cl bottle-conditioned versions of its four beers but we do not know when it will open.

Walrave

As with De Ryck (above), the brewery has no official tap (Du: *proeflokaal*) but its hometown of Laarne, east of Ghent, is absolutely awash

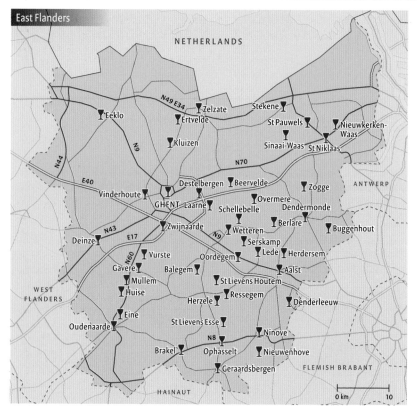

East Flanders

NETHERLANDS

Eeklo · N49 E34 · Zelzate · Stekene · St Pauwels · Nieuwkerken-Waas · Ertvelde · N9 · Kluizen · Sinaai-Waas · St Niklaas · N44 · N70 · E40 · Vinderhoute · Destelbergen · Beervelde · Zogge · ANTWERP · GHENT · Laarne · Overmere · Dendermonde · Schellebelle · N43 · E17 · Zwijnaarde · Wetteren · Berlare · Buggenhout · Deinze · N60 · Serskamp · Vurste · Oordegem · Lede · Herdersem · Gavere · Balegem · Aalst · Mullem · St Lievens Houtem · WEST FLANDERS · Huise · Herzele · Ressegem · Denderleeuw · Eine · St Lievens Esse · Ninove · Oudenaarde · N8 · Nieuwenhove · Brakel · Ophasselt · Geraardsbergen · FLEMISH BRABANT · HAINAUT · 0 km 10

with street corner locals, much-loved by flat-capped gentlemen of a certain age. This is the Flemish café heartland and it would be wrong to single one out as the best. We have rarely encountered these beers elsewhere.

AALST

🚄 Aalst *[IR]*

Large town (pop. 76,000) on the river Dender between Ghent and Brussels. A good base for touring and an interesting place in its own right. Its most famous building is the restored 13th century Aldermen's House (Du: *Schepenhuis*), with its 15th century belfry. St Martinus' church is worth a look too. Aalst is said to be at the centre of Belgium's smaller hop-growing area, though we have never seen hops growing. Its deliciously absurd annual three-day carnival ends on Shrove Tuesday and features onions.

Hotel tips: the **Keizershof★★★**, 15 Korte Nieuwstraat (**T** 053 77 44 11; **F** 78 00 97; www. keizershof-hotel.com) is a comfortable hotel with enough weekend deals to make it affordable much of the time; the **Station★★**, 14 Albert Liénartstraat (**T** 053 77 58 20; **F** 053 78 14 69) offers faded grandeur and good value; the **Lange Muur★**, 13 Stationsplein (**T** 053 77 37 46; **F** 053 78 53 90) is a low cost hotel situated above a reasonable Chinese restaurant, next to the station.

Babbelaer

3 Klapstraat   **T** 053 77 58 96

Five minutes' walk from the Grote Markt, off Pontstraat, a hundred metres beyond St. Martinus' church. Delightfully well-behaved, atmospheric place in a strange mix of styles, from religious via front parlour to Burgundian. Framed art on the walls. 60 beers including strength in authentic gueuze, regional beers and better Trappists. The menu (to 01.00, later at weekends) is on the tapas principle with fifteen different small-plate snacks on demand. Sausage is sold by the centimetre. Round the corner, the **Refuge** (10 Houtmarkt – T 053 41 03 64 – closed Fr; Sa 18.00–22.00; Su 12.00–21.30; others 11.30–15.00; 17.00–21.30) is a nice little restaurant with a beery flavour.

CLOSED SUNDAY

Wed 18.00 onwards; *Other days* 16.00 onwards

Bergenhof

4 Stationsplein   T 053 41 70 82

A simple café in front of the railway station, run with great professionalism. It gets better and better in its own quiet way. The list of 70 beers including most of the Trappists, several authentic gueuzes and some nice finds for the area, is said to have improved further according to recent reports. There is a stock of cellar-aged beers for the cognoscenti. Small snacks only. May close in the first half of June. Seats outside in summer. Please keep us up to date.

CLOSED MONDAY

Sun 10.00–13.00; 17.00–23.00
Other days 10.00–23.00

Capucientje

99 Kapucienenlaan   T 053 70 06 36

On the ring road, eight hundred metres clockwise from the Fox (below). A smart and stylish, high-ceilinged corner house that attracts a reassuringly middle-aged crowd. The main business is drinking beer and chatting. The list of 100 beers is strong on regionals from all parts of the country. Food stops at *mattetaart* and dry sausage. Small roadside terrace at the front and a function room for hire at the back.

CLOSED MONDAY

Sun 09.00–13.00; 17.00 onwards
Other days 11.00 onwards

Fox

60 Parklaan   T 053 77 43 46

Not convenient for the town but the roads to and from the motorway all converge on the massive traffic roundabout fifty metres away. Turn to go anticlockwise on the ring road to find this supposedly English-style pub. Really. Fake beams, fake handpulls, the works. 70 beers include de Dolle Brouwers. Good plates of food. A smart, cosmopolitan saloon bar that grows in confidence every year. Families welcome to come and eat.

CLOSED MONDAY; *Sat* 16.00 onwards;
Sun 14.00 onwards; *Other days* 11.00–02.00

Kastanjehof

12 Keizersplein   T 053 78 59 80

Opposite police HQ, beyond Hopmarkt from Grote Markt. Somehow if they did not tell you, you could guess that Yvette and Winnie have run this definitively lived-in long bar since 1981. Collections of things gather in corners or hang from the ceiling. Like cowbells and enamel Coca-Cola ashtrays. Above the bar are fifty pewter tankards. There are potted plants and monster sized goldfish. We liked the composite picture of James Dean, Marilyn Monroe and Humphrey Bogart being served drinks by Elvis Presley. 70 beers from a safe list with good regionals. No food.

CLOSED SUNDAY

Sat 06.30 onwards; *Mon–Fri* 08.00 onwards

BALEGEM

12km S of Ghent on N465
🚃 Balegem Dorp *[Denderleeuw–Zottegem]*

Small town in the middle of a rambling parish, in cycling country.

Soetekoeke

14 Issegem   T 09 324 88 74

Head out of town towards Oosterzele and after a kilometre, with luck, you will see the "Sweet Cake" signposted off to your left. This former farmhouse, with a small courtyard and large bar, boasts 80 beers, quite a few single malt whiskies and a good line in food. Good atmosphere, we are told.

CLOSED MONDAY & TUESDAY

Other days 11.30 onwards

BEERVELDE

8km E of Ghent off E17 exit 11
Small, unremarkable town in commuterland.

Mazure

163 Toleindestraat   **T** 09 355 39 76

One kilometre out of town on the road to
Lokeren. An attractive roadside tavern that
looks tiny but expands impossibly inside.
The small bar area branches into a large open
room with basic furnishings, exposed brick
and wooden beams. There is a small enclosed
beer garden at the back, with trees. 60 beers
include quite a lot from Huyghe and other
East Flanders producers, plus Hanssens, Dolle
Brouwers and Friart. Basic snacks include pasta.
CLOSED TUESDAY & WEDNESDAY
Sun 11.00 onwards; *Other days* 15.00 onwards

BERLARE

10km N of Aalst on N467
Schoonarde *[Wetteren–Dendermonde]* – 1km
Relaxed commuter town near the Schelde.

Oud Brughuys

55 Brugstraat   **T** 052 42 69 32

An old tollhouse by the riverside cycleway on
the Schelde's north bank, near the N467 road-
bridge. Refurbished to a high standard, with a
small terrace at the back. Just under 60 beers,
well-presented and with friendly service.
A good-looking menu (daily 12.00–14.00;
18.00–23.00) uses local ingredients and varies
with the seasons. Two kilometres down river
towards Dendermonde is the **Waterhoek** (23
Waterhoek – **T** 052 42 56 76 – closed Tu&We;
others from 11.30), a café with fifty beers and
a meaty menu, next to a small ferry crossing.
CLOSED MONDAY; CLOSED TUESDAY *(Oct–Apr)*
Fri & Sat 11.30–01.00; *Other days* 11.30–24.00

BRAKEL

12km ESE of Oudenaaarde on N8
Lierde *[Zottegem–Geraardsbergen]* – 5km
Small busy market town (pop. 14,000), on the
road from Oudenarde to Geraardsbergen.

Louvre

48 Neerstraat   **T** 055 42 13 24

One hundred metres north of the town
centre on the road to Ninove. A simple but
smart modern street corner café with a clear
and knowledgeable interest in beer. The list
of 100 includes everything from the town's
microbrewery, de Graal, plus Ellezelloise and
other Wallonian regionals. Likes seasonal
beers too. Food (11.00 onwards) is above
average pasta, pizza, omelettes and stuff,
plus chicory in season.
CLOSED MONDAY & TUESDAY
Sun 10.00–22.00; *Other days* 10.00–19.00

BUGGENHOUT

15km NE of Aalst off N17
Buggenhout *[Dendermonde–Mechelen]*

Commuter belt town (pop. 13,000) surrounded by woods that are popular for walking and
cycling. Site of a modern miracle in 2002 when
the two independent breweries in the town
both invented the idea of fermenting strong
pale ales by the *méthode Champenoise* at the
very same moment in history. Whoever
would have thought it possible?

Groene Wandeling

245 Kasteelstraat   **T** 052 34 04 56

Typical roadside taverne near the centre of the
woodland area, one and a half kilometres
south of the town. Verandah and enclosed
terrace outside. Large loungey saloon inside.
75 beers including many from local breweries.
Extensive snack menu and more substantial
meals from across the board.
CLOSED THURSDAY
Mon–Wed 11.00–23.00; *Fri–Sun* 11.00–01.00

DEINZE

18km SW of Ghent on N35 & N43
Deinze *[Ghent–Kortrijk or Lichtervelde]*

Industrial town on the banks of the Leie, half
way between Kortrijk and Ghent.

Saga

82 Markt **T** 09 380 88 60

Two hundred metres from the big church in
the centre of town, along the extended
rectangular car park that is the old market
square. An Art Deco café that leans towards
neo-Gothic. Specialises in regional beers,
New World wines and Scotch whiskies. The
small dark front bar has an impressive frieze
and monstrous black marble fireplace
worthy of a mausoleum. The rear conservatory
leads to a garden and terrace. The beer list of
70 favours longer-established micros. Food
is nibbles only. Also opens on Wednesday
morning.

CLOSED MONDAY; CLOSED SUNDAY (Sep–Jun)
Tue 18.00 onwards; Other days 16.00 onwards

DENDERLEEUW

8km SE of Aalst on N208
Denderleeuw [IR]

Strangely concocted market town (pop.
17,000) on the Brabant border on the
opposite bank of the Dender to Liedekerke.

Heeren van Liedekercke

33 Kasteelstraat **T** 053 68 08 88
E heerenvanliederkercke@belgacom.net

One of our favourite café-restaurants in all of
Belgium. The creation of Tom and Joost De
Four, whose combined culinary and cellar-
management skills have created a splendid
eating house with a wonderful beer list in a
most unpromising position. Logically you
would have thought that if a river goes
between two towns in different provinces it
would make sense to call it the boundary.
But the "Gentlemen of Liederkerke", while
on the Liedekerke (Brabant) side of the river
finds itself in Denderleeuw and East Flanders.
Here they do everything well, though at busy
times you may be dining in a leisurely way so
allow lots of time. The décor is more lumber-
jack than gentlemanly, though there is always
the cellar bar downstairs and a large terrace
extending into the garden in summer. The
list of over 300 beers is strong on everything,
though the regional brews and lambic beers
are the most impressive. They have about
fifty cellar-aged beers too. The beer menu is
well-written and helpful. Beer is stored in a
temperature-controlled cellar. The menu
ranges from small snacks to five-course haute
cuisine, with excellent presentation and a
willingness to experiment with some unusual
ingredients. If you are in for the long haul you
might consider the lambic-based aperitif.
Consider booking, especially on weekend
evenings and Sunday lunch. Outside is a
grassed beer garden and children's play area.
May close for two weeks in September.

CLOSED TUESDAY & WEDNESDAY
Mon 11.30–14.00 (Sep–Jun)
Other days 11.30 onwards

DENDERMONDE

12km NNE of Aalst on N47
Dendermonde [IR]

Market town (pop. 43,000) at the place where
the Dender flows into the Schelde. Negative-
ly adjusted by the Germans after the fall of
Antwerp in 1914. Some of the buildings in the
ornate Grote Markt are careful reconstruc-
tions. There are two paintings by Van Dyck in
the impressive Gothic Church of Our Lady.
The Begijnhof of St. Alexius, just off Oude Vest,
rewards a visit too.

Oude Vest

62 Oude Vest **T** 052 21 72 68

A daytime specialist beer café in the main
shopping street of the newer part of the town
centre. A good place for cosy nooks and an
open fire. Its name means the "Old Jacket",
which is a cool pub name in English. Inside is
classy latter-day rustic, outside is a small
streetside terrace. Serious expansion of the
beer list means it has reached nearly 200 but
brought with it the deletion of food. May
close for a fortnight in August and a week at
Easter. If you need to eat, try the
Ommeganck (18 Grote Markt – closed Wed),
which has good cooking and forty beers.

CLOSED SUNDAY; Mon 08.00–19.00
Thu 15.00–19.00; Other days 10.00–19.00

DESTELBERGEN

5km E of Ghent on N445
🚆 Gent Dampoort *[IR]* – 5km

Small suburban town (pop. 18,000),
just off the Ghent ring road R4 exit 4.

Reinaert

51 Reinaertweg   **T** 09 228 03 49

On the N447 Heusden road out of the town.
When one of Belgium's longest standing
specialist beer cafés, the Schippershuis,
closed in 2001 this handsome old coaching
inn opened on the main road nearby.
Set in the wetlands near to the Schelde it is
a simple cycle ride from Ghent. Inside is a
well-run split-level lounge with efficient
service. There is a garden at the back. The
proficient list of 80 beers has few surprises.
Food is commended, with a good range of
regional dishes.
CLOSED MONDAY
CLOSED TUESDAY *(Oct–Apr)*
Other days 11.00 onwards

DIKKELVENNE

15km SSW of Ghent on N452
🚆 Gavere-Asper *[Ghent–Oudenaarde]* – 4km
Small hillside town just above the Schelde.

Betoverde Maan

20 Kerkstraat   **T** 09 390 81 20

The "Enchanted Moon" only enchants at
weekends and is mainly a music café,
with the emphasis on a better class of
20th century popular lilts. The 55 beers are
incidental but include everything from the
Contreras brewery at the top of the hill,
plus Ellezelloise and Achouffe. Food is
limited to pasta and those foldover pizza
things. There is a flattish cycle/walking route
from the pub to the station.
CLOSED MONDAY TO THURSDAY
Fri–Sun 17.00 onwards

EEKLO

20km NW of Ghent off N9
🚆 Eeklo *[Eeklo–Ghent]*

Workaday town (pop. 19,000), on the old road
from Bruges to Ghent. St. Vincent's church
has one of the highest spires in the country.
The Stoomcentrum railway museum in
Maldegem runs a steam engine to here and
back in the summer.

Irish Pub

93 Oostveldstraat   **T** 09 378 47 01

Outside of Ireland and its cultural enclaves,
the concept of the Irish pub strikes the
Guide as an excuse to sell dull beers
and bad food as if they are Celtic icons.
Fortunately Eeklo's version is nothing
like that. This long heavily wooded bar in
the grounds of a small castle on the road
out to Oosteeklo serves an adequate list
of 60 beers and basic bar snacks. West of
the town beyond the largely useless ring
road, is the **Stadhuis van Raverschoot**
(14 Raverschoot, Adegem – closed
Mo&Tu, Sep–Jun; others from 11.00), a
canalside tavern with good food, a safe
children's play area and over forty beers.
CLOSED MONDAY TO WEDNESDAY *(Oct–Easter)*
Thu 18.00 onwards *(Oct–Easter)*
Other days 14.00 onwards

EINE

14km SSW of Ghent off N60
🚆 Eine *[Ghent–Oudenaarde]*
See Brewery cafés above: Cnudde.

ERTVELDE

15km N of Ghent off R4 & E34, on N448

Small market town, just off the extended
Ghent ring road. Home to the Van Steenberge
brewery and a café with the status of a beer
museum (see Beer Tourism).

Maple

50 Stoepestraat **T** 09 344 46 14

On the main N448 as it rolls into town directly off the E34 trunk road. Despite an increasingly urban setting, this is a country café close to a 16th century chapel that takes pride in its rustic atmosphere. This includes the friendly welcome to strangers. The beer list has settled at around 60, includes a good range of Trappists and some gueuzes. Various snacks but not full meals. They have regular top quality beer tastings.

CLOSED TUESDAY & WEDNESDAY

Sat 15.00 onwards; *Sun* 10.00 onwards
Other days 16.00 onwards

GERAARDSBERGEN

20km SSW of Aalst off N42

Geraardsbergen *[IR]*

Pleasant town (pop. 31,000) in the southern Flemish countryside, awash with minor forms of eccentricity. Its station is the end of the line for four different country routes, to Ghent, Aalst, Mons and Enghien. This makes it a good touring base. The town is built around the Oudenberg, one of Flanders' few hills. The cobbled lane from the sloping market square to the top of the hill is known to professional cyclists as the Wall. The square's St Bartholemew's church is a 19th century rebuild. At 13.00 daily it chimes the first four lines of "Oh Danny Boy". The town hall is from the same era, recreating neo-Gothic, but the Manneken Pis next to it is 15th century, making it two centuries older than the young upstart in Brussels. A plethora of piddling statuettes perch on poles along the town's streets. On Ash Wednesday there is a festival featuring a costumed parade at the end of which a local dignitary drains a silver goblet of wine containing a live fish. The audience then pelt each other with thousands of sugared buns. The local delicacy is a strangely tasty curd pastry called a *mattetaart*. We dare you to stay away.

Hotel tip: the **Grupello**★★★, 17 Verhaegenlaan (**T** 054 41 60 07; **F** 054 41 13 45; www. hotel-grupello.be) is a good value hotel, conveniently close to the station, with great breakfasts, a sound bistro and fifty safe beers.

Remembering Hell's Pils

Geraardsbergen's local museum at 26 Collegestraat includes a collection dedicated to the activities of the Concordia brewery, which closed in 1983. It is a classic example of one man's efforts to preserve the memory of an institution.

Johnny de Nie started collecting material in 1994 and has bought Concordia-related gear in Belgium, France and the Netherlands. The brewery made the legendary Hell's Pils, which featured in a memorable photo from the first edition of Michael Jackson's "Beers of the World". Their other famous beer was Arista and their cafés were once the toast of Geraardsbergen.

Eendracht

9 Markt **T** 054 41 82 80

The "Union" is a large, wood-panelled café in the market square, on the same side as the tourist office. Stocks 60 beers including Ellezelloise and Boon. These are accompanied by a range of hot and cold traditional snacks (not Su&Mo; others 12.00–14.30 & 18.00–22.00), such as cured raw bacon, smoked salmon and mixed fish. There are three billiards tables at the rear and a large terrace out front. On the opposite side of the square is the **Presse** (50 Markt – closed Wed; others from 09.30), an old-fashioned café with good *mattetaart*, fifty beers and a large collection of old beer bottles.

CLOSED TUESDAY

Mon 09.00–14.00; *Other days* 09.00 onwards

Saf

13 Stationsplein **T** 054 41 24 02

The Saf is in the long thin square between the railway station and our hotel tip. Its single, deep, wood-panelled bar expands at the rear to make it far larger than it appears. The easy-going atmosphere of a well-worn bar, plus usually efficient service. A separate room houses five billiard tables. The range of around 130 beers is less than in its heyday but remains strong on abbey beers and East Flanders regionals. The landlord runs a beer warehouse (www.sint-adriaans.be) and commissions the interesting St. Adriaans blond and dark beers. Cheese and pâté of the same name are available too, along with a wide range of bar snacks (16.00–01.00) that include steaks and brochettes.

CLOSED TUESDAY; *Sat & Sun* 11.00 onwards
Other days 16.00 onwards

GHENT

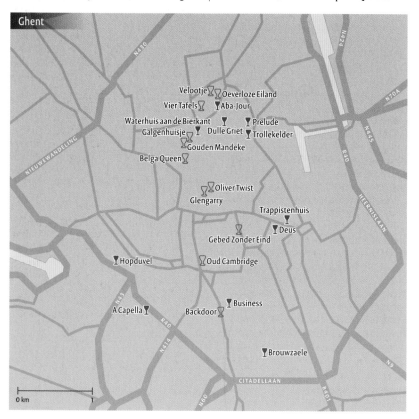

Gent-St.-Pieters *[IC]* & Gent–Dampoort *[IR]*

Ghent (Du: *Gent*; Fr: *Gand*) is the third largest city in Belgium (pop. 222,000) and the provincial capital of East Flanders. Not as important as Brussels, not as honeypot pretty as Bruges and lacking Antwerp's rugged features, it was traditionally the least visited of Flanders' big four cities. Get in quick before this changes.

Historically, Ghent is a city of neighbourhoods, its layout owing much to the fusion of seven previously separate market towns along two rivers. It was once among the most powerful city states in Europe. Jan van Gent was so famous that he even made it into Shakespeare as John of Gaunt. Hapsburg Emperor Charles V was born here in 1500.

If you want a memorable moment, sit on the quayside opposite Graslei and watch the sun set over Europe's most beautiful inland harbour, the oldest parts of which date from the 11th century.

The city's other famous buildings are the cathedral of St.Baaf, 's Gravensteen castle and the Town Hall (Du: *Stadhuis*), in that order. Most of the rest can be appreciated on a walking tour starting around Vrijdagmarkt, the largest of the squares in the town centre. Note Ons Huis, the Stalinesque HQ of the

198

Union of Socialist Workers. If you like your architecture Gothic, go sick for a month.

Two excellent art galleries are housed side by side in Citadel Park, out near St. Pieters' station – the Museum of Fine Arts and the Municipal Museum of Contemporary Art (SMAK). The Bijloke Museum on Godshuizenlaan tells the story of cloistered old Ghent, while the Museum of Industrial Archaeology and Textiles in Minnemeers, just north of the old centre, brings the story up to date.

Gravensteen castle has a museum dedicated to what the English translation calls "Court Paraphernalia". The French translation calls this "objects of justice", while the Dutch original appears to read "correction weapons". Enjoy seeing just how unpleasant it is possible to be.

The city's beer scene is really coming alive. Blame the 43,000 students who live here, a tiny proportion of whom attend the two schools of brewing.

Fortunately for visitors, Ghent's infrastructure is no longer honed to keep visitors at bay. New hotels have been fitted in cleverly all over the centre and the notoriously fractured transport network now verges on logical and useful. A good city map is still essential and may come free with the city attractions guide. As a general rule, Ghent's tourist attractions close on Monday.

Hotel tips: Ghent's hotel scene has improved a lot, though it is still wise to book ahead. Most central hotels are either expensive or part of a chain. Experienced budget travellers can try the **Flandria**★, 3 Barrestraat (**T** 09 223 06 26; **F** 09 233 77 89), or else just off centre near the **Trappistenhuis** (below) is the **Eden**★★, 24 Zuidstationstraat (**T** 09 223 51 51; **F** 09 233 34 57). Small family-run hotels offering a generally better deal are found out near St. Pieters station. The excellent **Astoria**★★★, 39 Achilles Musschestraat (**T** 09 222 84 13; **F** 09 220 47 87) is a personal favourite. Alternatively the **Ascona**★★★, 105 Voskenlaan (**T** 09 221 27 56; **F** 09 221 47 01), or the **Adoma**★★, 19 St.Denijslaan (**T** 09 222 65 50; **F** 02 245 09 37) should suffice.

Aba-Jour

20 Oudberg   **T** 09 234 07 29

The first proper beer café in the Patershol area of old Ghent, near to 's Gravensteen castle on the banks of the Leie. The name is French for "Lampshade". This long dark candle-lit saloon has an enclosed terrace overlooking the river at the back. The list of 70 is strong on Trappists and lambics but lacks strength elsewhere. Good reports about the food (to 24.00 weekdays; 01.00 weekends), especially steaks and chicken dishes. Nowhere near as atmospheric as its sister pub in Vurste (below) but a good find nonetheless.
Sat&Sun 15.00 onwards; *Other days* 11.00–01.00

A Capella

33 Godshuizenlaan   **T** 09 233 77 76

Opposite the Bijlokemuseum on the inner ring road, halfway from St Pieters Station to the city centre. This restored gentleman's residence with its elaborate portico is a quiet, comfortable retreat aimed at the more decadent drinker. Candle-lit and comfortable, but friendly and welcoming. There is a terrace at the back. The kitchen produces good, up-market cooking from a fresh menu daily (12.00–14.30 & 18.00–22.00). Wash this down with a well-chosen list of 55 beers that includes Westvleteren, Boon and several East Flanders regionals.   *Daily* 11.00–02.00

Backdoor

26 St. Amandstraat

You can tell from the fact that this place's sign contains the words "Rock-on café" that some readers may feel rather too cellar-aged or otherwise well-kept to chill out with the regulars here. Nevertheless there are 100 beers on the menu and while the music is often live it is not always loud. Get the drift on www.backdoorgent.be and celebrate the fact that Ghentish yoof is becoming beer savvy.   CLOSED SUNDAY
Fri–Sat 21.00 onwards
Other days 16.00 onwards

Brouwzaele

17 Ter Plaeten   **T** 09 224 33 92

The best looking beer café in the St. Pieters-plein area, on the canalside back route from the city centre to the station. Opposite the Kinepolis cinema. The interesting and stylish design is unchanged for fifteen years, featuring a huge circular bar canopy made from the copper lid of a real brewing kettle. The beer list of just over 100 is solid but unsurprising. The kitchen (11.30–14.00 & 18.00–23.00) serves up steaks, scampi and *Gentse stooverij*, a beef stew cooked in three beers. Alternatively try the dry sausage.
Daily 11.00–03.00

Deus

128 Vlaanderenstraat   **T** 09 233 66 06

A high-ceilinged street corner café-restaurant in light wood and glass. The triangular main room looks out onto two streets, while the bar area is virtually secluded. Opposite the main bus station and close to Ghent's rather half-hearted and dilapidated red light district. The list of 180 beers includes an excellent range of lambics, virtually every Trappist and a solid list of regionals. There is a large wine list too. Food (12.00–14.30; 18.00–22.00) dominates at times, stretching to pasta, salads, fish, steaks and daily specials. There is also a menu of smaller snacks (12.00–18.00). Hit the ground running in 2003 and getting better all the time.
Sun 18.00–24.00; *Other days* 12.00–24.00

Dulle Griet

50 Vrijdagmarkt   **T** 09 224 24 55

On the largest square in the old town. Named after a 16-ton iron cannon seen on Grootkanon-plein on the way to the Zuivel bridge. Its balls are aimed mainly at younger drinkers and it is unashamedly loud and busy most weekends. That said, it is possible to have a quieter drink at other times in what is essentially an atmospheric old pub. Claims to sell over two hundred beers, though they appear to have no list and we reckon 140 is more realistic. Food stops at cheese and ham sandwiches. A dizzying spiral staircase leads to upstairs

toilets. There is a small terrace on the square in summer. Sunday opening hours vary as much as the temperament of the staff, all modes available from open to impenetrable.
Sun 12.00–19.00; *Mon* 16.30–01.00
Other days 12.00–01.00

Hopduvel

10 Rokerelsstraat   **T** 09 225 37 29

From St. Pieters station the "Hop Devel" is a ten-minute saunter down Koning Albertlaan and Groot Britanniëlaan, left into Martelaars-laan then third right. From painful memory we know is a complicated half-hour walk from the centre. Do a taxi if you have to, but get here. Imagine a tiny old pub frontage in Coronation Street thirty years ago and you have the outside. Indoors, it is like Dr Who's Tardis, far bigger than it ought to be. Multiple rooms on two floors and a covered garden at the back. All adorned with old breweriana. Stocks up to 200 beers including the locally commissioned Stropken, a few from Contreras and other East Flanders brewers plus good lambics. Food (12.00–14.00 & 18.00–23.00) ranges from light snacks to substantial grills. Salmon, *côte à l'os*, warm goat's cheese salad and scampi brochettes are all worth trying. Service can be lugubrious.   *Daily* 11.30–01.00

Prelude

13 Bij St. Jacobs   **T** 09 225 04 04

Just off the city centre in a square of bizarrely numbered old buildings set around a church. A modern café that is arty enough to stave off charges of being chainstore. There is a small terrace outside. The beer list has risen to 80 and is strong on Trappists and brown ales. The usual bar snacks (12.00–14.00 & 18.00–22.00) are pleasant enough. A good place to be for the antiques market on Friday, Saturday and Sunday afternoons. May close in the first week of February and for most of July.
CLOSED TUESDAY; *Other days* 08.30 onwards

Trappistenhuis

164 Brabantdam   **T** 09 224 29 37

Brabantdam starts in the centre of town as a classy shopping street then does sleeze before becoming rather ordinary as it approaches St. Annaplein. Bedding in as one of Ghent's best beer houses, in what is inexplicably a preserved building. The intelligent list of 150 beers is served in civilised surroundings. Lots of breweriana and a library of beer books, in an open-plan multi-room, split-level design with an open fire. Strong on less common regional, particularly from small Wallonian brewers such as Abbaye des Rocs, Vapeur, Silenrieux and Fantôme. Good on winter ales too. Prides itself on its Trappists. Sharp efficient service is also friendly. Small snacks only. May close for the first half of August. *Sun* 18.00 onwards; *Sat* 14.00 onwards *Other days* 11.00–02.00

Trollekelder

17 Bij St. Jacobs   **T** 09 223 76 96

The "Trolls' Cellar" is in the same square as Prelude (above) on the opposite side of St. Jacob's church. Apart from the rather off-putting window display of cow-eyed midgets with Don King haircuts, the connection with trolls is imprecise. Note the painting in the main room and the strangely shaped noses of the audience. There are two storeys of wooden bar area, draped in hop garlands. Very candlelight and quiet conversation, this is often the beer café that visitors to Ghent remember with most affection. The beer list reaches 140 and includes regional, lambic and better Trappist beers. Food is now limited to cheese and sausage. They take a three-week break each summer.

CLOSED MONDAY; *Other days* 16.00–03 00

Waterhuis aan de Bierkant

9 Groentenmarkt   **T** 09 225 06 80

On the city bank of the Leie river at the hub of the city's new appreciation of itself, the "Waterhouse on the Beerside", has become a Ghent institution. Inside is a cosy, candle-lit old bar with views of the river. There is a slowly evolving list of around 130 beers with strength in regionals. A house beer called Gandavum Dry Hopping comes from Proef to owner Mario's specifications. Upstairs is the Gentse Poppentheater (puppet theatre), which plays on some evenings. The popular

riverside terrace, passed by trams, bicycles and boats but no cars, is now served also by a bistro called **Eethuisje**, with which the bar has connections. There is also a genever café called the **Dreupelkot** (12 Groentenmarkt – daily from 16.00).   *Daily* 11.00–02.00

OTHER GHENT CAFÉS:

On the direct route from Sint Pieters Station to the centre the **Oud Cambridge** (69 Neder-kouter) is a neat street-corner lounge bar with fifty beers. In a parallel street **Gebed Zonder Eind** (13 Walpoortstraat) is a seriously classy, low-key food café with forty beers and a good range of tasty vegetarian snacks.

If you are arriving from Dampoort Station, check out the **Verdronken Land** (57 Steendam – **T** 09 233 35 15 – Sa&Su from 17.00, others from 11.00), which seems to be growing a good list of unusual and well-priced ales from smaller breweries.

In the old centre, the **Glengarry** (32 St. Baafsplein) masquerades as a Scottish pub but in reality is a high-vaulted cellar sampling room for Belgium's top whisky pundit, Bob Minnekeer, to show off over two hundred top single malts and a couple of dozen beers.

The **Belga Queen** (10 Graslei – **T** 09 280 01 00 – daily 12.00–03.00) is a designer super-bar, on Europe's most beautiful inland quay, with thirty beers including draught Boon Lambiek and a few other specials. The expensive food (12.00–14.30; 19.00–24.00) is excellent but the best bit is the doors of the upstairs toilets. The **Galgenhuisje** (5 Groentenmarkt – **T** 09 233 42 51 – daily from 11.00) is the smallest bar in Ghent but hides a restaurant, the Galgenkelder (12.00–14.15 & 19.00–22.00), in 13th century cellars that were once the city's condemned cells. Between the last two places and facing the river, is the **Gouden Mandeke** (9 Pensmarkt – Sa&Su from 15.00; others from 11.00), an atmospheric boozer with forty beers.

The **Vier Tafels** (6 Plotersgracht) is a restaurant across the river in the Patershol, stocking just under forty beers from independent breweries to serve with international dishes reworked Belgian style. Finally, and saving the best till last, the Patershol hides

two other gems. The **Oeverloze Eiland** (19 Oudberg), on the opposite side of the street to Aba-Jour (above) is a seriously civilised place to sip Trappist beer, champagne or malt whisky, while indulging in tiny snacks and educated conversation. While virtually unsigned in a side alley round the corner is the plainly absurd and somewhat spooky **Velootje** (2 Kalversteeg – daily from 18.00), the cobwebbed apotheosis of brown café antiquity, hung with rusting bicycles, and brass candelabrae and needing a roaring log fire in June. Stick with Pater Lieven and prayer.

HERDERSEM

4km NNE of Aalst off N406
Aalst [IR] – 4km

An extension of greater Aalst in a semi-rural area off the road to Dendermonde.

Surprise
18 Aartstraat   **T** 053 78 89 93

The opening hours may suggest a hobby café but actually the main business here is a drinks warehouse. Off the Dendermonde road at Gijzegem, follow signs towards the town and Aartstraat will be on your left. They have 100 beers in stock but may only tell you about thirty. Bar snacks. Child friendly garden. They have a museum of 5,000 pig-related items.
CLOSED TUESDAY TO THURSDAY
Sat 10.00–18.00; *Sun* 10.00–13.00
Other days 18.00–21.00

HERZELE

12km WSW of Aalst on N46
Herzele [Zottegem–Denderleeuw]
See Brewery cafés above: De Ryck.

HUISE

20km SSW of Ghent off N60
Zingem [Ghent-Oudenaarde] – 5km

Attractive well-preserved village just off the Ghent to Oudenaarde road, with an imposing parish church. A good area for rambling.

Gans
40 Kloosterstraat   **T** 09 384 90 25

After a long run in our Belgian Top Ten, the "Goose" is probably the country café most swooned over by Guide readers. To find it follow the Nazareth road out of the village centre. Do not expect spectacular décor or amazing antiquity. The open log fire and scrub-top tables, the unhurried but welcoming atmosphere and even the forgivable linoleum floors have done-it-for-years written all over them. The beer list of over 300 is focussed entirely on Belgian specials and includes several that are out of current production. There is an enclosed grassy yard at the back and some limited play facilities for children. Although beer appreciation and nattering are the mainstays of business, the café's other claim to fame is its pancakes and home-made apple tart. There are other large snacks and the occasional barbecue has been known. They play pétanque in the garden. The couple who run the place are as authentic as their pub and demonstrate their priorities by closing for a fortnight in July/August. Opens at 14.00 on other Saturdays in high summer.
CLOSED MONDAY TO THURSDAY
Fri 18.00–01.00; *Sat* 16.00–02.00
Sun 10.30–13.30; 15.00–23.00

KLUIZEN

10km N of Ghent, off N458 and R4
Sleidinge [Ghent-Eeklo] – 5km

Large suburban village just off the ring road, near the greater Ghent docklands. The 55 bus from Gent-St.-Pieters station to Zelzate takes you to Kluizen Hoogstraat.

Bierkamer
30 Vaartstraat West   **T** 09 343 87 33

North of the village, off the road to Ertvelde. Gerten Broun has it in mind to create a classic beer café. Certainly he has started well. After training at Ghent's Waterhuis aan de Bierkant (above), he opened the "Beer Room" in summer 2004 with a reasonable list of beers from nearby Van Steenberge and friends. Since then the list has grown to 100 and

LEDE

3km NW of Aalst on N442

Aalst [IR] – 4km

Small suburban market town (pop. 17,000) with a bit of everything.

Hof te Puttens

20 Wichelsestraat **T** 053 80 51 30

A weekend-only art gallery, sculpture exhibition, café-restaurant and peacock shriekery. This place has been going for donkeys years, two hundred metres off the Wichelen road, at the edge of town before the railway tracks. 100 beers with particular strength in gueuze and Trappists. Food (to 21.00) ranges from simple bar snacks to full resaurant service and can be exquisite. The paintings are often for sale. Opens on bank holidays, plus other days by agreement. In the town centre, the **Bonten Os** (20 Molenbergstraat – closed Tu&We; others from 11.00) is a beautiful old farmhouse with good food, over forty beers and a nice garden.

CLOSED MONDAY TO THURSDAY
CLOSED FRIDAY (Oct–Apr)
Fri 19.00–22.00 (May–Sep); Sat & Sun 12.00–22.00

MULLEM

20km SSW of Ghent off N60

Zingem [Ghent–Oudenaarde] – 3km

Quiet, well-preserved village in a conservation area, becoming a honeypot for sentimentalists. Just off the main road from Ghent to Oudenaarde. On several long-distance rambling and cycling routes.

Kroon

15 Mullemplein **T** 09 384 28 20

Attractive traditional country pub set in the tiny square of this manicured village. The "Crown" is a deceptively large low-slung building. The affable atmosphere of the front bar attracts farmers, villagers and tourists. There are a couple of small rooms to expand into if it gets full and a large, plain dining room at the back. The beer list of over 100 is

features more interesting microbreweries like Hopperd, Blaugies, Fantôme, Regenboog and others. Sample these while surrounded by a collection of vaguely matching antiques and bric à brac. Although there is no cooking, with a couple of days notice they will present a ten-cheese platter for groups of four. Rave reviews so far. Opening times are evolving.

CLOSED TUESDAY TO THURSDAY
Fri & Sat 11.30 onwards (Easter to mid-Oct)
Other days 15.00 onwards

LAARNE

7km E of Ghent off R4 exit 5.

Wetteren [Ghent–Aalst or Dendermonde] – 5km

See Brewery cafés above: Walrave.

strong on Trappists. There is a good wine list too. The snack menu includes special omelettes and salads, plus a dish of the day. The rear garden is a sun-trap with a safe, enclosed children's play area.

CLOSED MONDAY TO WEDNESDAY
Sun 10.30 onwards; *Sat* 16.00 onwards
Other days 18.00 onwards

NIEUWENHOVE

9km ENE of Geraardsbergen
Appelterre *[Geraardsbergen–Denderleeuw]* – 5km

Village in the hinterland between the Flemish Ardennes and Payottenland.

Hocus Pocus

12 Nieuwenhovestraat   T 054 24 02 38

We first spotted the couple that run this place when they had a café in Payottenland. That place was interesting, this one is top quality. A multi-roomed village taverne, it offers a beer list of 90 and rising, an excellent menu and a new take on health- and witch-related decor. The beer list includes brews from Girardin, Boon, Ellezelloise, Géants, de Graal and others. The menu features local organic ingredients, strong vegetarian options and skilled home cooking. Unusually they have a smoke-free restaurant. There is a large garden outside and in case the health message really gets to you we think they hire bicycles but not broomsticks.

CLOSED TUESDAY & WEDNESDAY
Sun 11.30–23.00; *Other days* 11.00–23.30

NIEUWKERKEN-WAAS

5km NE of St. Niklaas on N451
Nieuwkerken-Waas *[St. Niklaas–Antwerp]*
Post-war Waasland town.

Dorsvlegel

155 Heihoekstraat   T 037 66 29 35

Three hundred metres out of the village in the direction of the E17, turning right. Said to stock 75 beers and serve mussels, ribs and burgers. A good pub for families, with a children's playground and games area at the back and convenient for De Ster recreation park. Up-to-date reports welcome.

CLOSED MONDAY; *Other days* 11.00 onwards

NINOVE

9km S of Aalst on N28 & N8
Ninove *[Denderleeuw–Geraardsbergen]*

Old market town on the River Dender. A possible base for touring Payottenland. Home to the excellent Slaghmuylder brewery.

Hotel tip: the Croone★★, 49 Geraardbergse-straat (T 054 33 30 03; F 054 32 55 88) is a friendly, family-run hotel with a large bar stocking the local ales.

Keizer

9 Burchtdam   T 054 32 48 48

Just south of the river in the town centre. Built in 1776, its large front room is nowadays arranged around an impressive oblong table, with raised seating and scrubtop tables in alcoves around the room. There are more intimate areas to the side and rear of the bar. 60 beers include Slaghmuylder, plus Boon lambics. Food is limited to sandwiches. There is a small streetside terrace in summer. Closes Sunday afternoon. Several other bars in the town centre show a beery interest and often stock the Cam lambics. Two worth trying are **Beurs** (2 Langemuntstraat – closed Sat & Sun; others from 08.00), a real community pub and **Gambrinus** (7 Oudstrijdersplein), which is more of a bistro.

CLOSED WEDNESDAY
Tue 09.30–14.00; *Other days* 11.00 onwards

OORDEGEM

9km W of Aalst on N9

Village on the old road from Ghent to Aalst. Hot on goat tourism. Has an impressive windmill on the Aalst road.

Bij den Bok

153 Grote Steenweg   **T** 09 369 16 83

The legacy of a classic Flemish eccentric, who had a passion for beer-drinking goats. Hence an otherwise easily missed roadside café on the main road through this workaday town becomes worthy of consideration for a night out. The beer list tops 60 and of course includes Leute Bokbier from Van Steenberge. Snacks are limited. In the small square by the church, the delightfully stripy **Lam Gods** (3 Oordegemdorp – closed Mon; Fr–Su from 10.00; others from 14.00) lists fifty beers.

CLOSED MONDAY TO THURSDAY
Other days 14.00 onwards

OPHASSELT

7km N of Geraardsbergen on N8
🚉 Schendelbeke *[Geraardsbergen–Denderleeuw]* – 4km
Village on the old road from Ninove to Brakel.

Bildeken

25 Leopoldlaan   **T** 054 51 82 72

Tantalising tips have reached us about what sounds like a great little café-bistro with 100 or more beers, a good menu and child-friendly outside play area. Said to close in the last half of September. More reports please.

CLOSED WEDNESDAY
Tue 12.00–14.00 *(Sep–Jun)*; *Others* 12.00 onwards

OUDENAARDE

16km SSW of Ghent off N60
🚉 Oudenaarde *[IR]*

On the Schelde, thirty kilometres upstream from Ghent, with direct trains from Ghent, Kortrijk and Denderleeuw. Oudenaarde (pop. 27,000) made its name in the 16th and 17th century for its verdure tapestries, featuring plants and flowers. The perversely ornate Town Hall (Du: *Stadhuis*) is late Gothic, pre-Baroque style and rather nice. There is a permanent tapestry exhibition in the Cloth Hall (Du: *Lakenhalle*) next door. Winston Churchill's ancestor, the Duke of Marlborough,

tonked the French here in 1708. Until recently the town was also famed for its oak-aged brown ales, now largely deceased.

Hotel tip: the Zalm★★★, 4 Hoogstraat (**T** 055 31 13 14; **F** 055 31 84 40) is a friendly, family-run hotel that was revamped a few years ago, bringing modern, functional bedrooms in contrast to ornate public areas.

Cridts

58 Markt   **T** 055 31 17 78

With rumours of brewing possibly returning to the old Liefmans plant in the town, the Guide feels obliged to continue mentioning the place. On the main square, this typical small town café-tea-room was once owned by the defunct Clarysse brewery. Since its closure the beer list has risen to 50. The restaurant (11.30–22.00) is increasingly serious, with a commendably short menu, leaning fishwards. The towns other nice-looking places are the **Clokke** (30 Markt), with good food and the best view of the town hall and the **Carillon** (49 Markt – closed Mon; others from 10.00), which badly needs an injection of flair and effort before it takes its natural place as the town's most attractive café.

CLOSED FRIDAY
Thu 06.45–18.00; *Other days* 09.00 onwards

OVERMERE

10km E of Ghent on N445 & N407

A pretty typical East Flanders market town blessed by Donkmeer lake and the Nieuwdonk recreation and watersports park.

Elvira

255 Donklaan   **T** 09 367 06 82

On the N467 towards Berlare, in the old village of Donk, that is now part of Overmere. At the urban end of the water park. This splendid, hundred-year-old, family-run café-restaurant seems to do everything well. 80 beers include some unusually good regionals. Food (11.30–14.00 & 18.00–22.00), under the auspices of masterchef Sven Bogaert, consists of a full bar menu or a restaurant offering anything up to a seven course à la carte dining extravaganza. One speciality is *danseresjes*, which we believe is fresh-water eel from the lake. After lunch you can hire a canoe, rowing boat or pedalo. A splendid day out. **CLOSED TUESDAY** Mon 10.15–18.00; *Other days* 10.15–23.45

RESSEGEM

10km WSW of Aalst off N46
Herzele *[Geraardsbergen–Denderleeuw]* – 4km Village near Herzele, the home of De Ryck brewery and Herzeele Castle.

Galerie 21

21 Blauwstraat **T** 053 62 40 37

Modern bistro in a quiet village, looking somewhat out of place in a classy sort of way. It has a small gallery of the owner's own paintings, a photography exhibition and collection of statues. The beer list of 55 features over a dozen lambics. Bills itself as a talking café (Du: *praatcafé*) and likes to buzz to the sound of human beings communicating. Pasta and pancakes, scampi and snails.
CLOSED MONDAY TO WEDNESDAY (*Sep–Jun*) *Thu & Fri* 17.00 onwards (*Sep–Jun*) *Other days* 14.00 onwards

SCHELLEBELLE

10km ESE of Ghent on the N416
Schellebelle *[Wetteren–Aalst or Dendermonde]* – 2km
Small town on the south bank of the Schelde.

Veer

2 Hoogstraat **T** 09 369 29 76

At the end of the high street in the centre of town, ten minutes' walk from the station. Smart upscale bar with no-smoking and children's areas housed in a striking 17th century building. Caters for everyone, from the old boys playing cards to families escaping shopping expeditions. It has built up a list of over 90 beers including a few unusual 75cl bottles. Bar meals (Fri–Sun) include *waterzooi*, pasta and *vispannetje*. There are pancakes on other evenings. Two outside terraces for sunlight and shade.
CLOSED WEDNESDAY; *Tue* 19.00 onwards *Sun* 10.30 onwards; *Other days* 14.00 onwards

SERSKAMP

10km NW of Aalst off N412 & N416
Serskamp *[Wetteren–Aalst]*
Village off the beaten track in a major commuter belt.

Eirekluts

6 Biesakker **T** 09 369 88 48

Four hundred metres from the neo-Gothic church of St. Dennis. From the station, it is two left turns off the road into the village. The name means, roughly, "Scrambled Egg". Smallish old-fangled bar inside and a larger terrace outdoors. Nearly 140 beers, including all Trappists and a surprising range of lambics. Good wine list too. Bar snacks include pancakes, summer and winter salads, croques, pasta and of course egg dishes. There is a glorified sandpit for younger children. Opens at 15.00 in summer.
CLOSED TUESDAY & WEDNESDAY *Sun* 11.30 onwards; *Other days* 16.00 onwards

SINAAI-WAAS

8km W of St. Niklaas off N70
Small old Waasland town popular with commuters.

Ster

78 Dries **T** 03 772 1679

A typical small-town taverne on the main square, smoothed down to a timeless operation. Not a great beer specialist though its list reaches 55 and includes some house beers that we think come from Van Steenberge. On the other hand the food (11.30–22.00) is top notch, with fresh ingredients and changing specials daily.
CLOSED WEDNESDAY
CLOSED THURSDAY (*Oct–Apr*)
Other days 11.00–01.00

SINT LIEVENS ESSE

15km SW of Aalst off N8 & N42
Small country town off the road from Ghent to the Ardennes, home of the Van Den Bossche brewery.

Fonteintje

45 Gentweg T 054 50 03 77

On the N42 Zottegem to Geraardsbergen road, two kilometres from the town centre. A smart, attractive, well-managed, solid, brick-built inn with a large terrace and two well-kept gardens. The open plan modern main bar is split into smaller areas. There is a wood-burning fire and fully antlered stag's head. A conservatory at the back overlooks an attractive, lawned garden and the "Little Fountain" after which it is named. There are 170 beers on a well-designed list that includes many regionals and abbey beers, plus everything from Van Den Bossche. The menu stretches from light snacks to big steaks via fish and local specialities. May close for two weeks in mid-September.
CLOSED TUESDAY & WEDNESDAY
Other days 12.00–14.00; 16.00 onwards

Tramstatie

30 Kauwstraat T 054 50 21 04

At the other end of town, on the road to St. Antelinks. The "Tram Station" is a striking building that was once exactly what it is called. Nowadays it is all floral curtains, tablecloths and old brewery posters. The high-ceilinged main bar has a fireplace and stove. The list of 110 beers includes a bit of everything. The conservatory restaurant offers steaks, fish dishes and some local dishes, including some cooked in beer. There are pancakes too. Opens on Mondays (from 18.00) in July & August.
CLOSED MONDAY TO WEDNESDAY
Thu 18.00 onwards
Fri & Sat 17.00 onwards; *Sun* 12.00 onwards

SINT LIEVENS HOUTEM

12km WSW of Aalst off N42
Herzele [*Geraardsbergen–Denderleeuw*] – 4km

Small market town at the meeting point of three long-distance footpaths.

Gouden Leeuw

56 Marktplein T 053 62 25 94

On the second largest market square in Belgium, so they say. A typical town pub, now boasting a small hotel wing – no details. Stocks 70 beers. Home-made specials and a growing snacks list, plus their own ice cream. Large terrace at the front except on market days. Out the back is a bouncy castle and ball bath (ask a parent). We assume they get their beers from the Pede warehouse in Doelstraat (see Beer Shops & warehouses), opposite which is a plain café called the **Graantje**.
CLOSED MONDAY; *Other days* 08.30 onwards

Groene Dal

9 Cotthem T 09 360 69 19

From Marktplein take the road signposted Zottegem. After eight hundred metres on the left, just after the town boundary, a lane called Cotthem branches left across the fields. Six hundred metres down this are two contrasting cafés. The "Greendale" is straight out of a posh magazine, with huge conservatories, a nice garden, lacquered ornaments and lace trimmings. Its 70 beers accompany a fine-looking menu that features a variety of house specials.
CLOSED MONDAY; *Other days* 11.30–23.00

Pikardijn

6 Cotthem T 09 360 51 28

On the other side of the road is an equally well-managed country pub of an entirely different genre. This splendid multi-roomed alehouse keeps a list of 220 beers, including Contreras and a large range of 75cl bottles, some very rare and unusual. Helpful advice comes from the beer list and the owners. Inside are several small rooms decorated with breweriana, including a poignant notice of sale for "a modern brewery and lemonade manufacturer of St. Lievens Houtem", dated ten weeks after D-Day. Old wooden furnishings and candles on the table. There is a covered terrace, garden and children's play areas. A variety of hot and cold snacks includes brochettes in various sauces. One of Belgium's best country pubs. May open on Wednesdays and Thursdays in high summer.

CLOSED MONDAY TO THURSDAY
Fri 18.00 onwards; *Sat* 16.00 onwards
Sun 12.00 onwards

SINT NIKLAAS

Off E17 exits 14 & 15
🚃 St. Niklaas *[IR]*

St. Niklaas (pop. 68,000) is the commercial centre of the Waasland area. The Grote Markt is dominated by the ornate Stadhuis and its forty-metre high tower, the Parochiehuis and the Old Gaol (Du: *Cipierage*). Just off the square, St. Niklaaskerk and newer Onze-Lieve-Vrouwkerk are worth a peek. The presence here of the Zythos national beer festival in March of each year has yet to impact greatly on the beer scene.

Tropical
1 Hospitaalstraat   **T** 03 766 35 17

From Grote Markt take Apostelstraat into Warburgstraat and then Hospitaalstraat. It is close to the Maria Midelares hospital. A great little single-room street corner café with warm yellow walls and lots of old breweriana. Includes a collection of beer bottles and an enamel sign promising "Extra Special Slag", which is only funny in English. The beer list of 90 includes the better Trappists, some authentic lambic beers and a wide range of better regionals. The knowledgeable young owner is happy to chat in English to visiting beer lovers. Food is limited to simple snacks. Note the early closing. May close for the first three weeks of July and to date has not opened during the Zythos festival.

CLOSED MONDAY (*all year*)
CLOSED SATURDAY & SUNDAY (*Jan–Apr*)
Sun 14.00–20.00; *Other days* 11.00–20.00

SINT PAUWELS

20km W of Antwerp on N403
Village on the main road from St. Niklaas to the Dutch border.

Grouwesteen
11 Grouwesteenstraat   **T** 037 76 66 06

This may be the last time we include this veteran beer café. The "Grey Stone", a converted farmhouse with a covered veranda, recently became a weekend café and dropped its list to 50, so we fear it is on the way out. Entering the town from the north, turn right at the church and you will eventually find Grouwesteenstraat on your left.

CLOSED MONDAY TO THURSDAY
Other days 12.00 onwards

STEKENE

10km NW of St. Niklaas on N41

Small Waasland town (pop. 17,000) with a 13th century church, and a town hall that looks like the Magic Castle at Disneyland Paris.

Filosoof
20 Polenlaan   **T** 03 779 95 49

Just off the main square in the direction of St. Gillis-Waas. Mildly eccentric single room café, split into three distinct sections. The covered patio can feel like drinking in a garden centre. The beer list of 53 would not get into the Guide elsewhere but scrapes in because this is Waasland and nobody has taken the serious beer café plunge yet. Interest in food is expanding.
Daily 10.30 onwards

VINDERHOUTE

6km NW of Ghent on N9, off R4
🚃 Drongen *[Ghent–Aalter]* – 4km
Small industrial town off the Ghent ring road.

Gloriette
93 Gavergrachtstraat   **T** 09 227 94 54

Postally in Drongen but easier to find by taking the Drongen road south out of Vinderhoute and turning right onto Gaversgrachtstraat. A rather ornate weekend café with a homely feel. Stocks over 70 beers. Serves up good snacks and "Grandmother style" cooking.

More reports please.
CLOSED MONDAY TO THURSDAY
Fri & Sat 15.00 onwards
Sun 10.00–12.30; 14.30–22.00

VURSTE

10 km S of Ghent off N60
🚃 Eke-Nazareth *[Ghent–Oudenaarde]* – 5km
Commuter village south of Ghent.

Gulzigen Bok
48 Gentweg   **T** 09 384 75 72

The "Gluttonous Goat" is a real gem. Created from a minimally converted farmhouse, its single dining and drinking area has the feel of a village school assembly room with a few rickety-rackety tables and chairs. Old photographs, a few agricultural implements and a dab of art adorn the walls. The beer list of 80 includes the local Contreras, some good West Flanders regionals, lots of lambics and more. Food includes salads, pasta, scampi, steaks and daily specials, plus a children's menu. This is the country seat of the people who own the Aba-Jour in Ghent (above). Thoroughly recommended. There is a garden at the back.
CLOSED MONDAY TO WEDNESDAY
Thu 18.00 onwards; *Fri–Sun* 11.00 onwards

WETTEREN

10km ESE of Ghent off E40 exit 17
🚃 Wetteren *[Ghent–Aalst or Dendermonde]*

Commuter town (pop. 22,000) near Ghent, on the banks of the Schelde. A few kilometres to the north is the Kasteel van Laarne, 17th century stately home inside, moated 12th century castle outside.

Bloemenlust
61 Smetledestraat   **T** 09 369 10 30

The "Flower Madness" is in an urban villa in an upmarket residential road off the Smetlede highway on the outskirts of town. It was once the residence of a top florist and its bar room is a redesign of the reception rooms of a private house. There is a small garden and children's play area outside. The list of beers reaches 180 and includes many unusual regionals. Its knowledgeable owner runs a beer club. Ask for room temperature beers if you prefer them that way. Food includes single plate meals, pancakes and home-made ice creams.   CLOSED THURSDAY (*Sep–Jun*)
Fri 17.00 onwards (*Sep–Jun*)
Other days 11.00 onwards

Warande
14 Warandelaan   **T** 09 369 06 49

In a château-like building in a park, this airy modern café does the catering for the three swimming pools, tennis courts, mini-golf and children's playground. This is the bar that keeps André Paeleman from brewing most of his beers. Turn immediately right out of the station and keep straight on until you find a large municipal park to your left. It is around eight hundred metres in all. The beer list now tops 100 and includes several authentic gueuzes and the Paeleman brews commissioned from Van Steenberge. Food is, well, a leisure complex menu. There is live music on the first Saturday in the month. For top nosh, opposite the station the **Ouden Post** (6 Stationsplein – closed Tu–Th; Fr&Sa from 15.45; others from 10.45) is a restaurant with a beautifully restored interior recalling the old posting inns of yesteryear. It also serves just under forty beers, including some serious gueuze.
Sun 09.30–22.00; *Wed* 12.00–24.00
Thu & Sat 1.00–02.00
Other days 11.00–14.00; 17.00–02.00

ZELZATE

13km NNW of Ghent off the R4 & E34

Market town (pop. 13,000) at the northern end of Ghent's port, which is linked to the Schelde by various sea canals. A long-standing victim of the renovations to the Bruges to Antwerp trunk road (E43) and the northern loop of the R4 Ghent ring road. Proposed site of the Museum van Eddy Wally, which we hope will be a worthy shrine to the "Voice of Europe".

The Warande in Wetteren

Pare-Choc

25 Franz Wittoucklaan **T** 09 342 92 22

In the middle of the old town centre, on the east side of the Ghent-Terneuzen sea canal, at the corner of Grote Markt. An all-singing, all-dancing, long-established town centre café with a flair for décor that is well over the top, from Twenties Tropicana to American retro. We like the petrol pump. The range of over 120 beers is serious and includes Westvleteren but is part of a broader package of amusement. This includes full meals, though we have not sampled.

CLOSED TUESDAY
Other days 10.00 onwards

ZOGGE

5km N of Dendermonde on N446
🚃 Zele *[Dendermonde–Lokeren]* – 3km

Old village in the Schelde valley.

Kurosa

136 Heirbaan **T** 052 48 08 82

A new-fangled old-fangled weekend beer café on the old road from Dendermonde to Waasmunster. Building a beer list from a start of 50, accompanied by retro décor and home-made snacks. We think they have branched out into bigger cooking but you

may gather we need more reports please.

CLOSED MONDAY TO THURSDAY
Sun 16.00–24.00; *Fri & Sat* 20.00 onwards

ZWIJNAARDE

4km S of Ghent off E40 exit 15
🚃 Gent-St.-Pieters *[IC]* – 3km

Satellite town, just to the south of Ghent.

Zwarte Fles

2b Joachim Schayckstraat **T** 09 221 53 35

The "Black Bottle" is a building of classic proportions, on the old village square. It is owned by St. Pieter's Abbey in Ghent and has been a specialist beer café for decades. Inside the main bar is broken up into alcoves, cleverly designed to use natural light on its terrace and in a winter garden. Its legendary beer list has cut back in recent years to just over 80 with more emphasis on draught beers served through the impressive row of copper taps. The kitchen (12.00–14.00 & 17.00–24.00) serves eel cooked in ten different ways. Mussels, steaks, lamb cutlets and frogs legs also feature. In the afternoon there are pancakes and waffles. Closes for three weeks in early September.

CLOSED MONDAY; CLOSED TUESDAY (*Sep–Apr*)
Tue 17.00 onwards (*May–Sep*)
Other days 11.30 onwards

Flemish Brabant

POPULATION (2002): **1,020.000**
MAIN TOWN: **Leuven** (88,000)
TOURISM WEBSITE: **www.vlaamsbrabant.be** (*Dutch only – follow Ontspannen*).

FLEMISH BRABANT (Du: *Vlaams-Brabant*) is the larger, northern chunk of the old province of Brabant. Much of its western half is part of greater Brussels, its once fertile plains strafed by the commercial spurs of the city. Of most interest to beer lovers is the sprawl of semi-rural villages immediately west and south of the capital, called Payottenland (Du: *Pajottenland*; Fr: *La Payotte*).

Payottenland is the centre of lambic brewing. The River Senne, a modest stream that runs through the area and on under Brussels, is to beers of spontaneous fermentation what the Spey is to Scotch whiskey. For more about the area and its traditional cafés see Lambic Country on page 225.

The province's administrative centre and largest city is Leuven (Fr: *Louvain*), home to the corporate HQ of global beer maker InBev and to Flanders' leading university. Most visitors remember it for the magnificent Gothic architecture of its old centre.

The area east of Leuven is Hageland. The traditional rolling fields of old Brabant are more in evidence here, especially when you get off the main highways into farming country where fruit crops include the modest revival of Belgian wine-making.

All but one of the world's official lambic brewers and blenders lie in the province – Drie Fonteinen, Girardin, Boon, Mort Subite (SCAM), Timmermans, Lindemans, De Troch, Belle Vue (InBev), Hanssens and de Cam.

At the opposite end of the spectrum are InBev's lager brewery at Leuven and ale brewery at Hoegaarden. Heineken's only Belgian holding, Affligem, lies between Brussels and Aalst and two of Belgium's largest independents, Haacht and Palm also brew here.

BREWERIES: **Affligem** (Heineken), *Opwijk*; **Angerik**, *Zellik*; **Belle Vue** (InBev), *Sint-Pieters-Leeuw*; **Boon**, *Lembeek*; **De Block**, *Peizegem-Merchtem*; **De Troch**, *Ternat*; **Domus**, *Leuven*; **Drie Fonteinen**, *Beersel*; **Duysters**, *Diest*; **Girardin**, *Sint-Ulriks-Kapelle*; **Haacht**, *Boortmeerbeek*; **Hoegaarden** (InBev), *Hoegaarden*; **Interbrew** (InBev), *Leuven*; **Lindemans**, *Vlezenbeek*; **Mort Subite** (SCAM), *Kobbegem*; **Palm**, *Steenhuffel*; **Schuur**, *Linden*; **Sint Pieters**, *Sint-Pieters-Leeuw*; **Timmermans**, *Itterbeek*.

OTHER BEER MAKERS: **de Cam**, *Gooik*; **Hanssens**, *Dworp* (gueuze blenders).

BREWERY CAFÉS

Affligem
Although it is not strictly the brewery tap, the **Affligem Cultureel Centrum** (6 Abdijstraat, Affligem – **T** 052 21 33 04 – Sa&Su all year, Th&Fr (Jun–Sep) from 12.00) at the 11th century Benedictine abbey of Affligem is run in the style of the Trappist brewery taps.

de Cam
Housed in a museum of folk art in the centre of Gooik, the **Cam** (67a Dorpsstraat, Gooik – daily from 11.00) is a typical, traditional bar that is in fact less than ten years old. The draught lambic and kriekenlambic are served via handpumps into crocks. There is also an excellent selection of authentic gueuzes and krieks from other brewers and a few other beers. The menu (11.30–14.00 & 17.30–20.30) is written in Dutch, plus a very local dialect. The brewer leads tours of the blending "cave" on Sunday afternoons.

Left: Leuven's Gothic Town Hall   213

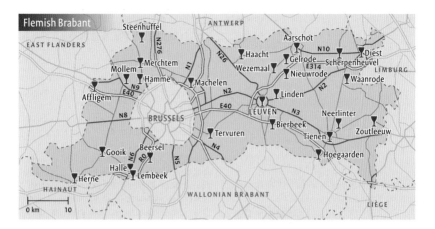

Domus

Belgium's longest surviving brewpub, in Leuven, still serves enough beers to warrant an entry in its own right (below), though sadly its own beers are now rarely made on the premises.

Drie Fonteinen

The world-famous Drie Fonteinen (3 Hermann Teirlinckplein, Beersel – **T** 02 331 06 52; **F** 02 331 07 03 – closed Tu&We; others 10.30–22.30) is a classic café-restaurant of the 1950s, built on the main village square at a time when Belgium was emerging from the deprivations of war into an era of greater confidence. This is one of the essential visits on any serious beer tour of Belgium. Until relatively recently the "Three Fountains" underplayed its role in the beer world, preferring to concentrate on its established place as a sound local restaurant with a well-regarded kitchen. Nowadays the beer side is more obvious, with draught lambic, faro and cherry lambic joining various vintages of the bottled beers. Its essentially plain Fifties interior is maturing into posh rustic, with lambic accoutrements such as porcelain crocks and handpulls taking over the bar. The menu ranges from simple snacks, through plainly cooked dishes to more traditional cooking with or without beer in the recipes. The main salon seats over a hundred and there is an equally pleasant, large room at the back for functions and overspill. There is an outdoor terrace at the back in summer. Despite this it can get still crowded in season and booking is recommended for Friday and Saturday nights and Sunday lunch. You can also buy beers to take away at the brewery counter round the corner at 2a Hoogstraat (Th–Sa 09.00–19.00). Closes over Christmas and New Year.

Duysters

The brewery's tasting café, the **Loterbol** (58a Michel Theysstraat, Diest) is open on the first Satuwrday of the month (16.00–24.00). As well as its own beers in best order, a range of Trappist beers, distributed by the parent company, is available.

Haacht

The **Brouwershof** (10 Provinciesteenweg, Wespelaar – daily 11.00–24.00) is the nearest thing to a brewery tap and serves their main beer, Primus, unfiltered on draught, in the manner of a German Zwickelbier.

Hoegaarden

The **Kouterhof** (24 Stoopkensstraat – daily from 11.00) serves all the plant's beers plus a menu of snacks and larger dishes cooked with the beers. Brewery visits are down to three a week.

Mort Subite

Bang next door to the brewery, in Kobbegem's main square is the **Wit Paard** (3 Lierput – **T** 02 452 65 15 – closed Tu; others from 10.30). This simple local café is in its fifth generation of family ownership. Mort Subite's gentle nudge towards traditionalising their products is reflected with the arrival of Oude Gueuze. No draught authentic lambic yet. Food is soup.

Palm

Opposite the brewery in Steenhuffel, the **Brouwershuis** (2 Sint Niklaasstraat – closed Tu; others 11.00-19.00, 21.00 May–Sep) on the market square, has unfiltered, unpasteurised Palm on handpump, along with draught lambic from Boon. All Palm's other beers are available too, plus elaborate food, of good quality in large quantities.

AARSCHOT

12km NE of Leuven off E314 exit 22.
Aarschot *[IR]*

Market town (pop. 12,000) known as the "Pearl of Hageland", the economic centre of this partially industrialised agricultural area.

Belang

6 Gasthuisstraat   T 016 57 17 13

Just off the road out of town to Herselt, after the Demer bridge. Quite rustic for an urban café. First and foremost a beer house. Welcomes strangers, good atmosphere. Over 100 beers including most of the regulars. No food as far as we are aware. More reports please.
CLOSED SUNDAY & MONDAY
Other days 11.00 onwards

AFFLIGEM

8km ESE of Aalst off N9
See Brewery cafés: Affligem (above).

BEERSEL

10km SSW of Brussels off R0 (A8) exit 19
Beersel *[Halle–Mechelen or Vilvoorde (Mon–Fri)]*

For fuller details of the delights of this Payottenland village, see Lambic Country on page 225. See also Brewery cafés above: Drie Fonteinen.

Centrum

11 Steenweg op Ukkel   T 02 331 06 15

In the centre of the village this classic small town hotel is being slowly renovated. But beware that progress is coming at different rates. The cosiest bar in town, with its wood-panelled walls and great atmosphere is well ahead, as is its cellar, with a revitalised beer list of over 120. The underused restaurant area has its moments too, with a menu featuring rabbit with prunes, *stoofvlees* and stoemp. We cannot however yet recommend the accommodation, which needed a lot of work. There is a nice terrace at the back and undoubtedly this is a place of great potential.
Daily 06.30–23.00

Oude Pruim

87 Steenweg op Ukkel   T 02 331 05 59

The broadest range of beers in the village is now at this excellent old lambic taverne. The list of 50 includes draught lambic from Girardin, all their bottled beers and others from Boon and Dupont. The food (10.00–22.00) is impressive too. The *schepkaas*, a stinking cheese served with fresh rolls, raw onion and lots of radish has received great praise but there are steaks, fish and omelettes too, plus game in season. Closes over Christmas and New Year.
CLOSED WEDNESDAY & THURSDAY
Other days 09.00 onwards

BIERBEEK

6km SE of Leuven off E40 exit 23
Vertrijk *[Leuven–Landen]* – 5km

Small commuter town, just off the Brussels to Liège motorway.

Molen

14 Dorpstraat   T 016 46 01 65

The "Mill" is built on the foundations of a former windmill, opposite the church in the centre of this suburban village. There is a handsome dark wood bar, with Belgian billiards and a ceramic tiled old stove. Stocks around 70 beers, including Hanssens, most

Trappists and many regionals. Food is limited to simple snacks. There is a small pavement terrace at the front and a children's play area largely hidden at the rear. They have a room for parties. Opens at 10.00 in summer.

CLOSED TUESDAY; *Other days* 11.00 onwards

DIEST

30km ENE of Leuven on N10

🚋 Diest *[Hasselt–Aarchot]*

Pleasant old market town (pop. 22,000) on the Limburg border. The station is a kilometre from the centre. There are impressive buildings around the Grote Markt and a delightful statue of a brewer at the end of Brouwerijstraat. Possibly the nicest looking nunnery (Du: *begijnhof*) in Belgium were it not for the church. Many cafés are in historic buildings.

Hotel tip: the town's most reliable hotel is the posh but affordable, family-run **Fransche Croon★★★**, 26 Leuvensestraat (**T** 013 31 45 40; **F** 013 33 31 59; www.defranschecroon.be).

Celt

32 Antwerpsestraat   **T** 013 29 08 85

Conveniently close to the station, this Belgian variant on an Oirish theme pub has few of the ghastly manifestations of pseudo-culture that smear the others of its ilk. Instead this is a chatty, affable, comfortable drinks café with a real touch of class. Beyond the obligatory imitations of Dublin's finest lies an intelligent list of 60 beers, including a good set of Trappists, lambics from Cantillon, de Cam, Drie Fonteinen and Boon and ales the Duysters brewery two blocks away. No food as far as we are aware.

CLOSED MONDAY
Other days 11.30 onwards

Ons Te Huis

11 Zoutstraat   **T** 013 31 35 35

The sad demise of the Grenadier, which had graced every edition of the Guide until ill-health forced its closure, prompted the owner of this excellent establishment to pep up his efforts to bring a range of top beers to his cellars. At the time of our last visit the range had topped 150, with a clear intention to continue collecting unusual and better quality ales, with perpetual changes but loyalty to Duysters, Kerkom and Ellezelloise. You will find it down the lane that runs between the big church and town hall to the quiet back route to and from the station. No food though they will put on bread and cheese for groups.

CLOSED MONDAY
Wed 07.00 onwards
Other days 09.30 onwards

OTHER DIEST CAFÉS:

Within the old nunnery (Du: *begijnhof*) is **Gasthof 1618** (18 Kerkstraat Begijnhof – **T** 013 33 32 40 – Mo–Fr from 15.00; Sa&Su from 12.00), a beautiful grand scale café-restaurant with a pedestrian beer list that flirts with better beers from time to time. The Duysters brewery café (see Brewery cafés: Duysters, above) is rarely open but if you want to try their beers the most reliable outlet is the **Haasken** (11 Grote Markt – **T** 013 31 13 40), which has them all on draught or in bottle, and serves reasonable food till late.

GOOIK

20km WSW of Brussels off N285

Village on the outskirts of Payottenland that is home to Belgium's newest gueuze blender (see Brewery cafés above: de Cam).

Groene Poort

31 Dorpstraat   **T** 02 532 10 21

A traditional taverne with a dark, old-fashioned interior, in the centre of the village. Not far from the De Cam museum. A pleasant courtyard at the back leads to a grassed area and outside toilets. The list of 60 beers includes draught lambic bottled beer from Girardin, plus several from Boon. Good bar food (12.00–22.00) is reported too.

CLOSED TUESDAY; *Other days* 11.00 onwards

Haas

6 Wijngaardbosstraat **T** 054 33 45 98

Built in 1870 on the road out of Gooik village towards Lombeek church. The "Hare" is a lovely rural café with a list of 80 unusually inexpensive beers. These include a draught lambic, authentic gueuze from Boon and Girardin, and regionals from Ellezelloise and Slaghmuylder. Limited snacks include traditional accompaniments. Enjoy them in the garden in the summer. There is a children's play area amid the goats and chickens. A few kilometres south of here you might check out the **Vijfde Wiel** (1 Kerkstraat, Oetingen – Sa&Su from 09.00; Mon from 16.00; others from 11.00), an old-style village café with a rising interest in beer.

CLOSED THURSDAY

CLOSED WEDNESDAY (Oct–Apr)

Fri 14.00 onwards; Other days 11.00 onwards

HALLE

15km SSW of Brussels off A8

🚃 Halle [IR]

A bustling market town (pop. 34,000) on the banks of the River Senne. The Basilica of St. Martin in Grote Markt is 14th century Gothic. There is a mid-Lent carnival. A good out-of-town base for Brussels and a trip round Payottenland. The Streekproductencentrum (3a Poststraat) is an excellent place to buy locally made lambics, wines and genevers.

Hotel tip: the highly professional **Elèveurs** ★★★, 136 Basiliekstraat (**T** 02 361 13 40; **F** 02 361 24 62; www.les-eleveurs.be) is convenient for the station and the town centre and offers sumptuous dining as well as plush accommodation.

Cambrinus

16 Bergensesteenweg **T** 02 361 43 83

A few metres off the main pedestrian street through the town, at the very beginning of the old road to Mons. There is a distinctly Dutch feel to this large one-roomed café, with carpets on the tables, fresh herring most days in summer and, er, plastic tulips.

Has a streetside terrace in good weather. Stocks 60 beers, including Westvleteren and Boon. Not much food. Usually closed for most of October.

CLOSED MONDAY; Other days 10.00 onwards

OTHER HALLE CAFÉS:

This frustrating market town has numerous cafés with beer lists in the forty to fifty bracket. In the main square the **Met** (3 Grote Markt – **T** 02 356 58 32 – closed Mo; Su 14.00–01.00; Fr&Sa 10.00–03.00; others 10.00–01.00) is a smart old local boozer with a tiled floor, lots of carved wood and a marble bar. The **Triangle** (25 Basiliekstraat – Su 11.00–23.00; others 08.00-23.00) has more food and most of the Silly beers. The **Monico** (15 Beestenmarkt) is also worth a try. The best food is at a disused maltings just off the centre of town called the **Mouterij** (20 Meiboom – **T** 02 356 50 87 – closed Tu; Su from 11.00; others 11.30–15.00 & from 18.00, not Mo).

HAMME

8km NW of Brussels off RO exit 9

🚃 Zellik [Brussels–Dendermonde] – 5km

Suburban town clumped along the old highway from Brussels to Merchtem.

Lindenhoeve

139 Lindestraat **T** 02 460 20 37

Lindestraat runs from the Merchtem highway through the old village centre and over the fields on to Kobbegem. This old farmhouse overlooks the first meadows at the edge of the village. Despite the suburban setting, there is a really rustic feel to the main bar and verandah. Young and old lambic from Girardin feature on a thoughtful beer list of 60 or so. The most prominent food are grilled on the open fire, though there are excellent salads and a variety of other dishes to be had. A superb place to end a days' cycle ride through Payottenland.

CLOSED MONDAY & TUESDAY

Other days 11.00 onwards

HERNE

20km WSW of Brussels on N255
🚂 Enghien *[IR]* – 3km

Fonteintje

69 Steenweg naar Asse　**T** 02 396 09 61

Postally in Herne but closer to Enghien (Du: *Edingen*) on the N285, near the hamlet of Koklane. Impressively large one-room café that we saw whistle up a hundred portions of spaghetti for a passing motorcycle convention. The beer list has ambitions and nudges 60 when they are all in stock.

CLOSED MONDAY
Sun 11.30 onwards; *Other days* 18.00 onwards

HOEGAARDEN

19km SE of Leuven off E40 exit 25
🚂 Tienen *[Leuven–Landen]* – 5km

See Brewery cafés above: Hoegaarden.

LEMBEEK

15km SSW of Brussels off E429 exit 22
🚂 Lembeek *[Halle–Braine Le Comte]*

Small Payottenland town, next to Halle at the southern end of lambic land. Home to the Boon brewery.

Kring

15 Stevens Dewaelplein　**T** 02 356 68 75

The café you end up in after touring the town's Boon brewery. Next to the church, in the village centre with a pleasant terrace in summer. A good example of a typical Belgian small town café. The beer list of 70 includes Kerkom and Ellezelloise, as well as everything from Boon. Basic bar snacks. They have a room for hire at the back.

CLOSED MONDAY
Other days 10.00 onwards

Below: *The Kring in Lembeek.*

LEUVEN

🚆 Leuven *[IC]*

Large university town (pop. 88,000) and provincial capital, twenty kilometres east of Brussels. You will need a doctorate before you can master the one-way system, so try to arrive by train and do the rest by muscle power. It was here that the Counts of Louvain declared themselves Dukes of Brabant in the 12th century. The University was founded in 1425 and is still a centre of influence in Flemish political life. Its acrimonious separation from its French-speaking half in 1968 threatened the stability of the nation in no small way. The Grote Markt is astonishing at night, its recently cleaned, ornately carved Gothic town hall and St. Pieter's cathedral carefully lit. The city's simply named arterial roads all spread out from here.

Hotel tips: the **Royale**★, 6 Martelarenplein (**T** 016 22 12 52; **F** 016 29 52 52; **www.laroyale. be**) and the **Mille Colonnes**★, 5 Martelaren-plein (**T** 016 22 86 21; **F** 016 22 04 34; **http:// millecolonnes.telenet.be**) are both big and basic but bang opposite the station and cheap. Slightly up-market is **Jackson's**★★, 110 Brusselsestraat (**T** 016 20 24 92; **F** 016 23 13 29; **www.hoteljacksons.be**) – no relation – a typical small town hotel just off the road from the station to the centre.

Blauwe Kater
1 Hallengang

At the end of a blind alley off the street that becomes Naamsestraat. The "Blue Cats" is a noisy, scruffy jazz and blues café that some will loathe. Its list of 65 beers is strong on regionals and Trappists. You pay a bit over the odds in order to listen to the most extraordinary collection of blues and jazz recordings this side of Chicago, some of astounding rarity. Live gigs are irregular and usually crowded. No food. There are a few seats in the alley.
Daily 19.00 onwards

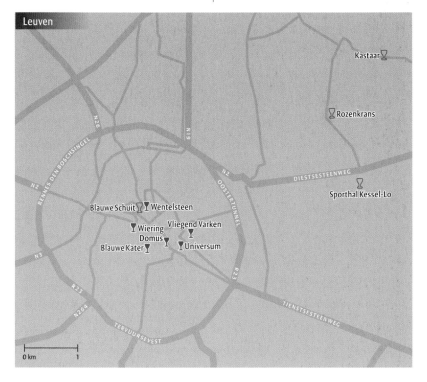

Domus

8 Tiensestraat   **T** 016 20 14 49

On one of the main streets that branch off the Sint Pieter's roundabout in the town centre. When it opened in the mid 1980s this was Belgium's first brewpub in decades. The now largely disused brewhouse is at the back of the extensive courtyard. The bars are large, modern, split-level and loungey. The beer list of 55 includes the remaining house brew and the ones that others brew for them. Service is slick, though the Gargantuan snack menu (11.00–24.00) leans towards the mundane. The restaurant menu (11.30–22.30) is a bit better. American breakfast is served until noon. Occasional live music in the courtyard includes Sunday afternoon concerts between May and September.   CLOSED MONDAY
Fri & Sat 09.00–02.00; *Other days* 09.00–01.00

Universum

26 Herbert Hooverplein   **T** 016 20 07 50

This great barn of a place, loosely based on a 15th century building, five hundred metres out of town along Tiensestraat is a popular student haunt in term time. Despite its absurd opening hours it is often found buzzing. The beer list has now stabilised around 65, including a lot of Trappists but no wow factor. Sells a lot of Rodenbach Grand Cru. Food is large bar snacks and includes chicory in ham in season.
Fri 06.00–04.00; *Other days* 07.00–04.00

Vliegend Varken

24 Bogaardenstraat   **T** 016 20 68 57

An old brown café that appears to be going red in stages as some sort of refurbishment. Some breweriana, wall seating, a brown-tiled floor and an old chimney pipe left on the wall. One main room with a bar, plus another smaller room at the back with a couple of games machines. There is a small pool room upstairs. Note the "Flying Pigs" after which it is named. The beer list tops 80 and includes Westvleteren and the better Trappists, numerous regionals but no serious lambics. Basic bar snacks (to 22.00). Middle class thirty-something music. The younger element leaves it alone until later.
CLOSED SATURDAY
Sun 20.00 onwards; *Other days* 18.00 onwards

Wentelsteen

6d Busleidengang   **T** 016 23 96 48

This high-ceilinged grand café appears to be studying for a degree in fine arts. Just off Vismarkt, which in turn is just off the city centre, in a courtyard by the Trilingue College. The beer list nearly reaches 60, with an emphasis on safer regionals. Bistro food is a cut above most of the other Guide entries. The pictures on the wall are often for sale. The extraordinary library of board games is not, though you can play them. Good atmosphere, even when the grand piano slips into concert mode.
Sun 14.00 onwards; *Other days* 11.00 onwards

Wiering

2 Wieringstraat   **T** 016 29 15 45

If you leave the bottom of Grote Markt on Brusselsestraat, Weiringstraat is the second on your left. Hidden at the back of the building on the corner is this curious split-level café that was nearly seen off by a disastrous fire in 2003. Instead it was recreated virtually intact but for the quirky wall hangings, which will take a while to build up again. Stocks a range of 60 beers. The well-practiced menu (12.00–23.00) of hefty snacks, includes grilled meats and scampi cooked in a dozen different ways. The cellar has gone no-smoking, appropriately.
Daily 11.30 onwards

OTHER LEUVEN CAFÉS:

On the same square as Wentelsteen (above), the **Blauwe Schuit** (16 Vismarkt – daily 11.00–02.00) is a loose-limbed café in French Colonial style, with a bamboo garden that seems to survive Brabantine winters.

If you fancy a short trip out of town to the city boundary then take Diestsesteenweg from the back of the station to Kessel-Lo. A right will take you down Rerum Novarumlaan to the swimming pool at **Sporthal Kessel-Lo** (6 Stadionlaan) and its surprisingly beery café. Alternatively if you take the next left into Molenlaan, you will come Vlierbeek Abbey and the highly atmospheric old **Rozenkrans** (14 Abdij Vlierbeek – **T** 016 25 63 03 – closed Mo; Tu&We 15.00-24.00; others from 11.00), which often stocks the rare Schuur beers and bizarrely makes a spaghetti sauce with Westmalle Tripel. Eight hundred metres beyond the abbey is the **Kastaar** (218 Schoolbergenstraat – **T** 016 25 61 76 – daily from 16.00) a delightful rustic brown café. All have forty to fifty beers.

LINDEN

6km ENE of Leuven off N2
🚃 Leuven *[IC]* – 5km
Suburban village off the old road from Leuven to Diest.

Hof

17 Gemeentestraat   **T** 016 62 07 39

Deceptively large Art Deco café in the unlikely setting of the off-road centre of a main road village. In the same family for five generations. Huge terrace outside. The list of 60 beers usually includes something from Cantillon and a beer or two from Schuur. Light snacks only but available till 23.00.
CLOSED WEDNESDAY; *Sat&Sun* 11.00 onwards
Other days 16.00 onwards

MACHELEN

10km NE of Brussels, off R0, exit 5.
🚃 Vilvoorde *[Mechelen–Brussels or Halle]* – 3km
Small, dull commuter town (pop. 14,000), one exit anticlockwise round the Brussels Ring from Zaventem airport.

Nova

19 Kerklaan   **T** 02 252 04 87

Large single-room café in the centre of town, near the church that dominates the main square. Lots of exposed wooden beams and a tiled floor. Old maps of Belgium on the walls. The beer list of 60 is safe and includes a house beer of unknown origin. Standard basic bar snacks include pasta and salads, waffles and ice cream. There is a small, enclosed pavement terrace. They have a function room for hire.
CLOSED WEDNESDAY
Other days 10.00 onwards

MERCHTEM

15km NW of Brussels on N211
🚃 Merchtem *[Brussels–Dendermonde]*
Small town (pop. 18,000) in suburbia, once former home of the Martinas brewery that made Ginder Ale famous.

Merchtemse Poort

2 Nieuwstraat   **T** 052 37 21 58

Near the centre of town a short walk from the big church. A smallish, single room street-corner café with a lived-in feel, slowly building

up a beery interest list. The list of 70 can include Westvleteren, Van den Bossche, lots of Trappists and some Boon. Food includes omelettes, croques, pasta and ice cream. One stop up the line at Opwijk the **Obstakel** (10 Schoolstraat – **T** 052 35 07 71) is up and coming for lambics, including draught Girardin, and a few other specials on a list of forty.
Wed 18.00 onwards; *Other days* 10.00 onwards

MOLLEM

12km NW of Brussels off N9
🚃 Mollem [Brussels–Dendermonde]

Old Payottenland village, enhanced by a couple of industrial estates.

Toren
13 Dorp   **T** 02 452 81 24

The "Towers" is an excellent village tavern owned by the same people as the Lindenhoeve in Hamme (above). Its beer list hits 60. The wide-ranging menu (*Fr&Sa* to 23.00; *others* to 22.00) features good cooking skills. Unusual wall adornments include vivid dissections of the human alimentary tract. Seats outside at the back. Easily reached from Brussels by train and also has a classic little lambic café on the other side of the church called the **Rie van Mollem** (see Lambic Country).
CLOSED MONDAY & THURSDAY
Sat 18.00 onwards; *Other days* 11.00 onwards

NEERLINTER

6km NE of Tienen, off N3 & N29

One of a number of old villages in the Hageland parish of Linter.

Timeless
46a Heidestraat   **T** 016 47 46 91

More reports please on this modern bistro-style café, found in a hamlet to the north of the village. Appears to enjoy a good reputation for food and to stock over 70 beers.
CLOSED TUESDAY & WEDNESDAY
Other days 11.00 onwards

NIEUWRODE

17km NW of Leuven off E314 exit 22
🚃 Aarschot [IR] – 4km

Straggling village just off the motorway.

Hoger-Op
31 Rot   **T** 016 56 42 63

Immediately south of the motorway exit take a highly unpromising right down Veelieden-straat and zig-zag your way to the the T-junction, where you turn right onto Rot. A much cared for country café, with glass top tables, flower vases and loyal locals, confused by visiting foreigners. Popular with billiards players, walkers and cyclists discovering Hageland. A breeding ground for champion cyclists and homing pigeons. Stocks around 120 beers, strong on Flemish regionals. Food includes a stewpot, pancakes and ice creams. May close for August.   CLOSED WEDNESDAY
Other days 10.00 onwards

SCHERPENHEUVEL

6km W of Diest on N10
🚃 Testelt [Aarschot–Hasselt] – 5km

Compact market town (pop. 20,000) on the old road from Aarschot to Diest, with a monstrous basilica, now the Jubilee Church Museum, at it heart. A good place to buy religious relics and sticks of rock. To confuse travellers it is often signposted Montaigue in French and Scherpenheuvel-Zichem in Dutch.

Molenhuis
2 Noordervest   **T** 013 29 07 56

Typical corner pub just off the Aarschot road as it leaves the town centre. An old-style café with a terrace overlooking one of the town's car parks. A place where the world drifts in and out. Two rooms, the larger featuring an old stove with ceramic decoration. Nearly 60 beers including Kerkom and a sound array of abbey beers. Omelettes, sandwiches, *vispannetje* and chicory with ham.
CLOSED WEDNESDAY
Fri & Sat 09.00–24.00; *Other days* 09.00–22.00

STEENHUFFEL

🚃 Londerzeel [Dendermonde–Mechelen] – 5km
See Brewery cafés above: Palm.

TERVUREN

This small town (pop. 20,000) on the eastern outskirts of Brussels, not far off Exit 1 of the Brussels Ring has a huge, predominantly British, ex-pat community because it is home to the British School of Brussels. A specialist beer café here would fill a serious gap in the market. It used to have the old Melydries on the Markt but this was sold nearly fifteen years ago. Intensive campaigning efforts by local British beer nuts have yet to reap serious rewards. We believe the best of the bunch are still the **Engel** (21 Kerkstraat) and the **Narixa** (67 Hoornzeelstraat). If any locals spot progess, tell us via **BelgiumGBG@aol.com** and we will be delighted to arrange loads of free publicity.

TIENEN

19km ESE of Leuven on N3 & N29
🚃 Tienen [Leuven–Landen]
Market town in western Brabant. The sugar capital of Belgium and, joyous surprise, there is a sugar museum to prove it.

Loft
11 Spiegelstraat ☏ 016 76 56 45

A most attractive bar in a modern professional style with smart service. In the town centre, down a side street between the Grote Markt and the Veemarkt. Newspapers on poles, soft lighting, Belgian cooking, smart ambience and pot plants. The list of 130 beers is still developing. Also stocks the largest variety of soft drinks we have ever seen. There is an outside terrace in summer. A discreetly separate family area at the back keeps the little darlings from annoying grown-ups without making their owners feel socially excluded.
CLOSED THURSDAY
Fri–Sun 10.00–23.00; Other days 11.00–21.00

WAANRODE

20km ENE of Leuven off N29

Large village three kilometres south of the E314 motorway (exit 24), half way between Leuven and Hasselt.

Jagershof
53 Grote Vreunte ☏ 016 77 72 29

Heading south from the motorway, turn left into the village and carry on with faith. Eventually you will spot the "Hunter's Lodge" on your left. This single-room village bar from the late Fifties, attracts customers of all ages. Quietly obsessed with great beers, especially of the Trappist variety. The list of 70 beers leans towards the unusual. No food. They have a Trappist beer festival on the first weekend in August to coincide with the village's floral festival and featuring some of the abbeys' in-house beers. May close second half September and for a week in March.
CLOSED MONDAY & TUESDAY
Other days 14.00 onwards

WEZEMAAL

10km NNE of Leuven on N19 near E314 exit 21
🚃 Wezemaal [Leuven–Aarschot] – 1km

Small town or large village with a big church.

Wisemaele
28 Steenweg op Nieuwrode ☏ 016 58 11 46

A quietly special café on the road from the church towards Nieuwrode. A single room with light wood furnishings and a tiled floor wraps itself round a central bar. A list of 80 beers includes de Dolle Brouwers, Anker and a few commissioned beers such as Ne Janneman and Drakson. No food here but you can make up for that at the town's other little gem, the **Ster Bij Boeres** (6 Kerkstraat – closed Mo; others 10.30–01.00). This beautifully restored 17th century inn near the church supplements some well-made and highly commended local dishes with fifty beers, local Hageland wines and top coffee.
Daily 10.00 onwards

ZOUTLEEUW

30km E of Leuven off N3
🚉 St Truiden *[Landen–Hasselt]* – 5km

Small east Brabantine town (pop. 8,000) off
the old road from Leuven to Aachen. Notable
for the enormous church of St. Leonardus,
which has a tabernacle boasting two hundred
figures from the Old Testament.

Leeuwenaar

16 Ridderstraat **T** 011 78 31 46

One hundred metres down a street that runs
off from the church. A convivial lived-in local
café on a street corner, with a small terrace
up front and a quiet area at the back. Stocks
60 beers on a list that is above average. Basic
bar snacks only. A more foody café that is on
its way up is the **Mirakel** (111 Ossenwegstraat
– **T** 011 69 89 19 – closed Tu; others from 11.00).
Reports welcome. **CLOSED WEDNESDAY**
Other days 11.00 onwards

Diagnosing old gueuze and kriek

It is still possible to strike lucky at times in cafés and discover a bottle of ancient gueuze or
lambic. Some of these old beers can remain drinkable for decades.

The old system of "labelling" involved daubing a white sash mark on the bottle to indicate a
gueuze and a pink sash mark to show a kriek. The maker's name was not discovered until the
cork was revealed.

In addition to beers from the remaining producers you may encounter the following:

De Koninck (Dworp): stopped making their own in 1977, though the now deceased De Neve
brewery (Schepdaal) re-labelled beers for them until 1992, and the Boon brewery still does.

De Vits (Asse) stopped making beers in 1977.

De Vits (Lembeek) is the brewery that was superseded by Boon in 1977.

Moriau (St Pieters-Leeuw) stopped making their own beers in 1981. De Neve carried on
making beers for them until 1992. More recently Boon brewery has also done this for them,
utilising small volumes of Kriek steeped specially by them.

Mosselmans (Dworp) stopped making their renowned kriek in 1976.

Troch Artur (Schepdaal) stopped making beers in 1978, though Lindemans continued some
bottling for them for a few years.

Van Den Houtte (Groot Bijgaarden) stopped making beers in 1977.

Van Malder (Anderlecht – Brussels) stopped making beers in 1986.

Wets (Sint Genesius Rode): stopped making their own in 1980, though Girardin still
produced beers for them until 1993.

(With thanks to Frank Boon)

Lambic country

If a beer traveller were to construct a perfect list of ten things to do before they died, a pilgrimage to the home of the lambic brewers and gueuze blenders of Brussels and Payotten-land would have to be in there, with a strong chance of taking pole position.

The Guide extols the virtues of spontaneous-ly fermented beers elsewhere (see Belgian Beer Styles, page 66). The other half of the package is the extraordinary array of cafés that concentrate on selling these most unusual and traditional of beers.

An essential toolkit for planning a trip to this area is the brilliantly written, unendingly enthralling and thoroughly superb *LambicLand* (Tim Webb, Chris Pollard & Joris Pattyn; £5.95 from www.booksaboutbeer.com; Cogan & Mater, 64 pp), which provides details of every known surviving lambic café in Payottenland and Brussels, plus all the information you will need to plan a longer stay.

By kind permission of Cogan & Mater we provide here a version for day-trippers.

Payottenland is a semi-rural patchwork of suburbia and small-holdings, just west of Brussels. It does not lend itself easily to self-promotion. Criss-crossed by motorways and trainlines, its old rustic face pock-marked by industrial estates and factories, Payottenland is the Belgian compromise writ large.

A hiker could traverse the area from north to south or east to west in a day. With a bicycle it is even easier. The slower your pace, the more you are likely to appreciate the contradictions and contrasts of this quietly unusual part of the world.

Having paid homage at the temple of Cantillon in Brussels and maybe taken in a few of its lambic cafés, the second phase of your initiation should begin in the suburban village of Beersel.

BEERSEL is eight kilometres south of Brussels off the E19 exit 19, on the Halle to Mechelen train line (weekdays only). The only official tourism in this superficially dreary village is its heavily moated 14th century castle. However, the real jewel in Beersel's crown is the wonderful **Drie Fonteinen** café-restaurant, lambic brewery, kriek steeper and gueuze blender (see Flemish Brabant: Brewery cafés).

Beersel's only hotel is the appropriately named **Centrum** (11 Steenweg op Ukkel – **T** 02 331 06 15; **F** 02 378 34 61 – daily 06.30–23.00). If the provincial government wants to do Beersel a big favour it will fund the major renovations required to turn its 21 bedrooms into the natural base for touring lambic country. Until then, make do with its cosy, tile-floored, panel-walled bar serving draught lambic and oude gueuze, and a menu that includes rabbit in prunes, *stoofvlees* and *stoemp*.

Two other cafés down the street warrant a visit. The increasingly excellent **Oud Pruim** has a full entry (see Flemish Brabant). At the more basic **Camping** (75 Steenweg op Ukkel – closed We; others 11.00–22.00) supporters of SK Beersel football club share space with the pigeon fanciers' club, and those on a tight budget can pitch a tent.

Sadly, the Drie Bronnen (13 Hoogstraat), which used to steep its own cherry lambic, has closed, as has the Bierhuis Oud Beersel (228 Laarheidestraat), former brewery tap of the now defunct Oud Beersel lambic brewery.

The hill from Beersel descends steeply to the Senne at Lot. The ascent on the other side towards **SINT PIETERS LEEUW** is gentle in comparison. Behind its church you will find **Herberg Moriau** (30 Rink – closed We; Th from 12.00; others from 09.30), which was formerly the base for Moriau gueuze blenders and which still influences a gueuze and a kriek from the Boon brewery.

Your next stop involves deciding your direction in more ways than one. Take the Vlezenbeek road and before you leave town you will find the **Watermolen** (34 Victor Nonnenstraat – **T** 02 377 19 91), a gourmet restaurant with a country house feel that stocks virtually every top bottled lambic to accompany splendid lunches (*Tu–Su* 12.00–14.30) and dinners (*Tu–Sa* 19.00–21.00).

Alternatively the Pepingen road will take you out of town to the ugliest TV mast in Belgium, near the base of which is the **Oude Smis van Mekingen** (10 J B Cardijnstraat – daily 07.30–20.00; closed Su 13.00–16.00), a classic front-room lambic café with gunmetal, enamel, linoleum and several generations of owner. They do not come more rustic that this, even if you are just twenty kilometres from the headquarters of the European Union.

If you like the Oude Smis and are on a

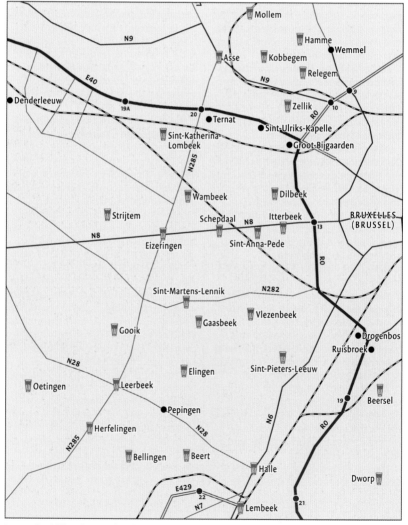

Payottenland villages known to have lambic cafés.

bicycle then a side trip becomes feasible to another simple classic in the village centre of **ELINGEN**. The **Meyts-Polle** (24 Zwarte Molenstraat – closed We & Th; others from 07.00) will surely close when madame decides that she has used her nutcrackers for the last time to uncork a bottle of gueuze.

The village of **VLEZENBEEK** too has a rural classic, a kilometre down a blind road that begins at its church as Zeypestraat. The **Kiek** (22 Donstraat closed Mo; others 08.00–20.00) is a place where farm labourers still quaff pitchers of cool draught lambic brought from the cellar in a large jug and refilled at the table.

If it is Sunday then plot a visit to the **Verzekering Tegen de Grote Dorst** at **EIZERINGEN** (see Beer Museums) for the tourist version of a working lunch. Otherwise take in the castle at **GAASBEEK**, a village with numerous cafés in different styles, on the way to the next compulsory visit.

Whichever route you take, your next stop should be **SCHEPDAAL**, where the **Rare Vos** (22 Marktplein – **T** 02 569 20 86 – closed Tu & We all year, Mo (*Jan–Apr*); others 10.30–22.00) begs your attention. On the sloping market square, this wonderful old tavern with its old-fashioned public bar and dining rooms has been doing things in its own way for decades. Cooking is hearty and traditional, from steaks and mussels to horsemeat stew cooked in gueuze, rabbit and pigeon dishes and simpler snacks. As well as a draught lambic they stock a draught kriek in summer and have their own house beer called Rare Vos, a unique draught lambic from Girardin with elements of faro that ends up with a similar character to an oak-aged ale.

Heading north from Schepdaal redbrick terraces swiftly give way to country lanes, which bring you to the village of **WAMBEEK**. Here you will encounter another fine Belgian phenomenon, the hugely popular café-restaurant at the back end of nowhere. The **Voet van Keizer Karel** (41a Klapscheutstraat – **T** 02 582 77 72 – closed Mo–We; Th from 18.00; Sa from 15.00; others from 12.00) serves draught lambic deep in toad and bat country, on a blind lane south of the village. Despite its isolation, its restaurant (Su to 21.00;

others to 23.00) is so popular that on most Sunday lunchtimes you will need to book.

To reach northern Payottenland take the road through Ternat, across the E40 at junction 20 and on towards **ASSE**. Before you reach the town you will see the **Koekoek** (200 Edingsesteenweg – closed Tu; others 09.30–19.30; closed Su 12.00–14.30), a delightful, neat roadside pub with a kitchen garden set amidst woodland and meadow. If the draught lambic here does not sustain you on your climb into town, the **Sedan** (191 Edingsesteenweg – closed Mo; others 10.00–22.00) can offer Boon's better bottled beers and a haircut.

Heading north you are now nearing journey's end. The town of Asse has numerous possibilities for trying draught lambic beers. However, when you reach its railway station you have one more decision to make.

On the Dendermonde train your first stop is **MOLLEM**, where the village church almost hides a café that is unannounced by any sign. Its actual name is the **Bij Rie van Mollem** (6 Dorp – Su variable; others 11.00–13.00 & from 18.00). This remarkable place is really a bar in the front room of a working farm, as gentlemen in need of certain facilities will discover.

On the Brussels train the first stop is **ZELLIK** where the delightfully simple **Zwaan** (539 Gentsesteenweg – daily 09.00–21.00) sits on the main road, defiantly unaware of an advancing tide called suburban Brussels, which devours the local culture one mouthful at a time.

The Zwaan is perhaps the place that most clearly tells the story of lambic and its traditions. When its owners eventually retire, will they sell it as a cheap small business that pays little for an eighty-four hour week, or as an expensive plot for development of much-desired apartment or office space? Which would you do?

A tourist slogan perhaps – "Visit Lambicland, while stocks last".

With thanks to Chris Pollard and Cogan & Mater Limited (www.booksaboutbeer.com).

Hainaut

POPULATION (2002): **1,280,000**
MAIN TOWNS: **Charleroi** (201,000), **Mons** (90,000),
   La Louvière (77,000), **Tournai** (67,000) and **Mouscron** (52,000)
TOURISM WEBSITE: **www.hainaut.be**

HAINAUT is Belgium's many facetted south-western province and for beer lovers, a current focus of great interest.

The central belt of Hainaut was for many years Belgium's economic powerhouse, with much mining, steel-making and other heavy industry. As in other parts of western Europe the post-industrial rationalisation of the last quarter of the 20th century hit it hard, not least its provincial capital, Charleroi.

With the end of mining an older landscape re-emerged, littered with the impressive remnants of an industrial past. Grassed over slagheaps from the old Borinage coalfield, stretch southwest from Mons to the French border, supporting new woodland, while the spaces between are reclaimed by agriculture. Newcomers arrive to buy and renovate houses, recreating country life for the first time since the 19th century.

Industrial archaeology dominates by sheer scale along the Canal du Centre around La Louvière. The magnificent technical wizardry of old lives on through 20th century sloping locks and canal lifts at Ronquières and Strèpy-Thieu.

But there is elegance too. The baroque châteaux of Beloeil and Attre are Belgium's Versailles and Blenheim on a lesser scale. Even the cathedral city of Tournai is beginning to acknowledge the inevitability of tourism.

Although Mons was caught in a pocket of intense fighting throughout the 1914–18 war, it has yet to display its military past in the same way as West Flanders. As much if not more attention is paid to Binche, where the Shrove Tuesday carnival has been going over the top for so long it has given words like "binge" to a number of European languages.

In contrast, southern Hainaut, the so-called Boot (Fr: *Botte*), is virtually depopulated.

At the western end of the Ardennes, with gently rolling downs and stuttering forestry it too is trying to plan its way out of economic problems.

The brewing scene in Hainaut is going places. Assistance from local and regional government has persuaded many smaller breweries to join forces. It is no coincidence that many breweries have improved their facilities for welcoming visitors to their gates.

The Grimbergen brand from the Union near Charleroi and the Trappist beers from Chimay may be the province's best-known but for excellence look elsewhere. Dupont brews beautiful ales, many from organic ingredients. The barley wines of Dubuisson deserve greater international recognition under whatever name. The beers that St. Feuillien brew at Le Roeulx are becoming exemplary.

Among the newer brewers, Géants and Abbaye des Rocs produce increasingly confident brews while Ellezelloise, Blaugies and de Ranke are now among the best beer-makers in Belgium. For eccentricity with authenticity can anyone top Vapeur?

BREWERIES: **Abbaye des Rocs**, *Montignies-sur-Roc*; **Augrenoise**, *Casteau*; **Authentique**, *Blaton*; **Barbiot**, *Ville-sur-Haine*; **Binchoise**, *Binche*; **Blaugies**, *Blaugies*; **Brasse-Temps**, *Mons*; **Brootcoorens**, *Erquelinnes*; **Brunehaut**, *Rongy*; **Caulier**, *Péruwelz*; **Cazeau**, *Templeuve*; **Chimay**, *Forges-les-Chimay*; **Dubuisson**, *Pipaix*; **Dupont**, *Tourpes*; **Ecaussinnes**, *Ecaussinnes-d'Enghien*; **Ellezelloise**, *Ellezelles*; **Frasnoise**, *Frasnes-Lez-Buissenal*; **Géants**, *Irchonwelz*; **Monts**, *Wodecq*; **de Ranke**, *Dottignies*; **Saint Feuillien**, *Le Roeulx*; **Silly**, *Silly*; **Union** (SCAM), *Charleroi* (Jumet); **Val de Sambre**, *Gozée*; **Vapeur**, *Pipaix*.

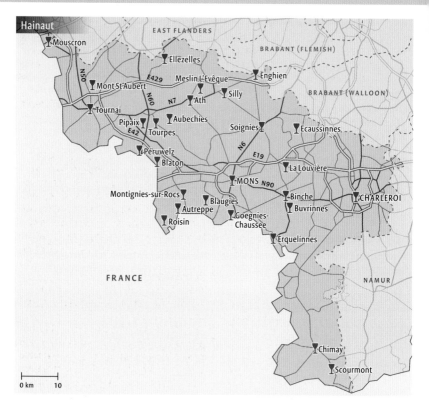

BREWERY CAFÉS

Authentique

This new microbrewery confidently expects to have its sampling room (5 Rue de Condé, Blaton – **T** 069 58 07 78 – Fr–Su 10.00–18.00) up and running by summer 2005. Brewery tours will be de rigeur we suspect.

Binchoise

In the carnival town of Binche, the **Malterie des Remparts** (38 Rue Faubourg St. Paul; Fr from 19.00; Sa from 15.00; Su from 11.00) has expanded from a meagre tasting room to a full-blown brasserie, with an emphasis on local dishes. Based in the old maltings, its opening hours may be expanded further.

Blaugies

Three hundred metres from the French border, beyond the edge of Blaugies village, this splendid craft brewery now has its own café-restaurant called the **Fourquet** (435 Rue de la Frontière – **T** 065 69 00 79; **F** 065 69 00 70 – closed Mo&Tu; others 11.00–23.00). Real no-holds-barred cooking (12.00–14.00; 18.00–21.30) includes an open grill in the middle of the bar area and premium quality meats. All housed in the relaxed and casual setting of a modern barn conversion. Beers available include the finest from near neighbours. You can hire a 30-place seminar room and a 9-bedroom hotel is promised. On Whitsun weekend the whole village opens its doors, including the brewery.

Brasse-Temps

The second in this chain of house breweries opened in Spring 2003 at Mons. The **Brasse-Temps** (Complexe Imagix, 1 Boulevard Initialis, Mons – Sa 14.00–24.00; others 11.00–24.00) is an American-style brewpub with loads of food (Su 11.30–22.30; others

11.30–14.30; 18.00–22.30) in the cinema complex of a huge commercial development at the western edge of the town, just off the road to Jemeppes. Beers include others from the Dubuisson group.

Caulier

This tall purpose-built modern brewery sits above a drinks warehouse and coffee supplier, on the same site as a petrol station, butcher's shop, greengrocery and hairdresser. Its three-storey open-plan taphouse, **Taverne Caulier** (134 Rue Sondeville, Péruwelz – closed Mo–We; Th 11.00–18.30; Fr&Sa 11.00–22.00; Su 16.30–22.00) parallels the development on the other side of plate-glass windows. The panoramic view over local terraced houses is a bonus. We hear conflicting stories about food but all their beers are available.

Cazeau

The brewery (67 Rue de Cazeau, Templeuve – **T** 0476 60 55 48) is open for the sale of beer on Friday evenings (16.00–19.00).

Chimay

The Abbey Notre Dame de Scourmont is six kilometres south of Chimay town. Its grounds and outbuildings may be visited (Tu–Fr 10.00 & 13.30). The abbey's beers, cheeses and Pinot aperitif may also be tried in two nearby brasseries. The **Auberge de Poteaupré** (5 Rue de Poteaupré – **T** 060 21 14 33 – closed Mo (Sep–Jun): others 10.00–22.00) is the official brewery tap and is on the main road. It has recently been upgraded, adding seven bedrooms and a simple menu. It is also the only official outlet for Chimay Dorée, the light beer brewed for the fathers and brewery workers. The **Ferme des Quatre Saisons** (8b Rue de Scourmont – Tu&We 11.00–19.00; others 11.00–22.00) is privately owned but works closely with the brewery. It has a large garden with a safe play area at the back and a small shop selling all things Chimay.

Dubuisson

A large modern café-restaurant called **Trolls & Bush** (28 Chaussée de Mons, Pipaix – **T** 069 64 78 68 – closed Mo; others 11.00–24.00) was recently built onto this rural brewhouse. Its attractive large, modern, stylish, bar stocks most of the beers from the Dubuisson group, including the two brewpubs. Food (12.00–15.00; 19.00–22.00) includes light snacks and bar meals. A shop sells brewery merchandise including bottles of the special brews like Prestige, that are rarely available elsewhere.

Dupont

Opposite the brewery gates, the **Caves Dupont** (Rue Basse, Tourpes – closed We; others from 09.30) is an excellent one-bar village pub with some good movie memorabilia and a rustic outlook. It serves up most of the Dupont beers, with extra helpings of rural authenticity. On the last weekend of September the whole village opens its doors, including the brewery and it cheese factory.

Ecaussinnes

The **Brasserie d'Ecaussinnes** (118 Rue Restaumont, Ecaussinnes – closed Jan; Sa&Su 14.00–22.00; Fr 18.00–22.00 May–Sep; Th&Fr 14.00–22.00 Jul&Aug) is based in an old farm just off the road from Ecaussinnes d'Enghien to Naast, just beyond the roundabout at the town boundary. They specialise in banqueting and other group visiting but many casual visitors drop in too for the restaurant and sampling café. Happy to do brewery tours when they are quiet but don't bank on it when there are coaches in the car park.

Ellezelloise

On a hill above this unremarkable small market town in rural north Hainaut an old farm looks down on Ellezelles and its surrounding countryside. Signposted off the road to Oudenaarde, the **Brasserie** (75 Guinaumont – daily 09.00–19.00; closed 12.00–15.00 Su) is a wood-lined tasting salon with a large outside terrace. This is very much a working brewery, so if you roll up just after breakfast expecting pukkah waiters in waistcoats to attend your every need you will be disappointed. Brewery tours and helpful assistance are more likely in the afternoon.

Géants

At Irchonwelz, on the outskirts of Ath, this above-average new brewery opens the gates of its impressive 13th century castle on Sunday afternoons (15.00–19.00) between June and August. There are seats in the courtyard and a sampling room inside. The brewery can usually be seen at some point.

Silly

By the time we are published it is likely that the **Brasserie** (1 Place Communale, Silly), bang next door to the brewery in the village centre will have completed its impressive revamp and be open for trade again. Meanwhile the best of the rest is the **Tonne** (19 Place Communale – closed Tu; others from 14.00) a lively all-comers boozer and general village amenity, just up the way.

Vapeur

This deliciously eccentric old steam brewery opens its sampling room on Sundays at 11.00 until it seems sensible to shut. We suggest you ring ahead to confirm. With advance notice there are eating possibilities.

ATH

20km NNW of Mons on N7
🚃 Ath [IR]
See Brewery cafés: Géants (above).

AUBECHIES

20km WNW of Mons off N526

Small village that is home to an important archaeological site and an Iron Age museum. Just up the road from the château and gardens of Beloeil (daily Apr–Nov), one of Belgium's most beautiful buildings. It remains privately owned by the De Ligne family, the sort of don't-mess-with-me aristocracy that traces its lineage back to the Holy Roman Empire.

Curoir

23 Rue du Croquet   ☏ 069 67 13 11

This smart converted farmhouse café-restaurant in the heart of the village only opens at weekends. Exposed brickwork and black, stone-tiled floor, massive bellows, potted plants and some older bits. Candle-

light, wood fires and helpful service. The beer list of 60 usually includes some newer local breweries. There is a good menu of snacks and well-prepared meals. Family-friendly and well-organised. We regret we missed the opening times.

CLOSED MONDAY TO THURSDAY

AUTREPPE

12 km SW of Mons off N548

Hamlet in the unexpectedly beautiful countryside between Dour and the French border. Great cycling country if you like hills.

Passe Tout Outre

1 Rue Chevauchoir   ☏ 065 75 90 59

A converted farmhouse at a country crossroads, which alternates between being a restaurant and a rural tavern. Inside the single large bare-brick saloon is broken into discreet areas. At the back is a large terrace with a children's playground, pétanque pitch and a huge garden with bits to explore. The beer list tops 100 and includes the full range Abbaye des Rocs and Blaugies plus much from other Wallonian brewers. There are local cider and perry (Fr: poiré) too. Food (12.00–14.00 & 18.00–22.00) is good, ranging from omelettes, croques, salads and local dishes to a changing list of à la carte main courses (not Sun pm) and a good cheese board. Opens for dinner reservations only on Sunday lunchtime.

CLOSED MONDAY & TUESDAY
Other days 17.00 onwards
Thu&Fri 12.00–14.00 also

BINCHE

16km ESE of Mons on N90 & N55
🚃 Binche [La Louvière–Binche]

Binche is the seat of the kings of Carnival. This rather dull market town (pop. 32,000) comes alive for a round-the-clock celebration on Shrove Tuesday (Fr: Mardi Gras) with a parade that was the original for New Orleans. Half of Hainaut takes to the streets, gaudily costumed as unlikely characters with symbolic roles. Less famous but there all year round is its beautiful old-fashioned railway station.

Petit Mousse

15 Avenue Charles Deliège **T** 064 77 52 52

Binche has finally acquired a café that intends to specialise in beer. At the bottom of the lacklustre main square cross the traffic lights and it is on your left. Long and loud, drawing a broad clientele. The list so far is 55 with no clear theme and only a few from Binchoise. Bar snacks too. Stays open later at weekends. If it is not to your taste, the cutest and classiest bar in town is the **Côte de Chez Boule** (13 Rue St. Paul) just off the top of Grand Place, which is on the way to the Binchoise brewery. See also Brewery cafés: Binchoise (above).

CLOSED MONDAY; *Other days* 09.00–24.00

BLATON

15km WNW of Mons off E42 exit 28
🚉 Blaton *[Tournai–St. Ghislain]* See Brewery cafés: Authentique (above).

BLAUGIES

14km SW of Mons off N549

Small village near the French border, made up of scattered hamlets. Home to the Blaugies brewery (see Brewery cafés above).

Aulnes

20 Rue Planche à l'Aulne **T** 065 65 91 15

An attractive converted farmstead at the rural edge of the village, thankfully signposted from the main roads. Majors on food and appeals to the more mature diner. Utterly *Belgique*, from its tablecloths to the wickerwork high-back chairs. There is an open range and grill next to the bar. Food appears to be available all day. The beer list now tops 100 with strength in 75cl Wallonian ales. The enclosed courtyard leads to a second building for parties. May close for four weeks from late August.

CLOSED MONDAY; *Other days* 11.00 onwards

Saline

39 Rue Ropaix **T** 065 63 12 20

Theoretically in Petit Dour, near Dour, but more part of the Blaugies collective of hamlets. This roadside relais has gone from strength to strength in recent years. Its intelligent list of 60 beers gets more interesting every time we visit. As well as the local brews from Blaugies and Abbaye des Rocs you can find beers from all over Belgium. The menu (12.00–15.00; 17.30–21.30) includes a wide range of homemade local snacks, salads and larger meals, including a sweet chestnut tart called *flamiche aux marolles* and a meat, vegetable and cheese casserole called *payelles*. The décor will not win prizes yet but there is a large roadside terrace and its popularity with the locals says a lot.

CLOSED WEDNESDAY

Tue 10.30–20.30; *Other days* 11.00 onwards

BUVRINNES

3km SE of Binche off N55
🚉 Binche *[La Louvière–Binche]* – 3km

A string of settlements south of Binche.

Fermette Des Pins

39 Rue de Lustre **T** 064 34 17 18

"Pine Tree Farm" is an isolated farmhouse brasserie just south of Binche. From the N55 as it leaves Binche in the direction of Beaumont is is signed (just) down Rue Basse Egypte or Rue Long Faulx, after the Gendarmerie. The beer list of 70 includes Dupont, Binchoise and Achouffe. Depending on the season you can lunch al fresco in the garden or dine semi-formally in front of an open wood-fire. The cooking runs from regular bar snacks like omelettes and waffles through solid restaurant fare to an adventurous five-course gastronomic menu. Service is polite, attentive and informative. They can cater for large parties with notice.

CLOSED TUESDAY & WEDNESDAY

Other days 11.00 onwards

CHARLEROI

🚃 Charleroi Sud *[IC]*

Large industrial city (pop. 201,000) at the heart of the old mining and steel-making area known as the Black Country (Fr: *Pays Noire*). It was briefly a popular destination for British budget travellers when Ryanair dubbed its airport, somewhat optimisticly, "Brussels South". Sadly all but the Prestwick flights are suspended, so the convenient public bus link with Charleroi Sud railway station, on the banks of the Sambre is quieter nowadays. A couple of cheap hotels (below) across the footbridge from the station, plus several good bars and restaurants have made Charleroi an easy overnight stay. The city centre divides into the Lower Town by the river and station, and the Upper Town, up the hill around the messy but popular Place du Manège. The Stalinesque but visitable museum of fine art (Fr: *Musée des Beaux Arts*) and the attractive but deserted Place Charles II are in the latter. The city also hosts Belgium's national exhibition centre (Fr: *Palais des Expositions*).

Hotel tips: the Ibis★★, 12 Quai de Flandres (**T** 071 20 60 60; **F** 071 70 21 91) offers cloned international adequacy, while the **Buisset**★★, 1 Place Buisset (**T** 071 31 45 88; **F** 071 31 34 14) is cheaper, individual and more basic.

Corto

12 Rue de Montigny

This cellar bar, just off the bottom of the pedestrianised hill that leads up to Place Charles II currently offers the best beer range in town though not the largest. It has the edge for its range of regional brews and interesting micros. Officially billed as a *rhumerie* it also stocks numerous rums from small producers for consumption neat or in cocktails. No food. Children tolerated till late if behaved. Loud music that goes live at weekends. Weekday opening 13.00 in July & August.

CLOSED MONDAY

Tue–Fri 11.00 onwards; *Sat&Sun* 15.00 onwards

Cuvé à Bière

68 Boulevard Jacques Bertrand
T 071 32 68 41

This long, deep, modern café with a tiny terrace, on the Place du Manège, near the Fine Arts Museum has some interesting neighbours. The "Vat of Beer" was accidentally omitted from the last edition of the Guide – sorry. For many years it has offered the largest range of beers in town, the list falling just short of 70. Binchoise, Caulier and Dupont are as interesting as it gets. Basic snacks only. Can get noisy late in the evening.
Daily 10.00 onwards

Templiers

7 Place du Manège   **T** 071 32 18 36

The city's most traditional café is on the opposite side of the square to our previous entry, separated by a car park and about sixty years. Professional service, scrub-top tables and that quiet confidence that comes with being a bastion of the community. Although the beer list stops just short of 50, it usually includes an authentic gueuze and other unusual finds for the area. Lunchtime food only (Mo–Fr 12.00–15.00), though they serve mussels on Friday evenings in winter.
Daily 10.00 onwards

OTHER CHARLEROI CAFÉS:

Two other cafés around Place du Manège deserve a mention. The **Excellence** (6 Place du Manège – *daily* 10.30–24.00), is a bright modern bistro with fifty safe beers, friendly service and reliable large snacks. The **Terrasse** (82 Boulevard Jacques Bertrand – *daily* 09.30–01.00), is a modern dark wood and shiny brass tavern with forty safe beers. Nearer to the station, the **Mille Colonnes** (6 Rue de Marchienne) stocks around forty-five beers and serves large snacks.

Opening hours in Belgian cafés change all the time. If you spot a set of fixed opening hours posted in a café that are different from the ones we state, let us know on BelgiumGBG@aol.com.

CHIMAY

45km SSE of Mons on N99 & N53

The ancient town of Chimay gives the impression of being self-contained. This is fitting as for centuries it was effectively owned and run by a local family, the De Croys. Their museum in the Château de Chimay, off Grande Place, should be visited (Apr–Oct) if only for its baroque gem of a concert hall and the fact that you may be taken round by a member of the family, with pride. Nowadays the town is more famous for its monastic beers, which actually hail from well south of here.

Casino

27 Place des Ormeaux
T 060 21 49 80

On the main route through town just off the centre, with its own football pitch and netball court. This classy remake of the old casino has glass-top gaming tables, Art Deco lighting, natty furnishings and a collection of black and white photographs of the area. 50 beers include everything from the abbey. Big food (12.00–14.30 & 19.00–22.30) features *escavêches Chimaciennes*, plus steaks and grills. In the town centre, the **Vieux Chimay** (22 Grande Place) is worth a peek for being a café cum tobacconist's and pizza-to-go emporium, though with a shrinking list of frozen beers.
Mon 08.00–16.00; *Other days* 08.00–24.00

ECAUSSINNES

25km NE of Mons off N532
 Ecaussinnes [*Braine-le-Comte–Manage or La Louvière*] – 2km

One of those quietly mad little Belgian towns (pop. 9,500), created by the merger of two villages, Ecaussinnes-d'Enghien and Ecaussinnes-Lalaing. The former is home to the Ecaussinnes brewery (see Brewery cafés above). A well-preserved 14th century castle replaced the 12th century ruin seen on the hill. Rubens' sister, Blandine, is buried in the local church. On the Monday of Pentecost, those seeking marriage gather for an annual fair in the main square, giving a new meaning to "being on the market". But if you get off on modern wonders of the world, the sight for you is the sloping lock of Ronquières, northwest of the town. Built in 1963, the principle is that two tanks of water, each three hundred metres long, counterbalance each other as they move ships up and down a kilometre and a half incline, a height of seventy metres. In summer you can visit the control tower and examine the whole thing by boat.

Vieux Moulin

1 Rue du Moulin   **T** 067 48 50 95

At the edge of Ecaussinnes-Lalaing, the eastern part of town. From its small market place go downhill, across the stream and turn right, to find this attractive converted farmhouse and barn. Choose between a large terrace outdoors and high-ceilinged beer halls inside. Stocks over 100 beers on an excellent list, that features Caracole, Binchoise, Ellezelloise, Achouffe and others. The full menu can include mussels cooked in more sauces than you thought existed and a chance to commission the salad of your dreams.
CLOSED MONDAY & TUESDAY
Wed&Thu 16.00 onwards (*Sep–May*)
Other days 11.00 onwards

OTHER ECAUSSINNES CAFÉS:

On the way from back to the market square you will pass the **Ronce** (12 Place des Comtes Van Der Burch – closed Tu; Mo&Th 11.00–15.00; others 11.00 onwards), a local-boozer-cum-restaurant, stocking forty beers with many from Ecaussinnes and St. Feuillien.

If you are going to Ronquières, the **Tour Glacée** (4 Route Baccara) at the foot of the sloping lock has well over forty beers from Dubuisson, St. Feuillien and others, plus loads of food.

ELLEZELLES

20km NNE of Tournai on N57
See Brewery cafés above: Ellezelloise.

ENGHIEN

25km SW of Brussels off E429 exit 26
🚃 Enghien *[IR]*

Another strange town (Du: *Edingen*) full of tall
19th century buildings on mediaeval streets.
Bang on the linguistic divide, it is one of the
few places outside Brussels to sign bilingually.

Rembrandt

1 Rue de Bruxelles   T 02 395 74 14

Six hundred metres from the station, in the
shadow of the massive church of St. Nicholas.
A typical town-centre meeting place and
general centre of conviviality, with a small
terrace outside. The unusual addition is an
eclectic beer list of 180, for which they deserve
more fame. The Double d'Enghien beers
from Silly are there along with many from
better-established microbreweries, though
a lot were missing on a recent visit. Plates of
tête de veau, tête pressée and Belgian cheese.
Mon&Tue 07.00–18.30; *Other days* 07.00–22.00

ERQUELINNES

20km SE of Mons on N55
🚃 Erquelinnes *[Charleroi-Jeumont(F)]*

Small industrial border town (pop. 10,000)
on the milk train route into north-east France.
Home to Brootcoorens brewery.

Commerce

338 Rue Roi Albert 1er   T 071 55 50 95

On a smartly re-ordered street bang opposite
the station. This large, airy corner café stocks
80 beers, highlighting the complete works
of Alain Brootcoorens, plus some other
Wallonian micros. Food is limited to pasta
and ice cream. They have a couple of fine
Belgian billiards tables. Mind your manners
because the local judo and karate clubs
meet here.
CLOSED SUNDAY
Other days 10.30–20.30

GOEGNIES-CHAUSSÉE

12km S of Mons on N563
🚃 Quévy *[Mons–Quévy]* – 3km

A border town in the real sense. One side of
the road is in Belgium and the other in France.
The cost of road signs is shared but in case
you think anyone intends to be grown-up
about this, the French spell their side *Gognies*.
You can work out the respective national
sales tax differences by spotting what shops
are on which side of the street.

Brunehault

52 Chaussée Brunehault   T 065 56 83 96

Brasserie and tavern on the Belgian side of
the street, with a wide-ranging snack menu
and a safe list of 60 interesting-enough beers.
Large open terrace at the front and a tidy,
tile-floored saloon bar indoors. Unmistakably
Belgian and genuinely different from the
French cafés across the street. No dogs.
CLOSED MONDAY
Other days 10.00 onwards

LA LOUVIÈRE

14km WNW of Charleroi off E42 exit 19
🚃 La Louvière-Centre & Sud *[IR]*

Old industrial city (pop. 77,000), rediscovering
a role for itself since coalmining subsided in
the Seventies. Surrounded by some remarkable
reminders of the industrial world, particularly
associated with the Canal du Centre. If you
have wheels, head for the hundred-year-old
hydraulic barge lifts at Houdeng-Goegnies
and Bracquenies, on the outskirts of the town.
Equally awesome in a different way is the
canal lift that replaced them at Strépy-Thieu.
Boat trips from Bracquenies may be possible.
At Houdeng-Aimeries, visit the Écomusée
Régionale du Centre (2B Rue St. Patrice) to get
the feel of an old Belgian mining community
and the Musée de la Mine to get the history
of mining.

Grain de Sel

30 Rue Albert 1er   T 064 67 74 97

Just off the main square in a semi-pedestrianised shopping street. A surprisingly pleasant small brasserie with an even smaller streetside terrace. 60 beers with virtually no rubbish, on a list of mainly Wallonian ales. Good salads, omelettes and single-plate meals, with steaks and goose liver. Somewhat in contrast with its workaday surroundings but the best place in the area to take lunch or end the day, particularly if you are embarking on some serious industrial tourism.

Daily 10.00 onwards

MESLIN L'EVÊQUE

25km NNW of Mons on N7

Off the old road from Ath to Enghien. On our way into the village a farm was selling eggs, potatoes and "rabbits for the table". Fairly near the Château d'Attre, Louis XV in style but with gardens spanning the river Dender that are distinctively British. Attre's furnishings are largely original and give a good impression of aristocratic life centuries ago.

Lanterne

36 Rue de la Sille   T 068 56 80 76

Six hundred metres beyond the village square, approached from the main road. Easily mistaken for a modern executive home. Run with great aplomb by a pleasant and straightforward couple. The remarkably good list of 65 beers includes Géants, Ellezelloise, Dupont and Silly. Evening snacks (18.30–21.30) get as far as kebabs and pasta and make a brief appearance on Sunday lunchtimes. From Monday to Thursday this is the village hair salon.

CLOSED MONDAY TO THURSDAY

Fri & Sat 15.00–01.00; *Sun* 10.30–01.00

God's presence in the café

MONS

Mons [IC]

Mons (Du: *Bergen*) is the provincial capital (pop. 90,000). A typical Belgian town draped over a small hill and arranged around its quietly impressive Grand'Place. Not so long ago, it was the main town of the Borinage, a fact marked by the strange, pudding-like hills around the edges of the town that are former slag heaps.

Mons was the site of a significant German victory early in the 1914–18 war. It was immortalised by a fake news story that an angel had appeared in the sky and so shocked the German infantry that the French and British forces were able to escape. The victory put the town on the front line for three years.

Mons faired little better in the 1939–45 war, when another German occupation exposed it to many bombing raids. At least the French and British troops fought alongside each other on these occasions. This was an advance on 1709, when a British army under the Duke of Marlborough, er, liberated the town from the French.

Despite all this history, the tourist potential here is woefully neglectfully. The main attractions are a few low-key museums in and near the Town Hall (Fr: *Hôtel de Ville*) and the nightlife around the Grand'Place. Top spot in our view is the stewed whelk stall, which for no particularly good reason has camped here every weekend for the last thirty years. We consider it a national treasure.

Hotel tips: a couple of coachloads and the town is full, so book ahead. Infotel★★★, 32 Rue d'Havré (**T** 065 40 18 30; **F** 065 35 62 24) is modern and functional, with a private car park; St.Georges★★, 15 Rue des Clercs (**T** 065 31 16 29; **F** 065 31 86 71) is central, with an Alsacienne theme that may stretch to beers from Alsace micros; Etna★, 1 Place Leopold (**T** 065 39 93 93; **F** 065 33 81 94) is basic but clean and bang opposite the station.

Cervoise

25 Grand'Place   **T** 065 31 46 06

There are about a dozen cafés on the Grand' Place. This one has the most impressive beer list. A long thin café where beer is the main attraction, though they do enough food to keep you in your seat. Privately owned by young Wallonian beer nuts, who seem unaware of the beer world outside Mons. They are also keen on cooling their beers so demand them *temperée* if you want a fuller flavour. The list of 150 is remarkably safe for its length. Food (11.30–14.30 & 18.30–22.00) includes pasta, salads, steaks, *escavêches* and a few vegetarian options. They have a terrace on the square.

Daily 08.00 onwards

Excelsior

29 Grand'Place   **T** 065 36 34 52

The most elegant brasserie on the Grand'Place is a classic of its kind. On the corner of Rue des Clercs, with substantial seating outside. Inside is more jacket than T-shirt. Brightly lit, wood-panelled with parquet flooring, tapering at the far end to a bar without seats. This is a classic design. Panoramic windows open onto the terrace with a good view of the square. Upstairs there is an equally well-appointed room for dining, private parties and busy times. The ever-changing beer list of over 100 is intelligent and interesting, featuring Flemish brewers like Van Eecke alongside Binchoise, Abbaye des Rocs, Géants, St. Feuillien and even Augrenoise. The best food (12.00–14.30 & 18.00–23.00, not Su pm) among our entries with a full menu of local and national dishes, including fish, steaks and local variations on "grandmother cooking". Special teas and coffees too.

Sat & Sun 11.00 onwards (Sep–Jun)
Other days 09.00 onwards

Maison Des Brasseurs

3 Grand'Place   **T** 065 35 18 28

On the opposite side of the square the "Brewers' House" is a large, open-plan, high-ceilinged café with murals on the walls and a brew kettle lid over the bar. It too has a terrace on the square. The beer list has nudged up to 55 and often includes St.Feuillien, Abbaye des Rocs, Ellezelloise and Dupont. Food is less impressive and limited to standard bar snacks.

Daily 09.00 onwards

Paysan

52 Rue de la Chaussée   **T** 065 31 85 87

The "Peasant" is a daytime café on the cobbled street that runs between Excelsior (above) and the station. Its long, thin, mirror-walled bar leads to a raised non-smoking area at the back. The TV is mainly for the sports channels but keeps itself contained. The list of 56 beers includes Dupont and Caulier among others. Basic snacks and ices only.

Sun 14.30–19.30;   *Other days* 08.00–19.30

OTHER MONS CAFÉS:

The **Ropieur** (14 Grand'Place), at the far end of Grand'Place is a small, personable street corner café with an overflow room upstairs. Its beer list stays around forty but usually includes several Wallonian ales in large bottles. Two other places around the square that have appealed to readers are the café-restaurant **Copenhagen** (11 Grand'Place – **T** 065 33 56 20) and the **Central** (18 Grand'Place – **T** 065 35 51 12), both of which have increased their beer lists to nearly fifty for 2005. See also Brewery cafés: Brasse-Temps (above).

MONTIGNIES-SUR-ROC

18km WSW of Mons off N549

Attractive old village with a huge green. Home to the Abbaye des Rocs brewery.

Château

7 Place Fulgence Masson   **T** 065 75 03 72

The "Castle" stands at the top of an unusual, village green shaded by mature trees. The setting could be one for a fine old English inn. This substantially proportioned pub is the centre of its local community for young and old. The part-time tourist office operates from one of its outhouses. Serves 60 beers including everything Belgian from the village brewery, Abbaye des Rocs, plus many from Hainaut's other breweries. Small snacks only. Closes from 14.00 to 16.30 on Sunday.

CLOSED TUESDAY;   *Other days* 11.00 onwards

MONT ST. AUBERT

5km N of Tournai off N48

Hilltop village with excellent views over Tournai and western Hainaut. Awkward to get to but worth the effort. Five minutes off the E42 exit 33 if you take the right route.

Belle Vue

4b Rue du Curé   **T** 069 22 88 65

Simple village brasserie enjoying a *belle vue* of the surrounding countryside. We know it is still there but have no word on its opening times or on whether it maintains a list of 70 beers including Caulier, Ellezelloise and Brunehaut and the like. They used to be hot on cooking over hot stones at the table. More (any!) reports please.

MOUSCRON

Mouscron *[IR]*

Mouscron (Du: *Moeskroen*) is what happened to Belgium when the industrial belt of greater Lille spewed out through a hole in the French border and made a town (pop. 52,000). Contiguous with the French communities of Tourcoing and Roubaix. Hit by the post-industrial vacuum it is now beginning to pick itself up after some bad years.

Belle Époque

30 Grand Place   **T** 056 34 08 03

On the old main square of this post-industrial market town. Positively arty for its setting. Professionally run in a sort of grand café style, with a small terrace in summer. 55 beers, with nothing local. Good *plats du jour* and other snacks. Tea dances on Sunday afternoons.

Daily 11.00 onwards

Ours

72 Rue de Tourcoing   **T** 056 33 04 87

This all-purpose, optimistic brasserie sits at the top of the high street in defiance of its surroundings. Its confident atmosphere is as French as it is Belgian. The large covered terrace overlooks the road junction. The inner area has high-backed seats round sturdy tables bar style. The list tops 55 on a good day. There is a massive range of bars snacks from baguettes and tartines to *carbonnade flamande*, *hôchepot*, rabbit cassoulet in Trappist beer, chicory au gratin and beef tongue in a tomato sauce.   *Daily* 11.00 onwards

PÉRUWELZ

20km SE of Tournai on N60
🚆 Péruwelz *[Tournai–St. Ghislain]*

Lived-in, small north Hainaut town (pop. 17,000) that is home to Caulier brewery (see Brewery cafés above). Come by train and see the old-fashioned station before it falls down. Wandering the streets you will find them awash with a plethora of small shops and businesses. This is the type of community that in the UK or US would have had its guts ripped out years ago by moronic town planning, at the behest of some soulless property development scoundrels.

Ménestrel
6 Grand Place

Bills itself as a theatre café and as the "Provincial Museum of Beer", though we have been unable to establish the basis of either claim. Rather this is an old-fashioned brown café on the town's rather understated main square. The official beer list has around 60 choices though we are assured there are 200 in stock. Quite how one gets to know what these are is unclear. Just keep picking names out of the Guide we guess. Regular music gigs in the evening. No food.

Sat 11.00 onwards
Sun 16.00 onwards
Other days 10.00 onwards

PIPAIX

12km east of Tournai off N7
🚆 Leuze *[Tournai–Ath]* – 4km
See brewery cafés: Dubuisson (above).

ROISIN

24km SW of Mons on N553

Border village in a picturesque part of southwestern Hainaut.

Etangs du Château
16 Rue du Château de Roisin   **T** 065 75 02 25

Large modern café off the village centre, on the way into a camping, caravanning and fishing complex. There are gardens, trout lakes and a large children's play area. The spacious terrace and plain bar accompany a surprisingly ambitious restaurant. The beer list reaches a solid 60. Light snacks are available all day (10.00–22.00) with major food in the restaurant every evening (not Su). They are connected with a beer shop down the road (*Tu–Su* 09.00–12.30; *We–Sa* 14.00–19.00).
CLOSED MONDAY & TUESDAY (*Sep–Jun*)
CLOSED WEDNESDAY & THURSDAY (*Dec–Feb*)
Other days 10.00 onwards

SCOURMONT

8km S of Chimay off N589
See Brewery cafés: Chimay (above).

SILLY

12km E of Ath off N57
🚆 Silly *[Ath – Enghien]* – 2km
See Brewery cafés: Silly (above).

SOIGNIES

18km NNE of Mons on N6
🚆 Soignies *[Mons–Braine-le-Comte]*

Pleasant small market town (pop. 24,000) on the old road from Brussels to Mons.

Régence
4 Rue de Mons   **T** 067 33 09 27

A pukkah, air-conditioned, single-room town-centre café just off the main square, opposite the large Romanesque church of St Vincent. Small terrace outside. Its list of 60 beers includes Dupont and Achouffe. Excellent range of salads and bar meals (12.00–14.00 & 18.00–21.00), such as cassoulet of duck confit, grilled *andouillette*, home-made *escavêche*, *tarte al d'jotte* and *flamiches* with goats cheese or sweet chestnuts. Closes on Sundays between 13.30 and 15.00.

CLOSED MONDAY
Other days 11.30 onwards

TOURNAI

🚃 Tournai *[IR]*

Tournai (pop. 67,000) is now officially the most boring town in all Wallonia in which to drink beer – the Guide says so! Things had been pretty rough for some years but the final nail in the coffin was the closure and sale of the long-serving Cave à Bière. When sold it made way for a comedy club – we understand the need.

There is a magnificence to Tournai (Du: *Doornik*), a city dominated by the presence of its 800-year-old Cathedral of Our Lady (Fr: *Cathédrale Notre-Dame*), a UNESCO World Heritage site. This dwarfs the old town by day and on dark nights hovers like an alien craft, silhouetted by powerful spotlights against the cloudbase.

The tragedy of its beerlessness is that Tournai is at the western end of the Hainaut beer belt. From here you can cycle to Enghien in a day and comfortably take in visits to or peeks at the outside of Dupont, Dubuisson, Vapeur, Géants and Silly on the way. Relatively short detours could add Caulier and Authentique, or Ellezelloise and Monts.

So where is the recognition of this? Or is such local excellence the sort of thing for other, wiser populations to appreciate?

If fate condemns you to be here we suggest that you frequent the excellent Moine Austère beer shop (see Beer Shops & Warehouses) and drink indoors, venturing out only to seek news of great developments to tell the Guide about on **BelgiumGBG@aol.com**.

Hotel tip: Aux Armes de Tournay★, 24 Place de Lille (**T** 069 22 67 23; **F** 069 22 70 35) is basic but comfortable and convenient for both the Grand Place and the ring road.

OTHER TOURNAI CAFÉS:

That a city with such a prominent role in Belgian history should have such a dull beer culture is a tragedy. The Grand Place, which locals use for practice in case they ever get a scratch entry in the Monaco Grand Prix, hosts the best of the rest, which are currently the **Quatre Saisons** (68 Grand Place – closed Mo), the **Beffroi** (15 Grand Place) and the **Impératrice** (128 Rue des Maux). Each stocks around forty beers. As for any others, you may get some suggestions at the towns only other beery highspot, the Moine Austère beer shop (see Beer Shops & Warehouses). If you have better luck, please let us know.

TOURPES

16km E of Tournai on N526
🚃 Leuze *[Tournai–Ath]* – 4km
See Brewery cafés: Dupont (above).

STELLA ARTOIS

Au Vieil Aubel

Restaurant Taverne

33 Spa →
25 Liège →
15 Verviers →
7 Battice →
Julémont 8 →

Liège

POPULATION (2002): 1,020,000
MAIN TOWNS: **Liège** (184,000), **Seraing** (60,000) and **Verviers** (53,000)
TOURISM WEBSITE: www.ftpl.be

LIÈGE is Belgium's eastern province. Wedged between Germany in the east, the Netherlands to the north and Luxembourg to the south, it possesses some of the most fought over countryside in the world.

The north of the province has much urban sprawl radiating out from the city of Liège, along the Meuse valley, north to the towns where the six motorways meet and south as far as Verviers. We have seen blast furnaces still operating near here.

To the west of the Meuse is the plain of Brabant while to its south and east are the northern reaches of the Ardennes. Here the woodlands of the Ourthe and Amblève valleys meet the moorland nature reserves of the High Fens (Fr: *Hautes Fagnes*), and the province takes more than its fair share of outstanding natural beauty.

The small, German-speaking cantons around Eupen were part of Germany until 1921, when they were ceded to Belgium under the Treaty of Versailles. German is the official language here and area elects its own German-speaking members to the Wallonian and national parliaments.

The Grand Prix track at Francorchamps will amaze unsuspecting drivers on days when it still functions as public road, though the waters at nearby Spa are probably more dangerous. In winter, there are ski resorts round Sankt Vith, while the long distance footpaths of the German-Belgian nature reserve thrive in summer. This world is now more easily reached, since they opened the exhilarating underpasses beneath Liège.

The bad news is that the province's beer scene is second only to Wallonian Brabant in its tedium. The province is responsible for making Jupiler, the most popular beer in Belgium. For those with taste buds reporting to their brains the two small breweries in the north, Grain d'Orge and Val-Dieu should be more entertaining

> BREWERIES: **Bruyères**, *Jupille-sur-Meuse*; **Flo**, *Blehen*; **Grain d'Orge**, *Hombourg*; **Interbrew**, *Jupille-sur-Meuse* (InBev); **Val-Dieu**, *Aubel*.

BREWERY CAFÉS

Grain d'Orge

The eponymous brewery's café at Hombourg pre-dated it by five years and still manages a full entry in its own right (below).

Val-Dieu

The **Casse-Croûte** restaurant (225 Val-Dieu, Aubel – open daily) next to the brewery is a self-service cafeteria serving all the beers, in the mold of Achel. The abbey itself is worth a look.

AUBEL

20km ENE of Liège on N648

Small hill town just south of the Fouron (Du: *Voeren*). Home to the Val-Dieu brewery (see Brewery cafés above).

Vieil Aubel
2 Rue de Battice   **T** 087 68 71 40

A lovely little café-restaurant in the centre of the town. Its traditional interior dates in part from the 15th century. The two rooms consist of a cosy friendly bar and, a few steps down, a smaller, quieter dining room. A good menu

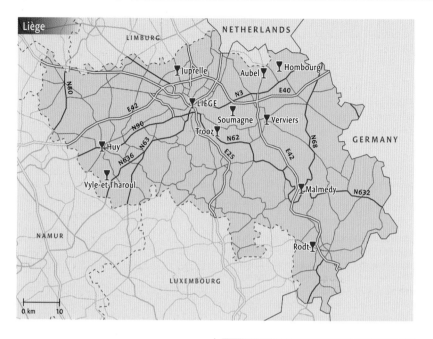

features home-prepared dishes using local ingredients, with some cuisine à la bière and surprisingly good mussels for this far inland. The beer list of 50 features the beers both Grain d'Orge and Val-Dieu. The **Berry** (22 Place Antoine Ernst) opposite the war memorial, is a simpler café with forty beers.
Monday 17.00 onwards; *Other days* 10.00 onwards

HOMBOURG

25km ENE of Liège on N608
Village in the hill country near the Dutch and German borders. On the edge of a triangle of land called New Moresnet, which between 1815 and 1919 was a neutral state in its own right, putting a strip of No Man's Land between Germany and Belgium. At the Three Stones (Fr: *Trois Bornes*) landmark, just beyond Gemmenich, you can walk through three countries in ten paces. The view from the Baudoin Tower next to it takes in Maastricht, Aachen and great swathes of the northern Ardennes.

Grain d'Orge
16 Centre   T 087 78 77 84

Large, friendly, village centre café, popular with locals, with a single open-plan bar and seats outside in summer. The bar front is in the style of a large copper brewing kettle. This was a beer café for several years before the brewery opened in 2002. Currently the list has dropped to 40 but of course includes all of those currently produced on the premises. Light snacks include pasta. There is open-top table football.
CLOSED TUESDAY
Mon 16.00 onwards; *Other days* 11.00 onwards

HUY

Halfway between Namur & Liège on N90
Huy [Liège–Namur]

To understand the full beauty of this ancient fortress town (pop. 18,000), approach it travelling upstream from Liège along the Meuse valley. The industrial monsters stop a few kilometres short, giving way to a community that owes its existence and amazing architecture to a pair of river bridges. Huy was besieged no fewer than thirty times during the last millennium. The early 18th century accounts for the stoneware overlooking the river. The scariest way to see the old town is from the *téléphérique* cable car that zooms along, several hundred feet in the air, on Saturday afternoons year-round and on most days in high summer. You can stop halfway, on top of the fort, if your heart is still functioning. There is free parking and a children's playgound at the out-of-town end on Rue Plaine de la Sarte. The Musée Communal in the Minim Brothers' cloister (Rue Vankeerberghen) gets good reviews.

Hotel tip: below the fortifications on the river, two minutes from the centre, the **Fort et sa Réserve★★**, 6 Chaussée Napoléon (**T** 085 21 24 03; **F** 085 23 18 42; www.hoteldufort.be) is a comfortable family-run hotel with an adequate restaurant.

Big Ben
8 Grand Place   **T** 085 23 15 83

The Guide wants some designer guru to come along to Huy and help it to gain some style. When they have finished with the townscape they can move onto the cafés. The Big Ben is another of those worthy places that is holding back its ambitions. In a corner of the sadly understated Grand Place where it has to plonk its terrace, well-placed for a walk around the largely neglected old quarter, this underlit, neatly furnished, family café is where the Simpsons mean the Flintstones and dream of chicken nuggets. It may have 130 beers and some halfway reasonable bar meals, including horse steak no less, but it needs a bit more class.   *Daily* 10.00–24.00

JUPRELLE

5km NNW of Liège on N20

Old industrial suburb off exit 33 of the E40 motorway as it skirts the north of Liège city, just beyond Rocourt.

Vaudrée Trois
13 Chaussée de Tongres   **T** 04 246 02 67

The insufficiently famous Vaudrée chain of brasseries brings light and happiness to the culturally starved Liègeois beer scene. If you want to see what it is all about but do not have the time to drop into the city itself then this is the Vaudrée for you. They would have had to try hard to find a worse setting for this third café, one kilometre north of the motorway junction on the road to Tongeren. Outside is a large, roadside terrace, while the modern lounge indoors replaced a dance club. This one only stocks 400 beers, of which two dozen are on draught. The list is big on abbey beers and stocks more proper gueuze than anywhere else in the province. The menu is as enormous as the beer list and includes ostrich, bison, kangaroo and springbok, plus live lobsters and oysters available at all times. For the really adventurous, the 74 bus rides between Place St.Lambert in Liège and Tongeren every hour. Taxis from the city centre take fifteen minutes and cost as many Euros each way. *Fri&Sat* 07.00 onwards; *Other days* 07.00–02.00

LIÈGE

🚄 Liège Guillemins *[IC]*

Officially the fifth largest city in Belgium (pop. 184,000), though if you include its conurbation it would be third. The provincial capital and an old seat of power.

Built on the back of heavy industry, its rusting blast furnaces still loom over the Meuse, like an old mariner intent on frightening the grandchildren with tales of ancient storms. The type of steel and chemical plants that constitute industrial archaeology in other parts of Europe, are still functioning here, extending up the Meuse for many kilometres. Predictions of their closure cause local politicians to judder.

For such an important place, cosmopolitan life is strangely subdued. Pompous buildings serve utilitarian functions. There is a sense of Liège having failed to notice that it lost its economic struggle against the move to a post-industrial age. It is as if nobody wants to tell it that the world has moved on.

Liègeois folk are portrayed as radical, independent and freethinking, awkward if you prefer, but terribly serious. George Simenon, the much-loved creator of French detective Maigret, hailed from here.

The city centre has its share of museums and churches. If you like your art modern, use the afternoon to visit the Musée d'Art Moderne at Parc de la Boverie on Outre-Meuse, the island in the river that is the city's artistic quarter. Paintings by Picasso, Monet, Magritte, Gauguin and others are hung alongside sculpture by Rodin. If you prefer your art older and angelic, try the collegiate church of St. Barthélemy in the Place of the same name. For a break from the traffic, try the parks around the Albert 1er bridge.

Considering its geographical position as the nearest Belgian city to the German ale-brewing capitals of Köln and Düsseldorf, and its political importance to Wallonia, Liège is embarassingly bereft of beer culture. Were it not for the Vaudrée lot it would have virtually none. Stranded readers seeking a greater diversity of cafés could risk culture shock and take the train to Maastricht, across the Dutch border, where they understand beer better.

Hotel tips: the cheaper hotels are congregated round the main railway station (Guillemins), which is easily reached from the motorway system and has a large safe car park. The best options remain the recently refurbished **Metropole**★★, 141 Rue des Guillemins (**T** 04 252 42 93; **F** 04 252 55 52; www.hotelmetropole.be) and the slightly more expensive, reliable and convenient **Univers**★★, 116 Rue des Guillemins (**T** 04 254 55 55; **F** 04 254 55 00), part of the Comfort Inn franchise.

Vaudrée Deux

149 Rue St. Gilles   **T** 04 223 18 80

The most central of this small chain of cafés is now so far ahead of the rest of Liège for beer selection that its existence is incomprehensible. Either it is an extreme example of niche marketing, drawing its custom from every last saddo in Liège who still likes decent beer, or else the rest of the city is missing a trick. The Guide believes it is the latter. Stepping

out of Guillemins station head straight on down Rue des Guillemins, take the first left down Dartois and a ten-minute walk brings you to Rue St. Gilles, an extension of Rue de la Cathédrale out of the city centre. Turn right and you will soon find this long, modern, café-restaurant and its amazing beer list on your right, opposite the chain's first beer shop. They claim to stock 900 beers here with twenty-four on tap. In years gone by the stocks tended to dwindle and quality was not always assured but latterly the whole chain has been re-invigorated with good results. The beer menu here takes a minimalist approach, though at least it is now broken down roughly into styles. Use the Guide. Foreign brews come from all corners of the globe with a bias towards the French-speaking world. Surprisingly for a café with one of the largest beer ranges in the world, there is a strong emphasis on food. Cooking is solid rather than brilliant but is available at most times. Service has improved in recent years, though the design of the café means that inevitably those sat opposite the long bar catch the waiters' attention more easily.

Fri & Sat 09.00–02.00; *Other days* 09.00–01.00

OTHER LIÈGE CAFÉS:

Not for the first time, the trip to check out the city's best beer cafés was accompanied by an optimistic list of over twenty new leads. The mood of previous tours with friends had turned so grisly that your heroic editor went alone this time. Two dozen cafés later he determined that this was really a job for a youngster. Liège cafés all serve about twenty beers with their stock dominated by the brands of the conglomerates. The great socialist city is doing its bit to support global capitalism.

A few cafés have half a dozen interesting beers from smaller independents but it is virtually impossible to find the province's own micros, such as Bruyères, Grain d'Orge or even Val-Dieu.

Round the cathedral area the **Saint Paul** (8 Rue St. Paul – **T** 04 223 72 17 – closed Su; others from 10.00) still boasts a lovely wooden fin de siècle interior and staff from central casting but now keeps just forty unadventurous beers. Fifty metres down the way the **Pôt au Lait** (9 Rue Soeurs de Hasque) internet café, courtyard bar and place-to-be-seen has a few better beers but not many. Apart from these the only bar to trouble the scorers was the **Point de Vue** (10 Place Verte – T 04 223 64 82), a pleasant café-restaurant just off the enormous Place de l'Opera, which stocks about forty beers including several from Val-Dieu, served cosily inside or noisily on the terrace.

Readers who hear about new beer cafés in the city are respectfully requested to keep them to themselves unless they have rock solid evidence that this is more than just a half-baked bit of gossip like all the other useless leads that keep descending on us.

LIÈGE (Angleur)

Angleur [IR]

South-eastern suburb on the way out towards Chaudefontaine and the south. The simplest way to get here is by train (three per hour) from Guillemins station. The public transport alternative is bus no. 26 from Place de la Republique Française. A taxi is worth considering, as visiting this obscure place is mandatory.

The extraordinary Vaudrée in Liège (Angleur) stays open all day, every day, for food and up to 900 beers.

Petit Vaudrée

182 Rue Vaudrée   T 04 367 04 86

This popular and successful local pub was the forerunner to the Vaudrée concept and the group's original café, though it actually left the line-up some while ago. One hundred metres down the same sidestreet as the next entry, this simple but busy street corner brasserie that has specialised in beer since 1978. The front bar, overlooks a small terrace and is mainly for drinking, while the back room is more foody. The list of 150 beers is populist but not without Wallonian highlights. Big café cooking (12.00–14.00 & 18.30–23.00, Fr&Sa 01.00) features large portions of beef, pork, lamb, trout, skate, salads, pasta and crêpes.
Daily 11.00 onwards

Vaudrée

109 Rue du Val Benoit
T 04 367 10 61   F 04 380 01 71

To find this unique beer emporium, leave Angleur railway station by the rear exit beyond platform six. Turn right, and the Vaudrée is at a street corner, two hundred metres on your left. Set in a part of greater Liège that has been concreted into the Seventies. The management has improved so much in recent years that we recommend large parties to ring ahead for seats. The big room is dining-only for much of the time. The semi-circular bar front is for drinking. The rest is a bit of both.

Said to stock over 900 beers though everyone seems to drink a regular brand. There is a problem with beers being out of stock and others can be well beyond their sell-by date. Some deliberately aged beers are stocked, as is a large array of ghastly fruit beers. A good selection of rare Scotch whiskies has been acquired. The non-stop kitchen served a similar menu to its younger brother in Liège centre. In this, the original 24/7 café, the kitchen and bar are supposed never to call time, though we have been threatening for fifteen years to take a large group for some four a.m. steak and trimmings one wet January Tuesday morning. We have yet to understand how they keep it so clean!

Daily 24 hours

MALMEDY

15km SSE of Verviers off E42 exit 10

A lively little market town (pop. 7,000) and economic centre. Dull tourism compared to the equally unbeery Stavelot or Spa but a nicer town and a good base from which to explore the eastern Ardennes and Hautes Fagnes. The only sights worth the candle are the Cathedral and the museum on Place de Rome devoted to the Cwarmê, the town's carnival held on the four days before Shrove Tuesday.

Hotel tip: in the town centre the Forge★★, 31 Rue Devant-les-Religieuses (T 080 79 95 95; F 080 75 75 99; www.hotel-la-forge.be) is small enough to be fun and offers excellent value.

Scotch

11 Place Albert 1er   T 080 33 06 41

Malmedy is the sort of regional centre that needs a proper beer café but until it gets one, we keep reaching for the Scotch. This comfortable, hard-working, old-style tavern is one of a dozen cafés on the town's main square. Its beer range nudges ever upwards, reaching 54 at our last visit. Trappists, Maredsous and Duchesse de Bourgogne are as good as it gets. A deep, cosy cave in which to waste away a lunchtime – bar snacks up to pasta. There is a summer terrace.

Daily 09.00 – 01.00

RODT

10km S of Malmedy off N675

A popular winter sports area near Sankt Vith, in German-speaking eastern Liège.

Hotel tip: the Buchenberg★, 98 Rodt (T 080 22 88 57; F 080 22 90 03) offers basic chalet accommodation throughout the year, attracting skiers in winter and hikers in summer.

Biermuseum

Ski Centrum am Tomberg
95 Rodt   T 080 22 63 01

Atop a sort of plateau surrounded by newly planted forest, just above the village. The museum is a collection of a few thousand beer bottles from around the globe in a chalet bar that has to earn a living outside the limited winter season. We would love to see them focus a bit on their strengths and instead of stocking 50 better-known brands, offer a good selection of winter beers in season and German brews in the summer.

CLOSED MONDAY TO FRIDAY (*School terms*)
Sat & Sun 09.00–19.00; *Other days* 11.00–19.00

SOUMAGNE

10km E of Liège on N621 & N604

Typical suburban town (pop. 12,000) just off the major motorway system and on the edge of proper countryside.

Plume

476 Rue de l'Egalité   T 04 377 52 37

From the motorway follow signs to Soumagne-Bas, where the Micheroux road meets the corner of Chaussée Colonel Josset, at the edge of town centre. The "Pen" is a surprisingly good, modern, multi-level, higgledy-piggledy drinking and eating emporium. The conservatory restaurant is like a small botanical garden extending into a covered terrace, spoilt only by its view of a busy road junction. The list of 130 beers includes numerous imports, such as Berliner Weissbier and Adelscott. There is a full restaurant menu and all-day snacks. Parking can be fun at busy times.

Fri & Sat 11.00–00.45; *Other days* 11.00–23.00

TROOZ

10km SE of Liège on N61
🚃 Trooz *[Liège–Verviers]*

The easternmost industrial village (pop. 7,600) of an urban sprawl south of Liège. Upstream from here along the Vesdre valley the landscape becomes rural for about ten kilometres before descending once more into the abyss at Pepinster.

Trooz

254 Grand Rue **T** 04 351 66 71

On the main road, about fifty metres from the station. This surprisingly classy café-restaurant revels in the personal touch and good taste of its owners. There is no beer list but a quick look at the fridge will give an idea of some of the range – others are available at cellar temperature. They stock around 55, with some interesting micro beers on draught. Enjoy the breweriana and classy café décor. The *petit restauration* and meals in the dining area (12.00–14.00; 18.00–21.30) are good too. Reasonable wine list.
CLOSED WEDNESDAY
Tue 09.30 – 15.00; *Other days* 09.30 onwards

VERVIERS

25km E of Liège
🚃 Verviers Central *[IR]*

Large market town (pop. 53,000) set in the valley of the River Vesdre, off the motorway from Liège to Luxembourg. Near the national parks along the German border and Moselle valley. Good shopping and a practical base for travelling the northern Ardennes.

Hotel tips: the **Ardennes**★★, 15 Place des Victoires (**T** 087 22 39 25; **F** 087 23 17 09) is conveniently close to the station and about the only cheaper option left in town, so reservation is recommended.

Red Ball

10 Pont St. Laurent **T** 087 33 39 50

Don't be put off by the absence of a bridge on Pont St. Laurent. It is one of the main shopping streets in the town centre, near the tourist office and the busy Place Verte. This unassuming, traditional terrace pub, with a small street terrace, has a real interest in beer and helpful staff. Wood panelling and cosy atmosphere, but not precious. The list of 120 beers includes Val-Dieu and other Wallonian regionals but also St. Bernardus. The menu is pretty substantial, particularly at lunchtime, with steaks and brochettes, plus *rognons Liègeois*, meatballs and brawn cooked in traditional and modern ways.
Mon–Sat 10.00 onwards; *Sun* 17.00 onwards

VYLE-ET-THAROUL

8km S of Huy off N641

Pleasant stone-built village in an attractive farming area, just south of the Meuse industrial belt. On a tourist trail called the Route Jolie vers l'Ardennes – literally the "Pretty Route to the Ardennes".

Merveille

1 Rue Pont de Vyle **T** 085 41 20 32

Just off the main road, shortly after the old railway bridge. Like the village itself, the "Marvel" is much improved in recent years. You can tell the original stone-built bar in this roadside café. The newer front room was just a battered verandah when the Guide's first edition was published back in 1992. Nowadays it has slate floor, a pitched roof and a bit of atmosphere. There is a new open terrace outside. The beer list of 80 includes beers from Caulier, du Bocq and Val de Sambre. The menu (12.00–21.00) includes cold meats, omelettes, croques, rolls, crêpes and waffles.
CLOSED MONDAY & TUESDAY *(Sep–Jun)*
Other days 12.00 onwards

Limburg

POPULATION (2002): **800,000**
MAIN TOWNS: **Hasselt** (69,000) and **Genk** (63,000)
TOURISM WEBSITE: wwwtoerismelimburg.be

LIMBURG is Belgium's north-eastern province. Traditionally a poor agricultural area with a few mineral deposits, in recent years it has developed into a place of forestry and footpaths, interspersed with the odd industrial belt. The northern half is part of the Kempen, a cross between fen and moorland. The southern half, the Haspengouw, is pleasant, fertile, undulating hill country.

In just twenty-five years Limburg has gone from being a no-go area for tourism to a major holiday area for people in search of exercise and eco-friendly pursuits. It all began with expansive projects like the Bokrijk Estate conversion and massive reforestation. Nowadays long, sometimes deserted country lanes through pine-scented woodland have replaced what was recently windswept barren fen.

Beyond Limburg's eastern border is an enclave surrounded by Liège province to the south and Dutch Limburg to the north, known as the Voeren (Fr: *Fourons*). This curious, pretty little area of undulating hills is said to be the most invaded area of land in the history of the world.

Limburg brewing has experienced a small revival in recent years. The province's best-known brand is the once ground-breaking now dull Alken Cristal. The biggest local presence is the family firm Martens, whose Sezoens defined a distinctively Limburger form of blond pale ale. The rising stars are the delightful farmstead brewery at Kerkom, whose Bink and Adelardus brands impress, and the newest Trappist brewery at the abbey in Achel.

BREWERIES: **Achel**, *Achel*; **Alken-Maes**, *Alken* (SCAM); **ter Dolen**, *Helchteren*; **Kerkom**, *Kerkom-Sint-Truiden*; **Martens**, *Bocholt*; **Sint Jozef**, *Opitter*.

BREWERY CAFÉS

Achel

Belgium's newest Trappist brewery is found 18km south of Eindhoven, signposted off the main N748. The **Gelagzaal Achel Trappist** (St. Benadictusabdij – **T** 011 80 07 69 – daily 11.00–18.00, May–Sep; others 12.00–17.00) is bang on the Dutch border. North from Achel village you travel through a housing estate and then across open country to this consecrated brewpub. The main room is a refectory, with as much café atmosphere as a municipal library, but there is a large sun-trap terrace outside with places to tie up your horse or chain your bicycle. There is also a beer shop (see Beer Shops and Warehouses).

ter Dolen

For secular abbey beers, try the **Kasteel Ter Doolen** (21 Eikendreef, Helchteren – closed Tu&We, Sep–May; closed Mo&Th, Oct–Mar; Fr from 18.00, Oct–Mar; Sa&Su from 13.00; others from 12.00). Head out of the town on the Eindhoven road and it is signposted to the right after six hundred metres. Situated in outbuildings of the old country seat of the Abbot of St. Truiden. Its excellent beers, pâté and cheese are delivered to scrubtop polished tables and peaceful rural ambience reigns across the courtyard and garden.

Kerkom

Belgium's cutest sampling café is the one used in winter at this delightful old farmhouse brewery (469 Naamsesteenweg, Kerkom-Sint Truiden – closed Mo; Tu–Fr, Nov–Mar; others 13.00–19.00, Nov–Mar; 12.00–19.00, Apr–Oct), south of St.Truiden on the N80. This recreation of a rustic brown café has a collection of

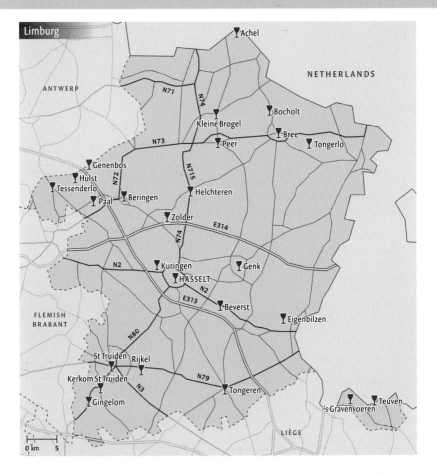

breweriana, tile floors, piano, stove, ancient bar and loads more. In summer they revert to the courtyard and a part of the old farmhouse on the opposite side. The tiny brewery is sometimes open for visitors. They have their own cheese.

Martens

The **Bierketel** (2 Reppelerweg, Bocholt – closed Th; others from 10.00) is bang opposite Martens brewery in the centre of town. It serves all the beers and bar snacks too.

Sint Jozef

The **Kieper** (2 Keyartstraat, Tongerlo – closed We&Th, Oct–Apr; others from 14.00, May–Sep; from 10.00, Oct–Apr) is a heavily wooded but relatively simple brewery tap. Postally in a

different village from the brewery, they are in practice less than a kilometre apart.

ACHEL

12km S of Eindhoven [NL] on the Dutch border
See Brewery cafés: Achel (above).

BERINGEN

15km NNW of Hasselt on N72 & N772, off E313 exit 26

🚄 Beringen [Hasselt–Lier] – 4km

Modern industrial town built around an old village.

Vijgeblad
8 Paalsesteenweg

"It's just a really nice place," said our normally articulate inspector. When pushed he added "like a modern brown café." Sofas, stove, old tiled floor, airy conservatory, small terrace at the back sort of thing. On the main N772 in the centre of the oldest part of town, easily accessible from the motorway. The list of 65 beers has included house beers commissioned from Kerkom. There are authentic lambics too. Food (11.30–21.00) runs from ciabattas via pasta to fish and steaks.
CLOSED MONDAY & TUESDAY
Wed 09.00 onwards; *Other days* 11.00 onwards

BEVERST

10km ESE of Hasselt on N2
🚆 Bilzen *[Hasselt–Liège]* – 5km
Small town on the old road to Maastricht.

Kleyne Laer
91 Holt　T 089 41 27 66

On the east side of town in what used to be the hamlet of Laer. This smoothly honed gem has been at it for years. We always come away with a good feeling. There are candles and religious statuettes in the lounge bar with classical music in the background. The garden is delightfully precise. A beer list of over 80 includes Achouffe, St. Jozef and Kerkom. Well-presented food (to 24.00) ranges from bacon and eggs to salmon, scampi and ribs. There is chicory in season and a great *côte à l'os*. Closes for the Easter holiday.
CLOSED WEDNESDAY; *Other days* 11.30–02.00

BOCHOLT

6km NNW of Bree on N76
See Brewery cafés: Martens (above).

BREE

28km NE of Hasselt off N73 & N76
Typical small Limburg town (pop. 14,000)

where the council has banned the use of what they term "mobile discobars" – they mean loud music blaring out of cars, bless them. On Fridays the market cuts the town off from the outside world.

Beeren
2 Bocholterstraat　T 089 46 47 64

In a cluster of cafés at a crossroads on the outskirts of town, found by taking Wittetorenstraat off the diminutive ring road. It will be on your right. This cross between a typical suburban British pub and a brown café is named after the family that has owned it since 1939. They will recommend beers from their changing list of 100. There is a beer tasting club on the last Thursday of the month. Food runs all day and includes pasta, pizza and scampi. In the town centre, the **Croon** (8 Vrijthof) claims sixty beers though we have only ever found forty.
CLOSED MONDAY; *Sun* 09.00 onwards
Tue 15.00 onwards; *Other days* 11.00 onwards

EIGENBILZEN

6km WNW of Maastricht [NL] off N2
Small town in international suburbia.

Briel
2 Bruulstraat　T 089 41 59 92

At the back of the church, off the little square at the centre of town. Well-used, lived-in café with a good local following. What you might call unpretentious but with classy ambitions. The beer list of over 50 features Limburger and Wallonian ales. In the plain, small-town restaurant at the back the emphasis is on local Haspengouw cookery.
CLOSED WEDNESDAY; *Other days* 09.00–01.00

GENENBOS

18km NW of Hasselt off E313 exit 25a
An old-rustic modern-industrial cluster off the Antwerp-Hasselt motorway. Not to be confused with a village of the same name off exit 27 a few kilometres south.

Celtic Art Gallery

4 Genebosstraat   **T** 013 67 13 73

From the motorway take the N73 and then first left into Bergstraat. The third left beyond the roundabout is Genebosstraat. In industrial estateland this multicultural, concert-throwing studio-gallery is adorned with original paintings for sale. The main room has an old tiled floor. There is a modern conservatory and a huge beer garden cum vegetable patch out the back. The beer list of around 50 includes most of the Limburg brewers plus Achouffe and Géants. No food spotted. Opens at 13.00 from November to April.

CLOSED WEDNESDAY
CLOSED MONDAY & TUESDAY (Nov–Apr)
Fri & Sat 11.00–23.00 ; *Others* 11.00–21.00

GENK

🚉 Genk [Hasselt–Genk]

Formerly the hub of the coal and minerals industry of the Kempen, transforming rapidly into a centre of modern commerce (pop. 63,000).

Trefpunt

23 Dieplaan   **T** 089 35 11 63

Coming out of the station, cross the road, head down the empty road and turn right at the buildings. The "Meeting Place" is on your left after a hundred metres. This modern-format, old-style café offers weekday sustenance to business folk in need of coffee, beer, food and somewhere to chat. Its changing list of over 50 beers usually has ter Dolen on draught. Interesting food includes good salads. A bit city life for Genk but you won't complain when you see the rest. More typical is **Bij de Waerd** (45 Stationsstraat) off Europalaan, with Dutch influence and fifty beers. It is also open at weekends.

CLOSED SATURDAY & SUNDAY
Mon–Fri 09.00–24.00

GINGELOM

24km SW of Hasselt on N80
🚉 Landen [IR] – 5km

Non-descript small town in Haspengouw blossom country.

Zesbunder

9 Schepen Beckersstraat   **T** 011 88 77 50

Turn off the main road at the Aldi supermarket. A pleasant and attractive all-round tavern with an up-market feel and convivial atmosphere. The beer list of 60 comes from across the courtyard. Nice terrace in the summer and a wood-burning stove in winter. Good at ribs. We would also like reports on a taverne called the **Pachthof** on the main street of Borlo (8 Thewitstraat), just east of here.

CLOSED TUESDAY
Sat 14.00 onwards; *Other days* 11.00 onwards

's GRAVENVOEREN

10km SSE of Maastricht [NL] off N608
🚉 Visé [Liège–Maastricht (NL)] – 5km

An attractive village in the linguisticly challenged Voeren enclave.

Hotel tip: the Blanckthys★★, 197 Klinkenberg (**T** 04 381 24 66; **F** 04 381 24 67) could now be the best option in the Voeren.

Swaen

188 Kinkenberg   **T** 04 381 33 50

The "Swan" is an excellent multi-roomed country village café with its own small museum of local life. Note the ancient range in the front bar. There is an English country-pub style terrace at the front and a courtyard to the rear. The list of around 60 beers includes brews from Val-Dieu and more distant regionals such as St. Bernardus. Regional cuisine includes local specialities like Herve cheese, smoked trout, tripe, stewed rabbit and various lamb dishes. There is dormitory accommodation for parties of up to fourteen, plus a room for private functions. Summer opening is 10.00.

CLOSED MONDAY; *Fri & Sat* 11.00–24.00
Sun 11.00–21.00; *Other days* 11.00–22.00

HASSELT

🚆 Hasselt *[IC]*

The provincial capital (pop. 69,000) is the most convenient travelling base for the Limburg area. Hasselt has its origins in mediaeval times and more of the old centre remains than guidebooks suggest. The city is home to Smeets, the largest genever distillery in Belgium and the National Jenever Museum (see Beer Tourism).

Northwest of the city is the Bokrijk Park estate and its open-air museum (Du: *Openluchtsmuseum*). Open daily from March to October, it occupies fourteen hundred acres and depicts Flemish life through the ages. Farm buildings, churches, workshops and houses have been transplanted into the grounds of Bokrijk castle. The site has a wildlife park, formal gardens and a nature reserve. There are buses and trains from the city centre. Free bus H3 goes to the city's Japanese gardens (Du: *Japanse Tuin*).

Every seven years comes the Kermesse, a festival in which the highlight is a giant called the Lounge Man, who goes round the street towing a barrel of warm pea soup, like if Brian Ferry did a shift for the Sally Army.

Hotel tips: Portmans★★★, 12 Minderbroedersstraat (☎ 011 26 32 80; F 011 26 32 81; www.walputsteeg.com) is a small, select town centre retreat. The **Century**★★, 1 Leopoldplein (☎ 011 22 47 99; F 011 23 18 24; www.century.be) and the **Pax**★★, 16 Grote Markt (☎ 011 22 38 75; F 011 24 21 37) are more basic but still comfortable. **Nieuwe Schoofs**★, 7 Stationplein (☎ 011 22 31 88; F 011 22 31 66; www.hoteldenieuweschoofs.be) is an acceptable B&B above a café opposite the station.

Hemelrijk

11 Hemelrijk ☎ 011 22 28 51

From the Grote Markt, locate St.Quintus Cathedral. Hemelrijk is behind it on the right before Zuivelmarkt. Its eponymous café, the "Kingdom of Heaven", which also bills itself in Latin as the "*Regnum Celestis*" is top right. A change of hands in 2001 led to a temporary panic that Limburg's top beer café would be going beerless. However, although it trans-

formed into an Italian restaurant its beer list actually increased to over 400, one of the best ranges in the country. We have received praise for the descriptions on an excellent beer menu and for the generally well-kept beers – sometimes a little too cold in summer. The range is well-balanced, and strong on regionals, Trappists, lambics and 75cl bottles. The all day Italian cooking bends a little towards the Flemish. Without question the best beer café in Limburg and in the national top ten.

Mon 16.00 onwards; *Other days* 12.00 onwards

OTHER HASSELT CAFÉS:

The **Augustina** (23 Leopoldplein) is a heavily muralled brasserie with forty beers and above average food. A rustic style restaurant called the **Windmolen** (46 Casterstraat) between the two ring roads on the Maastricht road, selling forty beers. If you are after genever, try the **Stookerijke** (Doktor Willemstraat – closed Mo; others from 11.00), which has eighty.

HELCHTEREN

20km N of Hasselt on N74
🚆 Zolder *[Hasselt–Lier]* – 5km
See Brewery cafés: Doolen (above).

HULST

18km NW of Hasselt off E313 exit 25a

Nondescript add-on to Tessenderlo, off the Antwerp–Hasselt motorway, awash with lorry parks.

Eikelhof

54 Eikelplein ☎ 013 66 83 70

An excellent modern beer café opposite the church in the unpromising setting of a residential square in this industrial village cum lorry park. The "Acorn Court" has a large open-plan main bar, with a billiards room at the back housing three full-size tables. Despite the obscure location, they are not phased by tourists dropping in from the motorway. The well laid out beer menu lists

85 brews including an impressive range of regionals and some micros. Food is pancakes and snacks, sometimes stretching to stews.
CLOSED TUESDAY; *Other days* 12.00 onwards

KERKOM-ST. TRUIDEN

5km S of St. Truiden on N80
St. Truiden *[Hasselt–Landen]* – 5km
See Brewery cafés: Kerkom (above).

KLEINE BROGEL

30km N of Hasselt off N74
Typically clean and neat Limburg town.

Wedelse Molen

250 Breugelweg   T 011 63 22 47

On the backroad to Overpelt, but closer to Kleine Brogel, on the banks of the Dommel. The "Water Mill" was working until 1957 and its mechanism still turns in the bar, which has some impressive beams in its original part. Changed hands in 2004 but we heard the beer list of 150, including brews from ter Dolen, de Dolle Brouwers and Kerkom has held up. There is a wide range of bar snacks and waffles. Spoilt only by cheapish furnishings and truly awful background music. Dancing on Saturday night. Sadly.
Daily 12.00 onwards

NEEROETEREN

12km NW of Genk on N757 & N773
Small modern town in the north-eastern corner.

Bakkemieske

61 Brugstraat

Well-managed roadside café a kilometre from the town centre on the road to Opoeteren, beyond the canal bridge. Attracts a lot of cyclists, families and bridge players. There is a kiddies' playground at the back with a little pond. Stocks 55 beers including most

Trappists and the beers from nearby Sint Jozef. The bar menu majors on buckwheat pancakes and the like.
CLOSED WEDNESDAY & THURSDAY
Sun 13.00 onwards
Other days 12.00–24.00

PAAL

15km NW Hasselt off E313 exit 26
Small town just off the motorway, with a big church.

Biertuin

143 Schaffensesteenweg   T 011 43 76 56

From the motorway take the N29 past Paal church and turn right into Schaffensesteenweg. It is some way to this spanking new, well-designed roadside café, which lies between the edge of town and open farmland. The owners seem to have chosen their favourite beers and put them on a single, well-described menu of 65 that includes authentic gueuzes, Trappists and regionals. Serious and casual cooking includes steaks, mussels, pork in Trappist beer, and others (to 22.00). Pancakes in the afternoons. There is a large garden and play area out the back. Back in town the **Stam** (41 St. Jansstraat – T 011 42 98 17 – closed Tu&We; Sa from 13.00; Su from 11.00; others from 18.00) still does its small town stuff, with snooker.
CLOSED WEDNESDAY
CLOSED THURSDAY (*Oct–Mar*)
Fri 16.00 onwards; *Other days* 11.00 onwards

PEER

33km NNE of Hasselt off N73
Small neat market town (pop. 13,000).

Torenhuis

40 Kerkstraat   T 011 63 19 57

The "Towers House" is opposite the base of the town's main church tower. Built in 1810, it was formerly the home of the town's first burgermeester but has been a café since 1966.

Witchcraft in the café

An elegant wooden interior features cane-sided armchairs, original oil paintings and a grandfather clock. There is a winter terrace cum restaurant at the back, a couple of smaller terraces and a billiards room downstairs. Always impresses first time visitors and gets better as the years pass. Stocks 60 beers including Martens, St. Jozef and ter Dolen. Serves a full menu (Sun all day, others 11.00–14.00 & 18.00–22.00), including good fish, steaks and ribs and the best *stoovlees* in Belgium. Opens at 07.00 on Mondays for the market.
CLOSED WEDNESDAY (Sep–Jun)
Fri & Sat 10.00–02.00
Sun 10.00–24.00; *Other days* 10.00–01.00

RIJKEL

5km E of St. Truiden off N79
St. Truiden [Hasselt–Landen] – 5km

Large village on various cycle routes, housing the VVV Haspengouw tourist HQ.

Oud Rycklen
33 Dionysius Vanleeuwenstraat
T 011 68 70 72

An extraordinary village taverne with a small front bar full of card players and other committed locals. The kitchen (11.30–13.30 & 17.00–21.30, 23.00 Fr&Sa) serves local snacks such as *roerei met hesp*, plus pasta, pancakes and waffles. There is a two-table snooker parlour at the side. 50 beers from Kerkom, Val-Dieu, Westvleteren and Achouffe, plus some authentic gueuzes. Fruit wines too.
CLOSED TUESDAY
Sun 10.00 onwards ; *Other days* 14.00 onwards

ST. TRUIDEN

15km SW of Hasselt on N3 & N80
St. Truiden [Hasselt–Landen]

Interesting market town (pop. 38,000) on the old road from Leuven to Liège. Built around a disappeared abbey founded by St. Trudo, whose unlikely legend is that every time he tried to build a church, an interfering old bat pulled it down. So he prayed hard and God kindly paralysed her. The usual grand civic buildings dominate the town, which also has numerous small museums and attractive churches. The strangest sight is Festraets Studio (24 Begijnhof), which houses the world's largest atomic clock and other creations by a local physicist.

Hotel tip: the Cicindria★★★, 6 Abdijstraat (T 011 68 13 44; F 011 67 41 38; www.cicindria-hotel.be) is conveniently central and affordably comfortable.

Eglantier
21 Stationstraat   T 011 68 60 29

Two hundred metres from the station on the way to the Grote Markt, the "Sweet Briar" is a restored turn of the century patrician's house. Mainly art deco with a tendency for café crème. Rather pleasant. Principally a beer café, with around 100 mainly better brews in stock. Food stretches to vol au vent (Du: *vidé*), rolls, lasagne and filling soups. Closed over Christmas and New Year and may close in the second half of July.
CLOSED SUNDAY & MONDAY
Other days 11.00 onwards

TESSENDERLO

20km NW of Hasselt on N725

257

Busy and attractive small town (pop. 15,000), near the borders with Antwerp and Brabant provinces. On Sundays try to catch the "black" market (Du: *Zwartemarkt*). Eight kilometres southwest is the picturesque Abbey of Averbode, founded in the 12th century, with a famous baroque church.

Hotel tip: the **Dravershof**★, 92 Schoterweg (**T** 013 66 16 10) is incredibly cheap and not that basic.

Paenhuys
1 Schoterweg   **T** 013 66 52 21

In the town centre, one hundred metres from the church on the road to Schoot. An ancient and modern café with a long-standing beer interest. The large open summer terrace is enclosed in winter. Stocks a solid and growing list of around 110 beers. There is a broad range of bar snacks including pasta and a good selection of fish specialities. Lots of ice cream too.
CLOSED THURSDAY
CLOSED WEDNESDAY (*Sep–Jun*)
Other days 11.00–02.00

15km SE of Maastricht [NL] off N648

Attractive village in the Voeren. Signposted off the N648 but virtually nowhere else.

Hotel tip: the **Kings Head**★★, 4 Dorpstraat (**T** 04 381 13 24; **F** 04 381 10 22) is about as English as Anderlecht FC, faintly mad but charming in its own way.

Moeder De Gans
6 Dorpstraat   **T** 04 381 22 85

Large, old country pub in an attractive setting, with elaborate terraces and gardens used to great effect in summer. Stocks around 60 beers including several cellar-aged Trappist brews on a separate list they may not tell you about. Makes its own damson genever, steeping the fruit in spirit in oak vats. Good range of bar food, including home-made apple pie. Gets like a food factory on Saturday nights. May open early in summer. The village's other café and our hotel tip are worth a peek.
CLOSED MONDAY; *Other days* 11.00 onwards

Home from home in Teuven

258

TONGEREN

🚃 Tongeren *[Hasselt–Liège]*

Old Roman town (pop. 30,000) from the days of the Belgae. Lots of cobbled streets and the sort of buildings that should appeal to the historically aware tourist.

Madrigal

8 St. Maternuswal **T** 012 23 88 45

Next to the fire station, on the corner of the road to Bilzen, from the outer side of what passes for the town's ring road, to the north of the centre. A well-run local boozer, with potted plants and low-back settles, all done in green. Slowly but surely becoming a specialist beer café. There is a small terrace at the side. Stocks around 90 beers. An unusual variety of bar snacks includes homemade shrimp croquettes, pizzas, frog's legs, snails and chilli. Further round the ring road on the way to Maastricht, the **Kroon** (123 Maastrichterstraat – **T** 012 39 19 38 – closed Mo; others from 09.30) has its supporters, as much for the Trappist beer ice cream as for the Westvleteren beers.

CLOSED WEDNESDAY; *Sat & Sun* 14.00 onwards
Other days 11.00 onwards

Rembrandt

11 Veemarkt **T** 012 23 41 89

Said to be the oldest café in Tongeren, which is the oldest town in Belgium. An excellent example of a brown café. A single, small L-shaped bar with a tiled floor, old fireplace and just five tables inside. The covered terrace on the square at the front holds many more. Extremely affable owners can chat away in good English. Food as far as croques, pasta and omelette. The well-written beer list nearly reaches 55 but is well above average, including Boon, Westvleteren, Rochefort and ter Dolen. The Sunday morning opening is for the antiques market that surrounds the place.

CLOSED MONDAY & TUESDAY
Sun 05.00–02.00; *Sat* 14.00–02.00
Other days 11.30–02.00

TONGERLO

7km SW of Bree on N721
See Brewery cafés: St. Jozef (above).

ZOLDER

10km N of Hasselt off N72
🚃 Zolder *[Hasselt–Lier]*

Nondescript small town (pop. 13,000) that is home to the international motorcycle racetrack.

Kuipke

60 Dorpsstraat **T** 011 53 71 02

Opposite the church, in the centre of town. A popular local café carrying a range of 60 beers. Closes on Monday and Tuesday in July. We hear of an interesting new café on the high street of a neighbouring town, called the **Gezellehuis** (25 Guido Gezellelaan, Heusden – closed We; Th from 16.00; others from 10.00), with forty beers.

Wed 12.30 onwards; *Other days* 10.30 onwards

Luxembourg

POPULATION (2002): **250,000**
MAIN TOWN: **Arlon** (23,000)
TOURISM WEBSITE: www.ftlb.be

Not to be confused with the neighbouring Grand Duchy of Luxembourg, of which it was once a part, Belgium's Luxembourg is its south-eastern province and the heart of the real Ardennes.

Its touristic potential is huge but history has condemned it to being a loose confederation of self-contained areas, their unofficial boundaries defined by the tributaries of the Meuse. Public transport and other components of infrastructure are as poor, with no fast trains outside the Brussels – Luxembourg line. Do not let this stop you from exploring but allow a little longer to get between places.

Apart from the splendid and sometimes spectacular landscape, the Ardennes is famed for its cuisine. Beyond the hams, sausages, pâtés and pies found stuffing the windows of the local pork butchers (Fr: *salaisons*), you will find excellent game in season.

The area has history too, from the 11th century crusader's castle at Bouillon to the memorials and rusting hardware left over from the Battle of the Ardennes in 1944. This was the German army's last offensive of the 1939–45 war and the largest ever land engagement of US forces, involving more troops than Gettysburg, Tet or Baghdad. Many towns display an American tank, to remind us why the European Union was formed.

The province's most famous beer is the Trappist pale ale from Orval, though the impish spiced beers from Achouffe also get around a lot. One of the most heartening aspects of compiling the Guide in the last fifteen years has been tracking the re-emergence of a beer culture in the province from the eccentricities of Fantôme to the excellence of Rulles. This is now a great area for beer travellers to explore.

BREWERIES: **Achouffe**, *Achouffe*; **Bouillon**, *Bouillon*; **Fantôme**, *Soy*; **Ferme au Chêne**, *Durbuy*; **Gigi**, *Gérouville*; **Millivertus**, *Toernich*; **Orval**, *Villers-devant-Orval*; **Rulles**, *Rulles*; **Sainte Hélène**, *Ethe*; **Saint Monon**, *Ambly*; **Trois Brasseurs**, *Athus*; **Trois Fourquets**, *Courtil*.

BREWERY CAFÉS

Achouffe

The tiny hamlet of Achouffe is five kilometres off exit 51 of the E25. The **Brasserie** (32 Rue du Village – closed We, Sep–Jun; others 09.00–21.00) is located at the back of the brewery. Enjoy excellent cooking while staring through a large glass panel at the increasingly impressive kit used to brew the stuff you are drinking.

Fantôme

The **Brasserie Fantôme** (8 Rue Préal, Soy – closed Mo-Fr, except school holidays; others from 10.30) is in a small farm on the road into town from Hotton. As with the beers you take them as you find them. The plain but oddly attractive bar has seats outside. All the beers of the moment are on sale and there may be dry sausage and cheese.

Ferme au Chêne

Durbuy, on the banks of the Ourthe, claims to be the smallest town in Belgium and is a honeypot for Japanese tourists. The **Ferme au Chêne** (115 Rue Comte d'Ursel – T 086 21 10 67 – closed Nov–Mar; closed Wed all year; others 10.00-20.00) is one of the smallest breweries in Belgium. Its beer is served and sold for take-away in the modern café, along with a few snacks, including the local *matoufé*, a variation on bacon and eggs. Out of season, phone ahead.

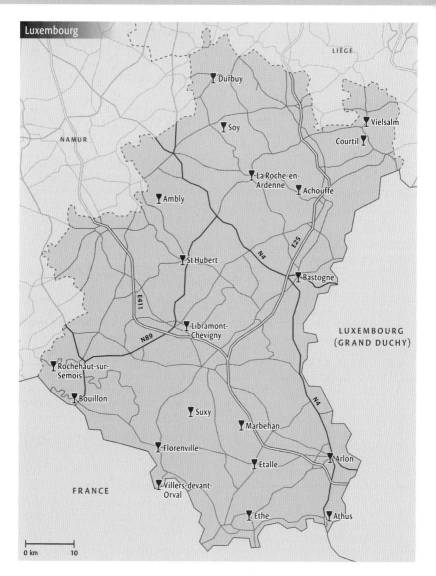

Luxembourg

LIÈGE

Durbuy

Soy

Vielsalm

NAMUR

Courtil

La Roche-en-Ardenne

Achouffe

Ambly

St Hubert

Bastogne

E25

N4

E411

N89

Libramont-Chevigny

LUXEMBOURG
(GRAND DUCHY)

Rochehaut-sur-Semois

N4

Bouillon

Suxy

Marbehan

Florenville

Etalle

Arlon

Villers-devant-Orval

FRANCE

Ethe

Athus

0 km   10

Orval

Orval is a working abbey at Villers-devant-Orval, six kilometres south of Florenville, near the French border. You may visit the ruins of the previous abbey and buy cheese and beer at its shop. The abbey's tavern, the **Ange Gardien** (3 Rue d'Orval – **T** 061 31 18 86 – closed Dec–Feb; closed Mo, Sep–Jun; others 11.30–19.30, 10.00–21.00 Jul–Aug), is a huge refectory-like café a few hundred metres short of the main gate. The beer served here is kept back at the brewery for longer bottle-conditioning. This is also the only outlet for the low gravity beer Petit Orval. There is a good range of snacks too, many featuring abbey produce. Stopping over in this beautiful spot is possible at the **Hostellerie d'Orval★** (14 Orval – **T** 061 31 43 65; **F** 061 32 00 92).

Rulles

There is no brewery tap but the **Buffet de la Gare** at nearby Marbehan railway station (8 Place de la Gare – **T** 063 41 15 54 – closed We; Su 10.00–15.00; others from 10.00) takes the rôle unofficially. Its landlord helps the brewer run the annual Brassigaume beer festival in the village (see Beer Events). As well as stocking Rulles beers you should get Ste. Hélène and about twenty others. Not your average station buffet, as witnessed by the adoring crowd of locals who come here to eat. Many of the trains on the Brussels-Luxembourg route stop here.

Saint Monon

This increasingly popular microbrewery has acquired a new tasting facility that opens most weekends through the year and all week in high summer (41 Rue Principale, Ambly – **T** 084 21 46 32 – closed Mo-Fr, Sep-Jun; others 11.00–18.00).

Trois Brasseurs

This French brewpub chain has only one Belgian incarnation to date, in Athus, near the borders with France and Luxembourg. The **Trois Brasseurs** (53 Rue de Rodange – daily from 16.00) is aimed mainly at the young, with an American-style menu, club nights, a casino complex and beers that are, well, unchallenging. Off the N88 to Rodange, near the centre of town.

Trois Fourquets

What a very Belgian concept to take a top quality restaurant and add a brewery. The **Trois Fourquets** (50 Courtil – **T** 080 64 38 39; **F** 080 64 38 80 – closed We&Th) is in the hamlet of Courtil, north of Gouvy in the northeast of the province. It has two separate eating options on the premises, a restaurant serving haute cuisine and a less expensive bistro. The two home-brewed ales are accompanied by a few from Achouffe. The Pils is from Simon, across the border.

ACHOUFFE

20km N of Bastogne off E25 exit 51
See Brewery cafés: Achouffe (above).

AMBLY

16km SSW of Marche-en-Famenne on N889
🚃 Forrières *[Libramont-Jemelle]* – 5km
See Brewery cafés: Saint-Monon (above).

ARLON

25km WNW of Luxembourg [L] on N4
🚃 Arlon *[Brussels-Luxembourg (L)]*

The provincial capital is little more than a market town (pop. 23,000) but can trace its origins back to Roman times. The Musée Luxembourgeoise (13 Rue des Martyrs) houses a few old remains. The town makes little of its history, ancient or modern, and frankly needs taking in hand by some benevolent tyrant in the tourist business.

Hotel tips: one of the best all-round hotels in the Guide is the **Peiffeschof★★★** (111 Chemin du Peiffeschof – **T** 063 41 00 50; **F** 063 22 44 05; **E** info@peiffeschof.be), two kilometres out of town by taxi on the way to the Luxembourg border. Superb food and hospitality, pleasant rooms with an Alpine chalet feel, plus a small range of local microbrewery beers for aficionados. Our in-town alternative demands an accomplished sense of humour. The astonishing **Ecu de Bourgogne★**, 9 Place de Léopold (**T** 063 22 02 22; **F** 063 23 27 54) must be the best business opportunity in all of Belgium. It is a superbly central, classically proportioned small-town hotel condemned to play Fawlty Towers without the humour, grace or respect. It takes the concept of customer care to new depths.

D'Alby

1 Rue du Marché au Beurre   **T** 063 21 64 47

On a corner of the Grand Place at the centre of the old town. A comfortable modern, lounge bar with a pleasant design and service that we have found friendly. Some say we are lucky. What is unquestioned is that since a tentative entry in our second edition, the beer list here has gone from strength to strength, such that it has become one of the best lists in the south. There were 150 beers at the time of our last visit, with a pan-Belgian

feel emerging. Considering the décor the absence of any food beyond basic bar snacks is surprising. There is an overflow bar upstairs with a good view of the square.
Mon–Thu 10.00–01.00
Fri & Sat 10.00–02.00; *Sun* 14.00–01.00

Forum

10 Rue des Capucins   **T** 063 22 08 84

In a backstreet parallel with the Grand Place. This unusual cellar bar looks as though it was constructed in a wine cellar of an ancient Roman villa, which it was. If you like bizarre aspects of café design, note the well in the corner of the front bar, with the illuminated view of water five metres below. Can get smoky but otherwise one of the best beer café atmospheres in the Ardennes. The list of 115 beers includes brews from Rulles, Binchoise and some foreign brewers. Food is limited to simple bar snacks.
Daily 12.00 onwards

OTHER ARLON CAFÉS:

The **Cigognes** (17 Rue de Diekirch – **T** 063 22 72 47) is a café frequented by market traders and locals, on one of the streets of Arlon's "inner ring", two minutes' walk from the centre. The range of beers is anyone's guess but it has definitely had its moments. Opening hours are liberal. Simon beers from the Grand Duchy and beers from St.Monon, Rulles, Ste. Hélène and new boy Millevertus manage to get into some local cafés.

ATHUS

12km S of Arlon off E411 exit 3
🚋 Athus *[Luxembourg (L) – Athus]* See Brewery cafés: Trois Brasseurs (above).

BASTOGNE

25km NNW of Arlon off E25 exits 53/54
🚋 Bastogne Nord *[Libramont–Bastogne]*

This small market town (pop. 13,000) found fame from conflict. The battle of the Ardennes is commemorated loudly at the American Mardasson Hill monument and museum on the outskirts of the town. In a vainglorious massacre of the English language usually reserved for presidential speeches, the fate of the final unsuccessful German offensive of the 1939–45 war is billed in terms that mistake battle for a game of football with shells. We find the silent, neat, grey, tree-shaded cemetery at Recogne, which is the resting place of 6,785 mainly unidentified German soldiers, a more suitable and engaging tribute.

Hotel tip: the Caprice★★, 25 Place MacAuliffe (**T** 061 21 81 40; **F** 061 21 82 01) is comfortably functional, child-friendly and pink inside, though the newly opened **Leo at Home★★**, 50 Place MacAuliffe (**T** 061 46 92 33) on the opposite side of the main square may give it a run for its money.

Lamborelle

19 Rue Lamborelle   **T** 061 21 80 55

Down a small pedestrian alleyway, just off Rue du Vivier, two blocks downhill from Place MacAuliffe. Dark and cosy with breweriana. Over 130 beers including many from better known Wallonian independents plus St.Monon and Bouillon. Small snacks are served all day, along with the occasional daily special. The music can get a bit enthusiastic. Our old entry for the town, **Bistro Leo** (8 Rue du Vivier) is still above average and does good food but sadly hovers below forty beers. Not that it bothers Leo, who seems to have the Bastogne catering franchise on everything including the Australian ice cream parlour!
CLOSED MONDAY; *Other days* 11.00 onwards

BOUILLON

On the far SW border with France, off N89

Attractive small town (pop. 6,000) on a loop of the River Semois, dominated by the 11th century ramparts of Godefroy de Bouillon's castle. Although upgraded in the reign of Louis XIV, several of its original rooms are hewn out of solid rock. The town has the appearance of a steep-banked creek on some rugged north European coastline, stacked with imposing early 20th century hotels and summer retreats. The rugged countryside round here makes for excellent walks. Cyclists should note that the eight-kilometre run into town from Corbillon is an exhilarating and visually alluring downhill-all-the-way do-it-before-you-die breeze.

Hotel tips: the town has numerous high quality hotels offering excellent value out of high summer. The **Alsace★★★**, 3 Faubourg de France (**T** 061 46 65 88; **F** 061 46 83 21; www.aubergedalsace.be) and the **Poste★★★**, 1 Rue de la France (**T** 061 46 51 51; **F** 061 46 51 65 – **E** info@hotelposte.be; www.hotelposte.be) are each particularly impressive.

Vieille Ardennes
9 Grand Rue   **T** 061 46 62 77

Pleasant, chatty, two-room street-corner café-restaurant on the castle side of the river, fifty metres from the Pont de Liège. The list of 60 beers evolves with time. Increasingly majors in plain but good Ardennaise cooking, ranging from simple bar snacks to three course meals. Opposite the Marché de Nathalie off-licence (see Beer shops & warehouse) and the Bouillon brewery. Sadly the town's other beer cafés have closed in recent years, though the foody and arty-in-a-blue-kind-of-way **Baratim** (12 Rue des Augustins) tries to stock some local beers on a list of over thirty.
CLOSED WEDNESDAY
Other days 10.00 onwards

COURTIL

25km NNE of Bastogne on N878 & N892
See Brewery cafés: Trois Fourquets (above).

DURBUY

10km NNE of Marche-en-Famenne on N833
🚃 Barvaux *[Jemelle–Liège]* – 5km
See Brewery cafés: Ferme au Chêne (above).

ETALLE

15km W of Arlon on N83
Small roadside town in the southern Ardennes.

Estalle
14 Place des Chasseurs Ardennais
T 063 45 62 80

On the main road from Arlon to Florenville, next to the church, with a small terrace at the front. A slowly improving sound local pub with enough beers, conversation and pub games to greet travellers with a Gaumaise welcome. Serves 45 beers including six Trappist ales and the local Gaumaise brews from Gigi. There are bar snacks. Opens from 16.00 on Tuesdays in the high season.
CLOSED TUESDAY
Fri & Sat 10.00–02.00; *Other days* 10.00–23.00

FORRIÈRES

10km SW of Rochefort on N849 & N889
🚃 Forrières *[Jemelle–Libramont]*
Railway village on the edge of the northern edge of the real Ardennes.

Estaminet
1 Rue des Allies   **T** 084 21 39 89

Discovered by accident, at the village high street, bang opposite the station. Trains often come here directly from Namur, Arlon and Luxembourg. Once a hotel but now just the village's main social centre. Confident, airy and popular. Stocks 90 beers, presumably as the personal passion of its owner. These include the local St Monon plus Bouillon, Ellezelloise and Val-Dieu. Food up to pasta and pizzas.   *Daily* 10.00 onwards

LA ROCHE-EN-ARDENNE

30km NNW of Bastogne on N89

Small market town on the banks of the Ourthe, said to be the capital of the Ardennes. Fierce fighting raged around the town in 1944, as recalled in a museum and by the presence of defunct American tanks. Teems with tourists on summer weekends, who pack its many restaurants and cafés. Visit out of season.

Hotel tips: the town is awash with hotels. The **Beau Rivage★★**, 26 Quai de l'Ourthe (**T** 084 41 12 41; **F** 084 41 12 42) has always been reliable.

Bronze

10 Place du Bronze   **T** 084 41 16 58

Large, multi-functional brasserie on the town's largest square at the hilly end of the main street. The hardest working of the town's cafés. The beer list reaches 60 and includes random highlights, not always in stock out of season. Food has expanded in recent years and now includes a full restaurant menu alongside a large selection of snacks and light meals.

CLOSED WEDNESDAY (*school terms*)
Fri & Sat 09.00–02.00; *Other days* 09.00–01.00

Venitien

28 Rue de l'Eglise   **T** 084 41 16 37

Comfortable high street corner café, one hundred metres from the river. Its beer list of 70 rises gently with the year and becomes more interesting, now assisted by a small beer shop next door that stocks twice the range. St. Monon and Fantôme usually feature. Minor snacks only and early closing except in high season. There is a small terrace. Between our two cafés is the **Ardennaise** (1 Rue du Pont – **T** 084 41 28 70 – daily 09.00–24.00) a good all round café with forty beers and good bar meals (10.30–22.00).

CLOSED MONDAY & TUESDAY (*Nov–Mar*)
Daily 10.00–23.00 (*Jul & Aug*); *others* 10.00–20.00

LIBRAMONT-CHEVIGNY

28km WSW of Bastogne off E411 exits 25/26
🚃 Libramont *[IR]*

Small town that acts as the main rail terminal for the southern Ardennes, being on the Brussels-Luxembourg main line. Untypically industrial for the region.

Lion Rouge

Place de la Gare   **T** 061 22 57 28

One of many cafés on the ground floor of an office and residential block opposite the railway station. Pretty basic but stocking 75 beers that are displayed above the bar. Simple bar snacks only. There is a small arcade of gaming machines at the back.

Mon–Fri 07.00–01.00
Sat 09.00–03.00; *Sun* 09.00–01.00

Yes

70 Grand Rue   **T** 061 23 48 23

On the main shopping street up in the town at the back of the station, just off the main road. A large, spotlessly clean, simple one-roomed modern brasserie with a small streetside terrace. It came as a surprise to owner Joel Clarenne that we consider his beer list the best in the Ardennes, with over 220 choices. His range of 75cl bottles and Wallonian regionals is probably the best we have seen in any café in Belgium. Flemish regionals are there too, plus most Trappists. The only weakness is lambics, which are from the commercial end of the spectrum. Food (11.00–22.00) is plentiful too, from cheese plates and spaghetti to salads, steaks and fish. Worth a major diversion.

Mon 11.00–14.30; *Other days* 11.00 onwards

MARBEHAN

24km WNW of Arlon on N897
🚃 Marbehan *[Libramont–Arlon]*

See Brewery cafés: Rulles (above).

ROCHEHAUT-SUR-SEMOIS

10km NW of Bouillon on N819

Beautiful small village, on a hill overlooking the Semois valley, in one of the most attractive parts of the Ardennes.

Hotel tip: the Auberge de la Ferme★★★
(**F** 061 46 10 01; www.aubergedelaferme.be) is the excellent small, family-run hotel that runs the Fermette (below).

Fermette

12 Rue de la Cense   **T** 061 46 10 00

Large and comfortable modern brasserie in an ancient building that is part of a family-owned complex at the heart of the village. This includes a good local food and drink shop and a heartily recommended, comfortable but good value auberge. Watch the community's business from the café terrace. The beer list of 50 includes St. Monon and a house beer from Caulier. Orval cheese, local

ham and omelettes are available all day, with a full menu (12.00–15.00; 18.00–22.00) of serious cooking that includes trout, wild boar, *choucroute* and excellent beef.
Daily 11.00–22.00

ST. HUBERT

28km W of Bastogne off N89

Pleasant market town just off the majestic but under-used N89 Ardennes highway. The Italianate church of St. Hubert dominates its main square. There are several good value small hotels and some excellent delicatessens. For unusual tourism go to Rédu, twelve kilometres to the west, which is Belgium's Hay-on-Wye or national capital of old books. Perhaps incongruously, it is also home to the European Space Center and museum.

Hotel tip: the **Luxembourg**★★, 7 Place du Marché (T 061 61 10 93; F 061 61 32 20) offers old town stability.

Caves de St. Hubert
13 Place du Marché   T 061 32 13 91

On the main street, beneath the "Légende de St. Hubert". A neat cellar bar in dark stone and glass, with no pretence of false traditions. The beer list of 60 is biased towards better producers such as Rulles, St. Monon and Achouffe. Food includes omelettes, tartines and pasta. The inner room, next to the bar, is non smoking. Plays the sort of young music older folk can tolerate. One to watch.
CLOSED MONDAY TO WEDNESDAY
Other days 11.30 onwards

SOY

11km NE of Marche-en-Famenne on N807
See Brewery cafés: Fantôme (above).

SUXY

30km WNW of Arlon on N894
Village in the rural boondocks at the heart of the largely destumped Forest of Chiny.

Stop
52 Rue Grande   T 061 31 56 43

Times change. Sadly the Stop is no longer a mad agglomeration of village supermarket, junk shop, bowling alley and local café. It has focussed its efforts on the last of these. This has been good for the beer list, now risen to over 70 and featuring many of the local brews plus numerous other highlights. Less good for the bowling alley, which sits, a bit disused-looking, laced precariously around the far side of the bar. A local campaign to preserve it would be good. Another UNESCO World Heritage site maybe? Still no prizes for décor but clearly doing well.
CLOSED THURSDAY
Fri & Sat 10.00–02.00; *Other days* 10.00–22.00

VIELSALM

12km SSW of Malmedy on N68
Vielsalm *[Liège–Gouvy]*

Small riverside market town in an area increasingly full of holiday parks, including the Ardennaise centre of the popular SunParks chain.

Escale
1 Avenue de la Salm   T 080 21 41 30

Modern one-room brasserie at the southern end of the small town centre, clearly serving the whole community. Television, music, screaming children, impassioned political debate, star-crossed lovers and drunk men moaning about the football, all in one space. An imaginative list of 120 beers features mainly independent breweries. A raised roadside terrace overlooks the main road. Food runs from basic bar meals to *carbonnade*, cassoulet of fish and chicory in bacon. Apologies for mislaying its opening hours. More reports welcome.

VILLERS-DEVANT-ORVAL

On the French border 8km SSE of Florenville on N86
See Brewery cafés: Orval (above).

Namur

POPULATION (2002): **460,000**
MAIN TOWN: **Namur** (106,000)
TOURISM WEBSITE: www.ftpn.be

NAMUR is Belgium's central southern province. With the exception of its capital, the city of Namur, it is largely rural. The area is dominated by river Meuse, which flows across the French border in the south to be joined by the Sambre at Namur and head on eastwards into Liège.

The north and west of the province are largely agricultural, with few tourist attractions, though the beer-commissioning abbeys of Maredsous and Floreffe are attractive. To the south and east, the western part of the Belgian Ardennes is famed for its caves and nature reserves.

Dinant has long been a base for touring the most attractive parts of the Meuse and Lesse valleys though its own facilities are too run-of-the-mill to retain the attention of tourists for long. While the Meuse remains an important conduit for industrial shipping, its use for pleasure craft is extremely limited.

South of Dinant public transport is thinly provided, even in the high season, so do not expect to get anywhere in a hurry. Those tempted to explore the beautiful valley of the Semois by bicycle should note that Eddie Merckx trained there. Take a bus map and plenty of patience, or a volunteer driver.

Readers will see from our listings that the province's café scene is dismal in parts. If you discover gems that we have missed let us know on BelgiumGBG@aol.com.

The best known breweries in the province are the long-established du Bocq, makers of the Gauloise beers and the still excellent Trappist brewery at the abbey of St. Rémy, near Rochefort. Of the smaller brewers, look out for the all-round excellence of Caracole and the unusual wheat beers of Silenrieux.

BREWERIES: **du Bocq**, *Purnode*; **Caracole**, *Falmignoul*; **Fagnes**, *Mariembourg*; **Lautenne**, *Lautenne*; **Mortals**, *Jamagne*; **Rochefort**, *Rochefort*; **Silenrieux**, *Silenrieux*.

BREWERY CAFÉS

du Bocq

The unofficial brewery tap is the **Place** (5 Grand Place, Purnode), near to the brewery in the centre of the village and selling all the its beers in pristine condition.

Caracole

We have conflicting reports about whether or not the rather nice tasting room and bar associated with the shop at the **Brasserie Caracole** (86 Côte Marie Thérèse, Famignoul) is open to the public or just reserved for brewery tours. We think it is open house all week in July and August, weekends only in June and September. Reports welcome.

Fagnes

South of Mariembourg, the **Brasserie des Fagnes** (26 Route de Nismes – **T** 060 31 39 19 – closed Mo; Tu–Th 15.00–21.00, Oct–Mar; others 10.00–21.00) is a tourist-orientated brewpub that does more marketing than brewing. The brewery can be seen clearly from the bar area but there is also a standing exhibit of a 19th century brewhouse. Light snacks include *escavêche* and others regional favourites. Large terrace and children's play area in summer. Open fires in winter.

Mortal's

In the hamlet of Jamagne, north of Philippeville this evolving hobby brewery

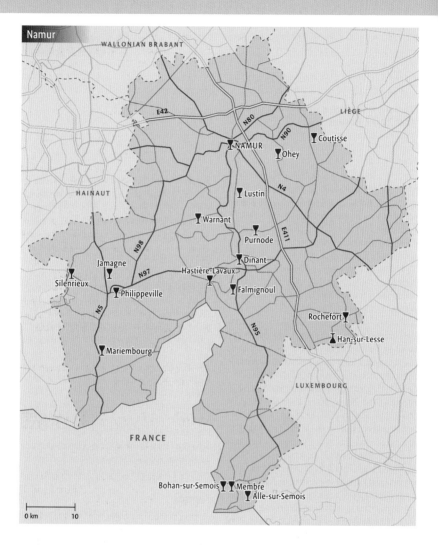

now runs a front room tasting café next to the brewery, which opens every Sunday (47 Belle Ruelle – 13.00–21.00) or by reservation. All currently available ales may be sampled or purchased for takeaway.

Rochefort

The Trappist brewery at Rochefort is the only one with no official brewery tap, though the excellent tavern-restaurant, the **Relais St. Remy** (140 Route de Ciney – **T&F** 084 21 39 09 – closed We; Tu 10.00–14.30 Sep–Jun; others

10.00–21.30) is rising in profile as the place to drink and to eat Rochefort beers. The *canard Trappist* is particularly fine. They keep a constant supply of room temperature beer in front of the bar for the cognoscenti.

Silenrieux

Even though Silenrieux is a small town it is easy to miss the **Chez L'Père Sarrasin** (1 Rue Noupre – **T** 071 79 64 07 – closed Mo; others from 10.00), a simple brasserie-restaurant, set back from the N978 Cerfontaine road.

Starters include *escavêche*, asparagus roulade, beetroot and tuna salad or scampi in garlic. Mains are more pasta, pizza and steaks. The brewery can be seen through internal windows. Could do with a major design overhaul.

BOHAN-SUR-SEMOIS

40km S of Dinant on N945

Small and picturesque town on the banks of the Semois near the French border in a popular tourist area.

Hotel tip: the **Dauby Dambroise**★, 76 Rue de Membre (☎ 061 50 01 59) is a pleasant pension with a small restaurant, mainly closed between New Year and Easter.

Ardennaise

16 Place Henri de la Lindi   ☎ 061 50 18 67

Apparently they do not have beer cafés in this part of the world because there is no demand. Yet when we last visited this brilliant example it was overflowing with customers of all ages, backgrounds and dress sense, clearly enjoying a spectacular beer list of over 250. In winter this weekend café is a thoroughly civilised beer saloon with chatty locals. In summer its street terrace burgeons with chat. There are six of the finest authentic gueuzes, an array of regional beers from the A Team – de Ranke, Ellezelloise, Dupont, Sint Bernardus, Van Eecke, Géants and Kerkom. They achieve the impossible by ignoring the trend. You will not find food beyond a portion of cheese but the ripple effect is such that the brasserie next door, the **Mel Bleu**, has added to its excellent range of *gauffres*, waffles and light lunches a healthily long beer list featuring numerous Canadian micros. Worth taking a long detour. CLOSED MONDAY TO FRIDAY (Sep–Jun) *Sat & Sun* 09.00–22.00

COUTISSE

15km E of Namur off N90

Hamlet on the little white road from Andenne to Haillot, at the point where the parishes of Andenne and Coutisse join.

Hotel tip: it does not pay to roll up on chance to the **Moulin Kevret**★★ (below). Always book ahead for accommodation and dinner. Letting rooms are growing in number and comfort but are still being renovated.

Moulin de Kevret

153 Rue de Haillot   ☎&F 085 84 49 33

Eight years' work has gone into renovating this 15th century watermill and small holding so far and they reckon there are four more to go. Not the easiest place to find but worth the effort. The official opening hours we quote are sound but others are negotiable, particularly if there is a group of you. This is a country living where two former top restaurateurs have parked themselves while they bring up their children. Enjoy 60 or so beers on a list concocted by cropping whatever they can. Food is at the discretion of la patronne, who can conjure anything from African to Thai as well as several versions of Belgian. Parties from six to sixty should decide their menu in advance. *Fri & Sat* 18.00 onwards; *Sun* 12.00 onwards Other times by arrangement

DINANT

20km S of Namur on A94 & N97 🚃 Dinant *[Namur–Dinant]*

Dinant is the old tourist centre of the Meuse Valley (pop. 13,000). Below a clifftop Citadel, the town marks its presence with the unmistakable onion dome of the Church of Notre Dame. And there the effort ends, which is a shame because the setting and surrounding countryside are very attractive. The *Grotte la Merveilleuse* on the Philippeville road, is less of a cave than those of Han-sur-Lesse but well worth worth visiting. Cruises go down the Meuse as far as the French border. Take the train to Anseremme and transfer to Houyet, twenty kilometres up river and you can barge or canoe it back in about five hours of gorgeous valley scenery, some bordering the Furfooz national park. Sadly, no Dinant café merits a full entry. The best for beer is probably the riverside **Brasseurs** (3 Rue

Albert Huybrechts – **T** 082 22 63 66). For staying and for eating your best bet is the dependable **Couronne** (1 Rue Adolfe Sax – **T** 082 22 24 41; **F** 082 22 70 31), opposite the onion-dome, a family-run hotel that dabbles in civilised ambience and good cooking plus a few beers.

FALMIGNOUL

10km S of Dinant on N95
See Brewery cafés above: Caracole.

HAN-SUR-LESSE

6km SW of Rochefort on N86

Another town desperately in need of a café that takes an interest in beer. Han exists entirely because of tourism, its whole economy built around the amazing *Grottes de Han*, its caves. The English writer Robert Graves once said of Shakespeare that "Despite all the people who like him, he is really an exceptionally fine playwright". And so it is with the caves at Han. Despite their popularity, they are worth a long detour, ideally avoiding the high summer hordes. From the town centre catch the rickety-rackety train for a ten-minute journey up the hill to the cave's mouth. Then open your own for much of the kilometre and a bit of stalactites, stalagmites and cleverly lit natural rock formations. At the end sit through a *son et lumière* before taking the boat ride an underground river, back to the real world. Allow ninety minutes. Take a light jumper even in high summer, plus waterproof shoes.

Then try to find lunch or supper in a café or restaurant with a decent beer list. We wish you luck. The Guide's staple has been the café at the hotel **Ardennes** (2 Rue des Grottes – **T** 084 37 72 20 – www.hansurlesse.be), which has an excellent terrace and bar menu and the best of a bad bunch of beer lists.

HASTIÈRE-LAVAUX

10km SW of Dinant on N96

Small village of several parts, straddling the Meuse at the first road bridge south from Dinant. The basilica is 11th century. You can reach here by bus from Dinant station. There are caves nearby at Pont d'Arcole (daily 09.00–19.00, Easter–Sep).

Pichet du Père Marlet
48 Rue Marcel Lespagne   **T** 082 64 51 60

At the bottom end of the high street, in a pleasant enough riverside town, "Father Marlet's Jug" is one of the longest established beer cafés in Wallonia, pre-dating the Guide by a decade or more. Its list of over 100 beers was featuring a wide range of 75cl bottles long before these came back into fashion. Its other claim to fame is its restaurant, where meat is grilled over an open fire, often in the bar. There is game in season. In the old days they would stay open non-stop for the whole weekend in summer but nowadays the pace is quieter. There is a small streetside terrace in summer. May close in the second half of November.
CLOSED MONDAY TO THURSDAY (*school terms*) *Fri* 18.00 onwards; *Other days* 11.00 onwards

JAMAGNE

4km N of Philippeville off N5
🚃 Philippeville [*Namur–Dinant*] – 4km
See Brewery cafés: Mortal's (above)

LUSTIN

12km S of Namur on N947
🚃 Lustin [*Namur–Dinant*]

Small village on top of a hill, overlooking the Meuse valley. Its railway station and beer café are down by the river.

Musée des Bières Belges
19 Rue de la Gare   **T** 081 41 11 02

This remarkable place is on the small valley road that runs alongside the railway line, close to the Meuse. Two trains an hour stop at the small halt one hundred metres away. Not so much a café as the active end of the museum of beer bottles and glasses (see Beer Tourism: Museums). The deal here is that you must buy a ticket to visit the museum and are then allowed to drink from a large range of current bottles and glasses. Parties are directed to one of the back rooms. Friends and interested beer lovers may sit at the small counter in the tiny front room to sample one of the many beers in stock. There is a small terrace outside. It is not yet clear whether Madame's recent retirement will mean that opening hours will be more restricted, though the yarning will.

CLOSED MONDAY TO THURSDAY (Sep–Jun) *Other days* 11.00–19.30

MARIEMBOURG

18km S of Phillippeville off N5
🚉 Mariembourg [*Charleroi–Couvin*]
See Brewery cafés: Fagnes (above).

NAMUR

🚉 Namur [*IC*]

A couple of years ago Namur (pop. 106,000) was saddled with the new Wallonian parliament, making it both the regional and provincial capital. It was chaotic enough without that.

Created at the place where the Sambre joins the Meuse, its main tourist attractions are found around the old Citadel. This sits on a hill approached through wooded parkland by winding road or else directly by cable car. It supports a sports stadium, open-air theatre, museums of forestry and of military history, a château and an amusement park. From here you can see the whole town and the confluence of its two rivers.

An excellent place for interesting shops, particularly in the pedestrianised areas of the older parts of town. Its main theatre is famous too.

Hotel tip: the **Tanneurs**★★★, 10 Rue des Tanneurs (**T** 081 23 19 99; **F** 081 26 14 32; www.tanneurs.com) is an amazingly converted old leather tanning factory with legendary food and rooms that range from student garrets to uniquely designerd multi-storey suites.

Bouffon du Roi

60 Rue de Bruxelles **T** 081 23 00 44

Turning right out of the station, Rue de Bruxelles is the road to the left at the the railway bridge. The "Court Jester" is a dark and cavernous long bar with a slate floor, paintings on the wall and candle-lit tables. The list of 70 beers is strong on triples, 75cl bottles and better-established Wallonian micros. There are excellent fruit wines from Profondeville, a few miles south of here, plus a range of whiskies, teas and coffees. Simple snacks only. They have a small library of beer books. Beer prices are hiked when there is live music.

Mon–Fri 08.00–01.00; *Sat & Sun* 18.00–01.00

Caves à Bieres

68 Rue Godfroid **T** 081 22 27 30

A recently opened beer café on the road that heads into the centre of town from the front of the station. Large, long-roomed bar in the modern style with prominent pinball machines. The opening beer list of nearly 60 includes brews from Géants, Dupont, Dubuisson, Lefèbvre and of course du Bocq. Lunchtime snacks (12.00–14.00) include sandwiches, pasta and other stuff. Stays open till 01.00 on Friday to Sunday.
Daily 11.30 onwards

Chapître

4 Rue du Seminaire **T** 081 22 69 60

At the blunt end of St Aubain's cathedral, five minutes walk from the station. The simplest of corner cafés but reeking of great *paysant* style. The superb ambience is created by candlelight, simple wooden furnishings and a handsome bar of the glass and carved wood variety. It has closed and re-opened since our last edition but new owners immediately shot the beer list up to 60 and brought to it as much class as the décor, with de Ranke, Dupont, Westvleteren and Slaghmuylder featuring. A *crêperie* will appear upstairs shortly. Opening hours may change.

CLOSED SUNDAY (*mostly*)
Sat 17.00 onwards; *Mon–Fri* 12.00–22.30

OTHER NAMUR CAFÉS:

At the bottom of Rue Emile Cuvelier, round Place du Theatre is the solid but unadventurous **Metropole** (1 Rue Emile Cuvelier), an attractive café with thirty-five beers, open till 21.00 most days. The area St. Aubain cathedral is spreading its wings. **Henry** (3 Place St. Aubain) is a good place for eats, with its attractive façade, elegant interior, slick service and thirty beers. Opposite, on the corner of Rue Lelièvre the **Fontaine** (Place St. Aubain) is building some better brews into its similar sized list. Brick walls, beamed ceiling and paintings of animal fables on plaster walls suggest it intends to do style.

OHEY

15km ESE of Namur on N921

Hilltop village south of Andenne, for the killing of cyclists by heart strain or heavy traffic.
Hotel tip: see Coutisse (above).

Engoran

9 Rue de Ciney **T** 085 61 22 22 **F** 085 61 37 79

A classic village institution at the highest point on the road, heading south from the village centre. It claims a mediaeval theme, which we think refers to the dark heavy furnishings. The beer list of around 60 punches above its weight thanks to the drinks centre next door, which we assume they own. Possibilities include St Monon, Silenrieux, Vapeur, Cantillon, Caracole and Achouffe, plus own label beers from Van Steenberge. The food gets good reports and there is a banqueting suite, called the Mon Joie. Beware the gaoled troll.
CLOSED MONDAY & TUESDAY
Sat 17.00–22.00; Other days 11.00–22.00

PHILIPPEVILLE

25km S of Charleroi on N5 & N40
 Philippeville [Charleroi–Couvin]

Isolated market town that comes alive on Saturday.

Philippe II

56 Rue de France **T** 071 66 68 60

A modern version of the typical street-corner local café, on the road in from the N5, two hundred metres short of the main square. The list of 60 beers is adventurous for the area but we have been unable to find out if it stocks the three new local breweries' beers. Small snacks. No terrace but there is a children's play area nearby. For grander fayre and usually a few unusual beers try the **Armes de Philippeville** (3 Place des Armes – **T** 071 66 62 41) in the market square, whose signature dish is rabbit in beer with nettles.

PURNODE

9km NNE of Dinant on N937
See Brewery cafés: du Bocq (above).

ROCHEFORT

25km ESE of Dinant on the N86

If ever there was a town in desperate need of a great beer café then surely this is it. The Abbaye Notre Dame de St. Rémy is the only brewing abbey that does not have a sampling café. Rochefort (population 12,000) is also as close as you will get in the western Ardennes to a transport hub. There are buses to the caves of Han-sur-Lesse and on to the railway station at Jemelle. This is the only town in the world to say to visitors "Yes we are named after an internationally acclaimed beer but we do not have a beer café." It has a ruined castle, the mediaeval château of Comtal and its own set of caves for people who do not like crowds, the Grottes de Rochefort. But no beer café.

Hotel tips: there is a lot of good-value accommodation around including a couple of gems out near the château, called the **Vieux Logis**★★, 71 Rue Jacquet (**T** 084 21 10 24; **F** 084 22 12 30) and the Fayette★, 87 Rue Jacquet (**T** 084 21 42 73).

There is also accommodation in the town centre, along with some very good eating opportunities. The best bar the town is probably at the **Luxembourg** (2 Place Albert 1er – **T** 084 21 31 68), an café-restaurant with accommodation and an effortless list of forty beers. Two of the town's cheap and cheerful hotel-restaurants, the **Central** (30 Place Albert 1er) and the **Limbourg** (21 Place Albert 1er) are equally docile.

SILENRIEUX

15km W of Phillippeville on N40.
See Brewery cafés: Silenrieux (above).

WARNANT

12km S of Namur off N92
🚃 Yvoir [Namur–Dinant] – 5km
Small village on the western side of the Meuse valley.

Marronniers

102 Rue de la Molignée   **T** 082 61 13 34

On the N971 as it bypasses the village on the way from Yvoir, on the Meuse, to Sosoye and the abbey of Maredsous. A pleasant, isolated roadside brasserie with a neat front bar. Still keeps around 60 beers according to our latest information. Its restaurant (12.00–14.30 & 18.30–21.00) offers set menus and à la carte dining that includes dishes brewed with the "local" Maredsous abbey beers. Down the way the abbey's huge refectory serves all the beers plus the bread and the cheese.

CLOSED TUESDAY & WEDNESDAY
Daily 10.30–23.00

In fond memory of Madame Thérèse Abeels, spirit of the Musée des Bières Belges in Lustin, who died in February 2006.

Wallonian Brabant

POPULATION (2002): 350,000
MAIN TOWNS: **Braine l'Alleud** (36,000) and **Wavre** (31,000)
TOURISM WEBSITE: www.brabantwallon.be

Wallonian Brabant (Fr: *Brabant-Wallonie*) is the smaller, more southerly slice of the old province of Brabant. It absorbs spikes of outer Brussels suburbia along its motorway junctions and train lines, ending up neither rural nor urban. It has the reputation for being the home of some serious money. You would never know from the state of its generally dowdy towns and dreary countryside.

More than any other province in Belgium, this is a disaster area for beer drinkers.

Unfortunately, it is also home to one of the country's biggest tourist attractions, the battlefield between Plaincenoit and Braine l'Alleud that the world called Waterloo. It was here in 1815 that a ragbag band of mercenaries under the leadership of a future British Prime Minister put an end to Napoleon's original plan for a single Europe and determined much of the shape of the present day continent.

There is history too in the old market towns of Nivelles, Ittre, Braine-le-Château and even the suburban sprawl of Tubize. But not much decent beer. For that you have to go to Louvain-la-Neuve, home to the south's most prominent university, created after an acrimonious split from the Flemish academics in Leuven. Imagine Milton Keynes if it had been cloned from the wartime workforce at Bletchley Park.

The province's only well-known beers come from the family-run Lefèbvre beer factory, famous for its Floreffe brands.

BREWERIES: **Brabant**, *Baisy-Thy*; **Brasse-Temps**, *Louvain-la-Neuve*; **Lefèbvre**, *Quenast*.

BREWERY CAFÉS

Brasse-Temps

In an area so lacking in specialist beer outlets it is ironic that the province's only brewpub, the **Brasse-Temps** (4 Place des Brabançons, Louvain-la-Neuve – closed Sa; Su 16.00–02.00; others 11.00–02.00) is bang opposite its only top-rate specialist beer café. For directions see below. The draught beers are brewed on the premises. Other Dubuisson beers are here too. Food is limited to soups, salads and pasta.

Lefèbvre

The brewery's home town of Quenast was responsible for making cobblestones. The museum of same is housed in what is *de facto* the brewery tap, the **Moulin d'Arenberg** (11 Rue Dr. Colson, Rebecq – closed Mo&Tu; others 14.00–24.00). You should get all their beers in this heavily timbered, smartly converted 17th century watermill, the larger of two on the riverbank. Rebecq is an attractive village. On Sunday afternoons from May to September a steam train goes from here to Rognon. The smaller mill gives flour-grinding demonstrations. The abbey of Floreffe is ten kilometres west of Namur.

JODOIGNE

9km SSW of Tienen on N29 & N240

Bustling but unremarkable market town, just south of the language divide, on the road from Charleroi to Tienen.

Retro

2 Avenue Fernand Charlot   T 010 81 03 42

A two-storey brasserie on the crossroads at the centre of town, intended to project a

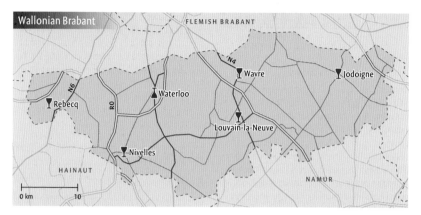

Thirties image. The beer list in the ground floor café reaches 50 on a good day and includes brews from Dupont, Ellezelloise and St. Feuillien. The restaurant upstairs offers a full range of meat and fish dishes, with lighter snacks available all day.
Daily 10.00 onwards

LOUVAIN-LA-NEUVE

20km SE of Brussels off N4 & E411 exit 8
🚆 Louvain-la-Neuve [Ottignies–Louvain-la-Neuve]

In the late Sixties the French-speaking half of the University of Leuven fell out big time their Flemish colleagues and in 1972 set up campus in a beetroot field near the industrial town of Ottignies. Here they constructed Belgium's first new town (pop. 25,000) for three hundred years. They called the place Louvain-la-Neuve, or "New Leuven" and created a special white paving stone called a *blanc de Bierges* to give the community a touch more class than its European equivalents. The residential, teaching and social facilities are clumped together in pseudo-suburbs. The Musée de Louvain-la-Neuve (1 Place Blaise Pascal) houses a collection of paintings bequeathed by a doctor in the days when they could afford the odd masterpiece. The town dies on Saturdays and in university holidays.

Hotel tips: the Relais★, 6 Rue de la Gare
(T 010 48 65 65; www.relais.ucl.ac.be) is a modern town-centre version of a sort of up-market hall of residence for travelling academics, with appropriately low prices.

Bretonne
1a Place des Brabançons   T 010 45 15 85

This modern estate-style café in the middle of a pedestrianised area at the centre of this campus town looks less like a beer bar than most but is probably in the Belgian top ten. Come by train – do not try to drive or even cycle. The station is on a special branch line from Ottignies. On exiting walk two blocks up the hill and down to your right is the small square that houses this oddly obsessive beer-café-cum-crêperie and the province's only brewpub (see Brewery cafés: Brasse-Temps above). The only sop to the rest of the genre it its use of chunky furniture. The design is everyday caff. Its terrace is a suntrap. The beer list of around 220 features over thirty 75cl bottles of Wallonian ales. The Flemish beers are sold under their French names wherever possible. Its other passion is pancakes (Fr: *crêpes*). They range from the sort with sugar and lemon juice via dozens of jam and honey versions and umpteen different mushroom recipes to masterpieces filled with lamb's kidneys in brown ale or coquilles St. Jacques in wheat beer. Seventy teas, fifty coffees, thirty cordials, countless ice creams. You get the message. Completist without being nerdy.
Daily 09.00–01.30

NIVELLES

Halfway between Brussels & Charleroi off E19 exit 19

🚉 Nivelles [Brussels–Charleroi]

Nivelles (Du: *Nijvel*) is a classically proportioned market town (pop. 24,000) that is home to many British and American ex-pats who work at the local SHAPE and NATO bases. The old town flows outwards from the Romanesque collegiate church of St. Gertrude in the enormous market square. This is largely a reconstruction of the original 11th century building and was badly bombed in the 1939–45 war.

Brasserie

13 Grand Place   T 067 21 95 08

Also known as Chez Maggie, this archetypal up-market town centre brasserie-taverne is a newcomer to the world of special beers. Its list sticks to safer indepependents like Silly, Caulier, Ellezelloise and St. Feuillien, who now hold the contract for supplying the town's Jean de Nivelles label beers. There is a large menu of good quality snacks and bar meals, including the local *tarte al djotte*, a heavy buckwheat and cheese pancake that it cholesterol's answer to the challenge of vegetarianism.
Daily 10.30 onwards

REBECQ

18km NW of Nivelles off E429 exit 24
🚉 Hennuyères [Halle–Manage]
See Brewery cafés: Lefèbvre (above).

WATERLOO

15km S of Brussels on N5, off R0 exit 27.
🚉 Waterloo [Braine l'Alleud–Brussels or Aalst]

39,000 troops were killed near here on 18th June 1815. The Battle of Waterloo was the turning point in the career of Napoleon Bonaparte. The British think they won it but in truth an international band of mercenaries, led by an Irishman, held out until the Prussians marched in from the wrong direction to seize the day.

The battlefield is ten kilometres south of the town, off exit 25 of the R0 motorway. Its attractions include a movie spectacular that is worth seeing, a panoramic painting that is not and an absurd but striking earthwork called the Butte du Lion. This last was constructed by French widows and you have to climb just 226 steps to conquer it. There is an annual re-enactment in mid-June.

Yet for all the historical brouhaha at the site and in the town, the place cannot muster one beer café worthy of the name. At the battlefield a single enterprise appears to have bought the catering rights and does not include beer in its world view of Belgium. The town is no better.

To mark this fact the Guide has put Waterloo forward as Belgium's entry to the competition for Europe's Least Beery Attraction (or ELBA). Motto: go there if you must but don't stay long.

WAVRE

25km S of Brussels off E411 exit 6
🚉 Wavre [Leuven–Ottignies]

The provincial capital (pop. 31,000) is the least impressive in Belgium, being more like a dowdy market town, with the Wednesday market its most endearing feature. A lot of big money lives round here but clearly it does not like quality beer. Your only reason to be here is take children to the Six Flags amusement park, formerly known as Walibi, two kilometres west of the town. The roller coaster, big wheel and famed indoor water centre will set you back €80 for a family of four.

Most of the bars round here are as dull as Norfolk rain. Best of the bunch is probably the **Hôtel de Ville** (Rue du Pont du Christ), which has forty beers including St. Bernardus and the Maredsous brands, plus the usual tavern trappings. Spot a potential full Guide entry and we will send you our next edition for free.

West Flanders

POPULATION (2002): **1,130,000**
MAIN TOWNS: **Bruges** (115,000), **Kortrijk** (75,000), **Ostend** (67,000) and **Roeselare** (54,000)
TOURISM WEBSITE: www.westtoer.be

WEST FLANDERS (Du: *West-Vlaanderen*; Fr: *Flandres Occidentale*) is Belgium's coastal province. It marks the westernmost corner of the country and as such is nearest geographical point to England. It is increasingly popular with British and French beer travellers, who are drawn to its history as well as its great beers and cafés.

The province's top tourist destination is the impressively preserved old cloth merchants' town of Bruges (Du: *Brugge*). Set in the drained marshland area of the Polders, this once great trading city now struts its stuff on the catwalk of top tourist destinations by simply being itself. Its streets buzz with smugly content hordes from all nations, pleased at having discovered such a cultured place in which to pass a few days.

The Belgian coastal resorts stretch sixty kilometres from De Panne to Knokke-Heist with hardly a break. The gentlefolk of late 19th century Europe considered its sandy beaches and broad promenades the height of fashion. A fast, efficient tram service runs its full length, linking easily to the rail terminals at Ostend and Blankenberge, and awkwardly to the ferry port at Zeebrugge. Its cultural capital is the port of Ostend. For the most impressive remnant of *fin de siècle* glamour, visit De Haan.

West Flanders was the site of much of the fighting in the 1914–18 war. The coastal town of Nieuwpoort was the northern end of a trench line that continued down the banks of the Ijzer, through Diksmuide to Ieper (Fr: *Ypres*) and on through Wallonia and France to the Swiss border.

In this quiet rural backwater, less than a century ago, Europe sacrificed a generation and proved that the squabbles of its inter-related Royal houses could no longer be resolved by military means. Stark memorials around Ieper and Diksmuide can still bring a chill to the cosily raised great-grandchildren of its survivors.

From the old textiles town of Kortrijk in the south, the gentle cycle ways along the Schelde to Oudenaarde could not be further removed.

The lay breweries around the hop town of Poperinge, St. Bernardus and Van Eecke brew big assertive ales in styles similar to the Trappist brewery at St. Sixtus abbey, near Westvleteren. God employs this place to show the world the potential of beer. They do not applaud compromise at de Dolle Brouwers either. Leroy makes insufficiently known lagers and Regenboog shows promise.

In the south the tradition is one of oak-aged ales, currently undergoing a revival in fortunes thanks to the tenacity of Verhaeghe, the re-investment in Rodenbach and the effects of awkward US importers demanding more authenticity to their sour brown ales.

BREWERIES: **Alvinne**, *Ingelmunster*; **Bavik**, *Bavikhove*; **de Bie**, *Loker*; **Bockor**, *Bellegem*; **Deca**, *Woesten*; **de Dolle Brouwers**, *Esen*; **'t Gaverhopke**, *Stasegem*; **Halve Maan**, *Bruges*; **Leroy**, *Boezinge*; **Liefmans**, *Dentergem*; **Old Bailey**, *St. Eloois-Winkel*; **Regenboog**, *Assebroek*; **Rodenbach**, *Roeselaere*; **Sint Bernardus**, *Watou*; **Strubbe**, *Ichtegem*; **Van Eecke**, *Watou*; **Van Honsebrouck**, *Ingelmunster*; **Verhaege**, *Vichte*; **Westvleteren**, *Westvleteren*.

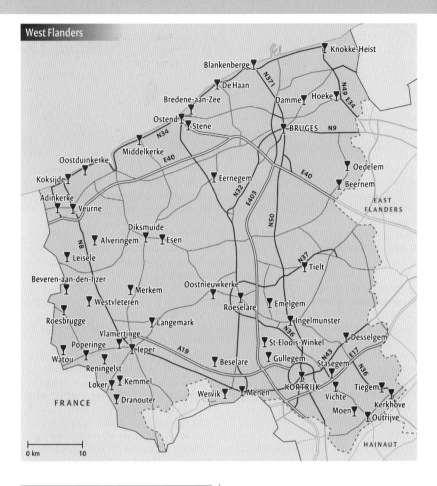

West Flanders

BREWERY CAFÉS

de Bie

The brewery moved a couple of years ago from a small hut in Watou to a handsome beer café called the **Hellekapelle** (171 Dikkebusstraat, Loker – **T** 057 44 85 44 – closed Mo–Th; Fr&Sa from 18.00; Su from 12.00). The name "Chapel of Hell" refers to a time when the church saw cafés as covens of debauchery and drunkenness. One reader described the décor as "elfin Buddhism meets the antiChrist". You have to see it to know what he means. Good food served till 22.00. There is an outside play area for children. All the brewery's beers are available on draught or in bottle.

De Dolle Brouwers

The brewery has a large plain tasting area open to the public at weekends (12b Roeselaerestraat, Esen – Sa 09.00–19.00; Su 14.00–19.00). Can be busy on Sundays, mainly because of the brewery tour (see Beer Tourism) and the fact that brewer Kris Herteleer opens up his increasingly impressive on-site art gallery to public view.

't Gaverhopke

This tiny brewery looks more like the village hall. Its tasting room (187 Steenbrugstraat, Stasegem – Sa&Su from 15.00) offers whichever of the six beers are in stock, plus snacks amounting to doorstep sandwiches. Also opens on bank holidays.

Old Bailey

West Flanders' first brewpub, in St. Eloois-Winkel (5 Kerkplein – closed We, plus Mo, Oct–Mar; others from 10.00). Surprisingly up-market for a small town bar, with good food and accommodation (**T** 056 50 07 28, **F** 056 50 96 49). Its underactive brewery is visible from outside and in.

Regenboog

No pub but they do have a shop (134 Astridlaan, Assebroek – closed Su&Mo; Sa 14.00–18.00; others 09.00–12.00 & 14.00–19.00). We assume this will continue after the projected move to Oudenaarde.

Rodenbach

We do not know if it is an official brewery-owned outlet but in the centre of Roeselare is the ultra-modern **Zalm** (24 Grote Markt – **T** 051 20 00 81 – closed We; Tu 07.00–16.00; Su from 11.00; others from 09.00). This replaced an old bar of the same name that had been closed some while. When it re-opened at the end of 2004 the surprise was a draught Rodenbach beer from the brewery's oak tuns called Oud Belegen Foederbier, apparently hand-pulled without carbonation. A couple of dozen other beers and food also feature.

Sint Bernardus

There is no tasting café at this brewery two kilometres south of Watou but, uniquely, the home of its former brewer, has been opened as a top rate pension. Stay at the **Brouwershuis** (23a Trappistenweg, Watou – **T** 057 38 88 60, **F** 057 38 80 71) for its charm, elegance and splendid breakfast. As a bonus the beers are available for guests to sample in the lounge and conservatory. There is a Belbus stop directly outside.

Van Eecke

Just next to the brewery in the centre of Watou, the **Brouwershof** (4 Douvieweg – **T** 057 48 76 16 – closed Tu, Oct–Jun; others from 09.00) is a small beer house under new ownership, where you can sample most of the beers from Van Eecke and Leroy of Boezinge. Needs to make more of its status.

Van Honsebrouck

The brewery is based in Ingelmunster town but the home of the Van Honsebrouck family is the castle, about 10km north of Kortrijk. Despite recent fire damage, this is still where you will find the brewery tap, the **Kasteelkelder** (closed Mo all year plus Tu–Fr, Oct–Easter; others from 14.00). Most of the beers are available, with a take home facility. There are also simple snacks made with the beer.

Verhaeghe

The best of Verhaeghe's own taverns in its hometown of Vichte is probably the **Hert** (Vichteplaats – closed Mo), which also does food. The best range of beers in the town, including their own, is at the **Watermolen** (22 Beukenhofstraat – closed Th; others from 16.00; Tu&We also 11.00–13.00), just down the street from the brewery, which does not.

Westvleteren

The simplest of Trappist breweries has the grandest of brewery taps. The **Vrede** (13 Donkerstraat – closed Fr; others from 10.00; to 20.00, Nov–Mar) is a great barn of a place that doubles as a conference centre, two kilometres from Westvelteren village, on the Hoppeland cycling route. Not a lot is on offer beyond three of the world's finest beers in tip-top condition. Food is limited to soup and basic sandwiches, plus *hommelpaptaart*, or "hop harvest quiche" in season and a bit of experimental beer-related stuff. A small shop sells the monastery's Port Salut style cheese and other authentic Trappist products. You are more likely to be able to buy the beers here than at the monastery's hole in the wall. May close for the first half of January and the latter half of September.

ADINKERKE

5km WNW of Veurne off E40 exit 1
🚃 De Panne *[De Panne–Lichtervelde]*

The first and last town on the coastal motorway to the Channel ports, just inland from De Panne and the western end of the coastal strip. Home to Plopsaland – we jest not – a magnificent entertainment if you have not yet had your seventh birthday.

Verloren Gernalen

3 Stationsplein   **T** 058 42 16 73

Bang opposite De Panne train station in the centre of Adinkerke village. An ideal first-and-last experience of the best of Belgian café life. A covered terrace is backed by a dining room and bar with an elegant but lived-in feel. The beer list edges ever closer to 60 with a good selection of regionals. The menu (12.00–20.30) stops short of full meals but includes salads, omelettes, rolls and a number of traditional bar snacks such as black pudding (Du: *bloedworst*) with apple sauce. Closes for January.
Mon & Tue 10.00 onwards
Other days 08.30 onwards

ALVERINGEM

6km SSE of Veurne off N8
Quiet West Flanders country town.

Brouwershof

40 Fortem   **T** 058 28 96 74

A nice old one-bar café in a traditional 19th century style, attached to the Snoek maltings and brewery museum (see Beer Tourism). Built in a deceased village brewhouse, by the Fortem bridge at the east end of town. Aims to serve at least one beer from every West Flanders brewery, reaching a total of 45, including a tafelbier for the kids. Small traditional snacks. Good range of tabletop café games. Down the way the **Potje Paté** (1

Kaatsspelstraat) makes and sells its own charcuterie and stocks a good list of thirty-five beers.
CLOSED MONDAY & TUESDAY
Wed–Sat 14.00 onwards (*Sep–Jun*)
Other days 10.30 onwards

BEERNEM

10km SE of Bruges off E40 exit 10
🚆 Beernem [*Bruges–Ghent*]
Pleasant enough small town (pop. 14,000) just off the motorway.

Zevende Hemel

5 Stationsplein   **T** 050 78 03 81

Bang next door to Beernem station, the "Seventh Heaven" seems intent on becoming one of Belgium's classic bars. Imagine a Bohemian version of Antwerp's Elfde Gebod with added taste. The bottled beer range started at 100 and is promised to double, with the intention of stocking most of the lambic beers. There appears to be investment from both Haacht and Grolsch. Food is rising in prominence. Children are not encouraged and they do not like large parties without advance warning. When you hear the Gregorian chant music, it is time to go home.
CLOSED MONDAY; *Fri & Sat* 11.00–03.00
Sun 11.00–21.00; *Other days* 11.00–01.00

BESELARE

18km W of Kortrijk off A19 exit 3
The village nearest to Bellewaerde amusement park with its killer rides and zoo. For a less stressful travel experience, try the reminders of front line carnage at Tyne Cot Cemetry, Hill 62 Sanctuary Wood Museum, Hooge Crater Museum or Hell Fire Corner.

Reutel

17 Reutelhoekstraat   **T** 057 46 79 77

A kilometre out of town, leaving by Oude Kortrijkstraat at a country crossroads. The beer list is 60 in winter, 90 in summer, usually including brews from de Bie. There is a small split-level bar inside and a larger terrace at the back. Basic but filling bar snacks include many for children. If you are after more substantial fare, head towards Moorslede, where the **Troubadour** (3 Marktplaats – **T** 051 63 55 96 – closed Mo; others from 10.00) serves fifty beers and good grills in faded elegance, or Dadizele, where the **Spaans Dak** (295 Dadizeelsestraat – **T** 056 50 99 80 – closed Tu&We) is a successful country tavern with a large steak and fish menu.

Daily 11.00 onwards

BEVEREN-AAN-DEN-IJZER

20km NW of Ieper on N364

One of those villages near the French border that got rebuilt to a new spec after 1918.

Beveren

20 Roesbruggestraat   **T** 057 30 05 73

A spotlessly clean, well-managed, modern style, one-room tavern with beams and exposed brickwork. On the main street near the church. Gather round the welcoming fireplace in winter. The list of 60 beers is strong on West Flanders brews. Food (Su 11.00–22.00; others 18.30–22.00) includes pasta, salads, steaks, fish and themed weekend specials. The overspill dining area has a cleverly designed sunken TV area for children, which keeps the noise down.

CLOSED MONDAY TO THURSDAY (*Sep–Jun*)
Fri & Sat 17.00 onwards
Other days 11.00 onwards

BLANKENBERGE

4 km W of Zeebrugge on the coast
Blankenberge [*Blankenberge–Bruges*]

Blankenberge (pop. 15,000) is the Belgian Bognor. Vauxhall Vectra man retires here to complain about the weather and his wife's advancing bunions. The yachts in the harbour are owned by people who actually sail them. The third largest and most crowded of the coastal resorts stretches over two kilometres

of dune and beach. In the holiday business since 1860, its seafront is one continuous run of apartment blocks, hotels, restaurants and cafés. The population rises six-fold in summer. It has an aquarium and casino.

Hotel tips: there are just over sixty in town. Try www.dekust.org. Deals vary in and out of season but are cheaper off the seafront. Train and tram links make it a possible base for touring the coast and the Bruges – Ghent – Brussels axis.

Brasseur

36 Leopoldstraat   **T** 050 41 41 34

On the street that links the Blankenberge Park tramstop to the western end of the promenade. Overlooks a busy public park and play area, in a line of similar-looking small pavement cafés. The covered terrace at the front is heated in winter. Stands out for its professional air as much as its beer list of 80, including St. Bernardus de Dolle Brouwers and the usual Trappists. Large snacks, pasta and salads. Winter opening hours depend on how many people are around, so ring.

CLOSED TUESDAY
CLOSED MONDAY & WEDNESDAY (*Nov–Mar*)
Other days 10.00 onwards

Luxembourg

75 Zeedijk   **T** 050 41 95 52

Long-standing specialist beer café, left out of the last edition on the grounds that it had been demolished. Unusually, when the new seaside apartment Residentie Luxembourg was completed the original owners re-instated it on the ground floor. Post-war furnishings are replaced by modern stuff and its cellar is smaller, which may account for a reduced beer range of 60. Needs more passion.

CLOSED THURSDAY (*Sep–Jun*)
Other days 10.00 onwards

Terminus

1 Leopold III Plein   **T** 050 41 19 45

Next to the main tram terminal, slap bang in the centre of town, about five hundred metres off the seafront. An all-round café for travellers and locals, in an archetypal post-war building, with a comfortable interior and a covered terrace. The list of 60 beers is good in West Flanders beers. Efficient service. Usual light snacks.

Daily 07.00 onwards

BREDENE-AAN-ZEE

2km E of Ostend on the coast

🚊 Oostende [*Ostend–Bruges*] – 3km

Snuck away behind the dunes, this pleasant seaside resort and its marina mark the recommencement of the coastal strip east of the many maritime activities of greater Ostend. Just off the coastal tram route. All the usual trappings of a modern resort and on the up.

Hotel tip: stay in Ostend – but campers should note that Camping KACB, 53b

Koningin Astridlaan, has a restaurant that serves haute cuisine, fine wines and a small select beer list.

Jonathan

52 Kapelstraat   **T** 059 32 55 37

On the main road that parallels the dual carriageway and tram route. Run by a couple of young guys who have a natural enthusiasm for beer without any of the usual geeky trappings. Their bright, simple, bistro-style café has a large and heavily umbrella'd roadside terrace. The place was named after Jonathan Livingstone Seagull because, well, it is. The list of 90 beers includes St Feuillien and Malheur. Snacks include omelettes and pasta. Table footie and pool. Closes sometimes in winter and stays open later in high summer.

Daily 08.00–22.00

Minnewater in Bruges.

BRUGES

Brugge *[IC]*

Brugge (pop. 115,000) is the largest, most famous and administratively most important town in West Flanders. To pronounce its Dutch name pitch halfway between "brewer" and "brook-her". To tell people where you are going for the weekend it is better to say Bruges.

Invest in a street map from the tourist office on Burg. Its one-way system, inside the ring road, is so complex that even seasoned Bruggophiles now park at the station and either walk or take the free bus to the centre.

Once a great merchant city and part of the Hanseatic League, traders came in mediaeval times from all over Europe to buy and sell cloth with their foreign counterparts. Its fortunes changed in the 16th century when silting of the Zwin river cut its links to the sea.

To balance its fortunes, the lack of a strategic river crossing saved it from war damage many times thereafter.

The final act of self-preservation was the decision in the late 1960s to knock down much of the old city walls to make way for a ring road. This kept most of the traffic out of the city centre and allowed tourism to develop. Bruges is now one of Europe's top five short break destinations and the only one without any great historical attractions.

It draws visitors by skillfully retaining the ambience of its merchant days in an unapologetically modern way. Set against a backcloth of imposing Flemish town houses and public buildings, Bruges oozes confident sophistication in carved stone. Put another way, Bruges is famous for being Bruges.

To avoid the crowds, think rain, February, weekday and evening.

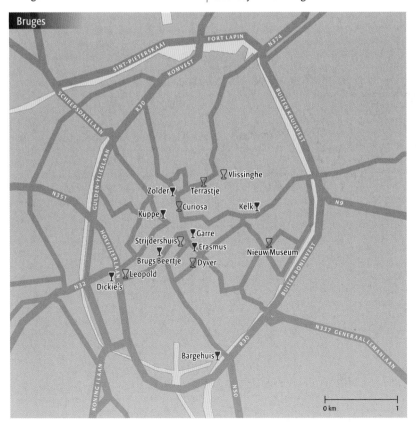

Bruges

Places worth a visit include the Memling Museum of 15th century Flemish paintings in Katelijnestraat and the Groeninge Museum of religious art and other treasures, on the banks of the Dyver Canal. The nunnery (Du: *begijnhof*) is also particularly attractive. English is spoken everywhere, French considerably less so. Enjoy.

Hotel tips: the Erasmus★★★ (see below; www.hotelerasmus.com) is compact, designer-modern and very beernut-friendly. Otherwise book in advance, on a package deal if needs be. Although it has ninety registered hotels, Bruges is frequently fully booked in summer and at weekends from April to October. At the popular hotels, travel agents usually get a better deal than private travellers. Check up-to-date availability of rooms on the official Bruges website at www.brugge.be/verblijf/internet.html. For out-of-town hotels try www.brugseommeland.be.

Bargehuis

2 Bargeweg   **T** 050 33 26 04

The burgeoning interest of mainly foreign tourists in quality Belgian beers is reflected in the growth of beer cafés in town. This one will appeal to parents with young children, who can sup their way through over 100 beers, including some unusual regionals, while the little darlings exercise in the huge sandpit and clog their arteries with chicken nuggets and similar. There are healthier meals too. Bargeweg runs from the Kathelijnepoort bridge, on the inner bank of the canal that rings the old town, to the picturesque Minnewater park, conveniently close to the station car parks.

CLOSED MONDAY; *Other days* 11.00 onwards

Brugs Beertje

5 Kemelstraat   **T** 050 33 96 16

The one and only, the original "Little Bruges Bear". You cannot call yourself a well-travelled beer lover until you have been here. This is the place that made us decide to create the Guide. Take Steenstraat west from Markt and at Simon Stevinplein turn right into Kemelstraat, to find this small, two-roomed café with its

rickety tables, well-worn ambience and virtual guarantee of meeting like-minded beer travellers from everywhere. The price of fame has been a decrease in the number of local drinkers at busy times though this remains first and foremost a pub for local people. The deal is that you receive properly poured beers in excellent condition and in return are asked your business by complete strangers. Nobody seriously believes you found the place by accident. When the two small rooms get full they may open the old function room at the back. The well-written beer list averages 250 from all over Belgium, with the local Regenboog a favourite. The best way to elicit Daisy's famous look of tolerance mixed with pity, is to ask for a Pils. Food is restricted to basic bar snacks. The original Bruges Bear is a small statue found, sometimes in costume, on the side of the Poortersloge building on the corner of Acadamiestraat. May close for two weeks in July and for a week around New Year.

CLOSED WEDNESDAY
Other days 16.00–01.00

Dickie's

16 Vrijdagmarkt   **T** 050 33 59 60

On the outer side of 't Zand, the large modern square at the top of Steenstraat that hosts the bricky new concert hall. Success provoked a redesign by the same people who did the makeover at the Botteltje in Ostend. The enigmatic Portuguese landlord has his moments and has upset a couple of readers but his list of 90 beers usually features splashes of extreme good taste. Until refurbishment the kitchen served proper tapas but this has made way for more regular grills (12.00–14.00 & 18.00–22.00). Home-constructed sangria and Dickie, the dachshund, remain.

CLOSED WEDNESDAY
Sun 16.00 onwards; *Other days* 10.30 onwards

Erasmus

35 Wollestraat   **T** 050 33 57 81   **F** 050 33 47 27

Wollestraat runs off the Markt. A hundred metres down on the left is the ever-changing front bar of this small hotel, which celebrated its twenty-fifth anniversary as a specialist beer

Daisy Claeys of 't Brugs Beertje

café in 2002. The beer list usually tops 120 and owner Tom Allewaerts is at an age when he likes to play. He especially likes experimenting with draught beers, obtaining versions that are not otherwise available. For example, the unsweetened version of Liefmans Kriek appears frequently. The décor is now distinctly modern, with classical music in the background. With a bit of luck the new design will stick. There are tables at the back overlooking the canal. The ever-changing cooking style appears to have found a level too, with the menu (12.00–15.30 & 18.00–22.00) containing a canny mix of new and old Flemish dishes from simple salads to wizardly creations in beer. Quality is good enough to suggest you book a table particularly in summer. The hotel has nine rooms and a good breakfast, at slightly above average prices, expected for this location. May close from mid-January to mid-February.

CLOSED MONDAY; *Other days* 12.00–24.00

Garre

1 De Garre   **T** 050 34 10 29

A *garre* is a small, blind alley usually built as a fire exit. This elegant café and sampling room opened in just such a location twenty years ago, off Breidelstraat, the cobbled way that runs between Markt and Burg. Simple and brightly lit, with exposed brickwork and a galleried upstairs room reached by the tight-wound stairwell. Sample your ales soberly in surroundings of understated elegance. Classical music and a selection of magazines add to a thoroughly civilised atmosphere. The rather expensive list of 130 beers includes a good range of West Flanders brews. The house beer is one of Van Steenberge's stronger efforts. Cheese and sausage only. May close for the last weeks of January and June.

Sat & Sun 11.00–01.00; *Other days* 12.00–24.00

Kelk

69 Langestraat   T 0473 73 34 60

A real warren of a place, just off the action beyond Burg. There are various claims about the beer list but we reckon it to be 80, including St. Bernardus, de Dolle Brouwers and others. Aimed more at locals than tourists, for a change. A bit tatty outside but there are plans to expand to include a beer shop and other schemes. Minor snacks only. The Dalmatian is deaf.

CLOSED MONDAY; *Other days* 16.00 onwards

Kuppe

19 Kuipersstraat   T 050 33 39 20

Off the Markt beyond Eiermarkt, opposite the Stadsschouwburg. Hovering between a specialist beer café and a young folks' haunt, with over 80 beers on a steadily more adventurous list that is good on West Flanders' brews. The music suggests it is aiming at a hair gel crowd, while the candles and stove imply greyer round the temples. Gel tends to win on weekend nights. Two of our top inspectors have directly opposed views about its merits. Help it to nudge it towards serious beeriness.

Mon–Fri 11.00 onwards
Sat & Sun 14.00 onwards

Zolder

53 Vlamingstraat   T 0477 24 49 05

Called the "Attic" it is actually a cellar bar. When you reach that part of Vlamingstraat that is so far off the Markt that it has become unfashionable, you will find this elegant abnormality on your left. Worth it in winter for its open fire and in summer for being far from the madding crowd. Brick and slate, serious and welcoming, civilised music includes jazz. The beer list of just over 60 punches well above its weight for having no weak spots and stocking the sort of excellent ales that its owner likes. There is a range of genevers too. Food is growing slowly but is mainly pasta and stew.

CLOSED TUESDAY
Sun 18.00 onwards; *Other days* 17.00 onwards

Just along from the Groeninge Museum, a few hundred metres from the Markt on a canal bank, is the **Dyver** (5 Dyver – T 050 33 60 69, F 050 34 78 78 – daily 11 .00–23.00) one of Belgium's top restaurants for cooking with beer. There is a lunchtime set menu (12.00–16.00) and evening à la carte (18.30–22.00) with beers to accompany each course. Perversely there is no beer list and they discourage choosing your own. The emphasis is on polished service, Baroque style and a menu that ranges from light modern to heavy traditional. It is always best to book. Reservations can be made in English.

The oldest and arguably the most traditional café interior is at the **Vlissinghe** (2a Blekersstraat – T 050 34 37 37 – closed Mo&Tu; others from 11.00; Su to 19.00), a heavyweight Flemish classic built in 1515 and once favoured by Van Dyck. Under thirty beers and off the beaten track but good enough to house Jan De Bruyne's Bieracademie presentations. In the same general direction is a smart local café called the **Terrastje** (45 Genthof – T 050 33 09 19 – open daily), pretty close to a full entry with forty-five beers and some good traditional Flemish cooking.

In the centre the **Strijdershuis** (14 Hallestraat – T 050 61 62 60 – closed Tu–Th; others 10.30–24.00) is a modern split-level café with cat litter terrace, good-looking food and over forty beers (including Strubbe and de Dolle Brouwers), one block off the Markt. An old friend, the **Curiosa** (22 Vlamingstraat – T 050 34 23 34 – closed Mo; others 11.00–24.00) has started to serve more beers again in its 16th century cellar bar with food (12.00–22.00). Over fifty at the last count but nothing seriously exciting.

Another old favourite that is on the way back but still off the beaten track is the **Nieuw Museum** (42 Hooistraat – T 050 33 12 80 – closed We; others from 18.00; plus Sa&Su 12.00–14.00) trying a beer list of over fifty to go with its large steaks cooked on an open fire.

At the less fashionable end of town around 't Zand, your best bet is probably the **Leopold** (26 't Zand – T 050 33 19 87) a decent bar with about forty beers.

BRUGGE (St. Andries)

Western suburb of Bruges on N367
🚃 Brugge [IC] – 3km
The bit of Bruges where the Belgians live.

Tuinbos

678 Gistelse Steenweg   T 050 38 05 99

This small roadside tavern, run by an enthusiastic couple, enjoys energetic support from local beer lovers, including its mature gentlemen's cycling club. For now you are likely to be the only tourist in the place though if its list of 150 expands any further it will on the international Grand Tour. Good range of Regenboog beers plus all the Trappists. Food stops at cheese and bread, plus local patés. Bus 5 from the station, Markt or 't Zand to Hermitage passes the front door.

CLOSED TUESDAY; *Other days* 10.00 onwards

DAMME

7km NE of Bruges off N374

Until the silting of the River Zwin, Damme was the seaport of Bruges and a major town in the wine trade. The view from the top of the church puts Flanders in proportion. In summer you can get here from Bruges by boat or bike.

Oude Speye

7 Kerkstraat   T 0474 41 26 57

One of the best new beer cafés in Belgium is this stylish but homely, high-ceilinged single room café in a typical, plush Damme townhouse in the main street. The front windows have an excellent view of the Stadhuis. The centrepiece is a large fireplace with sofas around it. The white paintwork and smart tiled floor still feel new but will wear in nicely. Started with a beer list of two hundred and rose within two years to 285. Beers from all over Belgium but particularly strong on lambics, Trappists and regionals. Food is limited to variations on hand-held toasted sandwiches, though Herve cheese with syrup was spotted. Opening hours can be erratic.

CLOSED MONDAY & TUESDAY *(Oct–Easter)*
Other days 12.00 onwards

DE HAAN

8km NE of Ostend on the coast

Up-market, seaside resort between Ostend and Blankenberge, which has been Agatha Christie'd by its town planners with attractive results. *Belle époque* enough to be called the Belgian Deauville, it is still sometimes referred to by its endearing French name of Coq-sur-Mer. The nearest coastal spot to SunParks De Haan holiday centre.

Hotel tips: there are just under thirty in all. Try www.dekust.org. **The Belle Vue★★★**, 5 Koninklijk Plein (T 059 23 34 39; F 059 23 75 22; **www.hotelbelleepoque.be**) is a good place for revived *fin de siécle*.

Torre

2 Hans Memlinglaan   T 059 23 65 32

The patio terrace at the front of the "Tower" backs onto tram stop De Haan aan Zee, twenty minutes from Ostend. If in doubt, it it the bright yellow building with the vermilion stripes! An arty modern café with candles on every table and Bauhaus-meets-Shaker furnishings. The clash of primary colours continues inside. Out of the other entrance is a smaller, quieter afternoon terrace. The changing list of 150 beers is nowadays hidden from view most of the time. If you can find a copy, it often features every style you can think of from around the country and is the most imaginative on the coast. You may find traditional gueuze and fruit beers, oak-aged old browns, Wallonian specials and virtually everything else. Fashion and business dictates that when evening comes the DJ rules, playing young person's music at a volume that can invade the space of more mature minds. Food (11.00–22.00) is gradually expanding, with salads and pasta the house specialities. Smaller snacks run later and there are pancakes in the afternoon. Charming owners apply active brainpower to the question of how to stay in business. Open every day in high summer. They have baby-changing facilities.

CLOSED MONDAY & TUESDAY
Other days 11.00 onwards

DESSELGEM

8km NE of Kortrijk on N43
Waregem *[Kortrijk–Deinze]* – 5km
Suburban village at the outer reaches of
greater Kortrijk.

Straetje Zonder Einde

212 Nieuwstraat
T 056 70 46 95

A smallish, weekend bistro and coffee house,
a kilometre out of the village on the back
road to St. Eloois-Vijve. The "Blind Alley"
may feel that way if you are on foot. 70 beers
on the list. Food reaches ribs and knuckles of
ham. Closes for the last week of August.
CLOSED MONDAY TO THURSDAY
Sun 11.00 onwards; *Fri & Sat* 17.00 onwards

DIKSMUIDE

20km N of Ieper on N35 & N369
Diksmuide *[De Panne–Lichtervelde]*
Diksmuide (pop.15,000) is on the River Ijzer,
the front line of the 1914–18 war. When the
shelling stopped they had to calculate its
location from a map. Its huge and haunting
IJzertoren memorial houses a museum of
Flemish patriotism, with the somewhat mixed
message that the quest for eternal peace is
made easier if you beat up the French. The
nearby Dodengang is a half-hearted reconstruction of the trenches that lined the west
bank of the river. A boat trip to Nieuwpoort,
or a bicycle ride to Ieper, runs through the
beautiful landscape that grew on the killing
fields of Europe. The altogether more normal
Westoria tourist hive offers multimedia
presentations about the local area.

Hotel tip: the small, privately owned **Vrede**
★★, 35 Grote Markt (**T** 051 50 00 38; **F** 051 51 06
21) will suit most requirements though the
Best Western chain's nearby **Pax**★★★, 2 Heilig
Hartplein (**T** 051 50 00 34; **F** 051 50 00 35) is
smarter.

Brouwershuys

19 Grote Markt   **T** 051 50 50 30

On the corner of the reconstructed Grote
Markt in one of the buildings erected in 1921
to imitate the grand townhouses that were
there before the conflict. An all-purpose
street corner café with a single bare brick and
stripped wood saloon bar. Smallish terrace
on the street outside. The list of 60 beers
includes de Dolle Brouwers from nearby Esen.
Minimal snacks. If it is rustic charm you are
after, head north on the N369 till you get to
Keiem and turn left onto Tervaetestraat. After
the Ijzer bridge you will find the **Tervaete**
(88 Ijzerdijk – Sa&Su from 11.00, Fr&Mo from
14.00), a delightful café with a riverside view,
slate and wood floor, candle-light, Ella
Fitzgerald and over forty better beers.
Home-made bread pudding too.
CLOSED WEDNESDAY
Mon 10.00–13.00 & 17.00 onwards
Sat 13.00 onwards; *Other days* 15.00 onwards

DRANOUTER

12km SW of Ieper on N322

Large village at the heart of Heuvelland, an
official agglomeration of eight villages at the
southwestern corner of the province. Set in
attractive rolling countryside that spills over
into French Flanders. It goes bananas on the
first full weekend of August when its international folk festival attracts up to 80,000 people.
Turns the place into a massive campsite, with
the village shops and cafés open 24/7.

Hotel tips: the Wulf★★, 1 Wulvestraat (**T&F**
057 44 56 67) is a 10-bedroom rustic but civilised converted farmhouse with good cooking
and several good beers, in a rural setting
south of the village. Halfway to Kemmel, on
Flanders' token hill, the **Hollemeersch**★★
(58 Lettingstraat – **T** 057 44 44 06; **F** 057 44 74
86) also has an above average range of beers.

Preekstoel

43 Zwartemolenstraat   **T** 057 44 69 52

On the lane that runs south from the village
centre, about a kilometre into the middle of

nowhere. The "Pulpit" is a class act. Traditional style furnishings, open log fire, black tiled floor and, er, a pulpit in the centre of the room. Just under 60 beers and rising, with emphasis on local regionals. There is an enormous range of home-made snacks and a smaller menu of steaks, fish and local specialities like hot pork tongue. The place to be when the festival is on – being eight hundred metres from the action it is usually empty, the locals having forsaken it too, on the assumption that it would be full.

CLOSED MONDAY TO THURSDAY (Sep–Jun)
Fri 18.00 onwards; *Other days* 14.00 onwards

Sarlinde

4 Hillestraat   **T** 057 44 87 65

Signposted from the village centre, about eight hundred metres away. A large dark bar with an even larger covered terrace overlooking a tree-lined garden and play area. Tends to stock around 120 beers from a slightly larger list that includes over twenty 75cl brews. Food is good value and good quality too. *Assiette Anglaise* is four types of ham with the local pickled brawn thrown in for good measure. Gets the folk festival full blast, as it is held in a nearby field. Opens at 12.00 from July to mid-September.

CLOSED THURSDAY (Oct–Jun)
Sat & Sun 12.00 onwards
Other days 18.00 onwards

OTHER DRANOUTER CAFÉS:

This part of Heuvelland would be one of the best rural pub crawls in Belgium if de Bie brewery had not crunched down the beer lists at **Kauwackers** (1 Kauwackerstraat) and **Tere Plekke** (21 Koudekotstraat) so that they are now restricted to house brews. At the top of the town, the bar of the **Musiekcentrum 't Folk** (234 Dikkebusstraat – **T** 057 44 69 33 – closed Wed&Thu, Sep–Jun) also stocks a good range of beers. If you want to think and travel laterally, pop over the French border to the **Ferme-Brasserie Beck** (Eecklestraete, Bailleul – **T** 03 28 49 03 90 in France – closed Mo–Fr; Sa from 19.00; Su from 17.00).

15km S of Ostend off N33

Typical small Flemish town, five minutes south of the E40 exit 5, off the Ostend to Torhout road.

Buuzestove

174 Stationsstraat   **T** 059 29 03 42

On the way into town from the N33. The Buuzestove is the name of the impressive piece of Leuven-made ironmongery that has blazed away in the middle of the front bar of this traditional small-town café for longer than anyone cares to remember. A specialist beer café for decades, ihe regular list is now down to 60 but its heart is still in the right place. Strubbe produce its dark, bittersweet house brew called Buuzestoveke. The food (from 12.00) has always been well above average here and they do impressive things with steaks, eel and giant prawns, scampi, scallops and frogs' legs, sometimes cooking on the open fire. There are terraces outside, back and front. May close for up to a month from the end of January.

CLOSED WEDNESDAY
Other days 11.00 onwards

6km ESE of Roeselare off N36
Izegem *[Lichtervelde–Kortrijk]*

Village in the suburban hinterland. Officially Emelgem has not existed since it was made formally part of Izegem in 1963. However, nobody asked the locals or told the map-makers and road sign writers.

Hotel tips: in Izegem, the **Park★★★**, 3 Papestraat (**T** 051 33 78 20; **F** 051 33 78 69; www.parkhotel-izegem.be) is the brand new business hotel next to the old Carpentier maltings, while the **Century★★**, 24 Nederweg (**T** 051 30 18 44; **F** 051 31 51 79) was equally modern forty years ago.

Kroegske

35 Vijfwegenstraat **T** 051 30 77 63

The Guide suggests the two hotels above because although there is no point in coming here for anything other than this café, we suspect that once you have arrived you will not be wanting to leave. To find it from Izegem station head over the bridge. Vijfwegenstraat is off the roundabout. The anonymous street of terraced houses gives the clear message that you have to be in the wrong place but you are not. The main room of this small and cosy, immensely civilised brown café is hung with plants and candle-lit. It is wrapped round a neat bar that stocks 450 beers from all over Belgium and beyond. There are cellar-aged beers too. The shortish menu features traditional cooking, much of it involving beer. There is a small garden at the back in summer. Cigars, pipes, dogs, babies, Pilsener and wheat beer are not allowed. The limited opening hours reflect the fact that the owners consider this their hobby. Closes on public holidays.

CLOSED MONDAY TO WEDNESDAY
Thu 19.00–24.00; *Fri & Sat* 19.00–01.00
Sun 17.00–22.00

ESEN

3km E of Diksmuide on N35
🚃 Diksmuide *[De Panne–Lichtervelde]* – 3km
See Brewery cafés: de Dolle Brouwers (above).

GULLEGEM

NW outskirts of Kortrijk off R8 exit 8.
🚃 Kortrijk *[IC]* – 4km
Suburb off the Kortrijk ring road. Take bus 748 bus from Kortrijk.

Danny tending the bar at the Kroegske.

Rusteel

168 Heulestraat   **T** 056 35 65 64

Large restored 16th century farmhouse in a suburban setting, not far off the ring road. Its many rooms look out over a cobbled courtyard, attractive garden and an unusual farm cum deer park. It has been a beer café since 1982. The list of 300 includes most popular brands in Belgium. Food is also wide ranging and popular Flemish – but no *frites*. Waiter service is sharp but courteous. They run a Friday night barbecue in summer. Sunday night closing is often 22.00. Families are made particularly welcome. Car parking is on the opposite side of the road, fifty metres away.

CLOSED TUESDAY

CLOSED MONDAY & WEDNESDAY (Sep–Jun)

Thu–Sat 16.00 onwards (Sep–Jun)

Other days 11.30 onwards

HOEKE

14km NE of Bruges just off E34

Knokke *[Knokke–Bruges]* – 5km

Waterside hamlet near the Dutch border, minimally signposted off the E34 just as it crosses the Damme-Sluis canal.

Hotel tip: the **Welkom**★★ (below) has ten bedrooms and self-catering apartments, making this a convenient stopover for northern Flanders.

Welkom

34 Damse Vaart Noord

T 050 60 24 92   **E** info@hotelwelkom.be

This smart but simple hotel on the banks of the Napoleon canal between Damme and Sluis has a single room canalside bar, broken into discreet areas. Its terrace overlooks the water. It can be a bleak setting in winter but a great spot in summer. Looks particularly inviting if you have just cycled the long, straight, tree-lined, canal path from Damme and Bruges. 80 beers and rising on a list that features de Dolle Brouwers, Malheur, St. Bernardus and others. Food includes the usual suspects, from small snacks to full meals. Closes two weeks in October.

CLOSED THURSDAY; *Other days* 10.00 onwards

IEPER

25km W of Kortrijk off N38

Ieper *[Kortrijk–Poperinge]*

To French speakers this market town (pop. 35,000) is Ypres. To the private soldiers who 90 years ago took the King's shilling it was "Wipers", the British communications centre during the 1914–18 war.

The Ypres Salient was a bulge in the trench line that ran around the town throughout the conflict. Expecting their advances to have a quick result, Europe's politicians and generals refused to believe the stalemate. The four battles of Ypres epitomised the catastrophe. A quarter of a million young men died in the third battle alone, known to history as Passendale.

To touch the unthinkable reality, visit the Menin Gate (Du: *Menenpoort*), where, at 20.00 every evening the road is closed while buglers sound Last Post in thanks for the sacrifices of so many strangers. Its cold marble and the 54,896 names of the disappeared sit in stark contrast to the town centre's coolly informative In Flanders Field Museum. The Ramparts Museum in Rijselstraat is more "hands on" and personal.

There are 160 cemeteries round here for the bodies of the recognised. Tours of the area's major sites manage respectfully and neatly to introduce the whole ghastly business. Most of this once rich cloth merchants' town was destroyed by artillery fire. Defiance and hope demanded the precise reconstruction of its imposing public buildings.

In 1938 the locals revived the ancient Cats Festival (Du: *Kattestoet*), omitting the bit of the original that involved hurling screaming moggies from the windows of the Cloth Hall (Du: *Lakenhalle*). The modern hoolie happens on the last Sunday in May.

Hotel tips: the Ariane★★★, 58 Slachthuisstraat 58 (**T** 057 21 82 18; **F** 057 21 87 99; www.ariane.be) got a rave review for quality comfort from one of our top inspectors; the **Old Tom**★★, 8 Grote Markt (**T** 057 20 15 41; **F** 057 21 91 20) is more standard beer traveller stuff.

Posterie

57 Rijselsestraat **T** 057 20 05 80

A survivor of five editions, the "Post Office" has been Ieper's top beer café for over fifteen years. Three hundred metres from the Grote Markt on the road to the Lille Gate (Du: *Rijselpoort*), this excellent tavern is entered though a small courtyard. The beer list of nearly 170 is strong on regional brews, many of which are also on sale at their shop (11.00– 19.00) near the front gate. The kitchen (11.30– 23.30) produces a wide range of traditional Flemish cooking, solid preparation for a day spent getting to understand the ghastly reality of armed combat. Further down the street, the **Klein Rijsel** (208 Rijselsestraat – **T** 057 20 02 36 – closed We; others 10.30–21.00) next to the Lille Gate, acts as the entrance to the Ramparts Museum. It has also developed the second best selection of beers in Ieper, with lots of Leroy and quite a few label beers.
CLOSED WEDNESDAY; *Other days* 11.00–02.00

INGELMUNSTER

14km N of Kortrijk on N50
🚉 Ingelmunster *[Kortrijk–Lichtervelde]*
See Brewery cafés: Van Honsebrouck (above).

KEMMEL

10km SSW of Ieper on N331 & N304

Village with an English sort of green, next to West Flanders' token hill, the Kemmelberg. This is topped by a monument to the fallen French foot soldiers of the battle of Kemmel.
Hotel tip: Kemmelberg★★★, 4 Berg (**T** 057 44 41 45; **F** 057 44 40 89).

Labyrint

29 Dries **T** 057 44 65 81

This café, games emporium, restaurant, Celtic archaeology museum, art gallery and labyrinthine maze complex falls below the Guide's strict inclusion criteria. However, the list of 40 contains little rubbish and features an excellent selection of West Flanders ales. There are excellent local snacks and fuller meals. Good facilities for children. Closes for two weeks in October or November.
CLOSED TUESDAY; *Other days* 10.00–22.00

KERKHOVE

12km SW of Oudenaarde on N8
🚉 Anzegem *[Kortrijk–Oudenaarde]* – 4km
Hamlet in the attractive Schelde valley.

The Labyrint at Kemmel.

Eenvoudig Bestaan

38 Krevelstraat   **T** 0475 58 24 56

Foody café off the N8 Oudenaarde to Avelgem road. The beer list of 60 includes brews from Achouffe, de Bie, Ellezelloise and St. Bernardus. It seems to have been built in a converted village chapel. More reports please.

CLOSED MONDAY

CLOSED TUESDAY & WEDNESDAY (Sep–Jun)

Thu & Fri 18.00–24.00

Sat 16.00–02.00; Other days 14.00–24.00

KNOKKE-HEIST

3km E of Zeebrugge on the coast

🚃 Knokke [Knokke-Bruges]

Knokke-Heist (pop. 33,000) is an amalgamation of four coastal villages – Heist, Duinbergen, Knokke and Het Zoute. The town gets posher as you near the Netherlands. The casino (from 15.00) houses Magritte's picture, The Enchanted Lands. To the east are the salt marshes of Het Zwin nature reserve – take wellies. This is the resort for the better off, though you will still need windbreaks on the beach.

Hotel tip: there are just under fifty in all. Try www.dekust.org.

Schildia

250 Zeedijk-Heist   **T** 050 51 50 58

At the Duinbergen end of Heist, on the seafront, nearest to the Heldenplein coastal tram stop. If you cycle up the coast from De Panne then of the four hundred or so sea front cafés you will have passed, this is the most serious about beer. Inside is a modern, comfortable lounge in the fashion of the best promenade restaurants. The terraced area across the street is good for dining al fresco while the children use bicycles and other wheeled weapons hired from local shops to mow down passing holidaymakers indiscriminately. The beer list of up to 200 has been strong on abbey beers ever since the beer bug first bit this place a quarter of a century ago. The food is well above average too, ranging from omelettes and single plate meals to steaks and mussels, with particular strength in seafood. One of the most reliable specialist beer cafés in Belgium. Opens at 10.00 in the high season.

CLOSED FROM MID-NOVEMBER TILL FEBRUARY

CLOSED WEDNESDAY (Sep–Jun)

Other days 11.00 onwards

OTHER KNOKKE-HEIST CAFÉS:

Knokke-Heist, like every place on the Belgian coast, is awash with cafés. Many stock thirty beers but remarkably few make beer a special interest. Given the high profile of beer in the tourist's list of reasons to come to Belgium, this observation is both sad and worrying. Up near the Royal Golf Club, **Put 19** (74 Sparrendreef) is a civilised bar with enough beers to be interesting. If you discover anything else, let us know on BelgiumGBG@aol.com.

KOKSIJDE

25km south west of Ostend on the coast

🚃 Veurne [De Panne–Lichtervelde] – 5km

Resort town near the western border of the coastline, next along from De Panne.

Belle Vue

383 Strandlaan   **T** 058 51 82 57

A typical large sea front brasserie on the promenade at the point where it meets the main street of the old village of St. Idesbald, now part of Koksijde. Lots of wood panelling and friendly service. Around 70 beers with a healthy interest in Wallonian ales from independents such as Brunehaut, Caulier, Dupont and others. Keen and beery owners. Usual mix of crêpes, light meals and ice creams but cassoulet, grilled salmon and steaks too.

CLOSED WEDNESDAY (Oct–Jun)

Other days 09.00–22.00

KORTRIJK

Kortrijk *[IC]*

Known to the Romans as Cortracum, Kortrijk (Fr: *Courtrai*) has been a centre of the textiles industry for five centuries. It is the largest town (pop. 75,000) in southern Flanders and was shelled heavily in the 1939–45 war. Some monuments survived, including the Broeltoren, twin towers that were part of the old town walls. There is a picturesque 17th century nunnery (Du: *begijnhof*) at the back of the church of Our Lady. The imposing St. Maartenskerk is worth a peek. Emnity with the French here goes back beyond the Battle of the Golden Spurs in 1302, when a band of Flemish peasants covered marshy ground with brushwood and induced the French noblemen's cavalry to charge. Drowned by the weight of their armour, the victims left enough spurs to fill the aisle of a local church. The St. Pol genever distillery (212 Gentsesteenweg – **T** 056 22 12 91) has a sampling room with a video and trips can be arranged with advance notice.

Hotel tip: the Groeninge★, 1a Groeningestraat (**T** 056 22 60 00; F 056 20 01 88; www.hotelgroeninge.be) does faded grandeur with limited charm; the **Damier**★★★ 14 Grote Markt (**T** 056 22 15 47; F 056 22 86 31; www.hoteldamier.be) is considerably nicer and affordable if you book through the website.

Boulevard

15 Groeningelaan   **T** not known

One of the most stylish new cafés in the Guide. Off the city centre, the summer sees chairs and tables set out among mature trees that line the boulevard. The wooden interior does art, quality music and lashings of good taste. Simple but elegant snacks on a clever menu will sustain you through the evening. A clever beer list of 100 and rising. Will we suspect never settle. Features lots of microbrewery beers and 75cl bottles. Not a lot of big brewery stuff. Opens at 16.30 if the weather is fine and life is good.

CLOSED WEDNESDAY & THURSDAY
Other days 18.00 onwards

Eirekedeire

31 Sint Jansstraat   **T** 056 51 84 64

This lovely old brown café, "full of tat and old radios", is at the edge of the pedestrianised centre near the root of Zwevegemstraat. This is where the local beer cognoscenti tend to hang out when they want to mingle with friends. Can get a bit cliquey but they don't bite. The list of around 75 beers includes large bottles of Dupont. Food is limited to pasta and chilli. There is a small terrace out front but we recommend languishing inside.

CLOSED MONDAY & TUESDAY
Other days 17.00 onwards

Klokke

12 Grote Markt   **T** 056 25 30 01

Third millennium bistro restaurant at the quietest end of the city's main square. There is a large terrace and a mezzanine floor that leads to a first floor function room. Minimalist grey and black décor with matching photography. A good feel despite its modernity. Above average food and list of nearly 70 beers, including a lot from Verhaeghe. This complements a menu that includes salads, large cold plates, pastas and some more adventurous dishes, done well. New world wines. Tends to close on bank holidays.

CLOSED TUESDAY; *Other days* 10.00 onwards

Mouterijtje

25a Kapucijnenstraat   **T** 056 20 14 14

Opposite the cinema on the other side of the Broeltoren bridge from the town centre. The "Little Maltings" is a converted malt store. Its bar is deep set but brightly lit and brick-vaulted. There is a small terrace on the street. The list of 100 beers has matured with time though adventurous it is not. There is a broad menu including brochettes, salmon fillet, baked monkfish, mussels, carbonade and frogs legs. Food is available until midnight and sometimes later.

CLOSED WEDNESDAY
Thu & Sat 17.00 onwards; *Sun* 11.30 onwards
Other days 11.30–14.30 & 17.00 onwards

Vlasblomme

4 Etienne Sabbelaan   **T** 056 21 60 32

Being the age-old centre of the linen trade, Kortrijk is home to the National Flax and Linen Museum and the "Flax Flower", its café and meeting centre. To find them head out on the old N50 Tournai road to where it crosses junction 2 of the E17. After two hundred metres on your left is Universiteitslaan, which leads to the museum at first right. Alternatively take the no. 13 bus from the station. You do not have to visit the museum to come here and enjoy the classic bits of café décor including a huge central fireplace, uplifted brick by brick from a bar in Bissegem and reconstructed here. Its list of 75 beers and good value cooking (12.00–14.00) have delighted readers who have made the trek. There are lighter meals in the evenings. Betweentimes snacks including a local sweet pastry called *kalletaart*. It may close for December. There is a non-smoking room.

CLOSED MONDAY
Tue–Thu 10.00–20.00 *(Sep–Jun)*
Sat 10.00–24.00
Other days 10.00–22.00

5km NNE of Ieper off N313
Ieper *[Kortrijk–Poperinge]* – 5km

Large village with plenty of space, deep in the West Flanders countrytside.

Koornbloem

19 Markt   **T** 0478 24 31 50

On the main square, opposite the church. A modern, split level interior of an older café. Nudging 60 beers at present but with intentions to go higher. Strong on West Flanders independents such as de Dolle Brouwers, St. Bernardus and de Bie. Light snacks are available too. There is a small terrace at the back. We will be interested to hear about progress.

CLOSED THURSDAY; *Wed* 10.15–14.00 *(Oct–Mar)*
Other days 10.15 onwards

On the French border, 12km from the coast Quiet border village less than ten minutes off the main road from Dunkerque to Lille.

Voshol

21 Leiseledorp   **T** 058 29 81 57

Next to the church, in the village centre. The "Fox Hole" sets the standards you should expect from a Flemish tavern. Smallish, with a comfortable country pub atmosphere and an open fire, it stocks 60 beers. Excellent food prepared in an open kitchen at the end of the lounge. At busy times you may have a problem coming just for a beer as they are dependent on the restaurant business for survival. Specialises in eel and mussels but competent in other fish and meat dishes. They offer a free breathalyser service on leaving. May close for two weeks before Easter.

CLOSED MONDAY TO THURSDAY *(Sep–Jun)*
Fri 19.00 onwards; *Other days* 11.00 onwards

12km SW of Ieper on N322
One of the eight villages that make up Heuvelland, near the French border. Home to de Bie brewery (see Brewery cafés: de Bie above).

Heksenstoel

1 Douanestraat   **T** 057 44 73 77

On the main street, one hundred metres up from de Bie brewery. A gem in wood and candlelight. Great understated décor. The sort of place that gets away with putting a double bass on the wall and garlanding it with hops. 70 beers from all over Belgium and a few from across the French border. Civilised music shapes the ambience without spoiling the conversation. Popular for its food, which ranges from grills to rabbit in Trois Monts ale. Thoroughly recommended.

CLOSED MONDAY & TUESDAY
CLOSED WEDNESDAY *(Oct–Easter)*
Thu–Sat 18.00 onwards
Other days 12.00 onwards

MERKEM

11km N of Ieper off N369
Village off the old main road, easily missed.

Kippe

70 Stationsstraat   T 051 54 40 48

Fifty metres off the road from Diksmuide to Ieper, turning off the more northerly feeder road. A pleasant open-plan tavern with its own art gallery and plenty of modern sculpture. Becoming darker with the passing years. A safe but solid beer list now reaches 90. Food is expanding too, though this is no restaurant pub. Background music is compulsory unless you drink in the garden at the front with its large children's play area, climbing frames and duck pond. Beware the chickens.
CLOSED TUESDAY; *Sat & Sun* 15.00 onwards
Other days 14.00 onwards

MIDDELKERKE

8km SW of Ostend on the coast

Dependable seaside resort (pop. 16,000) with a small casino and the usual watersports facilities. There is a seafront beer festival in mid June sponsored by a local drinks warehouse.

Hotel tip: Isaura★★, 86 Koninginnelaan
(T 059 30 38 13; F 059 31 04 11).

Iceberg

132 Zeedijk   T 059 30 48 79

On the sea front, nearest to tram stop Middelkerke Casino. A long-established, deep-set café fifty metres from the Casino. One of a dying breed of good value, superficially plain but subtly atmospheric promenade pubs. Stocks around 90 beers including many from West Flanders plus some better known brands from other independents. Under the same ownership for nearly forty years, with a personal collection of four hundred stone beer mugs on show. There is a small terrace. Food is limited to pasta and sandwiches. The **Watou** (271 Zeedijk – closed Wed) is a large

concrete bar towards the western end of the sea front serving mainly St. Bernardus and Bockor beers, plus big spaghetti.
CLOSED TUESDAY; *Other days* 09.00–23.00

MOEN

12 km SE of Kortrijk on N8
Small town near the Hainaut border.

St. Pietershof

6 Kraaibos   T 056 45 64 51

Our last edition excluded this remarkable rustic time-warp on the grounds that it had died. It appears it was only hibernating. Two kilometres north of the town, near the canal that links Kortrijk to the Schelde, thus on the Flanders cycleway (Du: *Vlaanderen fietsroute*). Down a track with a drawbridge, the "St. Peter's Court" is a beautifully chaotic farmhouse and small-holding with more poultry than patrons. Enjoy up to 90 beers sometimes including lambic from the cask. You may get ice cream, buckwheat pancakes and local cheeses too.
CLOSED TUESDAY TO THURSDAY (Sep–Jun)
Other days 15.00 onwards

OEDELEM

9km SE of Bruges on N33
🚆 Beernem *[Bruges–Ghent]* – 5km
Small town, five minutes off the E40 exit 10.

Kiosk

4 Markt   T 050 78 15 95

In the main square. A small, modern Flemish tavern with a terrace, in a small, Flemish town with ornate council buildings. It stocks 60 beers including the Reinaert range from Proef. Majors more on its excellent menu (11.30–21.30) specialising in salmon, Zeebrugge prawns, other seafood and steaks. All served to the sound of Bartok and Beethoven. It has been pottering on for five editions so far.
CLOSED TUESDAY & WEDNESDAY
Other days 11.30 onwards

OOSTDUINKERKE

24km W of Ostend on the coast

This part of the coastal strip does not have a real specialist beer café but it does have an excellent old-fashioned bar. The **Peerdevisschers** (4 Pastoor Schmitzstraat) is a way down Leopold II Laan, next to the fishery museum that chronicles the story of the horseback fishing trade. A delightful, traditional, high-ceilinged café with tablecloths and the largest pickled herrings in the world. Its tangy dark brown house beer is from Strubbe. On the seafront near the Oostduinkerke Bad tramstop the **Rubens** (442 Zeedijk) serves just under fifty expensive beers in its elegant lounge bar and summer sun terrace. Nearby, one of the smartest modern cafés on the seafront, the **Barkentijn** (461 Zeedijk) offers a solid list of nearly forty beers at better prices. The **Captain** (213 Leopold II Laan – closed Mon & Tue (Sep–Jun); others from 11.00) has a similar sized list with a few unusual finds for the area, such as Caulier and Van Den Bossche, plus solid bar snacks (12.00–14.00 & 18.00–20.00).

OOSTNIEUWKERKE

4km W of Roeselare on N36
🚃 Roeselare [Lichtervelde–Kortrijk] – 4km

Most

239 Roeselarestraat   **T** 051 20 25 17

A characterful, self-confident bar on the outskirts of the village, offering good value for money. A real locals' haunt with a good atmosphere, where strangers are made welcome despite the odd thick-accented, ribald comment. The stove in the centre of the room, like the floor, the hanging lamp and the landlord, has reached ample maturity. A rising interest in beer has thus far led to a list of 75 from mainly local breweries. Well-presented bar meals include excellent old-fashioned local pâté. There is a pleasant, well-established patio garden.

CLOSED WEDNESDAY
Other days 10.00 onwards

OSTEND

🚃 Oostende [Ostend – Bruges]

Ostend (Du: *Oostende*; Fr: *Ostende*) is Belgium's oldest port (pop. 67,000) and the terminal for ferries from Ramsgate. It remains the home of the deep sea fishing fleet, a naval base, a commercial dock and a shipyard.

Until 1834 this was a small fortified town on an unattractive coastline of salt marsh and dune. Then the newly created Belgian monarchy led the transformation of the coast by ordering the construction of sea dykes, drainage schemes and rail links to the rest of the world. In an era that worshipped the conquest of nature by civil engineering, the new Belgian riviera became a highly fashionable holiday venue. Nowhere more so that Ostend and Ter Streep, the fifteen kilometre stretch of dunes and sandy beaches that runs to the west.

Visitors remember Ostend for the line of seafood stalls that run along the front and the excellent restaurants on the opposite side of the road, from the railway station to the casino (from 15.00) in the Kursaal leisure complex.

Britain's reputation as a nation of drunken dough-brains put the normally welcoming Ostenders off English-speaking tourists for a while. We are slowly being forgiven, since the typical weekender profile changed from "chips and a Stella mate!" to "would a lightly chilled Duvel go well with your Sole Ostendaise, m'n'eer?"

Hotel tips: there are about sixty in all. The **Marion★★** (**F** 059 50 28 56; www.hotelmarion. be) with its twenty-four plain rooms and three plusher suites and excellent Botteltje café (see below) is the logical place for beer travellers. If it is full, try the **Thevenet★** (see below) or use www.dekust.org.

Botteltje

19 Louisastraat   **T** 059 70 09 28

Ostend's two best beer cafés are found on opposite sides of the street in what is now called the Louisa Quarter (Du: *Louisakwartier*). It is a ten-minute stroll from the station and ferry terminal. Turn right and walk past the seafood stalls on Visserskaai, eventually turning left into Langestraat. Louisastraat is fourth on the right. The "Little Bottle" is the ground floor bar of the Marion hotel, a legendary starting and ending point of many a Belgian beer trip. Success has allowed significant expansion. The beer list still hovers around 300 and features a good variety of brews from smaller independents like Regenboog and Boelens. They also buy in loads of winter beers and make some available all year round. Even experts can get helpful advice from the sideburns behind the bar! Its Lucullus restaurant (Tu–Sa 18.00–22.30) is uncompromisingly focussed on the best of Flemish seafood and steaks but is open to the possibility of cooking with beer. Auntie BBC is there for the homesick.

Mon 16.30–01.00; Fri & Sat 11.30–02.00
Other days 11.30–01.00

Ostens Bierhuus
14 Louisastraat   **T** 059 70 67 01

The beer list and decor at the "Ostend Beer House" is different enough from its near neighbour to guarantee most visitors will pop in for several at a natter. Tim Smith is as English as his name suggests but has been running this leading Belgian café for longer than either he or the Guide care to remember. There are usually around 150 beers. Relations with the neighbours are friendly. Although you would expect a strong British drinking contingent here, it is a testament to his longevity on the Ostend scene that in practice Tim's clientele is mainly local. No food, only nibbles. Closes 22.30 on Monday.

CLOSED TUESDAY; *Other days* 14.00 onwards

OTHER OSTEND CAFÉS:

The **Thevenet** (61 Koningstraat – **T** 059 70 10 35; **F** 059 80 94 19) is Ostend's other beery hotel, with a list that fluctuates from a dreary thirty via an acceptable fifty to a high of eighty with alarming regularity. The **Prince Rose** (26 Troonstraat – closed Tue; others from 11.00) is a modern café close to Henegouwenstraat tramstop, with a list of forty that includes some specials. The **Illusie** (19 Graaf de Smet de Naeyerlaan – closed Mon; others from 18.00) on the road to Bredene is an arty café with its own small theatre at the back of the bar room. Sadly its interest in special beers waxes and wanes, though on song it hits fifty.

OUTRIJVE

15km SE of Kortrijk on N353
Quiet town on the north bank of the Schelde.

Slietje
141 Heestertstraat   **T** 056 64 74 72

A weekend café at a country crossroads one kilometre north of the town on the small road to Heestert. The dark, bare-bricked, rustic interior is deceptively large but keeps a cosy feel. A wood stove burns in winter. The large courtyard caters well for families with young children in summer. The list of 80 beers includes Achouffe, de Dolle Brouwers and Van Eecke. Food includes pasta, salads, ribs, fish au gratin, waffles and pancakes. Another café worth finding is the **Narrenkoning** (8 St. Pietersstraat – closed Mo&Tu; Su 11.30, others from 17.00), in a lovely setting next to the parish church, close to the town end of Heestertsestraat. Forty beers, faintly mad décor and good home-made snacks.

CLOSED MONDAY TO THURSDAY
Fri 18.30 onwards; Sat 17.00 onwards
Sun 11.30 onwards

POPERINGE

10km W of Ieper off N38
Poperinge [Kortrijk–Poperinge]

The pleasant small market town (pop. 19,000) at the heart of Belgium's main hop-growing area. In September the surrounding countryside is dominated by four-metre-high hopbines strung up on rows of slanting trestles. The National Hop Museum (71 Gasthuisstraat) is found here and every three years there is an international carnival dedicated to the hop, the Hoppestoet, which fills the third weekend in September (see Beer Tourism). At the Talbot House (43 Gasthuisstraat) the Rev. Philip Clayton convened the Everyman's Club, offering soldiers of all ranks time out from fighting the 1914–18 war. The international Christian fellowship organisation Toc H, was created in its memory. You can still bunk down there in authentic style (T 057 33 32 28; www. talbothouse.be).

Hotel tips: the **Palace**★★ (below) is an excellent family-run small town hotel that is used to accommodating international beer travellers. Card-carrying CAMRA member get a 10% discount on any of the eleven rooms; if it is full the **Belfort**★★ (29 Grote Markt – T 057 33 88 88; F 057 33 74 75; www.hotelbelfort.be) has rooms, studio apartments and even a house for rent that sleeps up to ten.

Paix

20 Grote Markt T 057 33 95 78

At the narrower end of the market square is the "Peace", a modern café-restaurant with a terrace overlooking the square. Its good value range of over 100 beers includes a lot from West Flanders but also a good range from Dupont. The food side has taken off a lot more in recent years, with good salads, four types of eel and numerous steak options. There is a reasonably healthy children's menu and if that fails they make their own ice cream. There is a garden at the back with a slide and swings. Service can be slow.

CLOSED WEDNESDAY
Tue 10.00–17.00 (Sep–Jun); Other days 10.00–01.00

Palace

34 Ieperstraat T 057 33 30 93 F 057 33 35 35

Two hundred metres off Grote Markt and five minutes' walk from the station, Guy and Beatrijs Osteux-Beernaert's archetypal small-town family-run hotel is one of the best all-round places in the Guide. Its part Art Deco, part small town tavern saloon bar offers an excellent choice of beers. The official list hovers around 100 though others can and do appear when they get to know you. There is strength in lambics and local ales, though Guy likes to keep some above average lagers

too. Try the often-overlooked local Dortmunder, Kerelsbier Licht on draught. The more formal dining room serves a full restaurant menu (12.00–13.30 & 19.00–21.00) featuring top quality beef and more delicate Flemish cuisine, all served in a most civilised atmosphere. This is an ideal base for touring the Westhoek region of West Flanders. They run their own beer festival on the last full weekend of October (see Beer Tourism) in the incongruously massive function room at the back. As if to prove they have their priorities right, they close for three weeks in high summer to have their own holiday.

CLOSED WEDNESDAY
Sun 10.00–14.00; Other days 10.00–24.00

OTHER POPERINGE CAFÉS:

The Grote Markt is awash with cafés that serve around forty beers and feature the Watou breweries' beers. Try the **Belfort** (no. 29), the **Nieuwe Haene** (no. 33) and the **Oud Vlaenderen** (no.14). Just off the Grote Markt, down Guido Gezellestraat is the **Hommelzak** (10b Paardenmarkt – T 057 33 71 72 – closed Th; others from 11.00), a first storey bar with reasonable food and an enlarging list of over forty.

RENINGELST

10km WSW of Ieper on N304
🚌 Poperinge [Kortrijk–Poperinge] – 5km

Small town among the hop fields to the south of Poperinge.

Hotel tip: the **Diligence**★★, 4 Kasteelmolen-straat (T 057 44 79 39; F 057 44 79 40; www.de-diligence.com) is a small family-run hotel on the road to Klijte that hires out horses to guests and children, and accommodates those who bring their own.

Boerenhol

4 Driegoenstraat T 057 36 02 53

Out in the middle of nowhere, a kilometre east of the town. Take Pastoorstraat from the centre and proceed with faith into the deep countryside. A small and cosy weekend café that serves good home-prepared dishes.

Many of the 60 or so beers it stocks are local. Opens for groups and parties on request. In high summer opening times change to 15.00 onwards.

CLOSED MONDAY
CLOSED TUESDAY TO THURSDAY (Sep–Jun)
Sat 14.30–24.00; Sun 10.00–23.00
Other days 16.00–23.00

ROESBRUGGE

18km WNW of Ieper on N308

Small town on the Ijzer, close to the French border.

Rohardushof

1 Bergenstraa   **T** 057 30 10 16

Postally in Beveren-Kalsijde but found in practice at the edge of Roesbrugge on the Beveren road. This easily missed café with a good local following, shares its space with a chocolate shop, beer shop and a museum of pottery and folk art. Commissions a pleasant, dark house beer called Forte Bruin, similar in style to an English "old ale". This was once brewed by the surprisingly well-preserved Feys brewery in the town, which the landlord would love to revive and re-open. The beer list of 120 is eclectic. The short menu (12.00–14.00 & 18.00–22.00) has local specialities including a challenging *potjesvleesch*. Good range of café games. Beware the sex-crazed bite-sized dog.

CLOSED WEDNESDAY
Mon 15.00 onwards; Other days 10.00 onwards

ROESELARE

16km NNW of Kortrijk off E403 exit 6
🚌 Roeselare [Lichtervelde–Kortrijk]

Busy Flemish town (pop. 54,000) that is home to the world famous Rodenbach brewery.

Hotel tips: the old **Park Hotel**★★★ and the modern **Flanders Inn**★★★, 7a–8 Stationsplein (**T** 051 26 31 31; **E** info@parkhotel-roeselare. be; **www.parkhotel-roeselare.be**) are two equally smart halves of the same business, conveniently close to the station.

Koornbloem

118 Ooststraat   **T** 051 20 18 52

From the station head for town, turning left. At a small square you will find Ooststraat on your right. The Cornflower is two hundred metres on your left. A neat, modern café with a small pavement terrace. The beer list of 55 includes numerous middleweights including the locally matured Rodenbach beers. There are good bar snacks and single plate meals (11.30–14.30 & 17.30–21.30). See also Brewery cafés: Rodenbach (above).

CLOSED SUNDAY; Fri & Sat 10.00 onwards
Other days 10.00–20.00

SINT ELOOIS-WINKEL

10km NNW of Kortrijk off E403 exit 6
See Brewery cafés: Old Bailey (above).

STASEGEM

4km E of Kortrijk off R8 exit 4
🚌 Kortrijk [IC] – 4 km
See Brewery cafés: Gaverhopke (above).

STENE

4 km S of Ostend off N33, near E40 exit 5.
🚌 Oostende [Ostend–Bruges] – 4 km

Old village on the southern outskirts of modern Ostend. Bus 5 or 6 from the city centre.

Vlasschaard

5 Oudstrijdersplein   **T** 059 80 38 01

A smart rustic-style café by the church, in this not-quite-absorbed village near the Ostend town boundary. A good drinking bar, a dining room and a small terrace. Farming implements and garden tools on the ceiling, cloths on the tables. Nearly 80 beers and rising. There is a West Flanders emphasis but Rochefort too. A sound menu features mostly Flemish standards, though there are nine other restaurants within two hundred metres of the front door!

CLOSED MONDAY & TUESDAY
Other days 11.00 onwards

TIEGEM

12km E of Kortrijk on N36
🚏 Anzegem *[Kortrijk–Oudenaarde]* – 4km

Small town in an attractively undulating part of West Flanders that passes for mountainous terrain round here.

Vossenhol
22 Tiegemberg   **T** 056 68 06 00

From the town centre follow the N494 towards Anzegem until you reach a cluster of bars that exploit the view. A large, family friendly, bistro restaurant with an enclosed garden at the side overlooking a well-equipped, indestructible children's playground. 60 beers. Food (12.00–14.00 & 18.00–22.00) runs to scampi, steaks, salads and fish dishes. There are pancakes and waffles in the afternoon. In July & August weekday closing is later. CLOSED WEDNESDAY; *Sat* 16.00 onwards *Fri&Sun* 12.00 onwards; *Other days* 12.00–18.00

TIELT

22km NNE of Kortrijk on N35 & N37
🚏 Tielt *[Gent–Lichtervelde]*

Dull market town equidistant from Bruges, Ghent and Kortrijk.

Pado
68 Stationsstraat   **T** 051 40 71 91

Go off the beaten track to find this one – please! It is only a hundred metres from the station, albeit in what is possibly the most boring-looking town in Flanders. Despite its setting this is a top quality bar with a natty modern design in frosted glass and well-lit light wood. The adventurous beer list of 85 features a good selection of regionals, quite a few micros and a handful of ultra-specials. Genuine tapas (11.00–24.00) includes Serrano ham, home-marinaded olives, various anchovies, manchego cheese, chorizo and much else. This is a real find – you'll love it, we promise! CLOSED TUESDAY & WEDNESDAY
Other days 11.00–24.00

VEURNE

25km SW of Ostend off E40 exit 2
🚏 Veurne *[De Panne–Lichtervelde]*

A few miles from the North Sea coast and equidistant from the French border, Veurne (Fr: *Furnes*) is one of the so-called Polder towns (pop. 11,000). Its main attraction is the ornate Spanish architecture round the Grote Markt. The annual penitents' procession (Du: *Boetprocessie*) on the last Sunday in July, is a uniquely Belgian parade led by men dressed as sad Capucijn monks and carrying heavy wooden crosses. St. Walburga's church has a piece of the actual real cross, presented by Robert II of Flanders in thanks for his ship surviving a violent storm. In July and August there are carillon concerts (Wed 10.30; Sun 20.00). The International Museum of Bread, Rolls, Cakes and Icing is on Iepersesteenweg.

Hotel tips: the **Croonhof**★★, 9 Noordstraat (**T** 058 31 31 28; **F** 058 31 56 81) is a pleasant, family-run small town hotel with dabs of class.

Flandria
30 Grote Markt   **T** 058 31 11 74

Another survivor of five editions. Typical of one genre of market square café. There is a single, high-ceilinged, airy saloon bar and a cramped covered terrace on the pavement. Many of the 100 or so beers are from West Flanders. The menu is limited to bar snacks but includes numerous local specialities on the theme of designer brawn. Good attentive service.   CLOSED THURSDAY
Wed 09.00–18.00; *others* 09.00–24.00 (*May–Sep*) 09.00–22.00 (*Oct–Apr*)

OTHER VEURNE CAFÉS

The **Centrum** (33 Grote Markt) has a long beer list but is far from adventurous. The **Heksekotje** (12 Pannestraat), just off the main square, shows promise too, with a few micros getting a place on a list nudging fifty.

VICHTE

12km E of Kortrijk on N36 near E17 exit 4
🚃 Vichte [Kortrijk–Oudenaarde] – 1km
See Brewery cafés: Verhaeghe (above).

VLAMERTINGE

4km W of Ieper off N38
🚃 Ieper [Kortrijk–Poperinge] – 4km

Small town out among the war graves between Ieper and Poperinge.

Lido

184 Poperingseweg **T** 057 20 17 95

We are taking a chance by including this typical small town café. The number of beers available is not fully clear. The full range of Leroy and Van Eecke are certainly there and top Guide sleuths have had no difficulty staying entertained with more unusual brews. Typical of a dying breed of village bar with a bit extra. Interesting décor. Good plain cooking is reported.

CLOSED THURSDAY; *Other days* 10.00 onwards

WATOU

7km W of Poperinge

The so-called brewers' town of Watou lies close to to the French border and is easy to reach from Lille and the Channel ports. In fact there has never been more than a handful of breweries here despite the fact that this is hop country. The two that remain are among the best in the land – St. Bernardus and Van Eecke.

Although the parish has no specialist beer café, between here and the border village of Abele are numerous excellent places to enjoy beers in a variety of settings.

Hotel tips: modern, rather plain lodgings can be found in the village square at the hotel **Een Huis Tussen Dag en Morgen**★★ (15 Watouplein – **T&F** 057 38 88 24). But if you want a real treat, try the Brouwershuis (see Brewery cafés: St. Bernardus above).

In the village centre the two cafés of note are the delightfully simple **Brouwershof** (see Brewery cafés: Van Eecke above) and the anything-but-simple **Hommelhof** (17 Watouplein – **T** 057 38 80 24; **F** 057 38 85 90 – closed We; Tu 12.00–14.30; others 12.00–14.30 & 18.30–21.30). This attractively rustic restaurant is run by Stefaan Couttenye, one of the chefs who pioneered the promotion of cooking with beer. Everything is on offer from heavyweight grandmother cooking, via the local specialities of pickled meats to delicacies such as hopshoots (in the late spring). They have a menu in English. It also functions as a village café from 10.00 on summer mornings and in the afternoons, stocking every one of the village's ales.

South of the town, beyond the St. Bernardus brewery on Trappistenweg, are four cafés that could not be more different from each other. Signposted off to the left and set in Helleketel wood are the **Helleketel** (6 Vuileseulestraat – **T** 057 38 80 35), an atmospheric little pub next to a Belbus stop of the same name and the **Sparhof** (1 Stoppelweg – closed Th; others 12.00–14.00, except We & from 18.00) a rustic tavern with a full menu and nearly fifty beers. Signposted off to the right from Trappistenweg, and easily found from Abele high street is the **Hanekamp** (22 Hanekampweg – Fr&Sa 18.00–24.00; Su 12.00–23.00) a delightfully simple well-run cottage café of simple charms with around forty beers.

In Abele, if you turn left the road will take you to the extraordinary **Wally's Farm** (232 Abeelseweg – **T** 057 33 52 24 – closed Mo–Th, Sep–Jun; Fr&Sa from 19.00; others from 12.00), where Elvis impersonator and American dream nut Wally Merlevede pays homage to the king, when he is not supervising giant barbecues or tending his forty beers.

To get around without fear of the breathalyser, either investigate the Belbus options or else hire a bicycle from De Huurfiets, 6 Vijfhoekstraat (**T** 057 36 06 62), just off Watouplein. Another transport of delight is the horse-drawn covered wagon (Du: *huifkartochten*) that visits local places of interest, including breweries.

WERVIK

10km WSW of Kortrijk off A19 exit 2a
🚃 Wervik [Kortrijk–Poperinge]

A small old market town in the post-industrial sprawl along the French border southwest of Kortrijk.

Grooten Moriaen

63 Koestraat **T** 056 31 49 24

Fifty metres from the river that marks West Flanders' border with beloved France, is this street full of shell holes, put here to frighten off Renault drivers. Enveloped by the official National Museum of Tobacco (Du: *Tabaks-museum*) and approached by the unofficial national museum of potholes. Under a striking windmill sits this traditional style *fin de siècle* café with wonderful old bar fittings and rickety furniture. Another great Belgian pub in the middle of nowhere. 70 beers on our winter visit included three own label brands. No food spotted.

CLOSED WEDNESDAY; *Other days* 10.00 *onwards*

WESTVLETEREN

15km NW of Ieper off N8
See Brewery cafés: Westvleteren (above).

The Grooten Moriaan at Wervik.

Buying take-home beer

One advantage to Belgium's best beers being bottled is that you can take them home to enjoy at will. For tourists from the English-speaking world this avoids the usually extortionate rates of "sin tax" that afflict alcoholic drinks back home. Here we review the options for do-it-yourself beer importing.

The cross-Channel boozer-cruiser trade aims to score alcohol the drug, so there are remarkably few good outlets for top rate beers around the French Channel ports. The Guide has none to recommend.

There are four ways to buy beer for home consumption in Belgium – supermarkets, specialist beer shops, drinks warehouses and breweries. There is no tradition of off-licence chains. We cover the options for buying from breweries elsewhere in the Guide. Here we will concentrate on the others.

Supermarkets

Supermarkets are much the same the world over. Their advantages are usually easy access and sometimes lower prices. Their disadvantage as a source of beer is their lack of cellar care – a particular concern when buying beers that condition in the bottle.

Supermarkets also exert a negative effect on independent producers. While a large contract with a single customer with guaranteed pay dates is an obvious attraction to a small brewer, being behoven to the varying, exacting and compromising demands of that customer is not.

The big supermarket groups in Belgium are the French-owned Carrefour, which bought the loss-making, beer-loving Belgian-owned GB a couple of years back, the "family-owned" Colruyt group, the equally Belgian but now largely US-based Delhaize-De Leeuw group and the German Aldi & Lidl chains.

Delhaize and Carrefour are generally your best bets for beer but do not expect a connoisseurs' corner.

Specialist beer shops

Specialist beer shops tend to sell a huge range of individual bottles at around 60 per cent of café prices. These are the best places to find beers from newer and smaller brewers and the special stuff from larg producers.

Beware the tourist trap shops in cities like Bruges, Antwerp and Brussels, which know they can charge a little extra for convenience but sometimes take outrageous liberties on pricing.

Drinks warehouses

There is no equivalent to these businesses in most of the English-speaking world. This is where hometown Belgium buys its beers for home consumption. Most also supply the local licensed trade and. The general public are welcomed with varying degrees of enthusiasm.

They go by a variety of names. In Dutch the first half of the name tend to include *bier-*, *drink-* or *dranken-* and the latter half *-markt*, *-handel* or *-centrale*. The French prefer *négociants* and *dépositaires* and feature words like *boissons* and *depot*.

Every town will have one. A few specialise in top quality beers but most stock mainly the better-known naff brands plus a large range of soft drinks. Before the creation of InBev, Interbrew had been on a ruthless campaign of buying up or squeezing out the independent operators in this sector.

Drinks warehouses are where you buy the better-known classics by the case. They tend to have a drive-in facility or conveniently placed parking area. They will have trolleys for loading up your crates. Most are happy with selling mixed cases, say four lots of six beers, but the closer you get to single bottles the less happy they are.

Most expect to receive payment in cash or by cashcard. Remarkably few take credit cards

Where exactly is the check-out?

or foreign currency, so check before you enter.

With 40% of Belgian beer now going to export, bewildered owners are getting used to English-speaking customer wandering around, often carrying this book and knowing more about the beers than most Belgian customers and many of the staff.

A few tips

Do not walk into the store and expect to work out what you want from what is in front of you. These places dazzle the unwary, so take a rough shopping list.

Try not to rely on advice from shop assistants. Most are marketing victims.

Be wary of beers that show no "sell by" date as these are likely to have been brewed before 2001. Beers that do not show a real brewery of origin are likely to be label beers.

Deposits

Most bottles and crates have deposits that add to the price you pay. Deposits on large bottles (150cl and up) can be huge. Bottles with no deposit carry a recycling logo on their label.

Most places will take your empties back but may refuse to take cases if they do not deal with that brewery or if it has changed its case design.

You do not have to fill a case with empties to return it. Do not mix bottle types in a returned case though, as these are often refused. There are only five standard designs of bottle

in Belgium but there are a couple of dozen variants. Obscure types need taking back in their original cases.

Customs & Excise

Provided you paid the local beer taxes in Belgium there is no duty to pay on beer brought into another EU country, such as the UK or Ireland. However, it is illegal to sell beer on, for example, to your local pub or off licence or even to your mates.

Beer brought back must be for "personal consumption". In practice Customs officials allow around 100 litres per head provided you are plausible. Show them your well-thumbed copy of the Guide – they know us!

Beer on airplanes

For North America and Australasia the problem is the weight limit on planes and fear of breakages in the hold. Our experience of the latter is that while bottles, caps and corks are pretty sturdy, glass does not like to be up against glass. Using bubble-wrap or bottle socks is usually enough.

Unfortunately, although Belgian beer shops are generally well geared up to beer travellers and their foibles, designer wrapping for safe carriage has not yet arrived, so plan your campaign before you leave home and bring your own wrapping.

A few beer shops and warehouses will export directly to you but this is rare.

Recommended beer shops and warehouses

The distinction between a shop and a warehouse may be blurred. Some larger shops look and operate pretty much like warehouses and some trade warehouses have a shop out at the front. For that reason we lump all our listings together.

The outlets below are the best we have encountered thus far. The list is deliberately biased towards those convenient for the ports of departure to the UK and for ex-pat English-speaking communities. All have been reported by readers as being relatively foreigner friendly.

Tell us of better ones on BelgiumGBG@aol.com

ANTWERP

ANTWERP
Dorsvlegel
12 Oude Vaartplaats ⊤ 03 232 9754

This beer shop, out near the Rubens museum and associated with the Oud Arsenaal café, specialises in unusual brews and helpful service. *Daily 10.30–16.00.*

BAARLE HERTOG
Brouwershuis
42 Molenstraat ⊤ 014 69 94 03
www.beterbier.be

Longstanding, famous beer shop in a Belgian enclave surrounded by Dutch North Brabant. Usually helpful and knowledgeable. 700 beers, mainly Belgian with some Dutch micros. Has expanded to include a tasting room (see Antwerp). Ask for the authentic lambics, which are not always on show.
Closed Monday. Others 10.00–18.00.

ESSEN
De Caigny
79 Spijker ⊤ 03 667 71 71

Drinks warehouse near the Dutch border, stocking 400 beers at keen prices.
Su 10.00–13.00; others 09.30–18.00.

Van Oevelen
47A Moerkantsebaan ⊤ 03 667 23 06
E erik.vanmeel@proximedia.be
www.vanoevelen.be

Another of the same ilk, also stocking 400 beers, and welcoming the public and trade customers alike.
Closed Tuesday. Su 09.30–12.30; Sa 09.00–18.00; others 09.00–12.30; 13.30–18.30.

BRUSSELS

CITY CENTRE
Bier Tempel
56 Marché aux Herbes ⊤ 02 506 19 06

Excellent shop right opposite the main tourist information office. A bit pricey but not ridiculous for such a prime location. 100 beers at any one time and not afraid to experiment with the unusual and exceptional.
Glasses, T-shirts, gift packs and books also.
Daily 10.00–19.00, 21.00 in summer.

IXELLES
Beer Mania
174 Chaussée de Wavre ⊤ 02 512 17 88
E beermania@skynet.be www.beermania.be

The best specialist beer shop in the capital but off the tourist track. Stocks 400 beers. Particularly strong on new Wallonian producers. Also books, glasses, T-shirts, posters etc.

They run a worldwide export service accessible through their multi-lingual website. They will also ship for walk in customers. They have a tasting facility to help you choose. May stay open later – phone to confirm.
Closed Sunday (not Dec). Others 11.00–21.00

SBS Special Beer Service

13 Rue Eugène Cattoir   **T** 02 640 45 64

Beer wholesaler with a ground floor selection of sixty safer beers by the case and many more craft beers downstairs, many in 75cl bottles. The best of the Brussels drinks markets.
Closed Sunday. Mo 13.00–18.00; others 10.00–18.00

EAST FLANDERS

GHENT

Hopduvel

625 Coupure Links   **T** 09 225 20 68
E hopduvel@skynet.be   www.dehopduvel.be

Famous warehouse run by the indefatigable Marc van Liefferinge, who cannot understand why he gets so many British beer lovers turning up in their estate cars and transit vans. Good parking and loading. 400 beers. Books, glasses and souvenirs. Several own brand beers from Van Steenberge. Foreigner-friendly. What you see is what you get.
Closed Monday. Su 10.00–12.00; others 10.00–12.30 & 13.30–18.00.

MELLE

Bierhalle

36a Hovenierstraat   **T** 09 230 88 44
www.bierhalle.be

Drinks warehouse off the Ghent ring road, open to the public.
Closed Sunday. Mo 14.00–18.30; Sa 09.00–18.00; others 09.00–12.30 & 14.00–18.30.

OLSEN

Mimir

52 Grote Steenweg   **T** 09 388 43 73
E info@drankencentralemimir.be
www.drankencentralemimir.be

A good all-round drinks warehouse, making a name for itself on the old road from Kortrijk to Ghent (N43). Stocks around 350 beers.

Good parking. Ask nicely and they will help you pack the trunk.
Closed Monday. Su 09.00–12.00; others 09.00–12.15 & 13.30–18.30, 18.00 Sa.

OOSTAKKER

Dranken Geers

7 Ledergemstraat   **T** 09 251 05 83
E info@drankengeers.be
www.drankengeers.be

Large shop cum small store just off the R4 north-east of Ghent, stocking a range of around 500 beers. Mainly from independent breweries with particular strength in lambics and organic beers. Peruse the list on their English language website.
Closed Sunday. Sa 09.00–12.00 & 13.30–18.00; others 08.00–12.00 & 13.00–19.00.

ST. LIEVENS-HOUTEM

Pede

10 Doelstraat   **T** 053 626730

Warehouse in a very beery neck of the woods, stocking 300 beers. Closes for lunch.
Su 09.00–12.00; others 09.00–19.00.

FLEMISH BRABANT

AARSCHOT

Holemans

117 Langdorpsesteenweg   **T** 016 56 24 61
E jan.holemans@skynet.be
http://users.pandora.be/dvt/holemanse.htm

Although there is a beer shop here catering for single purchases Holemans is principally a warehouse. Do not be put off, as it is one of the best – much recommended by our Belgian contributors. Check their website for discount details in English. There is a range of over 450 beers at generally keen prices, with something special easy to find.
Closed Sunday & Monday. Sa 09.00–18.00; others 09.00–12.00 & 13.00–19.00.

HALLE

Streekproductencentrum

3a Poststraat   **T** 02 361 31 90
E info@streekproductencentrum.be
www.streekproductencentrum.be

A Payottenland produce shop with just under 200 beers on sale. Naturally it stocks a huge range of lambics, plus a goodly lot of organic beers. *Closed Sunday to Tuesday. Others 09.00–18.00.*

SINT PIETERS LEEUW

BVS

57–65 Georges Wittouckstraat   **T** 02 377 18 43
E w.depauw@b-v-s.be
The initials stand for Brewery of the Valley of the Senne, from the days when they used to make beer here. Nowadays they stock around 250, with strength in regional ales but sadly succumbing to mainly commercial lambics, Drie Fonteinen and Boon aside.
Opening hours not known.

HAINAUT

COMINES-WARNETON

Houblonnière

39 Rue des Combattantes   **T** 056 55 46 36
E lahoublonniere@skynet.be
www.lahoublonniere.be

One of many beer supermarkets stacked along the French border, not far from the Lille urban conurbation. Near Comines railway station. 400 beers, plus chocolates. Advance orders and international shipping can be organised via the website. Takes Visa and Mastercard.
Closed Sunday. Mo 14.00–18.30; others 09.00–12.00 & 14.00–18.30.

PLOEGSTEERT

Brasserie Vanuxeem

150 Rue d'Armentières
T 056 58 89 23   **F** 056 58 75 59

A beer shop-warehouse in that enclave of Hainaut that is surrounded on three sides by West Flanders and on the fourth by France. 500 beers but few from new producers. Often full of French beer lovers driving Citroën vans and estates. Commissions three house beers under the Queue de Charrue brand (see Brewers without Breweries). Takes major credit cards.
Closed Sunday. Mo–Th 09.00–12.00; 13.00–19.00; others 09.00–19.00.

TEMPLEUVE

Palais des Bières

40 Rue de Roubaix

A funny little beer shop with a drive-in warehouse that is more of a stacked yard. Said to stock 600 beers. Not the best organised shelves, poor on lambics but a good chance of finding the rare and bizarre here. Loads of T-shirts, caps, mirrors and other beery stuff. *Closed Monday. Su 09.00–12.00; others 09.00–12.00 & 14.00–18.30.*

TOURNAI

Moine Austère

8 Rue Dorez   **T** 069 84 00 92

Excellent beer shop, two hundred metres off the Grand'Place. Stock varies but can hit 300 beers. Closes for lunch – more so on Sunday. Friendly and helpful.
Closed Monday. Tu 14.00–18.00; others 10.00–18.00.

LIÈGE

AUBEL

Stassen Vin

2 Place Albert 1er   **T** 087 68 63 66
E stassen.vin@skynet.be   www.stassenvin.com

A privately owned supermarket of regional produce, wines and beer. Stocks about 300 brews in all, though the cheeses and *charcuterie* of the region are as big a draw. In true Belgian fashion it also sells bottling machines, synthetic corks and all manner of wooden casks. *Closed Sunday. Mo 09.00–12.30; others 09.00–18.00.*

BATTICE

Corman Collins

1a Rue de Xhéneumont
T 087 67 42 96   **F** 087 66 07 69
E info@corman-collins.be
www.corman-collins.be

This spacious shop not far off the E40 and E42 motorways stocks around 350 beers, including ten that are commissioned specially for them (see Brewers without Breweries). The attached warehouse is strictly for the drinks trade and deals mainly with deliveries. Helpful English website.   *Closed Sunday. Others 09.00–18.00.*

LIÈGE

Antre du Vaudrée

130 Rue St. Gilles

Opposite the Vaudrée II café just off the city centre and owned by the same people. This specialist beer and spirits shop opened in October 2004 with 550 beers. Perhaps the most publicity-shy outlet in Belgium. All reports (and any contacts details!) welcome. *Daily* 10.00–18.00.

LIMBURG

ACHEL

Voedingswinkel en Bierhal

Achelse Kluis   **T** 011 80 07 62

The grocery store at the Achel cloister, next to the newest of the Trappist breweries (see Independent Breweries and Limburg). Sells everything you need for daily living, plus a range of about 150 beers. Strong on both Trappist and abbey beers. *Lunchtime may vary. Closed Monday (Oct–Apr)* & *Sunday; others* 09.00–12.00 & 12.30–17.00.

MOL

Bierbron

79 Turnhoutsebaan   **T** 014 31 47 43

This specialist beer shop is helpfully close to the SunParks holiday centre. 150 beers include an unusually excellent range of lambics from Boon, Cantillon, Drie Fonteinen, Girardin, Hanssens and others. Takes credit cards. *Closed Monday.*

LUXEMBOURG

BOUILLON

Marché de Nathalie

6 Grand Rue

A well-stocked beer shop deep in the Ardennes, specialising in Wallonian ales though not exclusively. Sells around 300 beers plus drinking paraphernalia. Home to the Bouillon brewery (see Independent Breweries), for the moment. *Closed Mo–We (Sep–Jun); others* 09.00–18.30.

NAMUR

ANNEVOIE

Drink d'Annevoie

60 Chaussée de Namur   **T** 082 61 35 84

Small beer warehouse with 400+ special beers at keen prices. *Closed Sunday* & *Tuesday. Mo* 13.30–18.30; *others* 10.00–18.30.

COUVIN

Comptoir des Fagnes

34b Route Charlemagne   **T** 060 34 52 95
E comptoir@fagnes.be
www.comptoirdesfagnes.be

Large beer store on the N5, that welcomes serious beer buyers. Claims to stock the widest range of beers in Wallonia at around 600. Lots of other stuff from wines and spirits via chocolates, cheese and *charcuterie* to tobacco products. *Su*&*Mo* 09.30–12.00; *others* 09.30–12.00 & 14.00–18.00, 18.30 *Fr*&*Sa.*

WALLONIAN BRABANT

NIVELLES

62 Rue de Namur

OK you explorers, we are told that this unnamed shop stocks local produce including a wide range of 75cl bottles of Wallonian ales and is a five-minute walk from the station. Which may sound vague but remember this is a beer desert. More information gratefully received. *Closed Monday.*

WEST FLANDERS

ABELE

Noel Cuvelier's

30 Abelestationsplein   **T** 057 33 33 05

Farm shop near the French border, just off the rat run between Poperinge and the A25 dual carriageway Lille to the Channel coast. Charmingly rustic, with 300 beers, cheese, chocolate and seasonal vegetables. *Daily* 08.00–20.00.

KROMBEKE

Nevejan Drankcentrale

16 Graaf van Hoornweg   T 057 40 00 35

Drinks warehouse in a village north of Poperinge. Very much the local wholesaler but close enough to the French border to attract British visitors. 200 beers from the region, plus the classics. Special beers are becoming harder to find and this will be its last listing if the trend continues.

Closed Sunday. Sa 09.00–17.00; others 08.00–19.00.

MENEN

All Drinks

209 Wervikstraat   T 056 51 87 87

More like a beer supermarket than a warehouse. Near the French border stocks about 350 safer beers. Closes for lunch.

Closed Tuesday. Su 09.00–12.30; others 09.00–19.00.

OSTEND

Vanhoutte Depot

78 Hendrik Serruyslaan   T 059 31 15 15

A drinks shop with around 200 beers in stock, spotted opposite the back end of the Mercator ship on the town side. Fairly safe list but with some high spots at keen prices. Good wine stock too.   *Opening hours not known.*

ZEDELGEM

Rotsaert

28 Remi Claeysstraat   T 050 20 94 98
E patrick.rotsaert@tiscali.be

Specialist beer warehouse at the edge of an industrial estate just off the N32 – driving from Bruges turn right at the EPOS building and persevere. "Only" 250 beers but includes numerous rarities.

Closed Sunday. Sa 10.00–17.00; others 10.00–18.00.

Is this Belgium's top beer shop?

Not far off exit 20 of the E313 motorway between Antwerp and Hasselt is the workaday town of Grobbendonk. A few hundred metres from its centre, on the road to Viersel, looking for all the world like an undersized supermarket is one of the most extraordinary specialist beer shops in the world. **Willems Bierhandel** (26 Leopoldstraat – T 014 51 17 74; www.bierhandelwillems.be – closed Su&Tu; Sa 08.30–18.00; others 08.30–12.30, 13.30–19.00) has to be the ultimate place to go to find unusual Belgian beers. A good range of authentic lambics is backed up by a plethora of stuff from new micros, with an unusually good selection from down south.

Kris Herteleer, artist, brewer and driving force behind the Dolle Brouwers.

The beer scene in Luxembourg

The national motto of the Grand Duchy of Luxembourg is "Mir wölle bleiwe wat mir sin", which translates roughly as "We want to stay as we are". Thankfully for beer lovers the last five years have seen this vow broken many times.

A few unassailable facts suggest that the Grand Duchy should be a top country for beer. For a start, Luxemburgers drink more beer than anyone else in Europe bar the Germans and the Irish.

Then there is its geographical position, just over Belgium's south-eastern border. To its north and east is Germany, the land of twelve hundred breweries, seven thousand beers and the Reinheitsgebot purity law. Even the part of France adjoining its southern border is a well-known beer-making region.

So why is it that until recently the Grand Duchy had been such a tedious place for beer drinkers?

Its size matters and so does its business base. Luxembourg has a sleepover population of less than half a million and takes up only 2,590 square kilometres. Its *raison d'être* in modern Europe is its mandarin but essentially wealth-obscuring tax laws.

Although it used to have an industrial belt down south and still has a beautiful rural north reminiscent of the lower Alpine slopes, what Luxembourg does best is to allow international capitalists to avoid paying their fair contribution to the upkeep of their homelands. This may be why most of the money behind InBev is lodged here. For reasons that defy explanation, fat cats and their servants are satisfied by dull beer.

Recent developments

Until 1999 Luxembourg had three largish brewery companies and two small local ones, each concocting variants on indifferent pale lager.

In that year Mousel brewery, on the banks of the Alzette in the city of Luxembourg merged with the Diekirch brewery of Diekirch to form the Brasserie de Luxembourg Mousel-Diekirch. The Mousel plant promptly closed in celebration. The newly formed **Luxembourg** brewery then "came out" as an Interbrew subsidiary and remains part of InBev.

The largest of the remaining independent breweries is **Bofferding** of Bascharage. Imagine an obsessively clean producer of well-sculpted pale lagers, with enough bite to keep things interesting, and you will understand where they are coming from. Not a bad choice as house Pilsners.

The other two long-established breweries to survive are **Simon** of Wiltz in the agricultural north, and **Battin** of Esch-sur-Alzette in the once steel-making south.

Battin has buddied up with Bofferding for marketing purposes and continues to vie with them as to which company produces the best of Luxembourg's lagers. Simon meanwhile has started to get a teeny bit adventurous, expanding into stronger lagers and a wheat beer made from organic spelt.

Wanting to stay as it was came easily to Luxembourg brewing until 2000, when Jean Bollendorf started to build a brewhouse next to his restaurant in Redange, not far from the Belgian town of Arlon. The **Redange** craft brewery began by making some adventurous but initially rather ropy beers that were variants of wheat beer. In recent years quality has picked up markedly and the range has grown in range and confidence.

Then in 2002 an urban brewpub cum hotel set up next to a large *salaisons*, eight hundred metres down the road from the Bofferding brewery in Bascharage. The **Béierhaascht** would not look out of place in Germany or the US. For now it tends to produce draught beers in safer mainstream styles, though there have been a few experiments.

The following year saw the arrival of an eco-friendly rustic version of the same thing at Heinerscheid in the Ourdaller national park in the north of the country. The **Ourdaller** brewery produces a variety of draught and bottled beers featuring numerous grains. Its food and accommodation options are humble in comparison to Béierhaascht (think chalet rather than conference centre) but the principle is the same.

The Luxembourg beer revival has some way to go but there are signs of further improvement. Planning permission has been granted to construct a house brewery within the shell of the old Mousel brewery in Luxembourg city. And the seriously adventurous you can brew their own beer at the microbrewery housed in the Musée Nationale de l'Art Brassicole in Wiltz Castle and overseen by Simon brewery.

LUXEMBOURG BEERS TO LOOK OUT FOR

Battin

Battin Urtyp (5.5%) is the best of the regular brews, a crisp, well-constructed original-style Pilsener. **Battin Christmas** (5.5%) is a dark winter lager that has its fans.

Béierhaascht

Visit the brewery (below) to sample whatever is on. We found the light beer **Haaschtbéier Hell** (5.1%) the most impressive of the regular brews. *See more on* www.beierhaascht.lu.

Bofferding

Bofferding Lager Pils (4.8%) is the best of the country's standard draught lagers in our view. **Hausbéier** (5.2%) is an impressively characterful, slightly peppery lager in flip-top bottles for take-home year-round. **Bofferding Fréijoers Béier** (4.8%) is the impressive light lager for the early spring. **Bofferding Christmas Béier** (5.5%) is a dryish chestnut-amber lager, more reminiscent of autumn leaves rather than Christmas spices.

Luxembourg

Sadly Diekirch and Mousel brands are now the country's also-ran beers. The unfiltered version of the Mousel Pilsener is available at one or two cafés, literally, but may expand its circulation soon.

Ourdaller

The regular beers include **Héngeschter** (4.2%) draught Pilsener, the top-fermented **Kornelysbéier** (4.4% – summer only) that contains rye, **Wäissen Ourdaller** (4.6%) draught wheat beer made with malted spelt and **Wëllen Ourdaller** (6.8%), the bottled brown ale made with buckwheat. Follow its eco-friendly progress on www.cornelyshaff.lu.

Redange

All beers are made from organic ingredients and contain at least 20% wheat. **Okult No. 1 Blanche** (5.4%) is a Belgian-style wheat beer spiced with coriander and bitter orange, **Okult No. 2 Rousse** (5.4%) is modelled on a Bavarian bockbier, **Okult No.3 Blonde** (5.4%) is a blond lager aimed at the local market and **Quaffit** (6.2%), a British style three-grain stout. They have also started experimenting with high gravity seasonal beers such as **Mai-Bock** (7.2%), **Blanche au Sureau** (5.6%) and **Bock du Vendemiaire** (9%).

Simon

Simon Pils (4.8%) is the standard draught beer while **Simon Régal** (5.5%) is a smoother bottled blond lager. The joker in the pack is **Simon Dinkel** (4.8%), an unfiltered, unspiced, assertively grainy, dryish spelt beer. The other one the locals rave about is **Simon Noël** (6.5%), the dark Christmas lager.

THE CAFÉ SCENE

The Grand Duchy is about the same size as a typical Dutch or Belgian province. Its capital city is one of the most striking in the world, constructed above and along ancient rivers spanned by mighty viaducts. Much of its hilly hinterland is as twee as a waxed moustache. This is a land carefully constructed as a perfect setting for solid taverns and country inns.

So where are the great cafés then?

Well actually they are everywhere. The problem is that they all stock the same old international piffle Luxembourg style. One of the things that would give small Luxembourg brewers a real boost would be if some of the country's cafés and shops began to take pride in stocking beers.

Gaining the edge in the excellence stakes appears to consist more of cramming an extra bit of smokiness into that ham, lacing the sauerkraut with a few more caraway seeds or getting a drop more cream into the potatoes. The only highlights on the drinks list are the delightfully delicate wines of the small Luxembourg vineyards, to which many a frustrated beer lover has turned to experience something authentically local.

This is a great shame as Luxembourg has many attractions for the tourist. For example, one of our researchers found his mobile phone, which works well everywhere else in Europe, lost its signal everywhere more than a kilometre from the border.

LUXEMBOURG CAFÉS TO VISIT

Bascharage

The **Béierhaascht** (240 Route de Luxembourg – daily 11.00–24.00) is in the style of a German-style Gästhausbrauerei, like an American brewpub with rooms, on the main road through town. Its gleaming coppers and brewing paraphernalia must be visible from outer space. The incongruous but well-stocked smoked meats shop by the main entrance is the original business that spawned the project. In the huge modern bar and restaurant the cooking (daily 11.30-23.00) is based on heavy, carnivorous Lux-German, with the in-house pork specialities in pride of place of course. A good value daily special is usually available. The 28-bedroom three-star hotel (**T** 26 50 8550; **F** 26 50 8599; *www.beierhaascht.lu*) offers good value. There is a large beer garden in summer.

Heinerscheid

The newest of the Grand Duchy's three, very different brewpubs is based deep in the Ourdaller national park. The **Cornelyshaff** (37 Rue de Stavelot – **T** 269075 – closed Mo; others 10.00–24.00) is on the main road through the village, opposite the turning to Kalborn. The brand new no-expense-spared café-restaurant sells all the Ourdaller beers, plus plenty of other locally grown or made produce. The eight letting rooms offer good value. A shop sells local cheese, mustard, buckwheat noodles and rather disgusting pressed hemp oil! If you get here on the hourly bus 555 from Ettelbruck or Diekirch, you will pass the Radio Luxembourg transmitters.

Luxembourg

The Grand Duchy's capital (pop. 78,000) is a city with a spectacular natural beauty enhanced by the efforts of battlement architects. For the best view find the Hotel Grand Cravat, up in the old city. The prettiest part of town and the site of many of the more traditional cafés is Grund, down in the valley below the best of the preserved town walls. Just over the hill, passing a few the Magritte-style street lamps on the way is Clausen, with its collection of defunct breweries. Sadly, the capital's pubs are a blancmange of repetitive mediocrity. We have never found Simon or Battin beers here, let alone anything more exotic. The only vaguely unusual beer find is Mousel's Zwickelbéier, the unfiltered draught Pilsener found at two substantial old pubs that specialise in heavy Luxembourg cooking – the **Zeutsius** (71 Rue de Trèves – **T** 26 430031) and **Mousel's Cantine** (46 Montée de Clausen). Rumour has it that the latter café-restaurant won the award for moodiest service in Europe but that they couldn't be arsed to pick it up.

Mondorf-les-Bains

Just as we were going to press we heard that the Casino 2000 had opened an international beer bar called the **JP2B Jackpot Beer Bar** (daily 19.00–03.00) stocking 77 beers from around the globe. None sounded hugely exciting but it is a start.

Redange

The approach to Redange takes you through a beautiful and forested part of the country, interspersed with buildings of classical Luxembourgeois proportions. The **Brasserie** (61 Grand'Rue – closed Tu; others 11.00–01.00 – T 23 62 09 53) is just such a building, half way up the main street of this attractive hillside village. Considerable effort has gone into reclaiming this former brewery and turning it into a ground-breaking café-restaurant, though the bar remains pretty basic. The food gets good reviews but the restaurant does not always open in winter, when café opening hours may not hold either. Bus 518 goes to and from Ettelbruck and sometimes Diekirch. Bus 265 goes hourly between Redange and Luxembourg railway station. The town has no connection with Rédange station, which is near the French border.

Rumelange

This pleasantly lived-in town in the old industrial belt 25km south of the capital, is home to its country's only seriously special beer café, the **Café du Coin** (94 Grand'Rue – T 56 53 03 – closed Su; others 10.00–12.15; 15.30–01.00). On the main road out towards Esch and the national museum of mining, one kilometre up the hill from the train station. *Belle époque* in a neat and tidy kind of a way, with enough pedigree to be becoming a brown café. The beer list stands around a hundred with around 80 in stock at any one time. Tries to take beers from all the Luxembourg brewers but not reliably. Scotch whiskies include cask strength imports. Food is limited to cheese and charcuterie, with oysters on occasions. It must be a lonely

existence being the Grand Duchy's only specialist beer café. Encourage them.

Tourism for beer lovers

Be warned that this is a country that closes on Sunday and that getting around on Saturdays can be slow.

The city of Luxembourg has numerous smaller, cheaper hotels around the rather dowdy station area but no more than a couple nearer the action. None of the affordable ones is likely to impress. This city is for working in and looking at, rather than staying around.

A possible alternative base is Diekirch (pop. 6,000), a pleasant small town that is well-placed at the head of a branch line from Ettelbruck, to link into the national rail network. It has five hotels including the spick and span Parc★★★ (28 Avenue de la Gare; T 80 34 72; F 80 98 61; www.hotel-du-parc.lu), the deliciously understated Hiertz★★★ (1 Rue Clairefontaine; T 80 35 62; F 80 88 69) and the cheaper but highly acceptable Gare★★ (73 Avenue de la Gare; T 80 33 05; F 80 23 52).

Apart from its microbrewery for hire, we do not know what else goes on in the National Museum of the Brewing Art in Wiltz.

Buying beer to take home

The Grand Duchy ought to enjoy a thriving beer shop scene in view of its favourable tax regime. Sadly this is not the case.

A supermarket complex called the **Pall Center** (5 Rue d'Arlon, Oberpallen – closed Mo; Su 08.00-19.00; others 08.00-20.00), between the brewery at Redange and the Belgian border near Arlon, stocks everything they can get from Luxembourg, plus about 70 Belgian beers and a few German, though you will need your car.

One branch of the Delhaize chain (15-17 Route de Longwy, Bertrange) stocks around 60 Belgian beers and is accessible from Luxembourg city centre by bus – the City Concorde Mall route.

On the whole the Cactus chain of supermarkets is best for buying Luxembourg beers.

BREWERY
Cantillon

BEER
Lambic

GREAT BRITISH
BEER FESTIVAL
2003
5th AUGUST LONDON
OLYMPIA

ABV:
5.0%

Per Half: £1.50
Per Pint: £3.00

Belgian beer in the UK

The law conspires against the development of a respectable drinking culture in the UK. Stupid licensing hours in pubs for all age groups have led to the burgeoning of drinking clubs for the unrestricted young. High taxes on alcohol encourage drinks of little intrinsic worth that are cheap to make. Despite this a new breed of quality beer outlets is springing up across the UK. Here we highlight the best of Belgian ales.

MARK CAYGILL was so disappointed at being posted back to Britain from Brussels that his family allowed him to pull together this nationwide listing of some of the brightest and best of the breed.

The pubs, cafés, restaurants, hotels, off-licences, beer stores and other outlets listed here are not intended to be a comprehensive list but they do give a flavour of the sort of thing that enterprising people are achieving.

With thanks to **Jeremy Gray** for the information on London.

PUBS, RESTAURANTS AND SHOPS

NATIONAL

Cave Direct
20 Danson Mead, Welling, Kent DA16 1RU
www.belgianbeers.co.uk
T 020 8303 2261   **F** 020 8303 0180
E mail@cavedirect.co.uk

The original on-line and mail order specialist Belgian beer supplier, based in Kent but able to deliver anywhere in the UK (extra charges for Scotland, Wales and Northern Ireland). Minimum order £30.00 and one case. Around 120 beers in stock mainly from mainstream breweries but including the odd authentic gueuze, St. Bernardus, De Koninck, Orval, Achel, Rochefort and Maredsous brands too.

ALTRINCHAM
Small market town on the southern outskirts of Manchester.

Trappiste
40 Greenwood Street   **T** 0796 356 1335
www.letrappiste.com

Opposite the covered market in the town centre. A more authentic Belgian café than you will find in many towns in Belgium! Two-storey, with wooden floors and candlelight adding to the atmosphere. Table service only and strictly no perpendicular drinking. Other nods to the culture include continental licensing hours, posts of Tin Tin, Poirot and Jacques Brel and Belgian background music. 85 beers, including a dozen on tap, featuring Cantillon, Anker, Bosteels, Westmalle, Rochefort and Achel as permanent features. Regular guests can include UK rarities from Hanssens and Ellezelloise. The illustrated beer list gives useful tasting notes. The basic menu of mussels and chips is not always available, so ring ahead if you intend to dine. There is a pavement terrace on summer evenings.
Sat 12.30 onwards; *Sun* 19.00 onwards
Other days 18.00 onwards

BARNOLDSWICK
Typical south Lancashire town, a few of miles off the A56, between Burnley and Skipton.

Rainhall Drinks
18–22 Rainhall Road   **T** 01282 813374

On the way into the town from the A56. The last place on Earth you would expect to find an emporium of excellence but so what. Turn left at the lights into Rainhall Road and this excellent off license is fifty metres on your right. To find buried treasure head downstairs to the beer cellar. Well over three hundred beers from around the world with 100 Belgian. A solid list includes St. Bernardus, de Dolle Brouwers, Abbaye des Rocs and Dupont. Sampling on the premises is allowed though this is no café as yet. Thursday, Friday and Saturday evenings is best, so ring ahead.

BATTLE

East Sussex town that was the real site of the Battle of Hastings.

Café Belge

64a High Street   **T** 01424 772344
www.cafebelge.co.uk

One of a chain of five Belgian style café-restaurants based around Kent and East Sussex. All are primarily restaurants with a major Belgian theme. They cook mussels in fifty different ways, all with *frites*, but have more serious cooking too, as well as light lunches. Each stocks a range of 60 Belgian beers that cover the full gamut from a few better lagers via lightweight fruity stuff to serious brews that range from various Trappists via Bush and Karmeliet to include even Malheur Brut Reserve at times. Reservations via the website.

BEDFORD

Modern county town.

Wellington Arms

40–42 Wellington Street   **T** 01234 308033

Off the Broadway, north of the centre in the older part of town. Landlord Eric Mills seems to be on a personal quest to bring quality foreign beers to Bedfordshire. His stock of Belgians ales, often researched through self-sacrificing trips to Belgian beer festivals, can reach 50 and include Ellezelloise, de Graal, Drie Fonteinen, Abbaye des Rocs and Kerkom. *Sun* 12.00–22.30; *Other days* 12.00–23.00

BEXHILL-ON-SEA

Old seaside town on the East Sussex coast.

Café Belge

45 The Marina   **T** 01424 713513
See Battle (above).

BIRMINGHAM

England's second city (after Manchester) only discovered beer in the Eighties. Before that it believed in the long defunct M&B and Ansells, the fore-runners of Auntie Stella and Uncle Bud. So the fact it has any Belgian beer at all is encouraging.

The **Anchor** (Bradford Street – **T** 0121 622 4516) is a short walk from New Street station, past the old Bull Ring and new cow's arse (Selfridge's) in developing Digbeth. This pioneering real ale pub stocks a small but growing selection of Belgian ales including Floreffe, Val-Dieu and St Feuillien, with occasional treats such as Winter Koninck or Gouden Carolus Ambrio on tap.

The **Bartons Arms** (144 High Street, Aston – **T** 0121 333 5988) is probably the best of Birmingham's extravagant Victorian gin palaces, easily reached by bus 51 or 52 from the city centre. Upstairs was a former music hall that acted as a foil for the old Aston Hippodrome opposite. Now owned by an enterprising small brewery, a Belgian beer list that can include Piraat and even Westvleteren is the least of its many achievements. Thai food is recommended.

The best off-license in the city is **Stirchley Wines and Spirits** (1535–1537 Pershore Road, Stirchley – **T** 0121 459 9936 – Sun 18.00–22.30; others 12.00–23.00), about twenty minutes out of the centre, not far beyond BBC Pebble Mill on one of the main traffic arteries. Belgian regulars include Achouffe, St. Bernardus, Kerkom, Hanssens, Girardin, Corsendonk, Rodenbach, Verhaeghe and others. Good wines and whiskies too.

BRIGHTON

Sussex's little London on sea, with a dab of outrage and a pier.

Two pubs in the town carry a small but unusually high quality range of Belgian beers. Conveniently close to the railway station is the **Evening Star** (55–56 Surrey Street – **T** 01273 328931), a traditional boozer that backs up it's British real ales with about twenty Belgians, which may include beers from de Ranke, Ellezelloise, Cantillon and Girardin. The **Greys** (105 Southover Street – **T** 01273 680734) is equally traditional and sports a generally safer Belgian list that may include beers from Dupont, Rochefort and Verhaeghe. They have a policy of only one Rochefort 10 per customer.

BURNLEY

East Lancashire mill town held back from progress by an under-achieving football team.

Bridge Bierhuis

2 Bank Parade   **T** 01282 411304
www.bridgebierhuis.co.uk

Traditional, triangular shaped end-terrace boozer majoring on quality beer. As well as the obligatory range of real ales, the Bierhuis offers a solid list of around 40 Belgian brews. New beers are added on a regular basis and the list includes some rare UK finds such as Oeral, Bink, Malheur, Sloeber and Grottenbier. It opens on Tuesdays when Burnley play at home. For the wake, presumably.
CLOSED MONDAY & TUESDAY; *Sat* 11.00–23.00 *Sun* 12.00–22.30; *Other days* 12.00–23.00

The pub is supported by the **Hop & Vine Experience** (2 Victoria Road – **T** 01282 454970), an off-license opened in 2003, which has about 60 Belgian beers. No major surprises as yet but a number of good choices.

BURY ST. EDMUNDS

Ancient market town halfway between Cambridge and the North Sea, culturally as well as geographically. Home to the UK's smallest pub (the Nutshell) and largest independent brewery (Greene King).

Beer 2 Go

1a St Andrews Street South   **T** 01284 768534
www.beer2go.co.uk

Highly independent compact beer shop with around three hundred beers of which maybe 60 will come from Belgium. Abbaye des Rocs, Dupont, Kerkom, Dolen and Anker all feature in an ever-changing range.
CLOSED MONDAY
Sun 12.00–16.00; *Other days* 10.00–18.00

CAMBRIDGE

One of the world's great university towns, home to "silicon fen", the human genome project, numerous Nobel Prize winners and much of the vr-vr-vroom behind this book.

Bacchanalia

90 Mill Road   **T** 01223 315034

Formerly the Jug & Firkin, a cornerstone of the Cambridge sanity belt. Stocks beers from everywhere with up to 60 from Belgium, including some 75cl lambics and others. Always on the lookout for the unusual. Good on Dutch beers too. The other branch at 79 Victoria Road (**T** 01223 576 292) has a smaller selection.
Mon–Wed 11.00 – 20.00; *Thu–Sat* 11.00 – 21.00
Sun 12.00–14.00; 17.00–20.00

CANTERBURY

The county town of Kent, overly famed for its cathedral and insufficiently so for its cricket ground. Easily reached from most routes to and from the Dover ferries.

Café Belge

89 St. Dunstans Street   **T** 01227 768222
See Battle (above).

CHELMSFORD

Essex market town, sadly close to the A12 in the London commuter belt.

Onlyfinebeer

37 Broomfield Road   **T** 01245 255579
www.onlyfinebeer.co.uk

Situated in the West End area of Chelmsford, Onlyfinebeer is one of the UK's best off licenses. Stocking just over 1000 beers, it's range of Belgians stands at over 300, making it possibly the largest in the UK. Too many choices to pick out the highlights – get a good idea from the website. Offers home delivery over a wide area.
Sun 12.00–18.00; *Other days* 11.00–21.30

CHELTENHAM

Large Gloucestershire town, home to the horse-racing olympics, GCHQ and a College that makes Ladies.

Ken Sheather Wines

8 Mead Park   **T** 01242 231231
www.sheathers.co.uk

This is predominantly a quality wine merchant, in the Leckhampton area of Cheltenham. However, its owner takes a personal interest in the quality end of the Belgian beer market and stocks a range of around 70 from the likes of Boelens, Kerkom, Dolle Brouwers, Regenboog, Fantôme and Westvleteren. Well worth checking out for some rare UK finds.

CLOSED SUNDAY & MONDAY
Other days 10.00–18.00; *Sat* 10.00–13.00

COVENTRY

Ancient market town of naked Lady Godiva fame that was transformed by the car industry in the 1930s and again by the Luftwaffe ten years later. Its modern cathedral should be more famous.

Alexander Wines

112–114 Berkeley Road South   **T** 0247 667 3474
www.alexanderwines.co.uk

There has been an off-licence on the corner of Providence Street and Berkeley Street in the Earlsdon area of Coventry for over a century. The current one stocks three to four hundred beers, of which around 100 are Belgian. Check the website for a full list, which usually includes Dolle Brouwers, Friart, Silly, Slaghmuylder, Van Eecke and others on the best list in the Midlands.

Sun 12.00–14.30; 19.00–22.30
Other days 11.00–14.00; 17.30–22.30

CREWE

Market town in the industrial part of south Cheshire, best known as a railway junction.

Borough Arms

33 Earle Street   **T** 01270 254999

In centre of town, a full twenty minutes walk from the famous station, this genuine free house is a beacon of excellence. On top of their real ale selection they aim to stock up to seven Belgian beers on tap, backed up by another 50 in bottles. Mercifully free of noisy machines, a good place for friendly conversation. A framed Crewe Alexandra football shirt indicates the allegiances of the regulars, but nowhere is perfect.

Fri 15.00–23.00; *Sat* 12.00–16.00; 19.00–23.00
Sun 12.00–15.00; 19.00–22.30
Other days 19.00–23.00

CROYDON

Outer suburbia, on the way from central London to Gatwick airport.

Beer Circus

282 High Street   **T** 07910 095945
www.thebeercircus.co.uk

Inspired by the Bier Circus in Brussels, this unusual café, fifteen minutes walk from East Croydon railway station opened in May 2004. The main room is at street level, light and airy with an exposed stone floor and a growing collection of breweriana on its walls. Downstairs is more relaxed with a few tables and sofas. The highlight is an ambitious beer list of nearly three hundred, of which over 170 are Belgian. Quality German beers are also available. Prices are as yet very reasonable for the South-East. Highlights include Blaugies, Fantôme, Regenboog, de Ranke, Verhaeghe, Kerkom, Ellezelloise, de Dolle Brouwers, Cantillon, Cam, Drie Fonteinen, Girardin, Hanssens, and all the Trappist breweries on an ever-changing list that would guarantee top billing in Belgium itself. There is food too, though as yet as a secondary pursuit.

Sun 18.00–22.30; *Other days* 12.00–23.00

DARLINGTON

Formidable railway town in what was County Durham.

Binns

1–7 High Row   **T** 01325 462606

An unlikely location for the best range of Belgian beers in the North East. Binns is a department store at the end of Darlington's main shopping street. Its insufficiently famous off-licence is in its basement. Well over three hundred beers from around the world include about 80 from Belgium. Also strong on UK regionals and single malt whiskies. Clearly the creation of its manager, who cultivates his customers carefully.

Sat 09.00–18.00; *Sun* 11.00–17.00
Other days 09.00–17.30

EASTBOURNE

The archetype of South Coast decadence, to which bankers and other gentlefolk used to flock for a quiet retirement, before grey pound tourism was invented.

Café Belge

11–23 Grand Parade   T 01323 729967
See Battle (above).

FORTROSE

Village on the Black Isle of Cromarty, ten miles north-east of Inverness, the northernmost city in Scotland.

Anderson

Union Street   T 01381 620236
www.theanderson.co.uk

Guide regulars will know that we admire the obscure. And you don't get much more obscure than this. On the south side of Cromarty, which is neither black nor an island, the Anderson promotes fine living in an historic building at the centre of this picturesque seaside village. With the exception of the Clockwork in Glasgow (below) it has probably the best list of Belgian ales in Scotland, with up to 60 available. Likes to stock Trappist ales, including aged ones. There are also a hundred single malts, a menu based on local ingredients and nine en-suite bedrooms, in case the journey back is too long.

Sun 12.30–23.30; *Other days* 11.00–23.30

GLASGOW

Scotland's largest city, famed for football, ship-building on the Clyde, Charles Rennie Mackintosh's version of Art Nouveau and Billy Connolly. Where most cities would make do with a ring road, Glasgow runs a motorway through its centre.

Clockwork Beer Co.

1153–1155 Cathcart Road   T 0141 649 0184

Glasgow's first brew pub, opened in 1997 on the south side of the city. Catch a train from Central Station to Mount Florida, cross the footbridge and wander down the hill to Cathcart Road. Turn right and the Clockwork

is about 300 metres along on the left, close to Hampden Park, so full on international match days. The large open plan drinking area includes a rare no smoking section.
In a fabulous array of beers on the illustrated list at your table you should find 75 Belgians including Rochefort, Dubuisson, Orval, Cantillon and Boon. There is a huge range of single malts too in what must be Glasgow's premier quality drinking establishment. Recommended on days of the "Old Firm" (Celtic vs Rangers) match, as they do not show the match at all.

Sun 12.00–22.30; *Other days* 11.00–23.00

HALIFAX

Large mill town in West Yorkshire's Calder Valley. Just off 't M62.

Au Chocolat Belge

Unit 63, Rustic Gallery, Piece Hall
T 01422 363222
www.piecehall.info

Recently established Belgophile shop, inside the Piece Hall shopping centre. Majors in chocolates and beer, stocking around 75 of the latter.

CLOSED WEDNESDAY

Sun 10.30–17.00; *Other days* 10.00–17.00

KINGS LYNN

Large East Anglian town, close to the Norfolk – Cambridgeshire border.

Beers of Europe

Garage Lane, Setchey   T 01553 812000
www.beersofeurope.co.uk

Fantastic off-license at Setchey, just south of Kings Lynn. Well over a thousand beers in total, with over 300 from Belgium. It also runs an on-line mail order service that can deliver over a large area of the UK. Another place that can lay reasonable claim to the largest selection of Belgian beer in the UK. Beer glasses also available. As well as virtually all the safe beers, carries stocks of Vapeur, the Kapittel range from Van Eecke, Hanssens and even Lou Pepe from Cantillon.

Sun 10.00–16.00; *Other days* 09.00–18.00

KNARESBOROUGH

Picturesque North Yorkshire market town, birthplace of Mother Shipton a cave-dwelling prophet of doom. She predicted the world would end. It didn't, but we do have Miller Lite.

Beerritz

17 Market Place   **T** 01423 862850

On a corner of the market square. An off-license with close ties to the Beer Paradise warehouse in Tockwith (below). Stocks over two hundred beers, of which 50 are Belgian. Some glasses too.   *Daily* 10.00–22.00

LEEK

Picturesque market town in deepest Staffordshire.

Den Engel

23–25 St. Edward Street   **T** 01538 373751

An unusual location for one of the UK's longest standing traditional Belgian beer cafes. Authentic breweriana, wooden floors and a dash of eccentricity tell you that this genuinely Belgian style café is a bit special. Over 100 beers with several on tap are complimented by excellent food with a Flemish influence. This would still get into the Guide if it was in the middle of Bruges. The only English addition is a no smoking area. Worth a major detour.

Mon & Tue 19.00–23.00; *Wed & Thu* 17.00–23.00
Other days 12.00–15.00; 17.00–23.00

LEICESTER

Multi-cultural East Midlands city that is home to a solid rugby team, a wobbly soccer team, Gary Lineker and a local obsession with Belgian ales.

Café Bruxelles

90–92 High Street   **T** 0116 224 3013
www.cafebruxelles.co.uk

Built in 1903 and originally home to the Birmingham & Provincial Bank, this Belgian-style café bistro in the main shopping area exploits its heritage to imitate the ornate Brussels cafés of Horta and Art Nouveau. The tiled floor, hard wood furnishings, chandelier and ornate, hand painted domed ceiling would not look out of place just off Grand' Place. The list of 50 Belgian beers includes De Koninck on tap and bottled ales from Dupont, St. Feuillien, Abbaye Des Rocs, Achel and others. The food owes more to catering college than the Ilôt Sacré, though it is all edible and the ubiquitous mussels are there. The cellar bar (Fri & Sat only) may stay open till 01.00.

Other days 12.00–23.00; *Sun* 12.00–16.00

Criterion

44 Millstone Lane   **T** 0116 262 5418
www.mainlybeer.com

Owned by the same people as the Swan and Rushes (below), this plain looking Sixties pub not far from the Cathedral, near the Southways underpass is one of the last places you would expect one of Britain's best ranges of Belgian beer. The list is similar to its older sister's, though there is more food here, with home-baked Italian style pizzas the speciality of the house. It was the first UK pub to be nominated for Orval Embassy status.

Sun 12.00–22.30; *Other days* 11.00–23.00

Swan and Rushes

19 Infirmary Square   **T** 0116 233 9167
www.mainlybeer.com

From the city centre, follow the pedestrian signs for Leicester Royal Infirmary and De Montfort University and you should come across the Swan and Rushes by default. If you are a rugby fan the home of Leicester Tigers is just off the square down Welford Road. A traditional unassuming red brick British boozer, which happens to be almost triangular in shape. The range of up to 80 Belgian beers includes one of the best ranges of traditional lambic beers anywhere, including some of the best of Cantillon (like Lou Pepe), Drie Fonteinen and the very rare Girardin black label. Other rarities for the UK include XX Bitter, Bink, Vichtenaar, Grottenbier, Zatte Bie, Hercule and 75cl bottles from Blaugies, Dupont and Fantôme. The informative beer list will guide you through other glories from Germany, the Netherlands, France and some US micro-brewers, plus a range of UK real ales. Food is limited to lunchtime sandwiches and pub grub.

Sun 12.00–22.30; *Other days* 11.00–23.00

The Offie

142 Clarendon Park Road   **T** 0116 2302448
www.the-offie.co.uk

Established for over 30 years, the Offie is a superb off license in the Clarendon Park area of Leicester. In 2005 it was voted the Independent Beer Retailer of the Year. There are over 500 bottled beers available, of which around 150 are Belgian. A wide range of Belgian glasses are also stocked. A nationwide delivery service is offered and all major credit cards are accepted. See the full list and make orders on its website.
Sat 11.30–22.30; *Other days* 16.30–22.00

LIVERPOOL

Culturally unique port city with as many links to Dublin and New York as to the rest of the North West. Famous for producing musicians, comedians, footballers, politicians, playwrights, poets and drug barons.

Ship and Mitre

133 Dales Street   **T** 0151 236 0859
www.shipandmitre.co.uk

Popular pub with a mixed clientele, close to the Liverpool end of the Mersey Tunnel. An island bar serves two large and comfortable drinking areas. A well chosen list of just over 50 Belgian beers includes two on tap as well as bottled beers from Rochefort, Orval, Westmalle, Cantillon, Anker, Van Eecke, and Slaghmuylder. Good German and UK beers too. Decent affordable food is available at lunchtimes.
Sun 12.00–22.30; *Other days* 11.00–23.00

LONDON

The odd metropolis. If you don't know it, do pop in. Improving.

Belgo Centraal

50 Earlham Street, WC2   **T** 020 7813 2233
www.belgo-restaurants.com

The original Belgo chain is a shadow of its former self, though its flagship restaurant in Covent Garden still entertains with something of a cartoon version of Flemish cuisine and a list of 70 more mainstream beers. All are served in premises resembling the futuristic factory set of a black and white Fifties science fiction movie. The other branch at Chalk Farm (**Belgo Noord** - 72 Chalk Farm Road, NW1 – **T** 020 7267 0718 – *Sa* 12.00–23.30; *Su* 12.00–23.30; *others* 12.00–15.00, 18.00–23.00) and the three remaining cafés of its **Bierodrome** spin-off, at Islington (173 Upper Street, N1 – **T** 020 7226 5835 – *Sa&Su* 12.00–24.00; *others* 12.00–15.00, 18.00–23.00), Clapham (44–48 Clapham High Street, SW4 – **T** 020 7720 1118 – *Fr&Sa* 12.00–02.00; *others* 12.00–24.00) and Holborn (67 Kingsway, WC2 – **T** 020 7242 7469 – *closed Su*; *others* 12.00–23.00), have lesser lists. If they returned to the original plan of loads of top beers and authentic Belgian cooking they might turn a corner.   *Sun* 12.00–22.30
Fri & Sat 12.00–24.00; *Mon–Thu* 12.00–23.30

Dove

24–26 Broadway Market, Hackney E8
T 020 7275 7617
www.belgianbars.com

A wonderfully atmospheric, multi-room traditional style pub, with a strong Belgian theme. Take bus 48 from London Bridge or Liverpool Street, alighting at Mare Street, which runs parallel to Broadway Market area. The nearest train station is London Fields, and nearest tube Bethnal Green. Stocks the same 115 beers as the Dovetail (below). A wide range of good food is available, including an excellent Sunday lunch. *Open daily* 11.00–23.00

Dovetail

9 Jerusalem Passage, Farringdon EC1
T 020 7490 7321
www.belgianbars.com

Excellent café-pub with currently the widest selection of Belgian beers in central London. Belgian influences include lots of Tin-Tin posters on the walls. The list of 115 bottled and draught Belgian beers are generally safe but include interesting ones from Cantillon, Slaghmuylder, Mortgat, Boon, St. Feuillien and Malheur. Good food includes the chance to try wild boar cooked in gueuze and ostrich cooked with coriander and De Koninck. Nearest tube station is Farringdon.
CLOSED SUNDAY; *Other days* 12.00–23.00

Lowlander

36 Drury Lane, Covent Garden WC2
T 020 7379 7446
www.lowlander.com

Slap bang in the centre of the city, with prices as high as you would expect. The grand café experience comes to London. Table service, good food and a lively ambience. Nip upstairs for people-watching. Holds regular beer tastings. The list of up to 60 Belgian beers is boosted by the presence of some from better Dutch micros. Regulars include St. Feuillien, Malheur, Dubuisson, Achel and even de Graal. Deli style snacks are available all day, plus a fuller menu (*Sat&Sun* 12.00–22.00; *others* 12.00–15.00 & 18.00–22.00) of Belgian influenced dishes that can include mussels and *stoemp*.
Sun 12.00–22.30; *Other days* 11.00–23.00

Pitfield Beer Shop

14 Pitfield Street, N1   **T** 0207 739 3701
www.pitfieldbeershop.co.uk

This excellent off-licence can claim to be the best in London, with over 150 Belgian beers in a huge international range. Mainly pretty safe but Cantillon, Slaghmuylder, Rochefort and Westvleteren appear too. Reasonable prices for the capital. You can ordered via the website or just walk in. May be closing.
CLOSED SUNDAY & MONDAY
Sat 10.00–16.00; *Other days* 11.00–19.00

Quinns

65 Kentish Town Road, Kentish Town NW1
T 020 7267 8240

This friendly, family-run Irish bar is perhaps the most unlikely outpost for Belgian beer in the capital. A traditional welcoming pub, despite it's size, there are about 40 Belgian beers and a dozen Dutch ones. Highlights include Cantillon, de Dolle Brouwers, Dupont, St. Feuillien and ter Dolen. Very reasonable prices for London, with 75cl of Malheur Brut Reserve coming in just under a tenner.
Daily 11.00–23.00

Utobeer

Borough Market, Southwark SE1
T 0207 394 8601
www.utobeer.co.uk

Excellent off-licence, not far from London Bridge tube station. Stocks over 100 Belgian beers on a list that has started safe but, like the opening hours, has grown. Abbaye Des Rocs, Achouffe, Dupont, Cantillon and Val-Dieu are there. Belgian glassware and international brews too. Beer can be ordered via the website.
CLOSED SUNDAY TO WEDNESDAY
Thu & Fri 12.00–18.00; *Saturday* 09.00–16.00

White Horse

1–3 Parsons Green, SW6
T 020 7736 2115
www.whitehorsesw6.com

The White Horse holds iconic status in the London beer world for its ground-breaking work in promoting British and international beers to an alert London audience that wants a bit more than handpumps and engraved mirrors. The extras they get are anything up to 50 Belgian ales and dozens of others, excellent home-made, nicely created for, barbecues on the terrace and the most ruthless sneak thieves in Britain so hold onto your bags at all times. Rumour has it mastermind landlord Mark Dorber wants a new challenge but if anyone else takes the helm at the Horse they would be daft to change an award-winning formula.
Sun 12.00–22.30
Other days 11.00–23.00

Other good London bars include **Microbar** (14 Lavender Hill, SW11 – **T** 020 7228 5300), a stylish café not far from Clapham junction that specialises in micro-brewery beers from round the world and stocks around a dozen Belgians from de Graal, Fantôme and others. The **Dog & Bell** (116 Prince St, Deptford SE8 – **T** 020 8692 5664 – *daily* 12.00–23.00; *closed* 15.30–19.00 *Sun*) was CAMRA London Pub of the Year for 2004. Pull up an old church pew and enjoy good beer with tolerant locals in a cracking bar. Bar billiards, an open fire for winter or rear patio for summer. Only 20 Belgian beers but neatly chosen from good breweries. The Dublin-based brewery, **Porterhouse** has two London pubs in Covent Garden (21–22 Maiden Lane, WC2 – **T** 020 7379 7917) and Barnes (201a Castelnau,

SW13 – **T** 020 8748 4486) serving a couple of dozen Belgian beers on an eclectic international list. Both serve good food. The Barnes branch may have the best pub garden in London.

London off licences that may carry high numbers of Belgian beers may include **Nelson Wines** (168 Merton High Street, SW19 – **T** 0208 542 1558), **Pops 'n' Hops** (538 Holloway Road, N7 – **T** 0207 272 1729), **Selfridges** (400 Oxford Street – **T** 0207 3183679) and **Theatre of Wine** (75 Trafalgar Road, Greenwich – **T** 0208 858 6363). We suggest you ring ahead for opening times and to get an idea of what is in stock.

MANCHESTER

The unofficial capital of northern England, a booming cosmopolitan mess of a place, with loads of style, money, music and fun factor. Home to Coronation Street and Manchester United – one a longstanding soap opera and the other a popular TV drama about northern life.

Belgian Belly
514 Wilbraham Road, Chorlton-cum-Hardy
T 0161 860 6766
www.belgianbelly.com

Owned and run by the irrepressible Barker family, the Belly is a shop on a mission. Unlike most off licences they import direct and supply pubs and restaurants throughout the North West. There is also an on-line mail order service with regional delivery. Stocks an ever-changing range of about 100 Belgian beers, plus Belgian chocolates, cheeses and pâtés. They offer a beer and a bite at lunchtime too. An unswerving commitment to promoting small producers includes refusing to stock anything from the multi-nationals – not a bad move given InBev's recent closure of Manchester's Boddingtons brewery. Runs a comedy club and numerous functions in conjunction with Lloyds Hotel opposite. Most credit cards accepted. Opens on Sunday in the run up to Christmas.
CLOSED SUNDAY; *Other days* 09.00–18.00

Fringe
8 Swan Street   **T** 0161 835 3815

The best and longest standing outlet for Belgian beer in the city centre. Situated close to the junction of the A665 and A62 in the so-called Northern Quarter. Recently refurbished and full of character, Bar Fringe is loosely based on a Belgian brown café and has an ever-changing range of around 30 better Belgian beers, rising as high as 60 during the regular festivals. Over a hundred pass through each year. There is food (12.00–16.00 Sat & Sun; 12.00–18.00 other days), plus UK beers too. A secluded patio drinking area appears in summer.
Sun 12.00–22.30; *Other days* 12.00–23.00

Another city centre pub worth checking out is the **Knott** (374 Deansgate), a small pub that looks like it's been wedged into a railway arch. It smallish range of Belgian and German beers is helped down by an eclectic range of up-market food.

NANTWICH

Market town in Cheshire, close to the M6 motorway.

Bhurtpore
Wrenbury Road, Aston   **T** 01270 780917

In the village of Aston, five miles south of Nantwich off the A530. Named after a twice besieged town in British-occupied India where an English army did the usual beastly things to the natives to the greater glory of the Empire. Two centuries on, curries are the culinary speciality here in both bar and restaurant, while the really unusual feature is a stock of around 110 Belgian beers, with some UK rarities. A small range of Czech and German beers are also available. Children are welcome until 20.00 and there is live folk music on the third Tuesday of the month.
Sun 12.00–22.30
Other days 12.00–14.30; 18.30–23.00

PETERBOROUGH

Modern town in north Cambridgeshire, just off the A1(M). Hosts the biggest beer festival in the UK after the Great British Beer Festival.

Charters (T 01733 315700 – *Su* 12.00–22.30; *Fr&Sa* 11.00–02.00; *others* 11.00–23.00) is a converted Dutch barge moored permanently on the River Nene in the town centre, next to Town Bridge. Its twenty beers include Bink Bloesem, Bornem Trippel and Abbaye Des Rocs. Live jazz at weekends earns the 02.00 license. There is a Chinese restaurant on the upper deck. It is owned by the same people as the **Brewery Tap** (90 Westgate – T 01733 358500), which has a similar list but a smarter dress code. The **Coalheavers Arms** (5 Park Street, Woodston – T 01733 565664) is a recently refurbished back street gem that boasts a range of Belgian beers, though not loudly enough for us to know which they are.

SHEFFIELD

The capital of the socialist republic of South Yorkshire, home to two underachieving football clubs and the place that gave the world Wilkinson Sword and the Full Monty.

Devonshire Cat

Wellington Street   T 0114 279 6700
www.devonshirecat.co.uk

Sheffield's best beer pub is a smart affair in the Devonshire Green area of the city. Glass fronted design extends to a display cellar. A top international beer selection includes about 55 from Belgium. On the pricey side but you have to pay for quality. A solid list includes Arabier, Achel, Grottenbier and Hommelbier. Decent food too.
Sun 12.00–22.30; *Other days* 11.30 – 23.00

Three other pubs in Sheffield with small but interesting Belgian beer lists are all outside the city centre but reasonably close to one another. These are the **New Barrack Tavern** (601 Penistone Road – T 0114 234 0148), the **Kelham Island** (62 Russell Street – T 0114 272 2482) and the **Fat Cat** (23 Alma Street – T 0114 249 4801). Even if their Belgian beer lists wilt they offer a great little crawl.

SOUTH NORMANTON

Small, dull town in a former coal-mining area, in desperate need of a makeover. Conveniently close to the M1 (J28), on the Nottinghamshire/Derbyshire border.

White Hart

43 Church Street   T 01773 819000

The Guide likes this place. Lady from Mons meets man from Nottinghamshire, moves to UK and sets up an authentic Belgian café-restaurant on the high street of a discarded mining town, where many of the other pubs were boarded up years ago. La Tambouille Grillée, or "Roasted Grub" if you prefer, opened in January 2003 in the old White Hart. The single room bar area is complemented by a larger, high ceilinged restaurant offering Belgian cuisine with a French influence, including frogs legs and snails. The fish *waterzooi* is a particular favourite. There are around 80 Belgian beers on an excellent list, with all the beers from the beloved Blaugies brewery featuring simply because it is madame's local brewery back home. The idea is impossible, the reality is lovely and we implore you to drop in every time you go close to junction 28.
CLOSED MONDAY
Tue & Wed 19.00–23.00; *Thu & Fri* 16.00–23.00
Sat 12.00–23.00; *Sun* 12.00–22.30

SOUTHAMPTON

Thriving port and university city that is the unofficial capital of the south coast.

Bitter Virtue

70 Cambridge Road   T 023 8055 4881
E enquiries@bittervirtue.co.uk
www.bittervirtue.co.uk

Privately owned beer shop just off The Avenue, established in 1997. Stocks around 115 Belgian beers in a range of nearly three hundred in all. We know people who travel from as far away as Bristol to stock up here.
CLOSED MONDAY
Sun 10.30–14.00
Other days 10.30–20.30

SOWERBY BRIDGE

Small, attractive West Yorkshire town, on the outskirts of Halifax.

Alma

Four Lane Ends, Mill Bank   T 01422 823334

The Alma is set in the hills overlooking the town, in a picturesque part of Yorkshire, not far off the M62 (J24). Behind the dark stone façade, you are greeted by authentic stone flagged floors and a real fire. In summer, the beer garden offers superb views across the Calderdale valley. This is another place where Belgian beer would not normally be expected though 90 are stocked with at least one on tap. The well-read landlord knows his stuff. Lunchtime and evening meals (We–Su) are good value for money. Another place well worth the detour.

Sun 12.00–22.30; Other days 11.00–23.00

TOCKWITH

North Yorkshire village, five miles off the A1 near Wetherby.

Beer Paradise

Marston Moor Business Park   T 01423 359533
www.beerparadise.co.uk

To call this a shop is misleading. Beer Paradise is a unit on an industrial estate that serves the licensed trade and individual customers, very much in the way of a Belgian *drankenhandel* or beer warehouse. Marston Moor Industrial Estate is just outside the village of Tockwith. You may have to ring the bell if the doors are not open. Mainly trade but happy to welcome serious private buyers. Stocks about 160 Belgian beers, along with UK, German and American beers – see the website.

CLOSED SATURDAY & SUNDAY
Mon–Fri 09.00–17.00

TONGHAM

Village near Farnham, in leafy Surrey.

Hogs Back Brewery

Manor Farm, The Street   T 01252 784495
www.hogsback.co.uk

As well as brewing and selling their own excellent range of real ales, the Hogs Back brewery shop sells over three hundred bottled beers, of which 80 to 100 are Belgian, depending on time of year. If you ring ahead you might get a tour of the brewery (Wed–Fri evening or at weekends). Open every day except Christmas Day and New Years Day (Sun hours on Bank Holidays).

*Sun 10.00–16.00; Wed–Fri 10.00–20.30
Other days 10.00–18.00*

WESTCLIFF-ON-SEA

The respectable side of Southend. Birthplace of cricketer and commentator Trevor Bailey.

Beers Unlimited

500 London Road   T 01702 345474
www.beersunlimited.co.uk

Beer shop serving seaside Essex. Stocks over two hundred beers, of which around 55 are Belgian. The list is largely solid and predictable, but includes St. Bernardus and a few from Van Eecke. The Belgians increase for Christmas. Check the website.

CLOSED WEDNESDAY & SUNDAY
Other days 10.00–17.00

WEST MALLING

Old Kentish market town now part of outer London suburbia.

Café Belge

High Street   T 01732 843247
See Battle (above).

OTHER POSSIBLE UK OUTLETS

The 5,000 pubs included in the *CAMRA Good Beer Guide 2005* (£13.99 – CAMRA Books – ISBN 1-85249-196-5) are selected by local CAMRA members for the quality of their draught British ales. The following entries are noted as also stocking Belgian beers. In some cases this will mean that they stock a few better known beers on tap, while others will stock a broader range and some would justify a full listing in the section above. Your experiences will be gratefully received on BelgiumGBG@aol.com.

BEDFORDSHIRE
LUTON: **Bricklayers Arms**, 16–18 Hightown Road (**T** 01582 611017)
TODDINGTON: **Oddfellows Arms**, 2 Conger Lane (**T** 01525 872021)

CAMBRIDGESHIRE
CAMBRIDGE: **Live And Let Live**, 40 Mawson Road, (**T** 01223 460261)
LEIGHTON BROMSWOLD: **Green Man** (**T** 01480 890238)
HISTON: **Red Lion**, 27 High Street (**T** 01223 564437)

CHESHIRE
CONGLETON: **Beartown Tap**, 18 Willow Street (**T** 01260 270990)
WARRINGTON: **Wilkies Tavern**, 25 Church Street (**T** 01925 416564)

DERBYSHIRE
SHIRLAND: **Hay Inn**, 135 Main Road (**T** 01773 835383)

ESSEX
LITTLE TOTHAM: **Swan**, School Road (**T** 01621 892689)
STOW MARIES: Prince Of Wales, Woodham Road (**T** 01621 828971)

HAMPSHIRE
PORTSMOUTH: **Hole In The Wall**, 36 Great Southsea Street, Southsea (**T** 02392 298085)
SOUTHAMPTON: **New Inn**, 16 Bevois Valley Road (**T** 02380 335662)

HERTFORDSHIRE
HERONSGATE: **Land Of Liberty Peace And Plenty**, Long Lane (**T** 01923 282226)
ST. ALBANS: **Farmers Boy**, 134 London Road (**T** 01727 766702); **King Harry**, 2 King Harry Lane (**T** 01727 846904); and **Lower Red Lion**, 34–36 Fishpool Street (**T** 01727 855669)

KENT
DEAL: **Bohemian**, 47 Beach Street (**T** 01304 374843)
GILLINGHAM: **Frog And Toad**, 38 Burnt Oak Terrace (**T** 01634 852231)
RAMSGATE: **Brewhouse and Bakers**, 98 Harbour Parade (**T** 01843 594758); and **Comfort Inn**, Victoria Parade, East Cliff (**T** 01843 592345)
SANDGATE: **Clarendon**, Brewers Hill (**T** 01303 248684)
TONBRIDGE: **Cask & Glass**, 64 Priory Street (**T** 01732 359784)
TUNBRIDGE WELLS: **Sankeys**, 39 Mount Ephraim (**T** 01892 511422); and the **Bitter End** (off-licence), 107 Camden Road (**T** 01892 522918)

LANCASHIRE
LYTHAM ST. ANNES: **Taps**, 12 Henry Street (**T** 01253 736226)

LEICESTERSHIRE (Rutland)
OAKHAM: **Grainstore**, Station Approach (**T** 01572 770065)

LINCOLNSHIRE
GAINSBOROUGH: **Eight Jolly Brewers**, Silver Street (**T** 01427 677128)
STAMFORD: **Otters Pocket**, 20 All Saints Street (**T** 01780 755228)

LONDON
ISLINGTON, N1: **Barnsbury**, 209–211 Liverpool Road (**T** 020 7760 75519)
CLAPHAM: **Rose & Crown**, 2 The Polygon (**T** 020 7720 8265)
STREATHAM: **Hogshead**, 68–70 Streatham High Road (**T** 020 8696 7587)
BRENTFORD: **Magpie & Crown**, 128 High Street (**T** 020 8560 5658)
BROMLEY: **Bitter End** (off-licence), 139 Masons Hill (**T** 020 8466 6083)

MANCHESTER (Greater)
CHORLTON-CUM-HARDY: **Marble Beer House**, 57 Manchester Road (**T** 0161 8819206)
HEATON NORRIS: **Navigation**, 11 Manchester Road (**T** 0161 4806626)
SALFORD: **Crescent**, 18–21 Crescent (**T** 0161 7365600)
WIGAN: **Anvil**, Dorning Street (**T** 01942 239444)

MERSEYSIDE
LIVERPOOL: **Everyman**, 5-9 Hope Street (**T** 0151 7089545); and **Thomas Rigbys**, 23–25 Dale Street (**T** 0151 2363269)

NORFOLK
ALDBOROUGH: **Old Red Lion**, The Green (**T** 01263 761451)
GORLESTON-ON-SEA: **New Entertainer**, 80 Pier Plain (**T** 01493 441643)
NORWICH: **Fat Cat**, 49 West End Street (**T** 01603 624364)
OLD BUCKENHAM: **Gamekeeper**, The Green (**T** 01953 860397)

NORTHAMPTONSHIRE
NORTHAMPTON: **Malt Shovel Tavern**, 121 Bridge Street (**T** 01604 234212)

NOTTINGHAMSHIRE
NOTTINGHAM: **Vat & Fiddle**, 12–14 Queens Bridge Road (**T** 0115 985 0611); and **Plough**, 17 St. Peters Road, Radford (**T** 0115 942 2649)

OXFORDSHIRE
OXFORD: **Wharf House**, 14 Butterwyke Place (**T** 01865 246752)

SHROPSHIRE
TELFORD: **Station Hotel**, 42 Market Street (**T** 01952 612949)

SOMERSET
BATH: **Salamander**, 3 John Street (**T** 01225 428889)
CREWKERNE: **Old Stagecoach Inn**, Station Road (**T** 01460 72972)
NORTH FITZWARREN: **Cross Keys** (**T** 01823 333062)
WRANTAGE: **Canal Inn** (**T** 01823 480210)

STAFFORDSHIRE
KIDSGROVE: **Blue Bell**, 25 Hardingswood (**T** 01782 774052)
STOKE-ON-TRENT: **Malt 'n' Hops**, 295 King Street, Fenton (**T** 01782 313406)

SUFFOLK
LOWESTOFT: **Oak Tavern**, Crown Street West (**T** 01502 537246)

SUSSEX (East)
PORTSLADE: **Stanley Arms**, 47 Wolseley Road (**T** 01273 430234)

SUSSEX (West)
WORTHING: **Selden Arms**, 41 Lyndhurst Road (**T** 01903 234854)

WARWICKSHIRE
ATHERSTONE: **Church End Brewery Tap**, 109 Ridge Lane (**T** 01827 713080)
RUGBY: **Merchants Inn**, 5 Little Church Street (**T** 01788 571119)

WEST MIDLANDS
DUDLEY: **Fountain**, 8 Temple Street, Lower Gornal (**T** 01384 242777)

YORKSHIRE (North)
MANFIELD: **Crown Inn**, Vicars Lane (**T** 01325 374243)
NORTHALLERTON: **Tithe Bar**, 2 Friarage Street (**T** 01609 778482)
SCARBOROUGH: **Cricketers**, 119 North Marine Road (**T** 01723 365864); and **Indigo Alley**, 4 North Marine Road (**T** 01723 381900)
SOUTH COWTON: **Arden Arms**, Atley Hill (**T** 01325 378678)

YORKSHIRE (West)
BRADFORD: **Fighting Cocks**, 21–23 Preston Street (**T** 01274 726907)
LEEDS: **Reliance Bar**, 76–78 North Street (**T** 01132 956060)

IMPORTERS AND DISTRIBUTORS

Larger breweries like Moortgat have their own distribution companies in the UK. InBev inherited no distribution problem as Interbrew had bought the British brewing industry. Smaller independent Belgian breweries are reliant on a relatively small number of importers for supplying to the UK licensed trade. These are the ones we know about.

Beer Direct

10 Ferndale Close, Werrington
Stoke-on-Trent ST9 0PW   T&F 01782 303823
E sales@beerdirect.co.uk
www.beerdirect.co.uk

Small enough to be friendly and approachable but big enough to offer distribution through-out most of England and Wales. They import directly from Abbaye des Rocs, Anker, Dupont, Lefèbvre, St. Feuillien, Val-Dieu and Van Steenberge. They can also source and supply beers from about thirty others.

Beer Paradise

Unit 20, Centre Park
Marston Moor Business Park
Tockwith, York YO26 7QF
T 01423 359533   F 01423 359534
E sales@beerparadise.ltd.uk
www.beerparadise.ltd.uk

As well as selling direct to the public (see above) this enterprising warehouse runs a trade supply service nationwide for orders of fifteen cases and above. They can source around thirty breweries.

Belgian Belly

514 Wilbraham Road
Chorlton-cum-Hardy, Manchester M21 9AW
T 0161 860 6766
www.belgianbelly.com

Imports direct from a number of smaller ale and lambic producers and sells onto pubs, off licences and clubs in the North West.

Bierlijn

Kwakkelhutstraat 54
4814 KR Breda, Netherlands
F 0031 84 876 1391 (Netherlands)
E info@bierlijn.co.uk
www.bierlijn.co.uk
&

Belgian Beer Import Limited

PO Box 810, GU21 4WF
T 01483 740984 (UK – Bart Verhaghe)
E bartverhaeghe@btconnect.com

Although its head office is in the Netherlands, this energetically laid-back import-export company hunts quality beers from the smaller Belgian breweries for its sister operation in Woking, for trade deliveries throughout mainland Britain. Staunchly anti-big brewery in its stance, it encourages substitution of those products with small brewery alternatives. Beer festival supply is a speciality – organizers should approach the Dutch office for good advice on stocking. Currently it imports regularly from Abbaye des Rocs, Achilles, de Bie, Binchoise, Blaugies, Boelens, de Cam, Cantillon, De Ryck, de Dolle Brouwers, Drie Fonteinen, Dupont, Ellezelloise, Fantôme, Girardin, Graal, Hanssens, Kerkom, Paeleman, Proef, de Ranke, Regenboog, St. Monon, and Silenrieux. They have recently taken batches of Glazen Toren, Grain d'Orge and Rulles too.

James Clay & Sons

Unit 1, Grove Mills, Elland
West Yorkshire HX5 9DZ
T 01422 377560   F 01422 375100
E info@jamesclay.co.uk

Long-established beer merchant and importer of beers from many countries. From Belgium they can source beers from around twenty-five breweries including Achouffe, Affligem (Heineken), Boon, Bosteels, Cantillon, Chimay, De Koninck, De Troch, de Dolle Brouwers, Dubuisson, Gouden Boom, Huyghe, Liefmans, Lindemans, Malheur, Moortgat, Orval, Palm, Rochefort, Rodenbach, Silly, St. Bernardus, Slaghmuylder, Timmermans, Van Eecke, Van Honsebrouck & Westmalle for trade customers throughout England.

Consumer groups

Consumerism is a relatively new phenomenon. For the world of beer it began officially in the UK with the Society for the Protection of Beer from the Wood, which was a forerunner to CAMRA (the CAMpaign for Real Ale), founded in 1971.

There is no doubt that around the world beer lovers have been making their voices heard increasingly clearly. The message, for those that wish to hear it, is that they want to preserve and develop characterful, complex beers made in traditional and newer styles, without shortcuts.

After CAMRA, the first national consumer groups in mainland Europe were formed in the Netherlands (1981) and Belgium (1983). Since that time similar groups have sprung up all over Europe. Their equivalents are emerging in other countries too.

ZYTHOS

Zythos is the Belgian beer consumers' voice. The organisation is a confederation of local groups. Each tends to organise an annual local beer festival, brewery visits and social events throughout the year. The organisation still consists entirely of Flemish groups, which is bound to diminish its influence with the industry. Nonetheless some significant victories are being won.

Zythos campaigns on a variety of issues that threaten the survival of craft brewing in Belgium. It has shown itself to be capable of mounting major challenges to proposed changes in legislation about the use of oak-ageing in breweries (*successful*) and the closure of specialist maltings by Interbrew Belgium (*unsuccessful*). It is actively campaigning to improve beer labelling (see page 7).

Not always on the wagon.

Its predecessor the Objective BierProevers (OBP) had been founded in 1983 as the Flemish consumer's riposte to the collapsing heritage of traditional beer styles in Belgium and the mass closures of traditional breweries in the Seventies. Although the organisation was a success it had to be wound up in 2002 for complicated reasons relating to the personal liabilities of its founders.

Also for this reason Zythos is a confederate of local groups, which are listed below.

Members receive a quarterly magazine called Zytholoog, written in Dutch.

The downside to the new arrangements for foreigners is that there is no longer any national membership available. The thing to do is join a local group, either at one of the many beer festivals, or via the website (**www.zythos.be**). The cost of this varies depending on the group.

For annual membership of the Ostend group, De Oostendse Bierjutters, offers British membership. Send a cheque for £21.50 (2004), payable to John White, to:

John White
DOB UK Treasurer
2 Grasby Crescent
Grimsby DN37 9HE

Zythos local groups

Antwerp

Berlaar-Heikant	De Heikantse Bierliefhebbers	heikantse.bierliefhebbers@zythos.be
Essen	OBER (Objectieve Bierprovers Essense Regio)	ober@zythos.be
Geel	Onder 't Schuim	onder.tschuim@zythos.be
Mechelen	The Beer Brothers	the.beerbrothers@zythos.be
Putte	Putse Bierkliek	putse.bierkliek@zythos.be

Brabant (Flemish)

Aarschot	De Aarschotse Bierwegers	aarschotse.bierwegers@zythos.be
Leuven	Leuvense Biertherapeuten	leuvense.biertherapeuten@zythos.be
Payottenland	De Lambiekstoempers	lambiekstoempers@zythos.be

East Flanders

Aalst	OPA (Objectieve ProefAjuinen)	opa@zythos.be
Baardegem	BOBSA (Baardegemse Objectieve Bierproevers SA)	bobsa@zythos.be
Buggenhout	De Bierpallieters	bierpallieters@zythos.be
Dendermonde	Ros Beiaard Bierproevers	ros.beiaard.bierproevers@zythos.be
Hamme	De Hamse Bierwuitens	hamse.bierwuitensd@zythos.be
Sint Niklaas	Tussen Pot end Pint	tpp@zythos.be
Temse	De Objectieve Kaaischuimers	objectieve.kaaischuimers@zythos.be
Zele	De Schuimkragen	schuimkragen@zythos.be
Zottegem	BLES (Bierliefhebbers van de Egmontstede)	bles@zythos.be

Limburg

Bree	De Breese Bierpreevers	breese.bierpreevers@zythos.be
Hasselt	De Limburgse Biervrienden	limburgse.biervrienden@zythos.be

West Flanders

Ieper	De Ieperse Bierkatjes	ieperse.bierkatjes@zythos.be
Ostend	DOB (De Oostendse Bierjutters)	de.oostendse.bierjutters@zythos.be
Wevelgem	HOP (Heerlijk Objectief Proeven)	hop@zythos.be

THE EUROPEAN BEER CONSUMERS' UNION (EBCU)

As a response to the development of Europe-wide decision-making in the EU and the globalisation of the brewing industry, Europe's main beer consumer groups have joined together as the European Beer Consumers' Union (EBCU).

There are currently twelve members of this confederation. These are:

BELGIUM: **Zythos**
DENMARK: **Danøl**
ESTONIA: **EUBC**
FINLAND: **Olutliitto**
FRANCE: **ATPUB**
ITALY: **Unionbirrai**
NETHERLANDS: **PINT**
NORWAY: **NORØL**
POLAND: **Bractwo Piwne**
SWEDEN: **SO**
SWITZERLAND: **ABO**
UNITED KINGDOM: **CAMRA**

The group is encouraging moves to form a consumer coalition in Germany to bear fruit. One notable recent victory was the declaration of the city of Bamberg in northern Bavaria as a UNESCO World Heritage site for brewing.

CAMRA BRUSSELS

CAMRA's Belgian members congregate under the banner of CAMRA Brussels to enjoy regular trips to breweries, beer festivals and other events. Built around the indomitable figure of Stephen D'Arcy, who compiles and edits the constantly updated guide to the cafés of Brussels and elsewhere (see Guidebooks).

All meetings are advertised via the CAMRA monthly newspaper, What's Brewing. All sympathisers welcome.

More information from:

Stephen D'Arcy
16 Rue Willems (# 2013)
1210 Brussels

Websites

As well as the Zythos website (www.zythos.be), which has a message board mainly in Dutch, there are two other message boards that carry active correspondence on all matters pertaining to Belgian beer.

www.belgianstyle.com is home to the Babble Belt, a much-lurked virtual parliament of English-speaking Belgian beer lovers. Constructed by an American and moderated by a Brit, if something appears on the scene the Babblers will be the first to know about it and to have several opinions on its worth.

An amateur site moderated by a Flemish beer lover but almost entirely English language based is the Belgian Beer site at Yahoo.com. To become a member, log on to http://groups.yahoo.com/group/belgianbeer/ initially.

The top French site, with a special interest in Wallonian beers but covering all of Belgium is www.bierebel.com. This is also the site with the most reliable up-to-date listing of new beers and breweries.

Other beer lovers' websites worth a peek are the American international sites www.ratebeer.com, www.realbeer.com, and www.beeradvocate.com, and two UK-based sites www.bottledbeer.co.uk and www.beer-pages.com.

Index of places

Index of beers

To find a beer, trace it through this list of 600 or so brand names and then refer to the listing under the brewery section indicated in italicised brackets after it. In the few cases where we do not know the brewery of origin, refer to the company that commissioned it.

If the name is not here we refer you to page 90 and the list of 200 or so additional brands commissioned from the Proef brewery in Lochristi.

Books for Beer Lovers

CAMRA Books, the publishing arm of the Campaign for Real Ale, is the leading publisher of books on beer and pubs. Key titles include:

Good Beer Guide 2007
Editor: ROGER PROTZ

The Good Beer Guide is the only guide you will need to find the right pint, in the right place, every time. It's the original and the best independent guide to around 4,500 pubs throughout the UK; the Sun newspaper rated the 2004 edition in the top 20 books of all time! Now in its 34th year, this annual publication is a comprehensive and informative guide to the best real ale pubs in the UK, researched and written exclusively by CAMRA members and fully updated every year.

£14.99   ISBN 10: 1 85249 224 4   ISBN 13: 978 1 85249 224 3

300 Beers to Try Before You Die
ROGER PROTZ

300 beers from around the world, handpicked by award-winning journalist, author and broadcaster Roger Protz to try before you die! A comprehensive portfolio of top beers from the smallest microbreweries in the United States to family-run British breweries and the world's largest brands. This book is indispensable for both beer novices and aficionados.

£14.99   ISBN 10: 1 85249 213 9   ISBN 13: 978 1 85249 213 7

The Big Book of Beer
ADRIAN TIERNEY-JONES

Everything you could ever want to know about the world's favourite drink; this beautifully illustrated book is an eye-opener to the world of beer articulated by well-known beer experts and those who brew it. A perfect gift for the 'real beer' connoisseur.

£14.99   ISBN 10: 1 85249 212 0   ISBN 13: 978 1 85249 212 0

Good Beer Guide Germany
STEVE THOMAS

The first ever comprehensive region-by-region guide to Germany's brewers, beer and outlets. Includes more than 1,250 breweries, 1,000 brewery taps and 7,500 beers. Complete with useful travel information on how to get there, informative essays on German beer and brewing plus beer festival listings.

£16.99   ISBN 10: 1 85249 219 8   ISBN 13: 978 1 85249 219 9

Order these and other CAMRA books online at **www.camra.org.uk/books**, ask at your local bookstore, or contact: CAMRA, 230 Hatfield Road, St Albans, AL1 4LW. *Telephone* 01727 867201

It takes all sorts to Campaign for Real Ale

CAMRA, the Campaign for Real Ale, is an independent not-for-profit, volunteer-led consumer group. We actively campaign for full pints and more flexible licensing hours, as well as protecting the 'local' pub and lobbying government to champion pub-goers' rights.

CAMRA has 75,000 members from all ages and backgrounds, brought together by a common belief in the issues that CAMRA deals with and their love of good quality British beer. For just £18 a year, that's less than a pint a month, you can join CAMRA and enjoy the following benefits:

A monthly colour newspaper informing you about beer and pub news and detailing events and beer festivals around the country.

Free or reduced entry to over 140 national, regional and local beer festivals.

Money off many of our publications including the *Good Beer Guide* and the *Good Bottled Beer Guide*.

Access to a members-only section of our national website, **www.camra.org.uk** which gives up-to-the-minute news stories and includes a special offer section with regular features saving money on beer and trips away.

The opportunity to campaign to save pubs under threat of closure, for pubs to be open when people want to drink and a reduction in beer duty that will help Britain's brewing industry survive.

Log onto **www.camra.org.uk** for
CAMRA membership information.

CAMPAIGN
FOR
REAL ALE

Do you feel passionately about your pint? Then why not join CAMRA

Just fill in the application form (or a photocopy of it) and the Direct Debit form on the next page to receive three months' membership FREE!

If you wish to join but do not want to pay by Direct Debit, please fill in the application form below and send a cheque, payable to CAMRA, to CAMRA, 230 Hatfield Road, St Albans, Hertfordshire AL1 4LW.

Please tick appropriate box

☐ Single Membership (UK & EU) £18

☐ For under-26 Membership £10

☐ For 60 and over Membership £10

For partners' joint membership add £3 (for concessionary rates both members must be eligible for the membership rate).
Life membership information is available on request.

If you join by Direct Debit you will receive three months' membership extra, free!

Title _____ Surname _____

Forename(s) _____

Address _____

_____ Post Code _____

Date of Birth _____ E-mail address _____

Signature _____

Partner's details if required

Title _____ Surname _____

Forename(s) _____

Date of Birth _____ E-mail address _____

Please tick here ☐ if you would like to receive occasional e-mails from CAMRA (at no point will your details be released to a third party).

Find out more about CAMRA at **www.camra.org.uk**   *Telephone* 01727 867201

CAMPAIGN FOR REAL ALE

Instruction to your Bank or Building Society to pay by Direct Debit

DIRECT Debit

Please fill in the form and send to: Campaign for Real Ale Ltd. 230 Hatfield Road, St. Albans, Herts. AL1 4LW

Name and full postal address of your Bank or Building Society

To The Manager _____ Bank or Building Society

Address _____

Postcode _____

Name (s) of Account Holder (s)

_____

Bank or Building Society account number

_____

Branch Sort Code

_____

Reference Number

_____

Banks and Building Societies may not accept Direct Debit Instructions for some types of account

Originator's Identification Number

| 9 | 2 | 6 | 1 | 2 | 9 |

FOR CAMRA OFFICIAL USE ONLY
This is not part of the Instruction to your Bank or Building Society

Membership Number

Name

Postcode

Instruction to your Bank or Building Society

Please pay CAMRA Direct Debits from the account detailed on this Instruction subject to the safeguards assured by the Direct Debit Guarantee. I understand that this instruction may remain with CAMRA and, if so, will be passed electronically to my Bank/Building Society

Signature(s)

_____

Date

_____

✂ detached and retained this section

This Guarantee should be detached and retained by the payer.

DIRECT Debit

The Direct Debit Guarantee

- This Guarantee is offered by all Banks and Building Societies that take part in the Direct Debit Scheme. The efficiency and security of the Scheme is monitored and protected by your own Bank or Building Society.

- If the amounts to be paid or the payment dates change CAMRA will notify you 7 working days in advance of your account being debited or as otherwise agreed.

- If an error is made by CAMRA or your Bank or Building Society, you are guaranteed a full and immediate refund from your branch of the amount paid.

- You can cancel a Direct Debit at any time by writing to your Bank or Building Society. Please also send a copy of your letter to us.